Hard Press

THE MEMOIRS OF GENERAL THE BARON DE MARBOT.

Translated by Oliver.C.Colt

Table of Contents

4

Introduction.

General, later the Baron, Marbot, came from a family which might be described as landed gentry. His father served in the bodyguard of Louis XV and later in the Republican army. Marbot himself was a soldier from the age of 17 and fought in the wars of the Republic and the campaigns of Napoleon. His memoirs were written for his family and his intimate circle, without thought of publication, and it was not until after his death in 1854 that his family were persuaded to offer the manuscript to publishers.

This is not a meticulously researched historical document, but the reminiscences of an old soldier, writing of events which took place many years earlier and I suspect that like most of us when we try to recall things that happened forty years ago his memory was a trifle indistinct.

By far the greater part of his narrative has the ring of truth, but in my opinion there are places where his imagination has embroidered the facts. This is particularly so when it comes to some of his personal adventures. He also, in my view, describes as real, events in which he did not take part and which may be no more than popular rumour.

It has to be remembered that there were no inquisitive war correspondents attached to the "Grande Arme" and news was what was written in Napoleon's bulletins.

As an example of the kind of thing which raises a question in my mind, in his opening chapter he says that he was a very sturdy infant and that the only illness he ever suffered from was small-pox. This does not seem probable; an outbreak of small-pox in the family would be a disastrous occurrence, it is a disease with a high mortality and could not be dismissed as a childish complaint. He also goes on to describe how his head got stuck in the cat-hole, but in the original he claims that his face turned blue and that he was being strangled when his father removed the door from its hinges to extricate him. Anyone who has attempted to remove a door from its hinges knows that you cannot do so without opening the door and using at least a screwdriver. It is also an operation which is difficult to perform single-handed and with a small child stuck in it even more so. He says that he was about three or four at the time, and the long-term memory does not start developing in a child until around the age of four. I think it more than likely that that good Baron has a false recollection derived from being told of these goings on by his mother and truly believes that he remembers them. A misdiagnosis of small-pox would not be surprising given the inadequate state of medical knowledge and practice of the time.

I do not doubt that he ran great danger and was seriously injured at Eylau, but there are elements in his recital which although they enhance the drama and would pass muster with the lay reader, are open to criticism by anyone with a medical training. He says that while he was attempting to release the "Eagle" from its standard, a bullet passed through his hat without touching his head. As a result of this he claims that he found himself paralysed and unable to use his legs to urge his horse forward, although he remained mentally perfectly clear. He says that the passage of the bullet close to his head caused bleeding from his nose and ears and even from his eyes, signs which a clinician would regard as probably indicating a serious fracture of the base of the skull.

I am not a neurologist, but I can think of no neurological injury which would produce the type of paralysis which he describes except a high lesion of the spinal cord. What is more, within a few moments he is in the saddle of a galloping horse and I cannot imagine that anyone suffering from a form of paralysis could remain there for very long.

The thoughtful reader may also wonder how the soldier who robbed him as he lay unconscious could suppose that he was dead, an unconscious person is quite plainly breathing.

Could it be that having been rendered unconscious as a result of the fall from his horse, he has some degree of retrograde amnesia and has invented details to fill the gaps in his memory, or could it be that writing, as he was, for his family and friends, he was indulging in a little pardonable exaggeration.

In spite of these reservations the story he tells is full of life and interest, and gives a vivid impression of war as it was fought then, including all its horrors and disasters.

In this translation I have not deviated from the gist of events, but I have taken the liberty of making a variety of omissions and emendations, with the aim of adding credibility to some of the events, such as those noted above. I have also prefaced some of his anecdotes, which he retails as fact, with the words "It is believed that..." or something to that effect.

The campaigns can be followed by the use of a good atlas, but unfortunately the many upheavals which Europe has undergone since those days has resulted in many of the names of places being changed. The curious reader may well find maps dealing with the Napoleonic wars in any well stocked public library.

All translation requires some degree of paraphrase. What sounds well in one language may sound ridiculous if translated literally into another. I have endeavoured to produce a version of these memoirs acceptable to the English-speaking reader, whether I have succeeded or not only the reader can say.

Oliver.C.Colt

THE MEMOIRS OF GENERAL THE BARON DE MARBOT.

Translated by Oliver.C.Colt

Chap. 1.

I was born on the 18th August 1782 at my father's Chteau of Larivire, in the beautiful valley of Beaulieu, on the borders of Limousin and Quercy—now the department of Corrze—where my father owned a considerable property.

The family of Marbot was of noble origin, although for a long time they had not preceded their name by any title. To use a then current expression, they lived nobly, that is to say on the income from their estates, without engaging in any form of employment. They were allied to and joined in the society of several of the important families of the district.

I mention this because, at a time when the nobility were so haughty and powerful, it shows that the family had a social position of considerable standing.

My father was born in 1753. He had a rather fiery temperament, but he was so good-hearted that, after a first outburst, he always sought to make one forget any hasty words which he might have uttered. He was a fine figure of a man, very tall and well built, with handsome, manly features.

My grandfather had become a widower when my father was still at school. His house was run by one of his elderly cousins, the oldest of the demoiselles Oudinet of Beaulieu. She gave unstinting care to my grandfather, who, having become almost blind as a result of a flash of lightning, which had struck near him, no longer went out of his manor. Thus my father, when he reached manhood, faced by an infirm old man and an aunt devoted to his least wishes, could have played fast and loose with the family fortune. He did not, however, abuse his position, but as he had a great fancy for a military career, he accepted a proposal which was made to him by colonel the Marquis d'Estresse, a neighbour and close friend of the family, which was to have him enrolled in the bodyguard of the king, Louis XV.

Being under the auspices of the Marquis d'Estresse, he was received in a number of houses; notably that of lieutenant-general the Comte de Schomberg, the inspector-general of cavalry, who, recognising my father's worth, had him posted to his regiment of dragoons as captain, and took him as his aide-de-camp.

On the death of my grandfather my father was still unmarried, and his fortune, as well as his place in the Royal Bodyguard, put him in a position to choose a wife, without the likelihood of being refused.

There lived at that time, in the Chteau de Laval de Cre, about a league from Larivire, a family of noble rank but without much money, named de Certain. The head of this house was stricken by gout and so his affairs were managed by Madame de Certain, an admirable woman, who came from the noble family of de Verdal, who claim to have Saint Roch amongst the kinsfolk of their ancestors on the distaff side, a Verdal, so they say, having married a sister of the Saint at Montpellier. I do not know how much truth there is in this claim, but before the Revolution of 1789, there was, at the gateway of the old chteau of Gruniac, owned by the de Verdals, a stone bench, which was greatly venerated by the inhabitants of the nearby mountains, because, according to tradition, St. Roch, when he came to visit his sister, used to sit on this bench, from where one can view the countryside, which one cannot do from the chteau, which is a sort of fortress of the gloomiest kind.

The de Certains had three sons and a daughter, and as was the custom at that time they added to their family name that of some estate. Thus the eldest son was given the name Canrobert: this eldest son was, at the time of which I write, Chevalier de St. Louis and a captain in the infantry regiment of Penthivre; the second son who was called de L'Isle was a lieutenant in the same regiment; the third son, who had the surname La Coste served, like my father, in the Royal Bodyguard; the daughter was called *Mlle*. Du Puy, and she was my mother.

My father became a close friend of M. Certain de La Coste, and it would have been difficult to do otherwise, for quite apart from the three months which they spent in quarters at Versailles during their period of duty, the journeys which they made together, twice a year, were bound to make a bond between them.

At that time public coaches were very few in number, dirty, uncomfortable, and travelled by very short stages; also it was considered not at all fashionable to ride in them. So, gentry who were old or in poor health travelled by carriage, while the young and officers in the armed forces went on horseback. There was an established custom among the Bodyguard, which today would seem most peculiar. As these gentlemen did only three months on duty, and as in consequence the corps was split into four almost equal sections, those of them who lived in Brittany, the Auvergne, Limousin and other parts of the country where there were good small horses had bought a number of these at a price not exceeding 100 francs, which included the saddle and bridle. On a fixed day all the Bodyguards from the same province, who were called to go and take up their duties, would meet, on horseback, at an agreed spot and the cheerful caravanserai would take the road for Versailles.

They made twelve to fifteen leagues each day, sure of finding every evening, at an agreed and reasonable price, a good lodging and a good supper at the inns previously arranged as stopping places. They went happily on their way, talking, singing, putting up with bad weather or heat as they did with accidents and laughing at the stories which all, in turn, had to tell as they rode along.

The group grew in size by the arrival of Bodyguards from the provinces through which they passed until, at last, the various parties arrived from all parts of France to enter Versailles on the day on which their leave expired, and, in consequence, at the moment of departure of those guards whom they had come to relieve. Then each of these latter bought one of the ponies brought by the new arrivals, for which they paid 100 francs, and forming fresh groups they took to the road for their paternal chteaux, where they turned the horses out to grass for nine months, until they were taken back to Versailles and handed over to other comrades-in-arms.

My father, then, was a close friend of M. Certain de La Coste, who shared the same quarters and belonged, like him, to the company de Noailles. On their return to the country they saw much of each other, and he made the acquaintance of *Mlle*. Du Puy. *Mlle*. Du Puy was pretty and high spirited, and although she would have little in the way of dowry, and although several rich matches were offered to my father, he preferred *Mlle*. Du Puy, and he married her in 1776.

We were four brothers: the eldest Adolphe, myself the second, Thodore the third and Flix the last. There was a gap of about two years between our ages.

I was very sturdy and suffered only some minor illnesses, but when I was about three, I had an accident which I can still remember.

Because I had a rather turned-up nose and a round face, my father called me "pussy-cat". It needed no more than this to give a small child the desire to imitate a cat; so it was my greatest pleasure to go about on all fours, mewing. I was also in the habit of going up to the second floor of the chteau to join my father in a library, where he spent the hottest hours of the day. When he heard the "miaow" of his little cat, he came and opened the door and gave me a picture-book to look at while he continued his reading. These little sessions gave me infinite pleasure. One day, however, my visit was not so well received as usual. My father, perhaps absorbed in his book, did not open the door for his little cat. In vain, I redoubled my "miaows" in the most appealing tone which I could produce. The door remained closed. Then I saw, at floor level, an opening called a cat-hole, which is present in all the chteaux of the Midi, at the bottom of the doors, to allow cats free access. This route seemed, naturally, to be for me: I put my head through, but that was as far as I could go. I then tried to withdraw my head, but my head was stuck and I could go neither forward nor back, but I was so much identified with my rôle as a cat that instead of speaking, to let my father know my predicament, I "miaowed" at the top of my voice, like a cat that is angry, and it appears that I did so in such a natural tone that my father thought that I was playing, but suddenly the "miaows" became weaker, and turned into crying and you may imagine my father's concern when he realised what had happened. It was only with great difficulty that I was freed and carried, half unconscious, to my mother, who thinking I was injured was much distressed.

A surgeon was sent for, who proceeded to bleed me, and the sight of my own blood and the crowd of all the inhabitants of the chteau, gathered about my mother and me, made such a vivid impression on my young imagination that the event has remained for ever fixed in my memory.

Chap. 2.

While my childhood was rolling by peacefully, the storm of revolution which had been growling in the distance, drew ever nearer, and it was not long before it broke. We were in 1789.

The assembly of the States General stirred up all manner of passions, destroyed the tranquillity enjoyed by the province in which we lived and introduced divisions into all families, particularly into ours; for my father, who for a long time had railed against the abuses to which France was subjected, accepted, in principle, the improvements which were mooted, without foreseeing the atrocities to which these changes were going to lead; while his three brothers-in-law and all his friends rejected any innovation. This gave rise to animated discussions, of which I understood nothing, but which distressed me because I saw my mother in tears as she tried to keep the peace between her brothers and her husband. For my part, although I did not understand what was going on, I naturally took sides with my father.

The Constituent Assembly had revoked all feudal rents. My father possessed some of these which his father had purchased. He was the first to conform to the law. The peasantry who had been waiting to make up their minds until my father gave them a lead, refused to continue paying these rents once they knew what he had done.

Shortly after this, France having been divided into departments, my father was named administrator for the Corrze and then a member of the Legislative Assembly.

My mother's three brothers, and nearly all the nobility of the county had hurriedly emigrated. War seemed to be imminent, so, to persuade all citizens to take up arms, and also, perhaps, to find out up to what point they could count on the populace, the government arranged for the rumour to be spread throughout all the communes of France, that the "Brigands" led by the migrs, were coming to destroy all the new institutions. The tocsin was rung by all the churches; everyone armed themselves with whatever they could lay hands upon; a National Guard was organised; the country turned into an armed camp while it waited for these imaginary "Brigands" who, in every commune, were said to be in the one next door. Nothing ever appeared, but the effect remained: France found herself in arms and had shown that she was prepared to defend herself.

We children were then alone in the country with our mother. This alert, which was called "The day of fear" surprised me and would probably have alarmed me, had I not seen my mother remain so calm. I have always thought that my father had discreetly warned her of what was about to happen.

All went well at first, without any excess on the part of the peasants, who, in our part of the country, retained much respect for the ancient families; but soon, stirred up by demagogues from the towns, the country-dwellers invaded the houses of the nobles, under and to seize the title deeds of feudal rents, which they burned in a big bonfire. From the height of our terrace, we saw these ruffians, torches in their hands, running towards the Chteau d'Estresse, from which all the men had emigrated and which was occupied only by women. These were my mother's best friends, and so she was greatly upset by this spectacle. Her anxiety was redoubled by the arrival of her own aged mother, who had been driven out of her chteau, which was declared national property because of the emigration of her three sons...!

Up until then, my father's property had been respected; largely because his patriotism was known, and because, to give further proof of it, he had taken service in the army of the Pyrénées as captain in the Chasseurs des Montagnes, at the end of his term in the legislative assembly. But the revolutionary torrent swept over everyone; the house at St. Cr, which my father had bought ten years before, was confiscated and declared national property because the deed of sale had been signed privately and the seller had emigrated before ratifying the deal before a notary. My mother was given a few days to remove her linen, then the house was put up for auction and was bought by the president of the district who had himself arranged for its confiscation!

At last, the peasants, stirred up by some agitators from Beaulieu, came in a body to my father's chteau and insisted, though with some politeness, that they had to burn the deeds of feudal rents which we still had, and make sure that migrs were not concealed in the chteau.

My mother received them with fortitude, handed over the deeds and pointed out to them that, knowing her brothers to be sensible people, they should not suppose that they would emigrate only then to come back to France and hide in her chteau.

They accepted the correctness of this line of reasoning, ate and drank and having burned the deeds in the centre of the courtyard, they left without doing any further damage, shouting "Long live France and citizen Marbot!" And charging my mother to write to him to say that they liked him very much and that his family was quite safe among them.

In spite of this assurance, my mother felt that her position as the sister of migrs might expose her to a great deal of unpleasantness from which even her position as the wife of a defender of the country would not protect her. She decided to go away for the time being. She told me later that she took this step because she was convinced that the revolutionary storm would last only for some months. There were many people who thought this!

My grandmother had had seven brothers, all of whom, as was usual in the Verdal family had been soldiers and knights of St. Louis. One of them, a former battalion commander in the infantry regiment of Penthivre, had married, on retirement, the rich widow of counsellor of the parliament of Rennes. My mother decided to go and stay with her and was counting on taking me with her, when I was smitten by a number of large and very painful boils. It was impossible to travel with a child of eight in such a state, and my mother was in great perplexity. She was extricated by a worthy lady, *Mlle.* Mongalvi, who was much devoted to her and whose memory will always be dear to me. *Mlle.* Mongalvi lived at Turenne and ran boarding establishment for young ladies of which my mother had been one of the first

12

occupants. She offered to take me into her house for the few months of my mother's absence. My father's agreement having been obtained, I left and was installed there. "What!" you may say, "A boy amongst young ladies?" Well yes, but do not forget that I was a quiet, peaceable, obedient child, and I was only eight years old.

The boarders who stayed with *Mlle.* Mongalvi, where my mother had once been one of them, were young persons of some sixteen to twenty years of age; the youngest being at least fourteen, and were sensible enough to let me mingle with them.

On my arrival, all this little feminine flock gathered about me and received me with such cries of pleasure and warm caresses that, from the first instant, I thought myself lucky to have made this trip. I figured that it would not last long and I believe that, secretly, I even regretted that I would have only a short time to spend with these nice young ladies, who did everything to please me and argued as to who was to hold my hand.

However, my mother left and went to stay with my uncle. Events moved forward rapidly. The terror bathed France in blood. Civil war broke, out in the Vende and in Brittany. Travel there became absolutely impossible, so that my mother, who had thought to spend two or three months at Rennes, found herself stuck there for several years.

My father continued on active service in the Pyrénées and in Spain, where his ability and courage had raised him to the rank of divisional general; while I, having gone as a boarder for a few months, stayed for some four years, which were for me years of much happiness, clouded only, from time to time, by the memory of my parents; but the good Mlles. Mongalvi and their boarders would then redouble their kindness, to dispel those thoughts which now and then saddened me. I was spoiled beyond belief by the mistresses and the boarders; I had only to wish for something to obtain it. There was nothing too good or too fine for me. My health recovered completely. I was clean and fresh, so they vied with one another to cuddle me. During recreation, which took place in a vast enclosure, where there was a fine garden, with paddocks, vines and arbours, the young ladies would crown me and garland me with flowers, then placing me on a little litter covered with roses, they would take it in turns to carry me while they sang. At other times I would play prisoners base with them, having the privilege of always catching but never being caught. They would read stories to me and sing songs. They competed to do something for me.

I recall, that on hearing of the horrible execution of Louis XVI, *Mlle.* Mongalvi had all the boarders on their knees, to recite prayers for the repose of the soul of the unfortunate king. The indiscretion of any one of us could have brought down disaster on her head, but all the pupils were of an age to understand, and I felt that it was something I should not talk about; so no one knew anything about it. I stayed in this pleasant retreat until November 1793.

Chap. 3.

When I was eleven and a half years old, my father was given command of a camp which was set up at Toulouse. He took advantage of a few days leave to come and see me and to arrange his affairs, which he had not been able to do for several years. He came to Turenne, to the house of one of his friends, and hurried to my lodging. He was in the uniform of a general officer, with a big sabre, his hair cut short and unpowdered and sporting an enormous moustache, which was in remarkable contrast to the costume in which I was used to seeing him when we lived peacefully at Larivire.

I have said that my father, in spite of his stern masculine looks, was a kind man, and particularly toward children, whom he adored. I saw him again with the keenest transports of delight, and he overwhelmed me with caresses. He stayed for several days at Turenne; he warmly thanked the good mesdames Mongalvi for the truly maternal care they had taken of me; but when he asked me a few questions, it was easy for him to see that though I had a good knowledge of prayers and litanies and lots of hymns, my remaining education was limited to some notions of history, geography, and spelling. He considered also, that, being now in my twelfth year, it was not possible to leave me in a boarding establishment for young ladies, and that it was time to give me an education which was more masculine and more extensive. He had resolved therefore, to take me with him to Toulouse, to where he had also brought Adolphe, and to place us both in the military college of Sorze, the sole great establishment of this kind which the revolutionary turmoil had left standing.

I left, after bidding a tender farewell to my young friends. We headed for Cressensac, where we were joined by Captain Gault, my father's aide-de-camp. While the coach was being got ready, Spire, my father's old servant, who knew that his master intended to travel day and night, made up packages of food.

At this moment a new spectacle was presented to me: a mobile column, composed of gendarmes, national guards and volunteers, entered the town of Cressensac with a band playing at its head. I had never seen anything like it, and it seemed to me quite superb, but I was unable to understand why, in the midst of all these soldiers, there was a dozen coaches filled with old men, women and children, all of whom looked extremely sad. This sight infuriated my father. He drew back from the window and, striding about with his aide-de-camp, whom he could trust, I heard him burst out, "These miserable members of the convention have ruined the revolution which could have done so much good. There you see yet more innocent people who are being thrown into gaol because they are landowners or are related to migrs; it is disgusting!"

Why, you may ask, did my father continue to serve a government which he despised? It was because he thought that to confront the enemies of France was honourable, but did not mean that the military condoned the atrocities which the convention committed in the interior of the country.

What my father had said, had interested me in the people in the coaches. I gathered that they had been, that morning, seized from their chteaux and were being led away to the prisons of Souilhac. They were old men, women and children, and I was wondering to myself how these frail people could present any danger to the country, when I heard several of the children asking for food. One lady begged a national guard to let her get out to go and buy something to eat. He refused her, rudely, and when the lady produced an "assignat" and pleaded with him to go and buy some bread, he replied, "Do you take me for one of your former lackeys?" This brutality angered me. I had noticed that Spire had placed in the pockets of the coach, a number of bread-rolls in the centre of which was a sausage; I took two of these rolls, and drawing near to the coach holding the child prisoners, I threw them in, when the guards were not looking. The mothers and the children made signs to me of such gratitude that I resolved to give food to all the other prisoners, and piece by piece, I gave them all the provisions which Spire had made for the two days journey to Toulouse, which we were about to make. We left, at last, without Spire having any suspicion of the distribution which I had just made. The little prisoners blew me kisses and their parents waved to me; but no sooner were we some hundred paces from the post-house than my father, who had been in haste to get away from a spectacle which distressed him, and had not wished to eat at the inn, felt hungry, and asked for the provisions. Spire pointed to the pockets in which he had placed them. My father and M. Gault rummaged through all the interior of the coach, but found nothing. My father grew angry with Spire, who from the height of his seat, swore by all the saints that he had stuffed the coach with food for two days. I was somewhat embarrassed; however, I did not want poor Spire to be blamed any longer, so I admitted what I had done. I expected to be scolded for acting without authority, but my father put his arm round me in the most affectionate manner, and many years after he still spoke with pleasure of my conduct on this occasion.

From Cressensac to Toulouse the road was full of volunteers, going to join the army of the Pyrénées, and making the air ring with patriotic songs. I was charmed by this bustling spectacle and would have been happy had it not been for my physical suffering. I had never made a long journey by coach before, and I was sea-sick throughout the trip, which decided my father to stop every night to allow me some repose. I arrived at Toulouse feeling very tired, but the sight of my brother, from whom I had been parted for four or five years, gave me so much joy that I very soon recovered.

My father, with the rank of divisional general, commanding the camp situated at Miral, close to Toulouse, was entitled to a billet, and the municipality had assigned to him the fine town house of Ressguier, whose owner had emigrated. Madame de Ressguier and her son had retreated to the most distant rooms, and my father gave orders that the strictest regard was to be given to their unhappy position.

My father's house was much frequented. Every day there were visitors, and he had a great deal of expense, for although at that time a divisional general received eighteen rations of all kinds, and his aides-de-camp a similar amount, it was not enough. He had to buy a host of things and as the state gave to a general officer what it gave to a sous-lieutenant, that is eight francs a month in cash, the rest being made up in assignats, the value of which diminished daily, and as my father was very generous, entertained many of the officers from the camp, had numerous domestic servants (at that time called servitors), had eighteen horses, a coach, a box at the theatre *etc*...He spent the savings which he had accumulated at Larivire, and it was from the time of his re-entry into military service that the decline of his fortune began.

Although the "Terror" was now at its height and class distinction was greatly weakened in France, from whence all good manners seemed to have removed themselves forever, my father knew so well how to impose them on the many officers who came to his quarters, that the most perfect politeness ruled in his salon and at his table.

Among the officers employed at the camp, my father had taken a great liking to two, who were invited more often than the others. One was named Augereau and was the adjutant-general, that is to say colonel of the general staff, the other was Lannes, a lieutenant of Grenadiers, in a battalion of volunteers from the department of Gers.

They became Marshals of the Empire and I have been aide-de-camp to both of them.

At this period Augereau, after escaping from the prison of the Inquisition at Lisbon, had come to fight in the Vende, where he was noticed for his courage and his quality of leadership. He was an excellent tactician, a skill which he had learned in Prussia, where he had served for a considerable time in the Foot-guards of Frederick the Great; hence his nick-name of "The Big Prussian." He had an irreproachable military turn-out, spick and span, curled and powdered, with a long pig-tail, big, highly polished riding boots and withal, a very martial bearing. This smart appearance was the more remarkable because, at this time it was not something on which the French army could pride itself, being almost entirely made up of volunteers not used to wearing uniform and very careless of their grooming. However nobody made fun of Augereau about this, for he was known to be a brave and accomplished duelist, who had given even the celebrated Saint-George, the finest swordsman in France, a run for his money.

I have said that Augereau was a good tactician; because of this, my father had appointed him to direct the training of the battalions of new leves, of which the division was largely composed. These men came from Limousin, Auvergne, the Basque country, Quercy, Gers and Languedoc. Augereau trained them well, and in so doing he was unaware that he was laying the foundations of his own future fame, for these troops, which my father then commanded, formed later the famous Augereau division which did such fine things in the Pyrénées and in Italy.

Augereau came almost daily to my father's house, and seeing that he was appreciated, he devoted to him a friendship which never wavered and of which I felt the benefit after the death of my mother.

As for Lieutenant Lannes, he was a very lively young Gascon, intelligent and cheerful, without education or training but anxious to learn at a time when no one else was. He became a very good instructor, and since he was very vain, he accepted with the greatest delight the praises which my father lavished on him, and which he deserved. By way of recompense, he spoiled, as much as he could, his general's children.

One fine morning, my father received the order to strike his camp at Miral and to lead his division to join the army corps of General Dugommier, which was laying siege to Toulon, which the English had captured in a surprise attack. My father then said to me that it was not in a school for young ladies that I would learn what I needed to know; that I needed more serious studies and in consequence he was taking me, the next day, to the military college of Sorze, where he had already arranged a place for me and my brother. I was thunderstruck! Never to go back to my friends with the Mesdames Mongalvi? That seemed impossible!

The road was covered with troops and guns, which my father passed in review at Castelnaudary. This spectacle, which a few days earlier would have delighted me, now failed to lessen the anxiety which I felt about the teachers in whose presence I was about to find myself.

We stayed overnight at Castelnaudary, where my father learned of the evacuation of Toulon by the English (18th Dec 1793), and was ordered to go with his division, to the eastern Pyrénées. Whereupon he decided to deposit us, the very next day, at Sorze, to stay there for a few hours only, and to set off immediately for Perpignon.

On leaving Castelnaudary, my father ordered the coach to stop at a famous tree under which the Constable Montmorency had been taken prisoner by the troops of Louis XIII, following the defeat of the supporters of Gaston d'Orlans, who had rebelled against his brother. He chatted about this event with his aides-de-camp, and my brother— who was already well informed—took part in the conversation. As for me, I had only the vaguest notions of the general history of France and knew nothing of the details. It was the first time I had heard of the battle of Castelnaudary, of Gaston, of his revolt and of the capture and execution of the Constable de Montmorency. I realised that my father did not ask me any question on the subject because he was quite certain that I would be unable to reply. This made me feel ashamed, and I concluded that my father was right in taking me to the college to be educated. My regrets then changed into a resolution to learn all that I needed to know.

Nevertheless, my heart sank at the sight of the high sombre walls of the cloister in which I was to be enclosed. I was eleven years and four months old when I entered this establishment.

Chap. 4.

I shall now give you a brief history of the college of Sorze, as I had it from Dom Abal, a former vice principal, whom I saw often in Paris during the Empire.

When, under Louis XV, it was resolved to clear the Jesuits out of France, their defenders claimed that they alone knew how to educate children. The Benedictines, sworn enemies of the Jesuits, wished to prove that this was not so; but as it did not suit them, although they were studious and learned, to turn themselves into schoolmasters, they selected four of their houses to be turned into colleges, among which was Sorze. There they placed those members of the order who had the most aptitude for teaching, and who could, after working for several years, retire to other monasteries of the order. The new colleges prospered, Sorze in particular stood out, and the crowd of pupils, who hurried there from all parts, made a larger number of teachers necessary. The Benedictines attracted there many learned laymen, who established themselves, with their families, in the little town in which the monastery was situated. The children of these lay teachers, who attended the college free as day pupils, formed, later, a nursery of masters of all the arts and sciences. Eventually the ability to give lessons at a very reasonable cost led to the setting up of several boarding houses for young ladies, and the little town became remarkable in that its citizens, even the simple merchants, had an extended education and practised all the fine arts. A crowd of foreigners, principally English, Spanish and American, came to stay there, in order to be near their sons and daughters during their education.

The Benedictine order was, in general, made up of very easy-going men; they mixed with the world and entertained often, so they were well liked; something that was very useful to those at Sorze when the revolution broke out.

The Principal at that time was Dom Despaulx, a man of the highest integrity, but who, being unwilling to subscribe to the "civic oath" then exacted from the clergy, retired and spent several years in retreat, from where he was later called by the Emperor to fill one of the highest positions in the university.

All the other Benedictines at Sorze took the oath: Dom Ferlus became Principal and Dom Abal Vice-Principal, and the college, in spite of the revolutionary upheavals, continued to operate, following the excellent start which it had been given by Dom Despaulx.

Later, however, a law having been passed requiring the secularising of the monks and the sale of their property, the days of the college seemed numbered; but many of the most important men in the country had been educated there, and they wanted it to be there for their children; the inhabitants of the town, even the labourers and peasants, respected the good fathers and realised that the destruction of the college would result in the ruin of the area. So an arrangement was made whereby Dom Ferlus would become the owner of the college and the immense property which belonged to it. Nobody attended the auction, and the Principal became, at a very modest price, the owner of the huge monastery and the land which it owned. The administrators of the department gave him plenty of time to pay. Everyone lent him assignats which he repaid with some loads of wood; the vast farms of the estate furnished food for the college and, lacking money, Dom Ferlus paid the external teachers in provisions, which suited them very well at a time when famine was rife in France.

18

On the death of Dom Ferlus, the college passed into the hands of his brother Raymond Ferlus, a former Oration, now married, a third-rate poet and man of little capacity. The college went into decline when the restoration of 1814 allowed back the Jesuits, who were determined to wreak revenge on the Benedictines by destroying the edifice which the latter had erected on the ruins of their order.

The university took sides with the Jesuits. M. Raymond Ferlus handed over the college to his son-in-law, M. Bernard, a former artillery officer who had been one of my contempories. He knew nothing about running such an establishment, and, besides that, a host of other good colleges sprang up as rivals, and Sorze, losing its importance from day to day, became one of the most mediocre institutions of learning.

I return now to the time when I was at Sorze. I have told you how Dom Ferlus saved the college from ruin, and how, upheld by the care of this enlightened man, it was the only great establishment of its kind left standing by the revolution. The monks adopted lay clothing and the appellation "Citizen" replaced that of "Dom." Apart from that, nothing essential was changed in the college and it continued to exist peacefully in a corner of France, while the country was most cruelly being torn to pieces. I say that nothing essential had changed because the studies followed their usual course, and there was no breakdown of order, but it was impossible that the feverish agitation which reigned outside should not be felt in the college. I will say also that Dom Ferlus, with diplomatic skill, presented the appearance of approving of what he could not prevent. The walls therefore were covered with Republican slogans. It was forbidden to use the word "Monsieur". The pupils went to the dining hall or on walks, singing the Marseillaise or other Republican hymns; and as they heard continually of the achievements of our armies, in which some of the older pupils were even enrolled as volunteers, and as they were brought up in a military atmosphere, (since, even before the revolution, Sorze was a military college, where one learned drill, horse-riding, fortification, and so on), all this youth had, for some time, adopted a warrior-like stance and spirit which had led to a slackening of good manners. Added to which the uniform contributed greatly to give them a very strange aspect. The scholars wore big shoes, which were cleaned only every ten days, stockings of grey thread, plain brown trousers and jacket, no waistcoat, shirts undone, and covered with stains of ink and red pencil, no tie, nothing on the head, the hair in a pig-tail, often undone, and the hands....! Like those of a coal-heaver.

Imagine me, clean, polished, dressed in clothes of fine cloth, neat and tidy, thrown into the midst of seven hundred urchins, got up as imps, and who, on hearing a shout of "Here are some new ones!" left their games and came, in a mob to gather round us, staring as if we were strange animals.

My father embraced us and left...! I was in a state of utter despair! Here I was, alone, alone for the first time in my life, my brother being in the upper school while I was in the lower. We were in the middle of winter. It was very cold, but according to school rules, the pupils were never allowed a fire!

Nevertheless, the pupils at Sorze were well fed, especially for that time; for in spite of the famine which was sweeping France, the good administration of Dom Ferlus provided an abundance of food. The everyday fare was certainly all that could be desired for school-children. However the supper seemed to me to be most niggardly, and the sight of the dishes put before me disgusted me: but had I been offered ortolans, I would not have been tempted, my heart was so full. The meal finished as it had begun, with a patriotic song. We knelt down at the couplet of the Marseillaise which begins "Amour sacr de la patrie"...Then we filed out, as we had come in, to the sound of a drum, and we went to the dormitories.

The pupils of the upper school had each his own room, in which he was shut in for the night; those of the lower school slept four to a room, of which each angle contained a bed. I was put with Guiraud, Romestan and Lagarde, who were my companions at table, and almost as new as I was. I was quite happy with this. They had seemed to me to be nice children, which, in fact, they were. But I was taken aback when I saw the smallness of my bed, the thinness of the mattress, and what displeased me most, the iron bed-stead. I had never seen anything like it. However everything was very clean, and in spite of my dismay I slept soundly, worn out by the shocks to my system which I had suffered on this fateful day.

The next morning, the drum beat reveille, makinga horrible noise in the dormitories, which I thought was quite atrocious; but how do you think I felt when I saw that, while I was asleep, someone had removed my beautiful clothes, my fine stockings and my pretty shoes, and had replaced them by the coarse garments and heavy footwear of the school? I wept with rage.

Having told you of the first impressions which I experienced on my entry into the college, I shall spare you the recital of all the torments to which I was exposed during the next six months. I had been too pampered by the mesdames Mongalvi not to suffer mentally and physically in my new position. I became very depressed, and had my constitution been less robust, I should have become ill. This period was one of the most unhappy in my life. In the long run, however, work and familiarity enabled me to cope with the situation. I was very fond of the lessons in French literature, in geography, and above all, in history, and I made progress in these subjects. I became passable at Latin and mathematics and at horsemanship and fencing. I was an expert at fire-arms drill and took much pleasure in the manoeuvres of the school battalion which was commanded by a retired captain.

At the time when I entered the college, the convention was imposing its blood-stained sceptre over France. Representatives of the people, on various missions, infested the provinces, and almost all of these who were of any importance in the Midi came to visit Sorze, whose title of "Military Academy" sounded pleasing to their ears.

Citizen Ferlus had a particular talent for persuading them that they must maintain an establishment devoted to educating a numerous youth, "The hope of the country". So he obtained all that he wanted. Often they would send us great bundles of brushwood, destined to supply the army, our Principal having persuaded them that we were a part of it, and were, in effect, its nursery.

These Representatives were received and fted like Sovereigns. On their arrival, all the pupils were dressed in their military uniforms; the battalion was paraded before them; a guard was mounted at every gate as if in a military barracks. Little tableaux were enacted which exuded the purest patriotism; one sang national hymns, and when they visited the classes, particularly those of history, an occasion was always found to produce some tirade on the excellence of Republican government and the patriotic virtues which derived from it. I can remember, in this regard, an occasion when Representative Chabot, a former Capuchin, questioned me on Roman history. He asked me what I thought of Coriolanus, who finding himself wronged by his fellow citizens, forgetful of his former services, withdrew to the country of the Volscians, sworn enemies of the Romans. Dom Ferlus and the teachers feared greatly that I might approve of the Roman's conduct, but I blamed him, saying that a good citizen must never bear arms against his country, nor dream of any vengeance against her, no matter how justified his discontent. The representative was so pleased with my answer that he patted me on the back, and complemented the head of the college and the teachers on the sound principles which they inculcated in their pupils!

This little success did not diminish the dislike I had for these representatives. The actions of the convention filled me with horror. Young as I was, I had, already, enough sense to realise that it was not necessary to wallow in French blood in order to save the country, and that the guillotinades and massacres were appalling crimes.

I shall not discuss here the system of oppression which ruled, then, in our unhappy country; this is a matter of history; but I may say that however strong the colours used to paint the horrors of which these terrorists were capable, the picture will be less lurid than the reality. Perhaps the most surprising thing is the stupidity of the masses, who allowed themselves to be dominated by men, the greater part of whom lacked any ability: for whatever may have been said, almost all the members of the convention were of more than ordinary mediocrity and their boasted unanimity arose from the fear they had of one another, since in their anxiety to avoid being guillotined themselves, they agreed with anything which the ringleaders proposed.

I saw, during my exile in 1815, many members of the convention who like me were forced to leave France. They were completely lacking in back-bone, and assured me that they voted for the death of Louis XVI and a host of odious decrees solely to save their own skins. The memory of these times has convinced me that the worst form of government is that by the masses.

Chap. 5.

I reached the age of sixteen in August 1798. Six months later, towards the end of February, I left the college of Sorze.

21

My father had a friend named M. Dorignac, who offered to take me with him to the capital. It took us eight days to reach Paris, where we arrived in March 1799, on the day when the Odon theatre was burned down for the first time. The flames were visible far off on the Orleans road, and I thought, in my simplicity, that the light came from furnaces operating in the city. My father, at that time, occupied a fine mansion in the Faubourg-St-Honor road, number 87, on the corner with the little Rue Vert. I arrived there at dinner time: all the family were gathered there. It would be impossible for me to describe the joy which I felt at seeing them all together! This was one of the happiest days of my life!

We were now in the spring of 1799. The Republic still existed, and the government was now composed of the Directorate of five members, and two chambers, one of which was called the Council of Elders, and the other the Council of Five Hundred

My father entertained many members of society. There I made the acquaintance of his intimate friend, General Bernadotte, and some of the outstanding men of the period, such as Joseph and Lucien Bonaparte, and also Napper-Tandy, the Irish leader, who had taken refuge in France. At my mother's house I frequently saw Madame Bonaparte and sometimes Madame De Stal, already celebrated for her literary works.

I had been in Paris for only about a month, when the term of the legislature expired. It was necessary to hold new elections. My father, fed up with the constant wrangling of political life, and regretting that he was not taking any part in the army's achievements, declared that he would no longer accept nomination as a deputy, and that he wished to return to active service. Events turned out in his favour. On the assembly of the new Chambers there was a change of minister. General Bernadotte became minister for war. He had promised my father that he would send him to the army of the Rhine, and my father was about to set off for Mainz, when the directory, learning of the defeat suffered by the army of Italy, commanded by Scherer, appointed as his successor, General Joubert, who commanded the 17th division, (now the 1st,) in Paris.

This post having now become vacant, the directory, realising that its great political importance required that it should be filled by someone of capacity and determination, instructed the minister for war to offer it to my father. My father who had resigned from the legislature only to resume active service, turned the offer down; but on Bernadotte showing him the letter of appointment, already signed, and saying that as a friend, he begged him to accept, and as a minister, he ordered him, my father gave in, and the next day he went to install himself in the headquarters of the Paris division, situated, at that time in the Quai Voltaire, at the corner of the Rue de Saint-Pres, and which has since been demolished. My father took as his chief of staff his old friend Col. Mnard. I was delighted by all the military suite with which my father was surrounded. His headquarters were never empty of officers of all ranks. A squadron of cavalry, a battalion of infantry and six field-guns were stationed before his portals, and one saw a crowd of orderlies coming and going.

This seemed to me much more entertaining than the exercises and translations of Sorze.

France, and in particular Paris, were, at this time, in a state of much agitation. We were on the brink of catastrophe. The Russians, commanded by the celebrated Souwaroff, had just entered Italy, where our army had suffered a major defeat at Novi, where General Joubert had been killed. The victor, Souwaroff, was heading for our army of Switzerland, commanded by Massna.

We had few troops on the Rhine. The peace conference begun at Rastadt had broken down and our ambassadors had been assassinated; now all Germany was arming once more against us, and the Directory, fallen into disfavour, had neither troops nor the money to raise them. In order to procure funds it decreed a forced loan, which had the effect of turning everyone against it. All hopes were pinned on Massna's ability to stop the Russians and prevent them from entering France. The directory, impatient, sent him courier after courier, ordering him to join battle; but this latter-day Fabius, unwilling to risk the safety of his country, was waiting for some false move, on the part of his impetuous adversary, to give him the opportunity for victory.

At this point, I shall relate an anecdote which demonstrates on how fine a thread sometimes hangs the destiny of states and the reputation of generals. The directory, exasperated to see that Massna did not obey the repeated commands to engage in battle, resolved to relieve him of his post; but, as it was feared that this general would take no notice of the order and simply stuff it in his pocket, if it was sent by an ordinary courier, the minister for war was ordered to send a staff-officer, charged to deliver, publicly, to Massna his demotion, and to give to his chief of staff, Chrin, the official letter which would confirm him as commander-in-chief of the army.

When the minister told my father, in confidence, about these plans, my father disapproved, saying that it would be dangerous, on the eve of a decisive action, to deprive the army of Switzerland of a general in whom it had confidence, and give the command to a general who was more used to administration than the direction of troops in the field. In addition, the position of the armies might change; and he thought it essential that the mission was given to a man with enough wisdom to assess the state of affairs, and who would not hand Massna his dismissal on the eve of, or in the middle of a battle.

My father, eventually persuaded the minister to give the task to to see if the suppliers had delivered the number of horses stipulated in their contract, would proceed to Switzerland with the authority to retain or to hand out the order for the dismissal of Massna, and the installing of general Chrin, according to the circumstances which might lead him to judge whether this would be useful or dangerous. This was an enormous responsibility to confide to the prudence of a simple captain, but M. Gault fully justified the faith my father had in him.

Arriving at the headquarters of the army of Switzerland five days before the battle of Zurich, he found the troops so full of confidence in Massna, and Massna himself so calm and determined, that he had no doubts of success, and, maintaining the deepest silence about his secret powers, he took part in the battle of Zurich and then returned to Paris, without Massna suspecting that this modest captain had in his hands the authority which could have deprived him of the glory of one of the finest victories of the century.

Had Massna been rashly dismissed, this would probably have led to the defeat of General Chrin and the invasion of France by the Russians, followed by the Germans, and perhaps finally to the overrunning of Europe. General Chrin was killed at Zurich, without being aware of the intentions of the government towards him.

The victory of Zurich, although, it prevented the advance of the enemy into the country, gave the Directory only a momentary respite. The government was everywhere crumbling; no one had confidence in it. The treasury was bankrupt; the Vende and Brittany were in open revolt; the interior stripped of troops; the Midi in turmoil; the chamber of deputies squabbling among themselves, and with the executive. In short, the state was on the verge of disaster.

Everyone in politics recognised that a major change was necessary and inevitable; but although all agreed on this point, opinions differed as to the remedy to be employed. The old Republicans, who upheld the constitution of year III, then still in force, believed that it would be sufficient to change several members of the Directory. Two of them were removed and replaced by *mm*. Gohier and Moulins; but this was the feeblest of palliatives for the calamities which afflicted the country, and it continued to be shaken by anarchy.

It was then that several members of the Directory, amongst whom was the well-known Sieys, thought, as did many of the deputies and the great majority of the public, that to save France it was necessary to put the reins of government in the hands of someone resolute and already distinguished by services given to the state. It was realised, also, that this would have to be a soldier who had great influence in the army, and who was able, by re-arousing national enthusiasm, to lead our banners to victory and chase away the foreigners who were preparing to cross our frontiers.

To speak like this was to point to General Bonaparte, but at this moment he was in Egypt, and the need was pressing. Joubert had been killed in Italy. Messna, though famous for several victories, was an excellent general at the head of an army in the field, but in no way a politician. Bernadotte did not seem to have the capacity or the wisdom to repair the country's fortunes. The eyes of the reformers then turned to General Moreau; although the weakness of his character and his indecisive conduct on the 18th Fructidor raised some fears about his ability to govern. It is certain, however, that lacking an alternative, he was asked to head the party which intended to overthrow the Directory, and was offered the title of President or Consul. Moreau, a good fighting soldier, lacked political courage, and perhaps doubted his own ability to cope with affairs in such a mess as were those of France. Also he was self-centered and indolent and worried little about the future of the country, preferring the repose of private life to the agitation of politics. He refused the offer and retired to his estate of Grosbois, to devote himself to hunting, of which he was passionately fond.

Abandoned by the man of their choice, Sieys and those with him, who wished to change the form of the government, not feeling themselves to be sufficiently strong or popular to achieve their aim without the support of a general whose name would rally the army to their side, were forced to turn their thoughts to General Bonaparte. The leader of this enterprise, Sieys, flattered himself that, having been placed in power, Bonaparte would busy himself with the management and re-organising of the army, and leave to him the conduct of the government, of which he would be the master and Bonaparte but the nominal head. Events showed how badly he was mistaken.

Imbued with this notion, Sieys, through the intermission of the Corsican deputy, Salicetti, sent a reliable secret agent to Egypt, to inform General Bonaparte of the troubled state of France, and propose to him that he should come back and place himself at the head of the government. Having no doubt that Bonaparte would accept readily and return promptly to Europe, Sieys put everything in motion to assure the execution of the coup d'tat which he was planning.

It was easy for him to convince his fellow director, Roger-Duclos, that their power was slipping away daily, and that the country being on the brink of complete disorganisation, the public welfare, and their personal interests, demanded that they should take part in the establishment of a strong government, in which they would contrive to place themselves in a less precarious and more advantageous position.

Roger-Duclos promised his agreement to the proposed changes; but the other three directors, Barras, Gohier and Moulins were unwilling to give up their positions, so Sieys and the leaders of his party resolved to go over their heads, and to sacrifice them after the event.

However, it would be difficult, not to say dangerous, even with the presence of General Bonaparte, to overthrow the Directorate, change the constitution and establish a new government, without the support of the army, and, above all, that of the division which occupied Paris. To be able to rely on this, it was necessary to be sure of the co-operation of the minister for war and of the general commanding the 17th division.

President Sieys then sought to win over Bernadotte and my father, by having them sounded out by several deputies who were their friends and also supporters of Sieys's plans. I have learned since that my father replied to the vague overtures which were put to him on behalf of the crafty Sieys by saying that he agreed that the country's misfortunes demanded a drastic remedy, but that, having sworn to maintain the constitution of year III, he would not use the authority he had over his troops to lead them to its overthrow. He then went to Sieys and handed in his resignation as commander of the Paris division, and requested a posting to a division on active service. Sieys hastened to fall in with his wishes, being only too glad to get rid of a man whose devotion to what he saw as his duty, might abort the projected coup. The minister, Bernadotte followed my father's example, and was replaced by Dubois-Crance.

President Sieys was, for some days, at a loss to find a successor to my father. In the end, he gave the command to general Lefebvre, who, having recently been wounded in the army of the Rhine, was at that moment in the capital. Lefebvre was a former sergeant in the Guards, a brave soldier, a good, workmanlike general, provided that he was closely supervised, but credulous in the extreme, with no understanding of the political situation in France. So, by careful use of the words "Glory," "Motherland," and " Victory, " One could be sure of making him do whatever one wished. This was just the sort of commander that Sieys was looking for. He did not even take the trouble to win him over, or to warn him of what was about to happen, so sure was he that on the day Lefebvre would not resist the influence of General Bonaparte, and the cajoleries of the president of the directorate.

He had made an accurate assessment of Lefebvre, for on the 18th Brumaire, he placed himself and all his troops under the command of General Bonaparte, to march against the Directorate and the Councillors, to throw down the established government and create the Consulate. This action made him, later, one of the Emperor's greatest favourites. He was made a marshal, Duke of Danzig and senator and was showered with riches.

I have rapidly outlined these events, because they explain some of the reasons which led my father to Italy: a move which had such a profound effect on his destiny and mine.

Chap. 6.

After handing over his command to General Lefebvre, my father returned to his house in the Faubourg St. Honor and busied himself with preparations for his departure to Italy.

A man's destiny is often influenced by the smallest of events. My father and mother were very friendly with M. Barairon, the director of registration, and one day, when they were going to dine with him, they took me along. The talk was of my father's coming departure, and the progress of my two younger brothers. At last, M. Barairon asked, "And Marcellin, what are you going to make of him?" "A sailor," replied my father, "Captain Sibille has agreed to take him with him to Toulon." Then the good *Mme*. Barairon, towards whom I have always felt the warmest gratitude, observed to my father that the French navy was in complete disarray, that the poor state of the country's finances would not allow its rapid refurbishment, and, furthermore, its inferiority vis—vis the English navy was such that it would spend most of its time in harbour. She said that she could not think why he, a divisional general, would put his son into the navy, instead of placing him in a regiment, where the name and services of his father would make him welcome. She ended by saying, "Take him to Italy, sooner than send him to die of boredom, in a vessel shut up in Toulon harbour."

My father, who had been briefly enticed by Capt. Sibille's proposition, was too intelligent not to appreciate *Mme.* Barairon's reasoning. "Well then," he asked me, "Do you want to come to Italy with me and serve in the army?" I put my arms round him and accepted, with a joy which my mother shared, for she had not been in favour of my father's first idea.

As, at that time, there was no military academy, and one could join the army only as a private soldier, my father took me right away to the municipality of the first arrondissment, in the Place Beauvau, and had me enlisted in the 1st Hussars, (formerly the Bercheny), who were part of the division which he was going to command in Italy. It was September the 3rd, 1799.

My father took me to a tailor, who had the job of making official army uniforms, and ordered for me a complete outfit for a Hussar of the 1st. As well as all the arms and equipment.

```
There I was!....A soldier!.....And was I not happy?  But
my
happiness was somewhat lessened when I reflected that
this was going
to upset my brother Adolphe, two years older than me,
and still stuck
in college.  I then had the idea that I would not tell
Adolphe about
my enlistment without telling him, at the same time,
that I wanted to
spend with him the period which would have to pass
before my
departure.  I then asked my father if he would allow me
to be
installed close to Adolphe, at Sainte-Barbe, until the
day when we
would take the road for Italy.  My father understood the
reason for my
asking, and thought well of me for it.  He took me, the
next day to
stay with a M. Lanneau.
```

Can you imagine my arrival at college?...It was a recreation period. All games stopped. All the pupils, big and small, surrounded me. They vied with each other to touch part of my equipment....In short, the Hussar was a complete success!

The day of the departure arrived....I said farewell to my mother and my three brothers with the greatest sadness, in spite of the pleasure I felt on starting a military career.

Chap. 7.

After my father had accepted a command in Italy, a division became vacant in the army of the Rhine, which he would have preferred; but an inescapable fate drew him towards the country where he would find his grave.

One of his compatriots, and a personal friend, M. Lachze, whom I might call his evil genius, had for a long time been French consul at Leghorn and Genoa, where he had business interests. This wretched man, in order to lure my father to Italy, was forever painting the most exaggerated picture of the country's beauties, and pointing out the credit which might be gained by dealing successfully with the difficult situation in the army there, whereas there would be little opportunity to acquire distinction in the army of the Rhine, where all was well. My father was swayed by this specious reasoning, and believing that there was more merit in going to the more dangerous post, he persisted in his intention of going to Italy, in spite of the objections of my mother, who had a secret presentiment which made her wish for my father to go to the Rhine. This presentiment was not false. She never saw her husband again!

To his present aide-de-camp, Captain Gault, my father now added Maintenon family and had some ability and some education, which he very rarely employed; for in a stupid manner, which was then quite common, he swaggered about, forever cursing and swearing, and talking of running people through with his sabre. This bully-boy had only one virtue, very rare at this time: he was always turned out with the knowing anything about him, now much regretted it; but he could not send him back without upsetting his old friend, Augereau. Although my father disliked him, he thought, perhaps rightly, that a general should make use of the military qualities of an officer, without worrying too much about his personal manners; but, as he did not care job of taking his coaches and horses from Paris to Nice, having under his orders the old stud-groom, Spire, a highly responsible man, used to the management of stables. The stable was large: my father had fifteen horses, which with those of his aide-de-camp and of his chief-of-staff and his assistants, together with those for the wagons

They left a month before we did.

My father took in his coach the fatal M. Lachze, Captain Gault and me. Colonel Mnard, the chief-of- staff, followed, with one of his assistants, in a post-chaise. A big rascal, my father's valet, went ahead as a courier. We travelled in uniform. I had a fine forage cap which pleased me so much that I wore it all the time, but, as I put my head out of the coach window frequently, because the coach made me travel-sick, it so happened that during the night, when my companions were asleep, the cap fell into the road. The coach, drawn by six vigourous horses, was going at top speed. I did not dare have it stopped and so I lost my cap. A bad omen! But I was to suffer far worse things in the terrible campaign which we were about to undertake. This incident upset me a good deal, but I said nothing about it for fear of being chaffed about the way the new soldier was looking after his kit.

My father stopped at Mcon, at the house of an old friend. We spent twenty-four hours there and then continued our journey to Lyons. We were not more than a few leagues from there, and were changing horses at the post-house of Limonest, when we noticed that all the postilions had decorated their hats with tricolour ribbons, and that there were flags of the same colours hanging from all the windows. We asked the reason for this demonstration, and were told that General Bonaparte had just arrived in Lyons...!

My father, who was certain that Bonaparte was still in the depths of Egypt, treated this news as absurd, but he was taken aback when, having sent for the post master, who had just returned from Lyons, he was told, "I saw General Bonaparte, whom I know very well, because I served under his command in Italy. He is staying in some hotel in Lyon, and has with him his brother Louis, Generals Berthier, Lannes and Murat, as well as a great, number of officers, and a Mameluke."

This could hardly have been more positive; however the revolution had given rise to so many falsehoods, and factions had been so cunning in inventing stories which would serve their ends, that my father was still in doubt when we entered the suburbs of Lyon. All the houses were draped with flags. Fireworks were going off. The crowd filled the streets to the point of preventing our coach from moving. There was dancing in the public squares and the air rang with cries of "Vive Bonaparte. Saviour of the country!" It was evident that Bonaparte was indeed in Lyon. My father said, "I was well aware that he was to be sent for, but I did not think it would be so soon. The coup has been well organised, and there are great events to come. I feel sure that I was right to leave Paris. At least, in the army I can serve the country without taking part in a coup, which, however necessary, I find repugnant." Having said this, he fell into a deep reverie, which lasted for the long time it took us to work our way through the crowds to the hotel where our rooms had been prepared.

The nearer we got to the hotel, the thicker the crowd became, and when we reached the door we saw that it was hung about with Chinese lanterns and guarded by Grenadiers. It was here that General Bonaparte was staying, in rooms that had been booked a week before for my father.

Although quick-tempered, my father did not say a word when the hotelier, who had been compelled to obey the orders of the municipality, came with some embarrassment to make his excuses. The inn-keeper having added that he had arranged for our accommodation at another hotel....very good, though of second grade....and run by one of his relatives, my father simply asked Capt. Gault to tell the postilion to take us there.

When we arrived, we were met by our courier, a lively fellow, who, heated by the long journey he had just made and the numerous drinks he had downed at each post-house had complained most loudly when he found that the rooms booked for his master had been given to General Bonaparte. The latter's aides-de-camp hearing this uproar and learning the cause, went to warn their master that General Marbot had been displaced to make room for him, and, at the same time, General Bonaparte saw through his open window my father's two coaches pull up at the door.

He had not been aware, until then, of the shabby way in which my father had been treated; and as General Marbot, recently commandant of Paris, and now a divisional commander in Italy was too important a man to be treated unceremoniously, and also as General Bonaparte had good reason to make himself popular with everybody, he ordered one of his officers to go down straight away and ask General Marbot to come, as a fellow soldier, and share his accommodation. Then, seeing the coaches leave before his aide-de-camp could speak to my father, Bonaparte went immediately, on foot, to offer his regrets in person.

The crowd which followed him set up a great noise of cheering, which, as it drew near our hotel, should have warned us, but we had heard so much since coming to the town that it did not occur to one of us to look out of the window. We were all in the drawing-room where my father was striding up and down, deep in thought, when the valet-de-chambre, opening the double doors, announced, "The General Bonaparte."

On entering, he hurried to embrace my father, who received him very politely, but coolly. They had known each other for a long time.

The explanations about the lodgings could be disposed of in a few words between two such people, and so they were. They had much else to talk about; so they went alone into the bedroom, where they remained in conference for more than an hour.

During this time, the officers who had come with General Bonaparte chatted with us in the drawing-room. I never tired of examining their martial appearance, their sun-bronzed faces, their strange uniforms and their Turkish sabres, hung from cords. I listened with interest to their stories of the campaign in Egypt, and the battles which were fought there. I took pleasure in hearing them talk of such celebrated places as the Pyramids, the Nile, Cairo, Alexandria, Acre, the desert and so on. What delighted me most, however, was the sight of the young Mameluke, Rustum. He had stayed in the ante-chamber, where I went several times to admire his costume, which he showed me willingly. He already spoke reasonable French, and I never wearied of asking him questions.

General Lannes recalled having let me fire his pistols, when, in 1793, he was serving under my father in the camp at Miral. He was very friendly toward me, and neither of us then foresaw that one day I should be his aide-de-camp, and that he would die in my arms at Essling. General Murat came from the same region as we did, and as he had been a shop-assistant to a silk merchant at Saint-Cr during the period when

30

my family spent the winter there, he had often come to the house, bringing purchases to my mother. My father, also, had rendered him a number of services, for which he was always grateful. He gave me a hug, and reminded me that he had often held me in his arms, when I was an infant.

General Bonaparte and my father having come back into the room, they presented to one another the members of their suites. Generals Lannes and Murat were old acquaintances of my father, who welcomed them with great affability. He was a little distant with General Berthier, whom, however he had seen before, when he was in the bodyguard and Berthier was an engineer.

General Bonaparte, who knew my mother, asked me, very politely, for news of her. He complimented me most warmly on having, while yet so young, taken up a military career, and taking me gently by the ear, which was always the most flattering caress which he bestowed on those with whom he was pleased, he said to my father, "One day this will be a second General Marbot." This prediction came true, although at that time I had no expectation of it. However I was very proud of these words. It takes so very little to make a child feel pleased with himself.

When the visit was over, my father disclosed nothing of what had been said between him and General Bonaparte; but I learned later that Bonaparte, without stating his objectives clearly, had sought, by the most adroit cajolements, to win my father over to his side, and that, my father had always dodged the issue.

Disgusted at seeing the people of Lyon running in front of Bonaparte, as if he was already the sovereign of France, my father declared that he wanted to leave at dawn the next day; but as his coaches needed some repairs, he was forced to spend an entire day at Lyon. I profited from this to have a new forage cap made, and, enchanted with this purchase, I took no notice of the political conversations, about which, to tell the truth, I understood little.

My father went to return the visit he had received from General Bonaparte. They walked alone for a very long time in the hotel's little garden, while their suites remained respectfully at a distance. We saw them sometimes gesture with warmth, and at other times speak more calmly; then Bonaparte, with a wheedling look, went up to my father and put his arm through his in a friendly fashion, probably so that the officials who were in the courtyard and the many spectators who hung out of neighbouring windows might conclude that General Marbot agreed with the plans of General Bonaparte; for this crafty man neglected nothing to achieve his aims.

My father came away from this second conversation even more pensive than he had been after the first, and on coming back to the hotel, he ordered our departure for the next day. Unfortunately, the next day, General Bonaparte was to make an excursion round the town to inspect the heights suitable for fortification, and all the post-horses were reserved for him. I thought that at this blow my father would become angry, but he contented himself by saying, "There is the beginning of omnipotence." And told his staff to see if they could hire any horses, so keen was he to get away from the town and from the sights which offended him. No spare horses could be found. Then Col. Mnard, who was born in the Midi, and knew the district perfectly, observed that the road from Lyon to Avignon was in such a poor state of repair that the coaches might be badly damaged if they attempted it, and it would be better to embark them on the Rhne, the descent of which would offer us an enchanting spectacle. My father, who was no great lover of the picturesque, would, at any other time, have rejected this advice, but as it gave him the opportunity to leave the town a day earlier, he agreed to take to the Rhne.

Col. Mnard then hired a large boat, the coaches were put on board, and the next day, early in the morning, we all embarked: a decision which was very nearly the end of us.

It was autumn. The water was very low. All the time the boat touched and scraped along the bottom. One feared that it might be torn open. We slept the first night at Saint-Pray, next at Tain, and took two days to get as far down as the junction with the Drme. There we had much more water, and went along rapidly; but a dangerous high wind called the Mistral hit us when we were about a quarter league above the bridge known as Pont Saint-Esprit. The boatmen were unable to reach the bank. They lost their heads, and set themselves to praying instead of working, while a furious wind and a strong current were driving the boat towards the bridge! We were about to crash against the pier of the bridge and be sunk, when my father and all of us, taking up boat-hooks, hurried forward to fend off from the pier which we were about to strike.

The shock was so severe that it knocked us into the thwarts, but the push had changed the direction of the boat, which, by a miraculous piece of good fortune, shot through under the arch. The boatmen then recovered a little from their terror and resumed some sort of control of their boat; but the Mistral continued, and the two coaches offering a resistance to the wind made any manoeuvre almost impossible. At last, six leagues above Avignon, we went aground on a very large island, where the bow of the boat dug into the sand in such a way that it would not be possible to get it out without a gang of labourers, and we were listing over so far that we feared being swamped at any moment. We put some planks between the boat and the shore and, with the help of some rope, we all got ashore without accident, though with some difficulty.

There could be no thought of re-embarking in the very high wind,(although without rain), and so we pushed on into the interior of the island, which we thought at first was uninhabited; but eventually we came across a sort of farm, where we found some good folk who made us very welcome. We were dying of hunger, but it was impossible to go back to the boat for food, and all we had was a little bread.

We were told that the island was full of poultry, which was allowed to run wild, and which the peasants shot, when they wanted some. My father was very fond of shooting, and he needed some relaxation from his problems, so we borrowed guns from the peasants, some pitch-forks and sticks, and we set off on a hen shoot. We shot several, though it was not easy to hit them as they flew like pheasants. We also picked up many of their eggs in the woods. When we returned to the farm, we lit a big fire in the middle of a field, around which we set up a bivouac, while the valet, helped by the farmer, prepared the eggs and the chickens in a variety of ways. We supped well and then bedded down on some hay, no one daring to accept the beds which the good peasants offered us, as they seemed to us to be far from clean.

By day-break the wind had dropped, so all the peasants and the boatmen took spades and picks, and after several hours of hard work they got the boat afloat, enabling us to continue our journey towards Avignon, which we reached without any further accidents. Those that had befallen us were so embroidered in the telling, that the rumour reached Paris that my father and all his staff had been drowned.

The approach to Avignon, particularly when one comes down the Rhne, is very picturesque. The old Papal Chteau; the ramparts by which the city is surrounded; its numerous steeples and the Chteau de Villeneuve rising opposite, combine to make a fine prospect. At Avignon we met *Mme*. Mnard and one of her nieces, and we spent three days in the town, visiting the charming outskirts, including the fountain of Vaucluse. My father was in no hurry to leave, because in the Midi,had forced him to slow the pace of his march and my father did not wish to arrive before his horses.

From Avignon we headed for Aix, but when we reached Bompart, on the banks of the Durance, which, at that time, was crossed by a ferry, we found the river so swollen by flood, that it would not be possible to cross for at least five or six hours. We were debating whether to return to Avignon, when the operator of the ferry, a gentlemanly sort of person, who owned a charming little castle on the height some five hundred paces from the river bank, came and begged my father to rest there until the coaches could be embarked. He accepted, hoping that it would be for a few hours only; but it appeared that there had been heavy storms in the Alps, where the Durance has its source, for the river continued to rise all day, and we were compelled to accept lodging for the night, which was offered most cordially by the owner of the castle. The weather being fine we spent the day walking. It was a break in our travels which I enjoyed.

The next day, seeing that the flood-water was running even more rapidly than the evening before, our host, who was a devout Republican, and who knew the river well enough to judge that we would not be able to cross for twenty-four hours, hurried off, unknown to us, to the little town of Cavaillon, which is about two leagues from Bompart, on the same bank of the river. He had gone to inform all the "Patriots" of the locality that he had in his house divisional General Marbot. He then returned to the castle, where, an hour or so later, we saw the arrival of a cavalcade composed of the keenest "Patriots" of Cavaillon, who had come to beg my father to accept an invitation to a banquet, which they offered him in the name of all the notables of the town, "Always so staunchly Republican."

My father, who found these sort of occasions far from agreeable, at first refused; but these "Citoyens" were so insistent, saying that everything had been organised and that the guests had gathered, that my father gave in and went off to Cavaillon.

The best hotel had been decked with garlands, and was graced by the presence of the local dignitaries from the town and its outskirts. After an interminable number of compliments, we took our places at a table laden with the most exclusive dishes. Above all, there were ortolans, birds which thrive well in this part of the country.

A great many toasts were drunk. Virulent speeches were made, denouncing the "Enemies of liberty" and the dinner did not end until ten o'clock in the evening. It was a little late to return to Bompart, and anyway, my father could not with politeness leave his hosts the moment the meal was over. He decided then to spend the night at Cavaillon, and the rest of the evening was passed in rather noisy talk. Eventually, one by one, the guests went home and we were left alone.

The next morning, M. Gault asked the inn-keeper how much my father owed for his part in the immense feast of the night before, which he assumed was a communal meal in which each paid for his own share. The inn-keeper presented him with a bill of more than 1500 francs. The good "Patriots" not having paid a single sou!...We were told that though some had expressed a wish to pay, the great majority had replied that this would be "An insult to General Marbot"....!

Capt. Gault was furious at this procedure, but my father, who at first could not get over his astonishment, burst into laughter, and told the inn-keeper to go and collect the money at Bompart, to where we returned straight away, without saying a word of this to the chatelaine; whose servants we tipped handsomely, and then, taking advantage of the fall in the water level, we at last crossed the Durance and made our way to Aix.

Although I might not yet be of an age to discuss politics with my father, what I had heard him say led me to believe that his Republican ideas had been much modified over the preceding two years, and what he had experienced as a supposed guest of honour at Cavaillon had severely shaken them, but he did not display any ill-feeling on the subject of this banquet, and was even amused at the anger of M. Gault, who said repeatedly, "I am not surprised that, in spite of their cost, these scoundrels produced so many ortolans, and ordered so many bottles of good wine! "

After spending a night at Aix, we left for Nice. This was the last stage of our journey. While we were travelling through the mountain and the beautiful forest of Estérel, we encountered the Colonel of the 1st Hussars, who, escorted by an officer and several troopers, was taking some lame horses, returned by the army, back to the depot at Puy-en-Velay. This colonel was named M. Picart and had been given his command because of his administrative ability. He was sent frequently to the depot to arrange for the equipment of men and horses, which he then forwarded to the fighting units, where he appeared but rarely and did not stay for long.

34

When he saw Col. Picart, my father had the coach stopped and got out, and after presenting me to my colonel, he took him on one side, and asked him to name an intelligent and well educated non-commissioned officer who might be made my mentor. The Colonel named Sergeant Pertelay. My father made a note of the name, and we excellent hotel, with our coaches and horses in first-class order.

Chap. 8.

The town of Nice was full of troops, among which was a squadron of the 1st Hussars, to which regiment I belonged. In the absence of its colonel, the regiment was commanded by a Major Muller. On learning that the divisional general had arrived, Muller came to see my father, and it was agreed between them that, after a few days rest, I should begin my service in the seventh company, commanded by Capt. Mathis.

Although my father was very good to me, I was so much in awe of him that I was very shy in his presence, a shyness which he thought was greater than was really the case; he said I should have been a girl, and often called me madamoiselle Marcellin, which annoyed me very much, especially now that I was a Hussar. It was to overcome this shyness, that my father wished me to serve in the ranks, and in any case, as I have already said, one could not join the army except as a private soldier. My father, it is true, could have attached me to his personal staff, since my regiment was part of his division, but, quite apart from the notion which I have described above, he wanted me to learn how to saddle and bridle my own horse and to look after my arms and equipment; also, he did not want his son to enjoy the least privilege, as this would have had a bad effect on the rest of the troops. It was already enough that I was to be allowed to join a squadron without undergoing a long and wearisome period of training at the depot. I passed several days with my father and his staff, travelling about the district round Nice, which was very beautiful, but the moment for my entry into the squadron having arrived, my father asked Major Muller to send him Sergeant Pertelay.

Now, there were two brothers of this name in the regiment, both of them sergeants, but having nothing else, physically or mentally in common, the elder being something of a scamp, while the younger was thoroughly respectable. It was this latter whom the colonel had intended to appoint as my mentor, but in the short time which he and my father had spent together, Col. Picart had forgotten, when naming Pertelay, to add the younger: furthermore, this Pertelay was not in the part of the squadron which was stationed in Nice, while the elder was in the very company, the seventh, which I was about to join.

Major Muller believed that the colonel had named the elder to my father and that this wild character had been chosen to open the eyes of an innocent and shy young man, which I then was. So he sent us the elder Pertelay.

This example of the old type of Hussar was a rowdy, quarrelsome, swashbuckling, tippler, but also brave to the point of foolhardiness; for the rest, he was completely ignorant of anything that was not connected with his horse, his arms and his duties in the face of the enemy. Pertelay the younger, on the other hand, was quiet, polite, and well-educated. He was a handsome man and just as brave as his brother, and would surely have gone far had he not, while still very young, been killed in action.

Now to return to the elder. He arrived at my father's quarters, and what did we see? A fine fellow, very well turned out it is true, but with his shako tipped over one ear, his sabre trailing on the ground, his red face slashed by an immense scar, moustaches six inches long, which, stiffened by wax, curled up into his ears, two big plaits of hair, braided from his temples, which, escaping from his shako, hung down to his chest, and with all this an air...! An air of rakishness which was increased by his speech, which was rattled out in a sort of Franco-Alsatian patois. This last did not surprise my father, as he knew that the 1st Hussars were the former regiment of Bercheny, which in earlier days recruited only Germans, and where, until 1793, all the orders were given in German, which was the language generally used by the officers and men, almost all of whom came from the provinces bordering the Rhine. My father was however exceedingly surprised by the style and manner of my proposed mentor.

I learned later that he had hesitated to put me in the hands of this bravo, but M. Gault having reminded him that Colonel Picart had described him as the best N.C.O.in the squadron, he decided to try it. So off I went with Pertelay, who, taking me by the arm without ceremony, came to my room, showed me how to pack my kit into my valise, and conducted me to a small barracks, situated in a former monastery, and now occupied by a squadron of the 1st Hussars.

My mentor made me saddle and unsaddle the pretty little horse which my father had bought me; then he showed me how to put on my cloak and my arms, giving me a complete demonstration, and having decided that he had explained to me all that was necessary, he thought it time to go for dinner. My father, who wished me to eat with my mentor, had given us extra money to meet the expense.

Pertelay took me to a small inn, which was crammed with Hussars, Grenadiers and soldiers of every sort. We were served with a meal, and on the table was placed an enormous bottle of red wine of the most violent nature. Pertelay poured me a glassful. We clinked glasses. My man emptied his and I raised mine without putting it to my lips, for I had never drunk undiluted wine and I found the smell of this liquid disagreeable. I admitted this to my mentor, who shouted, in a stentorian voice, "Waiter! Bring some lemonade for this boy who never drinks wine." A gale of laughter swept through the room. I was mortified, but I could not bring myself to taste this wine, and as I did not dare to ask for water, I dined without a drink.

A soldier's apprenticeship has always been hard going. It was particularly so at the time of which I write. I had, therefore, some unhappy experiences to suffer. A thing I found unbearable was the requirement to share my bed with another Hussar. The regulations allotted only one bed for two soldiers. N.C.O.s alone were allowed to have a bed each. On the first night which I spent in the barracks, I had already gone to my bed when a tall, ungainly Hussar, who arrived an hour after the others, approached it, and seeing that it was occupied, he unhooked a lantern and stuck it under my nose to examine me more closely. Then he got undressed. As I watched him, I had no idea that he intended to get in beside me; but I was soon disillusioned, when he said to me roughly, "Shove over, conscript!" And got into the bed, taking up three-quarters of it, and began to snore loudly. I was unable to sleep a wink, largely because of the revolting odour arising from a large package which my comrade had placed under the bolster, to raise his head. I could not think what this could be, so to find out, I slid my hand gently toward this object and found it to be a leather apron impregnated with cobbler's wax, which shoemakers use to treat their thread. My amiable bed companion was one of the men employed by the regimental bootmaker. I was so disgusted that I got up, got dressed, and went to the stables where I bedded down on a heap of straw. The next day I told Pertelay of my misadventure, and he reported it to the sub-lieutenant commanding the platoon. He was a well-educated man named Leisteinschneider (in German, a stone-worker) who was later killed in action. He understood how painful it must be for me to have to sleep with a bootmaker, and he took it on himself to arrange for me to have a bed in the N.C.O's room, something which pleased me greatly.

Although the revolution had produced a great relaxation in the general turn-out of troops, the 1st Hussars had kept theirs exactly as it was when they were Bercheny's Hussars; so except for the physical differences imposed by nature, all troopers had to resemble one another in their appearance, and as the regiments of Hussars of that period had not only pig-tails, but long plaited tresses which hung from their temples and turned-up moustaches, it was the rule that everyone belonging to the regiment must have moustache, pig-tail and tresses. Now, as I had none of these things, my mentor took me to the regimental wig-maker where I bought a false pig-tail and tresses, which were attached to my own hair, already fairly long, as I had let it grow since my enlistment. These embellishments embarrassed me at first but I got used to them in a few days, and it pleased me to imagine that they gave me the appearance of a seasoned trooper. It was a different matter when it came to the moustache I had no more of a moustache than a girl, and as a hairless face would have spoiled the ranks of the squadron, Pertelay, as was the custom of Bercheny, took a pot of black wax, and with his thumb he gave me an enormous curling moustache, which covered my upper lip and reached almost to, my eyes. The shakos of the time did not have a vizor, so that, when I was on guard duty, or during an inspection, when one has to remain perfectly still, the Italian sun, shining hotly onto my face, sucked the moisture out of the wax of which my moustache was made, and, as it dried it pulled at my skin in a most disagreeable manner. However, I did not blink. I was a Hussar! A word that had for me an almost magical significance; besides which, having engaged in a military career, I understood very well that my first duty was to obey the regulations.

My father and part of his division were still in Nice, when we heard of the events of the 18th Brumaire, the overthrow of the Directorate and the establishment of the Consulate. My father had too much contempt for the Directorate to regret its downfall, but he feared that, intoxicated by power, General Bonaparte, after re-establishing order in France, would not restrict himself to the modest title of consul, and he predicted to us that in a short time he would aim to become king. My father was mistaken only in the title, four years later Napoleon made himself emperor.

Whatever his misgivings about the future, my father congratulated himself on not having been in Paris on the 18th Brumaire, and I believe that had he been there he might well have opposed the actions of General Bonaparte, but in the army, at the head of a division facing the enemy, he was content to adopt the passive obedience of the soldier. He even rejected proposals, which were made to him by a number of generals and colonels, to march on Paris at the head of their troops. "Who," he said to them, "will defend our frontiers if we abandon them? And what will become of France if, to the war against foreigners, we add the calamity of civil strife?" By these wise observations he calmed down the hot-heads; but he was, nonetheless, very disturbed by the coup which had just taken place: he adored his country and would have greatly preferred that it could have been saved without being submitted to the yoke of a dictator.

I have said that my father's principle reason for making me enlist as a lowly Hussar had been to rid me of the simple notions of a schoolboy, which had not been changed by my short acquaintance with the world of Paris. The result exceeded his expectations, for living amongst swaggering Hussars, and having as a mentor a sort of brigand who laughed at my innocence, I began to howl with the wolves, and for fear that I might be mocked for my timidity, I became a real devil. This, however, was not enough for me to be accepted into a sort of brotherhood, which under the name of the clique, had members in all the squadrons the 1st Hussars.

The clique was made up of all the biggest rogues, but, at the same time, some of the bravest men in the regiment. The members of the clique supported one another against all opposition, particularly in the face of the enemy. They called themselves the Jokers, and recognised one another by a notch cut into the metal of the first button on the right hand row of the pelisse and dolman. The officers were aware of the existence of the clique, but as its worst crimes were limited to the adroit theft of chickens or sheep, or some trick played on the local inhabitants, and as the Jokers were always at the forefront in any action, they turned a blind eye. I was young and feckless, and I longed desperately to belong to this raffish society, which I thought would raise my standing amongst my comrades; but it was in vain that I frequented the salle-d'armes to practice swordsmanship and the use of the pistol and carbine, and that I dug my elbows into anyone who got in my way: allowed my sabre to trail on the ground and tipped my shako over one ear, the members of the clique regarded me as a child and refused to admit me to their society. However, an unforeseen event led to my being accepted unanimously.

The army of Italy was at this time in Liguria and spread out on a front of more than sixty miles in length, the right of which was in the Gulf of Spezzia, beyond Genoa, and the left at Nice and Var, that is to say on the frontier of France. We had, therefore, the sea at our backs, and we faced Piedmont, which was occupied by the Austrian army, from which we were separated by that branch of the Apennines which runs from Var to Gavi: a bad position, in which the army ran the risk of being cut in two, which, in fact, happened some months later.

My father, having been ordered to concentrate his division at Savona, a small town, by the sea, ten leagues towards France from Genoa, set up his headquarters in the bishop's palace. The infantry was spread out among the market towns and villages of the neighbourhood to keep watch on the valleys from which emerged the roads which led to Piedmont. The 1st Hussars, who had come from Nice to Savona, were encamped on a plain known as the Madona. The outposts of the enemy were at Dego, four or five leagues from us, on the forward slopes of the Apennines, whose summits were covered in snow, whereas Savona and its surroundings enjoyed the mildest of climates.

Our encampment would have been delightful if the rations had been more plentiful; but there was at that time no main road from Nice to Genoa; the sea was covered by English warships, so the army had to live on what could be brought by detachments of mules along the Corniche, or by small boat-loads, which could slip unnoticed along the coast. These precarious supplies were scarcely enough to provide, from day to day, sufficient food to support the troops; but, happily, the country produced plenty of wine, which enabled them to bear their privations with more resignation.

One fine day I was walking along the beach with my mentor when we came on a "taverna," where there was a charming garden planted with orange and lemon trees, under which were tables at which sat soldiers of all kinds. He suggested that we went there, and although I had never overcome my distaste for wine, I agreed, simply to please him.

In those days the cavalryman's belt did not have a hook, so that when we went on foot, it was necessary to hold up the scabbard of the sabre with one's left hand, and one could allow the end to trail on the ground. This made a noise on the pavement, and looked rather dashing, so of course I had to adopt this way of doing things. Thus it happened that as we went into this garden, the end of my scabbard came in contact with the foot of an enormous horse-gunner, who was sprawled on his chair with his legs sticking out. The horse artillery had been formed at the beginning of the revolutionary wars from men taken from the companies of Grenadiers, who took advantage of the occasion to get rid of their most troublesome characters. The men of the flying artillery, as it was then called, were known for their dash, but also for their love of quarreling.

The one whose foot the end of my scabbard had touched, shouted to me in a very rude tone of voice, "Hussar, your sabre drags too much!" I was going to walk on without saying any thing, when master Pertelay, nudging me with his elbow, whispered, "Tell him to come and lift it up." So I said to the gunner "Come and lift it up then!" "That will be easy!" he replied. Then, at another whisper from Pertelay, "I'd like to see you do it!" I said. On these words, the gunner, or this Goliath, for he was at least six feet tall, sat up straight with a threatening air... But my mentor pushed himself between him and me. All the gunners who were in the garden came to support their comrade, but a crowd of Hussars gathered beside Pertelay and me. There was a lot of angry shouting with everyone talking at once; I thought there was going to be a general mele. However as the Hussars were in a majority of at least two to one, they took the matter the more calmly, while the gunners realised that if they started something they would get the worst of it, so in the end the giant was made to understand that in brushing his foot with my scabbard, I had in no way insulted him, and that should be the end of the matter.

During the tumult, however, a trumpeter from the artillery, of about twenty years of age, had offered me some insults, and in my indignation I had pushed him so roughly that he had fallen into a muddy ditch. It was agreed that this lad and I should fight a duel with our sabres.

We left the garden, followed by all the assistants, and found ourselves by the edge of the sea, on fine solid sand, ready for battle. Pertelay knew that I was quite a good swordsman; however he gave me some words of advice on how I should attack my adversary, and fastened the hilt of my sabre to my hand with a large handkerchief, which he rolled round my arm.

My father hated duelling. Not only because of his own conclusions about this barbarous custom, but also, I believe, because in his youth, when he was a member of the bodyguard, he had acted as second for a comrade of whom he was very fond, and who was killed in a duel over the most trivial matter. However that may be, when my father took command, he ordered the police to arrest anyone caught engaging in swordplay and bring them before him.

Although the trumpeter and I both knew of this order, we had, nevertheless, taken off our dolmans and taken up our sabres. I had my back to the town of Savona, my adversary was facing it, and we were about to begin our combat when I saw the trumpeter duck to one side, pick up his dolman and make off at top speed.

"Coward!....Runaway!" I shouted, and was about to, pursue him when two iron hands grasped me by the collar. I turned my head and found myself facing some eight to ten police! I understood then why my antagonist had cleared off, followed by all the assistants, including master Pertelay, whom I saw disappearing into the distance, as fast as their legs could carry them, for fear of being arrested and brought before the General.

There I was! Disarmed and a prisoner! I picked up my dolman, and looking very sheepish, followed my captors, to whom I had not given my name, as they led me to the Bishop's palace where my father was installed. He was at that moment with General Suchet, who had come to Savona to confer with him on service matters. They were walking in a gallery which overlooked the courtyard. The police put me up before General Marbot, without any idea that I was his son. The sergeant explained why I had been arrested. Then my father, looking very severe, gave me a lively dressing down, after which admonition, he said to the sergeant, "Take this Hussar to the citadel." I left without saying a word, and without General Suchet, who did not know me, suspecting that the scene he had just witnessed had taken place between a father and his son. It was not until the next day that he learned the truth, and he has often spoken to me since, with laughter, about the episode.

On my arrival at the citadel, an ancient Genoese building situated near the harbour, I was locked into a big room lit by a high window, which faced toward the sea. I recovered slowly from my fright. The reprimand which I had received seemed to me to be deserved; however I was less concerned at having disobeyed the General than I was at having upset my father. I passed the rest of the day sadly enough.

In the evening, an old ex-soldier of the Genoan force brought me a jug of water, a piece of ration bread, and a bale of straw, on which I lay down, without being able to eat. I could not go to sleep; at first because I was too upset, and later because of the arrival of some large rats, which ran about me and soon made off with my piece of bread. I was lying in the dark, a prey to my sad reflections, when, at about ten o'clock, I heard the bolts of my prison being drawn and I saw Spire, my father's old and faithful servant. He told me that after my despatch to the citadel, Capt. Gault, Col. Mnard, and all my father's officers had asked him to pardon me. The General had agreed, and had sent him, Spire, to find me and take the order for my release to the governor of the fort. I was taken before the governor, General Buget, an excellent man, who had lost an arm in battle. He knew me and was very fond of my father. He felt it his duty, after giving me back my sabre, to give me a long lecture, to which I listened patiently, but which made me reflect that I would get a much worse telling-off from my father. I did not have the courage to face this and decided to evade it, if that were possible. At last we were let out of the gates of the citadel. The night was dark, and Spire went in front with a lantern. As we walked through the narrow twisting streets, the good fellow, delighted to be bringing me back, recounted all the comforts which would await me at headquarters. "But," he said, "you must expect a severe ticking-off from your father." This last remark put an end to my doubts, and in order to let my father's anger cool off, I decided it would be better not to appear before him for a few days and that I would return to my bivouac at Madona. I could easily have slipped away without playing any trick on poor Spire; but fearing that he might be able to pursue me by the light of his lantern, I gave it a kick which sent it flying ten paces from him, and ran off while the good man, groping for his lantern, shouted, "Ah...! You little blighter! I shall tell your father!"

After wandering for some time in the deserted streets, I found at last the road to Madona, and made my way to the regimental camp. All the Hussars thought I was in prison. As soon as one of them recognised me by the light of the fires, I was surrounded and questioned. There was much laughter when I described how I had got away from Spire. The members of the clique were so satisfied with my behaviour that they decided unanimously to admit me into their society, which was preparing an expedition to go, that very night, to the gates of Dego and steal a herd of cattle which belonged to the Austrian army. The French Generals and even the corps commanders were obliged to ignore these raids, which, in the absence of regular rations, the soldiers carried out beyond the advance posts in order to obtain food. In each regiment the boldest soldiers had formed marauding bands who were marvellously skilled at finding out where supplies were being assembled for the enemy, and using ruse and audacity to lay hands on them.

A rascally horse-dealer had told the clique that a herd of cattle which he had sold to the Austrians was in a meadow a quarter of a league from Dego, and now sixty Hussars, armed only with their carbines, were on their way to capture it. Avoiding the main road, we went several leagues into the mountain by winding and atrociously rough tracks. We surprised five Croats, who had been left to guard the herd, asleep in a shed. To prevent them from going to waken the garrison at Dego, we tied them up and left them there. We drove away the herd without a shot being fired and returned to the camp, tired out, but delighted to have played such a successful trick on the enemy, and at the same time acquired some food.

This event illustrates the already wretched condition of the army of Italy, and demonstrates to what a state of disorganisation such neglect will bring troops; whose officers are obliged not only to tolerate these sort of expeditions, but to take advantage of the supplies they procure without seeming to know whence they come.

Chap. 9.

Happy in my military career, I had not even reached the rank of corporal when I was raised immediately to that of sergeant. This is how it came about.

On the left of my father's division was that commanded by General Sras, whose headquarters were at Finale. This division, which occupied the part of Liguria where the mountains are steepest, was composed solely of infantry, the cavalry being unable to operate, except in small detachments, on the few open spaces which at this point separate the shore of the Mediterranean from the mountains of Piedmont. General Sras, having been ordered to push forward with the greater part of his division to reconnoitre the area of Mount Santa-Giacomo, beyond which there were several valleys, wrote to my father requesting the loan of a detachment of fifty Hussars for this expedition; a request which could not be turned down. So my father agreed and named Lt. Leisteinschneider as commander of this detachment, of which my platoon was a part.

We left Madona to make our way to Finale. There was, at that time, only a very bad road along the sea coast, known as the Corniche. The lieutenant badly injured his foot as a result of a fall from his horse, and so the command passed to the next in seniority who was a sergeant named Canon, a handsome young man, capable and well-trained, and full of self-assurance.

General Sras, at the head of his division, advanced next day onto the snow-clad slopes of Mount Santa-Giacomo, where we encamped. He had intended to go forward the next day, with he almost certain expectation of making contact with the enemy; but in how great a number? On this subject the General had absolutely no information, and as his orders from the commander-in-chief were to reconnoitre the

Austrian positions at this point of the line, but not to engage in combat if he found the enemy in strength, General Sras reflected that if he advanced his infantry division into the middle of the mountains, where often one could not see enemy troops until one found oneself face to face with them at a bend in a gorge, he might be led, in spite of his wishes, into a major battle against superior forces, and obliged to carry out a dangerous retreat.

He decided therefore to proceed with caution, and to push out, three or four leagues in front of him, an advance party which could probe the country and, most importantly, take some prisoners, from whom he hoped to get some information; for the peasantry either knew nothing or would not talk. As a small body of infantry would be endangered if he advanced them too far, and as, also, men on foot would take too long to return with the information which he so urgently needed, it was to the fifty Hussars that he gave the task of going ahead and exploring the terrain. Then, as the country was very broken, he gave a map to our sergeant, briefed him, in front of the detachment and sent us off, two hours before daylight, repeating that it was essential that we went ahead until we made contact with the enemy outposts, from which he would very much like us to capture a few prisoners.

Sergeant Canon managed his detachment according to the book. He sent out a small advance-guard, put scouts on the flanks and took all the precautions usual in partisan warfare. When we had gone some two leagues from the camp, we came on a large inn. Our sergeant questioned the inn-keeper and was told that, a good hour's march away, was a body of Austrian troops, the size of which he did not know, though he knew that the leading regiment contained some very unpleasant Hussars, who had maltreated a number of the local inhabitants.

Having gathered this information, we set off once more, but hardly had we gone a hundred paces, when Sergeant Canon, writhing on his horse, declared that he had the most dreadful pain and could not go any further. He handed the command to Sergeant Pertelay, who was next in seniority. Pertelay, however pointed out that he was an Alsatian and was unable to read French, and could not, in consequence, understand the map or the written instructions given by the general. He did not wish to accept the command. All the other sergeants, old Bercheny Hussars, refused for the same reason, as did the corporals. In vain, as a matter of duty, I offered to read the general's instructions and explain our route on the map for any of the sergeants who would take over; they all refused anew; then, to my great surprise, these old sweats turned to me and said "Take command yourself. We'll follow you and obey all your orders."

The rest of the party expressed the same wish, and it was clear that if I refused, we would go no further and the honour of the regiment would be blemished; for it was essential that the general's orders were carried out, above all when it was perhaps a matter of avoiding a disaster for his division. So I accepted the command, but not without asking Sergeant Canon if he felt able to continue. At which point he began to complain once more, left us and returned to the inn. I promise you I thought he was really ill, but the men of the detachment, who knew him better, made some very disparaging remarks about him.

I think I can say, without boasting, that nature has endowed me with a good stock of courage. I might even add that there was a time when I enjoyed facing danger. My military record and the thirteen wounds I have received in the wars are, I believe, sufficient proof. So, on taking command of fifty men, placed under my orders in such extraordinary circumstances,—me, a simple Hussar, seventeen years of age—I resolved to prove to my comrades that if I had neither experience nor military talent, I was at least brave; and placing myself resolutely at their head I set off in the direction where I knew we would encounter the enemy.

We had been marching for a long time when our scouts spotted a peasant who was trying to hide. They hastened to capture him and bring him back. I questioned him. He came, it seemed, from four or five leagues away, and claimed that he had not seen any Austrian troops. I was sure he was lying, either from fear or from cunning, because we were very close to the enemy cantonments. I remembered then that I had read in a book about partisan warfare, which my father had given me to study, that to persuade the inhabitants of a country in which one is fighting to talk, it is sometimes necessary to frighten them. So I roughened my voice, and, trying to give my boyish face a ferocious look, I shouted, "What! You rascal! You have been wandering about in a country occupied by a great body of Austrian troops, and you claim you have seen nothing? You are a spy! Come on lads, let's shoot him right away."

I ordered four Hussars to dismount, indicating to them not to harm the fellow, who, finding himself held by the troopers whose carbines had just been loaded in front of him, was overcome by such terror that he swore that he would tell me all he knew. He was a servant in a monastery, who had been given a letter to take to relatives of the Prior, and he had been told that if he ran into the French, he was not to tell them where the Austrians were; but now that he was forced to speak, he told us that a league from us there were several regiments of the enemy billeted in the villages, and that about a hundred of Barco's Hussars were in a hamlet which was only a short distance away. Questioned about the defensive precautions taken by these Hussars, he said that before one reached the houses, they had posted a picket-guard which was in a garden surrounded by hedges, and that when he went through the hamlet, the remainder were preparing to water their horses at a little pond on the far side of the buildings.

Having received this information, I had now to make a plan of action. I wished to avoid passing the picket-guard who, being entrenched behind hedges, could not be attacked by cavalry, while the fire from their carbines would perhaps kill several of my men and give warning of our approach. To do this required that we go round the hamlet, so as to reach the pond, and fall, unexpectedly, on our enemies. But how were we to pass without being seen? I then ordered the peasant to lead us on a detour, and promised to set him free as soon as we reached the other side of the hamlet, which we could see: when he refused to do so, I had him taken by the scruff of the neck by one Hussar while another held a pistol to his ear, which made him

44

change his mind. He guided us very well; some large hedges hid our movements, and we got completely round the village to see, at the edge of a small pond, the Austrian squadron peacefully watering their horses. All the riders were carrying their arms, which is the usual practice for outposts, but those in command had neglected a precaution which is essential in war, that is, to allow only one troop at a time to unbridle their horses and enter the water, while the remainder stay on the bank ready to repel any attack. Confident that there were no French about and relying on the watchfulness of the guard posted at the entry to the village, the enemy commander had thought this precaution unnecessary. This was to be his downfall.

When I was some five hundred paces from the pond, I ordered the peasant to be released, who ran off as fast as his legs could carry him; then, sabre in hand, and having forbidden my comrades to utter any war-cry, I advanced at full gallop on the enemy Hussars, who did not see us until a moment before we arrived at the pond. The pond's banks were too high for the horses to climb out, and there was only one practicable way in, which was the one that served as the village drinking place. It is true that this was a wide area, but there were more than a hundred horsemen crowded together there, all with their bridles in their hands and their carbines slung, so unconcerned that some of them were singing. You may imagine their surprise!

I attacked them immediately with carbine fire, which killed several, wounded many and knocked out a lot of their horses. The confusion was total! Nevertheless, their captain, rallying some men who were nearest to the outlet, tried to force a passage to get out of the water, and opened fire on us, which although not sustained, wounded two of my men; they then engaged us, but Pertelay having killed the captain with a blow from his sabre, the rest crowded back into the pond. To escape from the carbine fire, many tried to reach the other bank; several lost their footing and a good number of men and horses were floundering in the water. Those who reached the other side found that their horses could not clamber up the steep edge and so they abandoned them, and pulling themselves up by the aid of trees growing along the bank, they fled in disorder into the countryside.

The twelve men of the picket-guard came running at the sound of firing. We attacked them with the sabre and they also took to flight. However there remained about thirty men still in the pond, afraid to try to escape because we occupied the only way out. They shouted to us that they were surrendering; I accepted this and as they came to the bank, made them throw down their arms. Most of these men and horses were wounded, but as I wished to have some trophy from our victory, I chose seventeen horses and riders who were fit, and placing them in the middle of the detachment,I abandoned the rest and went off at the gallop, going round the village, as before.

It was just as well that I made a rapid retreat, for as I had foreseen, the fugitives had run to warn the nearby troops who had already been alerted by the sound of gunfire, and within half an hour there were five hundred horsemen on the banks of the little pond and some thousands of infantrymen close behind them. We, however, were two leagues away, our wounded having been able to sustain a full gallop. We stopped for a short time on top of a hill to bandage their wounds, and we laughed to see in the distance several enemy columns following our trail, since we knew that they had no hope of catching us, because in their fear of falling into an ambush they were feeling their way forward very slowly. Being now out of danger, I gave Pertelay two of the best-mounted troopers and sent him off post-haste to inform general Sras of the success of our mission; then marshalling the detachment into good order, with our prisoners in the centre and well guarded, I set off at a slow trot down the road to the inn.

It would be impossible for me to describe the joy of my companions and the praises which they heaped on me during this journey. It could be summed up in these words, which in their minds was the highest commendation, "You are truly worthy to serve in Bercheny's Hussars, the finest regiment in the world."

Meanwhile, what had been happening at Santo-Giacomo during my absence? After several hours of waiting, General Sras, impatient for news, saw some smoke on the horizon; his aide-de-camp put his ear to a drum placed on the ground, a common expedient in wartime, and heard the distant sound of gunfire. General Sras was uneasy, and having no doubt that the cavalry detachment was at grips with the enemy, he took a regiment of infantry with him as far as the inn. When he arrived there, he saw, under the cart-shelter, a Hussar's horse tied up to the rail; it was Sergeant Canon's. The inn-keeper appeared and was questioned. He replied that the sergeant of Hussars had gone no further than the inn, and had been, for several hours, in the dining room. The General went in, and what did he find but Sergeant Canon asleep by the fireside with, in front of him, an enormous ham, two empty bottles and a coffee cup! The wretched sergeant was woken up; he attempted once more to make the excuse of a sudden indisposition, but the accusing remains of the formidable meal which he had just eaten, gave the lie to his claims of illness, so General Sras was very short with him. The General's anger was increasing at the thought that a detachment of fifty cavalrymen handed over to the command of a young soldier had probably been wiped out by the enemy, when Pertelay and the two troopers who were with him arrived at the gallop to announce our victory and the approaching arrival of seventeen prisoners. As General Sras, in spite of this happy outcome, continued to berate Sergeant Canon, Pertelay said to him, in his bluff outspoken way, "Don't scold him, mon General, he's such a coward that if he'd been in charge we wouldn't have succeeded!" A remark which did nothing to improve the awkward position of Sgt. Canon, who was now placed under arrest.

I arrived in the midst of these goings-on. General Sras broke poor Sgt. Canon, and made him take off his chevrons in front of a regiment of infantry and fifty Hussars. Then, coming to me, whose name he did not know, he said, "You have carried out successfully a mission which would normally be given only to an officer. I am sorry that the powers of a divisional commander do not allow me to promote you to sous-lieutenant, only the commander-in-chief can do that, and I shall ask him to, do so, but in the meantime I promote you to sergeant." He thereupon ordered his aide-de-camp to announce this in front of the detachment. In order to carry out this formality, the aide-de-camp had to ask my name, and it was only then that General

Sras learned that I was the son of his comrade, General Marbot. I was very pleased about this, because it demonstrated to my father that favouritism had nothing to do with my promotion.

Chap. 10.

The information which General Sras obtained from the prisoners having decided him to push forward, he ordered his division to come down from the heights of Mont Santa-Giacomo, and to encamp that evening near to the inn. The prisoners were sent to Finale, and as for the horses they belonged by rights to the Hussars. They were all of good quality, but, according to the custom of the time, which was aimed at favouring poorly mounted officers, captured horses were always sold for five louis. This was a fixed price and was paid in cash. As soon as the camp was established the sale began. General Sras, the officers of his staff, the colonels and battalion commanders of the regiments in his division soon took up our seventeen horses, which produced the sum of 85 louis. This was handed over to my detachment, who, not having had any pay for six months, were delighted with this windfall, for which they gave me the credit.

I had some money, so I did not pocket my share from the sale of the horses, but to celebrate my promotion, I bought from the inn-keeper two sheep, an enormous cheese and a load of wine, with which my detachment had a feast. This was one of the happiest days of my life.

General Sras, in his report to General Championet included a most flattering reference to my conduct, and said the same sort of thing to my father; so when, several days later, I brought the detachment back to Savona, my father welcomed me with the greatest show of affection. I was highly delighted; I rejoined the camp where all the regiment was united; my detachment had arrived there before me and had told of what we had done, giving me always the leading part in our success, so I was heartily welcomed by the officers and soldiers and also by my new comrades, the non-commissioned officers, who handed me my sergeant's stripes.

It was on this day that I met the younger Pertelay for the first time, he had come back from Genoa, where he had been stationed for some months. I became friendly with this excellent man, and regretted not having had him as my mentor at the beginning of my career, for he gave me much good advice, which steadied me up and made me break away from the wild men of the clique.

The commander-in-chief, Championet, intended to carry out some operations in the interior of Piedmont, but having very little in the way of cavalry, he ordered my father to send him the 1st Hussars, who could no longer stay at Madon, in any case, because of the shortage of fodder. I parted from my father with much regret and left with the regiment.

We went along the Corniche as far as Albenga. We crossed the Apennines, in spite of the snow, and entered the fertile plains of Piedmont. The commander-in-chief fought a number of actions in the area round Fossano, Novi and Mondovi, some of which were successful and others not.

In one of these actions I had the opportunity of seeing Brigadier-general Macard, a soldier of fortune whom the revolutionary upheavals had carried almost straight from the rank of trumpet-major to that of general! He was a good example of a type of officer created by luck and their personal courage who, although displaying much bravery before the enemy, were nevertheless incapable of occupying effectively a senior position because of their lack of education.

This extraordinary character, a veritable colossus, was well known for one peculiarity. When about to lead his troops in a charge against the enemy, it was his custom to shout "Let's go! I'll put on my animal dress." Then he took off his uniform, his jacket and shirt and retained only his plumed hat, his leather breeches and his big boots! Thus, naked to the waist, he displayed a torso almost as hairy as that of a bear, which gave him a very strange appearance indeed. Once in his animal dress, as he called it, General Macard, sabre in hand, hurled himself at the enemy horsemen, swearing like a pagan; but it so happened that he rarely reached any of them, for at the unexpected and terrible sight of this kind of giant, half naked and covered in hair rushing toward them uttering the most fearsome yells the enemy often fled in all directions, not knowing if they had to deal with a man or some extraordinary wild beast.

General Macord was entirely ignorant, which sometimes amused the more educated officers under his command. One day one of them came to ask permission to go into a neighbouring town to order a pair of boots. "Parbleu!" said the general, "This has come at just the right time; since you are going to the bootmaker, sit down and take the measurements of my boots and order a new pair for me." The officer, much surprised, said that he could not take the measurements as he had no idea how to do this, having never been a boot-maker. "What!" exclaimed the general loudly, "I see you sometimes spend whole days sketching and drawing lines opposite the mountains and when I ask what you are doing, you say you are measuring the mountains. How is it that you can measure objects which are more than a league away, and yet you cannot measure a pair of boots which are under your nose? Come on, take the measurements quickly and no more nonsense." The officer assured him that this was impossible. The general insisted; swore; got angry; and it was only with great difficulty that other officers, attracted by the noise, were able to put an end to this ridiculous scene. The general could never understand how a man who could measure mountains could not measure a pair of men's boots.

You should not think, as a result of this anecdote, that all the general officers in the army of Italy were like the good general Macord. Far from that, they contained in their number many men distinguished by their education and manners; but at this time there were still some senior officers who were completely out of place in the higher ranks of the army. They were being weeded out little by little.

The 1st Hussars took part in all the battles fought at this time in Piedmont, and suffered many losses in encounters with the Austrian heavy cavalry. After some marching and countermarching, and a series of almost daily minor engagements, General Championet, having concentrated the centre and left of his army between Coni and Mondovi, attacked, at the end of December, several divisions of the enemy army.

The encounter took place on a plain dotted with small hills and clumps of trees. The 1st Hussars, attached to General Beaumont's brigade, were positioned on the extreme right of the French army. As the number of officers and men who make up a squadron is laid down in the regulations, our regiment, having suffered casualties in the previous affairs, instead of putting four squadrons into the line could put only three; but having done this, there were some thirty men left over, of which five were sergeants. I was one of this number, as were both the Pertelays. We were formed into two sections and Pertelay the younger was put in command. General Beaumont merely instructed him to scout on the right flank of the army, and act as the situation seemed to require. We then left the regiment and went to explore the countryside.

In the meanwhile, a fierce battle commenced between the two armies, and an hour later, when we were returning to our own lines without having spotted anything on the flank, young Pertelay saw, opposite us, and consequently on the extreme left of the enemy line, a battery of eight guns whose fire was raking the French ranks. Very unwisely, this Austrian battery, in order to have a better field of fire, had advanced onto a small hillock some seven or eight hundred paces in front of the infantry division to which it belonged. The commander of this artillery believed that he was quite safe because the position he occupied dominated the whole French line, and he thought that if any troops set out to attack him, he would see them and would have time to regain the safety of the Austrian lines. He had not considered that a little clump of trees, close to where he was, could conceal a party of French troops, and had thought no more about it. But young Pertelay resolved to lead his men there, and from there to fall upon the Austrian battery.

Pertelay, knowing that on the battlefield no one takes much notice of a single horseman, explained his plan to us, which was for us to go individually, a detour by a sunken road, to arrive one by one behind the wood on the left of the enemy battery, and from there to make a sudden assault on it, without the fear of cannon-balls, because we would be approaching from the side. We would capture the guns and take them to the French lines. The first part of this plan was executed without the Austrian gunners noticing; we reached the back of the little wood, where we re-formed the sections. Pertelay put himself at our head. We went through the wood, and sabre in hand, threw ourselves on the enemy battery at the moment when it was directing a murderous fire on our troops. We sabred some of the gunners, but the rest hid under their ammunition wagons, where our sabres could not reach them. As instructed by Pertelay, we did not kill or wound the men on the limbers, but forced them at sword point to make their horses pull the guns toward the French lines. This order was obeyed in respect of six guns whose riders had remained on horseback, but the riders for the two other guns had dismounted, and although some of the Hussars took the horses by the bridle, they refused to move.

The enemy infantry were running to the aid of their battery; minutes seemed like hours to us; so young Pertelay, satisfied to have captured six guns, ordered us to leave the others and to head, with our booty, at the gallop, for the French lines.

This was a prudent measure, but it proved fatal to our leader, for hardly had we begun our retreat, when the gunners and their officers emerged from their hiding places under the wagons, loaded the two guns which we had not taken with grape-shot and discharged a hail of bullets into our backs.

You can well imagine that thirty horsemen and six artillery pieces, each drawn by six horses and ridden by three transport riders, all proceeding in a state of disorder, presented a target which the grape-shot could hardly miss. We had two sergeants and several Hussars killed or wounded, as well as two of the transport riders. Some of the horses were also put out of action, so that most of the teams were so disorganised that they could not move. Pertelay, keeping perfectly cool, ordered the traces of the dead or injured horses to be cut and Hussars to take the place of the dead transport riders, and we continued quickly on our way. However, the commander of the Austrian battery made use of the few minutes we had taken to do this to direct a second volley of grape-shot at us, which caused further casualties, but we were so resolved not to abandon the six guns which we had captured that we repaired the damage as well as we could, and kept on the move. We were already in touch with the French lines and out of the range of grape-shot, when the enemy artillery officer changed projectiles and fired two cannon-balls at us, one of which shattered the back of poor young Pertelay.

However, our attack on the Austrian battery and its outcome had been seen by the French generals who moved the line forward. The enemy drew back, which allowed the remnants of the 1st Hussars to revisit the area where our unfortunate comrades had fallen. Almost a third of the detachment were killed or wounded. There were five sergeants at the beginning of the action; three had perished; there remained only Pertelay the elder and myself. The poor fellow was wounded but suffered almost more mentally, for he adored his brother, whom we all bitterly regretted. While we were paying him our last respects and picking up the wounded, General Championet arrived with General Suchet, his chief-of-staff. The commander-in-chief had witnessed the actions of the platoon. He gathered us round the six guns which we had just captured, and after praising the courage with which we had rid the French army of a battery which was causing them the most grievous losses, he added that to reward us for having saved the lives of so many of our comrades, and contributed to the day's success, he intended to use the power which a recent decree of the First Consul had given him to award "Armes d'honneur" and that he would award three sabres of honour and one promotion to sous-lieutenant to the detachment, who should decide amongst themselves who the recipients should be. We then regretted even more keenly the loss of young Pertelay, who would have made such a fine officer.

The elder Pertelay, a corporal and a Hussar were awarded the sabres of honour, which, three years later gave the right to the Cross of the Legion of Honour. It remained to be decided which of us would be sous-lieutenant. All my comrades put my name forward, and the commander-in-chief, recalling that General Sras had written to him about my conduct at Santa-Giacomo, designated me sous-lieutenant...! I had been a sergeant for only a month! I have to admit, however, that during the capture of the guns, I had done no more than the rest of my companions; but as I have already said, these good Alsatians did not feel that they had the qualities to take command and become officers. They were unanimous in choosing me, and General Championet, as well as noting the favourable comments of General Sras, was perhaps also glad to be able to please my father.

My father, however, was less than pleased with what he considered to be my over-rapid promotion, and he wrote to me instructing me to refuse it. I would have obeyed; but my father had written in the same strain to General Suchet, the chief-of-staff, and this latter had replied that the commander-in-chief would be very put out to find that one of his divisional generals had taken it upon himself to disapprove of a promotion which he had made. My father then authorised me to accept, and I was gazetted sous-Lieutenant in December 1799.

I was one of the last officers promoted by General Championet, who, not being able to remain in Piedmont in the face of superior forces, was compelled to re-cross the Apennines and lead his army back to Liguria. He was greatly distressed to see his force breaking down, because he was not given enough supplies to support it, and he died two weeks after he had made me an officer. My father, who was now the most senior divisional general, was made provisional commander-in-chief of the army of Italy, whose headquarters were at Nice. He therefore went there and immediately sent back to Provence the few remaining cavalry, as there was no longer any fodder in Liguria. So the 1st Hussars went back to France, but my father kept me behind to become his aide-de-camp.

While we were at Nice, my father received an order from the war ministry to go and take command of the advance guard of the army of the Rhine, where his chief-of-staff Col. Mnard would join him. We were very pleased at this, since want of supplies had reduced the army of Italy to such a state of disorder that it seemed impossible that it could be kept in Liguria. My father was not sorry to be leaving an army which was disintegrating, and was likely to be pushed back across the Var and into France. He prepared to move as soon as General Massna, who had been nominated to replace him, had arrived. He sent M. Gault, his aide-de-camp, to Paris to buy maps and make various preparations for our operations on the Rhine. But fate had decreed otherwise, and my unfortunate father's grave was destined to be in Italy.

When Massna arrived he found no more than the shadow of an army: the soldiers, without pay and almost without clothing and footwear, existing on a quarter of the normal ration, were dying of malnutrition as well as an epidemic of disease, the result of the intolerable privations which they were suffering. The hospitals were full but had no medicines. Some groups of soldiers, and even whole regiments, were daily abandoning their posts and heading for the bridge across the Var, where they forced a passage to get into France and spread themselves over Provence, although saying that they were willing to return if they were given food! The generals were unable to remedy this appalling state of affairs. They became, daily more discouraged, and all were requesting leave or retiring on the grounds of ill-health. Massna had expected that he would be joined in Italy by several of the generals who had helped him to defeat the Russians in Switzerland, among them, Soult, Oudinot and Gazan, but none of them had yet arrived, and it was essential to do something about the serious situation.

Massna, who was born in La Turbie, a village in the little principality of Monaco, was one of the most crafty Italians that ever existed. He did not know my father, but he decided on their first meeting that he was a big-hearted man who loved his country, and, to persuade him to stay, he played on these sensitive areas, his generosity and his patriotism, suggesting to him how much nobler it would be for him to continue to serve in the unhappy army of Italy rather than go to the Rhine. He said that he would take the responsibility for the failure to carry out the orders given to my father by the government if he would agree to stay. My father, beguiled by these speeches and not wishing to leave the new commander in a mess, consented to remain with him. He did not doubt that his chief-of-staff, Col. Mnard, his friend, would also give up the idea of going to the Rhine; but this was not to be. Mnard stuck to the order he had been given, although he was assured that it would be cancelled if he wished. My father felt very badly about this desertion. Mnard hurried off to Paris, where he took the job of chief-of-staff to general Lefebvre.

My father went to Genoa, where he took command of the three divisions which composed the right wing of the army. Despite all the shortages, the winter carnival was quite gay in the town, the Italians being so pleasure-loving! We were lodged in the Centurione Palace, where we spent the end of the winter 1799-1800. My father had left Spire at Nice with the greater part of his baggage. He now took on Col. Sacleux as his chief-of-staff, an admirable man, a good soldier, with a very pleasant personality, if somewhat solemn and serious-minded. He had as his secretary a young man by the name of Colindo, the son of a banker, Signor Trepano of Parma, whom he had picked up after a series of adventures too long to relate here, who became my very good friend.

Early in the spring of 1800, my father was told that General Massna intended to give the command of the right wing to General Soult, who had just arrived, and was much my father's junior, and he was ordered to go back to Savona and head his old division, the third. My father obeyed, though his pride was hurt by this new posting.

Chap. 11.

A serious situation was developing in Italy. Massna had received some reinforcements; he had established a little order in his army, and the campaign of 1800, which led to the memorable siege of Genoa and the battle of Marengo, was about to begin.

52

The snows which covered the mountains separating the two armies having melted, the Austrians attacked us, and their first efforts were directed upon my father's division, the third, stationed at the right of the French line, which they wished to separate from the centre and the left by driving them back from Savona to Genoa.

As soon as hostilities commenced, my father and Col. Sacleux sent all the non-combatants to Genoa; Colindo was among them. As for me, I was thoroughly enjoying myself, exhilarated as I was by the sight of marching troops, the noisy movements of artillery and the excitement of a young soldier at the prospect of action. I was far from suspecting that this war would become so terrible and would cost me so dear.

My father's division, fiercely attacked by greatly superior forces, defended for two days positions at Cadibone and Montenotte, but eventually, seeing themselves on the point of being outflanked, they had to retire to Voltri, and from there to Genoa, where they shut themselves in, together with the two other divisions of the right wing.

I had heard all the well-informed generals deploring the circumstances which forced our separation from the centre and the left, but I had at that time so little understanding of the principles of warfare that I took no notice. I understood well enough that we had been defeated, but as I personally had overcome, before Montenotte, an officer of Burco's Hussars, and takingaking the plume from his shako, had fastened it proudly to the head-band of my bridle, it seemed to me that I was like a knight of the middle-ages returning laden with the spoils of the infidel.

My childish vanity was soon crushed by a dreadful event. During the retreat, and at a moment when my father was giving me an order to take, he was hit by a bullet in the left leg, which had been wounded once before, in the army of the Pyrénées. The injury was serious, and my father would have fallen from his horse if he had not leaned on me. I took him out of the battle area. His wound was dressed. I shed tears as I saw his blood flow, but he tried to calm me, saying that a soldier should have more courage. My father was carried to the Centurione Palace in Genoa, where he had lived during the preceding winter. Our three divisions having entered Genoa, the Austrians blockaded it by land, and the English by sea.

I can hardly bring myself to describe the sufferings of the garrison and the population of Genoa during the two months for which this siege lasted. Famine, fighting and an epidemic of typhus did immense damage. The garrison lost ten thousand men out of sixteen thousand, and there were collected from the streets, every day, seven or eight hundred of the bodies of the inhabitants, of every age, sex, and condition, which were taken behind the church of Carignan to an immense pit filled with quick-lime. The number of victims rose to more than thirty thousand.

For you to understand just how badly the lack of food was felt by the inhabitants, I should explain that the ancient rulers of Genoa, in order to control the populace, had from time immemorial exercised a monopoly over grain, flour and bread, which was operated by a vast establishment protected by cannons and guarded by soldiers, so that when the Doge or the Senate wished to prevent or put down a revolt, they closed the state ovens and reduced the people to starvation. Although by this time the constitution of Genoa had been greatly modified and the aristocracy now had very little influence, there was not, however a single private bakery, and the old system of making bread in the public ovens was still in operation. Now, these public bakeries, which normally provided for a population of a hundred and twenty thousand souls, were closed for forty-five days out of the sixty for which the siege lasted. Neither rich nor poor could buy bread. The little in the way of dried vegetables and rice which was in the shops had been bought up at the beginning of the siege at greatly inflated prices. The troops alone were given a small ration of a quarter of a pound of horse flesh and a quarter of a pound of what was called bread. This was a horrible mixture of various flours, bran, starch, chalk, linseed, oatmeal, rancid nuts and other evil substances. General Thibauld in his diary of the siege described as "Turf mixed with oil."

For forty five days neither bread nor meat was on sale to the public. The richest were able (at the start the siege only,) to buy some dried cod, figs and some other dried goods such as sugar. There was never any shortage of wine, oil and salt, but what use are they without solid food? All the dogs and cats in the town were eaten. A rat could fetch a high price! In the end the starvation became so appalling that when the French troops made a sortie, the inhabitants would follow them in a crowd out of the gates, and rich and poor, women, children and the old would start collecting grass, nettles, and leaves, which they would then cook with some salt. The Genoese government mowed the grass which grew on the ramparts, which was then cooked in the public squares and distributed to the wretched invalids, who had not the strength to go and find for themselves and prepare this crude dish. Even the soldiers cooked nettles and all sorts of herbage with their horse flesh. The richest and most distinguished families in the town envied them this meat, disgusting as it was, for the shortage of fodder had made nearly all the horses sick and even the flesh of those dying of disease was distributed.

During the latter part of the siege, the desperation of the people was something to fear. There were cries that, as in 1756 their fathers had massacred an Austrian army, they should now try to get rid of the French army in the same way; and that it was better to die fighting than to starve to death, after watching their wives and children perish. These threats of revolt were made more serious by the fact that if they were carried out, the English by sea and the Austrians by land would have rushed to join their efforts to those of the insurgents, and would have overwhelmed us.

Amid such dangers and calamities of all sorts, Massna remained immovable and calm, and to prevent any attempt at an uprising, he issued a proclamation that French troops had orders to open fire on any gathering of more than four people. Regiments camped in the squares and the principal streets. The avenues were occupied by cannon loaded with grape-shot. It being impossible for them to come together, the Genoese were unable to revolt.

It may seem surprising that Massna was so determined to hold on to a place where he could not feed the inhabitants and could scarcely maintain his own troops; but Genoa was, at that time, of great importance. Our army had been cut in two. The centre and the left wing had retired behind the Var. As long as Massna occupied Genoa, he kept part of the Austrian army occupied in besieging him and prevented them from employing all their forces against Provence.

Massna knew also that the First Consul was assembling at Dijon, Lyon, and Geneva, an army of reserve, with which he proposed to cross the Alps by the St. Bernard pass, to enter Italy and to surprise the Austrians by falling on their rear while they were directing their efforts at taking Genoa. We therefore had the greatest interest in holding the town for as long as possible. These were the orders of the First Consul, and were subsequently justified by events.

To return to the siege. When he heard that my father had been brought to Genoa, Colindo Trepano hurried to his bedside, and it was there that we met once more. He helped me most tenderly to care for my father, for which I am even more beholden to him because, in the midst of these calamities my father had no one about him. All his staff officers had been ordered to go and attend the commander-in-chief; soon rations were refused to our servants, who were forced to go and take up a musket and line up with the combatants to have a right to the miserable ration which was distributed to the soldiers. No exception was made, apart from a young valet, named Oudin, and a young stable-lad, who looked after the horses; but Oudin deserted us as soon as he knew that my father had typhus.

My father fell ill with this dreadful disease, and at a time when he was in the greatest need of care, there was no one with him except me, Colindo and the stable lad Bastide. We did our best to follow the doctor's instructions, we hardly slept, being endlessly busy massaging my father with camphorated oil and changing his bedclothes and linen.

My father could take no nourishment except soup and I had nothing with which to make it but rotten horse-meat. My heart was breaking.

Providence sent us some help. The huge buildings of the public ovens were next to the walls of the palace where we were living. The terraces were almost touching. It was on the immense terraces of the public ovens that the crushing and mixing took place of all sorts of chicken food which was added to the rotten flour to make the garrison's bread. The stable lad Bastide had noticed that when the workmen of the bakery left the terraces, they were invaded by horde of pigeons who had their nests in the various church towers of the town, and were in the habit of coming to pick up the small amounts of grain which had spilled onto the flagstones. Bastide, who was a very clever lad, crossed the narrow space which separated the terraces, and on that of the public ovens he set up snares and other devices with which he captured pigeons which we used to make soup for my father, who found it excellent, compared to that made from horse.

To the horrors of famine and typhus were added those of a merciless and unceasing war, for the French troops fought all day on land against the Austrians, and when nightfall put an end to the Austrian assaults, the English, Turkish, and Neapolitan fleets, which were protected by darkness from the port's cannons and the batteries on the coast, drew close to the town, into which they hurled a great number of bombs which did fearful damage.

The noise of the guns and the cries of the wounded and dying reached my father and greatly disturbed him. He lamented his inability to place himself at the head of the men of his division. This state of mind worsened his condition. He became more gravely ill from day to day, and progressively weaker. Colindo and I did not leave him for a moment. Eventually, one night when I was on my knees by his bedside, sponging his wound, he spoke to me, perfectly lucidly, and placed his hand caressingly on my head, saying, "Poor child, what will happen to him, alone and without support in the horrors of this terrible siege?" Then he mumbled some words, among which I could distinguish the name of my mother, dropped his arms and closed his eyes...

Although very young and without much length of service, I had seen many dead on various battlefields, and above all on the streets of Genoa; but they had fallen in the open, still in their clothes, which gave them a very different appearance to someone who had died in bed. I had never witnessed this last sad spectacle and I believed that my father had fallen asleep. Colindo knew the truth but had not the heart to tell me, so I was not aware of my error until some time later, when M. Lachze arrived and I saw him pull the sheet over my father's face, saying, "This is a dreadful loss for his family and friends". Only then did I understand that my father was dead.

My grief was so heartbroken that it touched even General Massna, a man not easily moved, particularly in the present situation when he had need of such resolution. The critical position in which he found himself drove him to behave toward me in a way which I thought atrocious, although now I would do the same in the same circumstances.

To avoid anything that could lower the morale of the troops, Massna had forbidden any funeral ceremonies, and as he knew that I had been unwilling to desert the mortal remains of my much-loved father, and thought it was my intention to go with him to his graveside, he feared that his troops might be adversely affected by the sight of a young officer, scarcely more than a boy, following, in tears, his father's bier. So he came the next day before dawn to the room where my father lay, and taking me by the hand, he led me twelve Grenadiers, accompanied only by one officer and Col. Sacleux, took the body in silence, and placed it in a provisional grave on the rampart facing the sea. It was only after this mournful ceremony was over that General Massna told me of it and explained his motives for this decision. I was overcome by misery. It seemed to me that I had lost my poor father for a second time; that he had been deprived of my last services. My protests were in vain and there was nothing I could do but go and pray by my father's grave. I did not know where it was, but Colindo had followed the burial party, and he led me there. This good young man gave me the most touching evidences of sympathy, and this at a time when everyone thought only of themselves.

Nearly all the officers of my father's staff had been killed or carried off by typhus. Out of the eleven which we were at the start support to his general's son, he lived alone in the town. M. Lachze abandoned me also. Only the good Col. Sacleux showed any interest in me, but having been given the command of a brigade, he was constantly outside the walls combatting the enemy. I stayed alone in the huge Centurione Palace with Colindo, Bastide, and the ancient concierge.

A week had scarcely passed since my father's death when General Massna, who needed a large number of officers in attendance because some were killed or wounded almost every day, ordered me to come and of those generals who were dead or unable to mount a horse. I obeyed. I followed the general all day in battle, and when I was not detained at headquarters, I went back to the Palace, and at nightfall, Colindo and I, passing among the dying and the dead bodies of men, women, and children which littered the streets, went to pray at my father's tomb.

The famine in the town continued to worsen. An order went out forbidding any officer from having more than one horse, the rest were to be butchered. There were several of my father's left and I was most unhappy at the thought of these poor beasts being killed. I managed to save their lives by proposing that I should give them to officers of the general staff in exchange for their worn out mounts, which I then sent to the butchery. These horses were later paid for by the state, on production of an order for their delivery. I have kept one of these orders as a curiosity; it bears the signature of General Oudinot, Massna's chief-of-staff.

The cruel loss which I had just suffered, the position in which I found myself, and the sight of the truly horrible scenes in which I was involved every day, taught me more in a short time than I would have learned in a number of happier years. I realised that the starvation and disaster of the siege had made egoists of all those who a few months before had been smothering my father with attention.

I had to find within myself the courage and resource not only for my own needs but to look after Colindo and Bastide. The most pressing requirement was to find something for them to eat, since they were given no food from the army stores. I had, it is true, as an officer, two rations of horse meat and two rations of bread, but all this added together did not amount to more than a pounds weight of very bad food, and we were three! We very rarely caught pigeons now, for their numbers had infinitely diminished.

In my position as aide-de-camp to the commander-in- chief, I was entitled to a place at his table, where once a day was served some bread, some roast horse and some chick peas; but I was so embittered at General Massna having deprived me of the sad consolation of attending my father's burial, that I could not bring myself to sit down at his table, although all my comrades were there and a place was reserved for me. But at last the wish to help my two unfortunate companions decided me to go and eat with the commander-in-chief. From then on Colindo and Bastide had each a quarter of a pound of horse meat and the same amount of bread. As for me, I did not have enough to eat, for the portions served at the general's table were exceedingly small, and I was worked hard. Often I had to lie on the ground to stop myself from fainting.

Providence came once more to our aid. Bastide had been born in the region of Cantal, and he had met, the previous winter, another Auvergnian whom he knew, and who was living in Genoa where he had a small business. Bastide went to visit this friend, and was surprised, on entering the house, to smell the odour which floats around a grocer's shop. Bastide remarked on this and asked his friend if he had some food. His friend admitted that he had, and begged Bastide to keep this a secret, since all food found in private hands was confiscated and taken to the army stores. The shrewd Bastide then offered to arrange the purchase of any surplus provisions by someone who would pay cash and would keep the secret inviolate. He came to tell me of his discovery. My father had left me some thousands of francs, so I bought, and brought back to our dwelling at night, a quantity of dried cod, cheese, figs, sugar, chocolate *etc.* All of which was extremely expensive, and the Auvergnian had most of my money. However I was happy to pay whatever he asked, for I heard daily at general headquarters suggestions that the siege would continue and the famine get worse. Sadly, this in fact happened. My joy at having procured some food was increased by the thought that I had thereby saved the life of my friend Colindo, who, without it, would have assuredly died of starvation, for he knew no one in the army except me and Col. Sacleux, who was shortly to be struck down by a dreadful misfortune.

Massna, attacked on all sides, seeing his troops worn down by continual battle and famine, forced to hold down a large population, driven to despair by hunger, found himself in a most critical position, and believed that to maintain good order in the army he needed to impose iron discipline. So any officer who did not execute his orders immediately was dismissed, under the power which the law gave at that time to the commander-in-chief.

Several examples of this kind had already been made when, during a sortie which we had pushed forward some six leagues from the town, the brigade commanded by Col. Sacleux was not in position at the time ordered in a valley where it was meant to block the passage of the Austrians, who thus escaped.

The commander-in-chief, furious at seeing his plans come to nothing, dismissed poor Col. Sacleux by publishing his dismissal in an order of the day. Sacleux may well not have understood what was expected of him, but he was a very brave man. Assuredly he would have blown his brains out, had he not been determined to restore his honour. He took up a musket and joined the ranks as a private soldier! He came to see us one day, Colindo and I were sore at heart to see this excellent man dressed as a simple infantryman. We said our good-byes to Sacleux who, after the surrender of the town, was restored to his rank of colonel at the request of Massna himself, who had been impressed by Sacleux's courage. But the following year, when peace had been made in Europe, Sacleux, perhaps wishing to rid himself completely of the stigma with which he had been so unjustly branded, asked to be posted to the war in Santa-Dominica, where he was killed at the moment when he was about to be promoted to brigadier-general! There are men who, in spite of their merits, have a cruel destiny; of which he was an example.

Chap. 12.

I shall discuss only briefly the conduct of the siege or blockade which we sustained. The fortifications of Genoa consisted at that time of a plain wall, flanked by towers; but what made the place well suited for defence was the fact that it is surrounded at a short distance by mountains, the summits and flanks of which are dotted with forts and strong-points. The Austrians continually attacked these positions. When they took one, we went to retake it, and the next day they came to take it again. If they managed to do so, we went to chase them out once more. There was an endless shuttling back and forth, with varying results, but in the end, we remained in control of the terrain. These encounters were often very fierce. In one of them, General Soult, who was General Massna's right hand man, was climbing up Monte Corona at the head of his men to retake a fort of that name, which we had lost the day before, when his knee was struck by a bullet at a moment when the enemy, who greatly outnumbered his party, were running down from the top of the mountain. It was impossible with the few troops we had at this point to resist the avalanche, and a retreat was called for. The soldiers carried General Soult for some way, on their muskets, but the intolerable pain which he suffered decided them that he should be left at the foot of a tree, where his brother and one of his aides-de-camp stayed with him to protect him from being attacked by the first enemy troops to arrive. Luckily there were among these some officers who had much respect for their illustrious prisoner.

The capture of General Soult having encouraged the Austrians, they pushed us back to the city wall, which they were preparing to attack when a heavy storm darkened the blue sky, which we had had since the beginning of the siege. The rain fell in torrents. The Austrians halted and most of them sought shelter in the blockhouses or under the trees. Then General Massna, one of whose principal gifts was the ability to turn to advantage the unforeseen incidents of warfare, addressed his men, rekindled their spirit, and having reinforced them with some troops from the town, he ordered them to fix bayonets and led them, at the height of the storm, against the erstwhile victorious Austrians who, taken by surprise, retired in disorder. Massna pursued them with such effect that he cut off some three thousand Grenadiers, who laid down their arms.

This was not the first time that we had taken numerous prisoners, for the total of those we had captured since the beginning of the siege amounted to more than eight thousand; but having no food for them, Massna had always sent them back, on the condition that they would not be used against us for a period of six months. Although the officers held religiously to their promise, the wretched soldiers, who went back to the Austrian camp ignorant of the undertaking that their leaders had made on their behalf, were transferred to other regiments and forced to fight against us once more. If they fell again into our hands, something that often happened, they were once more sent back and transferred anew; so that there were very many of these men who, on their own admission, had been captured four or five times. Massna, angered at the lack of good faith on the part of the Austrian generals, decided that this time he would retain both officers and men of the three thousand Grenadiers whom he had captured; and so that the duty of guarding them would not fall on his troops, he had the unfortunate prisoners loaded into floating hulks moored in the middle of the harbour with the guns of the harbour mole aimed at them. He then sent an envoy to General Ott, who commanded the Austrian troops before Genoa, to reproach him for his failure to keep his word, and to warn him that he did not consider himself bound to give the prisoners more than half the ration of the French soldier; but that he would agree to an arrangement which the Austrians might make with the British, whereby vessels might bring, every day, food for the prisoners, and not leave until they had seen it eaten, so that it could not be thought that Austrian general who may have hoped that a refusal would compel Massna to send back the three thousand soldiers, whom he probably intended to use again, turned down this philanthropic proposal, and Massna then carried out his threat.

The French ration was composed of a quarter of a pound of disgusting bread and an equal amount of horse flesh; the prisoners were given only half this amount! This was fifteen days before the end of the siege. For fifteen days, these poor devils remained on this regime!. Every two or three days Messna renewed his offer to the enemy general; he never accepted, perhaps out of obstinacy, or perhaps because the English admiral, Lord Kieth, was unwilling to employ his long-boats for fear, it is said, that they would bring typhus back to the fleet. However that may be, the wretched Austrians were left howling with rage and hunger in their floating prison. It was truly appalling! In the end, having eaten their boots and packs, and perhaps some dead bodies, they nearly all died of starvation! There were hardly more than seven or eight hundred left when the place was surrendered to our enemies. The Austrian soldiers, when they entered the town, hurried to the harbour and gave food to their compatriots with so little caution that many of them died as a result.

I have described this horrible episode, firstly as an example of the sort of ghastly event which war brings in its train, but principally to brand with shame the conduct and lack of good faith of the Austrian general, who forced soldiers who had been captured and released on parole, to take up arms against us once more, although he had promised to send them back to Germany.

In the course of the fighting which took place during the siege, I ran into a number of dangers but I shall limit myself to mentioning two of the more serious.

I have already said that the Austrians and the English took it in turns to keep us constantly in action. The first attacked us at dawn, on the landward side, and we fought them all day; at night, Lord Kieth's fleet would begin its bombardment, and try, under cover of darkness, to seize the harbour; which forced the garrison to keep a keen look-out on the seaward side, and prevented it from having any rest or relaxation. Now, one night, when the bombardment was more violent than usual, the commander-in-chief was warned that the light of Bengal flares burning on the beach had disclosed numerous boat loads of English soldiers heading for the harbour breakwater. Massna, his staff, and the squadron of guides which went everywhere with him, immediately mounted their horses. We were about a hundred and fifty to two hundred horsemen when, passing through a little square called Campetto, the general stopped to speak to an officer who was returning from the harbour. Someone shouted "Look out for bombs!" And at that moment, one fell onto the crowded square.

I and several others had pushed our horses under a balcony which overhung the door of an hotel, and it was on this balcony that the bomb fell. It reduced the balcony to rubble, and bounced onto the road, where it exploded with a fearful bang in the middle of the square, which was lit for an instant by its malevolent light, after which there was complete darkness. One expected many casualties. There was the most profound silence, which was broken by the voice of General Massna, asking if anyone was hurt. There was no reply, for by some miracle, not one of the horses or men had been hit by the flying fragments. As for those who, like me, had been under the balcony, we were covered with dust and bits of building material, but nobody was injured.

I have said that the English bombarded us only at night. However, one day, when they were celebrating some occasion or other, their ships, dressed overall, approached the town in broad daylight, and amused themselves by hurling at us a large number of projectiles. Those of our batteries which were in the best position to reply to this fire, were located near the breakwater on a big bastion in the form of a tower, known as the Lanterne. The general ordered me to take a message to the officer in charge of this battery, instructing him to direct all his efforts on an English brig, which had insolently anchored a short distance from the Lanterne. Our gunners fired with such accuracy that one of our large bombs fell on the English brig, piercing it from deck to keel so that it sank almost immediately. This so infuriated the English admiral that he had all his guns trained on the Lanterne, on which they now opened a violent fire. My mission being completed, I should have returned to Massna; but it is rightly said that young soldiers, not recognising danger, confront it more coolly than those with more experience. The spectacle of which I was a witness, I found very interesting. The platform of the Lanterne was floored with flagstones and was the size of a small courtyard. It was equipped with twelve cannons on enormous wooden mountings. Although it may be very difficult for ship at sea to aim its fire with sufficient accuracy to hit such a small target as was the platform of the Lanterne, the English managed to land several bombs there. As these bombs descended, the gunners took shelter behind or underneath the massive timbers of the gun mountings. I did the same; but this shelter was not entirely safe, because the flagstones presented a great resistance to the bombs, which, being unable to bury themselves, rolled unpredictably about the platform in all directions, and the fragments from their explosion could pass under or behind the mountings. It was, therefore, absurd to stay there when, like me, one was not obliged to do so. But I experienced a fearful pleasure, if one can describe it thus, in running here and there with the gunners whenever a bomb fell, and emerging with them as soon as the fragments from its explosion had settled. It was a game which could have cost me dear. One gunner had his legs broken, others were wounded by bomb fragments, lumps of metal which did terrible damage to anything they hit. One of them sliced through the thick timber baulk of a mounting behind which I was sheltering. However, I remained on the platform until Col. Mouton, who later became Marshal the Comte de Lobeau, and who, having served under my father, took an interest in me, while passing, caught sight of me. He came over to the Lanterne and ordered me sharply to come down and return to my post beside General Massna. He added, "You are still very young, but you should realise that, in war, it is stupid to expose yourself to needless danger. Would you be any better off if you had a leg smashed for no good reason?"

I never forgot this lesson, and I have often thought of the difference it would have made to my life, if I had lost a leg at the age of seventeen.

Chap. 13.

The courage and tenacity with which Massna had defended Genoa would have very important results. Major Franceschi, sent by Massna to contact the First Consul, had managed to slip through the enemy fleet at night, both in going and coming. On arriving back in Genoa he said that he had left Bonaparte descending the St. Bernard at the head of the army of reserve. Field-marshal Mlas was so convinced of the impossibility of bringing an army across the Alps, that while part of his force, under General Ott was blockading us, he had gone with the remainder fifty leagues away, to attack General Suchet on the Var. This gave the First Consul the opportunity to enter Italy without resistance, so that the army of reserve had reached Milan before the Austrians had ceased to regard its existence as imaginary. The First Consul, once in Italy, would have liked to go straight away to the aid of the town's brave garrison, but to do that it was necessary for him to unite all the elements of his force, such as the artillery and military supplies, whose passage across the Alps had proved extremely difficult. This delay gave Marshal Mlas the time to hurry with his main force from Nice in order to oppose Bonaparte, who was then unable to continue his march towards Genoa without defeating the Austrian army.

While Bonaparte and Mlas were engaged in marches and countermarches in preparation for a battle which would decide the destiny of France and Italy, the garrison of Genoa found itself reduced to its last extremity. The typhus epidemic was raging. The hospitals had become ghastly charnel houses; starvation was at its worst. Nearly all the horses had been eaten, and though for a long time the soldiers had had no more than half a pound of rotten food daily, the distribution for the following day was not assured. There was absolutely nothing left when, on the 15th Prairial Massna gathered all his generals and colonels together and announced that he had decided to attempt a breakout with those remaining men who were fit for duty, to try to reach Livorno; but his officers declared unanimously that the troops were no longer in a state to engage in combat, or even a simple march, unless they were given sufficient food to restore their strength, and the stores were completely empty! General Massna then considered that, having carried out the orders of the

First Consul and facilitated his entry into Italy, that it was his duty to save the remains of a garrison which had fought so valiantly, and which it was in the country's interest to preserve. He therefore resolved to treat for the evacuation of the place, for he would not allow the word capitulation to be uttered. The English admiral and General Ott had, for more than a month, been making proposals for a parley, which Massna had always turned down; but now, compelled by circumstance, he told them that he would accept. The conference took place in the little chapel which is situated in the middle of the bridge of Conegliano, and which is, as a result, between the sea and the French and Austrian lines. The French, English, and Austrian staffs occupied each end of the bridge. I was present at this most interesting event.

The foreign generals treated Massna with much respect and consideration, and although he demanded favourable conditions, Admiral Kieth said more than once that the defense had been so heroic that they did not wish to refuse them. It was then agreed that the garrison would not be made prisoners, that they could retain their weapons and could go to Nice, and that having reached there they would be free to engage in further hostilities.

Massna, who realised how important it was that the First Consul should not be led into making any false move because of his anxiety to go to the aid of Genoa, asked that the negotiations should permit the safe passage of two officers through the Austrian lines, whom he proposed to send to Bonaparte to inform him of the evacuation of the town by the French. General Ott opposed this because he intended to leave with some twenty-five thousand men of the blockading force to go and join Field-marshal Mlas, and he did not want these French officers to warn General Bonaparte of his movements. But Admiral Kieth overruled this objection. The treaty was about to be signed when, from far away, in the midst of the mountains, came the distant sound of gunfire. Massna held up his pen, saying, "That is the First Consul, who has arrived with his army." The foreign commanders were much taken aback, but after a long pause it was realised that the sound was that of thunder, and Massna appended his signature.

It is to be regretted that the garrison and its commander were deprived of the fame which would have been theirs if they had been able to hold Genoa until the arrival of Bonaparte; and furthermore, Massna would have liked to hold out for a few more days, to delay the departure of General Ott's men to join in the battle, which was inevitable, between the First Consul and Field-marshal Mlas. In the event, General Ott was unable to join the main Austrian army until the day after the battle of Marengo, the result of which might have been very different if the Austrians, whom we had great difficulty in overcoming, had had twenty-five thousand more men with which to oppose us. The Austrians took possession of Genoa on the 16th Prairial(May) after a siege which had lasted two whole months.

Massna, as has been said, considered it so important that the First Consul was informed immediately about the situation that he had demanded a safe conduct for two aides-de-camp, so that if any thing untoward befell one of them, the other could carry his despatch. As it would be useful if an officer going on such a mission spoke Italian, Massna chose a Major Graziani, an Italian who was in the French service, but being a most suspicious man, Massna feared that a foreigner might be corrupted by the Austrians and delay his journey, so he sent me to make sure that he made all possible haste. This precaution was unnecessary as Major Graziani was a man of probity who knew the urgency of his mission.

On the 16th Prairial we departed from Genoa where I left Colindo, whom I expected to collect in a few days time, as we knew that the First Consul's army was not very far away. Major Graziani and I reached it the next day at Milan.

General Bonaparte spoke to me with sympathy about the loss which I had suffered, and promised that he would be a father to me if I behaved myself well, a promise which he kept. He asked us endless questions about the events which had occurred in Genoa, and about the strength and movements of the Austrian forces we had come through to reach Milan; he kept us by him, and had horses provided for us from his stable, since we had travelled on post mules.

We followed the First Consul to Montebello and then to the battlefield of Marengo, where we were employed to carry his orders. I shall not go into any details about this battle, where I ran into no danger; one knows that we were on the brink of defeat, and might have fallen if General Ott's men had arrived in time to take part in the action. The First Consul, who feared that he might see them appear at any moment, was very anxious, and did not relax until our cavalry and the infantry of General Desaix, of whose death he was still unaware, had ensured victory by overwhelming the Grenadiers of General Zach. Seeing that the horse which I was riding was slightly wounded on a leg, he took me by the ear, and said, laughing, "I lend you my horses, and look what happens to them!" Major Graziani having died in 1812, I am the only French officer who was present at the siege of Genoa and the battle of Marengo.

After this memorable affair, I went back to Genoa, which the Austrians had left as a result of our victory at Marengo. There I we embarked on a French brig, which in twenty-four hours carried us to Nice. Some days later, a ship from Leghorn brought Colindo's mother, who had come in search of her son. This fine young man and I had come through some very rough times together, which had strengthened the friendship between us, but our paths were divergent and we had to part, albeit with much regret.

I have said earlier, that about the middle of the siege, Franceschi, carrying despatches from General Massna to the First Consul, had reached France by passing through the enemy fleet at night. He took with him the news of my father's death. My mother had thereupon nominated a council of guardians, who sent to the aged Spire, who was at Nice with the coach and my father's baggage, an order to sell everything and return to Paris, which he then did. There was now nothing to detain me on the banks of the Var, and I was in a hurry to rejoin my dear mother; but this was not so easy; public coaches were, at the time, very scarce; the one that ran from

Nice to Lyon went only every second day and was booked up for several weeks by sick or wounded officers, coming, like me, from Genoa.

officers and I decided to form a group to go to Grenoble on foot, crossing the foothills of the Alps by way of Grasse, Sisteron, Digne and Gap. Mules would carry our small amount of baggage, which would allow us to cover eight to ten leagues every day. Bastide was with me and was a great help to me, for I was not accustomed to making such long journeys on foot, and it was very hot. After eight days of very difficult walking, we reached Grenoble, from where we were able to take coaches to Lyon. It was with sorrow that I saw once more the town and the hotel where I had stayed with my father in happier times. I longed for and yet dreaded the reunion with my mother and my brothers. I fancied that they would ask me to account for what I had done with her husband and their father! I was returning alone, and had left him in his grave in a foreign land! I was very unhappy and had need of a friend who would understand and share my grief, abundance and good living, was madly jolly, which I found most wounding; so I decided to leave for Paris without him; but he claimed, now that I had no need of him, that it was his duty to deliver me to the arms of my mother, and I was forced to put up with his company as far as Paris, to where we went by mail coach.

There are scenes which are perhaps better left to the imagination, so I shall not attempt to describe my first heartbreaking meeting with my widowed mother and my brothers. You can picture it for yourselves.

My mother had a rather pretty country house at Carrire, near the forest of Saint-Germain. I spent two months there with her, my uncle Canrobert, who had returned from emigration, and an old knight of Malta, M. d'Estresse, a friend of my late father. Adolphe was not in Paris, he was in Rennes with Bernadotte, the commander-in-chief of the army of the west, but my younger brothers and M. Gault came to see us from time to time. In spite of the kindness and shows of affection which were lavished on me, I fell into a state of sombre melancholy, and my health deteriorated. I had suffered so much, physically and mentally! I became incapable of doing any work. Reading which I had always loved became insupportable. I spent the greater part of the day alone in the forest, where I lay in the shade absorbed in my sorrowful reflections. In the evenings, I accompanied my mother, my uncle, and the old knight on their usual walk along the bank of the Seine; but I took very little part in the conversation, and hid from them my sad thoughts, which revolved always about my poor father, dying for want of proper care. Although my condition alarmed my mother, Canrobert, and M. d'Estresse, they had the good sense not to make matters worse by any remarks which would have only irritated a sick mind, but they sought gradually to chase away the unhappy memories which were so affecting me by bringing forward the holidays of my two younger brothers, who came to live with us in the country. The presence of these two children, whom I dearly loved, eased my mind of its sorrows, by the care I took to make their stay at Carrire a happy one. I took them to Versailles, to Maisons and to Marly, and their childish happiness slowly brought back to life my spirits which had been so cruelly crushed by misfortune. Who could have thought that these two children, so lovely and full of life would soon be no more?

Chap. 14.

The end of the autumn of 1800 was approaching; my mother went back to Paris, my young brothers went back to school, and I was ordered to join Bernadotte at Rennes.

Bernadotte had been my father's best friend, and my father had helped him in various ways on many occasions. In recognition of the debt owed to my family, he had written to me saying that he had reserved a place for me as his aide-de-camp. I received this letter at Nice when I returned from Genoa, and on the strength of it, I refused an offer from General Massna to take me on as a permanent aide-de-camp, and to allow me to spend several months with my mother before joining him and the army of Italy.

My father had arranged that my brother Adolphe should continue his studies in order to enter the polytechnic; so he was not a soldier when my father died; but on hearing this sad news, he rebelled at the thought that his younger brother was already an officer, and had been in action, while he was still on a school bench. He gave up the studies required for the technical arms, and opted to join the infantry instead, which allowed him to leave school.

He was presented with a good opportunity. The government had ordered a new regiment to be raised in the department of the Seine. The officers for this regiment were to be selected by General Lefebvre, who, as you know, had replaced my father in command of the Paris division. General Lefebvre was only too pleased to do something for the son of one of his old companions who had died in the service of his country; he therefore awarded my brother the rank of sous-lieutenant in this new unit. So far, so good! But instead of going to join his company, and without waiting for my return from Genoa, Adolphe hurried off to General Bernadotte, who, without further ado, handed the vacant post to the first brother to arrive, as if it was the prize in a race! So when I went to join the general staff at Rennes, I learned that my brother had been gazetted as permanent aide-de-camp, and I was only a supernumerary, that is to say temporary. I was very disappointed, because, had I expected this, I would have accepted the proposal made by General Massna. But this opportunity had now passed. It was in vain that General Bernadotte assured me that he would obtain an increase in the establishment of his aides-de-camp, I did not think this likely, and was convinced that I would soon be moved elsewhere.

Bernadotte's staff was made up of officers who nearly all reached senior positions; four were already colonels. The most outstanding was, undoubtedly, Grard. He was very clever, brave and had a natural talent for warfare. He was under the command of Marshal Grouchy at Waterloo, and gave him some sound advice, which could have led us to victory. Out of the eleven aides-de-camp attached to Bernadotte's staff, two became marshals, three lieutenant-generals, four were brigadiers and one was killed in action.

66

In the winter of 1800, Portugal, backed by the English, had declared war on Spain, and the French government had resolved to support the latter. In consequence, troops were sent to Bayonne and Bordeaux, and the companies of Grenadiers who belonged to various regiments scattered throughout Brittany and the Vende were gathered together at Tours. This corps d'lite was intended to be the nucleus of the so-called army of Portugal, which Bernadotte was destined to command. The general had to move his headquarters to Tours; to where had to be sent all his horses and equipment, as well all that was required for the officers attached to his service. But the general, partly to receive his final orders from the First Consul and partly to take Madame Bernadotte back, had to go to Paris; and as it was customary in these circumstances during the absence of the general for the officers of his staff to be permitted to go and take leave of their families, it was decided that all the permanent aides could go to Paris, and that the supernumeraries would go to Tours with the baggage to supervise the servants, pay them every month, arrange with the supply commission for the distribution of forage, and the allotment of lodgings for the great number of men and horses. This disagreeable duty fell to me and my fellow supernumerary Lieutenant Maurin.

In the depths of winter and the most atrocious weather, we made on horseback the long eight days journey from Rennes to Tours, where we had all sorts of difficulties in setting up the headquarters. We had been told that we would not be there for much more than a fortnight, but we stayed there, bored stiff, for six weary months, while our comrades were disporting themselves in the capital. That was a foretaste of the unpleasant duties which fell to me as a supernumerary aide-de-camp. So ended the year 1800, during which I had undergone so much mental and physical suffering.

The town of Tours had many inhabitants, and there were many diversions; but although I received many invitations I did not accept any of them. Fortunately my time was fully occupied in looking after the large collection of men and horses, without which the isolation in which I lived would have been insupportable. The number of horses belonging to the commander-in-chief and the officers of his staff amounted to more than eighty, and all were at my disposal. I rode two or three every day, and went for some long rides round Tours, which although solitary, had for me much charm, and gave me gentle solace.

Chap. 15.

The First Consul now changed his mind about the army of Portugal. He gave the command to his brother-in-law, General Leclerc, and kept General Bernadotte in command of the army of the west. In consequence, the general staff, which my brother and the other aides-de-camp had just joined at Tours, was ordered to return to Brittany and betake itself to Brest, where the commander-in-chief was to be stationed. It is a long way from Tours to Brest, but the weather was fair, we were a young crowd, and the trip was great fun. I was unable to ride on horseback, because of an accidental injury to my hindquarters, so I rode in one of the commander-in-chief's coaches. We found him awaiting us at Brest.

The harbour at Brest held at that time not only a great number of French vessels, but also the Spanish fleet, commanded by Admiral Gravina, who was later killed at Trafalgar. When we arrived in Brest, the two allied fleets were expected to take to Ireland, General Bernadotte and a large invading force of French and Spanish troops; but while we awaited this expedition,—which never actually took place—the presence of so many army and naval officers greatly animated the town of Brest. The commander-in-chief, the admirals and several of the generals entertained daily. The troops of the two nations mingled on the best of terms, and I made the acquaintance of several Spanish officers.

We were thoroughly enjoying ourselves at Brest, when the commander-in-chief decided it would be a good idea to move his headquarters to Rennes, a dismal town, but more in the centre of his command. We had hardly arrived there when what I had foreseen happened. The First Consul cut the number of aides-de-camp allotted to the commander-in-chief. He was allowed only one colonel, five officers of lower rank and no additional officers. As a result I was told that I was to be posted to a regiment of light cavalry. I would have resigned myself to this, if it had been to return to the first Hussars, where I was known and whose uniform I wore; but it was more than a year since I had left the regiment, and I had been replaced, so I was ordered to join the 25th Chasseurs, who had just gone to Spain and were on the frontier with Portugal around Salamanca and Zamora. I felt increasingly bitter about the way I had been treated by General Bernadotte, for without his false promises I would have been an aide-de-camp to Messna and regained my place in the 1st Hussars.

So I was much discontented....But one must obey. Once I had got over my resentment—which does not last long at that age—I could not wait to get on the road and leave General Bernadotte, of whom I thought I had good reason to complain. I had very little money. My father had often lent money to Bernadotte, in particular when he bought the estate of Lagrange; but although he knew that, scarcely recovered from an injury, I was about to cross a large part of France and all of Spain and, what is more, had to buy a new uniform, he never offered to advance me a sou; and not for anything in the world would I have asked him to do so. Very luckily for me my mother had, at Rennes, an elderly uncle, M. de Verdal of Gruniac, a former major in the infantry of Ponthivre, with whom she had spent the first years of the revolution. This old man was a little eccentric, but very good-hearted; not only did he advance me the money which I desperately needed, but he gave it to me out of his own pocket.

Although, at this period, the Chasseurs wore the same dolman as the Hussars, theirs was green. I was foolish enough to shed a few tears when I had to discard the Bercheny uniform, and renounce the name of Hussar to become a Chasseur!

My farewell to General Bernadotte was somewhat cool; however he gave me letters of introduction to Lucien Bonaparte, our ambassador at Madrid, and to General Leclerc, our commander in Portugal.

On the day of my departure, all the aides-de-camp joined me in a farewell luncheon; then I set out with a heavy heart. I arrived at Nantes after two days of travel, dog tired, with a pain in my side, and quite sure that I would not be able to stand riding on horseback the four hundred and fifty leagues which I had to cover to reach the frontier of Portugal. By chance, however, I met in the house of an old acquaintance from Sorze, who lived in Nantes, a Spanish officer named Don Raphael, who was on his way to join his regimental depot at Estramadura. We agreed to travel together, and that I would be guide as far as the Pyrénées, after which he would take over.

We went by stage-coach through the Vende, where almost all the market towns and villages still bore the marks of fire although the civil war had been over for two years. These ruins made a sorry spectacle. We passed through La Rochelle, Rochefort and Bordeaux. From Bordeaux to Bayonne we rode in a sort of "Berlin" which never went at faster than a walking pace over the sands of Landes, so we often got out and walked alongside until we would stop to rest under a group of pine trees. Then, sitting in the shade, Don Raphael would take up his mandolin and sing. In this way we took six days to reach Bayonne.

Before crossing the Pyrénées, I had to report to the general commanding Bayonne. His name was General Ducos, an excellent man, who had served under my father. Out of concern for my safety, he wished to delay my entry into Spain for a few days, because he had just heard that a gang of robbers had plundered some travellers not far from the frontier. Even before the War of Independence and the Civil Wars, the Spanish character, at once both adventurous and lazy, had given them a noticeable taste for brigandage, and this taste was encouraged by the splitting up of the country into several kingdoms which once formed independent states, each with its own laws, usages, and frontiers. Some of these states imposed customs duties, some, such as Biscay and Navarre, did not; and the result was that the inhabitants of the customs-free countries constantly tried to smuggle dutiable goods into those whose frontiers were guarded by lines of armed and active customs officers. The smugglers, on their part, had, from time immemorial, formed bands, which employed force when cunning was insufficient, and whose occupation was not considered in any way dishonourable by the majority of Spaniards, who saw it as a just war against the imposition of customs. Preparing their expeditions, collecting intelligence, posting armed guards, hiding in the mountains, where they lie about smoking and sleeping, such is the life of the smugglers, who, as a result of the large profits to be made from a single operation, can live in comfortable idleness for several months. However, when the customs officers, with whom they have frequent skirmishes, have been victorious and confiscated their goods, these Spanish smugglers, reduced to extremes, think nothing of becoming highwaymen, a profession which they pursue with a certain magnanimity, since they never kill travellers, and always leave them the means to continue their journey. They had just done as much to an English family, and General Ducos, who wished to spare us the disagreeable experience of being robbed, had for this reason decided to delay our departure; but Don Raphael assured him that he knew enough about the habits of Spanish robbers to be certain that the safest time to travel in a province was just after a gang had committed some offence, because they then cleared off and hid for a while. So general Ducos allowed us to leave.

69

Draught-horses were at this time unknown in Spain, where all coaches, even the king's, were drawn by mules. There were no stage-coaches, and in the post-houses nothing but saddle horses. So that even the greatest of noblemen, who had their own coaches, were forced when they travelled to hire harness mules and go by short stages. The comfortably off took light carriages, which did not go more than ten leagues a day. The ordinary people attached themselves to caravanserais of donkey-men, who carried baggage in the same way as our carters, but no one travelled alone, partly for fear of robbers, and partly because of the mistrust with which a solitary traveller was regarded. After our arrival in Bayonne, Don Raphael, who was now in charge, said to me that as we were not such grandees that we could hire a coach, nor so poor that we had to join the donkey-men, there remained only two possibilities, either we rode on horseback or we took a seat in a carriage. Travelling on horseback, of which I have done so much, did not seem suitable, as we would have no means of carrying our baggage, so it was decided that we should go by carriage.

Don Raphael bargained with an individual who agreed to take us to Salamanca for 800 francs a head, and to lodge us and feed us on the way, at his own expense. This was double what a similar journey would have cost in France, and I had already spent a lot of money to get to Bayonne; but that was the price, and as there, was no other way for me to join my new regiment, I had to accept.

We left in an enormous and ancient four-wheeled carriage, in which three of the seats were occupied by a citizen of Cadiz, his wife and daughter, while a Benedictine Prior from the university of Salamanca completed the party.

Everything was new to me on this trip. Firstly, the harnessing, which greatly surprised me. The team consisted of six splendid mules, of which, to my astonishment, only the two on the shaft had bridles and reins, the remaining four went freely, guided only by the voices of the coachman and his "Zagal" who, agile as a squirrel, sometimes went for more than a league on foot, running beside his mules, which were at full trot, then, in a blink of an eye he would climb up on to the seat beside his master, only to get down and then up again; which he did twenty times a day; going round the coach and the harness to make sure that nothing was out of order, and while doing all this, singing to encourage his mules, each one of which he called by name. He never struck them, his voice alone being enough to urge on any mule which was not pulling its weight.

These activities, and in particular the man's singing, I found most entertaining. I also took a lively interest in what was said in the coach, for, although I did not speak Spanish, what I knew of Italian and Latin enabled me to understand much of what my fellow passengers were saying, to whom I replied in French, which they understood reasonably well. I did not smoke, but the five Spaniards, even the two ladies and the monk, soon lit up their cigars. We were all in good spirits. Don Raphael, the ladies, and even the fat monk sang together.

Normally we left in the morning. We stopped from one o'clock to three, to dine, rest the mules, and allow the heat of the day to pass, during which time one slept; what the Spanish call the siesta. Then we went on to our night stop. The meals were sufficiently plentiful, but the Spanish cuisine seemed to me, at first, to taste awful, however I got used to it; but I could never have got used to the horrible beds which we were offered at night in the pousadas or inns. They were really disgusting, and Don Raphael, who had just spent a year in France was forced to agree. To avoid this unpleasantness, on the first day of my arrival in Spain, I asked if I could sleep on a bale of straw. Sadly, I discovered that such a thing as a bale of straw was unknown in Spain, because, instead of threshing the sheaves of corn they have them trampled under foot by mules, which breaks the straw into short bits, scarcely as long as a finger. But I had the bright idea of filling a large cloth sack with this short straw, which I placed in a barn and slept on covered by my cloak; thus avoiding the vermin with which the beds and the rooms were infested. In the morning I emptied the sack and put it in the coach and each evening I refilled it so that I had a clean palliasse. Don Raphael followed my example.

We crossed the provinces of Navarre, Biscay and Alava, country of high mountains; then we crossed the Ebro and entered the immense plains of Castile. We passed through Burgos and Valladolid, and arrived, at last, after a journey lasting fifteen days, at Salamanca.

There, not without regret I parted from my good travelling companion, whom I was to meet once more in the same part of the world, during the War of Independence. General Leclerc was at Salamanca. He received me kindly, and even proposed that I should stay with him as a supernumerary aide-de-camp, but my recent experience had taught me that although the post of aide-de-camp offers one more freedom and comfort than regimental duty, this is only when one is on the establishment. As a supernumerary you are landed with all the unpleasant jobs, and you have only a very precarious position. I therefore turned down the favour which I was offered and asked to go and join my regiment. It was a good thing that I took this step, because, the following year, the general, having been given the command of the expedition to Santa Dominica, took with him, on his general staff, a lieutenant who had accepted the post which I had turned down, and all these officers and the general died of yellow fever.

I joined the 25th Chasseurs at Salamanca. The colonel was M. Moreau, an old officer and a very fine fellow. He gave me a warm welcome, as did my new comrades; and in a few days I was on the best of terms with everybody. I was introduced to the town's society, for at that time the presence of the French was highly acceptable to the Spanish, and completely opposite to what it became later. In 1801 we were their allies. We had come to fight for them against the Portuguese and the English, so we were treated as friends. The French officers were billeted with the wealthiest inhabitants and there was competition to have them. We were received everywhere. We were overwhelmed by invitations. Being thus admitted into the family life of the Spaniards, we learned more, in a short time, about their way of living than officers who came to the peninsula during the War of Independence could have learned in several years.

I was billeted in the home of a university professor, who had given me a very nice room looking out onto the handsome Salamanca square. My regimental duties were not very onerous and left me plenty of leisure time, which I used to study the Spanish language, which is, in my opinion, the most elegant and beautiful in Europe. It was at Salamanca that I saw, for the first time, the famous General Lasalle. He sold me a horse.

The fifteen thousand French troops sent to Spain with General Leclerc formed the right wing of the Spanish Grand Army, which was commanded by the "Prince de la Paix" and we were therefore under his orders. This man (Emmanuel Godoy) was the queen's favourite and was, in effect, the king. He came to revue us on one occasion. He seemed to me to be very pleased with himself, and although he was small and undistinguished looking, he was not lacking in charm and ability.

Godoy started the army moving, and our regiment went to Toro and then to Zamora. I was sorry to leave Salamanca at first, but we were as well received in other towns, particularly in Zamora, where I stayed in the house of a rich merchant who had a superb garden, where a numerous society would gather in the evenings to make music and pass part of the night in conversation amid groves of pomegranates myrtles and lemon trees. It is difficult to appreciate fully the beauties of nature if one has not experienced the delicious nights of the southern countries.

We had, however, to tear ourselves away from the pleasant life which we were leading to go and attack the Portuguese. We crossed the border: there were a few small engagements which all went our way: the French troops went to Viseu, while the Spanish came down the Tagus and reached Alantejo: we expected to enter Lisbon soon, as conquerors. But the Prince de la Paix, who had, without much reflection, called the French troops into the peninsula, now, also without much reflection, took fright at their presence, and to get rid of them he concluded, without the knowledge of the First Consul, a peace treaty with the Portuguese, which he cunningly had ratified by the French ambassador, Lucien Bonaparte. This greatly annoyed the First Consul, and caused, from that day, a rift between the two brothers.

The French troops stayed for several months longer in Portugal, until the beginning of 1802; then we returned to Spain and successively to our previous charming stations of Zamora, Toro and Salamanca, where we were always made welcome.

On this occasion I went through Spain on horseback with my regiment, and had no longer any need to avoid the verminous beds of the pousadas, since we were lodged each evening with the most respectable citizens. A route march, when one makes it with one's own regiment and in good weather, is not without a certain charm. One has a constant change of scene, without being separated from one's comrades; one sees the countryside in the greatest detail; we talk as we travel, we dine together, sometimes well, sometimes badly, and one is in a position to observe the customs of the inhabitants.

72

One of our pleasures was to watch in the evenings the Spaniards, shedding their usual lethargy, dance the fandango and the bolero with a perfection of grace and agility, even in the villages. The colonel offered them the use of his band, but they, quite rightly, preferred the guitar, the castanets, and a woman's voice; an accompaniment which gave the dance its national characteristics. These improvised dances, in the open air, engaged in by the working class in the towns as well as in the country, gave us so much pleasure, even as spectators, that we were sorry to leave them.

After more than a month on the road, we recrossed the Bidassoa, and although I had happy memories of my stay in Spain, it was with pleasure that I saw France once more.

Chap. 16.

At this period, regiments were responsible for their own remounts, and the colonel had been authorised to buy sixty horses which he hoped to procure, bit by bit, in French Navarre, while he was takingaking the regiment to Toulouse, where we were to form the garrison. But, for my sins, we arrived at Bayonne on the day of the town fair, and the place was full of horse-copers. The colonel arranged a deal with one of them, who provided all the horses the unit needed straight away. The dealer could not be paid immediately because the funds provided by the ministry would take a week to arrive. The colonel then ordered that an officer should remain behind in Bayonne, to receive this money and pay the supplier. I was picked for this wretched task, which landed me later in a most disagreeable situation, though at the time I saw only that I had been deprived of the pleasure of travelling with my comrades. However, in spite of my feelings, I had to obey orders.

To make it easier for me to rejoin the unit, the colonel decided that my horse should go with the regiment, and that after I had completed my mission, I should take the stage-coach to Toulouse. I knew several former pupils from Sorze who lived in Bayonne and who helped me to pass the time agreeably. The funds provided by the ministry arrived and I paid them out and was now free from all responsibility and ready to rejoin my regiment.

I had a cotton dolman, braided in the same material, and with silver buttons. I had had this strange costume made when I was on Bernadotte's staff, since it was the fashion there to wear this uniform when travelling in hot weather. I decided to wear this outfit on the journey to Toulouse, as I was not with my regiment, so I packed my uniform in my trunk and took it to the stage-coach, where I booked my seat and, unfortunately, paid in advance.

The coach was due to leave at five in the morning, so I told the porter at the hotel where I was staying to come and waken me at four, and the rascal having promised to do so, I went to bed without further ado. But he forgot; and when I opened my eyes, the sun was shining into the room and it was after eight o'clock...! What a disaster...! I was dumbfounded, and having cursed and upbraided the negligent porter, I had to think what I could do. The first difficulty was that the stage-coach ran only every second day, but that was not the major problem, which was that though the regiment had paid for my seat because I was on duty, they were not obliged to pay twice, and I had been stupid enough to pay for the whole journey in advance; so that if I took a new seat it would be at my own expense. Now at this time stage-coach fares were very costly, and I had very little money, and also, what was I to do for forty-eight hours in Bayonne, when all my belongings were on the coach...? I resolved to make the journey on foot.

I left the town without delay, and set off bravely on the road to Toulouse. I was lightly clad, and had nothing but my sabre, which I carried on my shoulder, so I covered the first stage briskly enough and spent the night at Peyrehorade.

The next day was a day of disaster. I intended to go as far as Orthez, and had already made half the journey when I was overtaken by one of these terrible storms which one has in the Midi. Rain mixed with hail fell in torrents, beating on my face; the road, already bad, became a morass in which I had the greatest difficulty in walking in boots with spurs; a chestnut tree near to me was struck by lighting.... No matter, I walked on with stoic resignation. But, behold....! In the midst of the storm I saw coming toward me two mounted gendarmes. You can easily imagine how I looked after paddling for two hours in the mud, dressed in my cotton breeches and dolman. The gendarmes belonged to the station at Peyrehorade, to which they were returning, but it seemed that they had lunched very well at Orthez, for they were somewhat drunk. The older of the two asked me for my papers; I gave him my travel permit, on which I was described as a sous-lieutenant of the 25th Chasseurs. "You! A sous-lieutenant?" shouted the gendarme, "you're too young to be an officer!" But read the description," I said, "and you will see that it says that I am not yet twenty years old. It is exact in every point." "That may be," he replied, "but it is a forgery; and the proof of that is that the Chasseur's uniform is green and you are wearing a yellow dolman. You are an escaped conscript, and I am arresting you." "All right," I said, "but when we get to Orthez and I see your lieutenant, I can easily prove that I am an officer and that this travel document is genuine."

I was not much worried by this arrest; but now the older gendarme said that he did not intend to go to Orthez. He belonged to the station at Peyrehorade, and I must follow him there. I said that I would do nothing of the kind, and that he could require this only if I had no papers, but as I had shown him my travel permit, he had no right to make me go back, and that it was his duty, according to the regulations, to accompany me to my destination, which was Orthez.

The younger gendarme, who was less full of wine, said that I was right. A lively dispute then broke out between the two of them. They hurled insults at one another and in the middle of the tempest which was all around us, they drew their sabres and charged furiously together. I was afraid I might be injured in this ridiculous combat, so I got into one of the huge ditches which ran along each side of the road, and although I was in water up to my waist, I climbed up onto the bordering field, from where I watched the two warriors skirmishing to get the better of one another.

Fortunately, the heavy, wet cloaks which they were wearing clung round their arms, and the horses, frightened by the thunder, would not go near each other, so that the riders could manage only a few ill directed blows. Eventually the older gendarme's horse fell, and he landed in the ditch. When he got out,covered in mire, he found that his saddle was broken and that he would have to continue his journey on foot; so he set out, after telling his companion that he was now responsible for the prisoner. Left alone with the more sensible of the two gendarmes, I pointed out to him that if I had anything to hide, it would be easy for me to make off into the country, as there was a large ditch between us which his horse could not cross, but that I would surrender myself to him since he had agreed not to make me go back. So I continued on my way, escorted by the gendarme, who was beginning to sober up. We had some conversation, and it became apparent that the fact that I had surrendered, when it would have been easy for me to run away, made him begin to think that I might be what I said I was. He would have let me go had he not been put in charge of me by his companion. He became more and more accommodating, and said he would not take me all the way to Orthez, but would consult the Mayor of Puyoo, which we were going to pass through.

My arrival was that of a malefactor: all the villagers, who had been driven back to the village by the storm, were at their doors and windows to see the criminal in the charge of the gendarme; however, the Mayor of Puyoo was a good, stout, sensible peasant, whom we found in his barn, threshing corn. As soon as he had read my travel permit, he said, gravely, to the gendarme, "Set this young man at liberty at once. You have no right to arrest him. An officer on a journey is designated by his documents, not by his clothes." Could Solomon have produced a better judgement? The good peasant did not stop at that, he wanted me to stay with him until the storm had passed and he offered me food. Then, while we were talking, he told me that he had once seen at Orthez a general whose name was Marbot. I told him that this was my father, and described him. Then the good man, whose name was Bordenave became even more solicitous and wanted to dry my clothes and offered me a bed for the night; but I thanked him and went on my way to Orthez, where I arrived at nightfall, completely worn out. The next day it was only with great difficulty that I could put my boots on, partly because they were wet and partly because my feet were swollen.

However I managed to drag myself as far as Pau, and being unable to go any further, I stayed there all day. I could find no other means of transport but the mail coach, and although the seats were very expensive, I took one as far as Gimont, where I was welcomed with open arms by M. Dorignac, a friend of my father, with whom I had spent several months after I left Sorze. I rested for a few days with his family, then I took a stage-coach to Toulouse. I had spent four times the cost of the seat which I had lost through the negligence of the hotel porter at Bayonne.

On my arrival at Toulouse I was going to look around for somewhere to live, but the colonel told me that he had arranged a place for me with one of his friends, an elderly doctor named M. Merlhes, whose name I shall never forget, because this worthy man and his numerous offspring were so good to me. During the two weeks I stayed with them, I was treated as a member of the family rather than as a boarder.

The regiment was up to strength and well mounted. We had many exercises which I found very interesting; though I sometimes found myself up before squadron commander Blancheville, an excellent officer, an old soldier from whom I learned to work with precision, and I owe much to him. Blancheville, before the revolution, had been on the staff of the gendarmes of Lunville. He was very well educated and took a great interest in young officers whom he thought capable of learning, and compelled them to study whether they liked it or not. As for the others, whom he called the block-heads, he simply shrugged his shoulders when they did not know their drill or made mistakes during exercises, but he never punished them for it. There were two or three sous-lieutenants whom he had picked out, they were *mm.* Gavoille, Dumonts and me. In our case he would not suffer an incorrectly given order, and punished us for the slightest mistake. As he was a very good fellow, when off duty we risked asking him why he treated us so severely. "Do you think I am so stupid that I would try to wash a black man white?" He replied, "Messers so and so are too old and lacking in talent to make it worth my while to try to improve them. As for you who have all that is required to succeed, you need to study, and study you shall!" I have never forgotten this reply, and I made use of it when I became a colonel. In fact old Blancheville had drawn our horoscopes accurately, Gavoille became a lieutenant-colonel, Dumonts a brigadier-general and I a divisional general.

On my arrival at Toulouse, I had exchanged the horse which I had bought in Spain for a delightful mount from Navarre. Now, it so happened that the prefect had arranged a race meeting in celebration of some fte or other, and Gavoille, who was a great lover of racing, had persuaded me to enter my horse. One day, when I was exercising my horse on a grass track, as he took a tight curve at full speed, he collided with the projecting wall of a garden and fell stone dead. My companions thought I had been killed or at least seriously injured, but by a miraculous piece of good luck I was unhurt. When I had been picked up, and saw my poor horse lying motionless, I was very upset, and went back sadly to my billet, where I confronted the realisation that I would have to buy another horse, and would have to ask my mother for the money to do so, although I knew she was very hard-up.

Comte Defermon, a minister of state and one of our trustees, was opposed to the sale of those properties which still belonged to us, because he foresaw that peace would increase the value of land. He considered, rightly, that they should be retained and creditors paid off gradually by rigid economy. This is one of the greatest obligations we owe to the good M. Defermon, the most sincere of my father's friends, and one for whose memory I have the deepest respect.

When my request for money to buy a new horse was submitted to the council of trustees, General Bernadotte, who was one of them, burst out laughing, saying that it was a good try and that the excuse was well chosen, and suggesting that my application was what now-a-days would be called a "con", but, fortunately my request was backed up by a letter from the colonel, and M. Defermon stated that he did not believe me capable of trying to obtain money by trickery. He was quite right in this, for although I had an allowance of only 600 francs, my pay of just 95 francs a month and a lodging allowance of 12 francs, I never had a penny of debt; something I have always regarded with horror.

I bought a new horse, which was not as good as the Navarrais, but the general inspections, which had been reintroduced by the First Consul, were approaching, and it was essential that I was quickly remounted, the more so because we were to be inspected by General Bourcier, who had the reputation of being a stern disciplinarian.

I was detailed to go with thirty men to form an escort for him. He welcomed me warmly and spoke of my father, whom he had known well, which, however, did not prevent him from putting me on a charge the following day. The way in which this came about is quite amusing.

would have been one of the most handsome men in the army if his calves had been in harmony with the rest of his person; but his legs were like stilts, which looked very odd in the tight breeches, called Hungarians, which were then worn by the Chasseurs. To get over this which completed his fine appearance. You will see how these calves got me into trouble, but they were not the only cause.

The regulations laid down that the tails of officer's horses should be left flowing, as were the tails of the trooper's horses. Our colonel, M. Moreau, was always perfectly mounted, but all his horses had their tails cut, and as he feared that General Bourcier—a stickler for the rules—would take him to task for setting a bad example to his officers, he had, for the time of the inspection, had false tails fitted to his horses which were so realistic that, unless one knew, one would think them natural. This was all very fine. We went on manoeuvres, to which General Bourcier had invited General Suchet, the inspector of infantry, and General Gudin, the commander of the territorial division, and was accompanied by a numerous and brilliant staff.

The exercises were very long. Almost all the movements, carried out at the gallop, ended with several charges at top speed. I was in was next to the captain that the colonel took up his position. They were therefore a couple of paces in front of me when the generals came to congratulate Colonel Moreau on the fine performance of his troops. But what did I then see?.... The extreme rapidity of the movements had deranged the accessories added to the turn-out of both had come adrift, the centre part, made of a pad of tow, was hanging down nearly to the ground and the hairs were spread over the horse's they had slipped round to the front, and could be seen as large lumps on his shins, which produced a somewhat bizarre effect, while the captain sat up proudly on his horse, as if to say "Look at me! See how handsome I am!"

One has little gravity at the age of twenty. Mine was unable to resist the grotesque spectacle in front of me, and in spite of the presence of no less than three generals, I was unable to stop myself from bursting into laughter, however much I tried. The inspecting general, not knowing the reason for my hilarity, called me out of the ranks to reprimand me, but to reach him I had to pass between the cursed tail and the new calves sported by the captain, and I again burst out laughing. I was then put under open arrest. The generals must have thought I was crazy, but as soon as they had gone, the officers of the regiment gathered round the colonel and Captain done, but in easier circumstances.

In the evening, the commandant Blancheville attended a reception given by Madame Gudin. General Bourcier, who was also there, having brought up the subject of what he called my escapade, M. Blancheville explained the reasons for my unseemly laughter, an explanation which gave rise to much amusement. The laughter was increased by the entry display himself in this brilliant society, without suspecting that he was one of the reasons for their hilarity. General Bourcier, appreciating that if he could not help laughing at a description of the sight which had greeted my eyes, it was natural enough that a young sous-lieutenant could not contain himself when confronted with this ridiculous spectacle, cancelled my arrest and sent someone to look for me. My arrival rekindled the laughter, which was increased going from person to person asking what it was all about, while everyone gazed at his calves.

Chap. 17.

Let us now turn to more serious matters. The Treaty of Lunville had been followed by the Peace of Amiens, which put an end to the war between France and England. The First Consul decided to profit from the tranquility of Europe and the freedom of the sea to despatch a large body of troops to Dominica, which he wished to recover from the control of the blacks led by Toussaint-Louverture, a man who, without being in open revolt against the French, nevertheless adopted an air of great independence. General Leclerc was to be in command of this expedition. This general was a capable officer who had fought successfully in Egypt and Italy; but his principal distinction was that he had married Pauline Bonaparte, the First Consul's sister. Leclerc was the son of a miller from Pontoise, if one can describe as a miller, a very rich mill owner who had a considerable business. The miller had given the best of educations to his son and also to his daughter, who married General Davout.

While General Leclerc was preparing for his departure, the First Consul concentrated in Brittany those troops which he had earmarked for the expedition, and these troops naturally came under the command of the commander-in-chief of the area, which was Bernadotte.

It is well known that there was always a great rivalry between the troops of the Rhine army and those of the army of Italy. The former were greatly attached to General Moreau, and did not care for General Bonaparte, whose elevation to the head of government they had witnessed with regret. For his part, the First Consul had a great liking for the soldiers who had fought with him in Italy and Egypt, and, although the breach with Moreau was not yet openly declared, he considered that it would be in his interest to remove to as far away as possible troops devoted to this general. In consequence, the troops selected for the expedition to Dominica were almost all taken from the army of the Rhine. These men, however were perfectly happy to find themselves in Brittany, under the command of Bernadotte, a former lieutenant of Moreau's who had almost always served with them on the Rhine.

The expeditionary force was to comprise eventually some forty thousand men. The army of the west proper consisted of a similar number, so that Bernadotte, whose command extended to cover all the departments between the mouth of the Gironde and that of the Seine, had for a time under his orders an army of eighty thousand men, of whom the majority were more attached to him than to the head of the consular government.

If General Bernadotte had had more strength of character, the First Consul would have regretted putting him in such a powerful position; for I can say today, as an historical fact which will harm no one, that Bernadotte plotted against the government of which Bonaparte was the head. I shall give some details about this conspiracy which were never known to the public, and perhaps not even to General Bonaparte himself.

Generals Bernadotte and Moreau, jealous of the elevated position of the First Consul, and dissatisfied with the small part he gave them in public affairs, had resolved to overthrow him, and place themselves at the head of the government in conjunction with a civil administrator or an enlightened magistrate. To achieve this aim, Bernadotte, who, it must be said, had a talent for making himself liked by both officers and men, went about the provinces of his command, reviewing troops and using every means to increase their attachment to him. Enticements of all sorts, money, promises of promotion, were employed among the junior officers, while secretly he denigrated the government of the First Consul to the seniors. Having sown disaffection amongst most of the regiments, it would not have been difficult to push them into revolt; particularly those destined for the expeditionary force, who regarded it as a sort of deportation.

Bernadotte had as chief of staff Brigadier-general Simon, a competent but rather colourless officer. His rank put him in a position to correspond daily with unit commanders, and he used it to make his office the centre of the conspiracy. A battalion commander named Foucart was at that time attached to General Simon, who made him his principal agent. Foucart, using the excuse of official duties, travelled from garrison to garrison organising a secret league, which was joined by almost all the colonels and a crowd of senior officers, who were turned against the First Consul by accusations that he aspired to royalty; something, it seems, that he had not yet considered.

It was agreed that the garrison of Rennes, composed of several regiments, would begin the movement, which would spread like a trail of gunpowder into all divisions of the army: and as it was necessary that in this garrison there should be one unit which would start things off and get the rest moving, the 82nd Line regiment was brought to Rennes. This regiment was commanded by Colonel Pinoteau, an energetic and capable man, very brave, but something of a hothead, although he appeared outwardly phlegmatic. He was a follower of Bernadotte and one of the most enthusiastic of the conspirators. He promised to deliver his regiment, where he was extremely popular.

Everything was ready for the explosion when Bernadotte, lacking resolve and aiming, like a true Gascon, to have a catspaw to pull his chestnuts from the fire, persuaded General Simon and the other principal conspirators that it was essential that he should be in Paris when the army of Brittany proclaimed the deposition of the consul, so that he would be in a position to seize immediately the reins of government, in association with General Moreau, with whom he was going to confer about the matter. In reality, Bernadotte wished not to be compromised if the attempt failed, while maintaining himself in a position to take advantage of any success, and General Simon and the other conspirators were blind enough not to see through this ruse. The day of the armed uprising was then agreed, but the man who should have led it, because he had organised it, had cunningly absented himself.

Before Bernadotte left for Paris, a proclamation had been drawn up, addressed to the people of France as well as to the army. Several thousand copies of this were to be stuck up on the day of the event. A bookseller in Rennes, introduced by General Simon and by Foucart into the conspiracy, had undertaken to print this proclamation himself. This ensured that the proclamation would be ready for use in Brittany, but Bernadotte wanted to have a large number of these posters in Paris, for it was important to spread them throughout the capital and to send them to all the provinces as soon as the army of the west had made its move against the government, and as there was a risk of discovery if an approach was made to a Paris printer, Bernadotte devised a method of acquiring a large number of posters without compromising himself. He told my brother Adolphe, who was his aide-de-camp, that he was authorised to accompany him to Paris, and that he was to bring his horse and his carriage in anticipation of a long stay. My brother was delighted, and having packed his personal effects into the lockers of the carriage, he instructed his servant to bring the carriage, unhurriedly, to Paris while he went there by stage-coach.

As soon as my brother had left, General Simon and Commandant brother's servant, opened the carriage lockers and took out the personal possessions, which they replaced by packets of the proclamation. Then, having closed everything up, they sent poor Joseph on his way, without any suspicion of what he was carrying.

However, the First Consul's police had got wind of something brewing in the army of Brittany, but without knowing exactly what was going on or who was involved. The minister of police thought it was his duty to inform the prefect of Rennes who was a M. Mounier, and by the most extraordinary chance the prefect received this despatch on the very day when the revolt was due to break out, during a parade at Rennes, at mid-day. It was now eleven-thirty!

The prefect, to whom the minister had given no positive information, thought that in order to obtain some, he could do no better,in the absence of the commanding general, than to consult his chief of staff. He therefore asked General Simon to come to his office, and showed him the ministerial despatch. General Simon, believing that all had been discovered, then foolishly lost his head.

He told the prefect that there was indeed a vast conspiracy in the army, in which he had, unfortunately, played a part, of which he now repented; and thereupon he disclosed all the plans of the conspirators, and named the leaders; adding that in a few minutes the troops gathered on the parade ground, at a signal from General Pinoteau, were going to proclaim the overthrow of the consular government!

You may imagine M. Mounier's astonishment, and the concern he felt at being in the presence of a culpable general who, though at first thrown into confusion, might recover himself and recollect that he had eighty thousand men under his command, of whom eight to ten thousand were at this moment gathered not far from the prefecture. The position in which M. Mounier found himself was critical, but he extricated himself adroitly.

The general commanding the gendarmerie, Virion, had been ordered by the government to put together at Rennes a body of unmounted gendarmes, for the formation of which every regiment had supplied some Grenadiers. These soldiers, having no unifying bonds, escaped, in consequence, from the influence of the colonels of the regiments, and recognised only the orders of their new leaders, those of the gendarmerie who, in accordance with the regulations, obeyed the instructions of the prefect. M. Mounier now sent for General Virion, telling him to bring all the gendarmes. Meanwhile, fearing that General Simon might change his mind and leave him to go and place himself at the head of his troops, he soothed him with honeyed words, assuring him that his repentance and his confession would mitigate his offence in the eyes of the First Consul, and persuaded him to hand over his sword and go to the Tour Labat with the gendarmes who had at that moment arrived in the courtyard. So now the prime mover in the revolt was in prison.

While this was going on at the prefecture, the troops assembled at the Place D'armes were awaiting the hour of the parade which would also be that of the beginning of the revolt. All the colonels were in the secret, and had promised their support except the commander of the 79th, M. Goddard, who it was hoped would follow the rest.

From what a slender thread hangs the destiny of empires! Pinoteau, a strong and determined man, was due to give the signal which his regiment, the 82nd, already drawn up in battle formation on the square, was impatiently awaiting; but Pinoteau, with Foucart, had been busy all morning arranging for the despatch of proclamations, and in their preoccupation he had forgotten to shave. Mid-day arrived. Colonel Pinoteau realising that he was unshaven, hurried to put this right; but while he was engaged in this operation, General Virion, escorted by a large number of gendarmes, burst into the room, seized his sword and declared him a prisoner. He was taken to the tower to join General Simon. A few minutes later and Colonel Pinoteau would have been at the head of ten thousand men, and would undoubtedly have succeeded in starting the revolt. But taken thus by surprise he could do nothing but surrender to force.

Having made this second arrest, Virion and the prefect sent an aide-de-camp to the parade ground to tell Colonel Goddard of the 79th that they had a communication for him from the First Consul. As soon as he arrived, they told him of the discovery of the conspiracy and the arrest of General Simon and Colonel Pinoteau, and persuaded him to unite with them in putting down the rebellion. Having agreed to this, Colonel Goddard returned to the parade ground without telling anyone what he had learned, and taking his battalion to the Tour Labat, he joined the battalion of gendarmes who were guarding it. Also there were the prefect and General Virion, who arranged for ammunition to be distributed to the loyal troops. They then awaited events.

Meanwhile, the officers of the regiments which were assembled on the parade ground, surprised at the sudden departure of the 79th, and not understanding why General Pinoteau was late, sent to his home, where they were told that he had been arrested and sent to the tower. They were told at the same time of the arrest of General Simon.

This put the cat among the pigeons. The officers of the various units got together; Commandant Foucart proposed that they should march immediately to free the two prisoners and carry on with the movement. This suggestion was received with acclamation, particularly from the 82nd, who worshipped Colonel Pinoteau. They hurried to the Tour Labat, but found it surrounded by four thousand gendarmes and the battalion of the 79th. The assailants were undoubtedly the more numerous, but they had no ammunition and if they had had any, many of them would have been reluctant to fire on their comrades, simply to make a change in the members of the government. General Virion and the Prefect addressed them and urged them to return to their duty. The soldiers hesitated, and seeing this, none of the officers dared to order a bayonet attack, which was the only action which remained possible. Gradually the regiments stood down, and returned one by one to their barracks. Commandant Foucart, left alone, was taken to the tower, along with the unfortunate printer.

On learning that the insurrection at Rennes had failed, all the officers of the other regiments of the army of Brittany disavowed it; but the First Consul was not taken in by their protestations, he brought forward the date of their embarkation for Dominica and the other islands of the Antilles, where nearly all of them died, either in the fighting or of yellow fever.

As soon as he had heard the first confessions of General Simon and before the situation was fully under control, M. Mounier had sent a despatch rider to the government, and the First Consul now considered whether he should have Bernadotte and Moreau arrested. However, he suspended this measure for lack of any evidence, and to get hold of some, he ordered the examination of any travellers coming from Brittany.

While all this was going on, the good Joseph arrived at Versailles in my brother's carriage, and much to his surprise, found himself seized by the gendarmerie, and, in spite of his protests, brought before the minister of police. On learning that the carriage which this man was driving belonged to one of Bernadotte's aides-de-camp, the minister, Fouch, had all the lockers searched and found them full of proclamations, in which Bernadotte and Moreau, after denouncing the First Consul in violent terms announced his fall and their accession to power.

Bonaparte, furious with these two officers, demanded their presence. Moreau told him that as he, Moreau,had no authority over the army of the west, he would accept no responsibility for the conduct of the regiments of which it was composed; and one has to admit that this was a valid objection. It however worsened the position of Bernadotte, who, as commander-in-chief of the troops assembled in Brittany, was responsible for maintaining good order and discipline amongst them; but not only had his army engaged in conspiracy, but his chief-of-staff was a leader in the enterprise. The rebel proclamations bore Bernadotte's signature, and more than one thousand copies of this document had just been found in a carriage belonging to his aide-de-camp. The First Consul thought that such evident proofs would flatten and confound Bernadotte; but he was dealing with a true Gascon, as devious as they come!

Bernadotte expressed surprise...indignation! He knew nothing...absolutely nothing! General Simon was a villain and so was Pinoteau! He defied anyone to produce the original proclamation bearing his signature! Was it his fault if some lunatic had arranged for his name to be printed at the foot of a proclamation which he utterly and completely rejected. As for the wicked originators of all these plots, he would be the first to demand their punishment.

Bernadotte had indeed contrived to get everything directed by General Simon, without giving him a single word in writing which might compromise himself, and had left himself in a position in which he could deny everything if, in the event of the plot failing, General Simon should accuse him of being a participant. The First Consul, though convinced of Bernadotte's guilt, had no solid evidence to go on, and his council of ministers concluded that it would not be feasible to bring charges against a general who was so popular in the country and the army. Sadly, these sort of considerations did not apply to my brother Adolphe. One fine night they came to my mother's house to arrest him, and this at a time when the poor woman was already overburdened with grief.

M. de Canrobert, her eldest brother, whom she had managed to have taken off the list of migrs, was living peaceably with her when he was picked out by a policeman as having been present at some gathering whose aim was the restoration of the previous government. He was taken to the Temple Prison, where he was detained for eleven months. My mother was taking every possible step to prove his innocence and obtain his liberty when she was struck by another terrible disaster.

My two younger brothers were pupils at the French Military School. This establishment had a huge park and a fine country house in the village of Vanves, not far from the banks of the Seine; and in the summer the pupils went there to pass some of their holidays, when those who had behaved well were allowed to bathe in the river. Now it so happened that, because of some student peccadillo, the headmaster had deprived the whole school of the pleasure of swimming; however my brother Theodore loved swimming, so he and some of his friends decided to go swimming without the knowledge of their masters. While the pupils were spread about the park playing, they went to an isolated spot where they climbed over the wall and, on a very hot day, they ran to the Seine, into which they jumped, bathed in perspiration. They were scarcely in the water, however, when they heard the college drum beating for dinner. Fearing that their escapade would be discovered by their absence from the refectory, they dressed hurriedly and rushed back by the way they had come, to arrive, breathless, at the start of the meal. In such circumstances, they should have eaten little or nothing, but schoolboys are heedless, and they ate as much as usual, with the result that they nearly all became ill. Theodore was particularly affected, and was taken to my mother's house desperately ill with pneumonia.

It was while she was going from the bedside of her mortally afflicted son to her brother's prison, that they came to arrest her first-born. An appalling situation for any mother. To make matters worse, poor Theodore died. He was eighteen years old, charming and handsome. I was desolated to hear of his death, for I was very fond of him. These dreadful misfortunes which, one after another, assailed my mother, impelled those who were my father's true friends to exert themselves on her behalf. A leading figure among them was M. Defermon, who worked almost daily with the First Consul, and who rarely failed to intercede for Adolphe and his widowed mother. Eventually, General Bonaparte said to him one day, that although he had a low opinion of Bernadotte's common sense, he did not believe that he was so lacking in judgement that in conspiring against the government, he would take into his confidence a twenty-one year old lieutenant; and besides that, General Simon had stated that it was he and Commandant Foucart who had put the proclamations in young Marbot's carriage, so that, if he was to blame at all, it was only to a very small extent. However, he, the First Consul, was not willing to release the aide-de-camp until Bernadotte came in person to ask him to do so.

When she heard of this decision taken by the First Consul, my mother hastened to Bernadotte's house and begged him to take the necessary step. He promised solemnly to do but the days and weeks rolled past without him doing anything. Eventually, he said to my mother, "What you are asKing of me will be extremely painful, but no matter, I owe this to the memory of your husband, as well as to the interest I have in your children. I shall go this very evening to see the First Consul and I shall call at your house after leaving the Tuileries. I am certain I shall be able to announce the release of your son."

One can imagine with what impatience my mother waited during this long day! Every coach she heard made her heart beat. But at last it struck eleven o'clock and Bernadotte had not appeared. My mother then went round to his house, and what do you suppose she was told?....That General Bernadotte and his wife had left, to take the waters at Plombires, and would not be back for two months! In spite of his promises, Bernadotte had left Paris without seeing the First Consul. Devastated, my mother wrote to General Bonaparte. M. Defermon, who undertook to deliver the letter, was so indignant at the conduct of General Bernadotte that he could not resist telling the First Consul how he had behaved toward us. "That," said the First Consul, "is the sort of thing I would expect!"

M. Defermon, Generals Mortier, Lefebvre and Murat then urged that my brother should be freed; observing that if he had been unaware of the conspiracy, it was unjust to keep him in prison, and even if he had known something about it, he could not be expected to carry tales about Bernadotte, whose aide-de-camp he was. This reasoning impressed the First Consul, who set my brother at liberty and sent him to Cherbourg, to join the 49th Line regiment, as he did not wish him to continue as aide-de-camp to Bernadotte.

Bonaparte, who had a very long memory, probably had engraved, somewhere in his head, the words, "Marbot. Aide-de-camp of Bernadotte. Conspiracy of Rennes." So my brother was never again looked on with favour, and some time later he was sent to Pondichery.

Adolphe had spent a month in prison; Commandant Foucart was there for a year. He was cashiered and ordered to leave France. He took refuge in Holland, where he lived miserably for thirty years on earnings from French lessons, which he was reduced to giving, as he had no personal fortune.

At last, in 1832, he thought to return to his native country, and during the siege of Anvers I saw, one day, come into my room, a sort of elderly schoolmaster, very threadbare; it was Foucart, I recognised him. He told me that he did not have a brass farthing! While I offered him some assistance, I could not help reflecting on the bizarre workings of fate. Here was a man who in 1802 was already a battalion commander, and whose courage and ability would have certainly carried him to the rank of general, if Colonel Pinoteau had not decided to shave at the moment when the conspiracy of Rennes was due to come to a head. I took Foucart to Marshal Grard, who also remembered him, and together we presented him to the Duc d'Orlans, who gave him a job in his library, at a salary of 2400 francs. He lived there for fifteen years.

As for General Simon and Colonel Pinoteau, they were imprisoned in the Isle de R for five or six years. Eventually, Bonaparte, having become Emperor, set them free. Pinoteau had been vegetating for some time in Rufec, his birthplace, when, in 1808, the Emperor, who was on his way to Spain, having stopped there to change horses, Pinoteau presented himself boldly before him and requested to be re-engaged in military service. The Emperor, who knew that he was an excellent officer, then placed him in command of a regiment, which he led faultlessly throughout the wars in Spain, so that after several campaigns, he was promoted to the rank of brigadier-general.

General Simon also returned to military service. He was in command of an infantry brigade in Massna's army when we invaded Portugal. At the battle of Busaco, where Massna made the mistake of mounting a frontal attack on the Duke of Wellington's army, which was in position on the heights of a mountain with a very difficult approach, Poor Simon, wishing, no doubt, to redeem himself and to make up for the time he had lost towards promotion, charged bravely at the head of his brigade, overcame every obstacle, clambered up the rocks under a hail of bullets, broke through the English line and was first into the enemy entrenchments. But, there, a bullet fired at close range shattered his jaw at the moment when the English second line drove back our troops, who were thrown down into the valley with considerable losses. The enemy found the unfortunate general lying in the redout among the dead and dying. His face was hardly recognisable as human. Wellington treated him with much respect, and as soon as he could be moved, he sent him to England as a prisoner of war. He was later permitted to return to France. But his terrible injury barred him from any further service. The Emperor gave him a pension, and one heard no more of him.

Chap. 18.

After the unhappy events which had just befallen her, my mother longed to re-unite her three remaining sons around her. My brother, having been ordered to join the expeditionary force which was being sent to India under the command of General Decaen, was given permission to spend two months with my mother; Flix was at the Military School, and a piece of good fortune brought me also to Paris.

The School of Cavalry was then at Versailles; every regiment sent there an officer and a non-commissioned officer, who, after completing their studies, returned to their unit to act as instructors. Now it so happened that at the moment when I was about to ask for permission to go to Paris, the lieutenant who had been at the School had completed the course, and the colonel proposed to send me to replace him. I accepted this with pleasure, for not only would it allow me to see my mother again, but it would ensure that for eighteen months I would be living only a short distance from her.

My preparations were soon made. I sold my horse and taking the stage-coach, I left the 25th Chasseurs, to which I was never to return; although not being aware of this at the time, my farewells to my comrades were lighthearted.

On my arrival in Paris, I found my mother greatly upset, not only on account of the cruel loss which we had just suffered, but also over the imminent departure of Adolphe for India, and the detention of my uncle Canrobert, which continued indefinitely.

We spent a month together as a family, at the end of which my elder brother had to report to Brest, where he was soon embarked for Pondichery in the "Marengo." As for me, I went to settle in at the School of Cavalry, whose barracks were in the great stables of Versailles.

I was lodged on the first floor, in apartments which had once been occupied by the Prince de Lambesc, the master of horse. I had a very big bedroom and an immense "salon" which looked out over the Avenue de Paris and the parade-ground. I was at first astonished that the most recently arrived pupil should be so well housed, but I soon learned that no one wanted this apartment because its huge size made it glacially cold, and few of the officer pupils could afford to keep a fire going. Happily I was not entirely without means. I had a good stove put in, and with a big screen, I made in this vast apartment a little room, which I furnished modestly, since all we were issued with was a table, a bed, and two chairs, which were quite out of place in the enormous space of my quarters. So I made myself reasonably comfortable until the return of spring, when the place seemed quite charming.

Although we were called pupils, you should not suppose that we were treated as students. We were allowed every freedom, too much freedom in fact. We were commanded by an old colonel, M. Maurice, whom we hardly ever saw, and who did not take part in anything. On three days in the week we had civilian horsemanship, under the celebrated equestrians Jardin and Coup, and we went there when it suited us. In the afternoon, an excellent veterinarian, M. Valois, ran a course on the care of horses; but no one compelled us to study with any diligence. The other three days were devoted to military matters. In the morning, military horsemanship, taught by the only two captains in the school, and in the afternoon, drill, also taught by them. Once this parade was finished, the captains disappeared and each student went his own way.

You will appreciate that it took a keen desire to learn, to get anywhere in a school so badly run; however most of the students made progress because, being destined to become instructors in their respective regiments, their self-respect made them fear not being up to the task. So they worked reasonably hard, but not as hard as one would as a schoolboy. As for behaviour, the staff took no interest in it. As long as the students caused no trouble in the establishment itself, they were allowed to do as they pleased. They came and went at all hours. They were subject to no rôle call. They ate in hotels, if it suited them, slept out, and even went to Paris without asking permission. The non-commissioned pupils had a little less liberty. Two moderately strict sergeants were in charge of them, who insisted that they were back by ten o'clock at night.

Each of us wore the uniform of his regiment, so that a gathering of the whole school presented an interesting sight, as when, on the first day of every month, we paraded in full dress in order to draw up the pay roll; then you could see the uniforms of all the French cavalry regiments.

As all these officers belonged to different units, and were thrown together only for the duration of the course, there could not exist between them the close fellowship which is one of the features of regimental life. We were too numerous (ninety) for there to be a bond between all. There were coteries but no union. I did not feel any need to socialise with my new comrades. I left every Saturday for Paris, where I spent the next day and most of Monday with my mother. There were at Versailles two old friends of my mother, from Rennes; the Comtesses de Chteauville, a pair of very respectable and well educated elderly ladies, who entertained only a select society. I went two or three times a week to spend an evening with them. The remaining evenings I employed in reading, which I have always greatly enjoyed, for if school sets a man on the road to education, he must get there by himself through reading. How pleasant it was, in the midst of a very harsh winter, to come back to my quarters after dinner, make up a good fire and there, alone, ensconced behind my screen and beside my little lamp, to read until eight or nine o'clock; then to go to bed, in order to save wood, and continue reading to midnight. In this way I re-read Tacitus and Xenophon and many of the classical Greek and Roman authors; I revised the history of Rome and of France, and the principle countries of Europe. My time, shared between my mother, my work at the school, a little good society and my beloved books, passed very agreeably.

I began the year 1803 at Versailles. Spring introduced some changes into my way of life. Each of the officers at the school was provided with a horse, so I devoted some of my evenings to taking long rides in the magnificent woods which surround Versailles, Marly, and Meudon.

During May, my mother was made very happy by the release of her eldest brother from the Temple prison, and the return to France of the other two, de l'Isle and de la Coste, who, having been struck off the list of migrs came to Paris.

The eldest of my mother's brothers, M. de Canrobert was a very pleasant, sensible man. He entered the service at a very young age, as a sous-lieutenant in the infantry of Ponthivre, and, under Lieutenant-general De Vaux, fought in all the campaigns of the war in Corsica, in which he distinguished himself. After the conquest of that country, he served out the twenty-four years which earned him the Cross of St. Louis. He was a captain when he married *Mlle*. Sanguinet and then retired to the Chteau of Laval de Cre.

Having become the father of a son and a daughter, M. de Canrobert was living happily in his manor when the revolution broke out in 1789. He was forced to emigrate to escape the scaffold, with which he was threatened, all his possessions were confiscated and sold, his wife was imprisoned with her two young children. My mother obtained permission to visit her unhappy sister-in-law, and found her in a cold, damp tower, stricken by a fever, which carried off, that very day, her young daughter. By dint of requests and supplications, my mother managed to obtain the release of her sister-in-law; but she died a few days later from the illness she had contracted in prison. My mother then took charge of the young boy, named Antoine. He was sent in turn to college and then to the military school, where he was one of their brightest pupils. Finally he became an infantry officer and was killed, bravely, on the field of battle, at Waterloo. My uncle was one of the first of the migrs who, under the consulate, were given permission to return to France. He recovered some part of his estate, and married again, this time to one of the daughters of M. Niocel, an old friend of the family.

M. Certain de l'Isle, the second of my mother's brothers, was one of the most handsome men in France. At the time of the revolution he was a lieutenant in the regiment of Ponthivre, in which were also serving his elder brother and several of his uncles. He took the same course as nearly all his comrades and emigrated in company with his younger brother, Certain de la Coste, who was in the King's bodyguard. After leaving France the two brothers stayed always together. They retreated first to the country of Baden, but their tranquility was soon disturbed: the French armies crossed the Rhine, and as all migrs who fell into their clutches were shot, by order of the Convention, the brothers were forced to hide hurriedly in the interior of Germany. Lack of money compelled them to travel on foot, which soon became too much for poor La Coste. They had great difficulty in finding lodgings, as everywhere was occupied by Austrian troops. La Coste became ill. His brother supported him. In this way they reached a little town in Wurtemberg, where they found a bed in a low class tavern. At daybreak they saw the Austrians leaving, and they were told that the French were about to occupy the town. La Coste, unable to move, urged de l'Isle to look to his own safety and to leave him to the care of Providence; but de l'Isle declared solemnly that he would not abandon his sick brother.

However two French volunteers arrived at the inn with a requisition for lodgings. The inn-keeper took them to the room occupied by my two uncles, whom he told that they would have to leave. It has been said, quite rightly, that during the Revolution, the honour of France took refuge in the army. The two soldiers, seeing that La Coste was ill, told the landlord that not only did they wish to keep him with them, but that they wanted a large room which was on the first floor, where they would establish themselves with my two uncles. In enemy country, the victor being the master, the inn-keeper obeyed the two French volunteers, who, during the two weeks in which their battalion was billeted in the town, took great care of Messers La Coste and de l'Isle, and even let them share in the good meals which their host was obliged to provide in accordance with the usages of war; and this comfortable regime, coupled with rest, restored to some extent, the health of La Coste.

When they left, the volunteers, who belonged to a battalion from the Gironde, wishing to give their new friends the means of passing through the French columns without being arrested, took from their uniforms the metal buttons which bore the name of their battalion, and attached them to the civilian clothing worn by my uncles, who could then pass themselves off as sutlers. With this new form of passport, they went through all the French cantonments without rousing any suspicion. They reached Prussia, and settled down in the town of Hall, where De l'Isle was able to give French lessons. They lived there peacefully until 1803, when my mother managed to have them struck of the list of migrs, and they returned to France after twelve years of exile.

Chap. 19.

Let us now return to Versailles. While I was on the course at the school of cavalry, great events were under way in Europe. England having broken the Treaty of Amiens, hostilities recommenced. The First Consul resolved to take the initiative by leading an army onto the soil of Great Britain, a daring and difficult undertaking, but not impossible. To put it into operation, Napoleon, who had just seized Hanover, the private property of the English monarchy, stationed on the coasts of the North Sea and the Channel, several army corps, and ordered the construction and assembly, at Boulogne and neighbouring ports, of an immense number of barges and flat-bottomed boats, on which he proposed to embark his troops.

All the armed forces were set in motion for this war. I regretted that I was not involved; and being destined to carry back to my regiment the knowledge I had acquired at the school, I saw myself condemned to spend several years in the depot with a whip in my hand, making recruits trot round on elderly horses, while my comrades were fighting at the head of troops which I had trained. I did not find this prospect very pleasant, but how was it to be changed? A regiment must always be fed with recruits, and it was certain that my colonel, having sent me to the school of cavalry to learn how to train these recruits, would not deprive himself of the services which I could render in this respect, and would keep me out of the fighting squadrons. One day, however, as I was walking down the Avenue de Paris, with my drill manual in my hand, I had a brilliant idea, which totally changed my destiny and contributed greatly to my promotion to the rank which I now occupy.

I had just learned that the First Consul, having fallen out with the court of Lisbon, had ordered the formation, at Bayonne, of an army corps destined to enter Portugal under the command of General Augereau. I knew that General Augereau owed some of his advancement to my father, under whose command he had served in the camp at Toulouse and in the Pyrénées, and although what I had experienced at Genoa after the death of my father had not given me a high opinion of the gratitude of mankind, I resolved to write to him and, having explained the predicament in which I found myself, ask him to extricate me by taking me on as one of his aides-de-camp.

Having written this letter, I sent it to my mother, to see if she approved. She not only approved, but knowing that Augereau was in Paris, she decided to take the letter to him herself. Augereau received the widow of his old friend with the greatest consideration; he immediately took his carriage and went to the War Ministry, and that same evening he handed to my mother my appointment as aide-de-camp. Thus a wish, which twenty-four hours earlier had seemed a dream, became a reality.

The following day I hurried to Paris to thank the general. He received me most kindly, and ordered me to join him at Bayonne, to where he was now going. It was now October, I had completed the first course at the school of cavalry and had little interest in starting on the second; so I was happy to leave Versailles, for I felt sure that I was starting on a new career, much more advantageous than that of a regimental instructor. I was quite right in thinking this, for nine years later I was a colonel, while those I had left at the school had hardly reached the rank of captain.

I reported promptly to Bayonne and took up my post as an aide-de-camp to the commander-in-chief. He was installed a quarter of a league from the town in the fine Chteau de Marac, in which the Emperor lived some years later. I was made very welcome by General Augereau and by my new comrades, his aides-de-camp, nearly all of whom had served under my father. This general staff, although it did not give to the army as many general officers as that of Bernadotte, was nevertheless very well made up. General Danzelot who was the chief-of-staff, was a highly capable man who later became the governor of the Ionian islands and then Martinique. His second in command was Colonel Albert, who at his death was general aide-de-camp to the Duc d'Orlans. The aides-de-camp were Colonel Sicard, who died at Heilsberg, Major Brame, who retired to Lille after the Peace of Tilsit, Major Massy, killed as a colonel at Moscow, Captain Chvetel and Lieutenant Mainville, the first of whom retired to his estate in Brittany and the second ended his career in Bayonne. I was the sixth and youngest of the aides-de-camp.

Finally the staff was completed by Dr. Raymond, who helped me greatly at Eylau, and Colonel Augereau, a half-brother of the general; a very quiet man, who later became a lieutenant general.

Chap. 20.

The greater part of the generals who made a name for themselves in the early wars of the revolution having sprung from the lower ranks of society, it has been supposed, wrongly, that they had received no education, and that they owed their success solely to their fighting ability. Augereau, in particular, has been very badly judged. He has been represented as boastful, hard, noisy and nasty. This is an error, for although he had a stormy youth, and fell into some political misconceptions, he was kind, polite and affectionate, and I can assure you that of the five marshals under whom I have served, it was he who did most to lessen the evils of war, who was most considerate toward the local populace and who treated his officers best, among whom he lived like a father among his children. It is true that he had a most irregular life, but before passing judgement you must consider the conditions which existed at the time.

Pierre Augereau was born in Paris in 1757. His father had an extensive business in the fruit trade and had acquired a large fortune, which allowed him to give his children a good education. His mother was born in Munich, and she had the good sense to speak nothing but German to her son, who, as a result spoke it perfectly; something he found most useful in his travels, and also during the wars.

Augereau was good-looking, large and well built. He loved all physical activities, at which he excelled. He was a good horseman and a fine swordsman. When he was seventeen his mother died, and one of her brothers who worked in the office of Monsieur (the king's brother) arranged for him to join the Carabiniers, of whom Monsieur was colonel in chief.

He spent several years at Saumur, where the Carabiniers were usually garrisoned, and where his efficiency and good conduct soon raised him to the rank of sergeant. Sadly, there was at this time a craze for duels. The reputation which Augereau had as an excellent swordsman compelled him to engage in several, for it was a great point among duelists not to accept that anyone was their superior; gentlemen, officers and soldiers fought for the most futile of reasons. It so happened that when

Augereau was on leave in Paris, the celebrated fencing master Saint-George, seeing him pass, said, in the presence of several swordsmen, there is one of the finest blades in France. Upon this, a sergeant of Dragoons named Belair, who claimed to be next to Saint-George in ability, wrote to Augereau saying that he would challenge him to fight unless he recognised the writer's superiority. Augereau having replied that he would do nothing of the sort, they met on the Champs-Elyses where Belair received a penetrating sword-thrust. He subsequently recovered and having left the service, he married and became the father of eight children, for whom he was unable to provide. So in the first days of the Empire it occurred to him to approach his old adversary, now a marshal. This man, whom I knew, was something of an original character; he presented himself before Augereau with a little violin under his arm, and said that as he had nothing to give his eight children for dinner, he would make them dance a quadrille to cheer them up, unless the marshal could put him in the way of providing a more substantial meal. Augereau recognised Belair, invited him to a meal, gave him some money and a few days later arranged for him to have a good job in the transport department. He also placed two of his sons in school. Conduct which requires no commentary.

Not all the duels which Augereau fought ended like this. As a result of an absurd custom, there existed an inveterate hatred between some units, the cause for which was buried in the past and often hardly known, but which, handed down from age to age, resulted in duels every time the units met. In this way the Gendarmes of Lunville and the Carabiniers had been at war for half a century, though they had not seen one another in this long period of time. At last, at the beginning of the reign of Louis XVI, they found themselves in the same camp at Compigne; whereupon, to show themselves no less brave than their forefathers, the Carabiniers and the Gendarmes decided to fight, and their determination was such that the officers thought it wiser to look the other way. However, to avoid too much bloodshed, it was agreed that there would be only one duel; each unit would select a combatant who would represent them, and after that there would be a truce. The Carabiniers chose their twelve best swordsmen, among whom was Augereau, and it was agreed that the defender of the regimental honour should be chosen by lot. On that day fate was more blind than usual, for it selected a sergeant by the name of Donnadieu, who had five children. Augereau observed that the name of a father of a family should not have been included in the draw, and asked if he might replace his comrade. Donnadieu declared that as his name had been chosen he would go forward. Augereau insisted, and this battle of generosity was ended only by the members of the meeting accepting Augereau's proposal. The name of the combatant chosen by the Gendarmes would soon be known and after that it was merely a matter of arranging for the two adversaries to meet, when a simulated quarrel would serve as a motive for the encounter.

Augereau had a fearsome opponent, an excellent swordsman, a professional duelist, who as a warm-up, awaiting the contest, had killed two sergeants of the Guards, on the days previously. Augereau, without allowing himself to be intimidated by the reputation of this bravo, went to the caf where he knew he was to appear, and while awaiting him sat down at a table. The Gendarme arrived, and when his opponent had been pointed out to him, he pulled aside his coat-tails, and sat down insolently on the table, his backside not a foot from Augereau's face. Augereau was drinking a cup of very hot coffee at the time and he gently eased back the opening, called the ventouse, which existed then at the back of a cavalryman's leather breeches, and poured the steaming liquid onto the the buttocks of the impudent Gendarme, who turned round in a fury! The quarrel having now been engaged upon, they went outside, followed by a crowd of Gendarmes and Carabiniers. As they went along, the ferocious Gendarme, to mock the man whom, he felt confident, would be his victim, asked Augereau, in a bantering tone, whether he would prefer to be buried in the town or in the country. "The country" replied Augereau, "I have always liked the open air." "Fine," said the gendarme, and, turning to his second, he said, "Put him with the other two I killed yesterday and the day before." This was not very encouraging, and anyone but Augereau might have been put out, but determined to sell his life dearly, he defended himself with such skill that his adversary lost his temper and made a false move, which allowed Augereau, who had remained calm, to run him through, saying that it was he who would be buried in the country.

The camp being ended, the Carabiniers returned to Saumur, where Augereau was peacefully continuing his military service when a disastrous event precipitated him into a life of high adventure.

A young officer of exalted birth, but with a very nasty temper, having found something to complain about concerning the grooming of horses, rounded on Augereau, and in an access of rage offered to strike him with his riding whip in front of the whole squadron. Augereau indignantly seized the officer's whip and threw it away, whereupon the latter, in a fury, drew his sword and confronted Augereau, saying, "Defend yourself!" Augereau restricted himself at first merely to parrying, but having been slightly wounded, he made a riposte and the officer fell dead.

The general, Comte de Malseigne, who commanded the Carabiniers in the name of Monsieur, was soon told of this affair, and although eye-witnesses agreed in saying that Augereau, provoked by the most unjustifiable attack, had legitimately defended himself, the general, who favoured Augereau, thought it would be wiser to get him out of the way. To do this he called on a Carabinier named Papon, a native of Geneva whose term of service was due to expire in a few days, and invited him to give his travel permit to Augereau, promising to give him another one later. Papon agreed to this, and Augereau was always most grateful to him, for when he arrived in Geneva, he learned that the court-martial, in spite of the evidence of the witnesses, had condemned him to death for raising his sword against an officer.

The Papon family had a business which exported a large number of watches to the east. Augereau decided to go with a representative whom they were sending there, and travelled with him to Greece, to the Ionian islands, to Constantinople and the shores of the Black Sea.

He was in the Crimea when a Russian colonel, guessing from his bearing that he had been a soldier, offered him the rank of sergeant.

Augereau accepted, and served for several years in the Russian army, which the famous Souwaroff commanded in a war against the Turks, and was wounded in the assault on Ismailoff.

When peace was made between the Porte and Russia, the regiment in which Augereau was serving was ordered to go to Poland; but he did not wish to stay any longer with the semi-barbarous Russians, so he deserted and went to Prussia, where he served at first in the regiment of Prince Henry, and then, on account of his height and good looks, he was posted to the famous guards of Frederick the Great. He was there for two years, and his captain had led him to hope for promotion, when one day the king, who was reviewing his guards stopped in front of him and said, "There is a fine looking Grenadier!....Where does he come from?" "He is French sire," came the reply. "Too bad," said Frederick, who had come to detest the French as much as he had once liked them. "Too bad. If he had been Swiss or German we could have made something of him".

Augereau, from then on, was convinced he would get nowhere in Prussia, since he had heard it from the lips of the king himself, and so he resolved to leave the country. This was a very difficult matter, because as soon as the desertion of a soldier was signalised by the firing of a cannon, the population set off in pursuit of him, in the hope of obtaining the promised reward, and the deserter when captured was invariably shot.

In order to avoid this fate and to regain his liberty, Augereau, who knew that a good one third of the guards, foreigners like himself, had only one wish, and that was to get out of Prussia, spoke with some sixty of the most daring, to whom he pointed out that a single deserter had no chance of escape, since it required only two or three men to arrest him, so that it was essential to leave in a body with arms and ammunition for defence. This is what they did, under the leadership of Augereau.

This determined group of men, attacked on their way by peasants, and even a detachment of soldiers, lost several of their company, but killed many of their adversaries, and in one night they reached a small area of the country of Saxony which is not more than ten leagues from Potsdam. Augereau went to Dresden, where he gave lessons in dancing and fencing, until the birth of the first Dauphin, the son of Louis XVI, an event which the government celebrated by granting an amnesty to all deserters, which allowed Augereau not only to return to Paris, but to rejoin the Carabiniers, his sentence having been quashed, and General de Malseigne having insisted that he was one of the finest N.C.O.s in the corps.

In 1788, the King of Naples, feeling the need to put his army on a good footing, requested the King of France to send him a number of officers and N.C.O.s to act as instructors, whom he undertook to promote to a rank above their present one on their arrival. Augereau was included in this party and was promoted to sous-lieutenant. He served there for several years, and had just been promoted to lieutenant, when he fell in love with the daughter of a Greek merchant. When her father refused his consent to the union, the two lovers were married in secret, and embarking on the first vessel they found about to leave, they went to Lisbon, where they lived peacefully for some time.

It was now the end of 1792; the French Revolution was spreading rapidly, and all the sovereign heads of Europe feared the introduction of these new principles into their states, and were suspicious of everything French. Augereau has often assured me that during his stay in Portugal he never said or did anything which could alarm the government, nevertheless, he was arrested and incarcerated in the prison of the Inquisition.

He had been languishing there for several months, when Madame Augereau, his wife, a woman of courage, saw come into the harbour a ship flying the tricolour. She went on board to give the captain a letter, informing the French government of the arbitrary arrest of her husband. The captain, although not a naval officer, went boldly to the Portuguese ministry and demanded the release of his compatriot; failing which, he said that he would declare war in the name of France. Whether the Portuguese believed this, or whether they realised that they had acted unjustly, they set Augereau free, and he and his wife went back to Havre in the ship of the gallant captain.

On his arrival in Paris, Augereau was designated captain, and was sent to the Vende, where by his advice and example he saved the army of the incompetent General Ronsin, which gained him the rank of battalion commander. Sick of fighting his fellow Frenchmen, Augereau asked to be posted to the Pyrénées, and was sent to the camp at Toulouse commanded by my father, who, recognising his ability, made him adjutant-general, (That is colonel of the general staff), and showed him many marks of affection, something which Augereau never forgot. Having become general, he distinguished himself in the wars in Spain and Italy, and in particular, at Castiglione.

On the eve of this battle, the French army, beset on all sides, found itself in a most critical position, and the commander-in-chief, Bonaparte, called a council of war; the only one he ever consulted. All the generals, even Massna, proposed a retreat, but Augereau, having explained what, in his opinion, could be done to get out of the situation, said, "Even if you all go, I shall stay here and will attack the enemy, with my division, at dawn." Bonaparte, impressed by the arguments which Augereau had put forward, then said that he would stay with him. After which there was no more talk of retreat, and the next day a brilliant victory, due in large part to the courage and tactical skill of Augereau, established, for a long time, the position of the French army in Italy. Bonaparte was always mindful of this day, and when, as Emperor, he created a new nobility, he named Augereau Duc de Castiglione.

When General Hoche died, Augereau replaced him in the army of the Rhine. After the establishment of the consulate, he was put in charge of an army composed of French and Dutch troops which fought the campaign of 1800 in Franconia, and won the battle of Burg-Eberach.

When peace had been declared, he bought the estate and chteau of La Houssaye. I may say, in regard to this purchase, that there has been much exaggeration of the fortunes of some generals of the army of Italy. Augereau, after having held for twenty years the rank of commander-in-chief, or of marshal, and having enjoyed for seven years a salary of two hundred thousand francs, and an award of twenty-five thousand francs, due to his Legion of Honour, left at his death an income of no more than forty-eight thousand francs.

There was never a man more generous, unselfish and obliging. I could give a number of examples, but will limit myself to two. General Bonaparte, after his elevation to the consulate, created a large unit of Guards, the infantry portion of which was placed under the command of General Lannes. Lannes was a distinguished soldier, but had no understanding of administration. Instead of conforming to the tariff laid down for the purchase of clothing, fabrics and other items, nothing was too good for him; so that the suppliers of clothing and equipment to the guards, delighted to be able to deal by mutual agreement with the manufacturers, (in order to get back-handers,) and believing that their malversations would be covered by the name of General Lannes, the friend of the First Consul, made uniforms in such luxurious style that when the accounts were drawn up, they exceeded by three hundred thousand francs the sum allowed by the ministerial regulations. The First Consul, who had resolved to restore order to the finances, and to compel commanders not to go beyond the permitted expenditure, decided to make an example. In spite of his affection for Lannes, and his certainty that not a centime had gone into his pocket, he held him responsible for the deficit of three hundred thousand francs, and gave him no more than eight days to pay this sum into the Guard's account, or face court-martial.

This uncompromising ruling had an excellent effect in putting an end to the extravagance which had got into unit accounting, but General Lannes, although he had recently married the daughter of a senator, had no hope of making this payment. When General Augereau heard of the fix in which his friend found himself, he went to his lawyer, drew out the sum required, and instructed his secretary to pay it into the Guard's account, in the name of General Lannes. When the First Consul heard of this, he warmly approved of what Augereau had done, and to put Lannes in a position to pay him back, he had him sent to Lisbon as ambassador, a very lucrative post.

Here is another example of Augereau's generosity. He was not a close friend of General Bernadotte, who had bought the estate of Lagrange, for which he expected to pay with his wife's dowry; but there was some delay in the transfer of this money, and his creditors were pressing him, so he asked Augereau to lend him two hundred thousand francs for five years. Augereau having agreed to this, Madame Bernadotte took it on herself to ask what rate of interest he would expect. He replied that although bankers and businessmen required interest on money which they lent, when a marshal was in the happy position of being able to help a comrade, he should not expect any reward but the pleasure of being of service. That is the man whom some have represented as being hard and avaricious. At this moment, I shall say nothing more about the life of Augereau, which will unroll itself in the course of my story, which will show up his faults as well as his fine qualities.

Chap. 21.

Let us now go back to Bayonne, where I had just joined Augereau's staff. The winter, in this part of the country, is very mild; which allowed us to train and exercise troops in preparation for an attack on the Portuguese. However, the court of Lisbon having conceded all that the French government required, we gave up the idea of crossing the Pyrénées, and General Augereau was ordered to go to Brest and take command of the 7th army corps, which was earmarked for an invasion of Ireland.

General Augereau's first wife, the Greek, being in Pau, he wished to visit her and take his leave of her, and he took with him three aides-de-camp, of which I was one.

Normally, a commander-in-chief had a squadron of "Guides", a detachment of which always escorted his carriage, as long as he was in a part of the country occupied by troops under his command. Bayonne did not yet have any "Guides," so they were replaced by a platoon of cavalry at each of the post-houses between Bayonne and Pau. These came from the regiment which I had just left, the 25th Chasseurs; so that from the carriage in which I was taking my ease, beside the Commander in Chief, I could see my former companions trotting beside the door. I did not take any pride in this, but I must admit that when we came to Puyoo, where you saw me arrive two years previously on foot, bedraggled and in the hands of the gendarmerie, I was weak enough to put on an air, and to make myself known to the worthy mayor, Bordenave, whom I presented to the commander-in-chief to whom I had told the story of what had happened to me in this commune in 1801; and as the brigade of gendarmes from Pyrehorade had joined the escort to Pau, I was able to recognise the two who had arrested me. The old mayor was sufficiently malicious to inform them that the officer whom they saw in the commander-in-chief's fine carriage was the same traveller whom they had taken for a deserter, although his papers were in order, and the good fellow was, at the same time, very proud of the judgement he had given on this occasion.

After a stay of twenty-four hours at Pau, we returned to Bayonne, from where the general despatched me and Mainville to Brest, in order to prepare his headquarters. We took seats in the mail-coach as far as Bordeaux; but there, owing to the lack of public transport, we were forced to take to the hacks of the posting houses, which of all means of travelling, is surely the most uncomfortable. It rained. The roads were appalling. The nights pitch dark; but in spite of this, we had to press on at the gallop, as our mission was urgent. Although I have never been a very good horseman, the fact that I was accustomed to riding, and a year spent in the riding school at Versailles, gave me enough assurance and stamina to drive on the dreadful screws which we were forced to mount. I got well enough through this apprenticeship in the trade of courier, in which, you will see later, I had to perfect myself; but it was not so with Mainville, so we took two days and two nights to reach Nantes, where he arrived bruised and worn out and incapable of continuing to ride at speed. However we could not leave the commander-in-chief without lodgings when he arrived at Brest, so it was agreed that I would go on ahead, and that Mainville would follow later by coach.

On my arrival, I rented the town house of M. Pasquier, the banker, brother of the Pasquier who had been chancellor and president of the house of peers. Mainville and several of my comrades came to join me a few days later, and helped to make the necessary arrangements for the commander-in-chief to maintain the sort of state expected of him.

We began the year 1804 at Brest. The 7th Corps was made up of two divisions of infantry and a brigade of cavalry; as these troops were not encamped but were billeted in the neighbouring communes, all the generals and their staffs stayed in Brest, where the anchorages and the harbour were packed with vessels of all sorts. The admirals and senior officers of the fleet were also in the town, and other officers came there every day, so that Brest afforded a most animated spectacle. Admiral Truguet and the commander-in-chief held a number of brilliant receptions, scenes that have often been the prelude to war.

In February General Augereau left for Paris, to where the First Consul had summoned him to discuss with him the plan for the invasion of Ireland. I went with him.

On our arrival in Paris, we found a very tense political situation. The Bourbons, who had hoped that in taking the reins of government, Bonaparte would support them, and would be prepared to play the part that General Monk had once played in England, when they discovered that he had no intention of restoring them to the throne, resolved to overthrow him. To this end they concocted a conspiracy which had as its leaders three well known men, although of very different character. These were General Pichegru, General Moreau and Georges Cadoudal.

Pichegru had taught Bonaparte mathematics at the college of Brienne, but he had left there to join the army. The revolution found him a sergeant in the artillery. His talent and courage raised him rapidly to the rank of general. It was he who achieved the conquest of Holland, in the middle of winter, but ambition was his downfall. He allowed himself to be seduced by agents of the Prince de Cond, and entered into correspondence with the Prince, who promised him great rewards and the title of "Constable" if he would use the influence which he had with the troops to establish Louis XVIII on the throne of his forefathers.

Chance, that great arbiter of human destiny, decreed that following a battle in which French troops, commanded by Moreau, had defeated the division of the Austrian General Kinglin, the latter's supply wagon was captured, which contained letters from Pichegru to the Prince de Cond. It was taken to Moreau, who was a friend of Pichegru, to whom he owed some of his promotion, and who concealed his discovery as long as Pichegru retained his influence; but Pichegru having become a representative of the people in the house of elders, where he continued to favour the Bourbons, was arrested with several of his colleagues. Whereupon Moreau hurriedly sent to the directorate the documents which incriminated Pichegru, and led to his deportation to the wilds of Guyana.

Pichegru contrived to escape from Guyana to America, from whence he went to England; where having no longer any need for secrecy, he put himself openly in the pay of Louis XVIII and aimed at the overthrow of the consular government. However, he could not pretend that, deprived of his rank, banished and absent from France for more than six years, he could any longer wield as much influence over the army as General Moreau, the victor of Hohenlinden, and on this account, very popular with the troops, of whom he was the inspector-general. Pichegru, then, out of devotion to the Bourbon cause, agreed to forget the reasons he had for disliking Moreau, and to unite with him for the triumph of the policy to which he was committed. Moreau, who was born in Brittany, was studying law at Rennes when the revolution of 1789 broke out. The students, young and turbulent, elected him as their leader, and when they formed a battalion of volunteers, they named Moreau as their commander. Having made his dbut in the profession of arms as a senior officer, he proved himself both courageous and competent, and was rapidly promoted to general and army commander. He won several battles, and conducted, in the face of Prince Charles of Austria, a justly celebrated retreat. But though a good soldier, Moreau lacked civic courage. We have seen him refuse to put himself at the head of the government, while Bonaparte was absent in Egypt, however, though he had helped the latter on the 18th Brumaire, he became envious of his power when he saw him raised to the position of First Consul, to the extent that he sought by all means to supplant him; driven on, it is said, by the jealousy felt by his wife and mother-in-law towards Josephine. Given this situation, it would not be difficult to persuade Moreau to conspire with Pichegru to overthrow the government.

A Breton, named Lajolais, an agent of Louis XVIII, and a friend of Moreau, became the intermediary between him and Pichegru; he travelled frequently between London and Paris, and it soon became evident to him that Moreau, while agreeing to the overthrow of Bonaparte, intended to keep power for himself, and not to hand it to the Bourbons. It was then thought that a meeting between him and Pichegru might lead him to change his mind, so Pichegru was landed on the coast of France from an English vessel at a spot near Trepot, and went to Paris, to where Georges Cadoudal had preceded him, along with M. de Rivire, the two Polignacs, and other royalists.

Georges Cadoudal was the youngest son of a miller from Morbihan; but as there was a bizarre custom, in that part of lower Brittany, whereby the last-born of a family inherited all the estate, Georges, whose father was comfortably off, had been given a certain amount of education. He was a short man, with wide shoulders and the heart of a tiger, whose audacity and courage had raised him to the high command of all the groups of "Chouans" in Brittany.

Since the pacification of Brittany he had lived in London; but his fanatical devotion to the house of Bourbon did not allow him any repose as long as the First Consul was at the head of the government. He formed a plan to kill him. Not by a clandestine assassination, but in broad daylight, by attacking him on the road to Saint-Cloud with a party of thirty or forty mounted "Chouans" well armed and wearing the uniform of the consular guard. This plan had the more chance of success, since, at this time, Bonaparte's escort was usually no more than four cavalrymen.

A meeting was arranged between Pichegru and Moreau; it took place at night, near the Church of La Madeleine, which was then being built. Moreau agreed to the deposition, and even the death of the First Consul, but he refused to consider the restoration of the Bourbons.

Bonaparte's secret police having warned him that there was underground plotting going on in Paris, he ordered the arrest of a number of former "Chouans" who were in the city. One of these gave some information which seriously compromised General Moreau, whose arrest was then agreed upon by the council of ministers.

This arrest initially created a very bad impression amongst the general public, because Cadoudal and Pichegru not having been arrested, no one believed they were in France, and it was said that Bonaparte had invented the conspiracy in order to get rid of Moreau. The government then had the strongest reasons to prove that Cadoudal and Pichegru were in Paris, and that they had met Moreau. All the barriers were closed for several days, and the most drastic punishment was decreed for anyone sheltering the conspirators. From that moment it became very difficult for them to find any place of safety, and soon Pichegru, M. de Rivire and the Polignacs fell into the hands of the police. These arrests began to convince the public of the reality of the conspiracy, and the capture of Georges Cadoudal dispelled any remaining doubts.

Cadoudal having stated in his interrogation that he had come with the intention of killing the First Consul, and that the conspiracy was backed by a prince of the royal family, the police started an investigation to discover the location of all the princes of the house of Bourbon. They found that the Prince D'Enghien, the grandson of the great Cond, had been living for some time at Ettenheim, a little town situated some leagues from the Rhine, in the country of Baden. It has never been proved that the Duc D'Enghien was involved in the conspiracy, but he certainly had, on several occasions, been imprudent enough to enter French territory. However that may be, the First Consul sent, secretly, and by night, a detachment of troops led by General Ordener, to the town of Ettenhiem, where they seized the Duc D'Enghien. He was taken immediately to Vincennes, where he was tried, condemned, and shot before the public was aware of his arrest.

This execution was greeted with general disapproval. It was held that had the prince been captured on French territory, he could have been tried under a law which in this case carried the death penalty, but that to go and seize him beyond the frontiers, in a foreign land, was a gross infringement of human rights.

It appeared, however, that the First Consul had not intended the execution of the prince, and had wished only to frighten the royalists who were conspiring against him; but that General Savary, the head of the gendarmerie, who had gone to Vincennes, took custody of the prince after sentence had been pronounced and in an excess of zeal, had him shot, in order, he said, to save the First Consul the trouble of ordering his death, or of sparing the life of so dangerous an enemy. Savary has since denied that he expressed such sentiments, but I have been assured by people who heard him that he did. Bonaparte is known to have blamed Savary for his hastiness, but the deed having been done, he had to accept the consequences.

General Pichegru, ashamed to be associated with assassins, and that the conqueror of Holland should stand in the dock with criminals, hanged himself in prison by his cravat. It has been claimed that he was strangled by Mamelukes of the Guard, but this is a fabrication. Bonaparte had no incentive to commit such a crime. It was more in his interest to have Pichegru disgraced before a public tribunal than to have him killed in secret.

Georges Cadoudal, condemned to death, along with several accomplices, was executed. The brothers Polignac, and M. de Rivire, who received the same sentence, had it commuted to life imprisonment. They were locked up in Vincennes, but after several years they obtained permission to live on parole in a nursing home. However, in 1814, on the approach of the allies, they left and went to join the Comte d'Artois in Franche-comt; then in 1815 they were most savage in their pursuit of the Bonapartists.

As for General Moreau, he was sentenced to two years detention. The First Consul pardoned him on condition that he went to the United States. He lived there in obscurity until 1813, when he went to Europe to range himself among the enemies of his country, and died fighting against the French; thus confirming all the accusations which were made against him at the time of Pichegru's conspiracy.

The French nation, weary of revolutions, and recognising the extent to which Bonaparte was needed for the maintenance of good order, chose to forget what was odious in the affair of the Duc d'Enghien, and raised Bonaparte to the throne, by declaring him Emperor on May 25th, 1804.

Almost all nations recognised the new sovereign of France. To mark the occasion, eighteen generals, selected from the most notable, were elevated to the dignity of Marshals of the Empire.

Chap. 22.

After the trial of Moreau, we returned to Brest, from where we shortly came back to Paris, as the marshal had to assist in the distribution of the decoration of the Legion d'Honneur, an award which the Emperor had recently instituted for the recognition of all sorts of meritorious actions. In this connection I recall an anecdote which was widely circulated at the time. In order to bestow the award on all these soldiers who had distinguished themselves in the Republican armies, the Emperor took into consideration all those who had been given Armes d'Honneur, and he selected a great number of these for the Legion d'Honneur, although several of them had returned to civilian life. M. de Narbonne, a returned migr, was living quietly in Paris in the Rue de Miromesnil, in the house next to my mother's, when, on the day that the medals were distributed, he discovered that his footman, a former soldier in Egypt, had just been decorated. Being about to dine, he sent for the footman and said to him, "It is not right that a recipient of the Legion d'Honneur should hand round plates; and it would be even less right that you should put aside your decoration to serve at table. Sit down with me and we shall dine together, and tomorrow you shall go to my country estate where you shall be a game-keeper. An occupation which is not incompatible with wearing your decoration."

When the Emperor was told of this display of good taste, he sent for M. de Narbonne, whom he had wanted to meet for a long time, having heard so much about his wit and intelligence, and was so pleased with him that he made him an aide-de-camp.

After distributing the crosses in Paris, the Emperor went, for the same purpose, to the camp at Boulogne, where the troops were drawn up in a semi-circle facing the sea. The ceremony was imposing. The Emperor appeared for the first time on a throne, surrounded by his marshals. The enthusiasm was indescribable! The English fleet who could see what was going on, sent several light vessels in an attempt to disrupt the event by a cannonade, but our coastal batteries briskly returned their fire.

There was a story current at the time which related that, after the ceremony was over, the Emperor was returning to Boulogne followed by his marshals and an immense retinue, when he stopped in the shelter of one of these batteries, and calling to Marmont, who had served in the artillery, said "Let us see if we can remember our old trade and land a bomb on that English brig." And dismissing the corporal who was in charge of the weapon, the Emperor aimed and fired at the vessel. The bomb brushed the vessel's sails and fell into the sea. Marmont tried but with no better fortune. The Emperor then recalled the corporal to his post and the latter took aim and fired with such effect that he landed a bomb on the brig, which promptly sank, to the great delight of the onlookers, whereupon Napoleon pinned a medal to the soldier's uniform. How much truth there is in this tale, I do not know. I shared in the favours being distributed on that day. I had been a sous-lieutenant for five and a half years, and had been through several campaigns. The Emperor, at the request of Augereau promoted me to lieutenant; but for a moment I thought he was going to refuse me this rank, for remembering that a Marbot had figured in the conspiracy of Rennes, he frowned when the marshal spoke up for me and, looking closely at me he said "Is it you who...?" "No sire, it is not me who!..." I replied. "Ah!" he said, "you are the one who was at Genoa and Marengo. I appoint you lieutenant."

The Emperor also granted me a place at the military school of Fontainebleau for my younger brother, Flix, and from that day on he no longer confused me with my elder brother for whom he always had antipathy, though Adolphe had done nothing to deserve it.

As the troops of 7th Corps were not concentrated in an encampment, Marshal Augereau's presence in Brest was of very little use; so he was given permission to spend the rest of the summer and the autumn at his fine estate of La Houssaye, near Tournan, in Brie. I even suspect that the Emperor preferred to have him there rather than in the depths of Brittany at the head of a large army. However, any doubts which the Emperor may have had about Augereau's loyalty were without foundation, and arose from the underground plots of a General S....

S.... was a brigadier-general serving in 7th Corps. A capable officer, but over-ambitious. He was regarded as untrustworthy by his fellow generals, who did not associate with him. Angered by this rejection, and bent on revenge, he sent to the Emperor a letter in which he denounced all the generals, as well as the marshal, as conspiring against the empire. Napoleon, to his credit, did not employ any secret means to ascertain the truth: he simply passed the general's letter on to Marshal Augereau. The marshal felt sure that nothing serious was going on in his army; however as he knew that several generals and colonels had engaged in some thoughtless talk, he resolved to put an end to this sort of thing. As he did not wish to jeopardize the career of those officers to whom he intended to deliver a rebuke, he thought it would be best if his words were carried by an aide-de-camp, and he chose to take me into his confidence for this important mission.

I left La Housaye in August, in very hot weather, and rode at full speed the one hundred and sixty leagues between the chteau and the town of Brest, and as many again on the way back. I stayed no more than twenty-four hours in the town, so I arrived back completely worn out, for I think that there is no more exhausting job than riding rapidly on horseback from post-house to post-house. I had found things a good deal more serious than the marshal had thought; there was, in fact a considerable ferment in the army, but the message I had brought calmed down the generals, almost all of whom were devoted to the marshal.

I was beginning to recover from my exertions when the marshal said to me one morning, that the generals wanted to denounce S.... as a spy. He added that it was absolutely essential that he sent one of his aides-de-camp, and he wanted to know if I felt able to make the journey again. He said he would not order me to go, but would leave it to me to decide whether I could do it or not. If it had been merely a matter of reward or even promotion, I think I would have refused the task, but it was a question of obliging my father's friend, who had welcomed me with so much kindness, so I said that I would be ready to go in an hour's time. I was worried that I might not be able to complete the journey, because of the extremely tiring nature of this form of travel; I rested for no more than two hours out of the twenty-four, when I flung myself down on a heap of straw in the post-house stables. It was fearfully hot weather, but I managed to reach Brest and return without accident, and had the satisfaction of being able to tell the marshal that the generals would limit themselves to expressing their mistrust of S....

General S... being now discredited, deserted and went to England, and is said to have wandered over Europe for twenty years before dying in poverty.

After my second return from Brest, the marshal rewarded me by putting me in direct contact with the Emperor. He sent me to Fontainebleau to meet Napoleon and conduct him to La Houssaye, where he was to spend a day in the company of several of his marshals. It was while walking with them and discussing his plans, and the manner in which he intended to uphold his dignity and theirs, that he presented each of them with a sum of money sufficient for them to purchase a mansion in Paris. Marshal Augereau bought that of Rochechouart, in the Rue Grenelle-St-Germain, which is today occupied by the ministry of information. The mansion was superb, but the marshal preferred to stay at La Houssaye, where he kept up a great state; for over and above his aides-de-camp, each of whom had his own apartments, the number of invited guests was always considerable. One enjoyed complete liberty; the marshal allowed his guests to do as they pleased, provided that no noise reached the wing of the chteau occupied by his wife.

This excellent woman, who had become a chronic invalid, lived very quietly, and appeared only rarely at the table or in the salon, but when she did, far from constraining our high spirits, she took pleasure in encouraging them.

She had with her two extraordinary lady companions. The first of these always wore men's clothing, and was known by the name of Sans-gene. She was the daughter of one of the leaders who, in 1793, defended Lyon against the forces of the convention. She escaped, with her father, both of them disguised as soldiers, and took refuge in the ranks of the 9th Dragoon regiment; where they assumed nommes de guerre and took part in campaigning.

Mlle. Sans-Gene, who combined with her masculine attire and appearance, a most manly courage, received several wounds, one of them at Castiglione, where her regiment was part of Augereau's division. General Bonaparte, who had often witnessed the prowess of this remarkable woman, when he became First Consul, gave her a pension and a position beside his wife; but life at court did not suit *Mlle.* San-Gene. She left *Mme.* Bonaparte, who by mutual consent handed her over to *Mme.* Augereau to whom she became secretary and reader. The second lady companion of *Mme.* Augereau was the widow of the sculptor Adam, and in spite of her eighty years was the life and soul of the chteau.

Noisy parties and practical jokes were the order of the day at this period of time, particularly at La Houssaye, whose proprietor was not happy unless he could see his guests and the younger members of his staff gay and animated. The marshal came back to Paris in November; the time for the coronation was drawing near and already the Pope, who had come for the ceremony, was at the Tuileries. A crowd of magistrates and deputations from various departments had collected in the capital, where also were all the colonels of the army, with detachments from their regiments, to whom the Emperor distributed, on the Champ de Mars, the eagles, which became so celebrated. Paris, resplendent, displayed a luxury hitherto unknown. The court of the new Emperor became the most brilliant in the world; everywhere were ftes, balls, and joyous assemblies.

The coronation took place on the 2nd December. I accompanied the marshal at this ceremony, which I shall not describe, since the details are so well known. Some days later the marshals held a ball in honour of the Emperor and Empress. There were eighteen marshals, and Marshal Duroc, although he was only Prefect of the Palace, joined with them, which made nineteen subscribers, each one of whom paid up 25,000 francs for the expenses of the event, which therefore cost 475000 francs. The ball took place in the great ballroom of the Opera, where never before had something so magnificent been seen. General Samson of the engineers was the organiser; the aides-de-camp acted as stewards, to welcome the guests and to distribute tickets. Everyone in Paris wanted one, so the aides were overwhelmed by letters and requests. I never had so many friends! Everything went off perfectly, and the Emperor appeared very pleased. So we ended the year 1804 in the midst of celebrations, and entered the year 1805, which was to be a year of many important events.

In order that his army could participate in the general jollifications, Marshal Augereau went to Brest, in spite of the rigours of winter, and gave a number of magnificent balls, at which he entertained a succession of officers, and even a good number of soldiers. At the beginning of spring, he returned to La Houssaye to await the moment for the invasion of England.

This expedition, which was regarded as chimerical, was, however, on the point of realisation. The presence of an English squadron of about fifteen ships, cruising endlessly in the Channel, made it impossible to transport a French army to England in boats and barges which would have sunk on the least contact with a larger vessel; but the Emperor could dispose of sixty ships of the line, either French or foreign, dispersed in the harbours of Brest, Lorient, Rochefort, Le Ferrol, and Cadiz; it was a matter of concentrating them, unexpectedly, in the Channel, and crushing, by a greatly superior force, the little English squadron, to become masters of the passage, if only for three days.

To achieve this, the Emperor ordered Admiral Villeneuve, the commander-in-chief of all these forces, to gather together, from the French and Spanish ports whatever ships were available, and head, not for Boulogne, but for Martinique, to where it was certain the English fleet would follow him. While the English were making their way to the Antilles, Villeneuve was to quit the islands, and returning round the north of Scotland, was to enter the eastern end of the channel with sixty ships, which would easily overcome the fifteen which the English maintained before Boulogne, and so put Napoleon in command of the crossing; while the English, on their arrival at the Antilles, would search around for Admiral Villeneuve's fleet, and thus waste valuable time.

A part of this fine plan was now put into action. Villeneuve left, with not sixty, but some thirty ships. He reached Martinique. The English, led astray, hurried to the

Antilles, which Admiral Villeneuve had left, but the French admiral, instead of returning via Scotland, made for Cadiz in order to pick up the Spanish fleet, as if thirty ships were not enough to overcome or chase away the fifteen English vessels!

That, however, is not all. Having arrived at Cadiz, Villeneuve spent a great deal of time repairing his ships; time during which the enemy fleet also returned to Europe, and established a patrolling force off Cadiz. In the end, the coming of the equinox gales having made sailing from this port difficult, Villeneuve found himself blockaded; so the ingenious plans of the Emperor came to nothing, and he, realising that the English would not be taken in a second time, gave up the idea of invading Britain, or at least postponed it indefinitely, and turned his attention to the continent.

Before I recount the principal events of this long war, and the part which I played in it, I must describe a terrible misfortune which befell the family.

My brother, Flix, who was at the military school of Fontainebleau, was a little short-sighted; he had, therefore, hesitated before taking up a military career; nevertheless, once embarked on it, he worked with such enthusiasm that he soon became a sergeant-major, a position difficult to maintain in a school. The pupils, an unruly lot, were in the habit of burying in the earth of the fortifications which they were digging, the implements which had been issued to them for the work. General Bellavene, the head of the school, a very strict man, ordered that the implements should be issued to the sergeant-majors, who would then be accountable for them.

One day, my brother, having seen a pupil bury a pick, rebuked him. The pupil replied very rudely and added that in a few days they would be leaving school, and being then the equal of his sergeant-major, he would demand satisfaction for the reprimand. My brother replied indignantly that there was no need to wait so long.

Lacking swords, they used compasses fixed to wooden batons: Jacqueminot, who later became a lieutenant-general, was my brother's second. My brother's poor eyesight put him at a disadvantage, but he succeeded in wounding his opponent, though he received in return a wound which penetrated his right arm. His companions dressed it secretly.

By an unhappy coincidence, the Emperor had come to Fontainebleau, and had decided to conduct manoeuvres for several hours, under a blazing sun. My poor brother, compelled to run without rest, his arm dragged down by the weight of his heavy musket, was overcome by the heat and his wound re-opened! He should have fallen out on the at the end of the session, would distribute the commissions of sous-lieutenant, so eagerly desired. Flix made superhuman efforts to resist, but at last his strength failed him and he collapsed and was carried away in a most serious condition.

General Bellavene sent an unfeeling message to my mother, saying that if she wished to see her son, she must come immediately, for he was dying. My mother was so distressed by this news, that she was unable to make the journey. I posted there as quickly as I could, but on my arrival I was told that my brother was dead. Marshal Augereau did all that he could for us, in these unhappy circumstances, and the Emperor sent the marshal of the palace, Duroc, to convey his condolences to my mother.

All too soon another source of sadness would come to afflict her; I would be forced to leave her, as war was about to break out on the continent.

At a time when it might have been thought that the Emperor had the greatest need to be at peace with the continental powers, in order to execute his design for the invasion of England, he issued a decree whereby he annexed the state of Genoa to France. This was greatly to the advantage of the English, who profited from this decision to frighten all the peoples of the continent, to whom they represented Napoleon as aspiring to become the master of the whole of Europe. Austria and Russia declared war on us, Prussia, more circumspect, made preparations, but as yet, said nothing.

The Emperor had no doubt foreseen these reactions, and a wish to see hostilities break out perhaps underlay his seizure of Genoa; for, despairing of ever seeing Villeneuve in control of the channel, he wanted a continental war to deflect the ridicule to which his proposed invasion, threatened for three years, but never put into action, might have exposed him by displaying his impotence in the face of England. The new coalition extricated him nicely from an awkward situation.

Three years under arms had had an excellent effect on our soldiers. France had never had an army so well trained, so well organised, so keen for action, nor a leader in control of so much power and such moral and material resources, who was so skillful in their employment. So Napoleon accepted the outbreak of war with pleasure, so confident was he of conquering his enemies, and of making use of their defeat to strengthen his position on the throne; for he knew the enthusiasm which the prospect of military triumph always stirred up in the martial French spirit.

Chap. 23.

The great army which the Emperor was about to set in motion against Austria, now had its back to that Empire, since the forces deployed on the coasts of the North Sea, the Channel and the Atlantic were facing England. On the right wing the 1st Corps, commanded by Bernadotte, occupied Hanover; the 2nd, under the orders of Marmont, was in Holland; the 3rd under Davout was in Bruges; the 4th, 5th and 6th commanded by Soult, Lannes and Ney, were encamped at Boulogne and in the surrounding district, while finally the 7th commanded by Augereau was in Brest, and formed the extreme left.

To break up this long cordon of troops and form them into a large body which could march toward Austria, it was necessary to effect an immense turn round from front to back. Each army had to make an about turn, in order to face Germany, and form columns, to march there by the shortest route. Thus the right wing became the left, and the left the right.

Obviously, to go from Hanover or Holland to the Danube, the 1st and 2nd Corps had a much shorter distance to travel than those who came from Boulogne, and they in turn were nearer than Augereau's corps, which, in order to go from Brest to the frontiers of Switzerland on the upper Rhine, had to cross the whole of France, a journey of some three hundred leagues. The troops were on the road for two months, marching in several columns; Marshal Augereau was the last to leave Brest, but he then went on ahead, and stopped first at Rennes and then successively at Alonon, Melun, Troyes and Langres, at which stops he inspected the various regiments, whose morale was raised by his presence. The weather was superb: I spent the two months travelling endlessly in an open carriage, from one column to another, carrying the marshal's orders to the generals, and was able to stop twice at Paris to see my mother. Our equipment had gone on in advance. I had a mediocre servant, but three excellent horses.

While the Grande Arme was wending its way towards the Rhine and the Danube, the French troops stationed in northern Italy, under the command of Massna, concentrated in the Milan area in order to attack the Austrians in the region of Venezia.

To transmit his orders to Massna, the Emperor was obliged to send his aides-de-camp through Switzerland, which remained neutral. Now it so happened that while Marshal Augereau was at Langres, an officer who was carrying Napoleon's despatches was thrown out of his carriage and broke his collar-bone. He was taken to Marshal Augereau whom he told that he was unable to continue his mission. The marshal, knowing how important it was that the Emperor's despatches should arrive in Italy without delay, entrusted me with the task of delivering them, and also of going through Huningue, where I was to pass on his order to have a bridge built over the Rhine at this spot. I was delighted to have this mission, as it meant that I would have an interesting journey and would be sure of rejoining 7th Corps before they were in action against the Austrians.

It did not take me long to reach Huningue and Basle; I went from there to Berne and on to Rapperschwill, where I left my carriage: then, on horseback and not without some danger, I crossed the Splgen pass, at that time almost impracticable. I entered Italy at Chiavenna, and joined Marshal Massna near Verona. I went off again without any delay, for Massna was as impatient to see me go with his replies to the Emperor as I was to rejoin Marshal Augereau before there was any fighting. However my return journey was not as rapid as my journey out, because a very heavy fall of snow had covered not only the mountains but also the valleys of Switzerland; it had begun to freeze hard, and horses slipped and fell at every step. It was only by offering 600 francs that I was able to find two guides who were prepared to cross the Splgen with me. It took us more than twelve hours to make the crossing, walking through snow sometimes up to our knees. The guides were on the point of refusing to go any further, saying that it was too dangerous, but I was young and venturesome, and I knew the importance of the despatches which the Emperor was awaiting.

I told my guides that even if they turned back, I would go on without them. Every profession has its code of honour; that of the guides consists principally in never abandoning the traveller committed to their care. Mine then went forward, and after some truly extraordinary exertions, we arrived at the large inn situated at the foot of the Splgen as night was falling. We would have undoubtedly died if we had been trapped on the mountain, for the path, which was barely discernable, was edged by precipices which the snow prevented us from seeing clearly. I was exhausted, but a sleep restored my strength, so I left at daybreak to reach Rapperschwill, where there were carriages and passable roads.

The worst of the journey was over; so, in spite of the snow and bitter cold, I reached Basle and then Heningue, where the 7th Corps was stationed, on the 19th October. The next day we began to cross the Rhine over a bridge of boats built for that purpose; for although there was, less than half a league away in the town of Basle, a stone bridge, the Emperor had ordered Marshal Augereau to respect the neutrality of Switzerland, a neutrality which they themselves broke, nine years later, by handing the bridge to the enemies of France in 1814.

Here I was then, involved once more in a war. It was now 1805, a year which for me heralded a long series of battles which lasted continuously for ten years, for it did not end until ten years later at Waterloo. However numerous the wars of the Empire might be, nearly all French soldiers enjoyed one or even several years of respite, either because they were in a garrison in France, or they were stationed in Italy or Germany when we were at war with Spain; but, as you will see, this did not happen to me; I was continually sent from north to south, and south to north, everywhere where there was fighting. I did not spend a single one of these ten years without coming under fire and without shedding my blood in some foreign country.

I do not intend to give, here, a detailed account of the campaign of 1805. I shall limit myself to recalling the principal events.

The Russians, who were marching to the aid of Austria, were still far away, when Field-marshal Mack, at the head of eighty thousand men, advanced, unwisely, into Bavaria, where he was defeated by Napoleon, who forced him to retreat to the fortress of Ulm, where he surrendered with the greater part of his army, of which only two corps escaped the disaster.

One of these, commanded by Prince Ferdinand, managed to reach Bohemia; the other, commanded by the elderly Field-marshal Jellachich, escaped into the Vorarlberg near Lake Constance, where, flanked by neutral Switzerland, it guarded the narrow passes of the Black Forest. It was these troops which Marshal Augereau was about to attack.

After crossing the Rhine at Huningue, 7th Corps found itself in the country of Baden, whose sovereign, along with those of Bavaria and Wurtemberg, had just concluded an alliance with Napoleon; so we were received as friends by the population of Brisgau. Field-marshal Jellachich had not dared to oppose the French in such open country, but awaited us beyond Freiburg, at the entrance to the Black Forest, the passage through which he expected us to effect only at the cost of much bloodshed. Above all, he hoped to stop us at the Val d'Enfer, a very long and narrow pass, dominated on both sides by sheer cliffs, and easy to defend. But the men of 7th Corps had now heard of the successes achieved by their comrades at Ulm and in Bavaria, and anxious to emulate them, they advanced through the Black Forest with such lan that they crossed through it in three days, in spite of the natural obstacles, the enemy resistance and the difficulty in finding food in this dreadful wilderness. The army finally broke out into fertile country and made camp around Donauschingen, a very pleasant town where there is the magnificent chteau of the ancient line of the princes of Furstenburg.

The marshal and his aides-de-camp were billeted in the chteau, in the courtyard of which is the source of the Danube; this great river demonstrates its power at the moment of its birth, for at the spot where it issues from the earth it already bears a boat.

The draught-horses for the guns and the supply wagons had been greatly fatigued by the passage through the rough and mountainous passes of the Black Forest, which a coating of frost had made even more difficult. It was therefore necessary to give them several days of rest; during which period the Austrian cavalry came from time to time to probe our outposts, which were positioned two leagues from the town; but this amounted to no more than some ineffectual fire which kept us on our toes, gave us some exercise in skirmishing, and allowed us to learn to recognise the various uniforms of the enemy. I saw, for the first time, the Uhlans of Prince Charles, Rosenberg's Dragoons and Blankenstein's Hussars.

The horses having recovered their strength, the army continued its march, and for several weeks we had a series of engagements which left us masters of Engen and Stockach.

Although I was very much involved in these various actions, I had only one accident, which, however, might have been serious. The ground was covered by snow, particularly round Stockach, where the enemy defended their position fiercely. The marshal ordered me to go and reconnoitre a spot to which he wanted to direct a column; I left at the gallop; the ground looked to me to be quite level, the snow, driven by the wind having hidden all the hollows, but suddenly my horse and I fell into a deep gully, up to our necks in snow. I was trying to get out, when two enemy Hussars appeared at the edge and fired their muskets at me. Fortunately, the snow in which my horse and I were floundering about prevented them from taking an accurate aim, and I came to no harm; but they were about to fire once more when some Chasseurs, which Marshal Augereau had sent to my aid, forced them to depart hurriedly. With some help I was able to get out of the ravine, but we had a great deal of difficulty in extricating my horse. As we were both unhurt, my comrades had a laugh at the strange appearance I presented after my bath of snow.

After we had gained control of the Vorarlberg, we captured Bregen,and drove Jellachich's Austrian corps to Lake Constance and the Tyrol. The enemy now sought the protection of the fortress of Feldkirch and its celebrated gorge, behind which they could defend themselves with advantage. We expected to have to fight a murderous battle to take this position when, to our astonishment, the Austrians offered to capitulate, an offer which Marshal Augereau was quick to accept.

During the meeting between the two marshals, the Austrian officers, humiliated by the reverse which their arms had just suffered, took malicious pleasure in giving us some very bad news which had been concealed up till this day, but which the Russians and Austrians had learned of from English sources. The Franco-Spanish fleet had been defeated by Lord Nelson on October 20th not far from Cadiz, at Cape Trafalgar. Villeneuve, our infelicitous admiral, who had failed to carry out the precise orders of Napoleon at a time when the appearance of a combined fleet in the Channel could have secured a safe passage for the troops assembled at Boulogne, learning that he was about to be replaced by Admiral Rosily, passed suddenly from an excess of circumspection to an excess of audacity. He left Cadiz and engaged in a battle which, had it turned out in our favour, would have been virtually useless, since the French army, instead of being at Boulogne to take advantage of such a success to embark for England, was two hundred leagues from the coast, fighting in Germany.

After a most desperate struggle, the fleets of France and Spain had been defeated by that of England, whose admiral, the famous Nelson, had been killed; taking to his grave a reputation as the finest seaman of the epoch. On our side we lost Rear-admiral Magon, a very fine officer. One of our vessels blew up; seventeen, as many French as Spanish, were captured. A severe storm which arose toward the end of the battle, lasted all night and the days following, and was on the verge of overwhelming both victors and vanquished, so that the English, concerned for their own safety, were forced to abandon nearly all the ships which they had captured from us; which were mostly taken back to Cadiz by the remains of their brave but unfortunate crews, though some were wrecked on the rock-bound coast.

It was during this battle that my excellent friend France d'Houdetot received a wound to his thigh which has left him with a limp. D'Houdetot, scarcely out of childhood was a naval cadet, and attached to the staff of Admiral Magon, a friend of my father. After the death of the admiral, the ship "The Algesiras," in which he served, was captured after a bloody encounter, and the English placed on board a prize crew of sixty men. But the storm separated the ship from the English fleet, and the prize crew realised that it was very unlikely that they could reach England, so they agreed to allow the French seamen to take the ship into Cadiz, with the stipulation that they would not be held as prisoners of war. The French flag was hoisted to identify the ship and the badly damaged vessel managed to reach Cadiz, though not without great difficulty. The ship which bore Admiral Villeneuve was captured and the unlucky admiral was taken to England, where he remained a prisoner for three years. Having been released on exchange, he decided to go to Paris, but, detained at Rennes, he committed suicide.

When Field-marshal Jellachich felt obliged to capitulate before the 7th French army corps, this decision seemed the more surprising since, even if defeated by us, he had the option of retiring into the Tyrol which was behind him, and whose inhabitants have for many centuries been greatly attached to the house of Austria. The thick snow which covered the country no doubt made movement difficult, but the difficulties presented would have been much greater for us, enemies of Austria, than for the troops of Jellachich, withdrawing through an Austrian province. However, if the old and hide-bound Field-marshal could not bring himself to campaign in winter, in the high mountains, his attitude was not shared by the officers under his command; for many of them condemned his pusillanimity, and spoke of rebelling against his authority. The most ardent of his opponents was General the Prince de Rohan, a French officer in the service of Austria, a bold and competent soldier. Marshal Augereau, fearing that Jellachich might take the advice offered by the Prince and retreat into the Tyrol where pursuit would be almost impossible, hastened to grant him all the conditions which he requested.

The terms of the capitulation were that the Austrian troops should lay down their arms, hand over their flags, standards, cannons and horses, but should not themselves be taken to France, and could withdraw to Bohemia after swearing not to bear arms against France for one year.

When he announced the capitulation in one of his army bulletins, the Emperor seemed a little disappointed that the Austrian soldiers had not been made prisoners of war; but he changed his mind when he realised that Marshal Augereau had no means of retaining them, as escape was so easy. In fact, during the night preceding the day when the Austrians were to lay down their arms, a revolt broke out in several brigades against Field-marshal Jellachich. The Prince de Rohan, refusing to accept the capitulation, left with his infantry division, and joined by some regiments from other divisions, he fled into the mountains, which he crossed, despite the rigours of the season: then by an audacious march, he bypassed the cantonments of Marshal Ney's troops, who occupied the towns of the Tyrol, and arriving between Verona and Venice, he fell on the rear of the French army of Italy, while this force, commanded by Massna was following on the tail of Prince Charles, who was retiring towards Friuli. The arrival of the Prince de Rohan in Venetian territory, when Massna was already in the far distance, could have had the most grave consequences; but fortunately a French army, coming from Naples, under the command of General Saint-Cyr, defeated the Prince and took him prisoner. He had, at least, submitted only to force, and was right in saying that if Jellachich had been there with all his troops, the Austrians might have defeated Saint-Cyr and opened a route for themselves back into Austria.

When a force capitulates, it is customary for the victor to send to each division a staff officer to take charge, as it were, and to conduct it on the day and at the hour appointed to the place where it is to lay down its arms. Those of my comrades who were sent to the Prince de Rohan were left behind by him in the camp which he quitted, for he carried out his retreat from an area behind the fortress of Feldkirch, and in a direction away from the French camp, so that he had little fear of being stopped; but the Austrian cavalry were not in a similar situation. They were in bivouac on a small area of open ground in front of Feldkirch, and opposite and a short distance from our outposts. I had been detailed to go to the Austrian cavalry and lead them to the agreed rendezvous; this brigade did not have a general, but was commanded by a colonel of Blankenstein's Hussars, an elderly Hungarian, brave and crafty, whose name, I regret, I cannot remember, for I think highly of him although he played me a most disagreeable trick.

On my arrival at the camp, the colonel had offered me the hospitality of his hut for the night, and we had agreed to set off at daybreak, to reach the spot indicated on the shore of Lake Constance, between the town of Bregenz and Lindau, at a distance of about three leagues. I was most astonished when, at about midnight, I heard the officers mounting their horses. I hurried out of the hut and saw that the squadrons were formed up and ready to move. I asked the reason for this hasty departure, and the old colonel replied, with cool deceit, that Field-marshal Jellachich feared that some jeering directed at the Austrian soldiers by the French, whose camp one would have to pass if one took the shortest route to the beach at Lindau, might lead to fighting between the troops of the two nations. Jellachich, in consultation with Marshal Augereau, had ordered the Austrian troops to make a long detour to the right so that they would avoid our camp and the town of Breganz, and would not come into contact with our soldiers. He added that as the route was very long and the road bad, the two commanders had advanced the time of departure by some hours; he was surprised that I had not been informed of this, but suggested that the written instructions had been held up at the advance posts, owing to some misunderstanding; he carried this deception so far as to send an officer to look for this despatch, wherever it might be. The explanation given by the colonel of the Blankensteins sounded so convincing that I did not say anything, although my instinct told me that this was a little irregular; but, alone in the midst of three thousand enemy cavalry, what could I do? It was better to appear confident than to seem to doubt the good faith of the Austrian brigade. As I was unaware of the flight of the Prince de Rohan's division, it did not enter my head that the commander of the cavalry intended to evade the capitulation. I rode alongside him, at the head of the column. The Austrian had made his arrangements for the avoidance of the French camps— whose fires could be seen—so well that we did not pass near any of them. But what the old colonel had not anticipated, and was unable to avoid, was an encounter with a flying patrol, which the French cavalry usually sent out into the countryside at night, some distance from an encampment: for suddenly there was a challenge, and we found ourselves in the presence of a large column of French cavalry, which was clearly visible in the moonlight. The Hungarian colonel, without seeming the least worried, said to me "This is work for you, as an aide-de-camp; kindly come with me and explain the situation to the commander of this French unit." We went forward. I gave the pass-word, and found myself in the presence of the 7th mounted Chasseurs, who, knowing that the Austrian troops were expected for the laying down of arms, and recognising me as one of Marshal Augereau's aides, made no difficulty about the passage of the brigade which I was conducting. The French commander, whose

113

troops had their sabres drawn, even took the trouble to have them sheathed, as witness to the good-will existing between the two columns, which went on their way for some distance, side by side. I closely questioned the officer in charge of the Chasseurs about the change in the time at which the Austrians were to move; but he knew nothing at all about it, something which did not raise any suspicion in my mind, for I knew that an order of this kind would not be distributed by the staff down to regimental level. So I continued to ride with the colonel for the rest of the night, finding, however that the detour we were making was very long, and the going very bad.

At last, at daybreak, the old colonel, seeing a patch of level ground, said to me, in a conversational tone of voice, that although he would soon be obliged to hand over the horses of the three regiments to the French, he wished to care for the poor animals up to the last, and to deliver them in good condition; In consequence he had ordered that they should be given a feed of oats. The brigade halted, formed up and dismounted; and when the horses had been tethered, the colonel, who alone remained on horseback, gathered in a circle around him the officers and men of the three regiments, and in a ringing voice which made the old warrior seem quite superb, he announced that the Prince de Rohan's division, preferring honour to a shameful safety, had refused to subscribe to the disgraceful capitulation whereby Field-marshal Jellachich had promised to hand over to the French, the flags and the arms of the Austrian troops, and had fled into the Tyrol; where he too would have led the brigade were it not for the fact that he feared that in that barren mountain country, there would not be enough fodder for so many horses. But now they had open country in front of them and having, by a ruse of which he was proud, gained a lead of six leagues over the French troops, he invited all those who had truly Austrian hearts to follow him across Germany to Moravia, where they could rejoin the army of their August sovereign, Francis II. Blankenstein's Hussars responded to this speech by their colonel with a resounding cheer of approval; but Rosenberg's Dragoons and the Uhlans of Prince Charles maintained a gloomy silence. As for me, although I did not yet know enough German to follow the colonel's words exactly, what I did understand, together with the tone of the orator and the position in which he found himself, allowed me to guess what was afoot, and I can promise you that I felt very crestfallen at having, although unwittingly, furthered the plans of this diabolical Hungarian.

A fearful tumult now arose in the immense circle by which I was surrounded, and I was able to appreciate the inconvenience stemming from the heterogeneous amalgamation of different peoples which makes up the Austrian Empire, and in consequence, the Austrian army. All the Hussars were Hungarian; the Blankensteins therefore approved the proposal made by a leader of their own nationality, but the Dragoons were German and the Uhlans were Polish; the Hungarian could make no nationalistic appeal to them, who, in this difficult situation listened only to their own officers; these officers declared that they thought themselves bound by the capitulation which Field-marshal Jellachich had signed and did not wish, by their departure, to worsen his position or that of their comrades who were already the hands of the French, who would be within their rights to send them all back to France as prisoners of war, if a part of the Austrian forces violated the agreement.

To this the colonel replied that when the Commander-in-Chief of an army looses his head, fails in his duty and delivers his troops to the enemy, his juniors have no need to consult anything but their courage and their devotion to their country. Then the colonel, brandishing his sabre in one hand, while with the other he seized the regimental standard, cried out, "Go then Dragoons! Go! Go! Yield to the French your dishonoured standards, and the arms which the Emperor gave us for his defence. As for us, the bold Hussars, we are off to rejoin our sovereign, to whom we can once more show with honour our unstained colours, and the swords of fearless soldiers!" Then, drawing close to me, and casting a look of disdain on the Uhlans and Dragoons, he added, "I am sure that if this young Frenchman found himself in our position and had to choose between your conduct and mine, he would take the more courageous course; for the French love honour and reputation as much as their country." Having said this, the old Hungarian sheathed his sabre, dug in his spurs, and leading his regiment at the gallop, he careered into the distance, where he soon disappeared. There was some truth in both the arguments which I had heard, but that of the old Hungarian seemed the more valid because it was in conformity with the interests of his country; I then secretly approved of his behaviour, but I could not, of course advise the Dragoons and Uhlans to follow his example; that would have been to step out of my rôle and fail in my duty. I maintained a strict neutrality in this discussion, and when the Hussars had left, I asked the colonels of the other two regiments to follow me, and we took the road for Lindau.

On the beach beside the lake, we found Marshals Augereau and Jellachich, as well as the French forces and the Austrian infantry regiments which had not followed the Prince de Rohan. On learning from me that the Blankenstein Hussars, having refused to recognise the capitulation, were heading for Moravia both marshals flew into a rage: Marshal Augereau because he feared that these Hussars might cause havoc in the rear of the French army, since the route which they would follow would take them through areas where the Emperor, in the course of his march on Vienna, had left many dressing stations full of wounded; artillery parks, *etc.* But the Hungarian colonel did not think it was part of his duty to advertise his presence by any surprise attack, as he was only too anxious to get out of a country bristling with French arms. By avoiding all our positions, moving always on minor roads, hiding by day in the woods and marching rapidly at night, he managed to reach the frontier of Moravia without trouble, and joined an Austrian army corps which occupied the area. As for the troops who remained with Field-marshal Jellachich, having laid down their arms, surrendered their flags and standards and handed over their horses, they became prisoners on parole for one year, and made off in dismal silence for the interior of Germany, to make their way sadly to Bohemia. I remembered, when I saw them, the valiant words of the old colonel, and I think I saw on the faces of many of these Uhlans and Dragoons a regret that they had not followed the old warrior, and an unhappiness when they compared the heroic position of the Blankensteins with their own humiliation.

Among the trophies which Jellachich's corps was forced to hand over were seventeen flags and two standards, which Marshal Augereau, as was usual, hastened to send to the Emperor, in the care of two aides-de-camp. Major Massy and I were detailed for this task, and we left the same evening in a fine carriage with, in front of us, a wagon containing the flags and standards, in the charge of an N.C.O. We headed for Vienna via Kempten, Brauneau, Munich, Lenz and Saint-Poelten. Some leagues before this last town, following the banks of the Danube, we admired the superb Abbey of Mlk, one of the richest in the world. It was here, four years later that I ran the greatest danger, and earned the praise of the Emperor, for having performed before his eyes the finest feat of arms of my military career; as you will see when we come to the campaign of 1809.

Chap. 24

In September 1805, the seven corps which made up the Grande Arme were on the march from their positions on the coast to the banks of the Danube. They were already in the countries of Baden and Wurtemberg when, on the 1st October, Napoleon, in person, crossed the Rhine at Strasburg. A part of the large force which the Russians were sending to the aid of Austria had at that moment arrived in Moravia, and the cabinet at Vienna should, with prudence, have waited until this powerful reinforcement had joined the Austrian army; but, carried away by an enthusiasm which they did not usually display, and which was inspired by Field-marshal Mack, it had despatched him, at the head of eighty thousand men, to attack Bavaria; the possession of which had been coveted by Austria for several centuries, and which French policy had always protected from invasion. The Elector of Bavaria, forced to abandon his state, took refuge with his family and his troops in Wurtzburg, from where he begged Napoleon for assistance. Napoleon entered into an alliance with him and with the rulers of Baden and Wurtzburg.

The Austrian army, under Mack, had already occupied Ulm, when Napoleon, having crossed the Danube at Donauwerth seized Augsburg and Munich. The French were now in the rear of Mack's force and had cut his communication with the Russians, who having reached Vienna, were advancing towards him by forced marches. The Field-marshal realised then, but too late, the error he had made in allowing himself to be encircled by French troops. He tried to break out, but was defeated successively in the battles of Wertingen, Gunzberg, and Elchingen, where Marshal Ney won fame. Under increasing pressure, Mack was forced to shut himself up in Ulm with all his army, less the corps of the Archduke Ferdinand and Jellachich who escaped, the former into Bohemia, and the latter to the region round Lake Constance. Ulm was then besieged by the Emperor. It was a place which, though not heavily fortified, could nevertheless have held out for a long time thanks to its position and its large garrison, and so given the Russians time to come to its relief. But Field-marshal Mack, passing from exalted over-confidence to a profound disheartenment, surrendered to Napoleon, who had now, in three weeks, scattered, captured, or destroyed eighty thousand Austrians and freed Bavaria, where he reinstalled the Elector. We shall see, in 1813, this favour repaid by the most odious treachery.

Being now the master of Bavaria, and rid of the presence of Mack's army, the Emperor increased the pace of his advance, down the right bank of the Danube towards Vienna. He captured Passau and then Linz, where he learned that 50,000 Russians, commanded by General Koutousoff, reinforced by 40,000 Austrians, whom General Kienmayer had collected, had crossed the Danube at Vienna and had taken up a position between Mlk and St. Poelten. He was told at the same time that the Austrian army commanded by Prince Charles had been defeated by Massna in the Venetian district and was retreating via the Friuli in the direction of Vienna; and lastly that the Archduke Jean was occupying the Tyrol with several divisions. Those two princes were therefore threatening the right of the French army, while it had the Russians in front of it. To protect himself against a flank attack, the Emperor, who already had Marshal Augereau's corps in the region of Bregenz, sent Maeshal Ney to attack Innsbruck and the Tyrol, and moved Marmont's corps to Loeben, in order to block Prince Charles' route from Italy. Having taken these wise precautions to protect his right flank, Napoleon, before advancing to meet the Russians, whose advance-guard had already clashed with ours at Amstetten, near to Steyer, wished to protect his left flank from any attack from those Austrians who had taken refuge in Bohemia, under the command of Archduke Ferdinand. To effect this he gave Marshal Mortier the infantry divisions of Generals Dupont and Gazan, and ordered him to cross the Danube by the bridges at Passau and Linz, and then proceed down the left bank of the river, while the bulk of the army went down the right. However, in order not to leave Marshal Mortier too isolated, Napoleon conceived the idea of gathering together on the Danube a great number of boats, which had been captured on the tributaries of the river, and forming a flotilla which, manned by men from the guard, could move down the river, keeping level with Mortier and making a link between the troops on both banks.

You may think it a little presumptuous of me to criticise one of the operations of a great captain, but I cannot refrain from commenting that the sending of Mortier to the left bank was a move which had not been sufficiently considered, and was an error which could have had very serious consequences. The Danube, Europe's largest river, is, after Passau, so wide in winter that from one bank one cannot discern a man standing on the other; it is also very deep and very fast-flowing, and it therefore provided a guarantee of perfect safety for the left flank of the French army as it marched down the right bank. Furthermore, any attack could be made only by the Archduke Ferdinand, coming from Bohemia; but he, very pleased to have escaped from the French before Ulm, had only a few troops, and they were mostly cavalry. Even if he had wished to do so, he had not the means to mount an attack which involved crossing an obstacle such as the Danube, into which he might be driven back. Whereas, by detaching two of his divisions and allowing them to be isolated across this immense river, Napoleon exposed them to the risk of being captured or exterminated. A disaster which might have been foreseen and which very nearly came about.

Field-marshal Koutousoff, had been awaiting the French with confidence, in a strong position at St. Poelten, because he believed that they were being pursued by the army of Mack; but when he heard of the surrender of this army at Ulm, he no longer felt himself strong enough to face Napoleon alone, and being unwilling to risk his troops to save the city of Vienna, he decided to put the barrier of the Danube between himself and the victor, so he crossed the river by the bridge at Krems, which he burned behind him.

He had scarcely arrived on the left bank with all his army, when he ran into the scouts of the Gazan division, which was proceeding from Dirnstein to Krems, with Marshal Mortier at its head. Koutousoff, having discovered the presence of a French corps isolated on the left bank, resolved to crush it, and to achieve this aim he attacked it head to head on the narrow road which ran along the river bank, while seizing control of the escarpments which overlook the Danube. He sent light troops to occupy Dirnstein to cut off the retreat of the Gazan division. The position of the division was made even more critical by the fact that the flotilla of boats had dropped back and there were only two little boats available, which made it impossible to bring reinforcements from the other bank.

Attacked in front and in the rear and on one of their flanks by enemies six times their number; shut in between the rocky escarpment occupied by the Russians and the depths of the Danube, the French soldiers, crowded on the narrow roadway, did not despair. The gallant Marshal Mortier set them an example, for, when it was suggested that he should take one of the boats and go over to the right bank, where he would be with the Grande Arme, and avoid giving the Russians the glory of capturing a marshal, he replied that he would die with his men, or escape over the dead bodies of the Russians!

A savage bayonet fight ensued: five thousand French were up against thirty thousand Russians: night came to add to the horrors of the combat: Gazan's division, massed in column, managed to regain Dirnstein at a moment when Dupont's division, which had remained behind opposite Mlk, alerted by the sound of gunfire, was running to their aid. Eventually the battlefield remained in French hands.

In this hand to hand fighting, where the bayonet was almost the only weapon used, our men, more adroit and agile than the giant Russians, had a great advantage; so the enemy losses amounted to some four thousand five hundred men, while ours were three thousand only. But had our divisions not been made up of seasoned soldiers, Mortier's corps would probably have been destroyed. The Emperor was well aware of this, and hastened to recall it to the right bank. What seems to me to be proof that he realised the mistake he had made in sending this corps across the river, is the fact that, although he generously rewarded the brave regiments which had fought at Dirnstein, the official bulletins scarcely mention this sanguinary affair, and it is as if one wished to conceal the results of this operation because one could find no military justification for it.

What further confirms me in the opinion which I have taken the liberty of expressing, is that in the campaign of 1809, the Emperor, when he found himself in a similar situation, did not send any troops across the river, but, keeping all his force together, he went with it to Vienna.

But let us return to the mission with which Major Massy and I were charged.

When we arrived in Vienna, Napoleon and the bulk of the army had already left the city, which they had seized without a shot being fired. The crossing of the Danube which it was necessary to effect in order to pursue the Russians and the Austrians who were retreating into Moravia, had not been disputed, thanks to a perhaps culpable deception which was carried out by Marshals Lannes and Murat. This incident, which had such a profound effect on this well-known campaign, deserves recounting.

The city of Vienna is situated on the right bank of the Danube: a small branch of that immense river passes through the city, but the main stream is half a league away; there the Danube contains a large number of islands which are connected by a long series of wooden bridges, terminated by one which, spanning the main arm of the river, reaches the left bank at a place named Spitz. The road to Moravia runs along this series of bridges. When the Austrians are opposing the crossing of a river, they have a very bad habit of leaving the bridges intact up to the very last moment, to give them a means of mounting a counter-attack against the enemy, who almost always does not allow them time to do so and takes from them the bridges which they have neglected to burn. This is what the French did during the campaign in Italy in 1796 at the memorable affairs of Lodi and Arcoli. But these examples had not served to correct the Austrians, for on leaving Vienna, which is not suited to defence, they retired to the other side of the Danube without destroying a single one of the bridges spanning this vast watercourse, and limited themselves to placing inflammable material on the platform of the main bridge, in order to set it alight when the French appeared. They had also established on the left bank, at the end of the bridge at Spitz, a powerful battery of artillery, as well as a division of six thousand men under the command of Prince D'Auersperg, a brave but not very intelligent officer. Now I must tell you that some days before the entry of the French into Vienna, the Emperor had received the Austrian general, Comte de Guilay, who came as an envoy to make peace overtures, which came to nothing. But hardly had the Emperor settled in the palace of Schoenbrunn, when General Guilay again appeared and spent more than an hour tte-a-tte with Napoleon. From this a rumour arose that an armistice had been arranged, a rumour which spread amongst the French regiments which were entering Vienna and the Austrians who were leaving to cross the Danube.

Murat and Lannes, whom the Emperor had ordered to secure the crossing of the Danube, placed Oudinot's Grenadiers behind a bushy plantation and went forward, accompanied only by some German-speaking officers. The enemy outposts withdrew, firing as they went. The French officers called out that there was an armistice, and continuing their progress, they crossed all the small bridges, without being held up. When they arrived at the main bridge, they renewed their assertion to the commander at Spitz, who did not dare to fire on two marshals, almost alone, who claimed that hostilities were suspended. However, before allowing them to go any further, he wanted to go and ask General Auersperg for orders, and while he did so, he left the post in charge of a sergeant. Lannes and Murat persuaded the sergeant that under the terms of the cease-fire, the bridge should be handed over to them, and that he should go with his men to join his officer on the left bank. The poor sergeant hesitated, he was edged back gently while the conversation continued, and by a slow but steady advance they reached, eventually, the end of the main bridge.

At this point an Austrian officer endeavored to set light to the incendiary material, but the torch was snatched from his hand, and he was told that he would be in serious trouble if he did any such thing. Next, the column of Oudinot's Grenadiers appeared and began to cross the bridge.... The Austrian gunners prepared to open fire, but the French marshals ran to the commander of the artillery and assured him that an armistice was in force, then, seating themselves on the guns, they requested the gunners to go and inform General Auersperg of their presence. General Auersperg eventually arrived and was about to order the gunners to open fire, although by now they and the Austrian troops were surrounded by the French Grenadiers, when the two marshals managed to convince him that there was a cease-fire, a principal condition of which was that the French should occupy the bridge. The unhappy general, fearing to compromise himself by the useless shedding of blood, lost his head to the point of leading away all the troops which he had been given to defend the bridges.

Without this error on the part of General Auersperg, the passage of the Danube could only have been carried out with great difficulty, and might even have been impossible; in which case Napoleon would have been unable to pursue the Russians and Austrians into Moravia, and would have failed in his campaign. That was the opinion at the time, and it was confirmed three years later when, the Austrians having burned the bridges, to secure a passage we were forced to fight the two battles of Essling and Wagram, which cost us more than thirty thousand men, whereas in 1805 Marshals Lannes and Murat took possession of the bridges without there being a single man wounded.

Was the stratagem they employed admissible? I have my doubts. I know that in war one eases one's conscience, and that any means may be employed to ensure victory and reduce loss of life, but in spite of these weighty considerations, I do not think that one can approve of the method used to seize the bridge at Spitz, and for my part I would not care to do the same in similar circumstances.

To conclude this episode, the credulity of General Auersperg was very severely punished. A court-martial condemned him to be cashiered, dragged through the streets of Vienna on a hurdle and finally put to death at the hands of the public executioner...! A similar sentence was passed on Field-marshal Mack, to punish him for his conduct at Ulm. But in both cases the death sentence was commuted to life imprisonment. They served ten years and were then released, but deprived of their position, expelled from the ranks of the nobility and rejected by their families, they died, both of them, shortly after they had been set at liberty.

The stratagem employed by Marshals Lannes and Murat having secured the crossing of the Danube, the Emperor Napoleon directed his army in pursuit of the Russians and the Austrians. Thus began the second phase of the campaign.

Chap. 25.

The Russian marshal Koutousoff was heading via Hollabrunn for Brno in Moravia, in order to join the second army which was led by the Emperor Alexander in person; but on approaching Hollabrunn, he was alarmed to discover that the troops of Lannes and Murat were already occupying the town and cutting off his means of retreat. To get out of this fix, the aged marshal, making use, in his turn, of trickery, sent General Prince Bagration as an envoy to Marshal Murat, whom he assured that an aide-de-camp of the Emperor was on his way to Napoleon in order to conclude an armistice, and that, without doubt, peace would shortly follow.

Prince Bagration was a very amiable man, he knew exactly how to flatter Murat, so that he in turn was deceived into accepting an armistice, in spite of the observations of Lannes, who wished to fight but had to obey Murat, who was his superior officer.

The truce lasted for thirty-six hours; and while Murat was inhaling the incense which the crafty Russian lavished on him, Koutousoff's army made a detour and concealing its movement behind a screen of low hills, escaped from danger, and went on to take up, beyond Hollabrunn, a strong position which opened the road to Moravia and assured his retreat and his junction with the second Russian army which was encamped between Znaim and Brno. Napoleon was still in the palace of Schoenbrunn, and was furiously angry when he heard that Murat had allowed himself to be bamboozled by Prince Bagration, and had accepted an armistice without his orders, and he commanded him to attack Koutousoff immediately.

Now the situation of the Russians had changed greatly to their advantage, so they repelled the French most vigorously. The town of Hollabrunn, taken and re-taken several times, set on fire by the mortars, filled with the dead and dying, remained finally in French possession. The Russians retired in the direction of Brno; our troops followed them and took possession of this town without a fight, although it was fortified and dominated by the well-known citadel of Spielberg.

The Russian armies and the remains of the Austrian troops were united in Moravia; the Emperor Napoleon, in order to deliver the final blow, arrived in Brno, the capital of the province.

My comrade Massy and I followed after him, but we moved slowly and with much difficulty, firstly because the post-horses were on their last legs, and then because of the great quantity of troops, guns, ammunition wagons, baggage, *etc.* with which the roads were obstructed. We were obliged to stop for twenty-four hours at Hollabrunn, while we waited for a passage to be cleared through the streets, destroyed by fire and littered with planks and beams and the debris of furniture, still alight. This unfortunate town had been so completely burned that we were unable to find a single house to provide shelter!

During our enforced stay, we were confronted and distressed by the most horrible and shocking spectacle. The wounded, mainly Russians, had taken refuge during the fighting in the houses which were soon set ablaze. All who could walk fled at the approach of this new danger, but the crippled and gravely injured were burned alive in the ruins! Many had attempted to escape the fire by crawling along the ground, but the flames had followed them into the streets,where one could see a multitude of these wretched victims half consumed by fire, some of them still breathing! The bodies of the men and horses killed in the battle had also been roasted, so that for several leagues around the town there was a sickening stench of burning flesh! ... There are countrysides and towns which because of their situation are destined to serve as battlefields, and Hollabrun is one of them, because it offers an excellent military position; thus it was that the damage done by the fire of 1805 had scarcely been repaired, when I saw the place again, four years later, once more on fire and littered with the half-roasted bodies of the dead and dying; as you will see from my description of the campaign of 1809.

Major Massy and I left this pestilential spot as soon as we could, and went on to Znaim, where, four years later I was to be wounded; and at last we reached the Emperor at Brunn (Brno), on November 22nd, ten days before the Battle of Austerlitz.

The day after our arrival, we completed our mission and handed over the flags with the ceremony laid down by the Emperor for solemn occasions of this kind; for he missed no opportunity of displaying to the troops anything which could raise their morale and enthusiasm.

The procedure was as follows:—Half an hour before the daily parade,—which took place at eleven o'clock outside whatever residence was serving as the Emperor's palace,—General Duroc, the Grand Marshal, sent to our billet a company of Grenadiers of the Guard, with bandsmen and drummers. The town of Brunn was full of French troops, and the soldiers, as we passed, celebrated with much cheering the victory of their comrades of 7th Corps. All the guard-posts accorded us military honours, and on our entry to the courtyard of the Emperor's quarters, the units formed up for the parade beat a salute, presented arms, and cried repeatedly "Vive L'Empereur!"

The aide-de-camp on duty came to receive us and to present us to Napoleon, to whom we were introduced, accompanied always by the N.C.O.s carrying the Austrian flags. The Emperor examined these various trophies, and after dismissing the N.C.O.s. he questioned us closely about the various actions which had been fought by Marshal Augereau and on all we had seen or learned on our long journey through a countryside which had been the theatre of war. Then he told us to await his instructions, and to join the imperial suite. The Grand Marshal Duroc took charge of the flags, for which he gave us a receipt in the regular manner, informed us that horses would be placed at our disposal and invited us, for the duration of our stay, to the table over which he presided.

The French army was now massed around and before Brunn. The Russian advance-guard occupied Austerlitz, while the bulk of their army was positioned round the town of Olmutz, where were also the Emperor Alexander of Russia and the Emperor of Austria. A battle seemed inevitable, but both sides being well aware that the outcome would have an immense bearing on the destiny of Europe, each hesitated to make a decisive move. Napoleon, usually so swift to act, waited for eleven days at Brunn before launching a major attack. It is, however, true that every day of waiting increased his forces by the arrival of great numbers of soldiers who had lagged behind because of illness or fatigue, and who having now recovered, hastened to rejoin their units. I recall that, in these circumstances, I told a white lie which could have ruined my military career.

Napoleon usually treated his officers with kindness, but there was one point on which he was perhaps too strict, for he held colonels responsible for keeping their units up to full strength, something it is very difficult to do during a campaign. It was in this matter that the Emperor was most often deceived, for the corps commanders were so afraid of displeasing him that they risked being committed to facing an enemy force disproportionate to their own numbers, rather than admit that sickness, fatigue and the need to forage for food had caused many soldiers to drop out. So Napoleon, in spite of his authority, never knew the exact number of combatants available to him on the day of battle.

Now it so happened that the Emperor, in the course of one of the endless trips he made to visit the various corps of the army, saw the mounted Chasseurs of his guard, who were moving to a different position. He was particularly fond of this regiment, of which his "guides" from Italy and Egypt formed the nucleus. The Emperor, whose experienced eye could estimate very exactly the strength of a column, noticing that their numbers were much reduced, took out of his pocket a little notebook, and, calling for General Morland, the commander of the mounted Chasseurs, he said to him in a stern voice, "Your regiment is down in my notes as having 1200 men, and although you have not been in action, you have no more than 800; what has happened to the others?" General Morland was a fine, brave fighting soldier, but he did not have a ready tongue, and being quite nonplussed, he said in his Franco-Alsatian dialect that he was short of only a small number of men. The Emperor maintained that he was about four hundred short, and to get to the truth of the matter he wanted to have an immediate count; but knowing that General Morland was very much liked by the officers of the imperial staff, he feared a cover-up, and thought he would be more likely to discover the truth by choosing an officer who did not belong to his entourage nor to the Chasseurs; so, seeing me, he ordered me to count the Chasseurs and to deliver to him personally a record of their numbers; having said which, he made off at the gallop. I began my task, which was made more easy because the troopers were riding past four abreast at walking pace.

Poor General Morland, who knew how close Napoleon's estimate was to the reality, was in a state of great agitation, for he foresaw that my report would call down on his head a severe reprimand. He hardly knew me, and did not dare to suggest that I might compromise myself to get him out of trouble. He was then sitting silently on his horse beside me, when, fortunately for him, his adjutant came to join him. This officer, named Fournier, had started his military career as an assistant surgeon, then, having become a surgeon-major, he felt that he had more of a vocation for the sabre than for the lancet, and had asked for and obtained permission to join the ranks of the combatant officers, and Morland, with whom he had served previously, arranged for him to join the Guard.

I had known Captain Fournier very well when he was still surgeon-major, and I was very much obliged to him, for not only had he dressed my father's wound when it was inflicted, but he had gone, like him, to Genoa, where, as long as my father lived, he had come several times a day to care for him: if the doctors charged with the duty of fighting the typhus epidemic had been as assiduous and zealous as Fournier, my father, perhaps, would not have died. I had often thought this, so I gave the warmest of welcomes to Fournier, whom I did not at first recognise in the pelisse of a captain of Chasseurs.

General Morland, seeing the pleasure we had in meeting one another, thought he might profit from our mutual friendship to persuade me not to reveal to the Emperor by how many men he was short. He took his adjutant aside and conferred with him for a time; then Fournier came, and in the name of our former friendship, he begged me to extricate General Morland from a most unpleasant situation by concealing from the Emperor the extent to which the regiment was under strength. I refused firmly and continued to count. The Emperor's estimate was very close, for there were only a few over eight hundred Chasseurs present, four hundred were missing.

I was about to leave to make my report, when General Morland and Captain Fournier renewed their pleas pointing out that the greater part of the men who had dropped behind for various reasons would rejoin them very shortly, and that it was not likely that Napoleon would engage in battle before the arrival of the divisions of Friant and Gudin, who were still at the gates of Vienna, thirty-six leagues from us and would take several days to reach us. In the interval more laggards would rejoin the unit. They added that the Emperor would be too busy to check my report. I could not pretend to myself that I was not being asked to deceive the Emperor, which was very wrong, but I felt also that I was under a great obligation to Captain Fournier for the truly tender care he had given to my dying father, I allowed myself therefore to be swayed and promised to conceal a large part of the truth.

I was scarcely alone when I realised the enormity of my error, but it was too late; the essential object now was to get out of the situation with the least harm possible. With this aim in view, I kept out of the way of the Emperor as long as he was on horseback, in case he went back to the bivouac of the Chasseurs, where their shortage of numbers striking him anew would give the lie to my report. I craftily did not return to the imperial quarters until night was approaching and Napoleon, having dismounted had gone to his apartment. Brought before him in order to make my report, I found him lying at full length on an immense map which was spread on the floor. As soon as he saw me, he called out "Well now! Marbot, how many Chasseurs are there in my guard? Are there twelve hundred as Morland claims?" "No sire" I replied."I counted only eleven hundred and twenty, that is a shortfall of eighty." "I was sure that there was a lot missing." said the Emperor, in a tone of voice which made it plain that he had expected a much larger deficit; and to be sure if there were no more than eighty men missing from a regiment of twelve hundred which had just come five hundred leagues in winter, sleeping almost every night in bivouac, that was a very small loss. So when, on going to dinner, the Emperor passed through the room where the senior officers of the guard were gathered, all he said to Morland was, "Now you see...you are short of eighty troopers; that is almost a squadron. With eighty of these men one could stop a Russian regiment! You must take care to see that men do not drop behind." Then, passing to the commander of the foot guards, whose numbers were also much reduced, Napoleon gave him a sharp reprimand. Morland, who thought himself lucky to have got away with no more than a few observations, came over to me, as soon as the Emperor was seated at table, and thanked me warmly. He told me that some thirty troopers had just arrived, and that a courier from Vienna had met more than a hundred between Znaim and Brunn, and many more this side of Hollabrunn, which meant that within forty-eight hours the regiment would have made up most of its deficiency. I wished for this as fervently as he did, for I was well aware of the difficult spot I had landed myself in out of my consideration for Fournier. I could not sleep that night for fear of the justifiable wrath of the Emperor, if he found out that I had lied to him.

I was even more dismayed the next day when Napoleon, in the course of his usual visit to his troops, started off in the direction of the Chasseur's bivouac, for a simple question put to an officer could expose everything; but just when I thought that I was done for, I heard the sound of the band of the Russian force, camped on the high ground of the Pratzen half a league from our position. I urged my horse forward towards the head of the numerous staff by whom the Emperor was accompanied, and getting as close to him as possible, I said in a loud voice, "I am sure there is something going on in the Russian camp, their band is playing a march".... The Emperor, who heard my remark, suddenly left the path which led to the Chasseur's bivouac, and headed towards Pratzen to see what was happening in the enemy advance-guard. He stayed a long time watching, and as night was approaching, he went back to Brunn without visiting the Chasseurs. For several days I was in a mortal panic, although I learned of the arrival of successive detachments of men, but at last the coming battle and the many preoccupations of the Emperor drove from his mind the idea of making the check which I so much feared. But I had learned my lesson; so when I became a colonel and was asked by the Emperor how many men were present in the squadrons of my regiment, I always gave the exact number.

Chap. 26.

If Napoleon was often deceived, he also used deception himself to further his projects, as can be shown by the tale of this diplomatic-military comedy, in which I played a part.

In order to understand this affair, which will give you the key to the intrigues which, the following year, gave rise to the war between Napoleon and the King of Prussia, we have to go back two months to the time when the French troops, having left the coast, were proceeding by rapid marches to the Danube. The shortest route which the first corps, commanded by Bernadotte, could take to reach Hanover, on the upper Danube, lay through Anspach. This little country belonged to Prussia, but as it was quite a long way from there, from which it was separated by a number of minor principalities, it had always been regarded in previous wars as being neutral territory, through which either party could pass, provided that they paid for any goods they required and refrained from any hostile action.

Things having been established on this footing, Austrian and French armies had often passed through the Margravate of Anspach, since the time of the Directory, without informing Prussia and without the latter raising any objection. Napoleon then, taking advantage of this convention, ordered Bernadotte to go through Anspach, which he did. However, the Queen of Prussia and her court, who detested Napoleon, on hearing of this, raised an outcry, claiming that Prussian territory had been violated, and took advantage of this event to rouse the nation and call loudly for war. The King of Prussia and his minister, Count Haugwitz, alone resisted the general clamour for action. This was in October 1805, when hostilities were about to break out between France and Austria, and the Russian armies were on their way to reinforce the latter. The queen and the young Prince Louis, the king's nephew, in an attempt to persuade the king to make common cause with the Austrians and Russians, arranged for the Emperor Alexander to come to Berlin, in the hope that his presence would influence Frederick-William.

Alexander arrived in the capital of Prussia on the 25th October. He was greeted with enthusiasm by the queen, Prince Louis and the supporters of war against France. The king, besieged on all sides, allowed himself to be persuaded, but only on the condition—advised by the old Prince of Brunswick, and Count Haugwitz—that his army should not be committed to a campaign until the outcome of the conflict between the French and the Austrians on the Danube had been determined. This partial adherence to their cause pleased neither Alexander nor the queen, but for the time being they could obtain nothing more explicit. A melodramatic scene was played out at Potsdam, where the Emperor of Russia and the King of Prussia, having descended, by the light of torches, into the sepulchral vaults of the palace, swore, in the presence of the court, eternal friendship, on the tomb of Frederick the Great; (an oath which did not prevent Alexander from incorporating into the Russian Empire, eighteen months later, one of the Prussian provinces, which Napoleon awarded him under the treaty of Tilsit, and this in the presence of his friend Frederick-William.) The Russian Emperor now went back to Moravia, to place himself at the head of his army, for Napoleon was advancing rapidly towards Vienna, which he shortly occupied.

When he heard of the King of Prussia's reluctance and the compact made at Potsdam, Napoleon, in order to deal with the Russians before the Prussians had made up their minds, installed himself for the encounter with the former in Brunn, where we now were.

It is said, quite rightly, that ambassadors are privileged spies. The King of Prussia, who heard daily of fresh victories won by Napoleon, was anxious to find out what the true position was between the warring parties; so he decided to send Count Haugwitz, his minister, to the French headquarters, with instructions to assess the situation. Now it was necessary to find an excuse for doing this, so he entrusted Count Haugwitz with a reply to a letter which Napoleon had sent to him, complaining about the agreement concluded between the Prussians and the Russians at Potsdam. Count Haugwitz arrived at Brunn some days before the Battle of Austerlitz, and would dearly have liked to stay there until he knew the result of the major engagement which was in prospect, in order to advise his sovereign to do nothing if we were victorious, or to attack us if we should be defeated. You do not have to be a soldier to see from a map what damage a Prussian army, coming from Breslau in Silesia, could do by going through Bohemia to fall on our rear around Regansberg.

As Napoleon knew that Count Haugwitz sent a courier every evening to Berlin, he decided that it would be by this means that he would inform the Prussians of the defeat of Field-marshal Jellachich's army corps, news of which had not yet reached them. This is how it was done.

Marshal of the Palace Duroc, after telling us what we were to do, had all the Austrian flags which we had brought from Bregenz secretly replaced in the lodgings which Massy and I occupied; then, some hours later, when the Emperor was in conversation with Count Haugwitz in his study, we re-enacted the ceremony of the handover of the flags in exactly the same way as it had been done on the first occasion. The Emperor hearing the band playing in the courtyard, feigned astonishment, and went to the windows followed by the ambassador. Seeing the flags carried by the N.C.O.s. he called for the duty aide-de-camp and asked him what was going on. The aide-de-camp having told him that we were two of Marshal Augereau's aides who had come to hand over to him the flags of Jellachich's Austrian corps captured at Bregenz, we were led inside; there Napoleon, without blinking an eyelid, and as if he had never seen us before, took the letter from Augereau, which had been re-sealed, and read it, although he had been aware of its contents for four days. Then he questioned us, making us go into the smallest details. Duroc had warned us to speak out loudly, as the ambassador was a little hard of hearing, this advice was of no use to Major Massy, who was the leader of the mission, since he was suffering from a cold and had almost completely lost his voice, so it was I who replied to the Emperor, and taking a lead from him, I painted in the most vivid colours the defeat of the Austrians, their despondency, and the enthusiasm of the French. Then, presenting the trophies one after the other, I named the Austrian regiments to which they had once belonged. I laid particular stress on two of them, because I knew that their capture would have a powerful effect on the ambassador, "Here," I said "is the flag of the infantry regiment of his Majesty the Emperor of Austria, and there is the standard of the Uhlans, commanded by the Archduke Charles, his brother." Napoleon's eyes twinkled, and he seemed to say, "Well done young man!" At last he dismissed us, and as we left we heard him say to the ambassador, "You see, monsieur le Comte, my armies are everywhere triumphant.... The Austrian army is no more, and soon the same fate will befall the Russians." Count Haugwitz seemed deeply impressed, and Duroc said to us, after we had left the room, "The count will write tonight to Berlin, to tell his government of the destruction of Jellachich's force, which will put a damper on the war party, and give the king new reasons for holding off. Which is what the Emperor very much wants."

This comedy having been played out, The Emperor, to be rid of a dangerous onlooker who could give an account of the disposition of his forces, suggested to Count Haugwitz that it was not very safe for him to remain between two armies which were about to come to blows, and persuaded him to go to Vienna to M. Tallyrand, his minister for foreign affairs, which he did that same evening.

The following day the Emperor said nothing to us about the scene which had been enacted the previous evening, but wishing, no doubt, to give some sign of his satisfaction with the manner in which we had played our parts, he asked Major Massy, kindly, about the progress of his cold, and he pinched my ear, which with him was a sort of caress.

Now the dnouement of the great drama was approaching and both sides were preparing for the coming struggle. Nearly all military authors so overload their narrative with details that they confuse the mind of the reader, to the extent that, in most of the published works on the wars of the Empire which I have read, I have been unable to understand the description of several of the battles in which I myself have taken part, and the various phases of which I know. I think that to preserve clarity in the description of an action, one needs to limit oneself to indicating the respective positions of the two armies, prior to the engagement, and to recounting only the principal and decisive events in the combat. This is what I shall attempt to do.

The coming battle is known as the Battle of Austerlitz, although it took place some distance from the village of that name: the reason for this is that, on the eve of the battle, the Emperors of Austria and Russia had slept in the Chteau of Austerlitz, out of which Napoleon drove them.

You will see on the map that a stream, the Goldbach, which rises on the far side of the road to Olmutz, flows into a pool called Menitz. This stream, which runs in a little valley with quite steep banks, separated the two armies. The right of the Austro-Russian forces lay on a wooded escarpment, situated behind the post-house of Posoritz, on the far side of the Olmutz road; their centre occupied Pratzen and the vast plateau of that name, and their left was near the meres of Satschan and the neighbouring marshes. The Emperor placed his left flank on a little hill, very difficult of access, which our men who had been in Egypt called the Santon (a holy man's grave) because it was surmounted by a small chapel, the roof of which had the appearance of a minaret. The French centre was near the pool of Kobolnitz, and the right was at Telnitz. The Emperor had put very few troops there in order to tempt the Russians into the marshy ground, where he had prepared their defeat by concealing in Gross-Raigern, on the road to Vienna, the corps of Marshal Davout.

On the 1st December, the eve of the battle, Napoleon left Brunn in the morning and spent all day examining the positions; in the evening he set up his headquarters behind the French centre, at a spot from where could be seen the camps of both armies and the area which would form their battlefield the next day. There was no building in the vicinity but a dilapidated barn, and it was there that were placed the Emperor's tables and maps, while he himself took up a position by a huge fire, surrounded by his numerous staff and his guards. Happily there was no snow, although it was very cold. I bedded down on the ground and fell into a deep sleep; but soon we had to remount our horses to accompany the Emperor, who was about to visit his troops. There was no moon, and the obscurity of the night was increased by a thick mist which made progress difficult. The troopers of the Emperor's escort had the idea of lighting torches made of pinewood and straw which were most useful. The soldiers, seeing the approach of a group of mounted men thus illuminated, could easily distinguish the imperial staff, and in an instant, as if by magic, one saw all our camp lit up by torches carried by the men who greeted the Emperor with cheer, made all the louder because the next day would be the anniversary of his coronation, a coincidence which seemed to them to be a good augury. The enemy must have been greatly astonished when, from the height of the neighbouring slope, they saw in the middle of the night, the light of sixty thousand torches and heard the repeated cheers of "Vive l'Empereur!" mingled with the sound of the regimental bands. All was gaiety, light and movement in our camp, while, on the Austro-Russian side, all was dark and silent.

The next day, the 2nd December, the cannons were heard at daybreak. We have seen that the Emperor had deployed few troops on his right wing; a bait which he dangled before the enemy, who would see the apparent possibility of taking Telnitz easily, and then crossing the Goldbach and going on to Gross-Raigern in order to control the road from Brunn to Vienna and so cut off our line of retreat. The Austro-Russians fell headlong into the trap, and, thinning out the rest of their line, they clumsily piled up a considerable force in the lower part of Telnitz, and in the narrow, marshy defiles around the meres of Satschan and Menitz. They thought, for some unknown reason, that Napoleon was considering withdrawing, without facing a battle, so to hasten this move they decided to attack us at the Santon on our left and at our centre before Puntowitz, so that, being defeated at these two points, and forced to retreat, we would find the road to Vienna cut by the Russian troops. But on our left Marshal Lannes not only repelled all the enemy attacks on the Santon, but drove them back across the Olmutz road as far as Blasiowitz, where the more level ground allowed Murat's cavalry to make several very effective charges, which compelled the Russians to retire hurriedly to the village of Austerlitz.

While our left was achieving this brilliant success, the centre, consisting of the troops of Marshals Soult and Bernadotte, who had been placed by the Emperor in the valley of the Goldbach where they were hidden by a thick mist, advanced towards the slope on which stood the village of Pratzen. It was at this moment that the bright "Sunshine of Austerlitz" appeared, the memory of which Napoleon was pleased so frequently to recall. Marshal Soult took not only the village of Pratzen but also the great plateau of that name, which is the high point of the surrounding country, and, in consequence, the key to the battlefield. Here took place, before the eyes of the Emperor, a very sharp engagement in which the Russians were defeated; but a battalion of the 4th Line regiment, commanded by Prince Joseph, Napoleon's brother, went too far in pursuit of the enemy and was charged and over-run by the horse-guards and Cuirassiers of the Grand-duke Constantin, the brother of Alexander, who captured their Eagle. A force of Russian cavalry advanced rapidly to support the momentary success of the horse-guards; but Napoleon sent against them the Mamelukes, the light cavalry and the mounted Grenadiers of his guard, led by Marshal Bessires and General Rapp, and a most sanguinary mele ensued. The Russian squadrons were overcome and driven back beyond the village of Austerlitz with great losses. Our cavalry captured many standards and prisoners, among whom was Prince Repnin, the commander of the horse-guards. This regiment, made up of the most glittering youth of the Russian nobility, suffered many casualties. The boastful threats which they had made concerning the French were known to our men, who in reply said that they would give the ladies of St. Petersburg something to cry about.

The painter Grard, in his picture of the Battle of Austerlitz, has taken as his subject the moment when General Rapp, leaving the battle, wounded and covered in his own and the enemies' blood, is presenting to the Emperor the flags which have been captured as well as Prince Repnin, his prisoner. I was present at this memorable scene, which the painter has reproduced with remarkable exactness. All the heads are portraits, even that of the brave trooper, who without complaining, though shot through the body, fell dead at the feet of the Emperor as he presented the standard which he had just captured. Napoleon, to honour the memory of this brave Chasseur, ordered the painter to include him in his composition. One can see also in this picture a Mameluke, who carries in one hand an enemy flag, and with the other holds the bridle of his wounded horse. This man, named Mustapha, known in the guards for his courage and ferocity, had set off, during the charge, in pursuit of the Grand-duke Constantin, who was only able to get rid of him by firing a pistol shot which mortally wounded his horse. Mustapha, grieved at having only a standard to offer the Emperor, said in his broken French, when he presented it, "Ah! If me catch Prince Constantin, me cut off head and bring to Emperor!" Napoleon replied indignantly, "You be quiet! You wicked savage!"

Let us now finish the story of the battle. While Marshals Lannes, Soult and Murat attacked the centre and right of the Austro-Russians and drove them back beyond the village of Austerlitz, the enemy left, having fallen into the trap which the Emperor had prepared for them, attacked the village of Telnitz and took possession of it, then, crossing the Goldbach, they prepared to occupy the road to Vienna; but they had greatly underestimated the skill of Napoleon in thinking that he would neglect to defend his route of retreat in case of misfortune. Marshal Davout's divisions were concealed in Gross-Regairn and from that point he fell on the Russians as soon as he saw that their massed troops were held up in the defiles between the meres of Telnitz, Menitz and the rivulet.

The Emperor, whom we left on the plateau of Pratzen, free of the right and centre of the enemy, who were retreating in disorder beyond Austerlitz, came down from the heights of Pratzen and hurried with Marshal Soult's corps and all his guard, infantry, cavalry and artillery, towards Telnitz; where he attacked in the rear the enemy

130

columns which Marshal Davout was attacking in front. From this moment, the cumbersome masses of the Austro-Russians, crammed together on the narrow pathways which ran alongside the Goldbach, finding themselves between two fires, fell into indescribable confusion. The ranks broke down and each man sought his own safety in flight. Some rushed into the marshes around the meres, but our infantry followed them; others tried to escape down the road which runs between the two meres, but our cavalry charged them with fearful slaughter; the largest body of men, principally Russians, tried to get across the frozen meres, and already a great number were on the ice of Lake Satschan when Napoleon ordered his gunners to fire on them. The ice broke in many places with a loud cracking sound and we saw a host of Russians with their horses wagons and guns slide slowly into the depths. The surface of the lake was covered with men and horses struggling amid the ice and water. A few were saved, helped by poles and ropes which our men held out to them from the bank, but many were drowned.

The number of combatants at the Emperor's disposal in this battle was sixty-eight thousand men. The Austro-Russians had ninety-two thousand. Our losses in killed and wounded were about eight thousand, the enemy stated that their losses in killed wounded and drowned amounted to fourteen thousand. We took eighteen thousand prisoners and captured one hundred and fifty cannons, as well as a great number of flags, standards, *etc.*

After giving orders to pursue the enemy in all directions, the Emperor went to his new headquarters in the post-house at Posoritz, on the Olmutz road. He was highly delighted as you may imagine, although he several times expressed regret that the only Eagle we had lost was that of the fourth line regiment, of which his brother, Prince Joseph, was colonel. The fact that this had been captured by the regiment of the Grand-duke Constantin, the Emperor of Russia's brother, made the loss even more annoying.

Napoleon soon had a great consolation; Prince Jean of Lichtenstein came, on behalf of the Emperor of Austria, to request a meeting, and Napoleon, realising that this would lead to peace and remove the fear of having the Prussians attack the French rear before he had rid himself of his present enemies, readily agreed to the proposal.

Of all the units of the Imperial Guard, the regiment of Mounted Chasseurs was the one which suffered the most casualties in the great charge made on the Pratzen plateau against the Russian Guard. My poor friend Fournier was killed, as was General Morland. It is said that Napoleon intended to have the body of General Morland interred in a mausoleum which he meant to have built in the centre of the Esplanade des Invalides, and that it was preserved in a cask of rum for that reason. But the mausoleum was never built, and it is alleged that the general's body was still in a room in the school of medicine when Napoleon lost his Empire in 1814.

I was not wounded at Austerlitz, although I was often exposed to danger, notably during the mele with the Russian cavalry on the Pratzen plateau. The Emperor had sent me to take some orders to General Rapp, whom I found it very difficult to reach amid the appalling confusion of the embattled soldiery. My horse was crushed up against that of a Russian horse-guard and our sabres were about to clash when we were separated by other combatants; I came away with a large bruise. However, the next day I ran into a more serious danger, one that one does not expect to meet on the field of battle.

On the morning of the 3rd of December, the day after the battle, the Emperor mounted his horse and went round all the places where action had taken place on the previous day. Having arrived at the mere of Satschan, Napoleon dismounted and was chatting round a fire with a number of marshals, when we saw, some hundred paces from the bank, a large slab of ice on which lay a poor Russian sergeant, who was unable to help himself because of a bullet wound in his thigh. Seeing the large group on the bank, the soldier raised his voice and pleaded for help, saying that when the fighting was over we were all brother soldiers. When his interpreter translated this, Napoleon was touched and ordered General Bertrand to do what he could to rescue the wretched Russian.

Several men of the escort, and even two staff officers, attempted to reach the Russian using two tree trunks which they pushed into the water, but they ended up by falling in with all their clothes on, and having difficulty in getting out. It then occurred to me to say that they should have entered the water naked, so that their movements would not be hampered, and they would not have to wear wet clothing. This observation was repeated to the Emperor, who said that I was right, and that the others had shown zeal without forethought. I have no wish to make myself out to be better than I am; I can assure you that, having just taken part in a battle where I had seen thousands of dead and dying, my emotions were blunted, I did not feel sufficiently philanthropic to risk pneumonia by struggling amongst the ice floes to save the life of an enemy soldier, however much I deplored his unhappy lot; but the Emperor's remark stung me into action, it seemed to me ridiculous that I should offer advice which I was not prepared to put into action. I jumped off my horse, stripped off my clothes and leapt into the lake.

I had been very active during the day, and was warm; the water felt bitterly cold, but I was young and vigourous, a very good swimmer, and encouraged by the presence of the Emperor, I was making towards the Russian, when my example and probably the praise I received from the Emperor, persuaded a lieutenant of artillery named Roumestain to come after me.

While he was undressing, I pushed on, but I had more difficulty than I had foreseen in forcing my way through the thin layer of new ice which was forming on the water, the sharp edges of which inflicted many scrapes and scratches. The officer who followed me was able to make use of the sort of path which I had made, and when he reached me, he volunteered to take the lead, to give me some relief. We eventually reached the large block of ice on which the Russian lay, but it was only with the greatest difficulty that we managed to push it near enough to the shore for the man to be rescued. We were both so cold and exhausted that we had to be lifted out of the water, and we were hardly able to stand. My good comrade Massy, who had watched me with much anxiety during this swim, had had the forethought to warm his horse's blanket before the fire, which he wrapped round me as soon as I was out of the water. After I had dried myself and dressed, I wanted to lie beside the fire, but Doctor Larrey was against this and told me to walk around, something I was unable to do without the aid of two troopers. The Emperor came to congratulate the two of us on the courage with which we had undertaken the rescue of the wounded Russian, and calling for his Mameluke, Roustan, whose horse was always loaded with provisions, he poured out for us a tot of rum each, and asked us, laughing, how we had enjoyed the bath.

As for the Russian sergeant, after his wound had been dressed by Doctor Larrey, Napoleon gave him several gold coins. He was wrapped in warm coverings and put in one of the houses of Telnitz which was acting as a dressing station; the next day he was taken to the hospital at Brunn. The poor lad blessed the Emperor as well as Roumestain and me, and wanted to kiss our hands. He was a Lithuanian, that is to say, born in a former province of Poland, which is now part of Russia. As soon as he had recovered, he announced that he wished now to serve no one but Napoleon. He was sent back to France with our own wounded and subsequently joined the Polish legion. In the end he became a sergeant in the lancers of the guard, and each time I met him, he gave me a warm greeting.

The ice-cold bath which I had taken and the almost superhuman efforts I had made to rescue the Russian could have cost me dear had I been less young and strongly built; for Lieutenant Roumestain, who did not possess the latter of these two advantages to the same extent, was taken that same evening with a severe chest infection. He had to be taken to the hospital at Brunn, where he spent several months between life and death. He never recovered completely, and his poor health forced him to resign from the service some years later.

As for me, although I felt very weak, I mounted my horse when the Emperor left to go to the chteau of Austerlitz, where his headquarters had been set up. Napoleon never went anywhere except at the gallop; in my bruised state this pace was hardly suitable, however I followed on, since night was approaching, and I feared to be left behind, and anyway, if I had ridden at a walk, I would have been overcome by the cold.

When I arrived at the courtyard of the chteau of Austerlitz, I had to be helped off my horse. A violent shivering took me, my teeth chattered and I felt very ill. Colonel Dahlmann, a major in the Mounted Chasseurs, who had just been promoted to replace Colonel Morland, remembering, no doubt, the service I had rendered to the latter, took, me into one of the chteau's barns, where he had established himself with his officers. There, after giving me some hot tea, his medical officer massaged me with warm oil, I was wrapped in several blankets and put into an enormous pile of hay with only my face exposed. A gentle warmth crept slowly back into my benumbed limbs; I slept very soundly and thanks to these ministrations and my twenty-three years, I awoke the next day fully recovered and able to mount my horse and to observe a spectacle of great interest.

The defeat suffered by the Russians had thrown their army into such confusion that all those who had escaped from the disaster of Austerlitz, hastened to Galicia to get out of reach of the victor. The rout was complete: the French took a great number of prisoners, and found the roads covered with cannons and abandoned baggage. The Emperor of Russia, who had believed he was marching to certain victory, withdrew, stricken with grief, and authorised his ally, Francis II to treat with Napoleon. In the evening following the battle, the Austrian Emperor, in order to save his country from total ruin, had sent a request for an interview to the French Emperor, and when Napoleon had agreed to this, he went to the village of Nasiedlowitz. The meeting took place on the 4th of December, near the Poleny mill, between the lines of the French and the Austrian outposts. I was at this memorable conference.

Napoleon left the chteau of Austerlitz early in the morning, accompanied by his large staff. He arrived first at the rendezvous, dismounted and strolled around until he saw the Emperor of Austria arrive. He went over to him and embraced him warmly.... A spectacle which might well inspire some philosophical reflection! A German Emperor coming to humble himself and solicit peace from a little Corsican gentleman, recently a second lieutenant of artillery, whose talents, good fortune and the courage of the French armies had raised to the pinnacle of power and made arbiter of the destiny of Europe.

Napoleon did not abuse the position in which the Austrian Emperor found himself; he was attentive and extremely polite, as far as could be judged from the distance which was respectfully maintained by the two general staffs. An armistice was arranged between the two sovereigns which stipulated that both parties should send plenipotentiaries to Brunn in order to negotiate a peace treaty between France and Austria. The two Emperors embraced once more on parting; the Germans returned to Nasiedlowitz, and Napoleon returned to spend the night at Austerlitz. He spent two days there, during which time he gave Major Massy and me our final audience, and charged us to tell Marshal Augereau all that we had seen; he gave us at the same time some despatches for the court of Bavaria, which had returned to Munich, and informed us that Marshal Augereau had left Bregenz and that we would find him at Ulm. We went back to Vienna and continued our journey, travelling day and night in spite of the heavy falls of snow.

I shall not go into any details of the political changes which resulted from the Battle of Austerlitz and the Peace of Presburg. The Emperor went to Vienna and from there to Munich, where he had to assist at the marriage of his step-son, Eugne de Beauharnais to the daughter of the King of Bavaria. It seems that the despatches which we carried to this court were concerning this marriage; for we could not have had a better reception. However, we stayed only a few hours in Munich and went on to Ulm, where we found Marshal Augereau and 7th Corps, and where we stayed for a fortnight.

In order to move 7th Corps gradually nearer to the electorate of Hesse, a close ally of Prussia, Napoleon ordered it to move to Heidelburg, where we arrived about the end of December and saw the beginning of the year 1806. After a short stay in this town, 7th Corps went to Darmstadt, the capital of the landgrave of Hesse-Darmstadt, a prince much attached to the King of Prussia by family ties as well as politics. Although this prince had, on accepting Hanover, concluded a treaty of alliance with Napoleon, he had done so with reluctance, and was suspicious of the approach of the French army.

Marshal Augereau, before taking his troops into the country of Darmstadt, considered it his duty to inform the landgrave, by letter, of his intentions, and he chose me to effect its delivery. The journey was one of only fifteen leagues; I made it in a night; but on my arrival at Darmstadt I found that the landgrave, to whom it had been suggested that the French intended to make him a prisoner, had left his residence and retired to another part of his state from where he could easily take refuge in Prussia. This created a difficulty for me, however, having heard that his wife was still in the palace, I asked to be presented to her.

The princess, whose person greatly resembled the portraits of the Empress Catherine of Russia, had, like her, a masculine character, great capability, and all the qualities necessary to control a vast empire. She also governed her husband as she did her states; she was a masterful woman, and when she saw the letter in my hands, addressed to the landgrave, she took it without further ado, as if it had been addressed her. She then told me quite frankly, that it had been on her advice that her husband had left on the approach of the French, but that she would arrange for him to come back if the marshal would give her an assurance that he did not have any orders to make an attempt on the liberty of the prince. I understood that the arrest and death of the Duc d'Enghien had frightened all those princes who thought that Napoleon might have some reason to complain about their alliances. I protested, as much as I could, the innocence of the French government's intentions, and offered to go back to Heidelburg and ask Marshal Augereau for the assurances which she required, an offer which she accepted.

I left, and returned the next day with a letter from the marshal, couched in such conciliatory terms that the landgravine, after saying that she relied on the honour of a French marshal, went immediately to Giessen, where the landgrave was, and brought him back to Darmstadt, where they both received Marshal Augereau most graciously, when he came to set up his headquarters in the town. The marshal was so grateful for the confidence which they had placed in him that several months later, when the Emperor gathered up all the little European states and reduced their number to thirty-two, out of which he formed the confederation of the Rhine, he not only contrived to preserve the landgravate but gained for the landgrave the title of Grand-Duke and an enlargement of his state which increased the population from scarcely five hundred thousand to over one million. Some months later, the new Grand-Duke allied his army to ours to combat the Russians, and requested that they should serve in Marshal Augereau's corps. The prince owed not only his preservation but his elevation to his wife's courage.

Although I was still very young, I thought that Napoleon had made a mistake in reducing the number of the little German principalities.

The fact is that in previous wars against France, the eight hundred princes of the Germanic region had been unable to act in unison; there were some who provided no more than a company, others only a platoon, and some just one soldier; so that a combination of all these different contingents made up an army wholly lacking cohesion, which broke up at the first reverse. But when Napoleon had reduced the number of the principalities to thirty-two, centralisation began to appear in the German forces. Those rulers who remained, with states increased in size, formed a small well-organised army. This result was what the Emperor had intended, in the expectation of using for his own ends all the military resources of the country; something which he was in fact able to do as long as we were successful. But on the first setback, the thirty-two sovereigns, by agreement among themselves, united in opposition to France, and their coalition with the Russians overthrew the Emperor Napoleon, who was thus punished for not following the ancient policies of the kings of France.

We spent part of the winter at Darmstadt, where there were ftes, balls and galas. The grand-duke's troops were commanded by a competent general named De Stoch. He had a son of my age, a charming young man with whom I struck up a close friendship, and to whom I shall refer again.

We were only some ten leagues from Frankfurt-on-main. This town, still free, and immensely rich as a result of its commerce, had been for a long time a hot-bed of all the plots contrived against France, and the place of origin of all the false stories about us which circulated in Germany. So that, the day after Austerlitz, and while the news was spreading that there had been an engagement, the result of which was not yet known, the inhabitants of Frankfurt were sure that the Russians had won, and several papers indulged their hatred to the point of saying that the disaster which had overtaken our army was so great that not a single Frenchman had survived!... The Emperor, to whom all this was reported, appeared to take no notice until, seeing the likelihood of a break with Prussia, he gradually moved his armies to the frontiers of that kingdom. Then, to punish the impertinence of the Frankfurters, he ordered Marshal Augereau to leave Darmstadt without warning, and to establish himself with his army corps in Frankfurt and its surroundings.

The Emperor decreed that the city, on the entry of our troops, should give, as a welcome, a louis d'or to each soldier, two to the corporals, three to the sergeants, ten to second lieutenants and so on! The inhabitants were also to lodge and feed the soldiers and pay messing expenses of six hundred francs daily for the marshal, four hundred for a divisional general, three hundred for a brigadier-general and two hundred for the colonels. The senate was instructed to pay every month, one million francs into the treasury in Paris. The authorities of Frankfurt, appalled by these exorbitant demands, hurried to the French envoy; but he replied "You claimed that not a single Frenchman escaped from the arms of the Russians; the Emperor Napoleon wishes to put you in a position to count the number making up a single

corps of his army. There are six more of the same size, and the guard to follow."
This reply plunged the inhabitants into consternation, for however great their wealth,
they would be ruined if this state of affairs continued for any length of time. But
Marshal Augereau made an appeal for clemency on behalf of the citizens, and he was
told he could act as he thought best; so he took it on himself to station in the town
only his general staff and one battalion. The remaining troops were spread around
other neighbouring principalities. The Frankfurters were greatly relieved by this, and
to show their gratitude to Marshal Augereau they treated him to a great number of
ftes. I was billeted with a rich merchant named M. Chamot. I spent nearly eight
months there, during which time he and his family looked after me very well.

Chap. 28.

While we were in Frankfurt, a very distressing event affecting an officer of 7th
Corps, landed me with a double mission, the first part of which was very unpleasant
and the second most agreeable, indeed brilliantly so.

As a result of a brain fever, Lieutenant N... of the 7th Chasseurs became completely
childish. Marshal Augereau detailed me to take him to Paris, first to Marshal Murat,
who had an interest in the matter, and then, if I was asked to do so, to the Quercy.
As I had not seen my mother since leaving for the campaign of Austerlitz, and I
knew that she was not far from St. Cr, in the Chteau de Bras, which my father had
bought shortly before his death, I welcomed with pleasure a mission which would
allow me not only to be of service to Marshal Murat but also to go and spend several
days with my mother. Marshal Augereau lent me a fine carriage and I set off on the
road to Paris. But the heat and insomnia so excited my poor companion that he went
from a state of idiocy to one of mania and nearly killed me with a blow from a coach
spanner. I have never made a more disagreeable journey. I arrived at last in Paris,
and I took Lieutenant N... to Murat, who was staying for the summer at the Chateau
de Neuilly. The marshal asked me to take the lieutenant to Quercy. I agreed to do
so, in the hope of being able to see my mother again, but I pointed out that I could
not leave for twenty-four hours, because Marshal Augereau had given me some
despatches for the Emperor, whom I was going to meet at Rambouillet, to where I
reported officially the same day.

I do not know what was in the despatches which I was carrying, but they made the
Emperor very thoughtful. He sent for M. de Tallyrand and left with him for Paris to
where he ordered me to follow him and present myself to Marshal Duroc that
evening.

I waited for a long time in one of the salons of the Tuileries, until Marshal Duroc,
coming out of the Emperor's study, the door of which was left half open, called for
an orderly officer to get ready set off on a long mission. But Napoleon called out,
"Duroc, that will not be necessary; we have Marbot here, who is going to rejoin
Augereau; he can push on to Berlin. Frankfurt is half way there." So Marshal Duroc
told me to prepare to go to Berlin with the Emperor's despatches. This was
disappointing as it meant that I had to give up all hope of seeing my mother; but I

had to resign myself. I hurried to Neuilly to tell Murat what had happened and as I believed that my new mission was very urgent, I returned to the Tuileries; but Marshal Duroc dismissed me until the next day. I was there at dawn: I was dismissed until evening; then the evening of the next day, and so on for more than a week. However, I remained patient, because each time I presented myself, Marshal Duroc kept me for only a minute, which allowed me time to get around Paris. I had been given quite a large sum of money for the purpose of buying myself new uniform, so as to appear well turned out before the king of Prussia, into whose hands I was personally to deliver a letter from the Emperor. You will understand that Napoleon neglected no detail when it came to enhancing the standing of the French army in the eyes of foreigners.

I left at last, after taking the despatches from the Emperor, who advised me that I should make sure that I carefully examined the Prussian troops, their bearing, their arms, their horses, *etc.* M. de Tallyrand gave me a packet for M. Laforest, the French ambassador in Berlin, to whose embassy I was to go. On my arrival at Maintz, which at that time was still part of French territory, I was told that Marshal Augereau was at Wiesbaden. I reported to him there and greatly surprised him by telling him that I was going to Berlin on the Emperor's orders. He congratulated me and told me to continue my journey. I travelled night and day, in superb July weather, and arrived in Berlin somewhat weary. At this period the Prussian roads were not yet metalled, one went almost always at walking pace over loose soil into which the coaches sank deeply, raising clouds of unbearable dust.

I was given a warm welcome by M. Laforest, at whose embassy I stayed. I was presented to the king and queen, and also to the princes and princesses. When the king received the letter from Napoleon, he seemed much affected. He was a fine figure of a man, with a benevolent expression, but lacking that animation which suggests a decisive character. The queen was really very pretty; she had only one blemish, she always wore a large scarf, in order, it was said, to conceal an ulcerated swelling on her neck. For the rest, she was graceful and her expression, calm and spiritual, was evidence of a firm personality.

I was very well received, and since the reply which I was to take back to the Emperor seemed so difficult to draft that it took more than a month, the queen was pleased to invite me to the balls and ftes which she gave during my stay.

Of all the members of the royal family, the one who treated me in the most friendly manner, or so it seemed, was Prince Louis, the king's nephew.

I had been warned that he hated the French, and in particular, their Emperor, but as he was passionately interested in military matters, he questioned me endlessly about the siege of Genoa, the battles of Marengo and Austerlitz and also about the organisation of our army. Prince Louis was a most handsome man, and in respect of spirit, ability and character, the only one of the royal family who bore any resemblance to Frederick the Great. I made the acquaintance of several members of the court, mainly with the officers whom I followed daily to parades and

138

manoeuvres. I spent my time in Berlin very pleasantly. The ambassador showed me much attention; but in the end I discovered that he wanted me to play, in a delicate affair, a rôle for which I was unsuited, so I became very reserved.

Now, let us examine the position of Prussia vis—vis France. The despatches which I had brought concerned this matter, as I later found out.

In accepting from Napoleon the gift of the electorate of Hanover, the patrimony of the English royal family, the cabinet in Berlin had alienated not only the anti-French party but almost all of the Prussian nation. Germanic pride was wounded by the victories won by the French over the Austrians, and Prussia feared that its commerce would be ruined by the war which had just been declared against it by the cabinet in London. The queen and Prince Louis made use of these turbulent emotions to persuade the king to make war on France by allying himself with Russia who, though abandoned by Austria, still hoped to take revenge for its defeat at Austerlitz. The Emperor of Russia was further encouraged in his plans by a Pole, his favourite aide-de-camp, Prince Czartoryski.

The anti-French party, which was growing daily, was not yet able to persuade the king to break with Napoleon; but aware that it was supported by Russia, this party redoubled its efforts, and profited adroitly from the mistakes made by Napoleon in placing his brother Louis on the throne of Holland, and nominating himself as protector of the confederacy of the Rhine: acts which were represented to the Prussian king as being steps on the path to the re-establishment of the empire of Charlemagne. Napoleon, it was said, wanted finally to reduce all the sovereigns of Germany to the status of vassals.

These assertions, though greatly exaggerated, had had a considerable influence on the king's thinking. His conduct toward France became from this time, more and more equivocal, and it was this that decided Napoleon to write to him personally, without going through the usual diplomatic channels, to ask "Are you for me or against me?" This was the tenor of the letter which I had given the king. His councillors who wished to gain time for the completion of their re-armament, delayed the reply, which was the reason for my long stay in Berlin.

At last, in August, there was a general explosion of ill-feeling towards France, and one saw the queen, Prince Louis, the nobility, the army and the general populace, noisily demanding war. The king allowed himself to become involved but, although determined to end the peace he still hoped to avoid hostilities, and it seems that in his reply to the Emperor he undertook to disarm if the latter would take back to France all the troops he had in Germany, which Napoleon was unwilling to do until Prussia had disarmed. So we were in a vicious circle which could be broken only by a war.

Before I left Berlin, I witnessed the frenzy to which hatred of Napoleon raised this normally placid people. The officers whom I knew no longer dared to speak to me or even to greet me. Several French people were insulted by the populace, and finally soldiers of the Royal Guard came boastfully to sharpen their sabres on the stone steps of the French embassy. I left hurriedly for Paris, taking with me much information on what was going on in Prussia. Passing through Frankfurt, I found Marshal Augereau very sad at having heard of the death of his wife, a good, excellent woman whose loss he felt deeply, and who was mourned by all the general staff, for she had been very kind to us.

On my arrival in Paris, I delivered to the Emperor the hand-written reply from the King of Prussia. After reading it, he questioned me on what I had seen in Berlin. When I told him that the soldiers of the guard had come to sharpen their sabres on the steps of the French embassy, he clapped his hand firmly on the hilt of his sword, exclaiming indignantly, "The insolent braggarts will soon learn that our arms are in good order!"

My mission now being over, I returned to Marshal Augereau, and spent all of September in Frankfurt where, while preparing ourselves for war, we entertained ourselves as best we could, for we thought that as nothing could be more uncertain than the life of a soldier, one should enjoy it as much as is possible.

Chap. 29.

While the different corps of the French army were approaching the banks of the Main, the Emperor arrived at Wurtzburg and crossed the Rhine with his Guard. The Prussians, for their part, were on the march, and going through Saxony, they compelled the elector to join forces with them. This enforced, and therefore unstable, alliance was the only one which the King of Prussia had in Germany. He was, it is true, expecting the arrival of the Russians, but their army was still in Poland behind the Niemen, more than one hundred and fifty leagues from the country where the destiny of Prussia was to be decided.

It is hard to believe the incompetence displayed, for seven years, by our enemies' governments. We saw, in 1805, the Austrians attack us on the Danube, and be defeated in isolation at Ulm, instead of waiting for Russia to join them and for Prussia to declare war on Napoleon. Now, in 1806, those same Prussians who, a year before, could have prevented the defeat of the Austro-Russians by joining them, not only declared war on us when we were at peace with Vienna, but repeated the mistake of attacking us without waiting for the Russians! Finally, in 1809, the Austrians renewed the war against Napoleon on their own, at a time when we were at peace with both Prussia and Russia! This lack of co-operation ensured a French victory. Sadly it was not so in 1813, when we were crushed by a coalition of our enemies.

In 1806 the King of Prussia was even more mistaken in taking to the field against Napoleon in the absence of the Russians, in that his troops, although well trained, were in no condition to be pitted against ours, because their composition and organisation were so bad.

In effect, at this time, Prussian captains were the owners of their company or squadron: men, horses, arms and clothing all belonged to them and the whole unit was hired out to the government for a fixed fee. Obviously, since all losses fell to their account, the captains had a great interest in sparing their companies, not only on the march but on the field of battle. As the number of men they were obliged to have was fixed and there was no conscription, they enrolled for money, first any Prussians who came forward, and then all the vagabonds of Europe, whom their recruiters enlisted in neighbouring states. But this was not enough, and the Prussian recruiters pressed many men into service, who having become soldiers against their will, were compelled to serve until they were too old to bear arms; then they were given a permit to beg, for Prussia could not afford to provide a home for old soldiers or a retirement pension. For the duration of their service these men had to be mixed with true Prussians, who had to constitute at least half of each company to prevent mutiny.

To maintain an army composed of such heterogeneous parts required an iron discipline; so the least fault was punished by beating. A large number of N.C.O.s, all of them Prussian, carried canes which they made use of frequently, and according to the current expression there was a cane for every seven men. The penalty for desertion by a foreign soldier was inevitably death. You can imagine the frightful position of these foreigners, who having enlisted in a moment of drunkenness, or been taken by force, found themselves far from their native land, under a glacial sky, condemned to be Prussian soldiers, that is slaves, for the rest of their lives! And what a life it was! Given scarcely enough to eat. Sleeping on straw. Thinly clad. Without greatcoats, even in the coldest winter, and paid a sum insufficient for their needs; they did not wait to beg until they had been given a permit on their discharge, for when they were not under the eyes of their superiors, they held out their hands, and there were several occasions both at Potsdam and Berlin when Grenadiers, even those at the palace gate, begged me for alms!

The Prussian-born officers were, in general, educated men, who performed their duties very well; but half of the officers, born outside the kingdom, were poor gentlemen from almost every country in Europe who had joined the army only to have a living, and lacking patriotism, were in no way devoted to Prussia, which the majority abandoned when there was any adversity. Finally, as promotion was only by length of service, the great majority of senior Prussian officers were old and infirm, and in no state to support the fatigues of war. It was an army thus composed and commanded which was to confront the victors of Italy, Egypt, Germany and Austerlitz. This was folly. But the cabinet in Berlin, recalling the victories which Frederick the Great had won with mercenary troops, hoped things would be the same. They forgot that times had changed.

On the 6th of October Marshal Augereau and 7th Corps left Frankfurt to head, with the rest of the Grande Arme, for the frontiers of Saxony, already occupied by the Prussians. The autumn was superb; it froze a little during the night, but by day there was brilliant sunshine. My little troupe was well organised; I had a good batman, Francois Woirland, a former soldier in the black legion, a real rascal and a great scrounger, but these are the best servants on a campaign, for with one of them one lacks for nothing. I had three excellent horses, good weapons, a little money and good health; so I stepped out gaily to face whatever the future might bring.

We went first to Aschaffenburg and from there to Wurtzburg, where we caught up with the Emperor, who ordered a march-past by the troops of 7th Corps, who were in good heart. Napoleon who kept a dossier about all the regiments, and who skillfully used to employ extracts from it to flatter the self-esteem of each unit, said when he saw the 44th line regiment, "Of all the units of the army you are the one with the most long service chevrons, so your three battalions I count as six!"...an announcement which was greeted by cheers. To the 7th, composed mostly of men from the lower Languedoc and the Pyrénées, the Emperor said, "There are the best marchers in the army, one never sees anyone fall behind, particularly when there is a battle to be fought." Then he added, laughingly, "But, to do you justice, I must say that you are the most brawling, thieving unit in the army!" "It's true! It's true!" replied the soldiers, each of whom had a duck, a chicken or a goose in his knapsack, an abuse which had to be tolerated, because, as I have told you, Napoleon's armies, once in the field, rarely received any rations, and had to live off the country as well as they could. This system had without doubt many defects, but it had one huge benefit, that of allowing us to move forward without being held up by convoys and supply lines, which gave us a great advantage over an enemy whose movements were subordinated to the cook-house, or the arrival of bread, and to the progress of herds of cattle, *etc*...etc.

From Wurtzburg, 7th Corps went to Coburg, where the marshal was lodged in the prince's palace. All his family had fled on our approach, except the celebrated Austrian Field-marshal, the Prince of Coburg. This old warrior, although he had fought for many years against the French, had enough confidence in the French character to await their coming, a confidence which was not misplaced, for Marshal Augereau sent him a guard of honour, returned promptly a visit he had received, and ordered that he was to be treated with the utmost respect.

We were not very far from the Prussians, whose king was at Erfurt. The queen was with him and rode up and down the ranks of the army on horseback, endeavouring to excite their ardour by her presence. Napoleon did not think that this was behaviour befitting a princess, and his bulletins made some wounding comments on the subject. The French and Prussian advance-guards met eventually, at Schleitz: where there took place, in view of the Emperor, a minor action in which the enemy were defeated; it was for them an ill-omened beginning.

That same day, Prince Louis, with a body of ten thousand men, found himself stationed in Saalfeld. This town is on the bank of the River Saale, in the middle of a plain which we could reach only by crossing some steep mountains. While Marshals Lannes' and Augereau's corps were moving toward Saalfeld through these mountains, Prince Louis, who had decided to await the French, should have occupied positions in this difficult country, full of narrow passes, where a few men could hold up a much greater number, but he failed to do this, probably because he was

142

convinced that the Prussian soldiers were infinitely better than the French. He carried this scorn for all precautions so far as to place part of his force in front of a marshy stream, which would make their retreat very difficult in the event of a reverse. Old General Muller, a Swiss in the service of Prussia, whom the king had attached to his nephew as a steadying influence, made some observations which the prince took very badly, adding that there was no need to take precautions to beat the French, all that was needed was to fall on them the moment they appeared.

They appeared in the morning on the 10th; Marshal Lannes' corps leading and Marshal Augereau's behind him. This last did not arrive in time to take part in the action where, as it happened, their presence was not needed, for Marshal Lannes' troops were more than sufficient.

While waiting for his corps to emerge onto the plain, Marshal Augereau, accompanied by his staff, went up onto a little hill which overlooked the open country, from where we could follow all stages of the action.

Prince Louis could still have retreated to join the Prussian corps which occupied Jena; but having been the leading instigator of the war he perhaps felt he should not do so without a fight. He was most cruelly punished for his temerity. Marshal Lannes, making use of the heights, at the foot of which Prince Louis had imprudently deployed his troops, first raked them with grape-shot from his artillery, and when this had demoralised them, he advanced several masses of infantry, which descending rapidly from the high ground, swept like a torrent onto the Prussian battalions and instantly overwhelmed them! Prince Louis, aghast, and probably aware of his mistake, hoped to repair it by putting himself at the head of his cavalry and impetuously attacking the 9th and 10th Hussars. He had at first some success, but our Hussars having made a new and furious charge, drove the Prussians back into the marshes, while their infantry fled in disorder.

In the middle of the mele, Prince Louis found himself engaged with a sous-officier of the 10th Hussars named Guindet, who summoned him to surrender; the prince replied with a slash of his sword which cut the sous-officier's face, who thereupon ran the prince through and killed him.

After the fight and the complete rout of the enemy, the prince's body having been recognised, Marshal Lannes had it carried with honour to the chteau of Saalfeld, where it was handed to the princely family of that name, who were allied to the royal house of Prussia, and in whose residence the prince had spent the previous day and evening, looking forward to the coming of the French, and even, it is said, giving a ball for the local ladies. Now he was returned to them, vanquished and dead!... The next morning I saw the prince's body, laid out on a marble table, all traces of blood had been cleaned away, he was naked to the waist, still wearing his leather britches and his boots. He seemed to be asleep. He was a truly fine looking man, and I could not help indulging in some sad reflections on the uncertainty of human affairs, when I saw the remains of this young man, born on the steps of a throne, and, but lately, so loved, so courted and so powerful!

The news of the prince's death spread consternation in the enemy army, and also throughout Prussia, where he was highly popular.

7th Corps spent the day of the 11th at Saalfeld. On the 12th we went to Neustadt, and on the 13th to Kehla, where we encountered some remains of the Prussian troops defeated at Saalfeld. When Marshal Augereau attacked them, they put up little resistance and laid down their arms. Amongst those captured was the regiment of Prince Henry in which Augereau had once served as a soldier, and since, unless one was of high birth, it was very difficult to become a senior officer in the Prussian army, and as sergeants never became second lieutenants, his former company still had the same captain and the same sergeant-major. Placed by a quirk of fate in the presence of his one-time soldier, now a marshal, the Prussian captain, who remembered Augereau perfectly well, acted as a man of discretion and spoke always to the marshal as if he had never seen him before. Augereau invited him to dinner and seated him next to himself, then, learning that the officer's baggage had been seized, he lent him all the money he needed and gave him letters of introduction to take to France. What must have passed through the captain's mind! But nothing can describe the astonishment of the old Prussian sergeant-major at seeing his former soldier covered with decorations, surrounded by a numerous staff and in command of an army corps! All of which seemed like a dream! The marshal was more expansive toward this man than he had been toward the captain. Addressing the sergeant by name, he shook him by the hand, and arranged for him to be given twenty-five louis for himself and two for every soldier who had been in the ranks with him and was still there. We thought this behaviour was in the best of taste.

The marshal had expected to sleep at Kehla, which is only three leagues from Jena; but just as night was falling 7th Corps was ordered to go immediately to this last town which the Emperor had just entered, at the head of his guard and the troops of Marshal Lannes, without striking a blow.

The Prussians had abandoned Jena in silence, but some candles, forgotten in the stables, had probably started the fire, the spreading flames of which were consuming part of the unfortunate town when Marshal Augereau's corps entered it at about midnight. It was a sorry spectacle to see the inhabitants, women and old people, half naked, carrying their children and seeking to escape by flight from the scene of destruction, while our soldiers, kept in their ranks by discipline and the nearness of the enemy, remained unmoved, their arms at the ready, regarding the fire as a small matter in comparison to the dangers they would soon have to face.

The part of the town through which our troops arrived was not affected by the fire and so they could move around freely, and while they were gathering in the squares and main streets, the marshal set up his headquarters in a nice looking mansion. I was about to enter, on returning from delivering an order, when I heard loud shrieks coming from a nearby house, the door of which was open. I hurried there and guided by the cries I found my way to a well-appointed apartment where I saw two charming girls, of about eighteen to twenty years of age, dressed only in their chemises, struggling against the advances of four or five soldiers from Hesse-

144

Darmstadt, belonging to the regiments which the landgrave had attached to the French troops of 7th Corps. Although these men, who were drunk, understood not a word of French, and I spoke little German, my appearance and my threats took them aback, and being used to beatings from their own officers, they made no retaliation to the kicks and cuffs which in my indignation I distributed freely in driving them downstairs. In this I was perhaps a little imprudent, for in the middle of the night, in a town in utter confusion there was a risk that they might turn on me and even kill me; but they ran away, and I put a platoon of the marshal's escort in one of the lower rooms.

I went up to the apartment where the two young girls had hurriedly dressed themselves, and was rewarded by their warmest expressions of gratitude. They were the daughters of a university professor, who had gone with his wife and the domestic staff to the aid of one of their sisters, who had recently given birth in that part of the town where the fire was raging, and they had been alone when the Hessian soldiers arrived. One of these young ladies said to me with great emotion, "You are going into battle at a time when you have just saved our honour. God will reward you, you may be sure that no harm will come to you." The father and the mother, who came back at this moment with the new mother and her child were at first much surprised to find me there; but when they learned the reason for my presence they too showered me with blessings. I tore myself away from the thanks of this grateful family to rejoin Marshal Augereau, who was reposing in the nearby mansion, awaiting the Emperor's orders.

Chap. 30.

The town of Jena is dominated by a height called the Landgrafenberg, at the foot of which runs the Saale River. The approaches to Jena are very precipitous, and at that time there was only one road, which ran to Wiemar via Muhlthal, a long and difficult pass, the outlet of which was covered by a small wood and guarded by Saxon troops, allies of the Prussians; a part of whose army was drawn up in line behind them at the distance of a cannon shot.

The Emperor, having only this one route by which he could reach his enemies, expected to suffer heavy losses in a frontal attack, for there seemed to be no way in which they could be outflanked. But Napoleon's lucky star once more came to his aid, in an unexpected way, which I do not believe has been related by any historian, although I can vouch for the truth of it happening.

We have seen that the King of Prussia compelled the elector of Saxony to join forces with him. The people of Saxony saw themselves, with regret, drawn into a war which could procure them no advantage in the future, and which for the present brought desolation to the countryside, which was the theatre for the hostilities. The Prussians were therefore detested in Saxony; and Jena, a Saxon town, shared in this detestation.

A priest who belonged to the town, angered at the fire which was consuming it, and regarding the Prussians as enemies of his king and fatherland, believed he could give Napoleon the means of clearing them out of the country, by showing him a little pathway by which a body of infantrymen might climb the steep slopes of the Landgrafenberg. He led there a platoon of light infantry and some officers of the general staff. The Prussians, who thought this pathway impracticable, had not bothered to guard it, but Napoleon thought differently. As a result of the report given him by his officers, he went up himself, guided by the Saxon cur, and accompanied by Marshal Lannes; he saw that, between the heights of the path and the plain occupied by the enemy, there was a small stony plateau, and he decided to concentrate there a body of troops who would sally from it, as if from a citadel, to attack the Prussians.

The undertaking would have been of unsurmountable difficulty for anyone but a Napoleon in command of French soldiers; but he ordered the tools used by the pioneers to be taken from the wagons of the engineers and the artillery and distributed to the infantry battalions, who worked in rotation for one hour each at widening and levelling the pathway, and when they had finished their task, each battalion formed up in silence on the Landgrafenberg, while another took its place. The work was carried on by the light of torches, whose flames were confused in the eyes of the enemy with the fires in Jena.

The nights are very long at this time of year, so that we were able to make the path accessible not only for foot-soldiers but also for the wagons of the artillery, with the result that, before daybreak, the corps of Marshals Lannes and Soult, the first division of Augereau's, as well as the foot guards, were massed on the Landgrafenberg. Never has the term massed been used with more exactitude, for the chest of each man was almost touching the back of the man in front of him; but the troops were so well disciplined that, in spite of the darkness and the crowding together of more than forty thousand men, there was not the least disorder; and although the enemy were occupying villages less than half a cannon shot away, they heard nothing.

On the morning of October 14th, a thick mist covered the countryside, which favoured our movements; Augereau's second division, making a diversionary attack, advanced from Jena via Muhlthal on the road to Weimar. As the enemy believed that this was the only way by which we could come from Jena, they had placed a considerable force there; but while they prepared to conduct a vigourous defence of this pass, Napoleon, bringing down from the Landgrafenberg the troops which he had accumulated there during the night, drew them up in battle order on the plain. A light breeze having dispersed the mist, which was followed by brilliant sunshine, the Prussians were stupefied to see the lines of the French army deployed opposite them and advancing to engage them in battle. They could not understand how we had got there when they thought we were down in the valley of Jena, with no other means of reaching them but the road to Wiemar, which they were guarding so thoroughly.

The battle began immediately and the first lines of the Prussians and Saxons, commanded by Prince Hohenlohe, were forced to retreat. They advanced their reserves, but we received a powerful reinforcement. Marshal Ney's corps and Murat's cavalry which had been held up in the pass, burst out into the plain and took part in the action. However a Prussian army corps commanded by General Ruchel stopped our columns for a time; but charged by French cavalry it was almost entirely wiped out and General Ruchel was killed.

Marshal Augereau's 1st division, coming down from the Landgrafenberg, joined with the 2nd, arriving from Muhlthal, and with the troops of Marshals Lannes and Soult, they proceeded down the road to Wiemar, capturing enemy positions as they went.

The Prussian infantry, whose poor composition I have already described, fought very badly, and the cavalry not much better. One saw them on several occasions advance, with loud shouts, towards our battalions; but, intimidated by their calm bearing, they never dared charge home; at a distance of fifty paces from our line they shamefully turned about, amid a hail of bullets and the jeers of our men.

The Saxons fought with courage; they resisted Marshal Augereau's corps for a long time, and it was not until after the retreat of the Prussian troops that, having formed themselves into two large squares, they began to withdraw while continuing to fire. Marshal Augereau admired the courage of the Saxons, and to prevent further loss of life, he had just sent an envoy to persuade them to surrender, since they had no longer any hope of relief, when Prince Murat arrived with his cavalry and mounted an attack with his Cuirassiers and dragoons, who charging impetuously the Saxon squares, overwhelmed them and forced them to lay down their arms. The next day, however, the Emperor set them at liberty and restored them to their sovereign, with whom he hastened to make peace.

All the Prussian troops who had fought before Jena, retreated in a complete rout along the road to Weimar, at whose gates the fugitives, their baggage and artillery had piled up, when suddenly the squadrons of the French cavalry appeared! At the sight of them, panic spread through the crowd of Prussians, who fled in utter disorder, leaving us with a great number of prisoners, flags, guns and baggage.

The town of Weimar, called by some the new Athens, was inhabited at this period by a great number of scholars, artists and distinguished authors, who had gathered there under the patronage of the ruling duke, an enlightened protector of the arts and sciences. The noise of guns, the passage of the fugitives and the entry of the victors caused a great stir in this peaceful and studious population; but Marshals Lannes and Soult maintained a firm discipline, and apart from having to provide food for the soldiers, the town suffered no outrage. The Prince of Weimar served in the Prussian army, nevertheless his palace, where the princess, his wife, was living, was respected and none of the marshals took up residence there.

Marshal Augereau's headquarters were established at the town gates, in the house of the prince's head gardener. All the inhabitants of the house having taken flight, the general staff found nothing to eat, and had to sup on some pineapples and plums from the hot-houses. This was a very light diet for people who, without food for twenty-four hours, had spent the preceding night on foot and all day fighting! But we were the victors, and that magical word enabled us to support all our privations.

The Emperor went back to sleep at Jena, where he learned of a success no less great than that which he had just achieved himself. The battle of Jena was a double battle, if one may use the expression, for neither the French nor the Prussian armies were united at Jena, they were each divided into two parts and fought two different battles: so that while the Emperor, at the head of the corps of Augereau, Lannes, Soult and Ney, his guard and the cavalry of Murat, was defeating the corps of Prince Hohenlohe and General Ruchel. The King of Prussia, at the head of his main army, commanded by the celebrated Prince of Brunswick, Marshals Mollendorf and Kalkreuth had left Weimar, and on their way to Naumburg had settled for the night at the village of Auerstadt, not far from the French corps of Davout and Bernadotte, who were in the villages around Naumburg. In order to rejoin the Emperor, who was at Apolda, in the plain beyond Jena, Davout and Bernadotte had to cross the Saale before Naumburg and traverse the narrow hilly pass of Kosen. Although Davout thought that the King of Prussia with the main body of his army was facing the Emperor, and not so close to him at Auerstadt, this vigilant warrior secured, during the night, the Kosen pass and its steep slopes which the King of Prussia and his marshals had neglected to occupy, thus making the same mistake as Prince Hohenlohe made at Jena in failing to guard the Landgrafenberg. The combined forces of Bernadotte and Davout did not amount to more than forty-four thousand men, while the King of Prussia had eighty thousand at Auerstadt.

From daybreak on the 14th, the two French marshals realised that they had to face much superior numbers; it was their duty then to act in unison. Davout, aware of this necessity, volunteered to put himself under the command of Bernadotte, but the latter jibbed at the idea of a shared victory, and unwilling to subordinate his personal interests to the welfare of his country, he decided to act on his Dornburg on the 13th, he decided to make his way there on the 14th, although Napoleon had written to him during the night to say that, if he was still in Naumburg, he should stay there and support Davout. Not finding the situation to his liking, Bernadotte left Davout to defend himself as best he could and, going down the Saale, he settled himself at Dornburg where, although he came across no enemies, he could see from the elevated position which he occupied, the desperate battle being fought by the gallant Davout some two leagues away. Meanwhile he ordered his men to set up their bivouacs and to start preparing a meal. His generals complained to him in vain at this culpable inaction; Bernadotte would not budge, so that Marshal Davout, with no more than twenty-five thousand men, comprising the divisions of Friant, Morland and Gudin, faced almost eighty thousand Prussians animated by the presence of their king.

The French, after emerging from the narrow pass of Kosen, formed up near the village of Hassenhausen; it was here that the real battle took place, because the Emperor was mistaken when he thought that he had before him at Jena the king and the bulk of the Prussian army. The action fought by Davout's men was one of the most terrible in our annals. His divisions, having successfully resisted all the attacks of the enemy infantry, formed into squares and repelled numerous cavalry charges, and not content with this, they advanced with such resolution that the Prussians fell back at every point leaving the ground strewn with dead and wounded. The Prince of Brunswick and General Schmettau were killed, Marshal Mollendorf was seriously wounded and taken prisoner.

The King of Prussia and his troops at first carried out their retreat towards Weimar in reasonably good order, hoping to rally there behind the forces of Prince Hohenlohe and General Ruchel, whom they supposed to have been victorious, while the latter, having been defeated by Napoleon, were for their part, on their way to seek support from the troops led by the king. Those two enormous masses of soldiers, beaten and demoralised, met on the road to Erfurt; it needed only the appearance of some French regiments to throw them into utter confusion. The rout was total, and was a just punishment for the bragging of the Prussian officers. The results of this victory were incalculable, and made us masters of almost all Prussia.

The Emperor showed his great satisfaction with Marshal Davout and with the divisions of Morand, Friant and Gudin by an order of the day, which was read out to all companies and even in the ambulances carrying the wounded. The following year Napoleon created Davout Duke of Auerstadt, although he had fought less there than in the village of Hassenhausen; but the King of Prussia had had his headquarters at Auerstadt, and the Prussians had given this name to the battle which the French called the battle of Jena.

The army expected to see Bernadotte severely punished, but he got away with a sharp reprimand; Napoleon was afraid of upsetting his brother Joseph, whose sister-in-law, *Mlle*. Clary, Bernadotte had just married. We shall see later how Bernadotte's behaviour during the battle of Auerstadt served, in a way, as a first step towards mounting the throne of Sweden.

I was not wounded at Jena, but I was tricked in a way that still rankles after forty years. At a time when Augereau's corps was attacking the Saxons, the marshal sent me to carry a message to General Durosnel, who commanded a brigade of Chasseurs, ordering him to charge the enemy cavalry. It was my job to guide the brigade along a route which I had already reconnoitred. I hurried away and put myself at the head of our Chasseurs, who threw themselves on the Saxon squadrons. The Saxons put up a stiff resistance and there was a general mele, but eventually our adversaries were forced to retreat with losses. Towards the end of the fighting, I found myself facing an officer of Hussars, wearing the white uniform of Prince Albert of Saxony's regiment. I held the point of my sabre against him and called on him to surrender, which he did, handing me his sword. As the fighting was over, I generously gave it back to him, as was the usual practice among officers in these circumstances, and I added that although his horse, under the conventions of war, belonged to me, I did not wish to deprive him of it. He gave me many thanks for this kind treatment and followed me as I returned to the marshal, very pleased with myself for bringing back a prisoner. But when we were about five hundred paces from the Chasseurs, this confounded Saxon officer, who was on my left, drew his sabre, wounded my horse on the shoulder and was about to strike me if I had not thrown myself on him. Although I had no sabre in my hand, our bodies were so close that he did not have room to swing his sabre at me, so he grabbed my epaulet, and pulled me off balance, my saddle slipped under my horse's belly and there I was with one leg in the air and my head hanging down, while the Saxon made off at full speed to rejoin the remains of the enemy army. I was furious, partly at the position I was in, and partly at the ingratitude with which this foreigner had repaid my courtesy. So when the Saxon army had been made prisoners, I went to look for my Hussar officer, to teach him a lesson, but he had disappeared.

I have said that the Duke of Hesse-Darmstadt, our new ally, had joined his troops to the Emperor's. This brigade had uniforms exactly like those of the Prussians, so several of their soldiers were killed or wounded mistakenly during the action. The young Lieutenant De Stoch, my friend, was on the point of meeting the same fate, and had already been seized by our Hussars, when, having seen me, he called out to me and I had him released.

The Emperor rewarded most generously the priest of Jena, and the elector of Saxony, having become king as a result of the victories of his ally Napoleon, rewarded him also; so that he lived very comfortably until 1814 when he took refuge in France to escape from the vengeance of the Prussians. They, however, had him taken up and shut away in a fortress where he spent two or three years. Eventually, the King of Saxony having interceded on his behalf with Louis XVIII, the latter reclaimed the priest on the grounds that he had been arrested without proper authority, and the Prussians having released him, he came to live in Paris. After the victory at Jena, the Emperor ordered a general pursuit of our enemies, and our columns took an enormous number of prisoners.

The King of Prussia had great difficulty in reaching Magdeburg and getting from there to Berlin, and it was said that the queen nearly fell into the hands of the scouts of our advance-guard.

It would take too long to detail all the disasters which befell the Prussian army; it is enough to say that of those troops who marched to attack the French, not a battalion escaped; they were all captured before the end of the month. The fortresses of Torgau, Erfurt and Wittemburg opened their gates to the victors who, having crossed the Elbe at several points—Augereau's corps crossing near Dessau—headed for Berlin.

Napoleon stopped at Potsdam, where he visited the tomb of Frederick the Great; then he went to Berlin where, contrary to his usual practice, he wished to make a triumphal entry. Marshal Davout's corps headed the procession; an honour to which it was entitled as it had done more fighting than the others. Then came Augereau's corps and then the guard.

Chap. 31.

On my return to Berlin which, when I had left it not long ago, had been so brilliant, I could not help having some sad reflections. The populace, then so self-confident, was now gloomy, downcast, and much afflicted, for the Prussians are very patriotic: they felt humiliated by the defeat of their army and the occupation of their country by the French; besides which almost every family had to mourn a relative or friend killed or captured in battle. I had every sympathy with their feelings; but I must confess that I experienced quite a different sentiment when I saw, entering Berlin as prisoners of war, walking sadly, dismounted and disarmed, the regiment of the so-called Noble Gendarmes; those same arrogant young officers who had so insolently come to sharpen their sabres on the steps of the French embassy!....Nothing could depict their shame and abasement at finding themselves defeated by those same Frenchmen whom they had boasted they would put to flight by their mere presence. They had asked that they might go round Berlin without entering it, to avoid the painful experience of filing as prisoners through the town where they were so well known and where the inhabitants had witnessed their bragging; but this is precisely why the Emperor ordered them to pass between two lines of French soldiers, who directed them down the road in which stood the French embassy. The inhabitants of Berlin did not disapprove of this little act of revenge, since they greatly disliked the Noble Gendarmes whom they accused of having pushed the king into the war.

Marshal Augereau was billeted outside the town, in the chteau of Bellevue, which belonged to Prince Ferdinand, the only one of Frederick the Great's brothers who was still living. This venerable old man, the father of Prince Louis who was recently killed at Saalefeld, was afflicted by grief made even more bitter by the fact that, against the opinion of all the court and also that of the son whom he mourned, he had strongly opposed the war, and had predicted the misfortunes which it would bring upon Prussia. Marshal Augereau thought it his duty to visit the prince, who had withdrawn to a dwelling in the town. He was received most politely; the unhappy father told the marshal that he had learned that his young son, Prince Auguste, the only one left to him, was at the town gate in a column of prisoners, and that he longed to embrace him before he was sent off to France. Since Prince Ferdinand's great age prevented him from going to look for his son, the marshal, sure that Napoleon would not object, told me to mount my horse right away, to go and find Prince Auguste, and to bring him back. Which I did.

The arrival of the young prince gave rise to the most moving scene. His elderly parents could not stop embracing this son, who recalled to them the loss of the other. To console them as much as lay within his power, the good marshal went to the Emperor's quarters and came back with authority for the young prince to remain, on parole, in the bosom of his family. A favour for which Prince Ferdinand was infinitely grateful.

The victory at Jena had had the most profound effect. Complete demoralisation had gripped not only the troops in the field, but the garrisons of the fortresses. Magdeburg surrendered without making any attempt at resistance; Spandau did the same; Stettin opened its gates to a division of cavalry, and the governor of Custrin sent boats across the Oder to fetch the French troops; who without this help would not have been able to take the place without several months of siege. Every day one heard of the surrender of some unit of the army or the capitulation of some fortress. The faulty organisation of the Prussian army became more evident than ever; the foreigners, in particular those who had been enlisted against their will, took the occasion to recover their liberty, and deserted in droves, or stayed behind to give themselves up to the French.

To the conquest of the Prussians, Napoleon added the confiscation of the states of the Elector of Hesse-Cassel, whose duplicity had earned him this punishment. This prince, who had been requested some time before the war to declare himself a supporter of either France or Prussia, lulled both parties with promises, with the intention of coming down on the side of the victor. An avaricious sovereign, the Elector had amassed a great fortune by selling his own people to the English, who used them to fight against the Americans in the War of Independence, in which many of them perished. Careless of his people's welfare, he had offered to join his troops to the French force on condition that the Emperor would cede to him the French American states. So no one was very sorry for the Elector, whose precipitous departure occasioned an event which is still not generally known.

Compelled to leave Hesse in a hurry, to take refuge in England, the Elector, who was regarded as one of the richest people in Europe, was unable to take with him all his wealth. So he sent for a Jew from Frankfurt by the name of Rothschild, a small-time banker and not well known, but respected for the scrupulous devotion with which he practised his religion: and it was this that decided the Elector to confide to his care some fifteen million in specie. The interest earned on this money was to belong to the banker, who was obliged to return only the capital.

When the palace of Cassel was occupied by our troops, agents of the French treasury seized a considerable quantity of valuables, mainly pictures, but did not find any money. It seemed impossible, however, that the Elector, in his hurried flight, had been able to take with him all his immense fortune. Now, as according to what are called the laws of war, the monies found in an enemy country belong to the victor, one wished to find out what had become of the treasure of Cassel. Information gathered on the subject disclosed that, before his departure, the Elector had spent a whole day with the Jew Rothschild. An imperial commission went to the latter's house, where his account books and his strong-boxes were minutely examined; but in vain, for no trace could be found of a deposit made by the Elector. Threats and intimidation produced no result, so the commission, convinced that no material interest would persuade a man so religious to perjure himself, wished to put him on oath. This he refused to accept. His arrest was considered but the Emperor was opposed to this act of violence because he thought it would be useless. Resort was then had to less honourable methods; it was proposed to the banker that he might retain half of the treasure if he would deliver the other half to the French administration; they would then give him a receipt for the full amount, accompanied by an order of seizure, proving that he had given way only to force and was thus shielded from any claim for restitution; but the upright Jew rejected this suggestion, and, tired of the struggle, they left him alone.

So the fifteen million remained in the hands of Rothschild from 1806 to the fall of the empire in 1814. Then, when the Elector had returned to his state, the Frankfurt banker handed over to him the exact sum which he had deposited. You may imagine how much interest might be earned by the sum of fifteen millions left in the hands of a Jewish Frankfurt banker for a period of eight years! It is from this time that dates the opulence of the House of the Brothers Rothschild, who owe to the probity of their founder the high financial standing which they enjoy today.

The Emperor, who was staying in the palace in Berlin, every day passed in revue the troops who arrived in succession in the town, to march from there to the Oder in pursuit of the enemy. It was while he was in Berlin that he performed a well known act of magnanimity in pardoning, for the Princess of Hatzfeld, her husband, who had used his position as burgomaster of Berlin to give the Prussian generals information about the movement of French troops; an act of espionage punishable by death. The generosity displayed by the Emperor on this occasion had a very good effect on the feelings of the Prussians.

During our stay in Berlin, I was pleasantly surprised by the arrival of my brother Adolphe, who, on learning of the fresh outbreak of hostilities on the continent of Europe had asked for and obtained from General Decaen, who commanded the French troops in India, permission to return to France, where he joined the Grande Arme. He was offered a position by General Lefebvre, but, mistakenly, in my opinion, he chose to serve as a supernumerary on the staff of Marshal Augereau, of which I was a member, a move which did neither of us any good.

I had also in Berlin another unexpected encounter. I was walking one evening with some friends along the Boulevard de Tilleuls, when I saw coming towards me a group of sous-officiers of the 1st Hussars. One of them broke away and ran to fall on my neck. It was my former tutor, the elder Pertelay who, with tears of joy cried "Te voil, mon petit!" The officers with whom I was, were at first astonished to see a sergeant-major so familiar with an officer; but their surprise vanished when I told them of my former relations with this old soldier, who, putting his arm round me, said to his companions, "It is I who made him what you now see before you!" And the good fellow was really convinced that I owed my present position to his teaching. So at dinner, which I stood him the next day, he overwhelmed me with inconsequential advice, which he believed to be very sensible and just the thing to perfect my military education. We shall meet this type of old Hussar again in Spain.

Napoleon, who was still in Berlin, was told of the surrender of the Prince Hohenlohe who, with sixteen thousand men, had laid down his arms at Prenzlow before the troops of Marshal Lannes and the cavalry of Murat. There was no other enemy corps in the field except that of General Blcher. This general, hard pressed by the divisions of Marshals Soult and Bernadotte, violated the neutrality of Lubeck, where he sought refuge; but the French pursued him, and Blcher, one of the most ardent supporters of the war against Napoleon, was forced to give himself up as a prisoner together with the sixteen thousand men under his command.

I must here tell you something remarkable, which shows how greatly chance influences the affairs of men and empires. We have seen Marshal Bernadotte failing in his duty and standing aside at Jena when Marshal Davout was fighting, not far from him, against infinitely superior forces. Well! This disgraceful conduct served to place him on the throne of Sweden. This is how it came about.

After the battle of Jena, the Emperor, although furious with Bernadotte, ordered him to pursue the enemy because the corps which he commanded, not having fired a shot, was in better shape for battle than those who had suffered losses. Bernadotte then set out on the track of the Prussians whom he defeated first at Halle and then at Lubeck, with the help of Marshal Soult. Now as chance would have it, at the very hour when the French were attacking Lubeck, some ships carrying a division of infantry which King Gustave IV of Sweden had sent to the aid of the Prussians entered the harbour. The Swedish troops had scarcely disembarked when, attacked by the French and abandoned by the Prussians, they were obliged to surrender to Bernadotte. Bernadotte, I can assure you, had, when he wished, the most engaging manner and very much wanted to appear before foreigners as a "Gentleman." To this end, he treated the Swedish officers in the most benevolent manner. After according them an honourable capitulation, he returned to them their horses and their baggage, saw to their needs and invited to his quarters the commander-in-chief, Count Moerner, as well as the generals and senior officers; he loaded them with kindnesses and courtesies to such an extent that, on their return to their country, they spread everywhere praise for the magnanimity of Marshal Bernadotte.

Some years later a revolution broke out in Sweden; King Gustave, whom a mental disorder had rendered unfit to rule, was removed from the throne and replaced by his aged uncle, the Duke of Sudermanie. As this new monarch had no children, the States Assembly, in order to designate a successor, chose the Prince of Holstein-Augustenburg, who took the title of Prince Royal. But he did not long enjoy this dignity, for he died in 1811 after a short illness, which was put down to poison. The states gathered once more to elect a new heir to the throne. They were hesitating between several German princes who put themselves forward as candidates when Count Moerner, one of the most influential members of the states, and the former commander of the Swedish division captured at Lubeck in 1806 by the French, proposed General Bernadotte, whose generous conduct he recalled. He praised also Bernadotte's military talents, and observed that the marshal was allied, through his wife, to Napoleon, whose support could be most useful to Sweden. A crowd of officers who had also been captured at Lubeck, joined their voices to that of General Moerner, and Bernadotte was elected almost unanimously as successor to the King of Sweden, and mounted the throne a few years later.

We shall see, further on, how Bernadotte, carried to the steps of a foreign throne by the fame which he had acquired at the head of French troops, displayed a lack of gratitude towards his native country. But now let us return to Prussia.

In one month the main forces of this kingdom, formerly in such a flourishing condition, had been destroyed by Napoleon, whose armies occupied the capital and the greater part of the provinces, and had already reached the Vistula, that great barrier between northern and central Europe. Marshal Augereau's corps remained for a fortnight in Berlin to reinforce the Guard during the long stay which the Emperor made in the town, and left about the middle of November, heading first for the Oder, which we crossed at Kostrzyn, and then on to the Vistula whose bank we reached at Bromburg (?Bydgoszcz). We were now in Poland, the poorest and nastiest country in Europe...! After the Oder, no more made roads: we marched on loose gravel or appalling mud. Most of the land was uncultivated and the few inhabitants we came across were dirty to a degree which defies the imagination. The weather which had been magnificent during October and the first part of November became frightful. We no longer saw the sun, it rained or snowed continually; food became short; no more wine, almost never any beer, and what there was atrociously bad; muddy water, no bread, and billets we had to share with cattle and pigs. The soldiers used to say, "How dare the Poles call this a country?"

The Emperor himself was disillusioned, for having come intending to rebuild Poland, he had hoped that the whole population of this vast country would rise as one man at the approach of the French army. But nobody budged...! In a vain attempt to rouse some Polish enthusiasm, the Emperor had invited the famous General Kosciusko, the leader of the last insurrection, to come and join him, but Kosciusko stayed peacefully in Switzerland, to where he had retired, and to the reproaches which were addressed to him, he replied that he knew the heedless and unstable character of his compatriots too well to hope that they would ever free themselves, even with French help. Unable to attract Kosciusko, the Emperor tried to make use of his renown by addressing to the Poles a proclamation in the name of this old warrior. Not one of them took up arms, although our troops occupied several provinces and even the capital. The Poles were not willing to rebel until Napoleon had declared the re-establishment of Poland, and he was not willing to do this until they had risen against their oppressors, which they did not do.

While 7th Corps was in Bromburg, Duroc, the grand marshal of the palace, arrived in the middle of the night at Marshal Augereau's headquarters. I was sent for and told to prepare myself to accompany Marshal Duroc, who was going as an envoy to the King of Prussia at Graudentz, and who needed an officer to replace his aide-de-camp, whom he had just sent to Posnan with despatches for the Emperor. I had been chosen because it was remembered that the previous August I had been on a mission to the Prussian court and that I knew almost all the officers and the court usages.

I was soon ready. The marshal of the palace took me in his carriage and we went down the left bank of the Vistula, occupied by French troops, to cross the river by ferry opposite Graudentz. We took lodgings in the town and then presented ourselves at the citadel, where all the royal family of Prussia had taken refuge after loosing four fifths of their state. The Vistula separated the two armies. The king seemed calm and resigned; the queen, whom I had seen not long ago looking so lovely, was greatly changed and seemed overcome by grief. She could not conceal from herself the fact that having urged the king to declare war, she was the principal cause of the misfortunes of her country, whose citizens raised their voices against her. The Emperor could not have sent a more acceptable envoy to the king than Marshal Duroc, who had held the post of ambassador in Berlin, and was well known to both the king and queen who appreciated his pleasant personality. I was too small a personage to be of any account; however the king and queen recognised me and greeted me with a few polite words.

I found the Prussian officers attached to the court had greatly modified the arrogant attitude they had displayed in August. Their recent defeat had changed their opinion of the French army; nevertheless I did not wish to take advantage of this and I carefully avoided mentioning Jena and our other victories. The affairs which Marshal Duroc had to discuss with the King of Prussia related to a letter which this monarch had sent to Napoleon, requesting a peace. The meeting lasted for two days which I occupied in reading, and walking on the gloomy parade ground of the fortress. I did not wish to go up onto the ramparts, although one enjoys from there an admirable view of the Vistula, for fear that I might be suspected of examining the defence works and armaments.

In the battles which had taken place from Jena to the Vistula, the Prussians had taken about a hundred of our men prisoner, whom they employed on the earthworks of the fortress in which they were confined. Marshal Duroc had charged me with the task of distributing some aid to these poor devils, who were doubly unhappy in that they could see from the height of the fortress the French troops from whom they were separated only by the Vistula. This proximity, and the comparison of their position with that of their comrades, free and happy on the left bank, led a French prisoner, one of the lite cavalrymen of the 3rd Dragoons by the name of Harpin, to attempt to escape. This was no easy matter, for one had first to get out of the fortress and then to cross the Vistula; but what cannot be achieved by a determined man? Harpin, who was employed by the master carpenter to pile timber, had made, secretly, a little raft; he had taken a long rope and, at night, had lowered the raft to the foot of the rampart, and had then descended himself by the same means. He had already put his raft in the water and was preparing to embark when he was surprised by a patrol, taken back to the fort and confined to a dungeon. The next day the Prussian commandant, in accordance with the common custom of the Prussian army, condemned Harpin to fifty strokes of the cane. It was useless for Harpin to claim that as a Frenchman he should not be subject to Prussian regulations, his status as a prisoner made this complaint void. He had already been taken to the wooden frame to which he was to be attached, and two soldiers were preparing to administer the flogging when, having gone to fetch a book from Marshal Duroc's coach, which was standing in the parade ground, I saw Harpin struggling with some Prussians who were trying to tie him up.

156

Indignant at the sight of a French soldier about to be subjected to a flogging, I ran towards him, my sabre in my hand, and threatened to kill the first man to strike a blow! ... Marshal Duroc's coach was guarded by one of Napoleon's couriers, known in every post house in Europe as "Moustache." This man, of herculean strength and the courage to face anything, had accompanied the Emperor on twenty fields of battle. When he saw me in the middle of the Prussians he hurried to me, and on my instructions, he fetched four loaded pistols which were in the coach. We untied Harpin; I armed him with two of the pistols and put him in the coach, where I placed "Moustache" next to him. I then told the commandant that as this coach belonged to the Emperor, whose arms it bore, it was a sacred place of safety for the French Dragoon, entry to which was forbidden to all Prussians under penalty of a bullet in the head, and I told Harpin and "Moustache" to fire on anyone who attempted to get into the coach. The commandant, seeing me so determined, abandoned his prisoner for the moment to go and get orders from his superiors. Then, leaving Harpin and "Moustache" in the coach with pistols in their hands, I went to the king's quarters and begged one of the aides-de-camp to go and tell Marshal Duroc that I needed to speak to him about a matter which could not wait. Duroc came out and I told him what had happened.

When he heard that they wanted to flog a French soldier, he shared my indignation. He returned to the king to whom he protested warmly, adding that if the sentence were to be carried out, the Emperor by way of reprisal would flog not only the soldiers but also the Prussian officers who were his prisoners. The king was a humane man; he ordered that the dragoon Harpin should be released, and to please Napoleon, from whom he was at that moment asking peace, he offered to Marshal Duroc to release to him all the prisoners if he would undertake to send back a similar number of Prussians. Duroc having accepted this offer, I went with one of the aides-de-camp to announce the news to the prisoners, who were overjoyed. We embarked them straight away and an hour later they were across the Vistula and amongst their brothers in arms.

Marshal Duroc and I left Graudentz the next night; he approved of my conduct and told me later that he had given an account of it to the Emperor, who also approved, and who warned the Prussians that if they flogged French soldiers he would have all Prussian officers who fell into his hands, shot!

I rejoined 7th Corps at Bromburg, and we went up the left bank of the Vistula towards Warsaw. Marshal Augereau's headquarters were established at Mallochiche. The Emperor arrived at Warsaw on the 19th December, and prepared to cross the Vistula. 7th Corps then went down the left bank once more to Utrata, where for the first time on this campaign we saw the Russian outposts on the opposite bank.

Chap. 32

The River Vistula is fast-flowing and very wide; one expected, because of this that the Emperor would halt his winter operations there and, protected by the river, would put his troops into winter quarters until the spring. This however was not to be. Marshal Davout's and Marshal Lannes' corps crossed the river at Warsaw, Marshal Augereau and his men crossed at Utrate, from where we went on to the banks of the Ukra, a tributary of the Bug and the Vistula. The entire French army having crossed this last river, found itself face to face with the Russians, against whom the Emperor ordered an attack on the 24th December. A thaw and rain made movement extremely difficult on the clay soil, for there are no metalled roads in this country.

I shall not describe all the actions which were fought that day to force a passage across the Bug; I shall restrict myself to saying that Marshal Augereau, given the task of securing the crossing of the Ukra, ordered General Desjardins to attack with his division, Kolozomb, and General Heudelet to attack Sochocyzn. The marshal directed the attack on Kolozomb in person. The Russians, after burning the bridge which had existed at this spot, had raised earthworks on the opposite bank which they defended with cannons and numerous infantry; but they had neglected to destroy a store of planks and beams which was on the right bank, at which we had arrived. Our sappers made use of this material to construct a temporary bridge in spite of a lively fire which killed several men of the 14th Line regiment, which was at the head of our columns.

The planks of the bridge were not yet fastened and were wobbling under the feet of our infantrymen, when the colonel of the 14th, M. Savary, brother of the Emperor's aide-de-camp, risked crossing on horseback, in order to put himself at the head of his men; but he had scarcely reached the bank when a Cossack, arriving at the gallop, plunged a lance into his heart and disappeared into the woods! This was the fifth colonel of the 14th who had been killed by the enemy! You will see later the fatal destiny which always accompanied this unfortunate regiment. The passage of the Ukra was secured, the guns captured and the Russians put to flight. Desjardins' division occupied Sochoczyn, where the enemy had repulsed the attack by Heudelet's division, a repulse which was of no consequence, as it was necessary only to secure one crossing. General Heudelet however, out of misplaced pride, had ordered the attack to be renewed and was once more driven off with the loss of some thirty men killed or wounded, among them a highly thought of engineer officer. I have always disapproved of the contempt for men's lives which sometimes leads generals to sacrifice them to their desire to see their names in the bulletins.

On the 25th of December, the day following the crossing of the Ukra, the Emperor, pushing the Russians before him, headed for Golymin, having with him the Guard, Murat's cavalry and the corps of Davout and Augereau, the last of whom led the column. Marshal Lannes went off in the direction of Pultusk. There were on this day some minor encounters with the enemy who were retreating with all speed. We slept in bivouac amongst the trees.

On the 26th, 7th Corps set out once more in pursuit of the Russians. We were at a time of year when the days are at their shortest, and in this part of Poland at the end of December, it starts to get dark about two-thirty in the afternoon. It was made more gloomy as we approached Golymin by a fall of snow mixed with rain. We had not seen the enemy since morning when, on our arrival at the village of Kuskowo, very close to Golymin, our scouts, who had seen in the obscurity a large body of troops which a marsh prevented them from approaching, came to warn Marshal Augereau, who ordered Colonel Albert to go and reconnoitre, escorted by twenty-five mounted Chasseurs, whom he placed under my command.

The mission was difficult for we were in the middle of a huge, bare plain where one could easily become lost. The ground, already muddy, was intersected by areas of bog which the poor light prevented us from seeing clearly; so we advanced with caution, and found ourselves within twenty-five paces of a line of troops. We thought at first that this must be Davout's corps, which we knew was in the neighbourhood, but as no one answered our challenge, we had no doubt that these were enemy troops. However, to make quite sure, Colonel Albert ordered me to send one of my best-mounted troopers up to the line which we could distinguish in the murk: for this task I picked a bemedalled corporal named Schmit, a man of proven courage. He, having gone alone to within ten paces of a regiment whose headgear he recognised as Russian, fired a shot from his carbine into the middle of it and came back smartly.

To account for the silence which the Russians had maintained up till then, I must tell you that this unit had become separated from the main body of the army, which it was trying to rejoin, and had lost its way in the vast plains, which it knew to be occupied by French troops who were heading for Golymin. The Russian generals, in the hope that they might pass close to us in the obscurity without being recognised, had forbidden their men to speak, and in the event of an attack, even the wounded were to make no outcry. This was an order which only Russian troops would have obeyed so punctiliously that when Colonel Albert, to warn Marshal Augereau that we were in the presence of the enemy, ordered the twenty-five troopers to fire, not a cry nor a word was heard, and no one fired back!

We then saw, in spite of the poor light, a body of about a hundred horsemen who were advancing silently to cut off our retreat. We should have made off at the gallop to rejoin our columns, but some of our troopers having become stuck in the mud, we were forced to proceed less rapidly, although pursued by the Russians, who fortunately had the same trouble as we did. A fire which had broken out in a nearby farm lit up the ground and the Russians began to gallop, which compelled us to do likewise. A new danger arose in that we had left from General Desjardins' division and were returning to General Heudelet's, who had not seen us leave and opened fire on us; so that we were being driven from behind by the Russians, while a hail of bullets in front wounded several of our men and some horses. It was no use shouting "We are French. Don't shoot!" The firing continued, and one cannot blame the officers who took us for the advance guard of a Russian column who were using French, which is widely understood among foreigners, in order to deceive them in the darkness which had now fallen. We were having a bad time, when it occurred to me to call out by name to the generals, colonels and battalion commanders of Heudelet's division, names which they would know could not be known to the enemy. This was a success and we were at last received into the French line.

The Russian generals, seeing that they were discovered and wishing to continue their retreat, took a measure of which I heartily approve, and one which in similar circumstances the French have never attempted to imitate. The Russians pointed all their guns at us, and having led away all the horses, they opened a violent fire to keep us at a distance. During this time they marched off their columns, and when the ammunition was finished, the gunners withdrew and left the guns to us. Was not this better than losing many men in an effort to save the guns, which would have been continually bogged down and slowed the retreat?

The fierce Russian cannonade became increasingly harmful when it started several fires in the villages, the spreading light of which enabled the Russian gunners to pick out the masses of our troops; in particular the dragoons and Cuirassiers led by Prince Murat, whose white cloaks made them a target. These units suffered more losses than the others, and one of our generals of the Dragoons was cut in two by a cannon-ball. Marshal Augereau, after taking Kuskowa, entered Golymin, which Marshal Davout was attacking from the other side. This town was being traversed at the time by the Russian columns, who, knowing that Marshal Lannes was marching to cut off their retreat by taking Pultusk, three leagues from there, were trying to reach that spot before he did at no matter what cost. So although our soldiers were firing on them at close range, they did not reply. To do so they would have had to stop, and minutes were too precious.

Each division and each regiment marched through our fusillade without a word and without slowing their pace for a moment...! The streets of Golymin were full of wounded and dying men, yet one did not hear a sound. It was forbidden! We might have been shooting at shadows, and it was only when our soldiers attacked with the bayonet that they convinced themselves that they were dealing with men. We took thousands of prisoners, while the remainder marched into the distance.

The marshals deliberated as to whether they should pursue the enemy, but the weather was so horrible and the night so dark once one left the neighbourhood of the fires, the men so soaked and exhausted, that it was decided that they should rest until the next day.

Golymin being crowded with dead, wounded, and discarded baggage, Marshals Murat and Augereau, together with some generals and their staffs, looking for somewhere to shelter from the glacial rain, established themselves in a huge stable which was near the town. There, those who could, lay on the dung heap in an attempt to get warm and to sleep, for we had been on horseback in the most frightful weather for twenty four hours or more. The marshals and all the colonels and brass-hats were naturally in the depths of the stable where it was warmer; as for me, a humble lieutenant, who came in last, I had to bed down near the doorway, where I was more or less sheltered from the rain, but exposed to the freezing wind, since the doorway had no door. The position was most uncomfortable and added to this I was dying of hunger, not having eaten since the previous evening. But my lucky star came once more to my aid. While the well sheltered senior officers were sleeping in the warm part of the stable, and the cold was preventing us lieutenants near the

160

doorway from doing the same, one of Prince Murat's servants arrived. I told him, in a low voice that his master was asleep; upon this he gave me a basket containing a roast goose, some bread and some wine, to give to the prince when he woke, and asked me to tell him that the mules with the provisions were expected to arrive in an hour's time. Having said which, he went off to await them.

Loaded with these provisions, I held council in undertones with Bro, Mainville, and Stoch, who, as badly placed as I, were shivering with cold and just as hungry. The conclusion reached in this deliberation was that as Prince Murat was asleep and as his provisions were due to arrive shortly, he would be able to have a meal when he woke; while we would be set on horseback and sent off in all directions without anyone asking if we had eaten or not; so without straining our consciences too much, we decided to demolish the contents of the basket, which we did with great rapidity. I don't know if this was pardonable, but what I do know is that I have had few meals which I enjoyed more.

While the troops who had been engaged at Golymin were resting, Napoleon, with all his Guard was wandering about on the plain, because, alerted by the sound of gunfire, the Emperor had hurriedly left the chteau where he was installed some two leagues from Golymin, with the intention of joining us by marching as the crow flies in the direction of the fires. But the ground was so soaked, the plain so intersected by bogs and the weather so awful, that it took him all night to make those two leagues, and he did not arrive on the field of battle until the fighting was long over.

On the same day as the fight at Golymin, Marshal Lannes, with no more than twenty thousand men, attacked at Pultusk some forty thousand Russians who were retreating, and inflicted immense losses on them without being able to stop them, so great was their superiority in numbers.

For the Emperor to have been able to pursue the Russians it would have required a frost to harden the ground which, on the contrary, was now so soft and sodden that one sank in at every step, and several men, notably the batman of an officer in 7th Corps, were drowned with their horses in the mud. It had now become impossible to move the artillery and to venture further into this unknown territory; besides which the troops lacked food and even boots, and they were extremely tired. These considerations decided Napoleon to place the whole army in cantonment in front of the Vistula, from the outskirts of Warsaw to the gates of Danzig. The soldiers, billeted in the villages, were at last sheltered from the weather, received some rations and were able to repair their equipment.

The Emperor returned to Warsaw to prepare for a new campaign. The divisions of Augereau's corps were spread in the villages around Plock, if one can give that name to a confused heap of lowly shacks, inhabited by unwashed Jews; but almost all the so-called towns in Poland are built like this and have similar inhabitants. The landowners, great and small, live in the country where they employ their peasants to cultivate their estates.

The marshal was lodged in Christka, a sort of chteau built of wood, as was customary in the country. He found in this manor some reasonable accommodation, while the aides-de-camp settled wherever they could in the rooms and barns. As for me, by ferreting around I found in the gardener's quarters a fairly good room with a fireplace; I settled in there with two friends, and leaving to the gardener and his family their very unsavoury beds, we made some out of planks and straw, on which we were very comfortable.

Chap. 33.

We celebrated at Christka the new year of 1807, which was very nearly the last year of my life. It, however, began very pleasantly for me, since the Emperor, who had not shown any favour to Augereau's staff during the Austerlitz campaign, fully repaired this oversight by heaping us with rewards. Colonel Albert was promoted to brigadier-general, Major Massy to lieutenant-colonel of the 44th Line regiment; several aides-de-camp were decorated; and finally the lieutenants, Bro, Mainville, and I, were made captains. This promotion gave me more than usual pleasure, since I had done nothing remarkable to earn it, and I was only twenty-four years old. Marshal Augereau, when he gave us our brevets of captain, said to Mainville, Bro, and me, "Let's see which of you three is the first to become a colonel." It was in fact I, who six years later commanded a regiment, while my comrades were still only captains: it is also true that in this period I had been wounded six times!

Once we had taken up winter quarters the enemy did the same, opposite to us but a considerable distance away. The Emperor expected that they would let us pass the winter in peace; however, our rest lasted only for a month; this sufficed but was not really enough.

The Russians, seeing the ground covered by snow and hardened by a very sharp frost, thought that this frigid weather would give the men from the north a great advantage over those from the south, unaccustomed to the severe cold. They resolved therefore to attack us, and in order to do this they moved, screened by the immense forest which lay between us, the greater part of the troops who faced us before Warsaw, down to the lower Vistula, opposite the cantonments of Bernadotte and Ney, whom they hoped to surprise and overrun by weight of numbers before the Emperor with the other army corps could come to their aid. But Bernadotte and Ney put up a stiff resistance, and the Emperor had sufficient time to mount an attack with a considerable force on the enemy rear who, seeing themselves at risk of being cut off from their operational base, retreated towards Konigsberg (Kaliningrad). We had therefore, on the 1st of February, to quit our billets where we were reasonably comfortable, and restarting the war, to go and sleep in the snow.

At the head of the central column, commanded by the Emperor in person, was Prince Murat's cavalry, then came Marshal Soult's corps, supported by that of Augereau, finally came the Imperial Guard . Marshal Davout's corps marched on the right flank of this huge column, and Marshal Ney's on the left. Such an agglomeration of troops heading for the same place soon strips the countryside of whatever food supplies are available, so we suffered much from hunger; only the Guard had wagons which carried food for distribution, the other corps lived on whatever they could find, that is to say they lacked practically everything.

I am not going to give any details of the actions which preceded the battle of Eylau, because Augereau's corps, which was in the second line, took no part in these various contacts, of which the most important occurred at Mohrungen, Bergfried, Guttstadt, and Valtersdorf. But at last, before the little town of Landsberg, the Russians, who had been chased for a week with a sword at their backs, decided to halt and make a stand. To do this, they placed eight lite battalions in an advantageous position, their right bounded by a village by the name of Hoff, their left by a thick wood, and their centre protected by a very steep-sided ravine, which could be crossed only by a narrow bridge. Eight cannons were placed in front of this line.

When the Emperor arrived opposite this position, he did not think it necessary to wait for the infantry of Marshal Soult, which was still several leagues behind, and attacked the Russians with some regiments of light cavalry who, dashing bravely over the bridge, crossed the ravine; but, assailed by gunfire and grapeshot, our squadrons were driven back in disorder into the gulch, from which they emerged with much difficulty. The Emperor, seeing the light cavalry repulsed, replaced them by a division of Dragoons, whose attack, received in the same manner as before, had a similar outcome. The Emperor then ordered the advance of General D'Hautpoul's terrible Cuirassiers, who crossed the bridge under a hail of grapeshot and fell on the Russian line with such ferocity that they literally flattened it. There then ensued the most frightful butchery; the Cuirassiers, enraged at the losses suffered by their comrades of the Hussars and Dragoons, almost entirely exterminated the eight Russian battalions, All were either killed or captured! The battlefield was a scene of horror. Never has a cavalry charge had such a devastating result. The Emperor demonstrated his satisfaction with the Cuirassiers by embracing their general before the whole division. General D'Hautpoul exclaimed, "To show myself worthy of this honour, I shall dedicate my life to your majesty." He kept his word, for the next day he was killed on the battlefield of Eylau. What an epoch! And what men!

The enemy army which, from a plateau beyond Landsberg, had witnessed the destruction of its rearguard, retired promptly towards Eylau, and we took possession of Landsberg. On the 7th February the Russian commander-in-chief, Benningsen, having decided to give battle, concentrated his army around Eylau, mainly in positions between us and the town. Murat's cavalry and Soult's infantry took these positions after fierce fighting, for the Russians held tenaciously to Ziegelhof, which dominates Eylau, as they wanted to make it the centre point of their line for the battle on the following day; but they were forced to retreat from the town. Night seemed to have put an end to this fighting, the prelude to the coming general action, when a fusillade of shots rang out in the streets of Eylau.

I know that military authors who have written about this campaign, claim that Napoleon ordered an attack because he did not want the town to remain in Russian hands; but I am sure that they are mistaken, and for the following reason:-

When the head of Marshal Augereau's column, coming down the road from Landsberg, drew near to Ziegelhof, the marshal climbed onto the plateau where the Emperor was already stationed, and I actually heard Napoleon say to Augereau, "It has been suggested to me that we should take Eylau this evening; but, apart from the fact that I don't like fighting at night, I do not wish to push my centre too far forward before the arrival of Davout on my right flank and Ney on my left. So I am going to wait for them until tomorrow on this plateau which, furbished with artillery, will provide a fine position for our infantry; then, when Davout and Ney are in the line, we shall march, together, against the enemy." Having said this, the Emperor ordered his bivouac to be set up at the foot of the Ziegelhof, and his guard to encamp around it.

But while Napoleon was explaining his plans to Marshal Augereau, who greatly approved of his prudence, the staff of the imperial palace, coming from Landsberg with their baggage and servants, arrived at our outposts, which were at the gates of Eylau, without anyone telling them to stop at Ziegelhof. These employees, used to seeing the imperial quarters very well guarded, and not having been warned that they were almost on top of the Russians, were interested only in selecting a good lodging for their master, and they set themselves up in the post-house, where they unpacked their equipment, stabled their horses, and began to cook. In the midst of these preparations they were attacked by a Russian patrol and would have been captured had it not been for the intervention of the guard which always accompanied the Emperor's baggage. At the sound of this outbreak of firing, the troops who were in position at the gates of the town ran to the rescue of Napoleon's equipment, which was already being pillaged by the Russian soldiers. The Russian generals, thinking that the French were attempting to seize Eylau, sent reinforcements to their side, and so a sanguinary battle was fought in the streets of the town, which ended up in our hands.

Although this attack had not been ordered by the Emperor, he saw no reason not to profit by it, and he set himself up in the Eylau post-house. The Guard and Soult's troops occupied the town which was surrounded by Murat's cavalry. Augereau's troops were positioned in Zehsen, a little hamlet in which we hoped to find some provisions, but the Russians had taken everything with them as they withdrew, so that our unhappy regiment, which had received no rations for eight days, had to make do with some potatoes and water. The equipment of the staff having been left at Landsberg, our supper was not as good as that of the soldiers, for we had no potatoes. Eventually, on the morning of the 8th, when we were about to mount our horses, one of the marshal's servants brought him some bread, and he, always generous, shared it out amongst his aides-de-camp. After this frugal meal, which for several of us was to be our last, the corps moved to the post to which it had been assigned by the Emperor.

In accordance with the plan which I explained when I started these memoirs, I shall not weary you with too detailed a description of the various phases of this terrible battle of Eylau, but will limit myself to the principal events.

On the morning of the 8th, the position of the two armies was as follows. The Russians had their left at Serpalten, their centre in front of Auklapen and their right at Schmoditten. They were awaiting the arrival of eight thousand Prussians, who were expected to go to Althoff where they would form the extreme right wing. The enemy's front line was protected by five hundred artillery pieces, of which a third at least were of large calibre. The French situation was much less favourable, since their two wings had not yet arrived. The Emperor had, at the start of the action, only a part of the force with which he had expected to do battle. Marshal Soult's corps was placed on the right and left of Eylau, the Guard in the town itself, and Augereau's corps between Eylau and Rothenen, opposite Serpalten. The enemy formed almost a semicircle about us, and the two armies occupied a terrain in which there were numerous ponds covered by snow, which neither side could see.

Neither Marshal Davout, who should have been on our right, towards Molwitten, nor Marshal Ney, who should have been on our left around Althoff, had yet appeared, when at daybreak, about eight in the morning, the Russians began the attack by a violent cannonade to which our gunners, though fewer in numbers, replied. Though fewer, they had the advantage, however of being much better trained than the Russians, and also of directing their fire at masses of men who had no cover, while the Russian cannon-balls mainly hit the walls of Eylau and Rothenen. Soon a strong enemy column advanced with the intention of capturing the town; it was vigorously repelled by the Guard and Marshal Soult's troops. At this moment, the Emperor heard, with much pleasure, that from the top of the church tower could be seen Davout's men arriving via Molwitten and marching towards Serpalten, from where they expelled the Russians and drove them back to Klein-Sausgarten.

The Russian commander, Benningsen, seeing his left beaten and his rear menaced by the audacious Davout, resolved to crush him, and directed the greater part of his force against him. It was then that Napoleon, with the object of preventing this movement by creating a diversion against the enemy centre, ordered Augereau to attack, although he foresaw the difficulties of this operation.

There are on the field of battle, circumstances when one must sacrifice some troops in order to preserve the great majority and ensure victory. General Corbineau, the Emperor's aide-de-camp, was killed by a cannon shot near to us while bringing to Marshal Augereau the order to advance. The marshal passed between Eylau and Rothenen and led his two divisions boldly against the enemy centre, and already the 14th Line regiment who made up our advance guard had seized the position which the Emperor had ordered to be taken and held at all costs, when the guns which formed a semi-circle about Augereau hurled out a storm of ball and grape-shot of hitherto unprecedented ferocity. In an instant, our two divisions were pulverised under this rain of iron! General Desjardins was killed and General Heudelet gravely wounded; however, they stood firm until the corps having been almost entirely destroyed, the remnants were compelled to retire to the cemetery of Eylau, with the exception of the 14th, who almost entirely surrounded by the enemy, remained on the little hill which they had occupied. The situation was made even worse by a gale of wind which blew a heavy snowfall into our faces, and reduced visibility to about fifteen paces, so that several French batteries opened fire on us, as well as the Russians. Marshal Augereau was wounded by a bullet.

The devotion of 7th Corps, however, produced a good result, for, relieved by our attack, Marshal Davout was able not only to maintain his position, but to take Klein-Sausgarten and even push his advance-guard as far as Kuschitten, in the enemy's rear. Then, in an attempt to deliver a knock-out blow, Napoleon despatched, between Eylau and Rothenen, the squadrons commanded by Murat. This terrifying mass fell on the Russian centre, overwhelming them, cutting them down with their sabres and throwing them into the greatest confusion. The valiant General D'Hautpoul was killed at the head of his Cuirassiers, as was General Dahlmann, who had succeeded General Morland in the command of the Chasseurs of the Guard. The success of our cavalry allowed us to carry the day. Eight thousand Prussians, escaped from pursuit by Marshal Ney, and arriving at Althoff, tried to mount a new attack by advancing, one does not quite know why, on Kuschitten instead of Eylau, but Davout drove them off, and the arrival of Ney's corps at Schmoditten towards the end of the day, made Benningsen fear that his line of communication would be cut, and so he ordered a retreat in the direction of Konigsberg, leaving the French masters of the horrible battlefield covered with dead and dying. Since the invention of gunpowder one has not seen such a terrible effect, for in relation to the numbers engaged at Eylau, in comparison to all the battles, ancient or modern, the proportion of losses was highest. The Russians had twenty-five thousand casualties, and although the figure for French losses has been given as ten thousand, it is my belief that it was at least twenty thousand. A total of forty-five thousand men, of whom more than half died!

Augereau's corps was almost entirely destroyed. Out of fifteen thousand combatants under arms at the beginning of the action, there remained by evening only three thousand, under the command of Lieutenant colonel Massy: the marshal, all the generals and all the colonels had been either killed or wounded.

It is difficult to understand why Benningsen, knowing that Davout and Ney had not yet arrived, did not take advantage of their absence to attack Eylau at daybreak with the numerous troops of the centre of his army, instead of using precious time in bombarding us; for his superior strength would certainly have made him master of the town before the arrival of Davout, and the Emperor would then have regretted having moved so far forward instead of consolidating his position on the plateau of Ziegelhof and awaiting the arrival of his flank forces, as he had intended the evening before.

The day after the battle the Emperor followed the Russians to the gates of Konigsberg; but that town was fortified and it was thought unwise to attack it with troops weakened by a sanguinary battle, and what is more, almost all the Russian army was in Konigsberg and the surrounding country.

Napoleon spent several days at Eylau, partly to collect the wounded and partly to reorganise his forces. The survivors of Augereau's corps were spread amongst other units and the marshal was given leave to return to France for the treatment of his wound. The Emperor, seeing that the bulk of the Russian army was now at a distance, put his troops into billets in the towns and villages in front of the lower Vistula. There was no interesting event during the rest of the winter, except the taking of Danzig by our troops. Hostilities in the open country would not begin again until the month of june, as we shall see later.

Chap. 34.

I did not want to interrupt the story of the battle of Eylau to tell you what happened to me in this terrible conflict; a sad tale, to understand which we must go back to the autumn of 1805 when the officers of the Grande Arme were equipping themselves in preparation for the Battle of Austerlitz. I had two good horses and was looking for a third of a better quality, a charger. This was something difficult to find, for although horses were infinitely cheaper than they are today, they were still expensive, and I did not have much money; but I had a piece of very good luck.

I ran into a German scholar, named M. d'Aister, whom I had known when he was teaching at Sorze; he was now tutor to the children of a rich Swiss banker, M. Scherer, who lived in Paris and was an associate of M. Finguerlin, who was a very wealthy man who kept up great state, and had a stable of many horses, amongst which was a charming mare called Lisette, an excellent animal from Mecklemberg, good-looking, swift as a stag, and so well schooled that a child could ride her. But this mare had a dreadful and fortunately rare vice: she bit like a bulldog, and attacked furiously anyone who displeased her, which decided M. Finguerlin to sell her. She was bought by *Mme.* de Lauriston, whose husband, an aide-de-camp to the Emperor, had written to her to ask her to buy him a charger.

M. Finguerlin, when he sold the mare, had omitted to mention her behaviour, and on the evening of her purchase, a groom, whom she had torn open, was found lying at her feet. *Mme.* de Lauriston was justly alarmed and demanded cancellation of the sale. Not only was this done, but the police, in order to prevent another such accident, required that a notice be fixed to Lisette's loose-box informing any potential buyer of her ferocity, and that any sale would be null and void unless the buyer declared in writing that he was aware of this notice.

As you may imagine, with such a recommendation, the mare was very difficult to sell; M. d'Aister told me that her owner was prepared to let her go for whatever was offered. I offered a thousand francs and M. Finguerlin handed Lisette over to me, although she had cost five thousand. For several months she gave me a great deal of trouble; it took four or five men to saddle her, and she could not be bridled without being blindfolded and having all four legs tied; but once on her back one found her a matchless ride.

However, since during the time I had owned her she had bitten several people, including me, I was thinking of getting rid of her, when, having taken into my service a man called Francis Woirland, who was scared of nothing, he, before approaching Lisette, about whose bad character I had warned him, armed himself with a very hot leg of roast mutton, and when she attempted to bite him, he offered this to her, which she seized in her teeth; but having burned her mouth and her tongue, the mare gave a cry and dropped the gigot, and from that moment she submitted herself to Woirland, whom she no longer dared to bite. I tried the same trick and achieved the same result. Lisette, as docile as a dog, allowed herself to be handled by myself and my servant; she even became a little more tractable with the grooms whom she saw every day, but woe betide any stranger passing too close to her. I could give many examples of her ferocity, but I shall limit myself to one.

While Marshal Augereau was staying at the chteau of Bellevue, near Berlin, the servants, having noticed that while they were at diner, someone was coming to steal the sacks of oats from the stable, asked Woirland to leave Lisette loose near the door. The thief arrived, slipped into the stable and was already carrying off one of the sacks when the mare grabbed him by the neck, dragged him into the yard and broke two of his ribs by trampling on him. People came running to the cries of the terrified thief, whom Lisette was unwilling to abandon until my servant and I persuaded her, for in her rage she would have savaged anyone else. The wickedness of this animal had got worse since the officer of the Saxon Hussars had treacherously stabbed her in the shoulder on the battlefield of Jena.

It was this mare that I was riding at the time when the remains of Marshal Augereau's corps, shattered by a hail of cannon and grape shot, were attempting to re-form in the area of the cemetery. You will recall that the 14th Line regiment had stayed alone on the little hill, which it might leave only if ordered to do so by the Emperor. The snow having stopped for a moment, one could see this gallant regiment almost completely surrounded by the enemy, waving its Eagle aloft to show that it still stood fast and needed help. The Emperor, touched by the devotion to duty of these brave men, decided to attempt their rescue; he told Marshal Augereau to send an officer with orders to them to quit the hillock, form a small square and withdraw towards us; while a brigade of cavalry would go to meet them and second their efforts.

This was before the great charge made by Murat and his cavalry, and it was almost impossible to carry out the Emperor's command because a swarm of Cossacks separated us from the 14th. It was clear that any officer sent towards the unfortunate regiment would be killed or captured before he got there. Nevertheless, an order is an order; and the marshal had to obey.

It was the custom, in the imperial army, for the aides to line up a few paces from their general, and the one in front went off first; when he had completed his mission, he joined the back of the queue, so that as each took his turn to carry orders, the dangers were shared equally. A brave captain of engineers, named Froissart, who, although not an aide-de-camp, was attached to the marshal's staff, was nearest to him and was sent off to carry the order to the 14th. He left at the gallop; we lost sight of him in the midst of the Cossacks and never saw him again, nor did we know what became of him.

The marshal, seeing that the 14th did not budge, sent another officer, named David. He suffered the same fate as Froissart, and we heard no more of him. It is likely that they were both killed, and having been stripped of their clothing their bodies were not recognisable among the many dead who covered the ground. For the third time the marshal called out "An officer to take orders "!...It was my turn.

When he saw before him the son of his old friend, and, I think I may dare to say, his favourite aide-de-camp, the good marshal's face fell and his eyes filled with tears, for he could not disguise from himself that he was sending me to an almost certain death; but the Emperor's order had to be obeyed; I was a soldier; no one else could take my place, I would not have allowed something so dishonourable. So I took off! Now, while prepared to sacrifice my life, I thought it my duty to take every precaution which might save it. I had noticed that the two officers who had gone before me had left with drawn sabres, which made me think that they intended to defend themselves against the Cossacks who would attack them during the ride. This intention was in my opinion ill-advised, for they would have been forced to stop and fight a multitude of enemies who, in the end, had overwhelmed them. I adopted a different approach, and leaving my sabre in its scabbard, I thought of myself as a rider who, to win the prize in a race, goes as fast as possible by the shortest route towards the winning post without taking any notice of what is to right or left of him during his passage. Now, my winning post being the hillock occupied by the 14th, I resolved to get there without paying any attention to the Cossacks, whom I blotted out of my thoughts.

This system worked perfectly. Lisette, light as a swallow, and flying rather than galloping, rushed through space, leaping over the piled up bodies of men and horses, over ditches and the broken mountings of guns, as well as the half-extinguished bivouac fires. Thousands of Cossacks were scattered about the plain. The first ones to see me behaved like hunters who, having raised a hare, mark its presence by shouts of "Yours! Yours!" But none of them tried to stop me, firstly because I was going so fast, and also perhaps because each one thought I would be caught by his comrades who were further on. In this way I escaped from them all and arrived at the 14th without either I or my excellent mare having suffered a scratch.

I found the 14th formed in a square on top of the hillock; but the slope of the ground was so gentle that the enemy cavalry had been able to carry out a number of charges, which had been vigorously repelled, so that they were surrounded by heap of the dead bodies of horses and Russian Dragoons, which formed a sort of rampart, and now made the position almost inaccessible to cavalry; for even with the aid of our infantrymen, I had great difficulty in getting over this bloody and frightful defence work, but at last I was inside the square.

Since the death of Colonel Savary, killed during the crossing of the Ukra, the 14th had been commanded by a battalion commander; when I gave this officer the order which I carried, for him to leave his position and try to rejoin the army corps, he replied that the enemy artillery which had been firing at them for an hour had occasioned such heavy losses that the handful of soldiers which he had left would inevitably be exterminated if they went down onto the level ground; and anyway there was no time to prepare for the execution of this movement, since a Russian column, coming to attack, was now close to us. "I can see no way of saving the regiment," said the battalion commander. "Go back to the Emperor and say good-bye to him from the 14th; and take back the Eagle which we can no longer defend."

The Eagles of the infantry were very heavy, and their weight was increased by the long thick pole of oak on which they were mounted. I was bending forward and attempting to detach the Eagle from its pole, when one of the many bullets which the Russians were firing at us went through the back part of my hat, very close to my head. The shock was made worse by the fact that the hat was held on by a strong leather strap which went under my chin, and so offered more resistance to the blow. I was partially stunned by this, and found myself unable to move.

However the column of Russian infantry was now climbing the hillock; they were Grenadiers, whose headgear, garnished with metal, looked like mitres. These men, full of liquor, flung themselves on the feeble remnants of the 14th, who defended themselves bravely with their bayonets, and even when the square was broken, formed themselves into little groups and continued for a long time the unequal struggle. In my confused state, I was unable to react in any way; I was attacked by a drunken Russian soldier, who thrust his bayonet into my left arm, and then, aiming another blow at me, lost his balance and missing his mark, he slashed Lisette's haunch.

The pain of this injury aroused her ferocious instincts, she grabbed the soldier with her teeth and tore away the greater part of his face,then, kicking and biting, she forced her way through the mele and taking the path by which we had come, she went off at the gallop in the direction of the Eylau cemetery while, thanks to the Hussar's saddle in which I was seated, I remained on her back.

As we approached Eylau a new danger arose. The snow had started to fall again and in the poor visibility a battalion of the Guard took me for a Russian and opened fire on me, but although my cloak and my saddle were hit, both I and my mare were untouched. Lisette, continuing to gallop, went through the three lines of infantry like a grass-snake through a hedge, but this last burst of speed drained her resources, she was losing a lot of blood because one of the big veins in her haunch had been cut, she collapsed suddenly and fell, throwing me to the ground, where I was rendered unconscious.

170

I must have remained in this state for about four hours, and I was not aroused by the great charge of Murat's ninety squadrons of cavalry, which went past me and perhaps over me. When I came to, this is the dreadful position in which I found myself. I was completely naked except for my hat and my right boot. A soldier of the transport section, believing me to be dead, had despoiled me, as was customary, and in an attempt to remove my boot, was dragging at my leg, with one foot on my stomach. I was able to raise the upper part of my body and to spit out some clots of blood, my face, shoulders and chest were badly bruised, and blood from my wounded arm reddened the rest of my body. I gazed around with haggard eyes, and must have been a horrible spectacle. The transport driver made off with my possessions before I could summon my wits and address a word to him. I was too dazed and weak to move, and unable to call for help. The cold was increasing and I had little hope of surviving without some form of miracle, and something like a miracle took place.

Marshal Augereau had a valet de chambre, named Pierre Dannel, a very intelligent boy, loyal, but inclined to be cheeky; and it so happened that while we were at Houssaye, Dannel, having spoken back to his master, had been given his notice. Desolated, Dannel begged me to intercede for him, which I did with so much zeal that he was reinstated in the marshal's good graces; since when the valet had been devoted to me. Dannel had taken it on himself to come from Landsberg, on the day of the battle, to bring some victuals to his master, which he had put in a very light wagon, able to go anywhere, and containing all the things that the marshal used most frequently. This little wagon was driven by a soldier who had served in the same transport unit as the man who had stripped me. This fellow, carrying my effects, was passing the wagon which was standing at the Eylau cemetery when, recognising his old friend, he went up to him to show him the lovely booty he had taken from a dead man.

Now, while we were in cantonments by the Vistula, the marshal having told Dannel to go to Warsaw to get some provisions, I asked him to take my pelisse and have the black astrakhan with which it was trimmed, removed and replaced by grey; a style newly adopted by the aides-de-camp of Prince Berthier, who set the fashion in the army. I was still the only one of Marshal Augereau's officers who had grey astrakhan.

Dannel, who was present when the transport driver displayed his booty, easily recognised my pelisse, which made him look more closely at the other belongings of the alleged dead man, amongst which he saw my watch, marked with my father's initials, for it had been his. The valet de chambre had no doubt that I had been killed, but mourning my death, he wished to see me for the last time, and having been led there by the transport driver, he found me alive!

This good fellow, to whom I owe my life, was overjoyed. He hurried to fetch my own servant and some orderlies, who carried me into a barn where they rubbed me down with rum, while they sent for Dr. Raymond. When he at last arrived, he dressed the wound in my arm and declared that the blood which I had lost would save me.

Soon I was surrounded by my comrades including my brother. A reward was given to the transport rider who had taken my clothes, which he handed over with good grace; but as they were soaked with blood and water, Marshal Augereau had me wrapped up in clothes of his own.

The Emperor had given permission for Augereau to return to Landsberg, but his wound made it impossible for him to ride a horse; so his aides-de-camp got hold of a sledge on which they mounted the body of a carriage. The marshal, who had decided not to abandon me, had me strapped in beside him, for I was too weak to sit upright.

Before I was picked up from the battlefield, I had seen my poor Lisette near to me. Her wound had stopped bleeding and she was back on her feet, eating some straw which had been used by soldiers in their bivouacs the previous night. My servant, who was very fond of Lisette, returned to look for her; he cut strips of clothing from a dead soldier and dressed the wound on her haunch, and got her fit enough to walk to Landsberg.

The commandant of the little garrison of the town, had had the good sense to prepare quarters for the wounded. The officers of the staff were put into a large and comfortable inn, so that instead of spending the night lying naked in the snow, I was tucked into a good bed and being looked after by my brother, my companions and the worthy Dr. Raymond. The doctor had to cut the boot which the soldier had tried to pull off, and even so, he had difficulty in getting it off because my foot had swollen so much. You will see, later that this could have cost me my leg, and perhaps even my life.

We stayed in Landsberg for thirty-six hours. The rest and the care given me restored my ability to move, and when, on the second day after the battle, Marshal Augereau set off for Warsaw, I was able, though still very weak, to travel on the sledge. The journey took eight days, because we moved only in short stages; I was recovering my strength little by little, but I was aware of an icy cold in my right foot.

On our arrival at Warsaw, I was put in a large house which had been reserved for the marshal, which suited me very well, as I was unable to get out of bed. The wound of my arm was healing, the bruising of my upper body was dispersing, and my skin was resuming its normal colour, however the doctor did not know why I could not get up, and hearing me complain about my leg, he decided to have a look at it, and what do you suppose he found? My foot had become gangrenous! An accident which had occurred many years ago was the cause of this. While I was at Sorze, my right foot had been pierced by the foil of a fencing opponent, which had lost its button. It seems that this injury had made my foot more sensitive to cold, and while I was lying on the snow it had become frostbitten, and not having been treated in time, gangrene had set in at the site of the old fencing injury, the area was covered by a scar the size of a five franc piece. The doctor looked with alarm at my foot, then, taking a bistoury, and having me held down by four servants, he picked off the scab and dug into my foot to remove the dead flesh, just as one would cut out the rotten part of an apple.

I suffered greatly, at first without complaining, though it was a different matter when the bistoury, having reached live tissue, exposed the muscles and bones, which one could see. The doctor then stood on a chair and having soaked a sponge in warm sweetened wine, he allowed it to fall, drop by drop into the hole he had made in my foot. The pain was intolerable! Nevertheless I had to endure for a week this fearful torture, but my leg was saved.

Today, when one is so prodigal with decorations and promotions, an officer who ran the risks which I had run in reaching the 14th regiment, would certainly be rewarded; but under the Empire this sort of devotion to duty was regarded as so normal that I was given no medal and never thought of asking for one.

A long rest having been judged necessary for the cure of Marshal Augereau's wound, the Emperor instructed him to go to France for treatment, and brought Marshal Massna from Italy; to whom my brother, Bro and several of my friends were appointed. Marshal Augereau took me with him, along with his secretary and Dr.Raymond. I had to be lifted in and out of the carriage, but otherwise I felt my health improve the further we got away from those frozen wastes to a more friendly climate. My mare spent the winter in the stables of M. de Launay, the administrator of army forage supplies.

The marshal went by way of Rawa to Silesia. As long as we were in dreadful Poland, where there are no metalled roads, it took twelve and sometimes sixteen horses to drag the coach out of the bogs and swamps through which we travelled. We went always at walking pace and it was not until we reached Germany that we found ourselves in a civilised country with proper roads. We stopped at Dresden, and spent ten or twelve days at Frankfurt-on-Main, from where we had marched the previous October to attack Prussia.

We finally reached Paris about the 15th of March. I could walk with much difficulty, and had my arm in a sling, and I still felt the effects of what I had been through, but the pleasure of seeing my mother once more, and the care she devoted to me, combined with the gentle influence of the returning spring, effected my cure.

Chap. 35.

I spent the end of March, all of April, and the first week of May in Paris. It was during this time that I got to know the Desbrires, a family of which my marriage was soon to make me a member. I had recovered my health, and I realised that I could not stay any longer in Paris. Marshal Augereau sent me to Marshal Lannes who took me willingly onto his staff.

The Emperor, in order to keep an eye on any moves which the enemy might be tempted to make during the winter, had settled himself in the middle of the cantonments of his troops, first at Osterode and then at the chteau of Finkenstein, from where, while planning a new campaign, he governed France and directed his ministers, who, every week, sent him their reports. The portfolios holding the various documents furnished by each ministry were collected every Wednesday by M. Dennie the elder, under-secretary of state for war, who sent them off on Thursdays in the charge of a junior official whose duty it was to deliver them into the hands of the Emperor. But this system worked very badly because most of these officials had never been out of France. They did not know a word of German, nor did they understand the currency or the regulations regarding posting in foreign countries, so they did not know how to manage matters once they had crossed the Rhine. In addition, these gentlemen, being unused to fatigue, soon found themselves overcome by that of a journey of more than three hundred leagues, which lasted continuously for ten days and ten nights. One of them was so incompetent as to allow his despatches to be stolen. Napoleon was so angry at this mishap that he sent a courier to Paris to tell M. Dennie not to give the portfolios in future to officials except those who knew Germany, and who, being able to support fatigue and privation, could carry out their duties more efficiently.

M. Dennie was having great difficulty in finding anyone to fill the post, when I turned up with a letter ordering me to report to Marshal Lannes. Delighted to have found someone to take the next lot of despatches, he warned me to be ready to leave on the coming Thursday, and gave me five thousand francs for expenses and the purchase of a carriage, which suited me very well, as I did not have much money to get me back to the army in the depths of Poland.

We left Paris about the 10th of May. Both my servant and I were armed, and if one of us left the coach the other remained on guard. We knew enough German to keep the postilions up to the mark, and as I was in uniform, they obeyed me with more alacrity than they would a civilian official. So that instead of taking the usual nine and a half or ten days over the journey, we made it in eight and a half.

The Emperor was delighted to have his despatches twenty-four hours earlier than expected, and after praising the keenness which had led me to ask to return to duty in spite of my recent wounds, he added that as I had been so efficient a courier, I could leave for Paris that same night to take back some other portfolios; a task which would not prevent me from taking part in the campaign, which could not restart before the beginning of June.

Although I had spent nothing like the five thousand francs which M. Dennie had given me, the marshal of the palace gave me the same sum to return to Paris, which I did as quickly as possible. I stayed no more than twenty-four hours in the capital, and left once more for Poland; the minister again gave me five thousand francs for this third journey; it was far more than was necessary, but that was how Napoleon wanted it. It is true that these trips were very tiring and very boring, even though the weather was fine. I was on the road day and night for nearly a month in the sole company of my servant.

I reported to the Emperor at Finkenstein, and was afraid that I might have to continue as postman until fighting broke out, when fortunately some replacements were found and the Emperor authorised me to go to Marshal Lannes, to whom I reported at Marienberg on the 25th May. He had with him Colonel Sicard, Augereau's aide-de-camp, who had been kind enough to take charge of my horses. It was with much pleasure that I saw once more my mare Lisette, who was fit enough for more service.

The fortress of Danzig, besieged by the French during the winter, had fallen into their hands. The return of the good weather soon saw campaigning recommence. The Russians attacked our cantonments on the 5th of June, and were sharply repulsed at every point. On the 10th there was a fierce encounter at Heilsberg which some historians describe as a battle. The enemy were once more defeated. I shall not go into any detail about this affair, since Marshal Lannes' corps took very little part in it, not having arrived until nightfall. We did, however, come under some heavy fire and Colonel Sicard was mortally wounded. He had already been wounded at Eylau, and although scarcely recovered from his injuries, had returned to take part in the renewed fighting. Before he died, the good colonel requested me to say his farewell to Marshal Augereau, and gave me a letter for his wife. I was very much upset by this painful scene.

The army now being in pursuit of the Russians, we passed through Eylau. The fields which we had left three months previously covered with snow and dead bodies, were now overspread by a delightful carpet of green, bedecked with flowers. What a contrast! How many soldiers lay beneath those verdant meadows? I went and sat at the place where I had fallen and been despoiled, and where I also would have died, had not a truly providential combination of circumstances come to my aid. Marshal Lannes wanted to see the hillock which the 14th had so valiantly defended. I took him there. Since the time of the battle, the enemy had been in occupation of the place; however, we found, still intact, the monument which all the corps of the French army had erected to the memory of their dead comrades of the 14th, thirty-six of whose officers had been buried in the same grave. This respect for the dead reflected honour on the Russians. I remained for a few moments on the spot where I had been hit by the bullet and wounded by the bayonet, and thought of the brave men who lay in the dust, and whose fate I had so nearly shared.

The Russians, having been defeated on the 10th of June at Heilsberg, retreated hastily and got a day ahead of the French who, by the evening of the 13th, were concentrated beyond Eylau, on the left bank of the Alle. The Russians occupied Bartenstein on the right bank of this river, which the two armies now descended on opposite sides.

Benningsen, whose stores of food and ammunition were in Konigsberg, where the Prussian corps was stationed, wanted to reach this town before the arrival of the French, but to do so he had to cross over onto the left bank of the Alle, where there were the French troops. The Russian commander hoped to reach Friedland sufficiently far ahead of the French to be able to cross the river before they could oppose him. The same reasons which made Benningsen wish to hold on to Konigsberg, made Napoleon wish to capture it. He had for several days constantly manoeuvred to out-flank the Russian left, and keep them away from the place, in the direction of which he had sent Murat, Soult and Davout to oppose the Russians if they arrived before us.

The Emperor, however, did not stick to this scheme, and foreseeing that the Russians would attempt to cross the Alle at Friedland, he aimed to occupy the town before they did, and on the night of the 13th-14th June, he despatched towards it the corps of Marshal Lannes and Mortier, and three divisions of cavalry. The rest of the army was to follow.

Marshal Lannes, who was in the van, with the Oudinot Grenadiers and a brigade of cavalry, having arrived at Posthenen, a league from Friedland, sent the 9th Hussars to reconnoitre the latter town. They were repulsed with losses, and daybreak revealed a large part of the Russian army massed on the opposite bank of the Alle on the high ground between Allenau and Friedland. They had begun to cross the old town bridge, beside which they had constructed two new ones.

The aim of the two armies was very easily understood. The Russians wanted to cross the Alle to get to Konigsberg, and the French wanted to stop them and drive them back across the river, which had very steep banks. The only crossing point was at Friedland. The Russians had difficulty in deploying from Friedland onto the open ground of the left bank, owing to the fact that the way out of the town was much restricted by a large lake, and by a stream called the Mill Stream, which ran in a very steep-sided ravine. To protect their crossing, the Russians had placed two strong batteries of guns on the right bank, which could cover the town and part of the land between Posthenen and Heinrichsdorf.

The Emperor was still at Eylau: the various corps marching towards Friedland were still several leagues away, when Marshal Lannes, having marched all night, arrived before the town. The marshal would have liked to attack the enemy immediately; but already they had thirty thousand men drawn up on the level ground before Friedland, and their lines, the right of which was opposite Heinrichsdorf, the centre at the mill stream, and the left at the village of Sortlack, were being endlessly reinforced; while Marshal Lannes had no more than ten thousand men; however, he deployed them skillfully in the village of Posthenen and the woods of Sortlack, from where he threatened the Russian's left flank, while with two divisions of cavalry he tried to stop their advance toward Heinrichsdorf, which lay on the route from Friedland to Konigsberg. There was a brisk exchange of fire before Mortier's corps arrived. Mortier, to dispute with the Russians the road to Konigsberg, while waiting for fresh reinforcements, occupied Heinrichsdorf and the area between this village and Posthenen. However, it was not possible that Lannes and Mortier with twenty-five thousand men could resist the seventy thousand Russians who would soon face them. The situation was becoming highly critical. Marshal Lannes sent a succession of officers to warn the Emperor to hasten the arrival of the army corps which he knew were coming up behind him. Mounted on my swift Lisette, I was the first to go. I met the Emperor as he was leaving Eylau; he was beaming with pleasure! He called me to his side, and as we galloped along, I had to explain to him what had happened before I left the battle. When I had finished my recital, the Emperor said to me, smiling, "Have you a good memory?" "Passable, Sir," I replied. "Well what anniversary is this, the 14th of June?" "Marengo" I said "Yes! Yes! The anniversary of Marengo," said the Emperor, "and I shall beat the Russians as I beat the Austrians!"

Napoleon was so convinced about this, that as he went along the columns, where the men greeted him with many cheers, he said to them repeatedly "Today is a lucky day, it is the anniversary of Marengo!"

Chap. 36.

It was after eleven o'clock when Napoleon arrived on the battlefield, where several corps had already come to join Lannes and Mortier. The remainder, including the Guard, were arriving one by one. Napoleon readjusted the line: Ney was on the right, positioned in the wood at Sortlack; Lannes and Mortier formed the centre, between Posthenen and Heinrichsdorf; the left stretched out beyond this last village. The heat was overpowering. The Emperor gave the troops an hour's rest, after which, at the signal of a volley by twenty-five guns, a general attack would begin. Marshal Ney's corps had the most difficult task, for they were to come out of their hiding place in the woods of Sortlack, fight their way into Friedland, which was filled with the main forces and reserves of the enemy, seize the bridges and thus cut off the Russian's way of retreat.

It is difficult to understand why Benningsen had placed his forces in front of the narrow exit from Friedland, and with their backs to the Alle with its steep banks, in the presence of the French who commanded the open country. The explanation given later by the Russian general was that having been a day ahead of Napoleon, he did not believe that the French troops could cover in twelve hours a distance which had taken his men twenty-four hours, and he had thought that Lannes' corps was an isolated advance-guard of the French army, which he could easily crush. When this illusion had been dissipated, it was too late to bring his army back to the other bank because the narrow defile at Friedland would have caused certain disaster, so he preferred to stand and fight.

At about one in the afternoon, the twenty-five guns at Posthenen, given the order by the Emperor, fired a volley, and battle was joined all along the line. At first our left and our centre moved very slowly to give the right, commanded by Ney, time to capture the town. The marshal, emerging from Sortlack wood, took the village of that name and advanced rapidly towards Friedland, sweeping aside everything in his path; but as they moved forward from the wood and the village of Sortlack to the first houses of Friedland, Ney's troops were exposed to the fire of the Russian batteries which, positioned behind the town on the heights of the opposite bank, caused them severe losses. This fire was made more dangerous by the fact that the gunners, separated from us by the river, could aim their guns in safety, knowing that our infantry could not attack them. This serious problem could have led to the failure of the attack on Friedland, but Napoleon overcame it by sending General Senarmont with fifty guns, which he placed on the left bank of the Alle, and subjected the Russian batteries to such heavy fire that they were soon silenced. As soon as the enemy fire had ceased, Marshal Ney resumed his advance, driving the Russians back into Friedland, and mingled in confusion with them, entered the streets of the unfortunate town, where the mortar bombs had started a huge fire.

A savage bayonet fight ensued in which the Russians, crammed together and scarcely able to move, suffered enormous losses! ... At last, in spite of their courage, they were compelled to retreat in disorder and seek refuge by crossing the bridges to the other bank; but General Senarmont had moved his guns into a position from which he could fire on the bridges, which he soon broke, after killing many of the Russians who were attempting to escape across them. All those who remained in Friedland were either killed, captured or drowned while trying to cross the river.

Up until this point, Napoleon had, so to speak, made his left and his centre mark time; he now moved them rapidly forward. General Gortschakoff, who commanded the centre and right wing of the enemy, attempted, bravely, to recapture the town, (which would have been of no use, because the bridges were down, although he did not know that). He charged at the head of his men into the burning Friedland; but driven out by Ney, who was occupying the town, and forced back into the open, he found himself confronting our centre, who drove him back to the Alle at Kloschenen. The Russians defended themselves heroically and refused to surrender although completely surrounded. Many of them were killed by our bayonets, the remainder rolled down the steep banks into the river, where a large number were drowned.

The extreme right of the enemy was composed mostly of cavalry who tried during the battle to capture or outflank the village of Heinrichsdorf; but driven off by our troops, they went back to the banks of the Alle, under the command of General Lambert, who, seeing that Friedland was in the hands of the French and that the Russian left and centre were defeated, gathered all he could of the regiments of the right wing and made off from the battlefield down the side of the Alle. Nightfall prevented the French from following, so his was the only body of Russian troops to escape the disaster.

Our victory was one of the most complete; we captured all the Russian guns; we did not take a many prisoners during the action, but a great many of the enemy were killed or wounded, amounting to more than twenty-six thousand; our losses were no more than three thousand dead and four or five thousand wounded. Of all the battles fought by the Emperor, this was the only one in which the number of his troops exceeded that of the enemy. The French strength was eighty thousand and the Russian's only seventy-five thousand. The remnants of the Russian army marched in disorder all night, and retired behind the River Pregal, having destroyed the bridges.

178

Marshals Soult, Davout and Murat had not been involved in the battle of Friedland, but their presence induced the Russians to abandon Konigsberg, which town our troops entered. We found there an immense store of all kinds of material.

I did not suffer any injury during the battle, though I ran into a number of dangers. You saw how I left Posthenen in the morning, on Marshal Lannes' orders, to go as quickly as possible to warm the Emperor that the Russians were crossing the Alle, and that a battle appeared imminent. Napoleon was at Eylau; I had therefore to make a journy of about six leagues to reach him, which would have presented no difficulty to my excellent mare if the road had been clear, but as it was congested by the troops of various units hurrying to the aid of Marshal Lannes at Friedland, there was no way in which I could gallop along it. I therefore went across country, which meant that Lisette, having had to jump hedges, fences and ditches, was already very tired when I met the Emperor, who was just leaving Eylau. However, I had, without a moment of rest, to return with him to Friedland, and although this time the troops moved to one side to let us pass, my poor mare, having galloped over twelve leagues altogether, six of them being across country, and in very hot weather, was utterly exhausted by the time I had rejoined Marshal Lannes on the battlefield. I realised that Lisette could not continue to carry me during the action, so, taking advantage of the rest which Napoleon allowed the troops, I set out to look for my servant, in order to change horses; but in the middle of such a large collection of troops there was not much hope of finding him. It was, in fact, impossible, and I went back to the staff still mounted on the weary Lisette.

Marshal Lannes and my comrades, who saw my problem, had advised me to dismount and allow my mare a few hour's rest, when I caught sight of a Hussar leading a horse which he had captured from the enemy. I took it over, and gave Lisette to one of the troopers of the marshal's escort, so that he could take her back behind the lines, let her have some food and hand her over to my servant, when he could find him. I then got astride my new mount, took my place among the aides-de-camp, and when it came to my turn, I went off.

I was, at first, very pleased with my fresh horse, until the time came when, Marshal Ney having gone into Friedland, Marshal Lannes sent me to warn him of an enemy movement. I had barely entered the town when this devil of a horse, which had behaved so well in the open country, finding itself in a little square, where all the houses were on fire and the street covered with burning planks and furniture, in the midst of which a number of bodies were being roasted, was so frightened by the sight of the flames and the smell of burning flesh that it would go neither forward nor back, and, digging in its heels, it remained motionless, snorting loudly, and no amount of spurring would persuade it to move. Now the Russians, having gained a momentary advantage, pushed our men back to the point where I was, and from the height of a church and some neighbouring houses, they were raining down bullets, while two guns which they carried with them fired grape-shot at the soldiers among whom I was.

Many men were killed around me, which recalled to my mind the position in which I had found myself at Eylau in the middle of the 14th. As I was not anxious to be wounded again and in any case, in staying where I was I was not carrying out my mission, I simply dismounted, and abandoning my infernal mount, I slipped through the houses to contact Marshal Ney at another spot, which was pointed out by some officers.

I was with him for some fifteen minutes; there were some bullets flying around, but nothing like so many as there had been at the place where I had left my mount. The Russians were eventually driven back at bayonet point and forced to retreat toward the bridges, whereupon Marshal Ney sent me to take the good news to Marshal Lannes. To get out of the town, I took the same route as I had taken to get in, and went through the little square where I had left my horse. It had been the scene of a fierce encounter which had left many dead and dying, among whom I saw my stubborn horse, its back broken by a cannon-ball, and its body riddled by bullets!.... From there I made for the outskirts in something of a hurry because the burning houses were collapsing on all sides and I was afraid of being buried beneath the debris. At last I got out of the town and reached the edge of the lake.

The heat of the day, added to that of the fire which was raging in the streets through which I had passed, had bathed me in sweat, and I was dropping with fatigue and hunger, for I had spent a night on horseback to come from Eylau to Friedland, I had galloped back to Eylau and returned to Friedland once more, and had not eaten since the previous evening. I was not looking forward, therefore, to crossing, under a blazing sun, the large area covered with high standing corn which separated me from Marshal Lannes. But once again I had a stroke of luck. General Grouchy's division of dragoons had been engaged not far away in a sharp encounter in which, although victorious, they had lost a number of men, and the colonels had, as was usual, collected the horses of the men who had been killed and put them in the hands of a detachment which would lead them away. I saw this body of men, of which every trooper was leading four or five horses and was taking them to the lake to drink.

I spoke to the officer in charge who, encumbered by all these led horses, was only too glad to let me have one, which I promised to return to his regiment in the evening. He picked out for me an excellent beast, which had been the mount of a sous-officier killed during the charge; astride of this horse, I returned rapidly to Posthenen.

I had hardly left the edge of the lake when it became the theatre of the most savage encounter, which was due to the desperate attempt made by Gortschakoff to reopen a way of retreat by capturing the road to Friedland which was held by Marshal Ney. Caught between the marshal's troops and those of our centre, who were now advancing, Gortschakoff's Russians defended themselves bravely amongst the houses bordering the lake; so that if I had stayed there, where I had thought of resting for a while, I would have landed in the middle of this fierce outbreak of fighting. I rejoined Marshal Lannes at the moment when he was moving towards the lake to attack the rear of the Russian troops whom Ney was driving away from the front of the town, and I was able to give him some useful information about the terrain on which we were fighting.

If the French army did not take many prisoners during the battle of Friedland, it was a different matter the next day and the days following; for the Russians, pursued with a bayonet at their backs, thrown into complete disorder and utterly exhausted, were abandoning their ranks and lying down in the fields, where we captured a great number. We also collected a large quantity of artillery. All those members of Benningsen's army who escaped hurried back across the Nieman, behind which was the Russian emperor who, perhaps recalling the danger to which he had been exposed at Austerlitz, had judged it unwise to assist in person at the battle of Friedland; and two days after our victory he hastened to ask Napoleon for an armistice, to which Napoleon agreed.

Three days after the battle the French army reached the town of Tilsit and the river Nieman, which at this point is only a few leagues from the frontiers of the Russian empire.

The rear of a victorious army presents a most dismal spectacle. The path of their advance is strewn with the dead, dying, and wounded, while the survivors, soon forgetting those comrades who have fallen in the fighting, rejoice in their success and go forward cheerfully to new adventures. Our men were delighted to see the Nieman, whose opposite bank was occupied by the remains of that Russian army which they had defeated in so many engagements; and where, in contrast to their own lighthearted songs, there reigned a mournful silence. Napoleon established himself at Tilsit, and his troops encamped around the town. The Nieman separated the two armies; the French occupied the left bank and the Russians the right.

The Emperor Alexander having requested a meeting with Napoleon, this took place on the 25th of June, in a pavilion on a raft anchored in the middle of the river, in sight of the two armies which lined the banks. It was a most imposing spectacle. The two emperors arrived, each from his own side, accompanied by only five of the principal officers of their armies. Marshal Lannes, who flattered himself that he should accompany the Emperor, saw himself displaced by Marshal Bessires, an intimate friend of Prince Murat; and he never forgave the marshals for depriving him of what he considered his right.

So Marshal Lannes stayed with us on the quay at Tilsit, from where we saw the two emperors embrace on meeting, which occasioned much cheering from both camps. The next day, the 26th, in the course of a second interview which took place once more in the pavilion on the Nieman, the Russian emperor presented to Napoleon his unfortunate friend, the King of Prussia. This prince whom the fortunes of war had stripped of a vast kingdom, leaving him only the small town of Memel and some miserable villages, maintained a bearing worthy of a descendant of Frederick the Great: Napoleon greeted him politely but coolly, for he considered that he had reason to complain of his conduct, and he planned to confiscate the greater part of his states.

To facilitate the meetings of the two Emperors, the town of Tilsit was declared neutral, and Napoleon handed over half of it to the Russian emperor, who set himself up there with his Guard. The two sovereigns spent some twenty days together, during which time they decided the fate of Europe. During these proceedings, the King of Prussia was relegated to the right bank, and had no quarters in Tilsit, which he visited but rarely. One day Napoleon went to call on the Queen of Prussia, who was said to be greatly distressed. He invited her to dine with him on the following day. She accepted the invitation, no doubt with little pleasure, but realising that at a time when peace was being sought it was necessary to take every measure to soften the heart of the victor.

Napoleon and the Queen of Prussia thoroughly detested one another: she had grossly insulted him in several proclamations, and he had returned the complement in his bulletins. Their meeting, however, did not display their mutual hatred; Napoleon was respectful and attentive, the queen gracious in her attempts to captivate her former enemy; attempts made all the more determinedly as she was not unaware that the peace treaty created—under the name of the kingdom of Westphalia—a new state, whose territory was to be provided by the electorate of Hesse, and by Prussia itself.

The Queen was resigned to the loss of several provinces, but she could not accept the loss of the fortified city of Magdeberg, possession of which was needed for the security of Prussia. For his part, Napoleon, who planned to nominate his brother Jrme as King of Westphalia, intended to add Magdeberg to this new state. It appears that, during the meal, the Queen deployed her not inconsiderable charms, and when Napoleon, to change the conversation, praised a superb rose which the Queen was wearing, she said to him, "Would your majesty not accept this rose in return for Magdeberg?" A more chivalrous person might have accepted, but Napoleon was too much of a realist to be won over by a pretty proposition. One may be sure that he restricted himself to admiring the beauty of the rose and also of the hand which proffered it, but he did not take the flower, which brought tears to the Queen's eyes. The conqueror, however, did not seem to notice. He kept Magdeberg and politely conducted the Queen to the boat which was to carry her to the opposite bank.

During our stay at Tilsit, Napoleon held a review of his Guard and the army in the presence of Alexander, who was impressed by the martial air and bearing of these troops. The Russian Emperor, in his turn, put on display some fine battalions of his Guard, but he did not dare to parade his line regiments, whose numbers had been so greatly reduced at Heilsberg and Friedland. As for the King of Prussia, of whose regiments there remained only the broken dbris, he did not exhibit them at all.

Napoleon drew up, with Russia and Prussia, a peace treaty in which the principal articles related to the creation of the kingdom of Westphalia for the benefit of Jrme Bonaparte. The elector of Saxony, now an ally and friend of France, was elevated to the dignity of king, and was awarded, in addition, the Grand Duchy of Warsaw, composed of a vast province of the former Poland, which was recovered from the

182

Russians. I shall not go into the less important articles of the treaty, which resulted in the re-establishment of peace between the great powers of continental Europe.

In elevating his brother to the throne of Westphalia, Napoleon added to the mistakes he had already made in awarding the kingdom of Naples to Joseph and that of Holland, Louis. The people of these countries felt humiliated at being ruled by foreigners who had not themselves done anything of importance and who were, in fact, nonentities, who had no merit except that of being Napoleon's brothers. The dislike and distrust which these new kings attracted contributed largely to the Emperor's downfall. The conduct of the King of Westphalia in particular made very many enemies for Napoleon.

Having concluded the treaty, the two Emperors parted with mutual assurances of friendship, which at the time seemed sincere.

Chap. 37.

The French army was spread out into the various provinces of Germany and Poland under the command of five marshals, in whose number Lannes had asked not to be included, since his ill-health required his return to France. If I had been his permanent aide-de-camp, I would have had to return with him, but I had an even better reason for going, and that was to rejoin Marshal Augereau, to whose staff I had not ceased to belong, my attachment to Marshal Lannes being only temporary. I made ready to return to Paris: I sold, as well as possible, my two horses, and I sent Lisette to the registrar-general, M. de Launey, who, having taken a liking to her, had asked me to let him have her when I had no further use for her. Her injuries and hard work had calmed her down, and I lent her to him for an indefinite period; he mounted his wife on her, and kept her for seven or eight years until she died a natural death.

During the twenty days which the Emperor had spent at Tilsit, he had despatched a great many officers, some to Paris, some to other parts of the empire, so that there were hardly any left available for duty. Napoleon did not want to take officers from their regiments, so he ordered a list to be made of all those who had joined the campaign voluntarily and those who did not belong to any army corps nor to the staff of any of the five marshals who were in command. I was included in this list, and felt sure that the Emperor, for whom I had already carried despatches, would choose me in preference to officers whom he did not know; and indeed, the Emperor sent for me on the 9th of July, and having given me some voluminous portfolios and some despatches for the King of Saxony, ordered me to go to Dresden and await him there. The Emperor intended to leave Tilsit that same day, but was going on a long detour to visit Konigsberg, Marienwerder, and Silesia, so that I would be several days ahead of him.

I crossed Prussia once more, and saw again several of our battlefields; I went through Berlin and arrived at Dresden two days before the Emperor. The court of Saxony was aware that a peace had been agreed, and that it raised the elector to the rank of king, and awarded him the Grand Duchy of Warsaw, but they did not yet know that the Emperor was to pass through Dresden on his way to Paris; it was I who gave this information to the new king.

You may imagine the result of this! ...Immediately the court, the town, and the army were thrown into a turmoil to organise a grand reception for the great Emperor who, after having so generously restored to liberty the Saxon troops captured at Jena, had loaded their sovereign with honours! I was received with enthusiasm; I was lodged in the chteau in a fine apartment, where I was magnificently cared for, and the king's aides-de-camp showed me round all the interesting sights of the palace and the town. Eventually the Emperor arrived, and in accordance with the protocol, which I already knew, I hurried to hand over the portfolios to M. Meneval, and to ask for the Emperor's further orders. These I found agreeable, for I was instructed to carry some fresh portfolios to Paris, and the Emperor gave me a letter which I was to deliver personally to the Empress Josephine. The marshal of the palace, M. Duroc, gave me eight thousand francs to cover the expense of the journey from Tilsit to Dresden and from Dresden to Paris. I took to the road in high spirits: I had just taken part in three fine campaigns, during which I had been promoted to captain, and had been noticed by the Emperor; we were about to enjoy the delights of peace, which would allow me to spend a long time with my mother; I was fully recovered; I had never had so much money; everything conspired to make me happy, and I was very happy.

I arrived at Frankfurt-on-main, where a lieutenant colonel of the Imperial Guard named M. de L... was in command. The Emperor had given me a letter for this officer, from whom he wanted, I think, some confidential information, for M. de L... was in touch with M. Savary, who ran the secret police. This colonel invited me to dine with him, after which he conducted me back to my coach; but as I got in I noticed a fair sized package which was not part of my despatches. I was about to call for my batman to get an explanation for this, when Colonel de L... stopped me, and told me, in an undertone, that the package contained some dresses in Berlin knitwear and other materials banned in France, and was destined for the Empress Josephine, who would be much obliged to me for bringing them to her! I recalled only too well the cruel anxieties I had suffered as a result of the false report which I had been persuaded to give the Emperor regarding the numerical strength of the "Chasseurs a Cheval" at Austerlitz, to consent to be engaged once more in some underhand business: so I flatly refused. To be sure I would have liked to please the Empress, but I was aware of the inflexible severity with which Napoleon treated those found guilty of smuggling, and after facing so many dangers, and shedding so much of my blood in battle, I had no wish to sacrifice whatever merit I had gained in the eyes of the Emperor by transgressing his laws in order to draw a smile of thanks from the Empress. To overcome my objections Colonel de L... pointed out that the package had several wrappings, of which the outermost, addressed to the minister for war, bore the seal of the 7th Light Infantry and the designation "Record of accounts." He was sure that the customs would not dare open such a package, the outer covering of which I could remove when I reached Paris and deliver the stuff to the Empress without being compromised; but in spite of all this fine reasoning, I absolutely refused to take part in this transaction and ordered the postilion to set off.

184

When we arrived at the post-house, half way between Frankfurt and Mainz, I took my batman to task for having taken into the coach this extra package; he replied that during dinner time, M. de L... himself had put these packages into the coach: he had supposed that they contained more despatches, and had not thought that he could refuse to accept them from the hands of the commanding officer in person. "Did you say packages?" I cried. "Were there then several? He took away only one." And now, rummaging amongst the Emperor's portfolios, I found a second package of contraband which the colonel had put into my trunk without my knowledge. I was taken aback by this trickery and was tempted to throw the dresses onto the highway. However I did not dare, and I continued my journey, determined that if the contraband was seized I would explain how it had been put into my coach, and by whom the stamp of the 7th Light Infantry had been put on the wrapping; for I had no wish to face the anger of Napoleon; but as this defence would have compromised the Empress,I decided that I would use it only as a last resort, and that I would make every effort to avoid my coach being examined. A stroke of luck and a little subterfuge got me out of this dilemma.

I arrived, very worried, at the bridge over the Rhine at Mainz, which separates Germany from France, and my anxiety was increased by the sight of the great collection of customs officers and soldiers in unifor, who were waiting round this frontier. When my carriage was stopped, in the usual manner, two men arrived simultaneously at the door; one was a customs officer, to carry out a search, and the other was an aide-de-camp to Marshal Kellerman, who was in command of the station, and who wanted to know if the Emperor was on his way. This is my chance! I thought to myself, and pretending not to notice the customs officer, I replied to the aide-de-camp, "The Emperor is coming behind me." This was no lie, he was indeed following me, but at an interval of two days...which I did not think it necessary to add.

My words were heard by all around me and threw them into a state of frenzied activity. The aide-de-camp went off across the bridge at the gallop, at risk of tumbling into the Rhine in his haste to warn Marshal Kellerman. The guard took up their arms. The customs men and their superiors tried to arrange themselves in the most military manner possible in order to look good in front of the Emperor and, as my carriage got in their way, they told the postilion to clear off....So there I was! Freed from their clutches!

I went on to the posting-house and quickly changed horses; but while this was being done, a violent storm broke over Mainz and the rain began to fall in torrents. It was five o'clock in the afternoon, dinner time; but on the news of the approaching arrival of the Emperor, the general alarm was beaten throughout the town; on which signal the marshal, generals, prefect, mayor, civil and military authorities, all threw down their napkins, and hastily donning their best clothes, they went in the pouring rain through the streams of water running in the streets to take up their posts; while I, who was the cause of all this commotion, was laughing my head off as I made off at full speed drawn by three good post-horses.

In view of the fact that the Empress was willing to disobey her august spouse by wearing clothes made of prohibited material, and that a colonel was willing to slip contraband into my coach without my knowledge, the trick which I had played seemed to me to be excusable. In any case, since it was June, the soakingaking which I had caused these Mainz officials to undergo would do no harm except to their clothes. When I was far from Mainz, I could still hear the sound of drums, and I learned afterwards that they had stayed up all night. The Emperor arrived two days later, but as he had had an accident to his coach, the good citizens of Mainz blamed that for the delay of which their fine clothes were the victims. I was heading swiftly and happily towards Paris, when a most disagreeable accident interrupted my progress, and turned my happiness to annoyance. You will understand that when a sovereign travels, it would be impossible to supply a change of horses for the numerous carriages which precede and follow him, if the staging posts were not reinforced by horses, known as "de tourne", brought from posts established on other routes. Now, as I was leaving Dombasle, a little town this side of Verdun, a confounded postilion "de tourne" who had arrived the night before, not having noticed a steep hill which one encounters after leaving the staging post, lost control of his horses during the descent and overturned my carriage, breaking the springs and the bodywork. To make matters worse, it was a Sunday and all the population had gone to a fête in a neighbouring village, so that I could not find a workman. Those that I found the next day were so unskillful that I had to spend two mortal days in this miserable place.

I was about to set out again when an outrider having announced the arrival of the Emperor, I took the liberty of stopping his coach to tell him of the accident which I had suffered. He laughed, took back the letter for the Empress which he had given me, and went on his way. I followed him to St. Cloud, from where, after giving the portfolios to the cabinet secretary, I went to my mother's home in Paris.

I took up once more my position as aide-de-camp to Marshal Augereau, a very easy task, as it consisted of going every month to spend one or two weeks at La Houssaye, where daily life was always so amusing. Thus rolled by the end of the summer and the autumn; during which time the Emperor's policies were leading towards fresh events and storms whose terrible commotions would nearly swallow me up; me, a very small personage, who, in his carefree youth, thought of nothing but enjoying life, after having seen death at such close quarters.

It has been rightly said that the Emperor was never so great and powerful as in 1807, when, after defeating the Austrians, the Russians and the Prussians, he had concluded a peace so favourable to France and to himself. But scarcely had Napoleon ended his war against the northern powers, when his evil genius drove him to undertake one even more terrible, in the south of Europe, in the Iberian peninsula.

End of Volume 1, The Memoirs of General the Baron de Marbot. Translated by Oliver.C.Colt

The Memoirs of General the Baron de Marbot. Translated by Oliver.C.Colt

Contents of Volume 2.

Volume 2.

Chap. 1.

My brother and the rest of Massna's aides-de-camp made haste to leave Spain and come to join us in Paris, where I remained all summer and the following autumn. I went each month to spend some days at the Chteau de Bonneuil, the home of M. and *Mme*. Desbrires. During my absence the Desbrires had been most friendly towards my mother, and on my return the affection I had felt for a long time for their daughter was increased, and I was shortly permitted to ask for her hand in marriage. The marriage was agreed, and I even had, for a time, the hope of being promoted to colonel before this important ceremony took place.

It was the accepted thing for the Emperor to sign the marriage contract of any of the colonels in the army, but he only very rarely accorded this favour to officers of lower rank, and they were required to inform the minister for war of the reasons which led them to ask for this distinction. I based my request on what the Emperor had said to me when I saw him on the eve of the battle of Marengo. He had said to me, speaking of my father who had died during the siege of Genoa, "If you behave yourself and follow in his footsteps, I, myself, will be your father." I added that since that day I had been wounded eight times, and was conscious that I had always done my duty.

The minister, Clarke, a very stern character, who almost always rejected requests of this sort, agreed that mine merited consideration, and promised me that he would submit it to his majesty. He kept his word, for a few days later I was ordered to report to the Emperor at the chteau of Compigne, and to bring with me the notary who held the contract of marriage; this was the good M. Mailand, with whom I set off in a post carriage.

When we arrived, the Emperor had gone hunting: not that he much enjoyed the sport, but he thought that he should copy the former kings of France. The signing was therefore put off until the next day, which greatly upset M. Mailand who was awaited in Paris. But what could one do?

On the following day we were presented to the Emperor, whom we found in the apartment where, twenty years later, I have so often served as aide-de-camp to princes of the House of Orlans. My contract was signed in the salon where later was signed that of the King of Belgium with Princess Louise, the daughter of King Louis-Phillipe of France.

During these short interviews, Napoleon was always very affable. He addressed some questions to the notary, asked me if my fiance was pretty, what was her dowry, *etc. etc.* On dismissing me he said that he would like to see me in a good position, and that he would soon reward me for my good services. For a moment I saw myself as a colonel, and this hope was reinforced when, on leaving the Imperial presence, I was accosted by General Mouton, Comte de Lobau, who assured me confidentially that the Emperor had put my name on a list of officers to whom he wished to give the command of a regiment. My pleasure on hearing this was increased by my knowledge that the Comte de Lobau, an aide-de-camp to Napoleon, was responsible under the minister for war, for military promotions. I returned to Paris full of joy and hope! I was married on the 14th November following.

I was happy in the bosom of my family, and expected every day my brevet as colonel, when I was told by the minister for war that I was to be posted as Major to the 1st regiment of Mounted Chasseurs, then in garrison in the depths of Germany. I was much downcast at this news, for it seemed to me most hurtful that I should be sent once more to serve as a simple squadron commander, a rank in which I had been wounded three times and had campaigned from Wagram to Portugal. I could not understand why I was being treated like this, after what the Emperor and the Comte de Lobau had said to me. It was the latter who gave me the key to this puzzle.

Massna, on his entry into Portugal, had fourteen aides-de-camp, of whom six were senior officers. Two of these, *mm.* Pelet and Casabianca, were made colonels during the campaign; they were senior to me and had amply fulfilled their duties. Their promotion seemed to make mine the more certain since I now became the most senior squadron commander on the staff. The man in the fifth place was M. Barain, who was a captain when I joined the staff. M. Barain had lost a hand at Wagram, and was promoted to major, which was fair; however, the Emperor in advancing him to this rank had designated him for work in the arsenals, work which can easily be done with an arm missing. Massna had expected that M. Barain would remove himself, but the latter insisted on going with him to Portugal, although he could not carry out any mission in such difficult country. No one thought therefore that he would get any further promotion.

It so happened, however, that M. Barain was a nephew of M. Francois de Nantes, the director of legal codification, who had found numerous positions for members of Massna's family. M. Francois de Nantes demanded in return that his nephew, Barain, should be recommended for the rank of colonel. The marshal, forced to choose between me and Barain, chose Barain. I learned from the Comte de Lobau that the Emperor was reluctant to sign, but that he eventually yielded to the insistence of the worthy director who had come to add weight personally to the only

190

request he had yet made on the behalf of his family. So Barain was promoted to colonel.

I have perhaps dwelt a little overmuch on this regrettable affair, but to assess my disappointment it is necessary to think back to the period in question and recall the important position occupied by battalion commanders in the imperial army, which resulted in several instances of colonels who refused promotion to general and asked only to be left in command of their regiments.

Massna sent me the following letter, the only reward for three campaigns fought and three wounds recieved under his command.

Paris. 24th November. 1811

My dear Marbot, I send you the service order which I have received on your behalf. I asked for promotion for you, as you are aware, and I am doubly disappointed that you did not obtain this and that I am also to lose you. I have been very satisfied with your services; a satisfaction which you are entitled to feel, regardless of any rewards which this may bring. Your record will always do you credit in the eyes of those under whose orders you may find yourself. Please believe, my dear Marbot, in my appreciation, my regrets and my sincere good wishes for you.

Massna.

I had not expected to meet Massna again, but his wife wrote to me saying that she wished to meet my wife, and inviting us both to dinner. I had always had the highest regard for the conduct of Madame Massna, particularly at Antibes, her home territory, where I met her for the first time, on my return from Genoa. So I accepted the invitation. Massna came up to me and once more expressed his regrets, and suggested that he might ask for my nomination as an officer of the Legion of Honour. I replied that as he had been unable to do anything for me when I was on his staff, and wounded before his eyes, I would not like to expose him to any further embarrassment, and that I would now seek advancement by my own efforts; then I lost myself in the crowd of guests.

This was my last contact with Massna, though I continued to visit his wife and his son, both of them my firm friends.

Chap. 2.

I shall now give you some details of Massna's career. Andr Massna was born on the 6th of May 1758 at La Turbie, a village in the little state of Monaco. His paternal grandfather was a respected tanner who had three sons: Jules, the father of the marshal, Augustin and Marcel. The first two of these went to Nice, where they set up a soap-works. Marcel went to France where he enlisted in the Royal-Italian regiment. When Jules died, leaving very little money and five children, three of them, amongst whom was the young Andr, were taken in charge by their uncle Augustin, who having taught them no more than to read and write, employed them in soap-making.

Andr, who was active and adventurous, could not adjust to the monotonous and laborious work of the factory, and at the age of thirteen he abandoned his uncle's home and embarked, secretly, as a cabin-boy, in a merchant ship; accompanied by one of his cousins named Bavastro, who became, during the wars of the empire, the most celebrated corsaire of the Mediterranean. As for Andr, having spent two years at sea and even made a voyage to America, he rebelled against the hard life and harsh treatment which were the lot of the seaman, and enlisted as a private soldier in the Royal-Italian regiment, under the auspices of his uncle Marcel, who had reached the rank of sergeant-major, and was soon to be commissioned. This Marcel Massna, whom I met in 1800, when he was commandant of the fortress at Antibes, was a serious and capable man, highly thought of by his Colonel, M. Chauvet d'Arlon. To help his nephew, he had him taught to speak and write reasonable French, and, in spite of some escapades, had him promoted to the rank of warrant-officer. He even held out some hope of a commission in the mounted constabulary, but Andr, tired of waiting, left at the end of his engagement.

Having gone back to civilian life, without any money, Andr joined forces once more once more with his cousin Bavastro, and taking advantage of the close proximity of the frontiers of France, Piedmont, the State of Genoa, and the sea, they embarked on smuggling on a grand scale, not only along the coast but across the mountains, the various passes through which he got to know extremely well; knowledge which he later found most useful when he was in command of troops in this part of the country. Hardened by the rough trade of smuggling, and compelled always to keep one jump ahead of the customs officers, Massna acquired, without being aware of it, an understanding of the principles of warfare, as well as the vigilance and activity without which one cannot become a good officer. Having by this means got together some capital, he married a French woman, *Mlle*. Lamarre, the daughter of an Antibes surgeon, and settled in this town, where he had built up a small business in olive oil and dried Provencal fruit, when the Revolution of 1789 broke out.

Influenced by his taste for arms, Massna left his wife and his shop and enrolled in the 1st battalion of volunteers from Var. His practical and theoretical knowledge of military matters earned him the rank of captain, and shortly after, that of major. Fighting soon broke out, and the courage and skill displayed by Massna elevated him rapidly to the ranks of colonel and brigadier-general. He was put in command of a camp called "the camp of a thousand pitchforks," in part of which was the 4th artillery company, commanded by Captain Napoleon Bonaparte, under whose orders he would serve later in Italy. Entrusted with the command of a column at the siege of Toulon, he distinguished himself by the capture of the forts Lartigues and Sainte-Catherine, which led to his promotion to divisional general. After the town had fallen, he joined his troops to the army of Italy where he was prominent in all the engagements which took place in the area between the shores of the Mediterranean and Piedmont; country which he knew so well. Intelligent, ceaselessly active, and of boundless courage, Massna, after some years of success, had already a high reputation, when a grave mistake nearly brought his career to an end.

At the beginning of the campaign of 1796, General Bonaparte had just become commander-in-chief of the army, which placed Massna, once his senior in rank, under his command. Massna, who always led the advance-guard, having defeated near Cairo (Cairo in Piedmont, not Cairo in Egypt. Ed.) an Austrian unit, learned that the enemy officers had planned a celebratory dinner in the inn of a nearby village which they had been forced to abandon. He conceived the notion, together with some brother officers, of taking advantage of this windfall, and left his division camped on the top of a fairly high mountain.

However the Austrians recovered their nerve, and charging back, they fell on the French camp at daybreak. Our soldiers, although taken by surprise, defended themselves bravely, but with no general in control, they were driven back to the edge of the plateau where they had spent the night, and, attacked by greatly superior forces, looked certain to suffer a major defeat when Massna, having with his sabre cut his way through the Austrian scouts, ran up a path which he knew of old and appeared in front of his troops who, in their indignation, received him with well-deserved cat-calls. The general, without taking too much notice, resumed command and proceeded to march his division to rejoin the main body of the army. It was then seen that a battalion placed the night before on an isolated hillock could not come down by any practicable route without coming under enfilading fire from the enemy. Massna scrambled quickly up the hillside on his hands and knees and went alone to the battalion where he addressed the men and assured them that he would get then out of this fix if they would follow his example. Ordering them to sheathe their bayonets, he sat on the snow at the edge of slope, and pushing himself by his hands, he slid to the bottom of the valley....All our soldiers, in fits of laughter, did the same, and in no time the whole battalion was gathered together, out of the range of the baffled Austrians. This method of descent, used by the peasants and mountain guides of Switzerland, had surely never before been used by a battalion of troops of the line. I have been assured by generals who were in Massna's division at the time that this incident actually occurred, and, nine years later, I was at the chteau of La Houssaye, when Marshal Augereau entertained the Emperor and all the marshals and I heard them joking with Massna about the new method of retreat which he had used on this occasion.

It seems that on the day that Massna was making use of this odd expedient, which he had often used in the days when he was a smuggler, Bonaparte, realising that he was very young to be appointed commander-in-chief, and feeling on that account that he should come down hard on any officer who failed in his duty, ordered Massna to be brought before a court-martial and accused of abandoning his post, which could result in a sentence of death or at the least cashiering!... But at the moment when the general was about to be arrested there began the famous battle of Montenotte, in which Massna's and Augereau's divisions took two thousand prisoners, four flags and five artillery pieces, and completely routed the Austrian army. After this triumph, to which Massna had largely contributed, there could not be any question of putting him on trial. His misdeeds were forgotten, and he was able to continue his splendid career.

Massna distinguished himself at Lodi, Milan, Verona, and Arcoli, in fact everywhere that he was in action, and in particular at the battle of Rivoli. When the preliminaries of a peace had been signed at Leoben, Massna who had contributed so much to our victories, was entrusted with the task of taking the draft treaty to the government. Paris welcomed him with the most lively expressions of admiration, wherever he went people crowded round him to gaze on the features of this famous warrior. But this triumph was soon eclipsed by his exaggerated love of money, which was always his principal weakness.

General Duphot, the French ambassador in Rome, had been assassinated in that city. A part of the army of Italy, under the command of Berthier was ordered to go and exact vengeance; but Berthier was recalled by Bonaparte who wanted to take him to Egypt, and his place as commander of the army in Rome was taken by Massna. Soon after the arrival of this general, who was already accused of procuring a great deal of money during the Italian campaigns of the previous year, the army complained that it was in a state of destitution, without clothing and almost without bread, while the administration, drawing millions from the Papal states, lived in luxury and abundance. The army turned against him and sent a deputation of one hundred officers to demand from Massna an account for the expenditure of this money. Whether he was unable to account for it or whether he refused to do so as a matter of discipline Massna would not give any explanation, and as the troops persisted in their demand, he was forced to leave Rome and give up his command.

As soon as he had returned to France, he put out a memorandum justifying his conduct, which was badly received by the public and by his colleagues to whom he had addressed it. What upset him most was that General Bonaparte left for Egypt without replying to a letter which he had written to him concerning the matter.

However, a new coalition of Russia, Austria, and England having declared war on France, hostilities recommenced. In such circumstances, Massna, although he had not cleared himself from the accusations brought against him, could not remain in obscurity; so the Directory, in order to make use of his military talents, hurriedly gave him command of the French army whose duty it was to defend Switzerland. Massna at first did very well; but having rashly attacked the dangerous defile of Feldkirch, in the Vorarlberg, he was driven off with losses by the Austrians.

This was a time when our army of the Rhine, commanded by Jourdan, had just been defeated at Stockach by Prince Charles of Austria, and the forces which we had in Italy, defeated at Novi by the Russians under Souvarow, had lost their commander-in-chief, Joubert, killed on the field of battle. The Austrians, ready to cross the Rhine, threatened Alsace and Lorraine; Italy was in the hands of the Russians, whom Souvarow was leading into Switzerland through the Saint-Gothard pass. France, on the point of being invaded over both its frontiers, at the Rhine and at the Alps, pinned all its hopes on Massna, and was not disappointed in her expectations.

194

As you already know, the Directory, impatient for action, threatened Massna with dismissal unless he engaged the enemy; but he was determined not to do so until circumstances gave him a superiority, however brief, over his opponent. At last this moment arrived. The maladroit General Korsakoff, a former favourite of Catherine II, had unwisely pushed on towards Zurich at the head of 50,000 Russians and Bavarians to await his commander-in-chief, Souvarow, who was on his way from Italy with 55,000 men. Before the arrival of Souvarow, Massna pounced like a lion on Korsakoff, surprising him in his camp at Zurich and driving him back to the Rhine after inflicting tremendous losses! Then, turning on Souvarow, whom the heroic resistance of General Molitor had held up for three days in the Saint-Gothard, he defeated him as he had defeated his lieutenant, Korsakoff.

As a result of these various engagements 30,000 of the enemy were killed or taken prisoner, fifteen flags and sixty guns were captured, the independence of Switzerland was secured, and France was delivered from an imminent invasion. This was Massna's finest (and cleanest) hour.

I have already told how Massna took charge of the disorganised army of Italy, which, after the death of General Championnet, had been briefly commanded by my father, and described his conduct of the defence of Genoa, which gave Napoleon the time to collect a force together, cross the Alps, and fight the battle of Marengo.

After this victory the First Consul, on his return to France, thought he could not commit the command of the army of Italy to a more illustrious officer than Massna; but in a few months there were complaints similar to those made by the army in Rome. The dissatisfaction was widespread, new taxes were levied and frequent unpaid! The First Consul, when he learned of this state of affairs, immediately and without explanation withdrew the command of the army from Massna, who returned to private life, where he showed his annoyance by refusing to vote in favour of Napoleon's life-consulship. He also did not present himself at the new court.

When Bonaparte mounted the imperial throne and rewarded the generals who had done most for the country, he included Massna in the first list of marshals, awarded him the grand cordon of the Legion of Honour, and created him head of the fourteenth cohort of the order, which he had just established. These dignities and the enormous emoluments which were attached to them overcame the resistance put up by Massna since he was deprived of the command of the army of Italy. He voted for the empire, went to the Tuileries and assisted at the coronation ceremony.

When a third coalition menaced France, in 1805, the Emperor gave Messna the task of defending, with forty thousand men, the northern part of Ital, against the attacks of the Archduke Charles of Austria, who had eighty thousand. This was a difficult operation; but not only did Massna hold Lombardy, but he pushed the enemy back beyond the Tagliamento, and by forcing Prince Charles to turn and face him at frequent intervals, he so delayed the Austrian general's progress that he was unable to arrive in time to save Vienna, nor to join the Russian army which Napoleon defeated at Austerlitz. Napoleon, however, did not seem to appreciate the services rendered by Massna on this campaign; he reproached him for not having acted with his usual vigour, which did not prevent him, after the treaty of Presberg, from instructing him to go and conquer the kingdom of Naples, on whose throne he wished to place his brother, Prince Joseph.

Within a month the French occupied the whole of the country except the fortified town of Gaete, which Massna took after a siege. But while he was directing the attack against this town, he suffered a loss which rendered him inconsolable. An enormous sum, which Massna claimed belonged to him, was confiscated by the Emperor!

Napoleon, who believed that the best way of forcing the English to ask for peace was to ruin their trade, to prevent their goods from entering the continent, ordered them to be seized and burned in all the countries under his control, that is to say more than half of Europe. But the desire for money is very powerful and business men are very crafty. A fool-proof system of smuggling had been devised. English merchants who were in the scheme, sent off a ship or ships full of merchandise which allowed themselves to be captured by one of our corsairs, who would then take it to one of the ports occupied by our troops, from Swedish Pomerania to the end of the kingdom of Naples. This first act having been carried out, it remained to get the goods ashore without confiscation, this had already been arranged. The immensely long coastline presented by the conquered countries could not be watched in its entirety by customs officers, so this function was carried out by soldiers under the command of the generals who were in charge of the kingdom or province occupied by our troops. So it required only an authorisation from one of them to permit the goods to be landed, after which the traders negotiated with the "protector." This was called a "licence."

The origin of this new form of commerce goes back to the days when Bernadotte was occupying Hamburg and a part of Denmark. He made a considerable amount of money in this way, and when he wanted to reward someone, he would give the person a licence, which could then be sold to a merchant. This practice spread, little by little, to all the coasts of Germany, Spain and mainly to Italy. It even got as far as the Emperor's court, where ladies and chamberlains were given licences by ministers. Napoleon was not told of this, but he knew, or suspected, that it went on. Nevertheless, in order not to interfere too drastically with the usages of the conquered countries, he tolerated this abuse outside France as long as it was carried on clandestinely, but if he discovered that someone had made immoderate profits from the illicit trade, he made them cough up. For example, when the Emperor heard that M. Michaux, the administrative head of Bernadotte's army, had lost, in one evening, 300,000 francs, in a Paris gaming house, he directed an aide-de-camp to write to him saying that the Invalides was in need of money, and that he was ordered to pay 300,000 francs into their account; which Michaux, who had made so much money from licences, hastened to do.

As you may imagine, Massna was not the last to engage in the business of selling licences. Together with General Solignac, his chief of staff, he flooded all the ports of Naples with them. When the Emperor was informed that Massna had deposited the sum of three million with a banker at Leghorn, who had taken at the same time 600,000 from General Solignac, he had a request sent to Massna for a loan of one million, and one for 200,000 francs from his chief of staff. Just one third of their illegal gains, which was not fleecing them too greatly. However, at the sight of this demand, Massna, bellowing as if he were being disembowelled, replied to Napoleon that as the poorest of the marshals, with a numerous family and crippling debts, he profoundly regretted that he could not send him anything! And general replied in similar terms.

They were congratulating themselves on having evaded these requests when, during the siege of Gaeta, the son of the Leghorn banker arrived to say that a French treasury inspector, escorted by a commissioner of police and a number of gendarmes, had arrived at his father's establishment and had demanded to see the accounts in which were recorded the deposits made by the marshal and general Solignac, stating that these sums belonged to the army, and had been entrusted to the two officers concerned, and that the Emperor demanded their immediate return, either in cash or negotiable bonds, and the cancellation of the receipts given to Massna and Solignac. A legal endorsement was given to this seizure which the banker, having nothing to lose, did not oppose.

It is impossible to describe Massna's fury on finding that he had been deprived of his fortune. It made him quite ill, but he did not dare to make any complaint when the Emperor, who was then in Poland, sent for him.

After the peace of Tilsit, the title of Duke of Rivoli and an award of 300,000 francs of income were a recompense for his services, but did not console him for what had been taken from him at Leghorn, for, in spite of his usual caution, he was heard to say on a number of occasions "I think it cruel that, while I was fighting in his interest, he had the gall to take the small savings I had banked at Leghorn!"

The invasion of Spain having sparked off a new war with Austria, the Emperor, threatened by these considerable forces, hurried back from the peninsula to go to Germany, to where he had already sent Massna. I have already described the part played by the marshal in the campaign of 1809. As a reward for his conduct at Essling and Wagram, the Emperor created him Prince of Essling and gave him an additional income of 500,000 francs, which was added to his previous award of 300,000 francs and his salary of 200,000 as marshal and army commander. The new prince had no more than that.

The campaigns of 1810 and 1811 in Spain and Portugal were Massna's last. They were not very happy; his morale had gone down and the two campaigns, instead of adding to his fame, lowered his reputation. The "Enfant chri de la victoire," as he had been named, suffered reverses where he could and should have been successful.

Massna was thin and bony, and of less than average height. His Italian features were full of expression. The bad sides to his character were hypocrisy, spite, harshness, and avarice. He had plenty of natural intelligence but his adventurous youth and the lowly position of his family had not encouraged him to study; he was totally lacking in what one calls education. In the heyday of his career he had a keen eye and a decisive mind and was not dismayed by a reverse. As he aged his caution began to verge on timidity, so anxious was he not to besmirch the reputation he had acquired. He hated reading, so he had no idea of what had been written on the principles of warfare, he acted intuitively, and Napoleon summed him up accurately when he said the Massna arrived on the battlefield without knowing what he was going to do, his actions were determined by circumstances.

It has been wrongly said that Massna was a stranger to flattery, and spoke his mind fearlessly even to the Emperor. Beneath his rough exterior Massna was a shrewd courtier. When in the course of a pheasant shoot, Napoleon had the misfortune to pepper Massna, injuring one of his eyes, Massna laid the blame on Berthier, although only Napoleon had fired a shot. Everyone understood perfectly the discretion of the courtier, and Massna was overwhelmed by attentions from the Emperor.

Although very miserly, the victor of Zurich would have given half his fortune to have been born in the France of the "Ancien Rgime" rather than on the left bank of the Var. Nothing displeased him more than the Italian termination to his name, of which he transformed the "a" to "e" in his signature. However the public did not adopt this change, and Massna he remained in spite of his efforts. The campaign in Portugal had so much weakened Massna physically and mentally, that he was obliged to seek rest and recuperation in the gentle climate of Nice, where he stayed for the whole of 1812; but Napoleon, returning from the disastrous invasion of Russia, and scouring Europe for further resources, thought that the name of Massna could still be of service, particularly in Provence. So he appointed him governor of the 8th military division.

When, in 1814, enemy forces invaded France, Massna, who, in any case, had few troops at his disposal, did nothing to arrest their progress, and on the 15th April he surrendered to the Duc d'Angoulme, who created him a Commander of Saint Louis, but would abroad, and had never become a naturalised French citizen! ... As if the victories of Rivoli, Zurich, the defence of Genoa, and a series of other successful actions on the behalf of France were not worth as much as naturalisation papers, given often to scheming foreigners for cash. The treatment given to Massna in these circumstances had a very adverse effect on sentiment in the public and the army, and was an additional source of the disenchantment of the nation with the government of Louis XVIII, which led to the return of the Emperor.

Napoleon disembarked near to Cannes on 1st March 1815 and set off immediately for Paris at the head of about a thousand Grenadiers of his Guard. The unexpectedness and swiftness of this invasion threw Massna into confusion. Nevertheless, he tried to stem the torrent by calling together some line regiments and activating the national guard of Marseilles and district; but having learned that the Duc d'Angoulme had surrendered and left the country, he sent his son to inform Louis XVIII that he could no longer rely on his support, and rallying to the imperial government, he hoisted the tricolour throughout the area and locked up the prefect of

Var, who still wanted to resist. By this conduct Massna alienated both the Royalists and the Bonapartists; so when the Emperor hurriedly summoned him to Paris, he greeted him very coolly.

When, soon afterwards, Napoleon made the great mistake of abdicating for the second time, following the battle of Waterloo, the Chamber of Representatives seized power and formed a provisional government whose first act was to invest Massna with the command of the national guard of Paris. It was hoped that, although his infirmities prevented him playing any active rôle, his name would inspire the populace to support the army in the defence of the capital, but when a council of war was assembled, Massna gave it as his opinion that Paris could not be defended! As a consequence an armistice was agreed with the enemy generals and the French army withdrew across the Loire, where it was disbanded.

Once the allies were masters of France, Louis XVIII, to punish Massna for having abandoned his cause after March 20th, included him among the judges who were to try Marshal Ney, hoping that out of enmity he would condemn his former colleague and so besmirch his good name; but Massna recused himself on the grounds that there had been disagreements between him and Marshal Ney in Portugal, and when this measure failed he joined with those judges who wanted Ney brought before the House of Peers. They had hoped to save him, but it would have been better if they had had the political courage to try him and acquit him....They did not dare! Ney was condemned and shot, but his blood did not pacify the Royalists, they became more implacable and soon pursued Massna himself.

The citizens of Marseilles, on whose behalf Massna had used his influence to obtain the freedom of their port, now denounced him to the Chamber of Deputies on the grounds of peculation. There was no evidence to support this charge, as Massna had never exacted any money in Provence, and the chamber, although known for its hatred of the leading figures of the empire, rejected the petition out of hand.

Massna, having escaped from the wave of reaction which was now sweeping the country, abandoned the stage on which he had played so brilliant a part, and retired to his chteau of Rueil, which had once belonged to Cardinal Richelieu, to end his splendid career in solitude and disgrace. He died on the 4th April 1817, at the age of fifty-nine.

At his death, the government had not sent the baton which is by custom placed on the bier of a marshal, so his son-in-law, General Reille, claimed this insignia from the minister for war, a fervent Royalist. When he received no reply to this reasonable request, in an act of courage, rare at the time, he let it be known to the court that if a baton did not arrive in time for his father-in-law's funeral, he would place ostentatiously on his coffin, the baton awarded to him by the Emperor. The government then decided that they would supply a baton after all.

I have touched on some of the blemishes which mar his career, but Massna more than compensated for them by the remarkable and heroic services he rendered to

France. He will be remembered as one of the great captains of an era which produced so many.

Chap. 3.

At the beginning of 1812, I was in Paris, with my young wife and our families. But the happiness which I enjoyed was lessened by the thought of my imminent departure. I was due to join the 1st Chasseurs Cheval as a squadron commander with the rank of Major. The chagrin which I felt at not having been promoted to Colonel, which I thought I deserved, was somewhat relieved when, having gone to the Tuileries to pay my new year respects, the Emperor sent an aide-de-camp to command my presence in his private quarters, where I found General Mouton, Comte de Lobau, who had always been on my side.

Napoleon appeared and told me in the most friendly manner that he had intended to give me a regiment, but that there were certain reasons which had led him to nominate Major Barain. He said that having promoted three of Massna's aides to Colonel he could not accord any more promotions to one general staff, but that he had not forgotten me and although he could not give me the nominal command, he would put me in the position of being, in effect, a regimental commander. "The commanding officer of the 23rd Mounted Chasseurs, M. de La Nougarde, has become so afflicted by gout that he can hardly mount a horse", the Emperor said, "but he is an excellent officer who has fought several campaigns with me, and I have a high regard for him. He has begged me to let him try to go once more on campaign and I do not wish to remove him from his regiment. However, I hear that this fine unit is going down hill in his hands so I am sending you as "Coadjutor" to M. de La Nougarde. You will be working for yourself, for if the Colonel recovers his health I shall promote him to general, and if not I shall transfer him to the gendarmes. In either case he will leave his regiment and you will become their colonel; so I repeat you will be working for your own benefit." This promise gave me renewed hope, and I was making ready to leave when the minister for war extended my leave until the end of March, which I found very acceptable.

The 23rd Chasseurs were stationed in Swedish Pomerania, so I had an enormous distance to travel, and as I wished to arrive before the expiration of my leave, I left Paris on the 15th of March, parting with much regret from my dear wife. I had bought a good barouche, in which, at the request of Marshal Mortier, I gave a seat to his nephew, Lieutenant Durbach, who belonged to the regiment which I was about to join. As my former servant, Woirland, had asked if he might stay in Spain, where he hoped to make his fortune running a canteen, I had replaced him, on my leaving Salamanca, by a Pole named Lorentz Schilkowski. This man, at one time an Austrian Uhlan, was not lacking intelligence, but, like all Poles he was a drunkard, and unlike the soldiers of that nation, he was as timid as a hare. Lorentz, however, as well as his native language, spoke passable French and fluent German and Russian, and for this reason he was most valuable to me in my travelling and campaigning in the north. I was nearing the Rhenish provinces, when on leaving Kaiserslauten at night, the postilion tipped my barouche into a pothole, where it was damaged. No one was hurt, but both M. Durbach and I agreed that this was a bad omen for soldiers who were about to face the enemy. However, after spending a day waiting for repairs to be made, we were able to get under way once more. Unfortunately the accident had so weakened the springs and the wheels that they broke six times during our journey, which delayed us considerably, and on occasions forced us to walk for several leagues in the snow. We arrived at last at the shores of the Baltic sea, where the 23rd Chasseurs were in garrison at Stralsund and Greifswald.

I found Colonel de La Nougarde to be an excellent officer, well-informed and capable, but so prematurely aged by gout that he was hardly able to sit on a horse, and went everywhere in a carriage, a most unsuitable method of transport for the commander of a regiment of light cavalry! He gave me an enthusiastic welcome, and after explaining the reasons which, in the interest of his career, made him stay with the regiment, he showed me a letter in which the Comte de Lobau informed him of the motives which had led the Emperor to attach me to him. M. de La Nougarde, far from being offended, saw this as another kindness on the part of the Emperor, and looked forward to being promoted to general or heading the gendarmerie. He counted, with my help, on completing at least part of the campaign, and on the realisation of his hopes at the first imperial revue. To make it clear that I shared the command, which was not in keeping with my rank as Major, he called together all the officers, in front of whom he provisionally delegated all his powers to me, until such time as he recovered his health, and instructed them to obey my orders without referring to him, since his illness often made it impossible for him to follow the regiment sufficiently closely to command it in person. An order of the day was issued along these lines, and from that day forward, except for the rank,I was virtually the commander of the regiment, and the regiment soon got into the habit of looking on me as their real leader.

Since that time, I have commanded several cavalry regiments, either as colonel or general. And I was for a long time inspector of this branch of the service; I can say with certainty that if I have seen units as good as the 23rd Chasseurs, I have never seen one better. It was not that the unit contained any outstanding personalities, such as I have seen sometimes in other regiments, but if there was not in the 23rd any one of remarkable talents, there was no one who did not maintain a high standard in carrying out his duties. There were no peaks, but there were no troughs; everyone kept in step. The officers were intelligent, well trained and well behaved. They lived together as true brothers-in-arms. The same applied to the N.C.O.s. And the troopers followed this good example. They were almost all old soldiers, veterans of Austerlitz, Jena, Friedland, Wagram, a fine body of men who came mostly from Normandy, Alsace, Lorraine and Franche-comte, provinces known for their martial spirit and their love of horses. The build and strength of these men was noticed by General Bourcier, who was in charge of remounts, and he supplied the regiment with horses which were bigger and more lively than the usual issue. A period of several years spent in the fertile land of Germany, had left both men and horses in splendid condition, and the regiment, when I took over, consisted of a thousand officers and men, well disciplined, calm and quiet in the face of the enemy.

I did not yet have a horse, so I went to Stralsund in the isle of Rugen, where they have excellent horses, and I bought several; I got some others from Rostock and ended with a stable of seven good beasts, which was not too many, as war with Russia appeared imminent. I had already forecast this during the summer of 1811, when I saw the great number of old soldiers whom the Emperor was taking from the regiments in the peninsula to reinforce his Old Guard. I had been confirmed in this opinion during my stay in Paris. There were, at first, some distant rumours of a rupture, which vanished quickly amid the entertainments and festivities of winter, but soon returned with increased insistence; and became almost certainties as a result of a serious event, the echoes of which reverberated throughout Europe.

The Emperor Alexander had had, since boyhood, a companion who was a young Russian nobleman, named Czernicheff, of whom he was very fond, and whom, when he came to the throne, he took as aide-de-camp.

In 1809, when Alexander, who was then an ally of Napoleon, was pretending, without actually doing so, to make war against Austria, whose country Napoleon had invaded, there arrived in Vienna Colonel the Comte de Czernicheff, on the ostensible mission to cement good relations between Napoleon and Alexander, but in reality to inform his sovereign of our success or failure, so that he could continue or break off his alliance with France according to circumstances.

Alexander's favourite received the friendliest of welcomes from Napoleon, whose side he never left during the parades and manoeuvres which preceded the battle of Essling, but when this bloody affair appeared to be in the balance, and a hail of bullets descended on the imperial general staff, M. de Czernicheff turned tail rapidly, and crossing the bridges over the Danube, he sought the safety of the palace of Schoenbrunn; and the day after the battle he took to the road for Petersburg, to announce, no doubt, the failure of our enterprise. Napoleon thought this behaviour most unbecoming, and made some jeering comments on the "bravery" of the Russian colonel. Nevertheless, after peace had been made with Austria, M. de Czernicheff came very often to Paris, where he spent part of the years 1810 and 1811. Handsome, courteous, likeable, highly deceitful and exquisitely polite, his title of aide-de-camp to the Russian emperor gave him entry not only to the court but also to the salons of high society, where he never discussed politics, and appeared to be interested only in the pursuit of women, where he was said to have considerable success. But toward the end of 1811, when new rumours of war began to circulate, the Paris police were informed that while appearing to be solely interested in pleasure, the Russian colonel was mixed up in some dubious political schemes, and he was put under close surveillance, when it was discovered that he had frequent meetings with M. X..., an employee of the ministry for war who had special responsibility for the situation reports concerning all the personel and material of the army, which were given to Napoleon every ten days. Not only had M. de Czernicheff been seen walking after midnight in the most secluded part of the Champs-Elysees with this man, but he had been observed, plainly dressed, slipping into the place where M. X... lived and spending several hours there.

The intimacy of someone so highly placed with a poor devil of clerk in the ministry for war being clear evidence that the former had seduced the latter to betray state secrets, the Emperor, highly indignant, ordered the arrest of M.Czernicheff, but Czernicheff, warned, it is said, by a woman, fled from Paris, and reached a nearby "relais" from where, taking unfrequented roads, he managed to reach the frontier, avoiding Maintz and Cologne to where the telegraph had transmitted the order for his seizure. As for the wretched clerk, he was apprehended at the moment when he was counting out the 300,000 francs which he had received for his act of treason. Compelled by the evidence to admit to his crime, he stated that another employee had also given information to the Russian, this man too was arrested, and the two of them were tried, convicted and shot. They died cursing Czernicheff, who they claimed had come to their attics to tempt them with a heap of gold which he increased whenever they hesitated. The Emperor had published in all the French newspapers a virulent denunciation of M. de Czernicheff, with some wounding observations which, although indirect, pointed to the emperor of Russia himself, for they recalled that the assassins of his father, Paul I, had not been punished by Alexander.

After these events, it was no longer possible to doubt that war was imminent, and although it had not been declared, both sides were openly preparing for it. The conduct of M. de Czernicheff was, in general, loudly denounced, but it had its secret supporters among the diplomatic community, who recalled that although Napoleon justly punished French citizens who sold their country's secrets to its enemies, he was not above corrupting foreign nationals who could give him useful information, particularly of a military nature.

Marshal Lannes told me,that in Vienna,in 1809, when hostilities were about to break out between France and Austria, whose armies were to be commanded by the Arch-Duke Charles, this prince was warned anonymously that a Major-general for whom he had a high regard and whom he was about to take on to his staff, had been bought by the French ambassador, General Andreossi, with whom he had frequent night-time meetings in a lonely house in the vast suburb of Leopoldstadt, the number of which was disclosed. Prince Charles thought so highly of this officer that he dismissed as an infamous calumny the anonymous accusation, and took no measures to determine the truth. The French ambassador had already asked for his passport and was due to leave Vienna in forty-eight hours time, when a second anonymous note informed the archduke that his assistant chief-of-staff, after working alone in his office, which contained the order of battle for the army, was going to have, on the following night, a last meeting with General Andreossi. The archduke, who wished to clear his mind of any suspicions which he might have,, in spite of himself, about an officer of whom he was fond, decided that he would prove, beyond doubt, that he was innocent. So, dressed very simply, and accompanied by only one aide-de-camp, he waited, after midnight, in the darkest part of the lane where the house in question was situated. After a short time the prince and his aide saw, with sadness, a man who in spite of his disguise was easily recognised as the assistant chief-of-staff, for whom, after an agreed signal, the door was opened. Soon he was followed by General Andreossi who was admitted in the same way. The meeting lasted for some hours, during which the archduke, no longer able to doubt the treachery of his assistant chief-of-staff, waited patiently outside the house, and when the door opened for General Andreossi and the Austrian general, who, came out together, they found themselves face to face with Prince Charles, who said aloud, "Good evening, Mr.Ambassador" and refraining from speaking to the assistant chief-of-staff, he shone the light from a lantern in his face.

The ambassador hurried away without saying a word, and as for the assistant chief-of-staff, seeing that he was caught in the act and knowing the fate which awaited him, he went to his house and blew his brains out with a pistol shot. This tragic event was hushed up by the Austrian government and not many people knew about it; it was announced that the assistant chief-of-staff had died of apoplexy. The French ambassador was said to have paid him two million.

While Napoleon was complaining bitterly about the means by which Colonel Czernicheff obtained information about our armies, General Lauriston, our ambassador in Petersburg, bought not only the most detailed information about the disposition of the Russian forces, but also the copper plates on which were engraved the immense map of the Muscovite empire. In spite of the great difficulties presented by the transport of this heavy mass of metal, the betrayal was so well organised and so lavishly paid for that these plates, stolen from the Russian archives, were taken from St.Petersburg to France without their disappearance being discovered by the police or the Russian customs. When the plates arrived in Paris the minister for war, when all the writing had been changed from Russian characters into French, had this fine map printed, and Napoleon ordered a copy to be sent to all the generals and commanders of light cavalry regiments. It was in this latter rank that I received one, which I contrived, with much difficulty to save during the retreat, for it forms a very big roll. Few people brought theirs back, but I still have mine.

Chap. 4.

The principal reason which led the Emperor to declare war on Russia was his desire to see the implementation of the treaty of Tilsit, whereby the Emperor Alexander agreed to close all the ports of his country to English traders, an undertaking which had never been properly carried out. Napoleon thought, rightly, that he could ruin the English, a manufacturing and trading nation, by preventing their commerce with the European continent; but the execution of this gigantic project offered so much difficulty, that it was only in France that the restrictions were enforced, and there the use of licences, to which I have referred above, made an enormous breach in the regulations. As for Italy, Germany and the Adriatic provinces, although the continental system was established by imperial decree, it was only implemented in theory, partly because of the extent of the coastline, and partly because of connivance and lack of surveillance by those responsible for the administration of these vast areas. So the Russian Emperor replied to the demands made by France by pointing to the state of affairs which was almost universal in Europe. The true cause, however, of the refusal of Alexander to accede to the demands of Napoleon, was that he feared that he would be assassinated in the same manner as his father, the Emperor Paul, who was accused firstly of having sullied the nation's reputation by allying himself to France and secondly of having destroyed Russian trade by declaring war on Britain. Alexander was aware that he had already given offence by the deference and friendliness which he had shown towards Napoleon at Tilsit and Erfurt, and he was anxious not to arouse more anger by cutting off all trade with England, the sole outlet whereby the Russian nobility could dispose of the products of their vast estates, and acquire a monetary income. The death of the Emperor Paul clearly showed the danger faced by Alexander, if he followed his father's example. An additional cause of fear was the fact that he was surrounded by the same officers who had surrounded his father, amongst whom was his chief-of-staff, Benningsen.

Napoleon did not take sufficiently into consideration these difficulties, when he threatened Alexander with war, unless he fell in with his wishes; although, when he learned of the losses and reverses suffered in Spain and Portugal, he seemed hesitant to engage in a conflict the outcome of which he deemed uncertain.

According to General Bertrand, Napoleon, on St. Helena said repeatedly that his only intention, to begin with, was to frighten Alexander into carrying out the terms of the treaty: "We were" he said, "like two opponents of equal ability, who are well able to fight, but being reluctant to do so, menace each other by threats and sabre-rattling, edging slowly forward, each hoping that his adversary will retreat rather than do battle"; but the Emperor's comparison was not exact, for one of these swordsmen had behind him a bottomless pit, ready to engulf him at the first backward step, so that having to choose between an ignominious death and a combat in which he might be successful he had to choose the latter. This was the situation in which Alexander found himself, a situation made worse by the influence exerted by the Englishman Wilson on General Benningsen and the officers of his staff. The Emperor Napoleon was still hesitant and seemed anxious to consult the sage opinions of Caulincourt, his former ambassador at St. Petersburg and those of a group of French officers who had lived for some time in Russia.

Among the latter was Lieutenant-colonel de Ponthon, who had been among a number of engineer officers who, after the Treaty of Tilsit had been posted, at the request of Alexander, to Russia, where they had spent several years. De Ponthon was a highly competent, but withal a very modest officer, he was attached to the topographic service, and did not think it was his place to offer his advice unasked, on the problems which would face an army at war in the Russian empire; but when he was questioned by the Emperor he felt it was his duty to tell the whole truth to the head of state, even at risk of displeasing him, so he described all the obstacles which would face this enterprise. The principal ones were the apathy and lack of co-operation between the Lithuanian states, subject for many years to Russia; the fanatical resistance to be expected from the people of Moscow; the scarcity of food and forage; the almost uninhabited areas which would have to be crossed; roads impassable for artillery after several hours of rain; but above all he stressed the rigour of the winter and the physical impossibility of conducting a war once the snow had begun to fall, which might be as early as the first days of October. Finally, at risk of giving offence and jeopardising his career, he begged Napoleon, for the sake of France and his own reputation, not to undertake this dangerous expedition, the calamitous outcome of which he now predicted. Having listened quietly to M. de Ponthon, the Emperor dismissed him without making any comment. For some days he appeared withdrawn and contemplative, and the rumour spread that the undertaking was off, but then M. Maret, Duc de Bassano, persuaded him to go back to his original intention, and assured him that Marshal Davout would be happy to move his large army of Germany to the banks of the Nieman, on the frontier of the Russian empire, in order to galvanise Alexander into action.

From this time on, although M. de Ponthon was in constant attendance as a member of the cabinet, the Emperor did not address a word to him during the advance from the Nieman to Moscow, and when, during the retreat, Napoleon was forced to admit to himself that the predictions of this admirable officer had been only too accurate, he avoided catching his eye. Nevertheless, he promoted him to the rank of colonel. . .

To return to the preparations which Napoleon was making to force the Russians, by hook or by crook, to comply with his wishes: from the month of April, the French troops stationed in Germany, as well as those of various princes of the Germanic confederation allied to France, were put into motion, and their march towards Poland was delayed only by the difficulty of finding forage for their numerous horses; the grass, and even the corn being scarcely out of the ground at this time in these northern countries. However, the Emperor left Paris on the 9th of May, and accompanied by the Empress, went to Dresden, where, awaiting him, were his father-in-law the Emperor of Austria, and almost all the German princes; attracted there, in some cases by the hope of having their domains extended, and in others by the fear of displeasing the arbiter of their destiny. The only absentee was the King of Prussia, who, not being included in the confederation of the Rhine, was not invited to this reunion and dared not turn up without the permission of Napoleon. He humbly requested this, and when it was obtained he hurried to Dresden to pay court to the all-powerful conqueror of Europe.

The protestations of fidelity and devotion which were lavished on Napoleon misled him into making a most serious error in the organisation of the contingents which were to make up the great army destined for the war against Russia. Instead of weakening the governments of Austria and Prussia, his former enemies, by demanding from them the greater part of their available troops, which, prudence would suggest should be placed in the van, not only to spare French lives, but to allow a watch to be kept on these new and undependable allies, Napoleon required no more than 30,000 men from each of these powers, and placed them on the two wings of his force. The Austrians under Prince Schwartzenberg on the right in Volhynie, and the Prussians, to whom he appointed as commander the French Marshal Macdonald, on the left, near the mouth of the Nieman. The centre was composed of French troops and those members of the German federation whose loyalty had been proved at Jena and Wagram.

There were discerning observers who were dismayed to see the wings of the army made up of foreigners, who, in the event of a reverse, could form two hostile armies in our rear, while the centre was embroiled in the heart of Russia. Not only that,

Austria who had an army of 200,000, placed only 30,000 at the disposal of Napoleon, and had 170,000 left with which to attack us in the event of failure, while Prussia, though less powerful, still had 60,000 men in reserve.

One is astonished that the Emperor was so little concerned about what he was leaving behind him; but his confidence was so great that when the King of Prussia requested him to allow his eldest son to join in the campaign as an imperial aide-de-camp, Napoleon turned him down, although the young prince would have been a valuable hostage to ensure the fidelity of his father.

While there was a succession of entertainments at Dresden, Napoleon's troops were wending their way through northern Germany. Already the army of Italy, having crossed the mountains of the Tyrol, was heading for Warsaw. The 1st, 2nd and 3rd Corps commanded by Davout, Oudinot and Ney, were passing through Prussia on their march to the Vistula. The states comprising the confederation of the Rhine had supplied their contingents, as had Austria and Prussia; it was noticeable, however that although the Austrian generals were happy to unite their flags with ours, the junior officers and the soldiers were reluctant to attack Russia, while the situation was reversed in the Prussian army, where the generals and Colonels felt humiliated by being compelled to serve under the command of their conqueror, while officers of lower rank and the soldiers, were pleased to have the opportunity of fighting alongside the French, and hoped to show that if they were defeated at Jena, it was not through any lack of courage on their part, but due to poor leadership by their superiors.

Napoleon had not only taken into the "Grande Arme" the troops of Austria and Prussia, but he had lowered the morale of the French forces by intermingling them with foreign contingents, so that the various Corps commanded by his marshals contained bodies of men from every part of Europe, Italians, Poles, Spaniards, Portuguese, Germans and Croatians. This admixture of races with different languages, cultures and interests, worked very poorly, and often hindered the efforts of the French troops. It was one of the principal causes of the reversals which we suffered.

Chap. 5.

Having left Dresden on the 29th of May, the Emperor made his way towards Poland via Danzig and the old Prussia, through which his troops were passing, whom he reviewed whenever he encountered them.

The army was now organised so that the 23rd Mounted Chasseurs were brigaded with the 24th. This brigade was commanded by General Castex and formed part of the 2nd Army Corps, commanded by Marshal Oudinet. I had known General Castex for a long time, an excellent officer, who treated me very well throughout the campaign. Marshal Oudinet had seen me at the siege of Genoa when I was with my father and also in Austria when I was aide-de-camp to Marshal Lannes, and was well disposed towards me.

On the 20th June, 2nd Corps was given the order to stop at Insterberg in order to be reviewed by the Emperor. These military ceremonies were awaited with impatience by those people who hoped to benefit from the awards distributed on the occasion by Napoleon. I was among this number. I felt sure that I would be promoted to the command of the regiment of which I was the acting commander, for apart from the promises given me by the Emperor, General Castex and Marshal Oudinothad had told me that they intended to propose me officially, and that Colonel Nougarde was to be posted, as general, to command of one of the huge remount depots, which would have to be set up in the rear of the army; but the bad luck which had, a few months earlier delayed my promotion to major , also held up my promotion to colonel.

At these reviews, the commanders of regiments were subjected to a rigourous cross-examination by the Emperor, particularly on the eve of a campaign; for apart from the usual questions about their strength in men and horses, their arms *etc.*, he would suddenly ask a number which were unforeseen and not always easy to answer. For example: "How many men from such and such a department have you received in the last two years? How many of your carbines come from Tulle and how many from Charleville? How many of your horses are from Normandy, from Brittany, from Germany? What is the average age of your men, your officers, your horses? How many men in this company have long-service chevrons? *etc...*etc."

These questions, which were always posed in an abrupt and demanding manner, and accompanied by a piercing look, disconcerted many colonels; but woe to him who hesitated to reply, he went into Napoleon's bad books. I was so well briefed that I was able to reply to all his questions, and, after complementing me on the fine turnout of the regiment, it looked as if the Emperor was going to promote me to colonel and M. de La Nougarde to general, when the latter, who with his limbs wrapped in flannel, had been hoisted onto horseback to follow from afar the movements of his regiment, which I commanded, hearing himself called for, came to Napoleon, and unwisely angered him by making a request on behalf of an officer, a member of his family, who was wholly undeserving. This roused a storm of which I suffered the consequences. The Emperor flew into a rage and ordered the Gendarmerie to clear the officer in question out of the army, and leaving M. de La Nougarde in dismay, he went off at the gallop. So M. de La Nougarde was not made a general.

Marshal Oudinot followed the Emperor to find out what was to happen to the 23rd, and was told "Major Marbot will continue to command them." Before reaching the rank of colonel I was destined to suffer yet another serious wound.

In fairness to M. de La Nougarde, I have to say that he expressed the liveliest remorse at having been the involuntary cause of the delay in my advancement. I was sorry for the difficult position in which this worthy man found himself, for he felt that he had forfeited the Emperor's confidence, and owing to his disability he had little hope of restoring himself by his conduct in the battles which were about to take place.

I was comforted by the fact that the Emperor, on the day of the review, had awarded all the promotions and the decorations which I had requested for the officers and other ranks of the 23rd, and as the gratitude for these favours is always directed to the commanding officer who has obtained them, the influence which I was beginning to have in the regiment was greatly increased and went some way to calm my regrets at not having been awarded substantive rank for the position which I occupied.

At about this time, I received a letter from Marshal Massna and another from his wife, the first recommending a M. Renique, and the second her son, Prosper. I was touched by this double approach and I responded by accepting the two captains into my regiment. However, Madame Massna did not carry out her intention, and Prosper Massna did not go to Russia. In any case he would not have been able to stand the harsh climate.

The army was soon to reach the frontier of the Russian empire, and see once more the river Nieman, where we had stopped in 1807. The Emperor positioned his troops on the left bank of this river as follows: on the extreme right was the Austrian Corps of Prince Schwartzenberg, on the border of Galicia near Drogitchin. On Schwartzenberg's left was King Jrme with two considerable army corps, between Bialystok and Grodno. Next to them was Prince Eugne de Beauharnais, with 80,000 men, at Prenn. The Emperor was in the centre, facing Kovno, with 220,000 men commanded by Murat, Oudinot, Ney, Lefebvre and Bessires. The Guard formed part of this immense body of troops. Finally, at Tilsit, Marshal Macdonald with 35,000 Prussians formed the left wing. Across the Nieman was the Russian army of about 400,000 men, commanded by the Emperor Alexander, or rather by Benningsen, his chief-of-staff. This force was divided into three parts, commanded by Generals Bagration, Barclay de Tolly and Wittgenstein.

Four historians have written about the campaign of 1812. The first of these was Labaume, a topographer, that is to say, belonging to a corps which although part of the armed forces never engaged in combat, and followed the army only to make maps. Labaume had never commanded troops and knew nothing of the practical side of war, so his judgements are almost always ill-founded and do an injustice to the French army. However, as the work apppeared shortly after the peace of 1814 and the re-establishment of Louis XVIII, partisan spirit and the desire for information about the terrible events of the Russian campaign gave it so much credence that no one tried to refute it, and the public came to accept its contents as the veritable truth.

The second book to be published was written by Colonel Boutourlin, an aide-de-camp to the Emperor Alexander. This, although expressing the Russian point of view, contained some worthwhile observations, and if there are some inaccuracies, it is because he did not have access to certain documents, for he is impartial and has done all he could to discover the truth. The work is generally esteemed as that of an honest man.

Labaume's book had already been forgotten when in 1825, following Napoleon's death, General de Sgur published a third story of the Russian campaign. The contents of this book distressed more than one survivor of the campaign, and even the Russians stigmatised it as a war novel. In spite of this, M. de Sgur enjoyed a great success, partly because of the purity and elegance of his style and partly because of the welcome the book was given by the court and the ultra-royalist party. The former officers of the imperial army, finding themselves under attack, appointed General Gourgaud to reply. He did so effectively, but with so much acerbity that it gave rise to a duel between him and M. de Sgur, in which M. de Sgur was wounded. One has to agree that if the latter was less than charitable towards Napoleon and his army, General Gourgaud accorded the Emperor too much praise, and refused to recognise any of his faults.

I have no intention of writing another history of the campaign of 1812, but I think I should relate the principal events, since they form an essential part of my life and times and several of them have a bearing on what happened to me; but in this brief resum I shall try to avoid the extremes embraced by Sgur and Gourgaud. I shall neither denigrate nor flatter, I shall be truthful.

At a time when the two powerful European empires were about to come to blows, England, a natural ally of Russia, had a duty to make every effort to help her to repel the invasion projected by Napoleon. By disbursing money to the Turkish ministers, the English cabinet was able to arrange a peace between the Sultan and Russia, which allowed the latter to recall the army which was on the frontier of Turkey, an army which played a highly important rle in the war. The English had also contrived a peace between the Emperor Alexander and Sweden, an ally of France, on whose goodwill Napoleon counted, the more so because Bernadotte had just been nominated as the heir apparent, and governed the country for the King, his adoptive father.

I have already explained how, through a bizarre sequence of events, Bernadotte was raised to the rank of heir presumptive to the crown of Sweden. The new Swedish prince, after announcing that he would always remain French at heart, allowed himself to be seduced or intimidated by the English, who could have easily overthrown him. He sacrificed the true interests of his adoptive country by submitting to the domination of England and allying himself with Russia in an interview with the Emperor Alexander. This meeting took place in Abo, a little town in Finland. The Russians had recently seized this province and they promised to compensate Sweden by the gift of Norway, which they intended to take from Denmark, which was a faithful ally of France. So Bernadotte, far from relying on our army to restore to him his provinces, accepted these Russian encroachments by ranging himself with her allies.

If Bernadotte had been willing to support us, the geographical position of Sweden could have been of great assistance to our common cause. The new prince did not, however, openly state his position, as he wanted to see who was going to be the victor, and he did not declare himself until the following year. Deprived of the aid of Turkey and Sweden, on whom he had relied to keep the Russian army occupied, Napoleon's only possible allies in the north were the Poles, but these turbulent people, whose forefathers had been unable to agree when they were an independent state, offered neither moral nor physical support.

In fact, Lithuania and the other provinces which formed more than a third of the former Poland, having been in Russian hands for almost forty years, had mostly forgotten their ancient constitution and had for a long time thought of themselves as Russian. The nobility sent their sons to join the army of the Czar, to whom they were too much attached by long custom to permit any hope that they would join the French. The same considerations applied to other Poles who in various divisions of their country had found themselves under the rule of Austria or Prussia. They were willing to march against Russia, but it was under the flags and under the command of their new sovereigns. They had neither love nor enthusiasm for the Emperor Napoleon, and feared to see their country devastated by war. The grand duchy of Warsaw, ceded in 1807 to the King of Saxony under the Treaty of Tilsit, was the only province of the ancient Poland which retained a spark of national spirit and was somewhat attached to France, but what was the use of this little state to the Grande Arme of Napoleon?

Napoleon, however, full of confidence in his army and in his own ability, decided to cross the Nieman, and so on the 23rd of June, accompanied by General Haxo and dressed in the uniform of a Polish soldier of his guard, he rode along its bank, and that same evening at ten o'clock, set in motion the crossing of the river by the pontoon bridges, the most important of which had been laid across the river opposite the little Russian town of Kovno, which our troops occupied without encountering any resistance.

Chap. 6.

At sunrise on the 24th we witnessed a most impressive spectacle. On the highest part of the left bank were the Emperor's tents. Around them, on the slopes of the hills and in the valleys, glittered the arms of a great concourse of men and horses. This mass, consisting of 250,000 soldiers split into three huge columns, streamed in perfect order towards the three bridges which had been thrown across the river, over which the different corps crossed to the right bank in a prearranged manner. On this same day the Nieman was crossed by our troops at other points, near Grodno, Pilony and Tilsit. I have seen a situation report, covered by notes written in Napoleon's hand, which gives the official strength of the force which crossed the Nieman as 325,000 men, of whom 155,400 were French and 170,000 allies, accompanied by 940 guns.

The regiment which I commanded formed part of 2nd Corps, commanded by Marshal Oudinot, which having crossed the bridge at Kovno headed immediately for Ianovo. The heat was overpowering. This, close to nightfall, led to a tremendous storm, and torrential rain, which drenched the roads and the countryside for more than fifty leagues around. Happily the army did not see this as a bad omen, as the soldiers considered violent thunder-storms were something to be expected in summer. The Russians too, every bit as superstitious as some of the French, had an unpropitious omen, for during the night of 23rd-24th of June the Emperor Alexander escaped with his life when, at a ball in Wilna, the floor of a room collapsed under the chair on which he was sitting, at the very hour when the first French boat, carrying a detachment of Napoleon's troops, reached the right bank of the Nieman and Russian soil. Be that as it may, the storm had made the air much cooler and the horses in bivouac suffered from this and also from eating wet grass and lying on muddy ground. So that the army lost several thousand from acute colic.

Beyond Kovnow there runs a little river called the Vilia, the bridge over which had been cut by the Russians. The storm had so swollen this tributary of the Nieman that Oudinot's scouts were held up. The Emperor arrived at the same moment as I did at the head of my regiment. He ordered the Polish lancers to see if the river was fordable, and in this process, one man was drowned; I took his name, it was Tzcinski. I mention this because the losses suffered by the Polish lancers in the crossing of the Vilia have been grossly exaggerated.

The Russians, however, retreated without waiting for the French army, which shortly occupied Wilna, the capital of Lithuania. It was near here that there took place a cavalry encounter in which Octave de Sgur, who had been with me on Massna's staff, was captured by the Russians while leading a squadron of the 8th Hussars which he commanded, he was the elder brother of General the Comte de Sgur. On the same day that the Emperor entered Wilna, Marshal Oudinot's troops came up against Wittgenstein's Russians at Wilkomir, where the first serious engagement of the campaign took place. I had not previously served under Oudinot, and this dbut confirmed the high opinion I had of his courage, without convincing me of his intelligence.

One of the greatest faults of the French at war, is to go, without reason, from the most meticulous caution to limitless confidence. Now, since the Russians had allowed us to cross the Nieman, invade Lithuania and occupy Wilna without opposition, it had become the done thing, amongst certain officers to say that the enemy would always retreat and would never stand and fight. Oudinot's staff and the marshal himself frequently stated this, and treated as fairy tales the information given by the peasants that there was a large body of Russian troops positioned in front of the little town of Wilkomir. This incredulity nearly resulted in disaster, as you will see.

The light cavalry, being the eyes of the army, while on the march, is always in front and on the flanks. My regiment then was less than a league ahead of the infantry, when, having gone a little way beyond Wilkomir without seeing any sign of the enemy, we were confronted by a forest of huge pine trees, through which the mounted men could move with ease but whose branches obscured the distant view. Fearing an ambush, I sent a single squadron, commanded by a very capable captain, to investigate. In about 15 minutes he came back and reported that he had seen an enemy army. I went to the edge of the forest from where I could see, at about a cannon shot from Wilkomir, behind a stream, a hill on which drawn up in battle order were 25 to 30 thousand Russian infantry, with cavalry and artillery.

You may be surprised that these troops did not have in front of them any outposts, pickets or scouts, but that is how the Russians operate when they are determined to defend a strong position. They allow the enemy to approach without any warning of the resistance they are about to meet, and it is only when the main body of their opponents comes within range that they open a ferocious fire with musketry and cannon, which can shatter the columns of their adversaries. It is a method which has often produced good results for the Russians; so General Wittgenstein had prepared this welcome for us.

The situation seemed to me to be so serious that to keep my regiment out of sight, I ordered them to go back into the forest while I myself hurried to warn Marshal Oudinot of the danger which lay ahead.

I found him in some open country, where having dismounted and halted his troops, he was peacefully eating his lunch in the midst of his staff. I expected that my report would shake him out of this false security, but he treated it with an air of disbelief, and clapping me on the shoulder he called out "Let's go! Marbot here has discovered thirty thousand men for us to thump." General Lorencez, the marshal's son-in-law and his chief-of-staff was the only one to take me seriously; he had once been aide-de-camp to Augereau and he had known me for a long time. He came to my defence saying that when the commander of a unit says "I have seen" he should be believed, and that to take no notice of information brought by an officer of the light cavalry was to court disaster. These observations made by his chief-of-staff caused the marshal to think, and he had started to question me about the enemy presence, which he still seemed to doubt, when a staff-captain by the name of Duplessis arrived, all out of breath, and announced that he had searched the whole area and had even been into the forest, and had seen not a single Russian. At this the marshal and his staff began laughing at my fears, which greatly upset me. Nevertheless I kept my mouth shut, certain that before very long the truth would become apparent.

Luncheon being over, the march got under way once more and I returned to my regiment, which formed the advance-guard. I led them through the trees as I had done previously, for I could see what was going to happen the moment we emerged opposite the enemy positions. In spite of what I had told him, the marshal decided to go down a wide, dead straight road which ran through the forest; but he had scarcely reached the edge of the trees when the enemy, seeing the large group formed by his staff, opened a running fire from their cannons which, placed opposite the road, could fire directly along it, throwing into disorder the gilded squadron, recently so full of themselves. Fortunately no one was hit by this fire, but the marshal's horse was killed, as was that of M. Duplessis and a number of others. I had been amply avenged, and I must confess, to my shame, that I had difficulty in hiding my satisfaction at seeing those who had scoffed at my report and treated as fantasy what I had said about the enemy presence,taking to their heels under a hail of shot and scrambling over ditches as best they could to seek shelter behind the great pine trees! The worthy General Lorencez, whom I had warned to stay in the forest, laughed heartily at this scene. In fairness to Oudinot, I must say that once remounted, he came and apologised for for his behaviour at luncheon, and asked me to brief him on the Russian positions, and point out a route through the forest which the infantry might take without being too much exposed to the enemy's guns.

Several officers of the 23rd who, like me, had been through the woodland in the morning, were detailed to guide the infantry divisions. Nevertheless, on their emerging from the trees they were subjected to a terrible cannonade, which could have been avoided if, having been warned of the Russian presence, there had been an attempt to turn one of their flanks, instead of making a frontal approach. As it was, we were now committed, once we emerged from the wood, to attacking the most heavily defended point and taking the bull by the horns.

However, our gallant soldiers engaged the enemy with such determination that they drove them from all their positions, and after two hours of fighting they began to retreat. This operation was not without danger, for, to carry it out, they had to go through the town and cross the bridge over a very steep-sided stream. This manoeuvre, always difficult to execute under fire, started off in an orderly fashion, but our light artillery, having taken up a position on a height which overlooked the town, by means of its gunfire soon produced disorder among the enemy columns, which broke ranks and rushed to the bridge. Once they had crossed the stream, instead of regrouping they fled helter-skelter over the open ground of the opposite bank, where the retreat soon became a rout! Only one regiment, that of Toula, stood its ground on the town side of the bridge. Marshal Oudinot very much wanted to force a passage across the bridge to complete his victory by pursuing the fugitives on the other side of the stream; but our infantry had hardly reached the suburbs, from where it would take them at least 15 minutes to reach the bridge,and time was precious.

My regiment, which had made a successful charge at the entrance to the town, had re-formed on the promenade, a short distance from the stream. The marshal sent word to me to bring them at the gallop and we had hardly arrived before he ordered me to charge the enemy battalions which were covering the bridge, then to cross the bridge and pursue the fugitives on the open ground of the opposite side. Experienced soldiers know how difficult it is for cavalry to overcome infantry, who are determined to defend themselves in the streets of a town. I was well aware of the dangers of the task which I had been given, but it had to be done, and without hesitation. I knew also that it is by his conduct in his first action that a commanding officer gains a good or a bad reputation amongst his men. My regiment was composed of battle-hardened troopers: I raised them to the gallop and, with me at their head, we fell on the Russian Grenadiers, who stood firm behind their bayonets. They were, however, overwhelmed by our first impetuous charge, and once their ranks had been penetrated, my terrible chasseurs, using the points of their sabres inflicted a frightful slaughter. The enemy retreated to the causeway of the bridge, where we followed them so closely that, on reaching the other side, they were unable to re-form, and our men got amongst them, killing all whom they could reach. When the Russian colonel was killed, his regiment, without leadership, lost heart and, seeing that the French skirmishers had now reached the bridge, they surrendered. I

214

lost seven men killed and some twenty wounded, but captured a flag and two thousand prisoners. After this action, we advanced onto the open ground where we took a great number of fugitives, several guns and many horses.

Marshal Oudinot had watched this action from a vantage point in the town, and he came to congratulate the regiment, for which he henceforth had a particular regard, which it well merited. I was proud to be in command of such men and when the marshal told me that he intended to recommend me for promotion to colonel, I was afraid that the Emperor would go back on his original plan, and post me to the first regiment which became vacant. How strange are the twists of fortune! The successful action at Wilkomir, where the 23rd earned such a fine reputation, nearly led on a later occasion to its destruction, because the courage which it had displayed at the time resulted in its being chosen to carry out a mission which was virtually impossible, which I shall describe shortly. Let us now return to Wilna, where the Emperor was beginning to meet with some of the difficulties which were to wreck his whole gigantic undertaking.

The first of these concerned the reorganisation of Lithuania, which we had just conquered. This had to be carried out in away which would please not only those provinces which were still occupied by Russia, but also those of the duchies of Posen and Galicia, which ancient treaties had incorporated into Prussia and Austria, Napoleon's allies, whom, for the time being, it was important not to offend.

The most committed of the noblemen who ruled the various parts of Poland proposed to Napoleon that they would raise all the provinces and place at his disposal more than 300,000 men on the day that he announced officially that all the partitions to which the country had been subjected were annulled, and that the kingdom of Poland was reconstituted. The Emperor, although he was aware of the benefits he would gain from such an armed uprising, could not conceal from himself the fact that its first result would be to involve him in war with Austria and Prussia, which rather than see themselves deprived of these huge and flourishing provinces would join their arms to those of Russia. Above all, he doubted the constancy of the Poles, who, after dragging him into war with the three most powerful of the northern nations, might perhaps fail to deliver their promised support. The Emperor therefore replied to these propositions that he would not recognise the kingdom of Poland until the inhabitants of these huge areas had shown themselves worthy of independence by rising against their oppressors. This now created a vicious circle, Napoleon would not recognise the kingdom of Poland until the Poles took action, and the Poles would not take any action until he did. An indication that Napoleon, in going to war with Russia, had no intention other than to enforce the continental blockade is the fact that he had not brought to the Nieman any arms or uniforms for the men which the Poles might have supplied.

Be that as it may, some influential noblemen, in an attempt to force Napoleon's hand, set up a National Diet in Warsaw, which was attended by a small number of deputies. The first act of this assembly was to proclaim the Reconstitution and Independence of the Ancient Kingdom of Poland. The echo of this patriotic declaration rang throughout all the provinces, whether Russian, Prussian or Austrian, and for several days it was believed that there would be an uprising which would probably favour Napoleon, but this unthinking exaltation did not last long among the Poles, of whom only a few hundred came to join us. The cooling off was so rapid that the town of Wilna and its surroundings could provide no more than twenty men to form a guard of honour for the Emperor. If the Poles had displayed at this time, a hundredth part of the energy and enthusiasm which they displayed during the insurrection of 1830-1831, they might have recovered their independence and their liberty, but, far from coming to the aid of the French troops, they denied them all necessities, and during this campaign our soldiers often had to take by force the food and forage which the inhabitants, and above all the nobles, hid from us, but handed over to the Russians, their persecutors. This partiality in favour of our enemies enraged our men and gave rise to some unpleasant scenes which M. de Sgur has stigmatised as disgraceful pillage! It is however impossible to prevent the weary and wretched soldiers who have received no issue of rations from commandeering the bread and the livestock which they need for their survival.

The need to maintain order in the provinces occupied by the army led the Emperor, in spite of everything, to appoint prefects and sub-prefects who were chosen from the most enlightened Poles, but their administration was illusory and no help to the French army. The main reason for the apathy of the Lithuanian Poles was the self-interested attachment of the nobility to the Russian government, which upheld their rights over their peasantry, to whom they feared the French might award their freedom, for all those Polish noblemen, who talked unceasingly about freedom, kept their peasants in the most brutish serfdom.

Although the concentration of French troops on their frontiers should have warned the Russians that hostilities were about to commence, they were nonetheless taken by surprise by the crossing of the Nieman, which they nowhere opposed. Their army began a retreat towards the Duna (Dvina) on the left bank of which they had prepared, at Drissa, an immense entrenched camp. From all parts the different French Corps followed the Russian columns. Prince Murat was in command of the cavalry of the advance-guard, and every evening he caught up with the Russian rear-guard; but after some skirmishing they made off during the night by forced marches, without it being possible to bring them to a decisive action.

Chap. 7.

During the first days of our invasion of Russia, the enemy had made the very serious mistake of allowing Napoleon to split their forces, so that the greater part of their army, led by the Emperor Alexander and Marshal Barclay, had been driven back to the Duna, while the remainder, commanded by Bagration, was on the upper Nieman around Mir, eighty leagues from the main body. Cut off in this way, Bagration tried to join the Emperor Alexander by going through Minsk; but Napoleon had entrusted the protection of Minsk to Marshal Davout, who vigorously repelled the Russians and drove them back to Bobruisk, which he knew was supposed to be guarded by Jrme Bonaparte, at the head of two corps , amounting to 60,000 men. Bagration was about to be forced to surrender when he was saved by the foolishness of Jrme, who had not accepted the advice which Davout had given him, and failing to recognise the superior wisdom of the experienced and successful marshal, had decided to go his own way, whereupon he manoeuvred his troops so ineptly that Bagration was able to escape from this first danger. Davout, however, followed him with his usual tenacity, and caught up with him on the road to Mohilew, where, although he had no more than 12,000 men, he attacked the 36,000 Russians and defeated them; though admittedly the Russians were surprised on an area of very broken ground which prevented them from making the best use of their superior numbers. Bagration was compelled to cross the Borysthenia much lower down at Novoi-Bychow, and being now out of reach of Davout he was able to rejoin the main Russian army at Smolensk.

During the marches and countermarches which Bagration undertook in his efforts to evade Davout, he surprised the brigade of French cavalry comannded by General Bordesoulle, and captured from him the whole of the 3rd Regiment of Chasseurs, whose colonel was my friend Saint-Mars.

The elimination of Bagration's force would have been of tremendous benefit to Napoleon, so his fury with King Jrme was unbounded. He ordered him to quit the army immediately and return to Westphalia, a rigourous but necessary measure, which had the effect of greatly damaging King Jrme's reputation in the army. However, one has to ask if he was entirely to blame? His major mistake was to think that his dignity as a sovereign should not permit him to accept the advice of a simple marshal, but Napoleon knew perfectly well that the young prince had never in his life commanded so much as a single battalion, nor taken part in the most minor skirmish, and yet he confided to his care an army of 60,000 men, and this at a somewhat critical juncture. General Junot, who replaced Jrme, was, before long, also guilty of a serious blunder.

It was around this time that the Russian emperor sent one of his ministers, Count Balachoff,to parley with Napoleon, who was still in Wilna. The purpose of this discussion has never been entirely clear; there were those who believed it was to arrange an armistice, but they were quickly disabused by the departure of the Count, and it appeared later that the English, who had a tremendous influence in the Russian court and the army, had taken umbrage at this mission, and fearing that Alexander might be considering coming to terms with Napoleon, they had loudly insisted that he should leave the army and return to St.Petersburg. Alexander accepted this proposal, but ensured that his brother, Constantine came with him. Left to themselves, and egged on by the Englishman Wilson, the Russian generals sought to wage war with a ferocity which might shake the French morale, so they ordered their troops to lay waste the country behind them as they withdrew, by burning all the houses and everything else which they could not carry away.

While Napoleon, from the central point of Wilna, was directing the various units of his army, the columns led by Murat, Ney, Montbrun, Nansouty and Oudinot had, on the 15th of July , reached the river Dvina. Oudinot, who had probably misunderstood the Emperor's orders, took the unusual step of going down the left bank of the river, while Wittgenstein and his men were going up the river on the other side. He arrived opposite Dvinaburg, an old walled town whose fortifications were in bad repair, where he hoped to capture the bridge and, having crossed to the other bank, to attack Wittgenstein from the rear. Wittgenstein, however, on leaving Dvinaburg, had left behind a strong garrison with numerous pieces of artillery. My regiment, as usual, constituted the advance-guard, which on this day was led by Marshal Oudinot himself.

The town of Dvinaburg is on the right bank of the river. We arrived on the left bank, where there is a considerable fortification which protects the bridge which links it to the town, from which it is separated by the river, which is very wide at this point. A quarter of a league from the fortifications, which Marshal Oudinot claimed were not equipped with cannon, I came on a Russian battalion, whose left flank was protected by the river and whose front was covered by the planks and hutments of an abandoned camp. In such a position the enemy was very difficult for cavalry to attack; however the Marshal ordered me to attack them. After I had left it to individual officers to make their way through the gaps between the huts, I ordered the charge, but the regiment had hardly gone a few paces, amid a shower of bullets from the Russian infantry, when the artillery, whose existence the Marshal had denied, thundered from the battlements, to which we were so close that the canisters of grape-shot were going over our heads before they had time to burst. A stray ball from one of them went through a fisherman's hut and broke the leg of the trumpeter who was sounding the charge by my side...I lost several men there. Marshal Oudinot, who had made a serious mistake in attacking a position which was protected by cannon, hoped to flush out the Russian infantry by sending in a Portuguese battalion which was ahead of our infantry; but these foreigners, former prisoners of war, who had been enlisted, somewhat unwillingly, into the French army, made little headway and we remained exposed. Seeing that Oudinot bore the enemy fire with courage but without giving any orders, I thought that if this state of affairs continued for a few minutes more, my regiment was going to wiped out, so I told my men to spread out and attack the enemy infantry in open order, with the double aim of driving them out of their position and preventing the gunners from firing for fear of hitting their own men who were intermingled with ours. Cut down by my troopers the defenders of the camp fled towards the bridgehead, but the garrison of this outpost was composed of recent recruits, who, fearing that we would follow the fugitives into the fortifications, hurriedly closed the gates; which compelled them to make for the pontoon bridge in an attempt to reach the other bank and the shelter of the town of Dvinaburg itself.

The bridge had no guard-rail. The pontoons wobbled. The river was deep and wide and I could see the armed garrison on the other side trying to close the gates. It seemed to me to be folly to advance any further. Thinking that the regiment had done enough, I had halted them when the Marshal arrived, shouting "Forward the twenty-third! Do as you did at Wilkomir! Cross the bridge! Force the gates! Seize the town!" General Lorencez tried in vain to persuade him that the difficulties were too great, and that a regiment of cavalry could not attack a fortress, however badly defended, if to get there they had to cross, two abreast, a third-rate pontoon bridge;

but the Marshal persisted, "They will be able to take advantage of the disorder and fears of the enemy" he said, and repeated his order to me to attack the town. I obeyed; but I was scarcely on the first span of the bridge, at the head of the leading section of my men, when the garrison, having managed to close the gates which led to the river, mounted the ramparts, from where they opened fire on us. The slender line which we presented offered a poor target for these inadequately trained men, so that their musket and cannon fire caused us fewer casualties than I had feared, but on hearing the fortress firing on us, the defenders of the bridgehead recovered their nerve and joined in the fray. Oudinot, seeing the 23rd caught between two fires, at the start of an unstable bridge across which it was impossible to advance, conveyed to me the order to retreat. The large gap which I had left between each section allowed them to turn round without too much confusion, however, two men and their horses fell into the river and were drowned. In order to regain the left bank we had to pass once more under the ramparts of the bridgehead, when we were exposed to a rolling fire which, fortunately, was aimed by unskilled militia, for if we had been up against trained marksmen, the regiment could have been wholly destroyed.

This unsuccessful action, so imprudently undertaken, cost me thirty men killed and many wounded, and it was to be hoped that the Marshal would be content with this fruitless effort, especially in view of the fact that the Emperor had not ordered him to take Dvinaburg; but, as soon as the infantry had arrived, he made a new assault on the bridgehead, which had now been reinforced by a company of Grenadiers, who, at the sound of firing had hurried from nearby billets, so that our troops were once more repelled with much greater losses than those suffered by the 23rd. When the Emperor heard of this abortive attack he placed the blame squarely on Marshal Oudinot.

At this time, my regiment was brigaded with the 24th Chasseurs, and General Castex, who commanded this brigade, had instituted an admirable routine in our method of operation. Each of the two regiments took it in turn to form, for twenty-four hours, the advance-guard if we were approaching the enemy, or the rear-guard if we were retreating, and to provide all the sentries, pickets and so on, while the other regiment marched peacefully along, recovering from the fatigues of the day before and preparing for those of the morrow, which did not prevent it from going to the aid of the unit on duty, if they came in contact with the enemy. This system, which was not in the regulations, had the great advantage of never separating the men from their officers or their comrades, or placing them under the orders of unknown commanders and mingling them with troopers of another regiment. Moreover, during the night, half of the brigade slept, while the other half watched over them. However, since no system is without its shortcomings, it could so happen, by chance, that it was the same regiment which was more often on duty when a serious engagement occurred, as happened to the 23rd at Wilkomir and Dvinaburg. It was the sort of luck which we had throughout the campaign, but we never complained. We came out of all these events well and were often envied by the 24th, who had fewer occasions on which to distinguish themselves.

While Oudinot was making his assault on Dvinaburg, the corps commanded by Ney, as well as the immense body of cavalry commanded by Murat, were proceeding up the left bank of the Dvina towards Polotsk, while Wittgenstein's Russian army followed the same route on the right bank. Being separated from the enemy by the river, our troops grew careless, and pitched their bivouacs in the French manner, much too close to its bank. Wittgenstein had noticed this and he allowed the bulk of the French force to draw ahead. The last unit in the line of march was Sbastiani's division, which had as its rear-guard the brigade commanded by General Saint-Genis, who had served as an officer in the army of Egypt, and who, although courageous, was not very bright. When he had reached a some way beyond the little town of Drouia, General Saint-Genis, on the orders of Sbastiani, put his troops into bivouac some two hundred paces from the river, which was believed to be uncrossable without boats. Wittgenstein, however, knew of a ford, and during the night he made use of it to send across the river a division of cavalry, which fell on the French troops and captured almost the entire brigade, including General Saint-Genis. This forced Sbastiani to hurry upstream with the rest of his division to make contact with the Corps commanded by Montbrun. After this swift raid, Wittgenstein recalled his troops and continued his march up the Dvina. The affair did Sbastiani's reputation a great deal of harm and drew down on his head the reproaches of the Emperor.

Shortly after this regrettable incident, Oudinot having been ordered to leave Dvinaburg and go up the river to rejoin Ney and Montbrun, his army corps took the same route as they had done and passed the town of Drouia. The Marshal intended to encamp his force some three leagues further on, but he feared that the enemy might use the ford to send across large parties of men to harass the great convoy which trailed behind him, so he decided that while he made off into the distance, with the main body of the troops, he would leave behind a regiment of General Castex's brigade in the position which had been occupied by General Saint-Genis, to watch the ford. As my regiment was on duty, there fell to it the dangerous task of remaining behind at Drouia on their own until the following morning. I knew that the greater part of Wittgenstein's force had gone up the river, but I could see that he had left behind, not far from the ford, two strong regiments of cavalry, a force more than sufficient to overcome me.

However much I might have wished to carry out the order to set up my bivouac on the spot used two days previously by Saint-Genis, this was impossible, for the ground was littered with more than two hundred bodies in a state of putrefaction, and to this major reason was linked another not less important. What I had seen and what I had learned about war had convinced me that the best means of defending a river against an enemy whose aim is not to establish himself on the bank which one occupies, is to keep the main body of one's troops well back from the river edge; firstly to have timely warning of the enemy's approach, and secondly, because, as it his intention to make a sudden raid and then retire smartly, he dare not go too far from the spot where he can cross back to the other side. So I settled the regiment half a league from the Dvina, on some slightly undulating ground. I left only some two-man sentinels on the bank, because, when it is purely a matter of observation, two men can see as much as a large picket. Several lines of troopers were placed one after the other between these sentinels and our bivouac, where, like a spider at the bottom of its web, I could be rapidly informed by these threads about what was going on in the area which it was my duty to guard. I had forbidden all fires and even the lighting of pipes, and had ordered complete silence.

The nights are extremely short in Russia in the month of July, but this one seemed very long to me, so afraid was I that I might be attacked during the hours of darkness by a force superior in strength to my own. Half of the men were in the saddle, the remainder were allowing their horses to graze but were ready to mount if given the signal. All seemed quiet on the opposite bank, when my Polish servant, who spoke Russian fluently, came to tell me that he had heard one old Jewish woman who lived in a nearby house say to another, "The lantern has been lit in the clock tower at Morki. The attack is going to begin." I had the two women brought to me, and questioned by Lorentz. They said that, as they were afraid of their village becoming a battleground for the two enemies, they had been alarmed to see the lamp lit in the bell tower of the church at Morki, which, the night before last had been the signal for the Russian troops to cross the ford and attack the French camp.

Although I was prepared for any eventuality, this was a piece of very useful information. At once the regiment was on horse, sabres in their hands. The sentinels by the river and the string of horsemen stretched across the plain passed from man to man, in low voices, the orders to come back. Two of the boldest sous-officiers, Prud'homme and Graft, went with Lieutenant Bertin to see what the enemy was doing. He came back shortly to say that a large column of Russian cavalry was crossing the ford, and that already there were some squadrons on our side of the river; but seemingly taken aback at not finding us camped at the same place as Saint-Genis they had halted, fearing, no doubt to go too far from their only means of retreat; then, having decided to go on, they were now approaching at a walk, and were not far off.

I immediately set fire to a huge haystack and to several barns which stood on some high ground, and by the light of the flames I could easily distinguish the enemy column, consisting of Grodno Hussars. I had with me about a thousand brave men, and with a cry of "Vive L'Empereur!" we charged at the gallop towards the Russians who, taken by surprise by this fierce and unexpected attack, turned tail and rushed in disorder to the ford. There they came face to face with a regiment of dragoons who, being part of their brigade had followed them and were just emerging from the river. This resulted in the most fearful confusion which enabled our men to kill many of the enemy and take many horses. The Russians tried to recross the ford in a mob to escape from the fire which my men aimed at them from the bank and a number of them were drowned. Our surprise attack had so startled the enemy who had thought to find us asleep, that they put up no resistance, and I was able to return to our bivouac without having to regret the death or wounding of any of our number. The break of day disclosed the field of battle covered by some hundreds of dead or wounded Russians. I left the wounded in the care of the inhabitants of the village near which we had spent the night, and took to the road to rejoin Marshal Oudinot, with whom I caught up that same evening. The Marshal gave me a hearty welcome and complemented the regiment on their conduct.

2nd Corps continued its march up the left bank of the Dvina and in three days arrived opposite Polotsk. There we learned that the Emperor had at last left Wilna, where he had spent twenty days, and was heading for Vitepsk, a town of some size, which he intended to make his new centre of operations.

On quitting Wilna, the Emperor had left the Duc de Bassano as governor of the province of Lithuania and General Hogendorp as military commander. Neither of these two officials was suited to organising the rear echelons of an army. The Duc de Bassano, a former diplomat and private secretary, knew nothing about administration, while the Dutchman Hogendorp, who spoke little French and had no idea of our military regulations and customs, was not likely to make much impression on those French who passed through Wilna or on the local nobility. So the resources available in Lithuania were of no help to our troops.

The town of Polotsk is situated on the right bank of the Dvina. Its houses are built of wood and it is dominated by a very large and splendid college, at that time occupied by the Jesuits, almost all of whom were French. It is surrounded by an earthwork fortification, having at one time undergone a siege during the war waged by Charles XII against Peter the Great. The corps commanded by Ney, Murat and Montbrun, in order to get from Drissa to Witepsk, had built a pontoon bridge across the Dvina, opposite Polotsk, which they left for Oudinot's corps, which was going to take the road for St.Petersburg. It was from here that 2nd Corps took a different direction to that of the Grande Arme, which we did not see again until the following winter, at the crossing of the Beresina.

It would require several volumes to describe the manoeuvres and the battles of that part of the army which followed the Emperor to Moscow. I shall therefore limit myself to describing the salient events as they occur.

On the 25th of July, there took place near to Ostrovno an advance-guard action, in which our infantry were successful, but where several regiments of cavalry were too hastily engaged by Murat. The 16th Chasseurs was amongst this number, and my brother, who commanded a squadron, was captured. He was taken far beyond Moscow to Sataroff, on the Volga, where he joined Colonel Saint-Mars and Octave de Sgur. They helped each other to bear the boredom of captivity, to which my brother was already accustomed, as he had spent several years in the prisons and hulks of Spain. The fortunes of war treated us both differently: Adolphe was captured three times but never wounded, while I was often wounded but never captured.

While the Emperor, now in control of Wilna, tried in vain to manoeuvre the Russian army into a decisive battle, Oudinot's corps, having crossed the Dvina at Polotsk, established itself in front of this town, facing the numerous troops of General Wittgenstein who formed the enemy right wing. Before I describe the events which took place on the banks of the Dvina, I should, perhaps, acquaint you with the composition of 2nd Corps.

Marshal Oudinot, who commanded the Corps, had under his orders no more than 44,000 men, divided into three divisions of infantry, commanded by Generals Legrand, Verdier and Merle. There were two brigades of light cavalry. The first, composed of the 23rd and the 24th regiments of Chasseurs, was commanded by General Castex, an excellent officer on all counts. The second was formed of the 7th and 20th Chasseurs and the 8th Polish Lancers, commanded by General Corbineau, a brave but dull-witted officer. These brigades were not combined into a single division, but were employed wherever the Marshal thought necessary.

The 24th Chasseurs, with which my regiment was brigaded, was a first class unit which would have done very well if there had been a bond of sympathy between the men and their commander. Unfortunately Colonel A... was very hard on his subordinates, who, for their part, disliked him. This state of affairs led General Castex to travel and camp with the 23rd, and to unite his field kitchen with mine, even though he had once served in the 24th. Colonel A..., big, skillful and always perfectly mounted, showed up well in engagements featuring the "arme blanche", but was thought not to be so keen on those in which fire-arms and artillery were involved. In spite of this, the Emperor recognised in him qualities which made him undoubtedly the best light cavalry officer in our European armies. No one had a better eye for country. Before he set out, he could predict where there would be obstacles not shown on the map, and where streams, roads and even paths would lead to, and deduce from enemy movements forecasts which were almost always correct. In all the aspects of war, great or small, he was remarkably adept. The Emperor had often used him for reconnaissance in the past and had recommended him to Marshal Oudinot, who frequently called him into consultation; with the result that many of the laborious and dangerous jobs fell to my regiment.

Chap. 8.

Hardly had the various army corps which had preceded us into Polotsk left to join the Emperor at Witepsk, when Oudinot, collecting his troops into a single immense column on the road to St.Petersburg, marched to attack Wittgenstein's army, which we believed was in a position some ten leagues from us, between two little towns named Sebej and Newel. At the end of the day we made our bivouac on the banks of the Drissa. This tributary of the Dvina is no more than a rivulet at the coaching inn of Siwotschina, where it is crossed by the main road to St.Petersburg and where, as there is no bridge, the Russian government has instead cut back the steep banks between which the stream runs to make a gently sloping approach and has paved its bed to the same width as the road, thus creating a passable ford. To the right and left of the ford, however, troops and vehicles cannot cross, because of the steepness of the banks. I mention this because, three days later this spot was the scene of a brisk engagement.

The next day, the 30th, my regiment being on duty, I took my place at the head of the advance-guard and followed by the whole army corps I crossed the ford through the Drissa. The heat was most oppressive, and in the dust-covered corn fields at the side of the road one could see two large areas where the grain had been flattened and crushed, as if a roller had been dragged over it, indicating the passage of a large column of infantry. Suddenly, near the coaching inn of Kliastitsoui these signs disappeared from the main road, and could be seen to the left on a wide side-road which led to Jacoubovo. It was evident that the enemy had turned off the road to Sebej at this point and was preparing to attack our left flank. This seemed to me to be a serious matter, so I halted our troops and sent a message to warn my general. The Marshal however, who usually kept in view of the advance-guard, had seen that I had halted. He came along at the gallop and in spite of the opinions of Generals Castex and Lorencez, he ordered me to continue up the main road. I had scarcely gone a league when I saw coming towards me a calische drawn by two post-horses....I stopped it and I saw a Russian officer who, overcome by the heat, was lying full-length on its floor. This young man, the son of the nobleman who owned the coaching inn of Kliastitsoui which I had just passed, was one of Wittgenstein's aides-de-camp, and was returning from St.Petersburg with the reply to some despatches which the general had sent to the government. You may imagine his surprise when, startled out of his sleep, he found himself surrounded by our bearded chasseurs, and saw not far away the numerous columns of French soldiers. He could not understand why he had not encountered Wittgenstein's army, or at least some of his scouts, between Sebej and the spot where we were; but his astonishment confirmed the opinion held by General Castex and me that Wittgenstein, to lay a trap for Oudinot, had suddenly quitted the road to St.Petersburg to attack the left flank and the rear of the French force. In fact, it was not long before we heard the sound of artillery and musket-fire.

Marshal Oudinot, although taken by surprise by this unexpected attack, extricated himself quite well from the tight spot in which he had landed himself. Ordering his columns to left face, he presented a line to the attacker, who was repulsed so vigourously that he did not care to renew the attack that day, and retired to Jakoubovo. Wittgenstein's cavalry had, however, enjoyed a considerable success, for they had captured, in the French rear, some thousand men and some of our equipment, amongst other things all our mobile forges. This was a serious loss, which was felt badly by the cavalry of 2nd Corps throughout the whole of the campaign. After this engagement, Oudinot's troops having taken up their position, Castex was ordered to return to Kliastitsoui to guard the point at which the road branched, where we were joined by General Maison's infantry. The Russian officer held prisoner in the house belonging to his father did us the honours with good grace.

In expectation of a major battle on the following day, the commanders of both armies had made their dispositions, and, at daybreak, the Russians attacked the inn at Kliastitsoui, which constituted the French right wing. Although in these circumstances both our regiments would be in action, the regiment on duty would be in the first rank, and it was the turn of the 24th Chasseurs. To avoid any possibility of hesitation, General Castex placed himself at the head of the regiment, and falling rapidly on the Russians, he overran them and took 400 prisoners without suffering many casualties. He was in the forefront of the attack, and his horse was killed by a bayonet thrust. In the resultant fall his foot had been trodden on, and he was unable for several days to lead the brigade. His place was taken by Colonel A....

The Russian battalions which the 24th had just defeated were immediately replaced by others which, emerging from Jacoubovo, marched rapidly towards us. The Marshal ordered A...to attack them, and we were told to advance, which we did without delay. Having arrived at the front line, we arranged ourselves in battle order and approached the Russians, who awaited us resolutely. As soon as we were within range, I ordered the charge... It was carried out with the greatest vigour, for my troopers, as well as displaying their usual courage, were aware that their comrades of the 24th were watching their every move. The Russians made what I consider to be the fatal mistake of discharging all their weapons at once by firing a volley, which, badly aimed, killed only a few men and horses. Continuous fire would have been much more devastating. They then needed to reload, but we did not give them time; our excellent horses, galloping at full speed, hit them with such force that many of them were knocked to the ground. A good number got to their feet and attempted to defend themselves with their bayonets against the sabres of our Chasseurs, but after suffering a great many casualties they fell back, then broke ranks, and a good number were killed or captured as they fled towards a cavalry regiment which had come to their aid. This was the Grodno Hussars.

I have noticed that when a unit has defeated another, it always maintains its superiority. I saw here a further proof of this, for the Chasseurs of the 23rd hurled themselves on the Grodno Hussars, as if they were easy prey, having previously beaten them soundly in a night battle at Drouia, and the Hussars, having recognised their enemy, took to their heels. This regiment, during the rest of the campaign, invariably faced the 23rd, who always retained their ascendancy. While these events were taking place on our right wing, the infantry on the left and in the centre had attacked the Russians who, defeated everywhere, abandoned the field of battle and at nightfall went to take up a position about a league away. Our army settled itself in the area which it occupied, between Jakoubovo and the road junction at Kliastitsoui. There was much celebration that night in the brigade bivouacs, on account of our victory. My regiment had captured the flag of the Tamboff infantry, and the 24th had also taken that of the Russian unit which they had overcome; but their satisfaction was diminished by the knowledge that two of their squadron commanders had been wounded, both of whom however, made a rapid recovery and served throughout the rest of the campaign.

When a unit endeavours to outflank an enemy it risks being itself outflanked. This is what happened to Wittgenstein, for on the night of the 29th, having left the St. Petersburg road to attack the left and rear of the French army, he had compromised his line of communication, which Oudinot could have cut completely if he taken full advantage of the victory achieved on the 30th. The Russian situation was made worse by the fact that while facing a victorious army which barred its line of retreat it learned that Marshal Macdonald, having crossed the Dvina and taken the fort of Dvinaberg, was advancing on the Russian rear. To get out of this difficulty,

Wittgenstein had, during the night after the battle, made a cross-country detour which took his army back on to the St.Petersburg road at a point beyond the inn at Kliastitsoui. Since, however, he was afraid that the French troops who were in that area might fall on his force during this flank move, he decided to prevent them from doing so by himself attacking them with superior strength, while the bulk of his army regained the route to St.Petersburg and reopened his communications with Sebej.

The next day, the 31st of July, my regiment came on duty at dawn, when it could be seen that part of the army which we had defeated the day before had avoided our right wing and was in full flight towards Sebej, while the remainder were about to attack us at Kliastitsoui. All of Marshal Oudinot's troops were immediately stood to, but while the generals were arranging them in battle order, a strong column of Russian Grenadiers attacked our allies, the Portuguese, and reduced them to complete disorder; they then turned on the large and solid coaching inn, an important point which they were about to take, when Marshal Oudinot, always in the forefront of any action, hurried to my regiment, which was already at the outposts, and ordered me to try to stop or at least slow down the enemy advance until the arrival of our infantry which was approaching rapidly. I took my regiment off at the gallop, and ordering the trumpeter to sound the charge, I struck the right of the enemy line obliquely, which greatly hindered the ability of their infantry and Grenadiers to fire on us, and they were about to be cut down, for they were already in disorder, when either spontaneously or under the orders of their officers, they made an about turn and ran for a large ditch which they had behind them. They all scrambled into it and from its cover they directed a continuous fire at us. Immediately I had six or seven men killed and some twenty wounded and I was hit by a stray ball in the left shoulder. My troopers had their blood up, but they could not attack men whom it was physically impossible to reach. At this moment Generak Maison arrived with his infantry and having ordered me to withdraw behind his columns, he attacked the ditch from both ends and all its defenders were either killed or made prisoner.

As for me, with a painful wound I was taken back to the inn and removed with difficulty from my horse. The good Dr. Parot, the regimental surgeon, came to dress my injury, but he had scarcely started this when he was forced to break off. There was a new Russian assault and a hail of ball fell about us, so that we had to remove ourselves out of range of the fire. The doctor found that my injury was serious and could have been fatal if the thick braiding of my epaulet, through which the ball had passed, had not deflected it and lessened its force. The blow had been sufficiently heavy to knock me back almost onto my horse's crupper, so that the officers and troopers who were following me thought I had been killed, and I would have fallen if my orderlies had not supported me. The dressing was very painful for the ball was embedded in the bone at the point where the upper arm joins the collar-bone. To get it out the wound had to be enlarged and you can still see the big scar.

I can promise you that if I had been already a colonel, I would have joined the many wounded who were being sent back to Polotsk, and after crossing the Dvina I would have sought some Lithuanian town where I might be cared for; but I was only a squadron commander and at any time the Emperor could arrive at Witepsk and hold a revue, at which he would award nothing except to those who were present bearing arms. This custom which at first may seem cruel, was based nevertheless on the interest of the service, for it encouraged the wounded not to remain in hospital any longer than was necessary, and to rejoin their units as soon as they were fit enough to do so. In view of the above, my success in action against the enemy, my recent wound received in combat and my devotion to the regiment, all compelled me not to go away; so I stayed in spite of the severe pain which I was suffering, and having put my arm in a sling as well as I could, and had myself hoisted onto horseback, I rejoined my regiment.

Chap. 9.

Since I had been wounded, things had changed considerably; our troops had defeated those of Wittgenstein and taken a great number of prisoners, but the Russians had reached the St. Petersburg road and were continuing their retreat to Sebej.

To get to this town from the inn at Kliastitsoui, one must cross the enormous marsh of Khodanui, in the middle of which the main road is raised on an embankment made of huge pine trees laid one next to another. On each side of this causeway is a ditch or rather a wide and deep canal, and there is no other route except by making an exceedingly long detour. The embankment is almost a league long, but of considerable width, so that, it being impossible to put flank guards in the marsh, the Russians marched in dense columns along this artificial road, beyond which our maps showed open country. Marshal Oudinot, aiming at further victory, had decided to follow them, and for this reason he had already despatched on the road to the marsh General Verdier's infantry, which was to be followed first by Castex's brigade of cavalry, then the whole army corps . My regiment had not yet joined the line when I returned to it.

When, in spite of my injury, I took up my place at their head, I received a general acclamation from both officers and men, which showed the affection and esteem in which these brave people held me; I was deeply touched by this, and even more so by the welcome I received from Major Fontaine. This officer, although both courageous and competent, was so unambitious that he had remained a captain for eighteen years, having refused promotion three times, which he had finally accepted only on a direct order from the Emperor.

So I once more took command of the 23rd, and began to cross the marsh behind General Verdier's division, at which the rear unit of the enemy column fired only a few long range shots while they were still on the causeway. When, however, our infantry reached the open country, they saw the Russian army deployed in battle formation, and were treated to a devastating barrage of artillery fire. Nevertheless, in spite of their losses the French battalions continued to advance. Soon they were all off the embankment and it was the turn of my regiment, at the head of the brigade, to reach the open ground. Colonel A... who was the temporary brigade commander was not there to give me orders, so I thought it right to remove my regiment from this dangerous spot and I led them off at the gallop as soon as the infantry gave me room;

however I had seven or eight men killed and a greater number wounded. The 24th, who followed me, also suffered many casualties. The same happened to General Legrand's infantry division; but as soon as they were formed up on the plain, Marshal Oudinot attacked the enemy lines, and they directed their artillery fire at several different points so that the exit from the marsh would have become less perilous for the remainder of the army, if Wittgenstein had not at that moment attacked with all his force the units which we had in the open. His superiority in numbers compelled us to give ground and we were driven back towards the causeway of the Khodanui. Fortunately the track was very wide, which allowed us to proceed by platoons. As soon as we left the plain the cavalry became more of a hindrance than a help. The marshal put us in front of the retreat; we were followed by Verdier's division, whose general had been very seriously wounded, and General Legrand's division made the rear-guard. The last brigade of this division, commanded by General Albert, had to fight a very sharp action while its last battalions were getting onto the causeway, but once they were formed into columns General Albert put eight artillery pieces at the tail end which kept up a continuous fire during the retreat, so it was the turn of the enemy to suffer heavy casualties. By contrast, the Russian artillery rarely discharged a shot because the guns had to be turned round to fire at us and then turned back to continue the pursuit, a lengthy and difficult operation on the causeway, so that they did us little damage.

The day was ending when the French troops, having crossed the marsh, repassed Kliastitsoui and found themselves once more on the banks of the Drissa, at the ford of Sivotschina which they had crossed in the morning to follow the Russians who had been defeated at Kliastitsoui. The Russians had their revenge, for having caused us seven or eight hundred casualties on the plain beyond the marsh they now had a sword at our backs. To put an end to the fighting and allow the army some rest, Marshal Oudinot led it across the ford to set up camp at Bieloe.

Night was falling when the outposts which had been left to watch the Drissa, reported that the enemy were crossing the river. The Marshal went there at once, and could see that eight Russian battalions with a battery of fourteen guns were setting up their bivouac on our side of the river, while the remainder of the army stayed on the other side, preparing no doubt to cross over and attack us on the morrow. This advance party was commanded by General Koulnieff, an enterprising officer but one who, like most of the Russian officers of the period drank to excess. It would seem that on this evening he had drunk more than usual, for it is otherwise difficult to explain why he made the grave error of coming, with no more than eight battalions to set up camp a short distance from an army of forty thousand men, and that in a most unfavourable position; for he had, some two hundred paces behind him, the Drissa, which could not be crossed except by the ford; not because of the depth of the water but because it ran between very steep banks fifteen to twenty feet high. Koulnieff had therefore no other line of retreat but the ford. Could it be that he hoped that his eight battalions and fourteen canons would be able, if defeated, to withdraw smartly across this one passage, in the face of an attack which might be launched at any moment by the French army from nearby Bieloe? The answer must be no, but general Koulnieff was in no state to consider the matter when he put his camp on the left bank of the river. It is perhaps surprising that Wittgenstein should have entrusted the command of his advance guard to Koulnieff, of whose intemperate habits he must have been aware.

While the head of the Russian column approached rashly to within such a short distance of us, a great confusion reigned, not among the troops, but among their leaders. Marshal Oudinot, although the bravest of men, lacked consistency, and passed rapidly from a plan of attack to one of a withdrawal. The losses which he had suffered towards the end of the day on the other side of the great marsh had thrown him into a state of perplexity, and he could not think how he was to carry out the Emperor's orders, which were to push Wittgenstein back at least as far as Sebej and Newel. He was therefore delighted to receive, during the night, a despatch informing him of the imminent arrival of a Bavarian corps commanded by General Saint-Cyr, which the Emperor was placing under his orders; but instead of awaiting this powerful reinforcement in his present sound position, Oudinot, advised by the general of artillery Dulauloy, wished to make contact with the Bavarians by withdrawing his army as far as Polotsk. This inexplicable notion was warmly opposed by the group of generals summoned by the Marshal. General Legrand said that although our success of the morning had been counter-balanced by the losses of the evening, the army was still in good heart and ready to advance, and that to retreat to Polotsk would damage their morale and present them to the Bavarians as a defeated force coming to seek refuge amongst them; an idea which would arouse indignation in all French bosoms. This vigourous speech by Legrand was acclaimed by all the generals and the Marshal then gave up the project of a retreat.

There remained the question of what to do the next day. General Legrand, with the authority of his seniority, long service and experience in warfare, proposed that they should take advantage of the serious error made by Koulnieff by attacking the advance-guard so imprudently placed without support on the bank which we occupied, and drive them back into the Drissa which they had behind them. This advice having been accepted by the Marshal and all the group, the execution of it was confided to General Legrand.

Oudinot's army was encamped in a forest of huge, widely spaced pines, beyond which there was a very extensive clearing. The boundaries of the wood took the form of a bow, the two ends of which reached the Drissa, which formed as it were the bow-string. The Russians had set up their bivouac very close to the river, opposite the ford. Their frontage was protected by fourteen artillery pieces. General Legrand wanted to take the enemy by surprise, so he ordered General Albert to send a regiment of infantry to each of the ends of the wood from where they could attack the camp from the flank, as soon as they heard the approach of the cavalry who, emerging from the woods in the centre of the bow would go bald-headed for the Russian battalions and drive them into the ravine. The task given to the cavalry was plainly the most dangerous, for not only had they to make a frontal attack on an enemy armed with 6000 muskets but would also be exposed to the fire of fourteen artillery pieces before they could reach their objective. It was, however, hoped that by a surprise attack, the Russians might be caught asleep, and put up little resistance.

You have seen that my regiment having come on duty on the morning of the 31st July at Kliastitsoui, had continued to serve for the whole of that day, and should, according to the regulations, have been relieved by the 24th at 1 A.M. on the 1st August, and it was this regiment whose duty it was to carry out the attack, while mine remained in reserve. There being only enough space in the clearing between the woods and the stream for one regiment of cavalry. However, Colonel A... went to Oudinot and suggested to him that there was a danger that while we were preparing to attack the troops in front of us, General Wittgenstein might send a strong column to our right which could cross the Drissa at another ford which probably existed some three leagues upstream from where we were, and gaining our rear could capture our wounded and our equipment; and that it would be a good idea to send a regiment of cavalry to keep an eye on this ford. The Marshal fell in with this suggestion and Colonel A... whose regiment had just come on duty, quickly ordered his men into the saddle and led them off on this expedition which he had thought up, leaving to the 23rd the dangers of the battle which was about to take place.

My regiment received with calm the news of the perilous mission which had been thrust upon them and welcomed the appearance of the Marshal and General Legrand when they came to supervise the preparations for this important attack which we were about to carry out.

At this time all the French regiments, with the exception of the Cuirassiers, had a company of Grenadiers known as the lite company, whose customary position was on the right of the line, a position which they held in the 23rd. General Legrand observed to the Marshal that as the enemy had placed their artillery in front of their centre, it was there that most danger would lie, and in order to avoid any hesitation which might compromise the whole operation, it would be advisable to attack this point with the lite company, which was composed of the most seasoned soldiers mounted on the best horses. It was in vain that I assured the Marshal that the regiment was in all respects as solid in one part as in another, he ordered me to put the lite company in the centre, which I then did. I next gathered the officers together and explained to them in low tones what we were to do, and warned them that, the better to surprise the enemy, I would give no preparatory commands and would simply order the charge when we were within close range of the enemy guns. Once everything had been arranged, the regiment left its bivouac, in complete silence, at the first faint light of dawn, and made its way without difficulty through the wood, the great trees of which were widely spaced, and arrived at the level clearing in which was the Russian encampment. I alone in the regiment had no sabre in my hand, for having only one hand which I could use, I needed that to hold the reins of my horse. You will understand that this was a very unpleasant situation for a cavalry officer about to engage the enemy.

However, I had chosen to go with my regiment and so I placed myself in front of the lite company, having beside me their gallant captain, M. Courteau, one of the finest of officers and one whom I valued most highly.

All was quiet in the Russian camp, towards which we advanced slowly and in silence, and my hopes of achieving a total surprise were increased by the fact that General Koulnieff not having brought any cavalry across the ford, we saw no mounted outposts, and could distinguish by the feeble light of their fires only a few infantry sentries, posted so close to the camp that between their warning and our sudden arrival the Russians would have little chance to prepare themselves for defence. Suddenly, however, two prowling and suspicious Cossack peasants appeared on horseback, some thirty paces from our line, and after regarding it for a moment they fled towards the camp, where it was obvious that they intended to give warning of our presence. This mischance was very unfortunate, because had it not been for that we would certainly have reached the Russians without losing a man; however since we were now discovered and were in any case nearing the spot where I had decided to increase the speed of our advance, I urged my horse into a gallop; the regiment did the same, and shortly I gave the order to sound the charge.

At this signal my gallant troopers and I launched ourselves at the enemy, upon whom we fell like a thunderbolt. The two Cossacks had, however, raised the alarm. The gunners, sleeping beside their guns, grabbed their slow matches, and fourteen canons belched grapeshot at the regiment. Thirty-seven men, of whom nineteen belonged to the lite company, were killed outright. The brave Captain Courteau was amongst them, as was Lieutenant Lallouette. The Russian gunners were attempting to reload their guns when they were cut down by our men. We had few wounded, almost all the injuries having been fatal. We had some forty. horses killed, mine was maimed by a heavy bullet but was able to carry me to the Russian camp where the soldiers, rudely awakened from their sleep, were rushing to take up their arms, but were being sabred by our troopers, whom I had ordered to get between them and the rows of muskets, so that few were able to reach one and fire at us. Then, alerted by the sound of gunfire, General Albert's two regiments of infantry ran from the wood to attack the two sides of the camp, bayoneting all who resisted. The Russians, in disorder, were unable to withstand this triple attack. Many of them, who having arrived at night had not been able to see the height of the river banks, tried to escape by this route and falling fifteen or twenty feet onto the rocks were injured and in many cases killed.

General Koulnieff, hardly awake, joined a group of two thousand men of whom about one third had muskets, and following mechanically this disorganised crowd he arrived at the ford, but I had given orders that this important spot should be occupied by five or six hundred horsemen, amongst whom were the lite company who, enraged at the loss of their captain, massacred most of the Russians. General Koulnieff, who had already been drinking, attacked Sergeant Legendre, who, thrusting his sabre into the Russian's neck, laid him dead at his feet. M. de. Sgur, in his story of the campaign of 1812, has General Koulnieff making a dying speech worthy of Homer. I was within a few feet of Sergeant Legendre when he drove his sabre into Koulnieff's throat, and I can certify that the General fell without uttering a word. The victory achieved by General Albert's infantry and the 23rd was complete. The enemy had at least 2000 men killed or wounded and we took around 4000 prisoners. The remainder perished by falling on the sharp rocks of the river.

Some of the most agile Russians managed to rejoin Wittgenstein who, when he heard of the sanguinary defeat of his advance-guard, began a retreat toward Sebej.

Marshal Oudinot, encouraged by the resounding success which he had just gained, decided to pursue the Russians, and took his army, as on the previous day, back across the Drissa to the right bank; but in order to give General Albert's infantry brigade and the 23rd Chasseurs an opportunity to recover from the effects of the fighting, he left them to keep watch on the field of battle at Sivotschina. I took advantage of this period of rest to carry out a ceremony rarely seen in war. This was to pay my last respects to those of our brave comrades who had lost their lives. They were laid, arranged by rank, in a large pit, with Captain Courteau and his lieutenant at their head. Then the fourteen canons, so gallantly captured by the 23rd, were placed before this military tomb.

Having completed this act of piety, I wished to dress my wound of the previous day, which was causing me a great deal of pain, and to do this I went to sit apart under a huge pine tree. There I saw a young battalion commander, who with his back against the trunk and held up by two Grenadiers, was painfully closing a little package on which a name was traced in his blood. This officer, who belonged to Albert's brigade, had suffered, during the attack on the Russian camp, an appalling bayonet wound which had slit open his abdomen from which the intestines were protruding, pierced in several places. Although some dressing had been applied the blood still flowed and the wound was mortal. The doomed man, who was well aware of this, had wished, before he died, to take leave of a lady whom he loved but did not know to whom he might entrust this precious message, when chance brought me there. We knew each other only by sight, but nonetheless, urged by the approach of death, he asked me, in a voice now faint, to do him two favours, then motioning the Grenadiers to one side he gave me the package, and saying, with tears in his eyes, "It is a portrait," he made me promise to deliver it secretly, with my own hands, if I was fortunate enough to return one day to Paris. "In any case" he added "there is no hurry, for it would be better if this was received long after I am gone". I promised to carry out this sad task which I was unable to do until two years later in 1814. The second request which he made I was able to carry out within some two hours. He was distressed to think that his body would be devoured by the wolves which abounded in the country and asked to be put beside the captain and the troopers of the 23rd, whose burial he had seen. This I promised, and when he died, not long after our unhappy meeting, I carried out this last wish.

Chap. 10.

Deeply moved by this unhappy event,I was meditating with much sadness, when I was awakened from my reveries by the distant sound of a sustained cannonade. The two armies were once more in action. Marshal Oudinot, after passing the inn at Kliastitsoui where I had been wounded the day before, had contacted the Russian rear-guard at the beginning of the marsh, the exit from which had been so disastrous for us on the previous day. He was determined to drive the enemy back, but they were not prepared to pass through this dangerous defile, and mounted a counter-offensive against the French troops who after suffering considerable losses retreated, followed by the Russians. One might have thought that Oudinot and Wittgenstein were playing a game of prisoner's base, advancing and retreating by turn. The news of this fresh retreat by Oudinot was given to us on the battlefield of Sivotschina by an aide-de-camp, who brought to General Albert the order to take his brigade together with the 23rd Chasseurs, two leagues to the rear, in the direction of Polotsk.

When it came to leaving, I was unwilling to part with the fourteen artillery pieces captured that morning by my regiment, and as the horses which pulled them had also fallen into our hands, they were harnessed up and we took the guns to our next bivouac, and on the night following to Polotsk, where it was not long before they played an effective part in the defence of that town.

Oudinot withdrew that same day to the ford at Sivotschina, which he had crossed in the morning in pursuit of Wittgenstein who bearing in mind the disaster which had overwhelmed his advance-guard at this place on the occasion, did not risk sending any isolated unit across to the bank which we occupied. So the two armies, separated by the Drissa, settled themselves for the night.

On the following day, the 2nd August, Oudinot having joined his units at Polotsk, hostilities ceased for a few days, as both sides were in need of a rest. We were rejoined by the good General Castex and also by the 24th Chasseurs, who were very angry with their Colonel for leading them away when it was their turn to attack the Russian camp. On their trip up the Drissa they had seen no sign of the enemy nor had they found any trace of the supposed ford.

After several days rest Wittgenstein led part of his troops towards the lower Dvina, from where Macdonald was threatening his right. When Marshal Oudinot followed the Russian army in that direction it turned to face him, and for a week or ten days there was a series of marches and countermarches, and several minor engagements which it would be too long and wearisome to describe, and which resulted only in the useless killing of men and the demonstration of the indecision of both commanders.

The most serious engagement during this short period took place on the 13th August near the magnificent monastery of Valensoui, built on the bank of the Svolna. This little river which has very muddy banks separated the French and the Russians, and it was obvious that whichever general attempted to force a crossing on such unfavourable terrain would come to grief. Neither Oudinot nor Wittgenstein had any intention of crossing the Svolna at this point; but instead of going to look for some other place where they could meet in combat, they took up positions on either side of this watercourse, as it were in mutual despite. Soon there was from both banks a lively cannonade which was totally useless as the troops on neither side could attack their adversaries and was no credit to either party.

However Wittgenstein, to protect the lives of his men, had restricted himself to posting some battalions of unmounted Chasseurs among the willows and reeds which bordered the stream, and had kept the bulk of his force out of the range of the French guns, whose brisk fire hit only some of his sharpshooters, while Oudinot, who had insisted, in spite of the sensible advice of several generals, on bringing his first line up to the Svolna suffered losses which he could have and should have avoided. The Russian artillery is nowhere as good as ours, but they used pieces called licornes, which had a range exceeding that of the French guns of the period, and it was these licornes which did the most damage among our troops.

Marshal Oudinot, in his belief that the enemy were going to cross the river, not only kept a division of infantry in position to repel them, but supported them with General Castex's cavalry, an unnecessary precaution, since a crossing of even a small river takes more time than is needed for the defenders to hurry into a position to oppose it. Nonetheless my regiment was exposed for twenty-four hours to the Russian fire, which killed or wounded several of my men.

During this confrontation in which the troops remained stationary for a long period, there arrived the aide-de-camp whom Oudinet had sent to Witepsk to report to the Emperor the result of the battles at Kliastitsoui and at Sivotschina. Napoleon who wanted to make it clear to the troops that he did not blame them for the lack of success in our operations, loaded 2nd Corps with rewards in the way of decorations and promotions, and then, turning to the cavalry, he awarded four Crosses of the Legion of Honour to each of the cavalry regiments. In the despatch announcing this news, Major-general the Prince Berthier added that in order to show his satisfaction with the conduct of the 23rd Chasseurs at Wilkomir, the bridge of Dvinaburg, the night battle at Drouia, Kliastitsoui and above all in the attack on the Russian camp at Sivotschina, the Emperor was awarding them, in addition to the four decorations given to the other regiments, fourteen decorations, one for each of the guns captured by them from Koulnieff's advance-guard, so that I had now eighteen crosses to distribute among my brave soldiers. The aide-de-camp had not brought the awards themselves, but the Major-general had added to his letter the request that the regimental commanders should draw up a list of recipients and forward it to him.

I assembled all the captains, and after taking their advice, I drew up my list, and presented it to Marshal Oudinot, asking at the same time if I might be allowed to announce the awards immediately to my regiment: "What, here, under fire?" "Yes, marshal, under fire. That enhances their value."

General Lorencez, who as chief of staff had written the report of the various actions, in which he had highly praised the 23rd, agreed with my suggestion and so the Marshal consented. The decorations would not arrive until later, but I had my servant look in my baggage for a piece of ribbon which I had in my portmanteau, and when it was found, and after it had been cut into eighteen pieces, I announced to the regiment the awards which the Emperor had presented, and calling out of the ranks each of the recipients in turn, I gave them a piece of the red ribbon, then so keenly wished for and so proudly worn, and which has since then been so diminished in value, almost prostituted, by handing it out indiscriminately to all and sundry.

This ceremony, conducted in the field and under fire, had a great effect, and the enthusiasm of the regiment was at its height when I announced the name of Sergeant Prud'homme, reputed justly to be the most intrepid and unassuming of the warriors of the 23rd. This brave survivor of many a fierce encounter, accepted with modesty his piece of ribbon, to the sound of loud acclamation from all the squadrons. A moment of well earned triumph. I shall never forget this moving scene which took place, as you know, within range of the enemy guns.

Sadly, there is no rose without its thorn. Two of the men who were included in my list had just been severely wounded. Sergeant Legendre, who had killed General Koulnieff, had an arm carried away, and Corporal Griffon had a leg smashed. The injured limbs were being amputated when I went to the dressing station to give them their decorations. At the sight of the ribbons they forgot for a moment their pain, but unhappily, Sergeant Legendre did not long survive his injury, though Griffon recovered and was sent back to France, where I saw him some years later in Les Invalides.

The 24th Chasseurs, who received only four decorations as opposed to the eighteen awarded to the 23rd, conceded that this was fair, but nevertheless they regretted that they had been deprived of the honour of taking the fourteen Russian guns at Sivotschina, even at the cost of suffering such casualties as ours, "We are soldiers" they said, "and must take our chances for better or worse." They blamed their colonel for providing them with what they called this let-out. Here was an army whose men actually clamoured for action.

You will doubtless wonder what I got out of all this, and the answer is nothing. The Emperor, before he removed Colonel de La Nougarde from the command of the regiment and either made him a general or head of a legion of gendarmes, wanted to know if his health would permit him to carry out the duties of either of these two ranks. As a consequence Marshal Oudinot was ordered to bring Colonel de La Nougarde before a medical board, whose conclusion was that he would never be able to mount a horse. In view of this, the Marshal authorised the Colonel's return to France, where he was given the command of a minor fortress. The unfortunate Colonel, before leaving Polotsk, where his infirmities had forced him to remain, wrote me a very touching letter in which he took his leave of the 23rd, and although he had never led the regiment into action, an event which increases the men's regard for their commander, his departure was justifiably regretted.

The regiment now being without a colonel, the Marshal expected to receive at any moment the order for my promotion to that rank, and quite frankly so did I. The Emperor had however moved away, and had left Witepsk to take Smolensk and from there to march on Moscow, and the work of his cabinet had been slowed by their preoccupation with military operations to such an extent that I was not gazetted Colonel until three months later.

Let us now return to the banks of the Svolna, which the French left hurriedly, after depositing some of their wounded in the monastery of Valensoui. Amongst those whom we lost was M. Casabianca, Colonel of the 11th light infantry regiment, who had served with me as aide-de-camp to Massna. He was a very fine officer whose promotion had been rapid; but his career was ended by a head injury received when he was visiting some of his men on the bank of the Svolna. He was dying when I saw him on a stretcher carried by some sappers. He recognised me and shaking my hand he observed that he was sorry to see our army corps so poorly managed. The poor fellow died that evening.

His last words were only too well founded, for our leader seemed to proceed without method or plan. After a success, he pursued Wittgenstein regardless of any obstacles and spoke of nothing less than driving him back as far as St.Petersburg, but at the least check he retreated swiftly and started seeing enemies everywhere. It was in this last state that he took his troops back to Polotsk, although they were displeased at being made to fall back before the Russians whom they had recently defeated in almost every encounter.

On the 15th of August, the Emperor's birthday, 2nd Corps arrived dejectedly at Polotsk, where we met with 6th Corps, formed of the two fine Bavarian divisions of General Wrde, which had a French general, Gouvion Saint-Cyr in overall command. The Emperor had sent this reinforcement of 8 to 10,000 men to Marshal Oudinot, who would have received it with more pleasure if he had not been afraid of the man in command.

Saint-Cyr was one of the most competent soldiers in Europe. A contemporary and rival of Moreau, Hoche, Kleber and Desaix, he had successfully commanded one wing of the French army of the Rhine at a time when Oudinot was scarcely a colonel or a brigade commander. I do not know anyone who could command troops in the field better than Saint-Cyr.

The son of a small landowner in Toul, he had studied to be a civil engineer, but he gave this up to become an actor in Paris, where he created the well-known rôle of "Robert,the Brigand Chief" In the City Theatre, where he was when the revolution of '89 broke out. Saint-Cyr joined a volunteer battalion, where he showed great courage and military talent. He soon became a divisional general and gained a number of victories. He was a tall man but looked more like a schoolmaster than a soldier, due in part perhaps to the habit adopted by the generals of the army of the Rhine of wearing neither uniform nor epaulets, but only a plain blue greatcoat.

One could not imagine anyone more self-controlled. The greatest dangers, setbacks, successes, or defeats, failed to rouse him to any show of emotion. He maintained an icy calm in all situations. It is obvious how useful such a temperament coupled with a taste for study and meditation, might be to a general officer, but Saint-Cyr had also some serious faults. Jealous of his comrades, he had been known to hold his troops back while, close to him, other divisions were decimated in a desperate struggle. He would then advance and profiting from the exhaustion of the enemy he would overcome them, and thus appear to have won the victory single-handed. Secondly, if Saint-Cyr was one of the best officers in the employment of troops in the field, he

236

was without doubt the one who took the least interest in their welfare. He never inquired if the men had food, clothing or footwear, or if their arms were in proper repair. He never held an inspection, nor visited the hospitals, nor even asked if there were any. In his opinion it was the duty of the colonels to see to all that. In short he wanted to be presented on the field of battle with regiments in fighting order, without troubling himself to see that they were kept in that condition. This sort of behaviour had not done Saint-Cyr any good. Wherever he served the soldiers, although acknowledging his military talents, regarded him without affection. His fellow officers dreaded working with him and the various governments which had taken power in France had employed him only out of necessity. The Emperor did the same, but he so much disliked Saint-Cyr that when he created the rank of marshal he left his name off the list of promotions, even though he had seen more service and shown more skill than most of those to whom Napoleon awarded the baton. Such was the man whom the Emperor had just placed under Oudinet's orders, to the great regret of the latter, who feared that he would be shown up by comparison with Saint-Cyr's superior talents.

On the 16th of August, the day on which my eldest son Alfred was born, the Russian army of some sixty thousand men attacked Oudinot, who, including the Bavarian unit led by Saint-Cyr, had fifty two thousand men under his command. In any other circumstances an engagement between one hundred and twelve thousand men would have been called a battle; but in 1812 the when the total number of combatants amounted to some six or seven hundred thousand, a fight involving one hundred thousand men was no more than an action, and it is this description which is given to the struggle at Polotsk between the Russian troops and those of Marshal Oudinot.

The town of Polotsk, built on the right bank of the Dvina, is surrounded by old earthen ramparts. Before the main frontage of the town the fields are divided by a large number of little ditches between which vegetables are grown. Although these obstacles are not impassable for artillery and cavalry, they hinder their movement. These gardens extend for less than half a league in front of the town, but on their left, on the bank of the Divna there is a large area of level ground. It is here that the Russian general should have attacked Polotsk, for it would have given him command of the frail and only pontoon bridge, which was our communication with the left bank from which we drew our ammunition and food supply. But Wittgenstein chose to make a frontal attack and directed his main force towards the gardens from where he hoped to scale the ramparts which, to tell the truth, were no more than easily climbed embankments, whose height, however, allowed them to dominate the ground in front of them. The attack was pressed home vigorously, but our infantry put up a stout defence among the gardens, while from the height of the ramparts the guns, among which were the fourteen captured by the 23rd at Sivotschina, ravaged the enemy ranks. The Russians fell back in disorder to reform themselves on the plain. Oudinot, instead of staying sensibly where he was, went after them and was in turn driven off with casualties. The greater part of the day was spent in this way, the Russians returning repeatedly to the attack, only to be driven back beyond the gardens by the French.

During these blood-stained comings and goings, what was General Saint-Cyr doing? He was following Oudinot about in silence, and when asked for his opinion he merely bowed and said "Monseigneur le Marachal" as if meaning since you have been made marshal, you must know more than me, a simple general. So you can sort this out for yourself.

Wittgenstein, having lost a great many men and despairing of gaining victory by continued attacks in the area of the gardens, ended up where he should have begun, by marching his troops towards the meadows which bordered the Dvina. Up until this time Oudinot had kept his twelve pounders and all his cavalry at this spot, as if they had nothing to do with the fighting; but the artillery general, Dulauloy, anxious about his guns, suggested to the Marshal that he should send not only the large calibre guns but also all the cavalry infantry. When Oudinot asked Saint-Cyr what he thought, instead of offering the sound advice that the artillery and the cavalry should stay where they were, on ground which allowed them to manoeuvre with ease and support the infantry, he only repeated his endless "Monseigneur le Marachal". In the end, Oudinot, in spite of the opinion of General Lorencez, his chief-of-staff, ordered the artillery and the cavalry to withdraw to the other side of the river. This ill-advised movement which looked like the prelude to a retreat and the total abandonment of Polotsk and the right bank, greatly displeased the troops who were involved, and lowered the morale of the infantry whose job it was to defend that part of the town which faced the open ground. The spirits of the Russians were, on the contrary, raised when they saw ten regiments of cavalry and several batteries of guns leaving the field of battle. In an effort to create confusion in this huge mass as it departed they brought forward and fired their licornes, the hollow ammunition of which acts first as a cannon-ball and then explodes like a mortar bomb. The regiments next to mine had several men killed or wounded. I was lucky enough to have none of my men hit though I lost some horses. My own horse was hit in the head and as it fell I went down with it and my injured shoulder struck hard on the ground, which was very painful. If the Russian gun had been elevated a bit more, it would have been I who was hit, fair and square, and my son would have been an orphan a few hours after first seeing the light of day.

The enemy now resumed their attack, and when, after crossing the bridge, we looked back to see what was happening on the bank which we had just left, we saw a disturbing spectacle. The French, Bavarian and Croatian infantry were fighting bravely and holding their own, but the Portuguese legion and the two Swiss regiments fled before the Russians, and did not stop until, having been driven into the river, they were in the water up to their knees. Then, forced to face the enemy or drown, they at last struck back, and by a constant barrage of fire they compelled the Russians to draw back a little. The commander of the French artillery, who had just crossed the Dvina with the cavalry, skillfully made use of the opportunity to be useful by bringing his guns to the river bank and directing a heavy fire across the stream at the enemy battalions drawn up on the opposite bank.

This powerful intervention having stopped Wittgenstein's men at this point, while the French, Bavarians and Croats drove them back elsewhere, the fighting eased up and an hour before the end of the day had degenerated into random firing. The Marshal, however could not escape the fact that he would have to continue fighting the next day; and so, preoccupied by a situation the outcome of which he could not predict, and ruffled by the obstinate silence of Saint-Cyr, he was walking his horse slowly, followed by only one aide-de-camp, among musketeers of his infantry, when enemy marksmen, seeing a rider with a plumed hat, took aim and put a ball through his arm.

The Marshal at once informed Saint-Cyr of the injury and handing to him the command of the army left him to sort matters out. He himself left the field, crossed the bridge, stopped for a few moments at the cavalry bivouac and quitting the army went to Lithuania in our rear, to have his wound cared for. We did not see him again for two months.

Chap. 11.

Saint-Cyr took up with a firm and skillful hand the reins of command, and in a few hours completely changed the look of things. Such is the influence of a man who is competent and who inspires confidence. Marshal Oudinot had left the army in a perilous state: part of his force driven back to the edge of the river, and the rest scattered amongst the gardens where they were firing at random: an inadequate lay-out of guns on the ramparts: the streets of the town cluttered with wagons, baggage, sutlers and wounded, all in complete confusion, while the troops had no means of retreat, should they be overcome, other than the pontoon bridge across the Dvina, a bridge which was very narrow and in such a bad state that the water was six inches over the planking of its platform. Finally, night was approaching and it was feared that the shooting would lead to a general action which might be disastrous in view of the disorder which ruled amongst the regiments of different nationalities.

General Saint-Cyr's first act was to order the withdrawal of those infantrymen who were in action, in the certainty that the tired enemy would do the same, as soon as they were no longer under attack.

The result was that soon the firing ceased on both sides. The troops were able to re-form and to have some rest, and further fighting was postponed until the next day. In order to put himself in a more favourable position, Saint-Cyr used the night to make preparations for the repulse of the enemy and to ensure a line of retreat, should it be necessary. With this aim, he gathered together all the corps commanders and after making clear to them the dangers of the situation, one of the more serious of which was the obstruction of the streets of the town and the approaches to the bridge, he ordered that the colonels, accompanied by several officers and with patrols, should go through the streets, sending those men of their regiments who were fit to their bivouac area, and all the wounded, sick, led horses, sutlers and carts to the other side of the bridge. General Saint-Cyr added that he would visit the town at daybreak and would suspend from duty any corps commander who had not carried out his instructions promptly. No excuse would be accepted. There was a rush to obey. The sick and wounded were carried to the left bank as well as everything which was not actually required for combat. That is to say all the impedimenta of the army. In this way the streets and the bridge were soon completely clear. The bridge was strengthened and the cavalry and guns brought back to the right bank and located in a suburb furthest from the enemy; and then, to improve his means of retreat, the prudent general had a second bridge made out of empty barrels and planks, which was for the sole use of the infantry. All these preparations having been completed before daylight, the army awaited its enemies with confidence. The latter, however, did not stir from their encampment on the open ground at the edge of the vast forest which surrounds Polotsk on the side opposite to the river.

General Saint-Cyr, who had expected to be attacked in the early morning, attributed the tranquillity which reigned in the Russian camp to the tremendous losses they had suffered the previous day. This may have been part of the reason, but the main cause of Wittgenstein's inactivity was that he expected the arrival, during the coming night, of a strong division of infantry and several squadrons of cavalry from St. Petersburg, and he had delayed his attack until he had received this powerful reinforcement so that he might the more easily defeat us on the day following.

Although the Polish nobles, the great landowners of the property round Polotsk, did not dare to support us openly, they did so in secret, and had no difficulty in providing us with spies. General Saint-Cyr, uneasy at what was going on in the Russian camp, arranged with one of these noblemen to have him send there one of his more enlightened vassals. The landowner sent to the Russian camp several cartloads of forage, and put amongst his carters his bailiff, dressed as a peasant. This man, who was highly intelligent, learned by chatting to Wittgenstein's soldiers that they were expecting a large body of troops. He even witnessed the arrival of some Cossacks and some cavalry, and was told that several battalions would arrive at the camp around midnight. Having gathered this information, the bailiff passed it to his master, who hurried to warn the commander of the French forces.

When he heard this news, Saint-Cyr determined to strike at Wittgenstein before the arrival of the expected reinforcements. But as he did not want to be involved in a long drawn-out affair, he warned his generals and corps commanders that he would not attack until six in the evening, so that, as night would put an end to the fighting, the Russians would be unable to exploit their success if things went their way. It is true that if we were victorious we would be unable to pursue the enemy in the dark, but Saint-Cyr had no intention of doing this, and for the moment wanted only to teach the Russians a lesson which would drive them away from Polotsk. As the French general aimed at taking the Russians by surprise, he ordered absolute calm to be maintained in the town and above all in the lines of outposts.

The day seemed very long. Everyone, even the General, in spite of his sang-froid, constantly looked at his watch. Having observed that, on the previous day, the absence of the French cavalry had allowed the Russians to drive our left wing almost into the Dvina, General Saint-Cyr, shortly before the attack, moved all his squadrons silently into a position behind some big buildings, on the other side of which lay the meadowland. It was on this level ground that the cavalry could manoeuvre to fall on the enemy right and give cover to the left wing of our infantry, of which the first two divisions were to attack the Russian camp while the third supported the cavalry and the remaining two formed the reserve and protected the town. All was ready when at last it was six o'clock, and the signal for the attack was given by the firing of a cannon, followed by a volley from all the French artillery which landed numerous projectiles on the enemy outposts and on the camp itself. At once our two first infantry divisions, led by the 23rd Light, fell on the Russian regiments positioned in the gardens, killing or capturing all whom they encountered and chasing the rest back to the camp, where they took many prisoners and captured several guns. This surprise attack, although carried out in broad daylight, was so successful that Wittgenstein was dining peacefully in a little country house near his camp when he was warned that French skirmishers were in the court-yard. He jumped out of a window and mounting a Cossack horse which happened to be there he galloped away to join his troops. Our skirmishers took some fine horses, documents, baggage wagons and wines belonging to the General also the silverware and some of the dinner laid on the table. An immense quantity of booty was seized in the camp by other units.

At the sound of this wholly unforeseen attack by the French, panic spread amongst our enemies, the majority of whom took to their heels without even picking up their weapons. The disorder was complete. No one was giving orders, even though the approach of our infantry was heralded by a fusillade of shots and the sound of the drums beating the charge. The scene seemed set for a resounding victory by the French troops, at whose head marched Saint-Cyr with his customary calm. However, in war an unexpected and often unimportant event can change a situation.

A large number of the enemy soldiers had reached in their flight the rear area of the camp, where was encamped the squadron of horse-guards which had arrived a few hours previously. This lite unit was made up of young men selected from the best of the nobility, and was led by a Major of proven courage, whose lan, it was said, was increased by generous draughts of liquor. When he saw what was happening, this officer leapt on his horse and followed by some hundred and twenty cuirassed riders, he rushed towards the French, whom he soon encountered. The first of our battalions which he attacked belonged to the 26th Light. They put up a vigourous resistance. The cavalry were repelled with casualties, and were rallying to prepare for a second charge when their Major, impatient at the time taken for the scattered horsemen to regain their ranks, abandoned the unsuccessful attack on the French battalion, and ordering his men to follow he led them at the gallop in open order through the camp, which was full of infantry, Portuguese, Swiss and even Bavarians, our allies, some of whom, dispersed by the victory itself, were trying to regroup while others were collecting the booty left by the Russians.

The cavalrymen killed or wounded many of these soldiers and threw the crowd into disarray. A disorderly withdrawal began which degenerated into a mass panic. Now, in a situation like this, soldiers can mistake for the enemy their own troops who are running to join them, so that, in a cloud of dust, it seems that they are being attacked by a large force, when in most cases it is only a handful of men. This is

241

what happened here. The horse-guards, scattered widely over the plain and pressing on without a backward look, seemed to the fugitives to be a massive force of cavalry, and so the confusion grew until it enveloped the Swiss battalion in the middle of which General Saint-Cyr had taken refuge. He was so much jostled by the mob that his horse fell into a ditch.

The General, who was clad in a simple blue greatcoat, without any badges of rank, lay motionless on the ground as the cavalry drew near, and they thinking he was either dead or only a humble civilian employee, passed by and continued their pursuit of the fugitives. One does not know how matters would have ended had not the gallant and quick-witted General Berckheim, at the head of the 4th Cuirassiers, charged down upon the Russian cavalry, who in spite of bravely defending themselves, were almost all killed or made prisoner. Their valiant Major was among the dead. The charge carried out by this handful of men could have had a dramatic result if it had been followed up, and this fine feat of arms goes to show once more that it is unexpected attacks by cavalry that have the best chance of success.

General Saint-Cyr, having been picked up by our Cuirassiers, ordered all the infantry divisions to advance immediately and attack the Russians before they could recover from their confusion. In this they were successful and the enemy were decisively beaten, losing many men and a number of guns.

While this infantry battle was taking place before Polotsk, another action was under way on their left, in the open plain which bordered the Dvina. As soon as the cannon shot gave the signal to engage, our cavalry regiments, led by Castex's brigade, advanced rapidly towards the enemy who, for their part, advanced towards us.

A major encounter seemed imminent, and the good General Castex said that although in spite of my recent injury, I had been able to command the regiment during the fighting round Sivotschina and Svolna, where it had been solely a matter of facing the fire of the infantry and the guns, it would not be the same today when in action against cavalry. During a charge I would be unable to defend myself since, with my one arm, I could not hold my horse's bridle and at the same time use my sabre. He therefore urged me to remain behind on this occasion, with the reserve division of infantry. I did not think that I should accept this well-meaning advice, and I expressed so vehemently my wish not to be removed from the regiment that the General gave way, but he arranged for me to have behind me six of the best cavalrymen, led by Sergeant Prud'homme, while at my side were four warrant officers, a trumpeter and my orderly Fousse, one of the finest soldiers in the regiment. Surrounded in this way, and placed in front of the centre of a squadron, I was sufficiently protected; besides, in an emergency, I would have dropped the reins to wield my sabre, which hung by its sword-knot from my right wrist.

The meadow was large enough to hold two regiments in battle order, so the 23rd and the 24th advanced in line. General Corbineau's brigade, consisting of three regiments was in the second line and the Cuirassiers followed, in reserve. The 24th, which was on my left, faced a body of Russian dragoons, while I was opposed to the

Cossacks of the Guard, recognisable by the red colour of their jackets and the fine quality of their horses which although they had arrived only a few hours ago did not appear in the least tired. We moved forward at the gallop, and when we were at a suitable distance from the enemy, General Castex ordered the charge and his whole brigade fell in one line on the Russians. By the violence of this attack, the 24th overwhelmed the dragoons who opposed them, but my regiment experienced more resistance from the Cossacks, a chosen band of men of superior stature, each armed with a 14 foot lance which he well knew how to use. Some of my Chasseurs were killed and many wounded, but once my gallant troopers had broken through this line bristling with steel they had the advantage, for the long lances are ineffective against cavalry when those carrying them are disorganised and closely engaged by adversaries who are armed with sabres which they can use with ease, while the lancers have great difficulty in presenting the point of their weapons. Thus the Cossacks were forced to turn their backs, whereupon my men slaughtered many of them and captured a large number of splendid horses.

We were about to follow up this success when our attention was drawn to a great tumult on our right, where we saw the plain covered with fugitives, for this was the moment when the Russian Chevalier-Gardes made their desperate attack. General Castex, thinking it would be unwise to advance any further when our centre appeared to be retreating in disorder, called for the rally to be sounded and the brigade came to a halt.

We had, however, scarcely re-formed our ranks when the Cossacks, emboldened by what was going on in the centre and burning to avenge their previous defeat, charged back on the attack and hurled themselves furiously on my squadrons, while the Grodno Hussars attacked the 24th. The Russians, driven back at every point by Castex's brigade, brought up successively their second and third line, whereupon Corbineau came to our assistance with the 7th and 20th Chasseurs and the 8th Lancers, and there ensued a great cavalry battle, the outcome of which hung in the balance. Both our own and the Russian Cuirassiers were advancing to join in when Wittgenstein, seeing his infantry beaten and hard pressed by ours, sent word to his cavalry to retire. They, however, were too hotly engaged for this command to be easily executed. In the event, Generals Castex and Corbineau, knowing that they would be supported by the Cuirassiers who were close behind them, committed in turn both their brigades against the Russians who were thrown into the greatest disorder and suffered heavy casualties.

On arriving at the other side of the wood where our victorious infantry and cavalry divisions were regrouping, General Saint-Cyr, seeing that night was approaching, called off the pursuit, and the troops returned to their bivouacs at Polotsk, which they had quitted a few hours earlier. During the fighting my wound had given me much pain, particularly when I had to gallop my horse. My inability to defend myself often put me in a difficult situation in which I might not have survived had I not been surrounded by a group of stalwarts who never let me out of their sight.

On one occasion, amongst others, I was pushed by the mob of combatants into a group of Cossacks, where to save myself I had to let go of the bridle and take up my sabre. I had, however, no need to use it, for seeing their commanding officer in danger all ranks of my escort furiously attacked the Cossacks who were now surrounding me, laid several of them in the dust and put the rest to flight. My orderly Fousse, the finest of Chasseurs, killed three of them and Warrent-Officer Joly two. So I came back safe and sound from this action, in which I had been determined to take part in order to encourage the regiment, and to show them afresh that as long as I could mount a horse it would be my honour to lead them when danger threatened. Both the officers and men of the regiment appreciated this, and the affection with which I was already regarded by them was increased, as you will see later, when I speak of the misfortunes of the great retreat.

Combat between cavalry units is infinitely less murderous than that involving the infantry, also the Russians are as a rule maladroit in the handling of their weapons, and their incompetent leaders do not always know how to employ their cavalry to best advantage. So that although my regiment was fighting the Cossacks of the Guard, considered one of the finest units in the Russian army, we did not suffer a great many casualties. I had eight or nine men killed and some thirty wounded; but amongst those last was Major Fontaine. This very fine officer was in the thick of the fighting when his horse was killed. His feet were entangled in the stirrups and he was trying to free himself with the help of some Chasseurs who had gone to help him when a Cossack officer, bursting through the group at the gallop, leaned dexterously from his saddle and dealt Fontaine a terrible sabre slash which blinded his left eye, damaged the other and split open his nose. However, as the Russian officer, proud of this exploit, was leaving the scene, one of our Chasseurs shot him in the back at six paces, so avenging his squadron commander. As soon as possible M.Fontaine's injury was dressed and he was taken to Polotsk to the Jesuit monastery, where I visited him that same evening. I admired the resignation with which this courageous soldier bore the pain and disability of becoming almost completely blind, since which time he has not been able to continue in active service. This was a great loss for the 23rd, in which he had been since its creation, liked and respected by all; I was much moved by his misfortune.

I was now the only senior officer in the regiment and I had to see to all the requirements of the service, which was a major task.

You may think that I have gone into too much detail about the various actions in which 2nd Corps was involved, but as I have said, I enjoy recalling the great conflicts in which I have taken part, and speak of these times with pleasure, for it then seems to me that I am once more in the field, surrounded by my brave companions, almost all of whom have now, alas, quitted this life.

To return to the present campaign: anyone but Saint-Cyr, after such a hard-fought action would have reviewed his troops to congratulate them on their success and enquire into their needs. Scarcely, however, had the last shot been fired, when Saint-Cyr shut himself up in the Jesuit monastery and spent all his days and part of the night playing his violin...a ruling passion from which only marching to attack the enemy could distract him. Generals Lorencez and Wrde, given the task of deploying the troops, sent two divisions of infantry and the Cuirassiers to the left bank of the Dvina. The third French division and the Bavarians stayed in Polotsk, where they were employed to build the fortifications of a vast entrenched camp, before acting as a support to the troops which from this important point were covering the left and rear of the "Grande Armee" on its march to Smolensk and on to Moscow. The light cavalry brigades of Castex and Corbineau were positioned two leagues in front of this camp, on the left bank of the Polota, a little river which joins the Dvina at Polotsk. My regiment went into bivouac near a village called Louchonski. The colonel of the 24th set up his a quarter of a league to the rear, covered by the 23rd. We stayed there for two months, during the first of which we did not go very far. When he heard of the victory won at Polotsk by Saint-Cyr, the Emperor sent him the baton o Imperial Marshalf. Instead of using the occasion to visit his troops, the new Marshal retired into even deeper seclusion, if that were possible. No one could approach the head of the army, which earned him the nick-name amongst the soldiers of the "Owl". More than this, although the huge monastery had more than a hundred rooms which would have been most useful for the wounded, he lived there alone, and considered it a great concession that he allowed senior officers who were wounded to be received in the outhouses. They were allowed to remain there for forty-eight hours, after which their comrades had to take them to the town. The cellars and granaries of the monastery were bursting with provisions amassed by the Jesuits; wine, beer oil, flour, *etc*. All were there in abundance; but the Marshal had taken charge of the keys of the store-rooms and nothing came from them, even for the hospitals. It was with the greatest difficulty that I obtained two bottles of wine for the injured Fontaine. The extraordinary thing was that the Marshal used hardly any of these provisions for himself, for he was a man of extreme sobriety, if also highly eccentric. The army complained loudly about his behaviour, and those same provisions which he refused to distribute to his troops were, two months later, consumed by flames and the Russians, when the French were forced to abandon the burning monastery and town.

Chap. 12.

While all this was going on at Polotsk and on the banks of the Drissa, the Emperor remained at Witepsk, from where he exercised overall control of the operations of the numerous units of the army. There are those who have reproached Napoleon with wasting too much time, first at Wilna, where he stayed for nineteen days, and then at Witepsk where he stayed for seventeen. They claim that these thirty-six days could have been better employed, particularly in a country where the summer is very short, and the rigours of winter begin to be felt about the end of September. This claim has some justice up to a point, but it should be remembered, firstly that the Emperor hoped that the Russians would request some compromise and, in the second place that it was necessary to concentrate once more all the units which had been scattered in the pursuit of Bagration. In addition it was essential to give some rest to the troops who, as well as their regular marches had to scour the countryside each evening, far from their bivouacs, in a search for food; because the Russians having burned all the stores as they retreated, it was impossible to make any daily distribution of rations. There was, however, for a long time a happy exception to this state of affairs, in the case of Davout's Corps. Davout was as good an administrator as he was a fighting soldier, and well before the crossing of the Nieman he had organised an immense convoy of little carts which followed his army. These carts carried biscuits, salted meat and vegetables and were drawn by oxen, a number of which could be slaughtered daily to provide food. This arrangement contributed greatly to keeping his men from straying from their ranks.

The Emperor left Witepsk on the 13th August, and moving further and further away from 2nd and 6th Corps, which he left at Polotsk under the command of Saint-Cyr, he went to Krasnoe, where a part of the Grande Arme faced the enemy. It was hoped that there would be a battle, but all that took place was a minor action against the Russian rear-guard, which was defeated and promptly withdrew. On the 15th of August, his birthday, the Emperor reviewed his troops, who welcomed him with enthusiasm. On the 16th the army reached Smolensk, a fortified town which the Russians call the holy of holies because they consider it to be the key to Moscow and the palladium of their empire. Ancient prophecies foretold disaster to Russia the day Smolensk was taken. This superstition, carefully nurtured by the government, dates from the time when Smolensk, situated on the Dnieper, was the furthest Muscovite frontier, from where they issued to make enormous conquests.

Murat and Ney, who were the first two to arrive before Smolensk, both thought, for some unknown reason, that the Russians had abandoned the place. The reports given to the Emperor having convinced him that this was the case, he ordered that the advance-guard should be sent into the town. The impatient Ney was waiting only for this command, he advanced toward the town gate escorted by a small body of Hussars, but suddenly a regiment of Cossacks, hidden by a fold in the ground covered by scrub, fell on our riders, drew them off and surrounded Marshal Ney, who was so hard pressed that a pistol shot fired at point blank range tore the collar of his coat. Fortunately the Domanget brigade hurried to the spot and freed the Marshal. The arrival of General Razout's infantry enabled Ney to get close enough to the town to convince himself that the Russians intended to defend it.

Seeing the ramparts armed with a great number of cannon, the artillery general, bl, a highly competent officer, advised the Emperor to by-pass the place by sending the Polish Corps commanded by Prince Poniatowski to cross the Dnieper two leagues further upstream; but Napoleon, accepting the advice of Ney, who assured him that Smolensk would be easily captured, gave the order to attack. Three army Corps, those of Davout, Ney and Poniatowski, launched an assault on the town from different directions. A murderous fire was poured down on them from the ramparts, and one even more deadly came from the batteries which the Russians had established on the opposite bank of the river. A most bloody struggle ensued; bullets, grape-shot and bombs decimated our troops, without the artillery being able to breach the walls. At last, as night was approaching, the enemy, who had bravely disputed every foot of ground, were driven back into the town itself, which they now prepared to abandon. Before they did so, however, they set all of it on fire. The Emperor thus saw an end to his hopes of capturing a town which was rightly supposed to be full of supplies. It was not until dawn the next day that the French entered the place, the streets of which were strewn with the dead bodies of Russians and smoking debris. The taking of Smolensk had cost us 12,000 men killed or wounded, an enormous loss which could have been avoided by crossing the Dnieper upstream, as had been proposed by General bl; for, seeing himself at risk of being cut off, General Barclay de Tolly, the enemy commander, would have evacuated the place and retired towards Moscow.

The Russians, after burning the bridge, halted for a short time on the heights of the right bank and then resumed their retreat on the road to Moscow. Marshal Ney followed them with his army corps, reinforced by Gudin's division which was detached from Davout's corps .

Not far from Smolensk, Marshal Ney caught up with the Russians as they passed, with all their baggage, through a narrow defile. A major engagement took place which could have been disasterous for the enemy if General Junot, who commanded 8th Corps and who had been slow in crossing the Dnieper two leagues above Smolensk, and who had then halted for forty-eight hours, had hastened to the sound of Ney's guns, which were no more than a league away. Although informed of the situation by Ney, Junot did not budge. He was then ordered, in the name of the Emperor to come to the assistance of Ney, but still he did not move.

Ney, facing greatly superior numbers, having engaged successively all the troops of his corps, ordered Gudin's division to take some strong positions held by the Russians. This order was executed with the greatest alacrity, but in the first wave the brave general fell mortally wounded. However, retaining his usual calm, and wishing to assure the success of the troops which he had so often led to victory, he appointed General Grard to take over the command, although he was the most junior brigade commander in the division.

Grard, at the head of the division attacked the enemy, and by ten in the evening, after losing 1800 men and killing some six thousand, he was master of the field of battle, from which the Russians made a hasty departure.

The next day the Emperor came to visit the troops who had fought so bravely; he rewarded them generously and promoted Grard to the rank of divisional general. Gudin died a few hours later.

If Junot had taken part in the action, he could have trapped the Russians in a narrow defile when, caught between two fires, they would have been forced to surrender, and thus brought the war to an end. One regretted the departure of King Jrme, whom Junot had replaced, for although a mediocre general, he would probably have gone to help Ney. We expected to see Junot severely punished, but he was one of Napoleon's earliest adherents and had supported him in all his campaigns, from the siege of Toulon in '93 to the present. The Emperor was fond of him and he forgave him. This was a pity, for it was becoming necessary to make an example.

When the Russian people heard of the fall of Smolensk, there was a general outcry against Barclay de Tolly. He was a German; the nation accused him of not putting enough effort into the war, and for the defence of ancient Muscovy they demanded a Muscovite general. Compelled to give way, Alexander handed the command of all the Russian armies to General Koutousoff, an elderly man of little ability, renowned only for his defeat at Austerlitz, but having the great merit, in the circumstances, of being an out and out Russian, which gave him a considerable influence in the eyes of the troops and the populace at large.

The French advance-guard, driving the enemy before it, had already passed Dorogobouje when, on the 24th of August, the Emperor decided to leave Smolensk. The heat was stifling; we marched on loose sand; there was insufficient food for such a large body of men and horses, for the Russians left nothing behind them but burning farms and villages. When the army entered Vyazma, this pretty town was in flames, and it was the same at Gzhatzk. The nearer we got to Moscow the fewer resources the countryside had to offer. Several men died and many horses. A few days later, the intolerable heat was succeeded by a cold rain which lasted until the 4th of September; autumn was approaching. The army was no more than six leagues from Mojaisk, the last town we had to take before reaching Moscow, when it was noticed that the strength of the enemy rear-guard had been considerably increased; an indication that a major battle was at last in prospect.

On the 5th, our advance-guard was briefly held up by a large Russian column, well entrenched on a small hill, garnished with a dozen guns. The 57th line regiment, which in the Italian campaign the Emperor had named the "Terrible", worthily upheld its reputation in capturing the redout and the enemy guns. We were already on the terrain upon which, forty-eight hours later, would be fought the battle which the Russians call Borodino and the French Moscow.

On the 6th, the Emperor announced in an order of the day that there would be a battle on the day following. The army welcomed this announcement with pleasure, in the hope that it would mean an end to their privations, for there had been no supply of rations for a month, and everyone had lived from hand to mouth. On both sides the evening was employed in taking up positions of readiness.

On the Russian side, Bagration, commanding 62,000 men was on the left wing; in the centre was the Hetman Platov with his Cossacks and 30,000 infantry in reserve; the right was made up of 70,000 men under the command of Barclay de Tolly, who was now the second in command, while the elderly General Koutousoff was the overall commander of all these troops, amounting to 162,000 men. The Emperor Napoleon had no more than 140,000, who were disposed as follows: Prince Eugne commanded the left wing, Marshal Davout the right, Marshal Ney the centre, King Murat the cavalry, while the Imperial Guard was in reserve.

The battle took place on the 7th of September; the weather was overcast and a cold wind raised clouds of dust. The Emperor, who was suffering from severe migraine, went down into a sort of ravine, where he spent the greater part of the day walking on foot. From this spot he could see only part of the battlefield, and to see its entirety he had to climb a nearby hillock, which he did only twice during the action. The Emperor has been blamed for his lack of activity, but it should be borne in mind that in the central position which he occupied with his reserves, he was able to receive frequent reports of events occurring at all points of the line, whereas if he had been on one wing or the other, the aides-de-camp, hurrying with urgent information over such broken ground, might not have been able to see him or known where to look for him. Also it must not be forgotten that the Emperor was ill and a strong and glacial wind prevented him from remaining on horseback.

I took no part in the battle of Moscow, so I shall refrain from going into any detail about the various manoeuvres carried out during this memorable action. I shall say only that after almost unheard of efforts the French succeeded in overcoming the most obstinate resistance of the Russians, and that the battle was one of the most bloody fought during the century. The two armies suffered casualties to a total of 50,000 dead or wounded. The French had 49 generals killed or wounded and 20,000 men put out of action. The Russian losses were a third greater. General Bagration, the best of their officers was killed, and by a bizarre turn of fate he happened to be the owner of the land on which the battle was fought. Twelve thousand horses were left on the field. The French took few prisoners, an indication of the courage and determination of the Russian resistance.

During the action there were several interesting episodes. When the Russian left had been twice driven back by the supreme efforts of Murat, Davout and Ney and had yet rallied for the third time and returned to the charge, Murat asked General Belliard to beg the Emperor to send part of his guard to secure a victory, failing which it would be necessary to fight another battle to beat the Russians. Napoleon was inclined to comply with this request, but Marshal Bessires, commandant of the Guard said to him "I shall permit myself to remind your majesty that you are at this moment some seven hundred leagues from France." Whether it was this observation or whether the Emperor thought that the battle had not reached the stage when he should commit his reserve, he refused the request. Two other demands of this kind met the same fate.

There was another remarkable incident which occurred in this battle so full of gallant deeds. The enemy front was covered by some high ground on which were redouts and redans and in particular, a crenelated fort armed with 80 guns. The French, after considerable losses had gained control of these field works but had not been able to retain the fort, and to regain it would be a very difficult task even for infantry. General Montbrun, who commanded the 2nd Cavalry Corps, had noticed, with the help of his field-glass, that the gate of the fort was not closed and that platoons of Russian soldiers were going through it. He also noticed that if one went round the side of the high ground, one could avoid the ramparts, ravines and rocks and lead a cavalry unit to the gate up a gentle slope suited to horses. General Montbrun proposed to get into the fort with his cavalry from the rear, while the infantry attacked the front. This hazardous operation having been approved by Murat and the Emperor, Montbrun was entrusted with its execution; but while the intrepid general was finalising his plan, he was killed by a cannon-ball. This was a great loss for the army, but it did not put an end to the project he had conceived, and the Emperor sent General Coulincourt to replace him.

One now saw something unheard of in the annals of war. A huge fort defended by numerous guns and several battalions of infantry attacked and taken by a column of cavalry. Coulincourt pressing ahead with a division of Cuirassiers, headed by their 5th regiment commanded by Colonel Christophe, broke through all those defending the approach to the fort, reached the gate, entered the interior and fell dead with a bullet through his head. Colonel Christophe and his troopers avenged their general by putting part of the garrison to the sword. The fort remained in their hands, which helped to assure a French victory.

Today, when the thirst for promotion has become insatiable, one would be astonished if, after such a feat, a colonel was not promoted; but during the Empire ambition was more modest. Christophe did not become a general until some years later, and never showed any discontent with this delay.

The Poles, usually so courageous, particularly those from the Grand Duchy of Warsaw commanded by Prince Poniatovski, fought so badly that the Emperor sent his major general to upbraid them. In this battle of Moscow, General Rapp was wounded for the twenty-first time.

Although the Russians had been defeated and forced to leave the field of battle, their generalissimo, Koutousoff, had the impudence to write to the Emperor Alexander claiming that he had just won a great victory over the French. This falsehood, which arrived in St.Petersburg on Alexander's birthday, gave rise to much rejoicing. A Te Deum was sung and Koutousoff was promoted to field-marshal. However it was not long before the truth was known and the joy turned to grief; but Koutousoff was now a field-marshal, which was what he wanted. Anyone but the timid Alexander would have severely punished the new field-marshal for this outrageous lie; but Koutousoff was needed, and so he remained head of the army.

Chap. 13.

The Russians, retreating towards Moscow, were contacted on the morning of the eighth, when there was a sharp cavalry engagement in which General Belliard was wounded. Napoleon spent three days at Mojaisk, partly to draw up the orders necessary in the circumstances and partly to reply to the back-log of despatches. One of these, which had arrived on the eve of the battle, had affected him greatly and had contributed to making him ill, for it announced that the so-called army of Portugal, commanded by Marshal Marmont, had suffered a severe defeat at Arpiles, near Salamanca, in Spain.

Marmont was one of Napoleon's mistakes. He had been one of Napoleon's companions at the college of Brienne and later in the artillery, and Napoleon took an interest in him. Misled by some success achieved by Marmont at school, the Emperor had a belief in the Marshal's military talents which his performance in the field never justified. In 1811, Marmont had replaced Massna as commander of the army of Portugal, proclaiming that he would defeat Wellington, but the contrary proved to be the case. Marmont, defeated, wounded, with his army in disarray and obliged to abandon several provinces, would have suffered even worse reverses if General Clausel had not come to his aid.

When he learned of this disaster, the Emperor must have reflected deeply on the present operation, for while he was about to enter Moscow at the head of his largest army, a thousand leagues away another army had just been defeated. By invading Russia was he about to lose Spain? Major Fabvier, who brought this despatch, volunteered to join in the battle for Moscow and was wounded in the assault on the great redout. It was a long way to come to be hit by a bullet.

On the 12th of September Napoleon left Mojaisk, and on the 15th he entered Moscow. This enormous city was deserted. General Rostopschine, its governor, had forced all the inhabitants to leave. This Rostopschine whom some have described as a hero, was a barbarian, who would shrink from nothing to achieve his aims. He had allowed the populace to strangle a number of foreign merchants, mainly the French, who were living in Moscow, on the sole grounds that they were suspected of hoping for the arrival of Napoleon's troops. Some days before the battle of Moscow, the Cossacks having captured about a hundred sick Frenchmen, Koutousoff sent them by a roundabout road to the governor of Moscow, who, regardless of their condition, left them for forty-eight hours without food and then paraded them triumphantly through the streets, where a number of these unfortunates collapsed and died of starvation. As this was happening, policemen read to the populace a proclamation by Rostopschine in which, to encourage them to take up arms, he declared that all the French were in a similar feeble state and would be easily overcome. When this disgusting performance was over, the majority of the soldiers still alive were killed by the mob, without Rostopschine doing anything to protect them.

The defeated Russian troops had only passed through Moscow, and had gone to re-group some thirty leagues from there, around Kalouga. Murat followed them with all his cavalry and several infantry corps. The Imperial Guard stayed in the town and Napoleon took up residence in the Kremlin, the ancient fortified palace of the Czars. Everything seemed peaceful, when, during the night 15th-16th September, some French and German merchants who had escaped the governor's attentions came to warn Napoleon's staff that the city was to be set on fire. This information was confirmed by a Russian policeman, who refused to carry out the orders of his superiors. He stated that before leaving Moscow, Rostopschine had thrown open all the prisons and released the prisoners and convicts, to whom he had given torches said to have been supplied by the British, and that these persons were lying hidden in the abandoned houses waiting for the signal. When the Emperor heard of this he instituted the strictest precautionary measures. Patrols went about the streets and killed a number of those caught setting fires alight, but it was too late; fire broke out in various parts of the city and spread rapidly owing to the fact that Rostopschine had taken away all the fire-fighting equipment. It was not long before the whole of Moscow was ablaze. The Emperor left the Kremlin and went to the chteau of

Peterskoe. He did not return until three days later, when the fire was beginning to subside for lack of fuel. I shall not go into any details about the fire itself, as there are several eye-witness accounts, but later I shall examine the consequences of this catastrophic conflagration.

Napoleon, who did not understand the position in which Alexander found himself, hoped always for some accommodation and eventually, tired of waiting, he decided to write to him personally. In the meantime the Russian army was being reorganised in the area of Kalouga, from where agents were sent to direct stray soldiers back to their units. It was estimated that there were about 15,000 of them concealed in the suburbs and able to wander about our bivouacs without being challenged. They sat round the fires with our men and ate with them, yet no one thought of making them prisoners. This was a great mistake, for they gradually returned to the Russian army, while our strength diminished daily owing to sickness and the increasing cold. We lost an enormous number of horses, which was thought due to the extraordinary efforts demanded by Murat from the cavalry, of which he was the commander. Murat, recalling the brilliant successes obtained against the Prussians in 1806 and 1807 by pursuing them closely, thought that the cavalry should be equal to any demands and should march twelve to fifteen leagues a day without worrying about the fatigue of the horses, the essential being to reach the enemy with at least some of the columns. However the climate, the shortage of rations and fodder, the long duration of the campaign and above all the tenacious resistance of the Russians had greatly changed the situation, so that by the time we reached Moscow, half our cavalrymen had no horses, and Murat managed to finish off the rest at Kalouga. Prince Murat was proud of his tall stature and his bravery; and being always decked out in strange but brilliant uniforms he had attracted the notice of the enemy, with whom he was pleased to parley, even exchanging gifts with the Cossack officers. Koutousoff took advantage of these meetings to encourage in the French the false hopes of a peace, hopes which Murat passed on to the Emperor. One day however, this enemy who claimed to be so weakened, arose, slipped into our cantonments and captured some supplies, a squadron of dragoons and a battalion of troops. After this Napoleon forbade, under pain of death, any communication with the Russians which he had not authorised.

The Emperor never entirely lost hope of concluding a peace. On the 4th of October he sent General Lauriston, his aide-de-camp, to General Koutousoff's headquarters. The cunning Russian showed General Lauriston a letter which he had addressed to the Emperor Alexander, urging him to agree to the French proposals, seeing that, as he alleged, the Russian army was in no state to continue the war. The officer carrying this despatch had hardly left for St. Petersburg, armed with a pass from Lauriston which would preserve him from attack by any of our men who were in the area between the two armies, when Koutousoff sent off a second aide-de-camp to his Emperor. This officer, having no French laissez-passer, was stopped by one of our patrols, taken prisoner and his despatches sent to Napoleon. The contents were the exact opposite to what had been shown to Lauriston. After imploring his sovereign not to treat with the French, he informed him that Admiral Tchitchakoff's army, freed from its duties on the frontier by the peace with Turkey, was moving towards Minsk in order to cut the French line of retreat. He also told Alexander of the discussions he had conducted freely with Murat, with the aim of encouraging the false sense of security entertained by the French in remaining in Moscow so late in the year.

When he saw this letter, Napoleon, realising that he had been tricked, fell into a furious rage, and is said to have contemplated marching on St.Petersburg; but beyond the diminished strength of the army and the rigours of the winter, which militated against such an undertaking, there were pressing reasons for the Emperor to get closer to Germany, in order to watch over that country and to see what was going on in France, where there had been a conspiracy whose leaders had been, for one day, in control of the capital. A fanatic, General Malet, had tossed a spark into Paris which could have started a fire, which, had he not encountered a man as far-seeing and energetic as Adjutant-major Laborde, might have put an end to the imperial government.

This was not heartening, and one can imagine the anxiety of Napoleon when he learned of the danger which had threatened his family and his government.

Chap. 14.

In Moscow, Napoleon's position grew worse daily. The cold was already bitter and only the French-born soldiers maintained their morale, but they composed no more than half the force which Napoleon had led into Russia. The remainder was made up of Germans, Swiss, Croats, Lombards, Romanians, Piedmontais, Spaniards and Portuguese. All these foreigners, who stayed loyal as long as the army was successful, now began to complain and led astray by the leaflets in various languages which the Russians spread widely through our camps, they deserted in droves to the enemy, who promised to repatriate them.

Added to this, the two wings of the Grande Arme, which consisted entirely of Austrians and Prussians, were now no longer in line with the centre as they had been at the beginning of the campaign, but were in our rear, ready to bar our way on the first command of their sovereigns, ancient and irreconcilable enemies of France. The position was critical, and although it would greatly hurt Napoleon's pride to display to the whole world that he had failed in his objective of imposing a peace on Alexander, the word "retreat" was at last uttered, but neither the Emperor nor the marshals nor anyone else thought of abandoning Russia and recrossing the Nieman; the idea was to go into winter quarters in the least unpleasant of the Polish provinces.

The evacuation of Moscow was agreed on in principle, but before taking this step, Napoleon, in a last endeavour to obtain a settlement, sent an emissary to Marshal Koutousoff, who did not make any response.

During these delays our army was melting away, day by day, and in blind overconfidence our outposts remained at risk in the province of Kalouga in untactical positions, when suddenly a wholly unforeseen event occurred which opened the eyes of the most incredulous and destroyed any illusions which the Emperor still had of achieving peace.

General Sbastiani, whom we saw allowing himself to be surprised at Drouia, had replaced General Montbrun as commander of the 2ndCavalry Corps, and although close to the enemy, he spent his days in his slippers, reading Italian poetry and carrying out no reconnaissance. Taking advantage of this negligence, Koutousoff attacked Sbastiani on the 18th of October, surrounded him and overwhelmed him by numbers, forcing him to abandon part of his artillery. Sbastiani's three divisions of cavalry, separated from the rest of Murat's troops were able to rejoin them only after fighting their way through several enemy battalions who stood in their way. In the course of this savage combat, Sbastiani displayed his valour, for he was a brave man, if a noticeably mediocre general. Something which will be demonstrated anew when we come to the campaign of 1813.

At the same time as he surprised Sbastiani, Koutousoff ordered an attack on Murat's lines, in which the Prince was slightly wounded. Having learned of this unsatisfactory affair, and on the same day been told of the arrival in the enemy camp of a reinforcement of ten thousand cavalry from the Russian army in Wallachia (The Russian border with the Turks, in southern Romania. Ed.) which the Austrians, our allies, had allowed to pass, the Emperor gave the order for the departure to begin on the following day.

In the morning of the 19th of October, the Emperor left Moscow, which he had entered on the 15th of September. His Majesty, the old guard and the bulk of the army took the road to Kalouga; Marshal Mortier and two divisions of the Young Guard remained behind for twenty-four hours to complete the destruction of the city and blow up the Kremlin, after which they brought up the rear of the march.

The army trailed behind it more than forty thousand carriages, which caused an obstruction whenever the road narrowed. When this was remarked on to the Emperor, he replied that each of these coaches could carry two wounded men and food for several, and that their number would gradually diminish. The employment of this philanthropic system could, I think, be objected to, on the grounds that the need to speed the march of a retreating army seems to me to outweigh all other considerations.

During the French occupation of Moscow, Murat and the cavalry corps had been stationed in part of the fertile province of Kalouga, but without seizing the town of that name. The Emperor wished to avoid passing through the area of the battle of Moscow (Borodino) and down the road to Mojaisk, which had been stripped of resources by the army on its approach to Moscow; and for this reason he took the road to Kalouga, from where he counted on getting to Smolensk through fertile and, as it were, unspoiled country, but at the end of several day's march, the army, which after joining with Murat's force amounted still to more than 100,000 men, found itself confronting the Russian army which occupied the little town of Malo-Iaroslawetz. The enemy was in an exceedingly strong position, nevertheless the

Emperor sent into the attack Prince Eugne, at the head of the Italian Corps and the French divisions of Morand and Gerard. Nothing could stand in the way of these men and they took the town after a long and murderous fight which cost us 4000 killed or wounded. Among the dead was General Delzons, a very fine officer.

The next day, the 24th of October, the Emperor, surprised at the degree of resistance he had encountered, and knowing that the whole Russian army barred his way, halted the march and spent three days considering what course he should follow.

On one occasion, during a reconnaissance of the enemy line, the Emperor nearly fell into their hands. There was a very thick fog, and suddenly shouts of "Hourra! Hourra!" were heard. It was a group of Cossacks who were emerging from a wood bordering the road, which they had been going through not twenty paces from the Emperor, knocking down and spearing anyone that they came across: but General Rapp rushed forward with the two squadrons of Chasseurs and mounted Grenadiers which went everywhere with the Emperor who, wielding their sabres, put the enemies to flight. It was during this encounter that M. Le Couteulx, my former companion on the staff of Marshal Lannes, and now an aide-de-camp to Prince Berthier, having armed himself with the lance belonging to a Cossack whom he had killed, was unwise enough to come back brandishing this weapon, and, furthermore, dressed in a pelisse and a fur hat which concealed the French uniform. A mounted Grenadier of the Guard mistook him for a Cossack officer, and seeing him heading towards the Emperor, went after him and slashed him across the body with his heavy sabre. In spite of this serious wound, M. Le Couteulx, placed in one of the Emperor's carriages, survived the cold and the exhaustion of the retreat, and managed to reach France.

The reconnaissance carried out by the Emperor had convinced him that it would be impossible to continue his march towards Kalouga without fighting a sanguinary battle against the large force commanded by Koutousoff. He decided, therefore, to reach Smolensk by taking the road leading through Mojaisk. The army then left the fertile countryside to take once more the now devastated route along which, marking their passage with fires and dead bodies, they had travelled in September. This movement by the Emperor left him, after ten weary days, no more than twelve leagues from Moscow, and caused the troops to feel increasing anxiety about the future. The weather turned much worse; Marshal Mortier rejoined the Emperor after having blown up the Kremlin.

The army saw once more Mojaisk and the battlefield of Borodino. The ground, furrowed by cannon-balls, was covered with the debris of helmets, cuirasses, wheels, weapons, fragments of uniform and thirty thousand bodies, partly eaten by wolves. The Emperor and the troops passed by quickly, casting a sad look at this immense graveyard.

After they had reached Vyazma the snow began to fall and a bitter wind to blow, which slowed their progress. Many of the vehicles were abandoned, and some thousands of men and horses perished of cold by the roadside. The flesh of the horses provided some nourishment for the men and also for the officers. The command of the rearguard passed successively from Davout to Prince Eugne and finally to Marshal Ney, who kept this unpleasant job for the rest of the campaign.

Smolensk was reached on the 1st of November. The Emperor had arranged for a great quantity of food clothing and footwear to be collected there, but those in charge of these supplies did not realise the state of disorganisation into which the army had fallen, and insisted on the paperwork and formalities of a normal distribution. This delay so exasperated the men, who were dying of cold and hunger, that they broke into the stores and took forcibly, whatever they could. With the result that some had too much, some enough and some nothing.

As long as the troops had maintained a proper order of march, the mixture of nationalities had given rise to no more than minor inconveniences, but once fatigue and privation had broken the ranks, discipline was lost. There was no way in which it could be maintained in a vast body of isolated individuals, lacking every necessity, walking on their own, without understanding why; for in this disorderly mass there ruled a veritable babel of tongues. A few regiments, mainly those in the Guard, held together. Almost all the troopers of the cavalry, having lost their horses, were formed into infantry battalions, and those of their officers who still were mounted were made into special squadrons, commanded by Generals Latour-Mauberg, Grouchy and Sbastiani, who acted as ordinary captains, while brigade commanders and colonels filled the post of sergeant and corporal. This resort alone, shows to what extremity the army was reduced.

In this critical position, the Emperor had counted on a strong division of troops of all arms, which General Baraguey d'Hilliers was supposed to bring to Smolensk; but, as we neared the town, we heard the General had laid down his arms before a Russian column, with the provision that he alone would not be made prisoner and would be allowed to rejoin the French army in order to explain his actions. The Emperor, however, refused to see Baraguey d'Hilliers and ordered him to return to France and to consider himself under arrest until he was brought before a court-martial. Baraguey d'Hilliers avoided court-martial by dying in Berlin, it was said, of despair.

This General was another of Napoleon's mistakes. He had been impressed by him at the time of the encampments at Boulogne when he had promised that he could train dragoons to serve either as cavalry or infantry. However, when this system was tried out in 1805, during the Austrian campaign, the Dragoons, now on foot and commanded by Baraguey d'Hilliers in person, were defeated at Wertingen before the eyes of the Emperor, and when placed once more on horseback, they once more suffered the same fate. It was several years before the unit recovered from the effects of this experiment. The originator of the system, having fallen from favour and hoping to re-establish himself by asking to come to Russia, had completed his downfall by capitulating without a struggle, and violating a decree stating that a commander forced to surrender should accompany his men into captivity, and forbidding him from negotiating terms favourable only to himself.

After spending several days at Smolensk, to allow stragglers to catch up with him, the Emperor went to Krasnoe, from where he despatched an officer to 2nd Corps, which was still by the Dvina and was now his only hope of safety.

The regiments of this corps, although they had not suffered the hardship and privation of those who had gone to Moscow, had however been more often in action against the enemy. Napoleon wishing to reward them by appointments to vacant positions, had brought to him for his approval a number of proposals for promotions, several of which related to me. One of these recommended me for the rank only of lieutenant-colonel and it was this that was put before the Emperor for his signature. I have it from General Grundler who, having been detailed to carry the despatch, found himself in the Emperor's office during the signing, that the Emperor scratched out with his own hand the words Lieutenant-colonel and wrote in the word Colonel, saying "I am paying off an old debt." So, on the 15th of November, I at last became Colonel of the 23rd Chasseurs, although I did not know it until some time later.

The painful retreat was resumed. The enemy, whose strength increased continually, cut off the corps of Prince Eugne, Davout and Ney from the rest of the army. The first two managed to fight their way through to join the Emperor, who was very distressed at the absence of Ney, of whom he had had no news for several days.

On the 19th of November Napoleon reached Orscha. It was now a month since he had left Moscow and there was still a hundred and twenty leagues to cover before reaching the Nieman. The cold was intense.

While the Emperor worried unhappily about the fate of his rear-guard and the gallant Marshal Ney, the latter was engaged in one of the finest feats of arms recorded in history. Leaving Smolensk on the morning of the 17th, after blowing up the ramparts, the Marshal had hardly begun his march when he was assailed by a myriad of the enemy, who attacked both flanks and the front and rear of his column.

Driving them off continually, Ney marched, surrounded by them for three days, to halt eventually before the dangerous pass of the Krasnoe ravine, beyond which could be seen a great mass of Russian troops and an array of guns which opened a lively and sustained fire.

Without being cast down by this unforeseen obstacle the Marshal took the bold decision to force a passage, and ordered the 48th of line, commanded by Colonel Pelet, to attack with the bayonet. At Ney's command, the French soldiers, although tired, hungry and numb with cold, rushed the Russian batteries and captured them. They were regained by the enemy and captured once more by our men but in the end they had to yield to the superiority in numbers. The 48th, shattered by grape-shot, was largely destroyed. Of the six hundred and fifty men who entered the ravine only about a hundred emerged. Colonel Pelet, gravely wounded was among them.

Night fell, and for the rearguard, all hope of rejoining the Emperor and the rest of the army seemed to be lost; but Ney had confidence in his men, and above all in himself. He ordered lines of fires to be lit, in order to keep the enemy in their camp, in the expectation of a renewed attack the next day, but he had decided to put the Dnieper between himself and the Russians and to entrust his fate and that of his troops to the strength of the ice covering the river. It was while he was trying to decide which was the shortest route to the river that a Russian colonel from Krasnoe arrived, as an envoy, and demanded that Ney should surrender. Ney was indignant, and as the officer was carrying no written instructions, he replied that he did not regard him as an envoy but as a spy who would be executed if he did not guide them to the nearest spot on the bank of the Dnieper. The Russian Colonel was forced to obey.

Ney immediately gave the order to quit the camp in silence, leaving behind the guns, wagons, baggage and those wounded unable to march with him; and helped by the darkness, he reached, after four hours, the banks of the Dnieper. The river was frozen over, but the ice was not everywhere thick enough to bear the weight of a number of men, so the Marshal sent his troops across one by one. Once over the river the troops thought they had reached safety, but dawn revealed an encampment of Cossacks. This was commanded by Hetman Platov who, as was his custom, had spent the evening drinking and was still asleep.

Discipline is so rigid in the Russian army that no one dared wake him nor take up arms without his orders, so the remains of Ney's Corps were able to pass within a league of the camp without being attacked. The Cossacks did not appear until the next day.

Under constant attack, the Marshal marched for three days along the winding bank of the Dnieper, which would lead him to Orscha, and on the 20th he at last saw this town where he hoped to find the Emperor and the army. He was, however, still separated from Orscha by a large area of open ground in which were many enemy troops, while the Cossacks were preparing to attack him from the rear. Taking up a good defensive position, he sent of a succession of officers to find out if the French were still in Orscha, failing which resistance would no longer be possible. One of these officers reached Orscha where the general headquarters still was. The Emperor was delighted to hear of the return of Marshal Ney, and to rescue him from his dangerous position he sent Prince Eugne and Marshal Mortier who drove off the enemy and brought back Ney and what remained of his unit.

The next day the Emperor continued the retreat. He was joined by troops under the command of Marshal Victor who had recently arrived from Germany, and he made contact with 2nd Corps, where Saint-Cyr had just returned the command to Marshal Oudinot.

Chap. 15.

As it is important to understand the events which led to the reunion of 2nd Corps with the army from which it had been separated since the start of the campaign, I must describe briefly what happened after the month of August, when, having defeated the Russians at Polotsk, Saint-Cyr set up near there an immense entrenched camp, protected by a part of his force, the remainder of which he spread out on both banks of the Dvina. The light cavalry provided cover for these cantonments and so, as I have already said, Castex's brigade, to which my regiment belonged, was stationed at Louchonski, on a little river named the Polota, from where we could keep an eye on the main roads leading from Sebej and Newel.

Wittgenstein's army, after its defeat, had retired beyond those towns, so that there was between the French and the Russians a space of more than twenty-five leagues of no-mans-land, into which both sides sent reconnaissance parties of cavalry, giving rise to unimportant skirmishes. For the rest, as the area round Polotsk was well supplied with forage and standing crops of grain, and as it seemed plain that we were in for a long stay, the French soldiers started to reap and thresh the corn, and grind it in the small hand-mills which are to be found in every peasant dwelling.

This process seemed to me to be too slow, so we repaired, with much difficulty, two water-mills, which stood by the Polota near Louchonski, and from that time on, a supply of bread for my regiment was assured. As for meat, the neighbouring woods were full of abandoned cattle; but as it was necessary to track them down every day, I had the idea of doing what I had seen done in Portugal, and that was to form a regimental herd. In a short time I had rounded up 7 or 8 hundred beasts which I put in the charge of some unmounted Chasseurs, to whom I gave local ponies, too small for military use. This herd, which I increased by frequent searches, lasted for several months and allowed me to make regular distributions of meat to the regiment, which maintained the men's health and earned me their gratitude for the care I took of them. I extended my care to the horses, for which we made big shelters, thatched with straw, and placed behind the men's huts, so that our bivouac was almost as comfortable as a regular camp in peacetime. The other unit commanders did the same sort of thing, but none of them had a regimental herd: their men lived from day to day.

While the French, Swiss, Croat and Portuguese regiments worked unceasingly to improve their conditions, the Bavarians alone made no effort to escape from want and sickness. It was in vain that General the Comte de Wrde tried to rouse them by pointing out how the French soldiers were building huts, reaping and threshing grain, milling it into flour, making ovens and baking bread, the wretched Bavarians, totally demoralised since they no longer were issued with regular rations, admired the work done by our men without attempting to imitate them. So they were dying like flies and there would have been none left if Marshal Saint-Cyr, shaking off for a moment his habitual indifference, had not persuaded the colonels of the other divisions to provide a daily supply of bread for the Bavarians. The light cavalry, stationed out in the country and near the woods, sent them some cattle.

However, these Germans, so feeble when it came to work, were brave enough in action against the enemy, but the moment the danger was over they relapsed into complete apathy. Nostalgia or home-sickness took them; they dragged themselves to Polotsk, and entering the hospitals established by their commanders, they asked for somewhere to die, and laying themselves on the straw, they never rose again. A great many died in this way and General de Wrde had to take into his wagon the flags of a number of regiments who had not sufficient men to defend them. And yet it was only September, the cold weather had not begun and on the contrary it was very mild. The other troops were in good heart and awaited cheerfully the outcome of events.

The men of my regiment were noted everywhere for their good health, which I attribute firstly to the quantity of bread and meat which I was able to give them and secondly to the liquor which I was able to obtain by an arrangement with the Jesuits of Polotsk. These good Fathers, all of them French, had a big farm at Louchonski, where there was a distillery for making grain spirit, but on the approach of war all the workers had fled back to the monastery, taking with them the stills and utensils, so that production had stopped, thus depriving the monastery of part of its revenue. The arrival of so many soldiers in the region had made alcoholic drinks so scarce and expensive that the owners of the canteens were undertaking a journey of several days to Wilna to obtain supplies. It occurred to me that I might be able to reach an agreement with the Jesuits whereby I would protect their distillery and have my men reap and thresh the necessary grain, in return for which my regiment would receive a daily share of the resulting product. My proposition was accepted by the monks, who benefitted greatly by being able to sell alcohol in the camps, while I had the advantage of being able to distribute a daily ration to my men who, since crossing the Nieman, had drunk nothing but water.

At first glance these details may seem pointless, but I am happy to recall them because the care I took of my men saved many of their lives and maintained the strength of the 23rd far above that of the other cavalry regiments in the corps, which earned me a token of his satisfaction from the Emperor which I shall refer to later.

Among the measures which I took are two which protected the lives of many of my troopers. The first of these was to insist that from the 15th of September they should each equip themselves with a sheepskin coat, many of which were to be found in abandoned peasant dwellings. Soldiers are like great children, for whom one must care sometimes against their will. Mine complained that these heavy pelisses were useless and overburdened their horses, but come October they were happy to put them on under their capes, and when it grew really cold they thanked me for having made them keep them.

The second step which I took was to send to the rear all those troopers who were without a mount, either because of enemy fire or because their horse had died for some other reason. A standing order required that these men should be sent to Lepel in Lithuania, to await horses which were to be sent from Warsaw. I was preparing to do this when I learned that Lepel was crammed with dismounted troopers, who were short of all supplies and had nothing to do because not a single remount had arrived there. So I took it on myself to send my dismounted men directly to Warsaw under the command of Captain Poitevin, who had been wounded. I knew that this was in breach of the regulations, but in a huge army, so far from its base and under such abnormal conditions, it was not possible for the general staff to attend to all the needs of the troops. Occasions therefore arose when a unit commander had to use his own judgement. General Castex, who could not give me official authorisation, having told me that he would close his eyes to what I was doing, I continued in this manner for as long as it was possible, so that in the end I had sent 250 men to Warsaw. After the campaign I found them once more on the Vistula, all in new uniforms, well equipped and well mounted and a welcome reinforcement for the regiment. The dismounted men from other regiments, amounting to some 9000, who had been sent to Lepel, caught unaware by the great retreat from Moscow, were almost all taken prisoner or died of cold on the roads. Yet it would have been so easy to have sent them during the summer and autumn to the remount depot at Warsaw, where there were plenty of horses but a shortage of riders.

I remained for a whole month resting at Louchonski, which helped to heal the wound I had received at Jakoubowo. We were very comfortable in our camp from the material point of view, but very worried about the events at Moscow, and it was only on rare occasions that we had news from France. At last I had a letter in which my dearest Angelique told me she had given birth to a boy. My joy at this was mixed with sadness, for I was a long way from my family, and although I could not foresee all the dangers to which I would soon be exposed, I could not pretend that there were not many obstacles to be overcome before our reunion.

About the middle of September, Marshal Saint-Cyr sent me on a rather delicate mission. It had two objectives: first to find out what the enemy were up to in the region round Newel and then to return via Lake Ozerichtchi in order to get in touch with Count Lubenski, one of the few Poles who were willing to do anything to shake off the Russian yoke. The Emperor who, although unwilling to proclaim the re-establishment of the former Poland, wanted to organise the areas already conquered into departments, had received many refusals from the noblemen to whom he had proposed to confide the administration; but having been assured of Count Lubenski's patriotism, His Majesty had nominated him Prefect of Witepsk. As this nobleman lived in an isolated spot outside the area under French control, it was difficult to inform him of his nomination and to ensure his safe arrival. Napoleon had therefore ordered that a body of light cavalry should be sent to the Count.

Detailed to undertake this mission, with three hundred men of my regiment, I picked the boldest and best-mounted men and having provided them with bread, cooked meat and vodka, as well as other necessities, I left the camp on the 14th of September, taking with me Lorentz to act as interpreter.

The life of a partisan is perilous and very tiring. One avoids the main roads and hides by day in the forest without daring to make a fire. One takes from a hamlet food and fodder to be eaten several leagues away to confuse enemy spies; one marches all night, sometimes arriving at different point from that intended, and one is constantly on the look-out. Such was the life I led when I found myself with no more than three hundred men, in a huge area which I did not know, out of touch with the French army and approaching that of the Russians, a numerous detachment of whom I might encounter at any time. It was a difficult situation, but I had confidence in myself and in the men who followed me, so I went forward resolutely, skirting by two or three leagues the road which runs from Polotsk to Newel.

Nothing much of interest happened to us. It is sufficient to say that thanks to the information given to us by the peasants, who hated the Russians, we made a tour round Newel, avoiding all the enemy positions, and after eight days, or rather eight nights, of marching we came to the shore of Lake Ozerichtchi, where there is the magnificent chteau which at that time belonged to Count Lubenski. I shall never forget the scene which greeted us on our arrival before this ancient and vast manor. It was a splendid autumn evening. The family of the Count had gathered to celebrate his birthday and to rejoice in the capture of Moscow by Napoleon, when some servants ran to announce that the chteau was surrounded by soldiers on horseback, who had posted sentries and guards and were now entering the courtyards. It was thought that these were the Russian police who had come to arrest the Count, and he, a man of great courage, was waiting calmly to be taken to the prison of St.Petersburg, when his son, who out of curiosity had opened a window, came to say that the troopers were speaking French.

On hearing this, the Count and his family followed by a crowd of servants rushed out of the chteau and gathered on an immense peristyle. When I mounted the steps, he advanced towards me with arms outstretched to embrace me, and declaimed in theatrical tones a most fulsome welcome. Not only did the Count embrace me, but his wife and daughters did the same, then the almoner, the tutors and governesses came to kiss my hand, and the domestic staff touched my knee with their lips. I was greatly astonished at these various honours, and accepted them with all the gravity I could muster. I had thought the whole performance was over when, at a word from the Count, they all knelt down and commenced to pray.

When we re-entered the chteau, I handed the Count his appointment as Prefect of Witepsk, adorned with the signature of the French Emperor, and asked him if he accepted it. "Yes". He cried, "and I am ready to go with you." The Countess was equally enthusiastic, and it was agreed that the Count with his eldest son and two servants would leave with me. I gave them an hour to get ready, which time was employed in giving my men a good supper, which they had to eat on horseback because of my fear of a surprise attack. Having said our farewells, we left to go and sleep in a forest four leagues from there, where we stayed hidden all the next day. At night we continued our march, but to put off our trail any of the enemy who might have been warned of our presence in the area, I took a different route to that by which I had come, and going by paths and at times across country, after five days I reached Polotsk. It was as well that I had taken a different route, because I learned later from some merchants who lived in Newel that the Russians had sent a regiment of Dragoons and 600 Cossacks to wait for me at the source of the Drissa, near a village I had passed on my way in.

After reporting to Marshal Saint-Cyr and presenting to him Count Lubenski, I went back to the camp at Louchonski, where I rejoined General Castex and the rest of my unit. My expedition had lasted for thirteen days, during which time we had suffered fatigue and privation; but I was bringing my men back in good shape. We had not been obliged to fight since any small bands of the enemy we did encounter fled when they saw us.

The journey which Count Lubenski had taken with us had allowed me to assess his character. He was a well educated man, capable and patriotic, but one whose enthusiasm was inclined to cloud his judgement when it came to considering how best to re-build Poland. Nevertheless, if all his compatriots had shown his vigour, and had taken up arms on the arrival of the French, Poland might have regained its freedom in 1812; but, with few exceptions, they remained profoundly apathetic.

After leaving Polotsk, the Count went to take up his post as prefect. He did not keep the position for long, for a month had hardly passed before the French army, having left Moscow passed through Witepsk on its retreat. Compelled by this disaster to abandon his prefecture and to shelter from the vengeance of the Russians, he took refuge in Galicia in Austrian Poland, where he had large landholdings. He lived there peacefully until 1830 when he returned to Russian Poland to take up arms against the Czar. I do not know what happened to him after this uprising, but I have been told by some of his countrymen that he went back to Galicia. He was a good patriot and a fine man.

A few days after our return to Louchonski, I was greatly surprised by the arrival of a detachment of thirty troopers belonging to my regiment. They had come from Mons and had in consequence travelled through Belgium, the Rhenish provinces, all of Germany and part of Prussia and Poland, and had come more than 400 leagues under the command of a simple N.C.O. However not a man had fallen out and not a horse was injured. That shows the sort of stuff of which the troopers of the 23rd were made.

Chap. 16.

On about the 12th of October, 2nd Corps which, since the 18th of August had been living in peace and plenty in and around Polotsk, had to prepare itself to run once more the dangers of war. We learned that Admiral Tchitchakoff, commander-in-chief of the Russian army in Walachia, having made peace with the Turks through the intervention of the English, was heading for Moghilew with the intention of getting in the rear of Napoleon who, still nursing the hope of concluding a treaty with Alexander, had not yet left Moscow. One might be astonished that Prince Schwartzenberg, who with thirty thousand Austrians, our allies, was supposed to be watching over the Russian forces in Walachia, had allowed them to pass, but that is what happened. Not only had the Austrians failed to block the road taken by the Russians, which they could have done, but instead of following behind them, they had stayed comfortably in their cantonments.

Napoleon had trusted too much in the good faith of the generals and ministers of his father-in-law, the Emperor of Austria, in giving them the responsibility of covering the right flank of the Grande Arme. Whatever excuses are offered, there can be, in my opinion, no escaping the fact that this was flagrant treachery on their part, and history will condemn them for it.

While on our right the Austrians were allowing passage to the Russian troops coming from Turkey, the Prussians who had so unwisely been placed on our left wing, were preparing to do a deal with the enemy, and that almost openly, without concealment from Marshal Macdonald, whom the Emperor had put at their head to ensure their fidelity. As soon as these foreigners learned that the occupation of Moscow had not led to a peace, they foresaw the disasters which would befall the French army, and all their enmity towards us was rekindled. They did not break out in open revolt, but Marshal Macdonald's orders were obeyed with reluctance, and the Prussians encamped near Riga could at any moment join Wittgenstein's Russians to crush 2nd Corps camped round Polotsk.

Plainly, Marshal Saint-Cyr's position was becoming difficult. He, however, did not seem perturbed, and as impassive as ever, he issued calmly and clearly the orders for an obstinate defence. All the infantry was concentrated in the town and the entrenched camp. Several bridges were added to those already uniting the two banks of the Dvina. The sick and the non-combatants were sent to Old Polotsk and Ekimania, which were fortified posts on the left bank. The Marshal did not consider he had enough troops to dispute the open ground with Wittgenstein, who had received powerful reinforcements from St.Petersburg, so he did not keep more than five squadrons with him, of which he took one from each regiment of light cavalry. The rest went over to the other bank.

On the 16th of October the enemy scouts appeared before Polotsk, the aspect of which had greatly changed, partly because of the huge, newly established, entrenched camp and partly because of the numerous fortifications which covered the open country. The biggest and strongest of these was a redoubt called the Bavarian. The unhappy remnant of General de Wrde's force asked if they might defend this redoubt, which they did with much courage.

The fighting began on the 17th and went on all day without Marshal Saint-Cyr being forced out of his position. This angered General Wittgenstein, who attributed the hold-up to his officers not having distinguished between the stronger and weaker of our defence works, and wishing to inspect them himself, he boldly approached them. This devotion to duty nearly cost him his life, for Major Curly, one of the finest officers in the army, having spotted the General, dashed forward leading a squadron of the 20th Chasseurs, who sabred some of the escort while he, forcing his way to General Wittgenstein, put the point of his sword to his throat and forced him to surrender.

Having effected the capture of the enemy commander, Major Curly should have retired swiftly, between two redoubts, and taken his prisoner into the entrenched camp; but the Major was too keen, and seeing that the General's escort was about to attempt his rescue, he thought it would be more creditable if he could keep his prisoner in spite of all their efforts. Wittgenstein then found himself in the middle of a group fighting for the possession of his person. In the course of the struggle Curly's horse was killed, several of our Chasseurs dismounted in order to pick up their leader, and in the confusion this created Wittgenstein made off at the gallop, calling for his men to follow.

When this event became generally known throughout the army, it gave rise to much debate. Some maintained that Major Curly should have killed Wittgenstein as soon as his escort returned to fight for his rescue, others thought that having accepted his surrender, Curly was not entitled to do so. Others again, thought that, having once surrendered, Wittgenstein should not have tried to escape. Whatever the rights or wrongs of these arguments may be, when Curly was presented to the Emperor during the crossing of the Beresina, where General Wittgenstein caused us many losses, Napoleon said to him, "This would probably not have happened if you had used your right to kill Wittgenstein at Polotsk, when the Russians were trying to take him from you." In spite of this reproach, merited or not, Curly became a colonel shortly after, and a general in 1814.

To return now to Polotsk where the enemy, repelled on the 17th, returned to the attack on the 18th in so much greater numbers that, after suffering very heavy losses, Wittgenstein's men captured the entrenched camp. Saint-Cyr, at the head of Legrand's and Maison's divisions drove them out at bayonet point. Seven times the Russians returned to the attack, and seven times the French and the Croats drove them off, to remain finally in control of all their positions.

Although now wounded, Saint-Cyr continued to direct his troops. His efforts were crowned with success, for the enemy left the field and retired into the nearby forest. 50,000 Russians had been defeated by 15,000 of our men. There was rejoicing in the French camp, but on the morning of the 19th we heard that General Steinghel with 14,000 Russians had just crossed the Dvina above Disna and was moving up the left bank to get behind Polotsk, seize the bridges and trap Saint-Cyr's force between his own and Wittgenstein's. Indeed it was not long before Steinghel's advance-guard appeared, heading for Ekimania, where there were the division of Cuirassiers and the regiments of Light Cavalry from each of which the Marshal had retained only one squadron at Polotsk.

At once we were all on horseback and we drove off the enemy who would in the end have gained the upper hand, for they were being strongly reinforced, while we had no infantry support until Saint-Cyr sent us three regiments taken from the divisions who were protecting Polotsk. However at this point Steinghel, who had only to make a little effort to reach the bridges, stopped short, while on the other side of the river Wittgenstein did the same. It seemed that the two Russian generals, after combining to draw up an excellent plan of attack, were unwilling to put it into operation. Each one leaving it to the other to overcome the French.

The French position was now highly critical, for on the right bank they were pressed back by an army three time their strength towards a town built entirely of wood and a sizeable river, with no means of retreat except the bridges which were threatened by Steinghel's troops on the left bank.

All the generals urged Saint-Cyr to order the evacuation of Polotsk, but he wanted to wait for nightfall, because he felt sure that the 50,000 Russians who faced him were waiting only for his first backward move to throw themselves on his weakened army and create a state of disorder in the ranks. So he stayed where he was and took advantage of the extraordinary inactivity of the enemy generals to wait for the onset of the dark, which was hastened, luckily, by a thick fog which prevented the three armies from seeing one another. The Marshal seized this favourable opportunity to effect his withdrawal.

The large number of guns and some cavalry squadrons who had remained on the right bank, had already crossed the bridges in silence, and the infantry were about to follow, their movement invisible to the enemy, when the men of Legrand's division, unwilling to leave their huts for the benefit of the Russians, set them on fire. The two other divisions, believing that this was an agreed signal, did the same and in an instant the whole line was aflame. This great conflagration having alerted the Russians to our retreat, all their guns opened up. Their mortars set fire to the suburbs and the town itself, toward which their columns charged. However, the French, mainly Maison's division, disputed every foot of ground, for the fires lit the place as if it were day.

Polotsk was burned to the ground. The losses on both sides were considerable. Nevertheless our retreat was carried out in an orderly fashion. We took with us those of our wounded whom it was possible to carry; the rest, together with a great many Russians, perished in the flames.

It seemed that there was a complete lack of co-operation between the leaders of the two enemy armies, for during this night of fighting Steinghel stayed peacefully in his camp, and made no more effort to support Wittgenstein than the latter had made to support him on the previous day. It was only when Saint-Cyr, after evacuating the place, had put himself beyond the reach of Wittgenstein by burning the bridges, that Steinghel, on the morning of the 20th, deployed his troops to attack us; but the French force was now united on the left bank, and Saint-Cyr mounted an assault against Steinghel, who was overcome with the loss of more than 2000 men killed or captured.

In the course of these fierce engagements, over four days and a night, the Russians had six generals and 10,000 men killed or wounded, while the losses of the French and their allies did not amount to more than 5,000, a huge difference which can be attributed to the superior firepower of our troops, particularly the artillery. The advantage which we had in respect of numbers was in part compensated for by the fact that the wounds which Marshal Saint-Cyr had suffered would deprive the army of a leader in whom it had entire confidence. It was necessary to replace him. The Comte de Wrde claimed that his position as commander in chief of the Bavarian Corps entitled him to command the French divisional generals, but they refused to obey a foreigner, so Saint-Cyr, although in much pain, agreed to remain in control of the two army corps and ordered a retreat towards Oula, in order to reach Smoliany and thus protect on one side the road from Orscha to Borisoff, by which the Emperor was returning from Moscow.

This retreat was so well organised that Wittgenstein and Steinghel who, after repairing the bridges across the Dvina, were following our trail with 50,000 men, did not dare to attack us, although we had no more than 12,000 combatants; and they advanced only fifteen leagues in eight days. As for the Comte de Wrde, his injured pride led him to refuse to accept instructions, so he marched off on his own with the thousand Bavarians which he had left and a brigade of French cavalry which he had acquired by subterfuge, having told General Corbineau that he had received orders to take it, which was not the case. His presumption was soon punished: he was attacked and defeated by a Russian division. He then retired without authorisation to Wilna, from where he reached the Nieman. The Corbineau brigade refused to go with him and returned to join the French army, for whom its return was a piece of good fortune, as you will see when we come to the crossing of the Beresena.

Ordered by the Emperor, Marshal Victor, Duc de Bellune, at the head of the 9th Army Corps consisting of 25,000 men, half of whom came from the Confederation of the Rhine, hurried from Smolensk to join Saint-Cyr for the purpose of driving Wittgenstein back across the Dvina. This project would have certainly been carried out if Saint-Cyr had been in overall command; but Victor was the more senior of the two marshals and Saint-Cyr was unwilling to serve under his orders, so the evening before their union which took place at Smoliany on the 31st of October, he declared that he could no longer continue the campaign and handing over the command to General Legrand, he set off to return to France. The departure of Saint-Cyr was regretted by the troops who, although they disliked him personally, gave him credit for his courage and his outstanding military talent. Saint-Cyr could have been a first class army commander if he had been less egoistic and if he had taken the trouble to gain the affection of officers and men by caring for their welfare. No man, however, is perfect.

Marshal Victor had no sooner gathered 9th and 2nd Corps under his command than chance offered him the opportunity of achieving a major victory. Wittgenstein, who was unaware of this union, relying on his superiority in numbers, had decided to attack us at a place where his line of retreat would be through some narrow defiles. It would only have required a combined effort from the two corps to destroy him, for our troops were now as numerous as his, were inspired by a better spirit and were keen for action; but Victor, doubtful perhaps of success on terrain which he was seeing for the first time, retreated during the night, and having reached Sienno he put the two units into cantonment in the district. The Russians also withdrew leaving only some Cossacks to keep an eye on us. This state of affairs which lasted for the first fortnight of November did the troops much good, for they lived well as the country offered many resources.

One day, Marshal Victor having been told that there was a considerable enemy force in the area of a certain village, ordered General Castex to send one of his units to reconnoitre the place. It was for me to go. We left at dusk and reached the village without any difficulty. It was situated in a hollow, in the middle of a huge dried marshland and was entirely peaceful, the inhabitants whom I interrogated with the aid of Lorentz said that they had not seen a Russian soldier in the past month, so I prepared to return to my base. However our return was not as trouble-free as our journey there had been.

Although there was no mist, the night was extremely dark and I was afraid of leading the regiment astray on the many embankments of the marsh, which I had to cross once more; so I took as a guide one of the villagers who seemed to me to be the least stupid. My column had been going along in good order for half an hour, when suddenly I saw camp fires on the slopes overlooking the marsh. I halted the column and sent two sous-officers to have a look. They reported that there was a large force barring our advance and another in our rear. I could now see fires between me and the village which I had just left and it appeared that I had landed, without knowing it, in the middle of an army corps which was making ready to bivouac for the night. The number of fires grew, and I estimated that there was a force of about 50,000 men present and I was in the middle of it, with 700 troopers. The odds were too great, and there seemed only one thing to do, and that was to gallop along the main embankment, on which we were, and taking the enemy by surprise, cut a path for ourselves with our sabres. Once free from the light of the fires, the darkness would prevent the enemy from following us. I made sure that all my troops knew what I proposed to do, and I have to admit that I was very uneasy, for the enemy infantry could take up their arms at the first cry of warning, and cause us many casualties.

I was in this state of anxiety when the peasant who was our guide burst into loud laughter, seconded by Lorentz. I asked them what they were about, but they did not know enough French to explain fully. Eventually, however, we understood that these were not camp fires but marsh fires, or will-of-the-wisp; something none of us had ever seen before; and so, relieved of one of the nastiest frights I have ever had, I returned to my camp.

Chap. 17.

After several days I was given a new mission, in which we would face not marsh fires but the muskets of the Russian dragoons. It happened that General Castex had gone to visit Marshal Victor, and the 24th was out on patrol, so that my regiment was alone in the camp when there arrived two peasants, one of whom I recognised as Captain Bourgoing, Oudinot's aide-de-camp.

The Marshal, who had gone to Wilna after he had been wounded at Polotsk on the 18th of August, having heard that Saint-Cyr had been wounded in his turn on the 18th of October, and had left the army, decided to rejoin 2nd Corps and take up its command.

Oudinot knew that his troops were somewhere in the region of Sienno and was heading for that town when, on arriving at Rasna, he was warned by a Polish priest that a body of Russian Dragoons and some Cossacks was roaming the area. The Marshal knew that there was a French cavalry unit at Zapol, so he wrote to the commander of this unit to request a strong escort, and sent the letter by Captain Bourgoing, who for additional safety disguised himself as a peasant. It was as well that he did so, for he had scarcely covered a league when he encountered a large detachment of enemy cavalry who, thinking that he was a local inhabitant, took no notice of him. Soon after this, Captain Bourgoing heard the sound of gunfire, and increased his pace towards Zapol.

As soon as I heard of the serious position in which the Marshal found himself, I left with my regiment at the trot to bring him help. It was a good thing that we arrived when we did, for although the Marshal, joined by his aides-de-camp and some dozen French soldiers, was barricaded in a stone house, he was on the point of being captured by the Dragoons when we arrived. When they saw us, the enemy mounted their horses and fled. My troopers went after them and managed to kill about twenty of them and take some prisoners. I had two men wounded. The marshal, glad to have escaped from the Russians, expressed his thanks, and I escorted him back to the French cantonments where he was out of danger.

At this period in time, it seemed that none of the marshals was prepared to recognise the right of seniority amongst themselves, for not one of them was willing to serve under the orders of his comrade, no matter how serious the situation. So as soon as Oudinot took command of the 2nd Corps, Victor, rather than remaining under his authority to join in combating Wittgenstein, took himself off with his 25,000 men to Kokhanov. Marshal Oudinot, left on his own, marched his men for several days round various parts of the province before setting up his headquarters at Tschereia, with his advance-guard at Loucoulm. It was here, during a minor action involving Castex's brigade that I received my promotion to colonel. If you recall that I had suffered, in the rank of major, a wound at Znaim in Moravia, two at Miranda de Corvo in Portugal, one at Jakoubowo, that I had fought in four campaigns in the same rank and that finally I had been in command of a regiment since the French entry into Russia, you may think that I had earned my new epaulets. I was grateful to the Emperor when I learned that he intended to keep me with the 23rd Chasseurs for whom I had great affection, and where I was liked and valued. In fact this decision was welcomed by all ranks, and the troops whom I had so often led into battle came, both officers and men, to tell me of their satisfaction at my remaining their commander. The good General Castex, who had always treated me as a brother, welcomed me in front of the regiment, and even the Colonel of the 24th, with whom I had few dealings, came to congratulate me with all his officers, whose respect I had acquired.

However, the situation of the French army grew worse by the day. General Schwartzenberg, the Austrian commander-in-chief whom Napoleon had placed on the right wing of his army, had, by an act of low treachery, allowed the troops belonging to Admiral Tchitchakoff to pass, and they had seized control of Minsk, from where they threatened our rear. The Emperor must now have much regretted that he had given the command of Lithuania to the Dutchman Hogendorf, his aide-de-camp who, having never been in action did not know what to do to save Minsk, where he could have easily have combined the 30,000 men of the Durette, Loison and Dombrowski divisions which had been placed at his disposal. The fall of Minsk, although a serious matter, was one to which the Emperor attached little importance, for he relied on crossing the Beresina at Borisoff, where there was a bridge, protected by a fort in good condition and manned by a Polish regiment. The Emperor was so confident about this that, in order to speed the march of his army he burned all his bridging equipment at Orscha. This was a disastrous mistake, for these pontoons would have assured us a quick crossing of the Beresina which, in the event, we had to effect at the cost of so much blood.

Despite his confidence in relation to the crossing, Napoleon, when he heard of the Russian occupation of Minsk, ordered Oudinot to proceed by forced marches to Borisoff; but we arrived there too late, because General Bronikovski who was in command of the fort, seeing himself surrounded by a numerous enemy, thought it would be a praiseworthy act to save his garrison. So instead of putting up a determined resistance, which would have given Oudinot the time to come to his help, he abandoned the fort, crossed the bridge to the left bank with all his men, and set out for Orscha to join Oudinot's corps, which he met on the road. The Marshal gave him a very rough reception and ordered him to return with us to Borisoff.

Not only were the town, the bridge across the Beresina and the fort which dominates it in the hands of Tchitchakoff, but the Admiral, carried away by this success and anxious to challenge the French, had marched from the town with the bulk of his army, the vanguard of which, consisting of a strong cavalry division, was led by General Lambert, the most competent of his lieutenants.

As the country was open Oudinot put ahead of his infantry the division of Cuirassiers, and ahead of them Castex's brigade of light cavalry.

It was about three leagues from Borisoff that the Russian advance-guard, going in the opposite direction to us, came up against our Cuirassiers, who having done little fighting during the campaign, had asked to be in the front line. At the sight of this fine regiment, still strong in numbers and well mounted, with their cuirasses gleaming in the sunlight, the Russian cavalry pulled up short; then, gathering their courage, they moved forward again, at which point our Cuirassiers, in a furious charge, overran them, killing or capturing about a thousand. Tchitchakoff, who had been assured that Napoleon's army was no more than a disorganised mass of men without arms, had not expected this display of vitality, and he beat a hurried retreat towards Berisoff.

It is well known that after putting in a charge, the big horses of the heavy cavalry, and above all those of the Cuirassiers, cannot continue to gallop for very long. So it was the 23rd and the 24th Chasseurs who took up the pursuit of the enemy, while the Cuirassiers followed in the second line, at a slower pace.

270

Tchitchakoff had not only made a mistake in attacking Oudinot but he had also brought with him all the baggage of his army, which filled more than fifteen hundred vehicles, so that the rapid retreat of the Russians caused such confusion that the two regiments of Castex's brigade often found themselves hindered by the carts which had been abandoned by the enemy. This confusion became even worse when we entered the town, where the streets were cluttered with baggage and draught horses, through which obstructions Russian soldiers, who had thrown away their arms, wove their way as they sought to rejoin their units. We managed to reach the centre of the town, but only after losing precious time, which allowed the Russians to cross the river.

Our orders were to reach the bridge and try to cross it at the same time as the fleeing Russians; but to do this one had to know where the bridge was, and none of us knew the town. My troopers brought me a Jew whom I questioned in German, but he either did not know, or pretended not to know the language, and I could get no information from him. I would have given a great deal to have had with me my Polish servant Lorentz to act as interpreter, but the coward had remained behind as soon as there was any fighting. So we had to comb the town until we eventually came to the Beresina. The river was not yet sufficiently frozen to permit one to cross on the ice, so it was necessary to use the bridge, but to take the bridge would require infantry, and our infantry was still three leagues from Borisoff. To take their place, Marshal Oudinot, who had arrived on the scene, ordered General Castex to dismount three quarters of the troopers of the two regiments, who armed with muskets could attack the bridge on foot. We left the horses in the nearby streets guarded by one or two men, and headed for the river behind General Castex who, on this perilous enterprise, wished to be at the head of his brigade.

The defeat suffered by the advance-guard had produced consternation in Tchitchakoff's army, the utmost disorder ruled on the side of the river which it occupied, where we could see a mass of fugitives disappearing into the distance; so although it had at first seemed to me that it would be extremely difficult for dismounted troopers, without bayonets, to force a passage over the bridge, and keep possession of it, I began to hope for a successful outcome, for the opposition was no more than a few musket shots. I therefore ordered that as soon as the first platoon reached the right bank it should occupy houses adjoining the bridge so that being in control of both ends we could defend it until the arrival of our infantry. Suddenly, however, the cannons of the fort thundered into action, covering the bridge with a hail of grape-shot, which forced our little group to fall back. A body of Russian sappers used this breathing space to set fire to the bridge, but as their presence prevented the gunners from firing, we took the opportunity to attack them, killing or throwing into the river the greater part of them. Our Chasseurs had already extinguished the fire when they were charged by a battalion of Russian Grenadiers, and driven at bayonet point off the bridge, which was soon set alight in many places and became a huge bonfire whose intense heat made both sides move away.

The French had now to give up hope of crossing the Beresina at this point, and their line of retreat was cut...This was for us a fatal calamity, and contributed largely to changing the face of Europe, by shaking the Emperor on his throne. Marshal Oudinot, once he saw that it was impossible to force a passage over the river at Borisoff, considered that it would be dangerous to have the town choked by the rest of his troops, so he ordered them to halt and set up camp while they were still some distance away. Castex's brigade stayed on its own in Borisoff and was forbidden to communicate with the other units, from which it was hoped to conceal for as long as possible the disastrous news of the burning of the bridge, which they did not hear about until forty-eight hours later.

Under the conventions of war, the enemy's baggage belongs to the captors. General Castex therefore authorised the troopers of my regiment and those of the 24th to help themselves to the booty contained in the 1500 wagons and carts abandoned by the Russians in their flight to the other side of the bridge. The quantity of goods was immense, but as it was a hundred times more than the brigade could carry, I called together all the men of my regiment and told them that as we were to make a long retreat, during which I would probably be unable to make the distributions of rations which I had done during all the campaign, I would advise them to provide themselves mainly with foodstuff, and think also about protection from the cold, I reminded them that an overloaded horse will not last for long, and that they should not weigh theirs down with articles of no use in war. "What is more", I told them, "I shall hold an inspection, and anything which is not food, clothing, or footwear will be rejected without exception". General Castex, to avoid all argument, had planted markers which divided the mass of vehicles into two parts, so that each regiment had its own area.

Oudinot's forces surrounded the town on three sides, the fourth was bounded by the Beresina, and there were a number of observation posts, so that our soldiers could examine the contents of the Russian carts in safety. It appeared that the officers of Tchitchakoff's army treated themselves well, for there was a profusion of hams, pastries, sausages, dried fish, smoked meat and wines of all sorts, plus an immense quantity of ships biscuits, rice, cheese, *etc*. Our men also took furs and strong footwear, which saved the lives of many of them. The Russian drivers had fled without taking their horses, almost all of which were of good quality. We took the best to replace those of which the troopers complained, and officers used some as pack-horses to carry the foodstuff which they had acquired.

The brigade spent another day in Borisoff, and as in spite of the precautions which had been taken, the news of the destruction of the bridge had spread throughout 2nd Corps, Marshal Oudinot, in order to allow all his troops to take advantage of the goods contained in the enemy vehicles, arranged that successive detachments from all the regiments might enter the town to take their share of the plunder. Notwithstanding the quantity of goods of all kinds taken by Oudinot's men, there remained enough for the numerous stragglers returning from Moscow on the following day.

The supreme command and indeed all officers who were able to appreciate the situation were extremely worried. We had before us the Beresina, on the opposite

272

bank of which were gathered Tchitchakoff's forces, our flanks were threatened by Wittgenstein, Koutousoff was on our tail, and except for the debris of the Guard and Oudinot's and Victor's corps, reduced now to a few thousand combatants, the rest of the Grande Arme, recently so splendid, was composed of sick men and soldiers without weapons, whom starvation had deprived of their former energy. Everything conspired against us; for although, owing to a drop in the temperature, Ney had been able, a few days previously, to escape across the frozen Nieman, we found the Beresina unfrozen, despite the bitter cold, and we had no pontoons with which to make a bridge.

On the 25th of November, the Emperor entered Borisoff, where Marshal Oudinot awaited him with the 6000 men he had left. Napoleon, and the officers of his staff were astonished at the good order and discipline which obtained in 2nd Corps, whose bearing contrasted so markedly with that of the wretched groups of men whom they were leading back from Moscow. Our troops were certainly not so smart as they would have been in barracks, but every man had his weapons and was quite prepared to use them. The Emperor was so impressed by their turn-out that he summoned all the colonels and told them to inform their regiments of his satisfaction with the way they had conducted themselves in the many savage actions which had been fought in the province of Polotsk.

Chap. 18.

You will recall that when the Bavarian General Comte de Wrde made his unauthorised departure from 2nd Corps, he took with him Corbineau's cavalry brigade, after assuring General Corbineau that he had orders to do so, which was not true. Well, this piece of trickery resulted in the saving of the Emperor and the remains of his Grande Arme.

General Corbineau, dragged unwillingly away from 2nd Corps, of which he was a part, had followed General Wrde as far as Gloubokoye, but there he had declared that he would go no further unless the Bavarian general showed him the order, which he claimed to have, instructing him to keep Corbineau with him. General Wrde was unable to do this, so Corbineau left him and headed for Dokshitsy and the headwater of the Beresina, then, going down the right bank of the river, he intended to reach Borisoff, cross the bridge and take the road to Orscha to look for Oudinot's Corps, which he thought was in the region of Bobr.

The Emperor, who had available the services of several thousand Poles belonging to the Duchy of Warsaw, has been blamed for not attaching, from the beginning of the campaign, some of them to every general or even every colonel to act as interpreters, for this would have avoided many mistakes. This was proved during the dangerous journey of several days which the Corbineau brigade had to undertake through unknown country, the language of whose inhabitants none of the Frenchmen could understand, for it so happened that among the three regiments which the General commanded was the 8th Polish Lancers, whose officers extracted from the local people all the necessary information. This was a tremendous help to Corbineau.

When he was about half a day's journey from Borisoff, some peasants told the Polish Lancers that Tchitchakoff's troops were occupying the town, information which dashed his hopes of crossing the Beresina; however these same peasants having persuaded him to turn round, led him to the village of Studianka, not far from Weselovo, four leagues above Borisoff, where there is a ford. The three regiments crossed the ford without loss and the General , going across country and avoiding some of Wittgenstein's troops who were moving towards Borisoff, eventually rejoined Oudinot on the 23rd of November at a place called Natscha.

This daring march undertaken by Corbineau was much to his credit, but more than that, it was a stroke of remarkable good fortune for the army, for the Emperor, realising the impossibility of re-building the bridge at Borisoff in the near future, resolved, after discussing the matter with Corbineau, to cross the Beresina at Studianka. Tchitchakoff, who had been told of the crossing at this point effected by Corbineau's brigade, had placed a strong division and many guns opposite Studianka, so Napoleon, to deceive him, employed a stratagem, which although very old, is almost always successful. He pretended that he was not interested in Studianka and that he intended to use one of two other fords which were below Borisoff, the most practicable of which was at the village of Oukolada. To this end he sent ostentatiously to the spot one of the still armed battalions, followed by a horde of stragglers, which the enemy might take for a full-strength division of infantry. At the tail of this column were numerous wagons, a few guns and the division of Cuirassiers. When they arrived at Oukolada these troops placed the guns in position, and did all they could to look as if they were about to build a bridge.

Told of these preparations, Tchitchakoff had no doubt that it was Napoleon's intention to cross the river at this point so as to reach the road to Minsk, which ran nearby. He therefore hurriedly sent down the right bank, to face Oukoloda, the entire garrison of Borisoff. Not only that, for some extraordinary reason, the Russian General, who had sufficient troops to protect both the upper and lower parts of the river, removed all of those which he had placed previously in a position to oppose a crossing at Studianka and sent them too down to Oukoloda. He had now abandoned the place where the Emperor intended to build a bridge, and had concentrated his force, uselessly, six leagues downstream.

In addition to the error of massing all his army below Borisoff, Tchitchakoff made a mistake which a sergeant would not have made, and one for which his government never forgave him. The town of Zembin, which is opposite to the ford at Studianka, is built on a vast marsh, through which runs the road to Wilna. The road goes over twenty-two wooden bridges which the Russian general could have easily reduced to cinders before leaving the district, as they were surrounded by many stacks of dry reeds. If Tchitchakoff had done this, the French army would have been left without hope. It would have served it nothing to have crossed the river, for it would have been halted by the deep marshland surrounding Zembin; but the Russian general left the bridges intact, and foolishly went down the Beresina with all his men, leaving only about fifty Cossacks to keep an eye on the ford.

274

While the Russians, taken in by Napoleon's subterfuge, were deserting the real point of attack, Napoleon gave his orders. Oudinot and his army Corps were to go by night to Studianka, and there arrange for the building of two bridges, before crossing to the right bank and occupying the area between the town of Zembin and the river. Marshal Victor, leaving Natscha, was to form the rear-guard. He was to drive before him all the stragglers, and was to try to hold Borisoff for a few hours before going to Studianka and crossing the bridges. Those were the Emperor's orders, the execution of which in detail was frustrated by events.

On the evening of the 25th, Corbineau's brigade, whose commander knew the area well, proceeded up the left bank of the Beresina towards Studianka, followed by Castex's brigade and several battalions of light infantry; after which came the bulk of 2nd Corps. We were sorry to leave Borisoff where we had spent two happy days. We had perhaps a presentiment of the bad times which were to come.

At daybreak on the 26th of November we arrived at Studianka, where there were no signs of any preparation for defence on the opposite bank, so that, had the Emperor not burned the bridging equipment a few days previously at Orscha, the army could have crossed immediately. The river, which some have described as huge, is more or less as wide as the Rue Royale in Paris where it passes the Ministry of Marine. As for its depth, it is enough to say that the three regiments of Corbineau's brigade had forded it seventy-two hours previously without accident, and did so again on the day of which I write. Their horses never lost their footing and had to swim only at two or three places. At this time the crossing presented only a few minor inconveniences to the cavalry the artillery and the carts, one of which was that the riders and carters were wet up to their knees, which was not insupportable because, regrettably the cold was not sufficiently severe to freeze the river, which would have been better for us. The second inconvenience which arose from the lack of frost was that the marshy ground which bordered the opposite bank of the river was so muddy that the saddle-horses had difficulty in crossing it and the carts could sink in to their axles.

Esprit de corps is certainly very praiseworthy, but it should be moderated or forgotten in difficult circumstances. This did not happen at the Beresina, where the commanders of the artillery and the engineers both demanded sole responsibility for building the bridges, and as neither would give way, nothing was being done. When the Emperor arrived on the 26th, he ended this quarrel by ordering that two bridges should be built, one by the artillery and one by the engineers. Immediately beams and battens were seized from the hovels of the village and the sappers and the gunners got to work. Those gallant men showed a devotion to duty which has not been sufficiently recognised. They went naked into the freezing water and worked for six or seven hours at a stretch, although there was not a drop of "eau de vie" to offer them, and they would be sleeping in a field covered by snow. Almost all of them died later, when the severe frosts came.

While the bridges were being built and while my regiment and all the troops of 2nd Corps were waiting on the left bank for the order to cross the river, the Emperor, walking rapidly, went from regiment to regiment, speaking to the men and officers.

He was accompanied by Murat. This brave and dashing officer who had so distinguished himself as the victorious French were advancing on Moscow, the proud Murat had been, so to speak, eclipsed since we had left that city, and during the retreat he had taken part in none of the fighting. One saw him following the Emperor in silence, as if he had nothing to do with what was going on in the army. He seemed to shed some of his torpor at the Beresina at the sight of the only troops who were still in good order, and who constituted the last hope of safety.

As Murat was very fond of the cavalry, and as of the many squadrons which had crossed the Nieman there remained none except those in Oudinot's corps, he urged the Emperor's footsteps in their direction.

Napoleon was delighted with the state of these units and of my regiment in particular, for it was now stronger than several of the brigades. I had more than 500 men on horseback, whereas the other colonels in the corps had scarcely 200, so I received some flattering comments from the Emperor, a great share of which was due to my officers and men.

It was at this time that I had the good fortune to be joined by Jean Dupont my brother's servant, a man of exemplary loyalty, devotion and courage. Left on his own after the capture of my brother early in the campaign, he had followed the 16th Chasseurs to Moscow and taken part in the retreat, while caring for my brother Adolphe's three horses, of which he had refused to sell a single one in spite of many offers. He reached me after five months of hunger and hardship, still carrying all my brother's effects, though he told me, with tears in his eyes, that having worn out his shoes and been reduced to walking barefoot in the snow, he had dared to take a pair of boots belonging to his master. I kept this admirable man in my service, and he was a great help to me when, some time later, I was wounded once more, in the midst of the most horrible days of the great retreat.

To return to the crossing of the Beresina. Not only did our horses cross the river without difficulty, but our "cantiniers" or sutlers, drove their carts across. This made me think that it might be possible, if one unharnessed some of the many carts which followed the army, to fix them in the river in a line, one after the other, to make a sort of causeway for the infantrymen, something which would greatly ease the flow of the mass of stragglers who the next day would be crowding round the entries to the bridges. This seemed to me to be such a good idea, that although I was wet to the waist, I recrossed the ford to offer it to the generals of the Imperial staff.

They accepted my suggestion, but made no attempt to pass it on to the Emperor. Eventually, General Lauristan, one of his aides-de-camp, said to me "I suggest that you yourself undertake the building of this footbridge, the usefulness of which you have so well explained". I replied to this wholly unacceptable proposition that I had at my disposal neither sappers nor infantrymen, nor tools, nor stakes, nor rope, and that in any case I could not leave my regiment, which being on the right bank, could be attacked at any time. I had offered him an idea which I thought was a good one, I could do no more and would now go back to my normal duties. Having said this I went back into the water and returned to the 23rd.

When the sappers and the gunners had finally completed the trestle bridges, they were crossed by the infantry and the artillery of Oudinot's corps, who, having reached the right bank, went to set up their bivouacs in a large wood, where the cavalry were ordered to join them. We could from there watch the main road from Minsk, down which Admiral Tchitchakoff had led his troops to the lower Beresina, and up which he would have to come to reach us, once he heard that we had crossed the river at Studianka.

On the evening of the 27th, the Emperor crossed the bridge with his guard and went to settle at a hamlet named Zawniski, where the cavalry were ordered to join him. The enemy had not appeared.

There has been much discussion about the disasters which occurred at the Beresina; but what no one has yet said is that the greater part of them could have been avoided if the general staff had paid more attention to their duty and had made use of the night 27th-28th to send over the bridge not only the baggage, but the thousands of stragglers who would be obstructing the passage the next day. It so happened that, after seeing my regiment well settled in their bivouac, I noticed the absence of the pack horse, which, as it carried the strong-box and the accounts of the regiment, could not be risked in the ford. I expected that its leader and the troopers of its escort had waited until the bridges were ready, but they had been so for some hours and yet these men had not arrived. Being somewhat worried about them, and the precious burden committed to their charge, I thought I would go in person and expedite their crossing, for I imagined that the bridges would be crowded. I hurried to the river where, to my great surprise, I found the bridges completely deserted. There was no one crossing them, although, by the bright moonlight, I could see not a hundred paces away, more than 50,000 stragglers or men cut off from their regiments, whom we called "rotisseurs". These men, seated calmly before huge fires, were grilling pieces of horse-flesh, little thinking that they were beside a river, the passage of which would, the next day, cost many of them their lives, whereas at present they could cross it unhindered in a few minutes, and prepare their supper on the other side. Furthermore, not one officer of the imperial household, not an aide-de-camp of the army general staff or that of a marshal was there to warn these unfortunate men and to drive them, if need be, to the bridges.

It was in this disorganised camp that I saw for the first time the soldiers returning from Moscow. It was a most distressing spectacle. All ranks were mixed together, no weapons, no military bearing! Soldiers, officers and even generals clad only in rags and having on their feet strips of leather or cloth roughly bound together with string. An immense throng in which were thrown together thousands of men of different nationalities gabbling all the languages of the European continent without any mutual understanding.

However, if one had used one of the regiments from Oudinot's corps or the Guard, which were still in good order, it would have been easy to herd this mass of men across the bridges, for, as I was returning to Zawniski, having with me only a few orderlies, I was able by persuasion and a bit of force to make several thousand of these wretched men cross to the right bank; but I had other duties to perform, and had to return to the regiment.

When I was passing by the general staff, and that of Marshal Oudinot, I reported the deserted state of the bridges and pointed out how easy it would be to bring the unarmed men across while there was no enemy opposition; all I got were evasive answers, each one claiming that it was a colleague's responsibility to see to such an operation.

On returning to the regimental bivouac, I was pleasantly surprised to see the corporal and the eight troopers who during the campaign had been in charge of our herd of cattle. These good fellows were desolate that the crowd of "rotisseurs" had set on their cattle, butchered and eaten them before their eyes without their being able to stop them. It was some consolation to the regiment that each trooper had taken from Borisoff enough food to last for twenty-five days.

My adjutant, M.Verdier, thought it his duty to go across the bridge to try to find the guardians of our accounts, but he got swallowed up in the crowd and was unable to get back. He was taken prisoner during the struggle on the next day , and I did not see him again for two years.

Chap. 19.

We now come to the most terrible event in the disastrous Russian campaign...to the crossing of the Beresina; which took place mainly on the 28th of November.

At dawn on this ill-fated day, the position of the two belligerents was as follows. On the left bank, Marshal Victor, having evacuated Borisoff during the night, had arrived at Studianka with 9th Corps, driving in front of him a mass of stragglers. He had left, to form his rear-guard, the infantry division of General Partouneaux, who had been told not to leave the town until two hours after him, and who should, in consequence, have sent out a small detachment of men, who could follow the main body and leave guides to signpost the route. He should also have sent an aide-de-camp to Studianka to reconnoitre the road and return to the division: but Partouneaux neglected all these precautions and simply marched off at the prescribed time. He came to a fork in the road, and he did not know which way to go. He must have been aware, since he had come from Borisoff, that the Beresina was on his left, and he should have concluded that to reach Studianka, at the side of this watercourse, it was the road on the left which he should take... but he did not do so, and following blindly some light infantry which had been ahead of him, he took the right hand road and landed in the middle of a large force of Wittgenstein's Russian troops.

278

Soon Partouneaux's division, completely surrounded, was forced, after a brave defence, to surrender. Meanwhile a simple battalion commander who was in charge of the divisional rear-guard, had the good sense to take the road to the left, by means of which he joined Marshal Victor at Studianka. The Marshal was greatly surprised to see the arrival of this battalion instead of the division of which it was the rear-guard, but his astonishment turned to dismay when he was attacked by Wittgenstein's Russians, whom he thought had been intercepted by Partouneaux. He could not then doubt that the General and all his regiments had been defeated and taken prisoner.

Fresh misfortunes awaited him, for the Russian General Koutousoff, who had been following Partouneaux from Borisoff with a strong body of troops, once he heard of his defeat, speeded up his march and came to join Wittgenstein in his attack on Marshal Victor. The Marshal, whose army corps had been reduced to 10,000 men, put up a stout resistance. His troops, even the Germans who were included among them, fought heroically though they were attacked by two armies, had their backs to the Beresina and had their movements hampered by the swarm of carts driven by undisciplined stragglers who were endeavouring, in a mob, to reach the river. Regardless of these circumstances they held off Koutousoff and Wittgenstein for the whole day.

While this confusion and fighting were going on at Studianka, the enemy, who aimed to gain control of both ends of the bridges, attacked Oudinet's Corps, which was in position before Zawniski, on the right bank. Some thirty thousand Russians, shouting loudly, advanced towards 2nd Corps, which was by now reduced to no more than eight thousand combatants. However, our men had not yet been in contact with those returning from Moscow, and had no idea of the disorder which ruled amongst them, so that their morale was excellent and Tchitchakoff was driven back before the very eyes of the Emperor, who arrived at that moment with a reserve of 3000 infantry and 1000 cavalry from the Old and the Young Guard . The Russians renewed their attack, and overran the Poles of the Legion of the Vistula. Marshal Oudinot was seriously wounded, and Napoleon sent Ney to replace him. General Condras, one of our best infantry officers, was killed. The gallant General Legrand received a dangerous wound.

The action took place in a wood of enormous pine trees. The enemy artillery could not therefore see our troops clearly, so that, although they kept up a vigourous bombardment, their cannon-balls did not hit us, but going over our heads, they broke off branches, some as thick as a man's body, which in their fall killed or injured a good number of our men and horses. As the trees were widely spaced, mounted men could move through them, although with some difficulty, despite which, Marshal Ney, on the approach of a strong Russian column, launched a charge against it with what remained of our division of Cuirassiers. This charge, carried out under such unusual conditions, was nevertheless one of the most brilliant which I have seen. Colonel Dubois, at the head of the 7th Cuirassiers, split the enemy column in two and took 2000 prisoners. The Russians, thrown into disarray, were pursued by the Light Cavalry and driven back to the village of Stakovo with great loss.

I was re-forming the ranks of my regiment, which had taken part in this engagement, when M. Alfred de Noailles, with whom I was friendly, arrived. He was returning from carrying an order from Prince Berthier, whose aide-de-camp he was; but instead of going back to the Marshal, he said as he left me, that he was going as far as the first houses of Stakovo to see what the enemy was doing. This curiosity proved fatal, for as he approached the village, he was surrounded by a group of Cossacks who knocked him off his horse and dragged him away by his collar while raining blows on him. I immediately sent a squadron to his aid, but this effort at rescue did not succeed, because a volley of fire from the houses prevented the troopers from getting into the village. Since that day nothing has been heard of M. de Noailles. It is likely that his superb furs and his uniform covered in gold braid having roused the cupidity of the Cossacks, he was murdered by these barbarians. M. de Noailles' family, knowing that I was the last person to speak to him, asked me for news about his disappearance, but I could tell them no more than what I have described. Alfred de Noailles was an excellent officer and a good friend.

This digression has diverted me from Tchitchakoff, who, after his defeat by Ney, did not dare to attack us again nor to leave the village of Stakovo for the rest of the day.

Having described briefly the position of the armies on the two banks of the Beresina, I shall tell you, in a few words what happened at the river itself during the fighting. The mass of unattached men who had had two nights and two days in which to cross the bridges, and who had, apathetically, failed to do so because they were not compelled, when Wittgenstein's cannon-balls began to fall among them, rushed in a body to get across. This huge multitude of men horses and carts piled up at the entrance to the bridges, trying to force their way on to them.... Many of those who missed the entrance were pushed by the crowd into the Beresina where most of them were drowned.

To add to the disaster, one of the bridges broke under the weight of the guns and the heavy ammunition wagons which followed them. Everyone then headed for the second bridge, where the crowd was so thick that strong men were unable to withstand the pressure and a large number were stifled to death. When they saw that it was impossible to cross the overcrowded bridges, many of the cart drivers urged their horses into the river, but this method of crossing which would have been very successful if it had been carried out in an orderly manner on the two preceding days, failed in the great majority of instances, because driving their carts in a tumultuous mob, they crashed into one another and turned over. Some, however reached the opposite side, but as no one had prepared an exit by smoothing the slope of the river bank, which the general staff should have seen to, few vehicles could climb out, and many more people perished there.

During the night of 28th 29th November, the Russian cannons added to these scenes of horror by bombarding the wretched men who were trying to cross the river, and finally at about nine in the evening there was a crowning disaster, when Marshal Victor began his withdrawal, and when his divisions, in battle order, arrived at the bridge, which they could cross only by dispersing the crowds which blocked their way ...We should perhaps draw a veil over these dreadful events.

At dawn on the 29th, all the vehicles remaining on the left bank were set on fire, and when finally General bl saw the Russians nearing the bridge, he set that on fire also. Several thousand unfortunates left at Studianka fell into the hands of Wittgenstein.

So ended the most terrible episode of the Russian campaign, an episode which would have been a great deal less terrible if we had made proper use of the time which the Russians allowed us after we had reached the Beresina. The army lost in this crossing 20 to 25,000 men.

Once this major obstacle had been crossed, the disorganised mass of men who had escaped from the disaster was still huge. They were directed to go along the road to Zembin. The Emperor and the Guard followed. Then came the remains of several regiments, and finally 2nd Corps, for whom Castex's brigade formed the last rear-guard.

I have already explained that the Zembin road, the only way left open for us, goes through an immense marsh by means of a great number of bridges which Tchitchakoff neglected to burn when he occupied this position a few days previously. We did not make the same mistake, for after the army had passed, the 24th Chasseurs and my regiment easily set them on fire by means of the stacks of dry reeds heaped up in the neighbourhood.

By ordering the burning of the bridges, the Emperor had hoped to rid himself for a long time of pursuit by the Russians, but fate was against us. The cold which at this time of year could have frozen the waters of the Beresina to give us a pathway across, had left the river running; but we had scarcely crossed over when there was sharp frost which froze it to the point where it would bear the weight of a cannon...and as it did the same to the marsh of Zembin, the burning of the bridges was of no value to us. The three Russian armies which we had left behind, could now pursue us without meeting any obstacle; but fortunately the pursuit was not very energetic, and Marshal Ney, who commanded the rear-guard and who had gathered together all the troops still capable of fighting, made frequent sallies against the enemy if they dared to approach too near.

Since Marshal Oudinot and General Legrand had been wounded, General Maison commanded 2nd Corps, which being, in spite of many losses, now numerically the strongest in the army, was always given the task of holding off the Russians. We kept them at a distance during the 30th of November and the 1st of December; but on the 2nd of December they pressed us so hard, in considerable numbers, that a serious engagement took place in which I received a wound, made even more dangerous because the temperature on that day registered 25 degrees of frost. I should perhaps limit myself to telling you that I was injured by a lance without going into further details, for they are so unpleasant that I still do not like to remember them.

However, I said I would tell the story of my life, and so this is what happened at Plechtchenitsoui.

It so happened that a Dutch banker named Van Berchem, with whom I had been a close friend at the college of Sorze, had sent to me at the start of the campaign his only son, who having become French by the incorporation of his country into the Empire, had enlisted in the 23rd, although he was barely sixteen years old...He was a fine and intelligent young man, and I made him my secretary, so that he went everywhere fifteen paces behind me with my orderlies. That is where he was on the day in question, when 2nd Corps, for whom my regiment was acting as rear-guard while crossing a vast open plain, saw coming towards them a mass of Russian cavalry, who quickly surrounded them and attacked them on all sides. General Maison deployed his troops with such skill that our squares repelled all the charges made by the enemy regular cavalry.

The Russians then sent in a swarm of Cossacks, who came impudently to attack with their lances the French officers who stood before their troops. Seeing this, Marshal Ney ordered general Maison to chase them off, using what remained of the division of Cuirassiers and also Corbineau's and Castex's brigades. My regiment, which was still numerically strong, was confronted by a tribe of Cossacks from the Black Sea, wearing tall astrakhan hats, and much better clad and mounted than the usual run of Cossacks. We engaged them, but as it is not their custom to stand and fight in line, they turned round and made off at the gallop. However, not knowing the locality they headed for an obstacle which is very unusual in these enormous plains, a large, deep gully, which owing to the perfect flatness of the surrounding country could not be distinguished from any distance. This pulled them up short, and seeing that they could not get across with their horses, they bunched together and turned to present to us their lances.

The ground, covered by frost, was very slippery, and our over-tired horses could not gallop without falling. There was, therefore, no question of a charge, and my line advanced at a trot towards the massed enemy, who remained motionless. Our sabres could touch their lances, but as they are thirteen or fourteen feet long, we could not reach our foes, who could not retreat for fear of falling into the gulch, and could not advance without encountering our swords. We were thus face to face, regarding one another when, in less time than it takes to tell, this is what happened.

Anxious to get to grips with the enemy, I shouted to my troops to grab some of the lances with their left hands and pushing them to one sided get into the middle of this crowd of men, where our short weapons would give us an enormous advantage over their long spears. To encourage them to obey, I wanted to set an example, so dodging several lances, I managed to reach the front rank of the enemy...My warrant officers and my orderlies followed me, and soon the whole regiment. There then ensued a general mle; but at the moment when it started, an old white-bearded Cossack, who was in the rear rank and separated from me by some of his comrades, lent forward and thrusting his lance skillfully between the horses he drove the sharp steel into my right knee, which it pierced, passing through beneath the kneecap.

Enraged by the pain of this injury, I was pushing my way towards the man to take my revenge, when I was confronted by two handsome youths of about eighteen to twenty, wearing a brilliant costume, covered with rich embroidery, who were the sons of the chieftain of this clan. They were accompanied by an elderly man who was some sort of tutor, but who was unarmed. The younger of his two pupils did not draw his sword, but elder did and attacked me furiously...I found him so immature and lacking strength that I did no more than disarm him, and taking his arm pushed him behind me, telling Van Berchem to look after him. I had hardly done this when a double explosion rang in my ears and the collar of my cape was torn by a ball. I turned round quickly, to see the young Cossack officer holding a pair of double-barrelled pistols with which he had treacherously tried to shoot me in the back and had blown out the brains of the unfortunate Van Berchem!

In a transport of rage I hurled myself at this rash stripling, who was already aiming his second pistol at me. Seeing death in my face, he seemed momentarily paralysed. He cried out some words in French. But I killed him.

Blood calls for blood. The sight of young Van Berchem lying dead at my feet, the act I had just carried out, the excitement of battle and the pain of my wound, combined to induce a sort of frenzy. I rushed at the younger of the Cossack officers and grabbing him by the throat I had already raised my sabre when his elderly mentor, to protect his charge, laid the length of his body on my horses neck in a manner which prevented me from striking a blow and called out, "Mercy! In the name of your mother, have mercy! He has done nothing!"

On hearing this appeal, in spite of the scenes around me, I seemed to see the white hand I knew so well, laid on the young man's breast and to hear my mother's gentle voice saying,"Be merciful". I lowered my sabre and sent the youth and his guardian to the rear.

I was so disturbed by what had happened that I would have been unable to give any further orders to the regiment if the fighting had continued for any length of time, but it was soon finished. Many of the Cossacks had been killed and the remainder, abandoning their horses, slid into the depths of the ravine, where a number died in the huge snow-drift which the wind had created.

In the evening following this affair, I questioned my prisoner and his guardian. I learned that the two youngsters were the sons of a powerful chieftain, who, having lost a leg at Austerlitz, hated the French so much that being unable to fight them himself, he had sent his two sons to do so. I thought it likely that, as a prisoner, the cold and misery would be fatal to the one survivor. I took pity on him and set both him and his venerable mentor at liberty. On taking his leave of me the latter said, "When she thinks of her eldest son, the mother of my two pupils will curse you, but when she sees the return of her youngest, she will bless you and the mother in whose name you spared him".

The vigour with which the Russian troops had been repulsed in this last contact having cooled their ardour, we did not see them again for two days, which allowed us to reach Molodechno; but if the enemy allowed us a momentary truce the cold increased its attack. The temperature fell to 27 degrees of frost. Men and horses were falling at every stride, frequently not to rise again. Notwithstanding, I remained with the debris of my regiment, in the midst of which I made my nightly bivouac in the snow. There was nowhere I could go to be better off. My gallant officers and men regarded their commanding officer as a living flag. They endeavoured to preserve me and offered me all the care which our appalling situation permitted. The wound to my knee prevented me from sitting astride my horse, and I had to rest my leg on my horse's neck to keep it straight, which made me get even colder. I was in great pain but there was nothing that could be done.

The road was lined with the dead and dying, our march was slow and silent. What remained of the guard formed a little square, in which travelled the Emperor's carriage, in which was also King Murat.

On the fifth of December, after dictating his twenty-ninth bulletin, which created stupefaction throughout all of France, the Emperor left the army at Smorgoni to return to Paris. He was nearly captured at Ochmiana by some Cossacks. The Emperor's departure greatly affected the morale of the troops. Some blamed him and accused him of abandoning them. Others approved saying that it was the only way to preserve France from civil war and invasion by our so-called allies, the majority of whom were waiting only for a favourable opportunity to turn against us, but who would not dare to make a move if they heard that Napoleon had returned to France, and was organising fresh military forces.

Chap. 20.

On his departure, the Emperor handed the command of the remains of the army to Murat, who in the circumstances proved unequal to the task, which it must be admitted was extremely difficult. The cold paralysed the mental and physical activity of everyone; all organisation had broken down. Marshal Victor refused to relieve 2nd Corps, who had formed the rear-guard since the Beresina, and Marshal Ney had, unwillingly, to keep it there. Each morning a multitude of dead were left in the bivouac where we had spent the night. I congratulated myself on having, in September, made my men equip themselves with sheepskin coats, a precaution which saved the lives of many of them. The same applied to the supplies of food which we had taken from Borisoff, for without these it would have been necessary to dispute with the starving hordes over the dead bodies of horses.

I may mention here that M. de Sgur claims that there were instances of cannibalism. I have to say that there were so many dead horses lying along the route that there was no need for anyone to resort to this. What is more, it would be a great mistake to think that the countryside was completely bare. There was shortage in localities close to the road, which had been stripped by the army on its march to Moscow but the army had passed in a torrent, without spreading out to the sides. Since then the

284

harvest had been gathered and the country had recovered somewhat, so that it was only necessary to go for one or two leagues from the road to find plenty. It is true, however, that only a well organised detachment could do this without being picked off by the parties of Cossacks which prowled around us.

I arranged, with some other colonels, the formation of foraging parties, who came back not only with bread and a few cattle, but with sledges loaded with salted meat, flour and oatmeal taken from villages which had not been abandoned by the peasantry. This proves that if the Duc de Bassano and General Hogendorp, to whom the Emperor had confided, in June, the administration of Lithuania, had done their job properly during the long period which they spent at Wilna, they could have created large storage depots; but they were interested only in supplying the town, without bothering about the troops.

On the 6th of December, the cold increased and the temperature fell to nearly minus thirty; so that this day was even more deadly than its predecessors, particularly for troops who had not been conditioned gradually to the climate. Amongst this number was the Gratien division, consisting of 12,000 conscripts, who left Wilna on the 4th to come in front of us. The sudden transition from warm barracks to a bivouac in twenty-nine and a half degrees of frost, within forty-eight hours was fatal to nearly all of them. The rigour of the season had an even more terrible effect on the 200 Neapolitan cavalrymen who formed King Murat's bodyguard. They also came to join us after a long stay in Wilna but they all died on the first night which they spent on the snow.

The remnants of the Germans, Italians, Spaniards, Croats and other foreigners whom we had led into Russia, saved their lives by means which the French found repugnant: they deserted, went to villages adjoining the road and awaited, in the warmth of their houses, the arrival of the enemy. This often took some time, for, surprisingly, the Russian soldiers, used to spending the winter in draught-free houses, warmed by continuously burning stoves, are more susceptible to the cold than the inhabitants of other parts of Europe, and their army suffered heavy losses; which explains the slowness of the pursuit.

We did not understand why Koutousoff and his generals did no more than follow us with a weak advance-guard, instead of attacking our flanks and going to the head of our column to cut off all means of retreat, but they were unable to carry out this manoeuvre, which would have finished us, because their soldiers suffered as much from the cold as we did, many of them dying as a result. The cold was so intense that one could see a sort of steam coming from one's eyes and ears, which froze on contact with the air and fell like grains of millet onto one's chest, and one had to stop frequently to rid the horses of huge icicles which were formed by their breath freezing on the bits of their bridles.

There were, however, thousands of Cossacks, attracted by the hope of plunder, who braved the seasonal bad weather and hung around our columns, even attacking places where they saw baggage, though a few shots would drive them off. Eventually, in order to harass us without running any danger, for we had been forced to abandon our artillery, they mounted light cannons on sledges, and used them to fire on our men, until they saw an armed detachment advancing towards them, when they took to their heels. These sneak attacks did little real damage, but they became very unpleasant because of their constant repetition. Many of the sick and wounded were taken and despoiled by these raiders, some of whom had acquired an immense amount of booty, and the greed for enrichment attracted new enemies, who came from the ranks of our allies: these were the Poles.

Marshal de Saxe, the son of one of their kings, said rightly that the Poles were the biggest thieves in the world, and would rob even their own parents, so, not surprisingly, those in our ranks showed little respect for the property of their allies. On the march or in bivouac, they stole anything they saw; but as no one trusted them, petty thieving became more difficult, so they decided to operate on a grand scale. They organised themselves into bands, and at night they would don peasant headgear and slip out of the bivouac to meet at an agreed spot, then they would return to the camp shouting the Cossack war-cry of "Hourra! Hourra!" which so frightened men whose morale had been broken, that many of them fled abandoning their possessions and food. The false Cossacks, after stealing all they could would return to the camp before daylight and become once more Poles, ready to become Cossacks again on the next night.

When this form of brigandage was disclosed, several generals and colonels decided to put a stop to it. General Maison kept such a close watch in the lines of 2nd Corps, that one fine night our guards surprised a group of about fifty Poles at the moment when they were about to play their rôle of Cossacks. Seeing that they were surrounded these bandits had the impudence to claim that they were just having a joke, but as this was not the time nor place for laughter, General Maison had them all shot out of hand. It was some time before we saw robbers of this kind again, but they reappeared later.

On the 9th of December, we arrived at Wilna, where there were some stores; but as the Duc de Bassano and General Hogendorp had left for the Nieman, there was no one to give orders, so that there, as at Smolensk, the officials demanded proper receipts for the issue of food and clothing, which was virtually impossible because of the disorganization of almost all the regiments. We lost some precious time in this way General Maison broke into several stores and his men took some supplies, but the remainder was taken the next day by the Russians. Soldiers from other corps wandered round the town in the hope of being taken in by the inhabitants, but the people who six months previously had welcomed the French with open arms, closed their doors to us when they saw us in distress. Only the Jews would accommodate those who could pay for temporary shelter.

Admitted neither to the stores nor to private houses, the majority of famished men headed for the hospitals where, although there was not enough food for all of them, they were at least sheltered from the piercing cold. This respite was enough to decide 20,000 sick and wounded, among whom were two hundred officers and eight generals, to go no further. They had reached the end of their physical and mental resources.

Lieutenant Hernoux, one of the most vigourous and brave officers in my regiment, was so overcome by what he had been through that he lay down on the snow, refusing to move, until he died. Several soldiers, of all ranks, blew their brains out, to escape from their suffering.

During the night 9th-10th December, in thirty degrees of frost, some Cossacks came and began shooting at the gates of Wilna. Many people thought this was the entire army of Koutousoff, and in a panic they fled from the town. I regret to say that King Murat was among them. He left without giving any orders, but Marshal Ney stayed and organised the retreat as best he could. We quitted Wilna on the morning of the 10th, leaving behind not only a great number of men, but also an artillery park and a part of the army's funds.

We had scarcely left the town when the infamous Jews turned on the men whom they had taken into their houses, stripped them of their clothes and threw them out naked into the snow. Some officers of the Russian advance-guard, which was entering the town, were so indignant at this behaviour that they killed a number of them.

In the midst of this chaos Marshal Ney had urged onto the road to Kowno all those whom he could stir into movement, but he had gone no more than a league when he came to the hill of Ponari. This small slope which in other circumstances the army would have hardly noticed, now became a most serious obstacle because the ice with which it was covered made it so slippery that the draught-horses were unable to drag up it the carts and wagons, so that what remained of the army's money would have fallen into the hands of the Cossacks had not Marshal Ney ordered that the wagons should be opened and the soldiers allowed to empty the strong-boxes. This sensible measure gave rise later to assertions that the men had robbed the Imperial treasury.

Several days before our arrival at Wilna, the intense cold having killed many of our horses and made the rest unfit to ride, my troopers all went on foot. I would have very much liked to join them but my injury prevented this, so I took to a sledge to which was harnessed one of my horses. This new method of transport gave me the idea that I might by this means save the sick men, of whom I had a considerable number. There is no dwelling in Russia so poor that it does not have a sledge, and it was not long before I had a hundred or so, each one drawn by a troop horse, carrying two sick men. This method of travel seemed to General Castex to be so convenient that he authorised me to put all my men on sledges. The commander of the 24th did the same and so the remains of the brigade became a sledge-borne unit.

You may think that in doing this we deprived ourselves of any means of defence, but you would be wrong, for we were much more mobile with the sleds, which could go anywhere, and whose shafts held up the horses, than we would have been in the saddle of animals which fell down all the time.

As the road was covered with abandoned muskets, each of our Chasseurs took two of them and an ample provision of cartridges, so that if any Cossacks dared to approach, they were met by a volume of fire which quickly drove them off. Our troopers could also fight on foot if need be. In the evening we formed a big square with our sledges, in the middle of which we lit our fires. Marshal Ney and General Maison often came to spend the night here, where they were secure, since the only enemies present were the Cossacks. This was undoubtedly the first time anyone had seen a rear-guard mounted on sledges; but it was a success in the prevailing conditions.

We continued to cover the retreat until, on the 13th of December, we saw the Nieman once more, and Kowno (Kaunas), the last town in Russia. It was at this spot that five months earlier we had entered the empire of the Czars. How greatly had our circumstances changed since then!...What appalling losses had we suffered!

On entering Kowno with the rear-guard, Marshal Ney found that the only garrison was a small battalion of Germans some 400 strong, whom he joined to the troops which he still had in order to defend the town for as long as possible, to give the sick and wounded the opportunity to cross into Prussia. When he heard that Ney had arrived, King Murat left for Gumbinnen.

On the 14th, Platov's Cossacks, followed by two battalions of Russian infantry, mounted on sledges together with several guns, appeared at Kovno which they attacked at a number of points; but Marshal Ney, helped by General Grard, held them off until nightfall, when he took us across the frozen Nieman, and was the last to leave Russian territory.

We were now in Prussia, an allied country... Marshal Ney, worn out and ill, regarding the campaign as finished left us and went to Gumbinnen, where there was a gathering of all the marshals. From that moment the army had no overall commander and each regiment made its own way into Prussia. The Russians, who were at war with this country, would have been entitled to follow us there, but satisfied with having re-conquered their territory, and not sure whether they should present themselves to the Prussians as friends or enemies, they decided to await instructions from their government, and halted at the Nieman. We took advantage of their hesitation to head for the towns of old Prussia.

The Germans are usually humane; many of them had relatives or friends in the regiments which had gone with us to Moscow. We were received well enough, and I can promise you that having slept for five months in the open, I was delighted to find myself in a warm room and a comfortable bed, but this sudden transition from a glacial bivouac to long-forgotten repose made me seriously ill. Nearly all the army were affected in this way. A number of them died, including Generals bl and Lariboisire, the artillery commanders.

In spite of the adequate reception given to us, the Prussians remembered their defeat at Jena, and the way in which Napoleon had treated them in 1807 when he seized part of their kingdom. Secretly they hated us and would have disarmed and captured us at the first signal from their King. Already General York, who led the numerous Prussian units which the Emperor had so unwisely placed on the left wing of the Grande Arme, and who were stationed between Tilsit and Riga, had made a pact with the Russians and had sent back Marshal Macdonald, whom, from some remnant of conscience, he did not dare to arrest.

The Prussians of all classes approved of General York's treachery, and as the provinces through which the sick and disarmed French soldiers were then passing were full of Prussian troops, it is probable that the inhabitants would have sought to take hold of them had it not been that they feared for their King, who was in Berlin, in the midst of a French army commanded by Marshal Augereau. This fear and the repudiation by the King (the most honest man in his kingdom) ofGeneral York, who was tried for treason and condemned to death, prevented a general uprising against the French. We profited from this to reach the Vistula and leave the country.

My regiment crossed the river near the fortress of Graudenz at the same place at which we had crossed on our way to Russia; but this time the crossing was much more dangerous because the thaw had already begun some leagues upstream and the ice was covered by about a foot of water and one could hear frightening crackings which heralded a general break-up. Added to which, it was in the middle of a dark night that I was given the order to cross the river immediately, for the General had just been informed that the King of Prussia had left Berlin and taken refuge in Silesia, in the midst of a considerable armed force. The populace becoming restless it was feared that they would rise against us as soon as the thaw prevented us from crossing the river. We had to get across at all costs, but this was a very dangerous operation, for the Vistula is quite wide at Graudenz, and there were many gaps in the ice which it was difficult to see by the light of the fires lit on both banks.

As there was no possibility of crossing with our sledges, we abandoned them. We led the horses and preceded by some men armed with poles to indicate the crevasses, we commenced the perilous journey. We had icy water half-way up our legs, which was not good for the sick and injured, but the physical discomfort was nothing compared to the anxiety produced by the cracking of the ice, which threatened at any moment to sink beneath our feet. The servant of one of my officers fell into a crevasse and did not reappear. We eventually reached the other side where we spent the night warming ourselves in some fishermen's huts, and the next day we witnessed a total thaw of the Vistula, which, had we delayed our crossing for a few hours, would have made us prisoners.

From the spot where we had crossed the Vistula, we made our way to the little town of Sweld, where my regiment had been in cantonment before the war, and it was there that I greeted the year 1813. The year which had ended was certainly the hardest of my life.

Chap. 21.

Let us now cast an eye rapidly over the reasons for the failure of the Russian campaign.

Undoubtedly the principal one of these was Napoleon's error in believing that he could make war in the north of Europe, before ending that which had been going on for a long time in Spain, where his armies were suffering serious reverses, at a time when he was preparing to invade Russian territory. The soldiers of French nationality, being thus spread from north to south, were in insufficient numbers everywhere. Napoleon thought he could supplement them by joining to their battalions those of his allies, but this was to dilute a good wine with muddy water. The quality of the French divisions was lowered, the allied troops were never better than mediocre, and it was they, who, during the retreat, sowed disorder in the Grande Arme.

A no less fatal cause of our defeat was the inadequacy, or indeed the total lack of organisation in the occupied countries. Instead of doing as we had done during the campaigns of Austerlitz, Jena and Friedland, and leaving behind the advancing army small bodies of troops which, stretching back in echelon, could keep in regular touch with one another to ensure tranquillity in our rear, to expedite the forwarding of munitions and individual soldiers and the departure of convoys of wounded, we unwisely pushed all our available forces towards Moscow, so that between that city and the Nieman, if one excepts Wilna and Smolensk, there was not one garrison, nor storage depot, nor hospital. Two hundred leagues of countryside were left to roving bands of Cossacks. The result of this was that men who had recovered from illness were unable to rejoin their units, and as there was no system of evacuation, we had to keep all the wounded from the battle for Moscow in the monastery of Kolotskoi for more than two months. They were still there at the time of the retreat and were nearly all taken prisoner, while those who felt able to follow the army died of exhaustion and cold on the roads. Finally, the retreating troops had no supply of stored food in a country which produces vast amounts of grain.

This lack of small garrisons in our rear was the reason why of the more than 100,000 prisoners taken by the French during the campaign, not a single one left Russia, because there was no way in which they could be passed back from hand to hand. All these prisoners escaped with ease and made their way back to the Russian army, which thus recovered some of its losses, while ours increased from day to day.

The absence of interpreters also contributed to our disasters, more than you might think. How, for example can one obtain information about an unknown country, if one cannot exchange a single word with the inhabitants? When, on the bank of the Beresina, General Partouneaux mistook the road, and instead of taking that leading to Studianka, took the one leading to General Wittgenstein's position, he had with him a peasant from Borisoff who, not knowing a word of French, tried to indicate by signs that the encampment was Russian, but, as he was not understood, through lack of an interpreter we lost a fine division of 7 or 8000 men.

290

In very similar circumstances, during October, the 3rd Lancers, taken by surprise, in spite of the advice of their guide, whom they did not understand, lost two hundred men. Now the Emperor had in his army some bodies of Polish cavalry, nearly all of whose officers and most of their N.C.O.s. spoke fluent Russian; but they were left in their regiments whereas some should have been taken, from each unit, and attached to generals and colonels, where they would have been extremely useful. I consider the provision of interpreters an important but often neglected element in military operations.

I have already commented on the major mistake that was made in forming the two wings of the army from the Prussian and Austrian contingents. The Emperor must have greatly regretted this, firstly on learning that the Austrians had given passage to the Russian army of Tchitchakoff, who then cut our line of retreat on the banks of the Beresina, and secondly when told of the treachery of General York, the head of the Prussian Corps. His regret must have increased further during and after the retreat, for if he had formed the two wings from French troops and had taken to Moscow the Austrians and Prussians, the two latter, having suffered their share of the hardships and the casualties would have been as much enfeebled as all the other corps, while Napoleon would have kept intact the French troops he had left on the two wings. I would go even further and say that to weaken Prussia and Austria Napoleon should have required from them contingents triple or quadruple the size of those which they contributed. It has been said with hindsight that neither of the two states would have complied with such a demand, but I disagree. The King of Prussia who had come to Dresden to beg the Emperor to accept his son as an aide-de-camp would not have dared to refuse, while Austria, in the hope of recovering some of the rich provinces which Napoleon had snatched from her would have done everything to satisfy him. The overconfidence which Napoleon had, in 1812, in the fidelity of those two states was his undoing.

It is often claimed that the fire of Moscow, for which praise is given to the courage and resolve of the Russian government and General Rostopschine, was the principal cause of the failure of the 1812 campaign. This assertion seems to me to be contestable. To begin with the destruction of Moscow was not so complete that there did not remain enough houses, palaces, churches and barracks to accommodate the entire army, and there is evidence of this in a report which I have seen in the hands of my friend General Gourgaud, who was then principal aide-de-camp to the Emperor. It was not therefore lack of shelter which forced the French to quit Moscow. Many people think that it was the fear of food shortage, but this is also erroneous, for reports made to the Emperor by M. le Comte Daru, the quartermaster-general of the army, show that even after the fire there was in the city an immense quantity of provisions, which would have supplied the army for six months, so it was not the prospect of starvation which decided the Emperor to retreat. These facts would appear to indicate that the Russian government had failed to achieve its aim, if this was indeed the aim it was pursuing; but in reality, its aim was quite different.

The court wished in fact to deliver a mortal blow to the ancient aristocracy of the Boyars by destroying the city which was the centre for their continual opposition.

The Russian government, although entirely despotic, has to pay much attention to the great nobles, whose displeasure has cost several emperors their lives. The richest and most powerful of these noblemen made Moscow the backdrop for their intrigues, so the government, more and more alarmed at the growth of the city, saw in the French invasion an opportunity for its destruction. General Rostopschine, who was one of the authors of this plan, was entrusted with its execution, the blame for which he later laid on the French. The aristocracy was not taken in, it accused the government so loudly and manifested so much discontent at the useless burning of its palaces that the Emperor Alexander, to avoid a personal catastrophe, was obliged not only to permit the rebuilding of the city, but to banish Rostopschine who, in spite of his protestations of patriotism, died in Paris, hated by the Russian nobility.

Whatever the motives may have been for the fire of Moscow, I think that its preservation would have been more harmful than useful to the French, for in order to control a city inhabited by some 300,000 citizens always ready to revolt, it would have been necessary to take from the army, and place as a garrison in Moscow, 50,000 men, who, when the time came to retreat, would have been assailed by the inhabitants, whereas the fire having driven out almost all the populace, a few patrols were enough to ensure tranquillity.

The only influence which Moscow had on the events of 1812 was due to the fact that Napoleon was unable to understand that Alexander could not sue for peace without being assassinated by his subjects, and believed that to leave the city without a treaty would be to admit that he was not able to hold on to it. The French Emperor insisted, therefore, on staying as long as possible in Moscow, where he wasted more than a month waiting in vain for a proposal of peace. This delay was fatal for it allowed the winter to become established before the French army could go into cantonments in Poland. Even if Moscow had been preserved intact it would not have made any difference; the disaster arose because the retreat was not prepared in advance and was carried out at the wrong time. It was not difficult to forecast that it would be very cold in Russia during the winter, but I repeat, the hope of a peace misled Napoleon and was the sole cause of his long stay in Moscow.

The losses suffered by the Grande Arme were enormous, but they have been exaggerated. I have already said that I have seen a situation report, covered with notes in Napoleon's hand, which gives the figure of those who crossed the Nieman as 325,000, of whom 155,000 were French. Reports issued in February 1813 gave the number of French who returned across the Nieman as 60,000, added to this figure can be that of 30,000 prisoners returned by the Russians after the peace of 1814. Giving a total loss of French lives of 65,000.

The loss inflicted on my regiment was in proportion much smaller. At the beginning of the campaign we had 1018 men in the ranks and we received 30 reinforcements at Polotsk, so that I took into Russia 1048 troopers. Of this number I had 109 killed, 77 taken prisoner, 65 injured and 104 missing. This amounted to a loss of 355 men, so that after the return of the men whom I had sent to Warsaw, the regiment, which from the bank of the Vistula had been sent beyond the Elbe to the principality of Dessau, had in the saddle 693 men, all of whom had fought in the Russian campaign.

When he saw this figure, the Emperor, who from Paris was supervising the reorganising of his army, thought it was a mistake, and sent the report back to me with an order to produce a corrected version. When I returned the same figure once more, he ordered General Sbastiani to go and inspect my regiment and give him a nominal roll of the men present. This operation having removed all doubt, and confirmed my report, I received a few days later a letter from the Major-general couched in the most flattering terms and addressed to all officers and N.C.O.s and particularly to me, in which Prince Berthier stated that he had been directed by the Emperor to express his Majesty's satisfaction at the care we had taken of our men's lives, and his praise for the conduct of all our officers and N.C.O.s.

After having had this letter read out before all the squadrons, I had intended to keep it as a precious memento for my family, but on further consideration, I decided that it would not be right to deprive the regiment of a document in which was expressed the Emperor's satisfaction with all its members, so I sent it to be included in the regimental archive. I have frequently repented of this, for scarcely a year had passed before the government of Louis XVIII was substituted for that of the Emperor, and the 23rd Chasseurs was combined with the 3rd. The archives of the two regiments were collected together, badly cared for, and after the total disbanding of the army in 1815, they disappeared into the yawning gulf of the war office. I tried in vain, after the revolution of 1830, to recover this letter, which was so flattering to my old regiment and to me, but it could not be found.

Chap. 22.

The year 1813 began very badly for France. The remains of our army, returning from Russia, had scarcely crossed the Vistula and started to reorganise, when the treachery of General York and the troops under his command forced us to retire beyond the Elbe, and shortly to abandon Berlin and all of Prussia, which rose against us, helped by the units which Napoleon had imprudently left there. The Russians speeded up their march as much as possible, and came to join the Prussians, whose King now declared war on the French Emperor.

Napoleon had in northern Germany no more than two divisions, commanded, it is true, by Augereau, but consisting mainly of conscripts. As for those French troops who had fought in Russia, once they were well fed and no longer slept on the snow, they recovered their strength, and could have been used oppose the enemy; but our cavalry were almost all without horses, very few infantrymen had kept their weapons, we had no artillery, the majority of the soldiers had no footwear and their uniform was in rags. The government had employed part of the year 1812 in making equipment of all sorts, but owing to the negligence of the war department, then in the hands of M. Lacue Comte de Cessac, no regiment received the clothing allotted to it. The conduct of the administration in these circumstances deserves some comment.

When a regimental depot had got together, at great expense, the numerous items required by its active battalions or squadrons, the administration arranged, with forwarding agents, the transport of the supplies as far as Mainz, which was then part of the Empire. These goods were in no danger while crossing France to the bank of the Rhine; however M. de Cessac ordered a detachment of troops to escort them as far as Mainz. There they were handed over to foreign agents, who were supposed to forward them to Magdeberg, Berlin, and the Vistula, without any French supervision. This undertaking was carried out with so much bad faith and delay that the packages containing the supplies of clothing and footwear took six to eight months to go from Mainz to the Vistula, a distance they should have covered in forty days.

This had been no more than a serious inconvenience when the French armies were in peaceful occupation of Germany and Poland, but it became a calamity after the Russian campaign. More than two hundred barges laden with supplies for our regiments were ice-bound in the Bromberg canal, near Nackel, when we passed this point in January 1813, but as there was, in this immense convoy, no French agent, and as the Prussian bargees already considered us as enemies, no one told us that these vessels were loaded with goods. The next day the Prussians took possession of this huge quantity of clothing and footwear and used it to equip several of the regiments they sent against us. Although the result of this was that the increasing cold killed a large number of French soldiers, there are those who boast of our efficient administration!

The lack of order in the French army's line of march as it went through Prussia was due principally to the ineptitude of Murat, who had assumed command after the departure of the Emperor, and later to the feebleness of Prince Eugne de Beauharnais, the Vice-Roi of Italy.

When the time came for us to re-cross the Elbe and enter the territory of the Confederation of the Rhine, the Emperor, before removing his troops from Poland and Prussia, wanted to facilitate a return to the offensive by leaving strong garrisons in the fortresses which could assure the crossing of the Vistula, the Oder and the Elbe, such as Thorn, Stettin, Magdeberg, Danzig, Dresden, *etc.*

This major decision on the part of the Emperor may be looked at in two ways. So it has been praised by some knowledgeable military observers and condemned by others.

The first party say that the need to provide a place of rest and safety for the numerous sick and wounded, which the army brought back from Russia, compelled the Emperor to occupy these fortresses, which, in addition, could store a massive amount of military equipment and foodstuffs. They add that these fortresses hindered enemy movements and by investing them, the enemy reduced the number of troops which could be actively employed against us; and finally that if the reinforcements which Napoleon was bringing from France and Germany enabled him to win a battle, the possession of the forts would help to ensure a new conquest of Prussia, which would bring us to the banks of the Vistula and force the Russians to return to their country.

In reply to this it is claimed that Napoleon weakened his army by breaking it up into so many scattered units who could not give each other mutual assistance; that it was not necessary to compromise the security of France in order to save a some thousands of sick and wounded, very few of whom would return to active service, and of whom nearly all died in the hospitals. It was also said that the regiments of Italians, Poles and Germans from the Confederation of the Rhine, which the Emperor mingled with the garrisons in order to lessen the requirement of French units, would not be much use; and in fact almost all the foreign troops fought very badly and ended up by going over to the enemy. Finally it was claimed that the occupation of the forts gave very little trouble to the Russian and Prussian armies, which, after blockading them with an observation force, could continue their march towards France. Which is what actually happened.

I find myself in agreement with latter of these two opinions, because it is evident that the forts could be of use to us only if we overcame the Russian and Prussian armies, which was a reason for concentrating our disposable manpower rather than dispersing it.

It might be said that as the enemy would no longer have to blockade the forts, they would thus have an increase in their manpower to match ours; but this is not so, for the enemy would have to leave strong garrisons in the forts which we abandoned, while we could make use of the men which were at present immobilised. I may add that the defence of these useless forts deprived the army in the field of the services of a number of experienced generals, among others, Marshal Davout, who alone was worth several divisions. I accept that during a campaign one must leave behind several brigades to guard places on which the safety of a country depends, such as Metz, Lille and Strasbourg, in the case of France, but the forts situated on the Vistula, the Oder and the Elbe, two or three hundred leagues from France were of only conditional importance, that is to say dependent on the success of our army in the field. When this did not come about, over eighty thousand men whom the Emperor had left in those garrisons in 1812 were obliged to surrender.

The position of France in the first months of 1813 was extremely critical, for in the south our armies in Spain had suffered some very serious reverses due to the weakening of their strength by the continual withdrawal of regiments, while the English ceaselessly sent reinforcements to Wellington, who had fought a brilliant campaign during 1812, and had captured Cuidad-Rodrigo, Badajoz and the fort of Salamanca, had won the battle of Arapiles, occupied Madrid and now threatened the Pyrénées.

In the north, the numerous battle-hardened soldiers whom Napoleon had led into Russia had nearly all died in action or of cold and starvation. The still intact Prussian army had just joined the Russians, and the Austrians were on the point of following their example. Finally, the sovereigns, and more importantly, the people of the Germanic Confederation, stirred up by the English, were wavering in their allegiance to France. The Prussian Baron Stein, an able and enterprising man, took this opportunity to publish a number of pamphlets in which he appealed to all Germans to shake off the yoke of Napoleon and regain their liberty. This appeal was readily received, as the passage, accommodation and maintenance of the French troops who had occupied Germany since 1806 had occasioned great expense, to which was added the confiscation of English merchandise as a result of Napoleon's continental blockade. The Confederation of the Rhine would have defected if the rulers of the various states of which it was composed had decided to listen to the wishes of their subjects; but none of them dared budge, so ingrained was their habit of obedience to the French Emperor, and so great their fear of seeing him arrive at any moment, to head the considerable forces which he was organising with such speed and building up constantly in Germany.

The greater part of the French nation still had the greatest confidence in Napoleon. Those who were well-informed blamed him, no doubt, for having the previous year led his army to Moscow, and in particular for having awaited the winter there, but the mass of the people, who were used to considering the Emperor as infallible and had no notion of the events of this campaign nor of the losses suffered by our men, saw only the glory which the occupation of Moscow reflected on our arms, and were more than willing to give the Emperor the means to heap victories round his eagles. Every department and every town gave patriotic gifts of horses, though the numerous levies of conscripts and money soon cooled this enthusiasm. Nevertheless the nation complied with reasonably good grace, and battalions and squadrons seemed to rise out of the ground, as if by some enchantment. It was remarkable that after all the levies of conscripts which had been made over the last twenty years, we had never recruited a finer body of men. There were several explanations for this.

To begin with, each of the eight hundred departments which then existed had, for several years, maintained a company of so-called departmental infantry, a sort of praetorian guard for the Prefects, who made a point of selecting men of a high physical standard for this duty. These men never left the principal towns of the department, where they were very well housed, fed and clad, and as they had very few duties to perform, they were able to build up their physical strength, for most of them led this life for six or seven years, during which time they were exercised regularly in the handling of arms, and in marches and manoeuvres. They lacked only the "baptism of fire" to become complete soldiers. These companies, depending on the importance of the department, were of 150 to 250 men. The Emperor sent them all to the army, where they were absorbed into the line regiments.

In the second place there was called into service a great number of conscripts from previous years, who had by protection, cunning or temporary illness obtained deferment, that is to say permission to remain at home until further orders. These older men were nearly all strong and vigourous.

These measures were legal; but what was not was the call-up of those who had already taken part in the ballot for conscription and whose names had not been drawn. These people, to whom this lottery had given the legal right to remain civilians, were nevertheless compelled to take up arms if they were less than thirty years old. This levy produced a large number of men fit to support the hardships of war. There was some objection raised to this measure, mainly in the Midi and the Vende, but the greater part of the contingent fell into line, so great was the habit of obedience. This meekness on the part of the populace enticed the government into practices even more illegal and more dangerous withal, in that they struck at the upper class; for after forcibly enlisting men who had been exempted by lot, the same measure was applied to those who had quite legally paid for a replacement, and they were forced into the army, although some families had been financially strained and even ruined in an attempt to save their sons, for at that time replacements cost from 12 to 20,000 francs, which had to be paid in cash. There were even young men who had been replaced two or three times, but who were still forced to go, and it was not unknown for one to find himself serving in the same company as the man he had paid to be his substitute. This injustice was the result of advice given by Clarke, the Minister for War and Savary, the Minister of Police , who persuaded the Emperor that to prevent any disturbance during the war, it was necessary to remove the sons of influential families from the country and put them in the army, to serve, in some respects, as hostages... To reduce somewhat the odium felt by the upper class towards this imposition, the Emperor created, under the name of "Guards of Honour", four regiments of light cavalry, specially reserved for young gentlemen of good family. These units, which were given a brilliant Hussar's uniform, were commanded by general officers.

To these more or less legal levies, the Emperor added the men produced by an early conscription and a number of battalions formed from the seamen, sailors and gunners of the navy, all trained men, used to handling arms and bored with the monotonous life in port, keen to join their comrades in the army. There were more than thirty thousand of these seamen, and it did not take long for them to become first class infantry soldiers. Finally the Emperor, obliged to use every means to rebuild his army, of which the greater part had perished in the frozen wastes of Russia, further weakened his forces in Spain by taking not only several thousands of men to make up his guard, but several brigades and entire divisions composed of old soldiers, accustomed to hardship and danger.

For their part, the Russians and particularly the Prussians, were preparing for war. The indefatigable Baron de Stein travelled the provinces, preaching a crusade against the French, and organising his "Tugenbond" whose members swore to take up arms for the liberation of Germany. This society, which stirred up so many enemies against us, operated openly in Prussia, which was already at war with the Emperor, and insinuated itself into the states and armies of the Confederation of the Rhine, despite the opposition of some sovereigns and with the tacit permission of others, to such an extent that almost the whole of Germany was, in secret, our enemy, and the contingents which were joined to our military forces were prepared to betray us at the first opportunity, as events would shortly show. These events would not have taken so long to come about if the German's natural laxity and sloth had not prevented them from acting sooner than they did, for the debris of the French army which crossed the Elbe in 1812 stayed peacefully in cantonment on the left bank of the river for the first four months of 1813, without being attacked by the Russians and Prussians who were stationed on the opposite bank, and who did not feel themselves strong enough to do so, although Prussia had mobilised its landwehr, made up of all fit men, and Bernadotte, forgetting that he was born a Frenchman, had declared war on us, and had joined his Swedish troops to those belonging to the enemies of his native country.

During the period which we spent on the left bank of the Elbe, although the army received continual reinforcements, there was still very little in the way of cavalry except for some regiments, one of which was mine, so we had been allotted as cantonments several communes and the two little towns of Brenha and Landsberg, in pleasant country near Magdeberg. While we were there I had a great disappointment. The Emperor wished to speed the organisation of the new levies and thought that for this purpose the temporary presence of unit commanders at their regimental depots would be useful. So he decided that all colonels should return to France except those who had a certain number of men in their unit, the number fixed for the cavalry was four hundred, and I had more than six hundred mounted men. I was therefore forced to stay behind, when I so much longed to embrace my wife and the child which she had given me during my absence.

To the disappointment which I felt was added another vexation, the good General Castex, whom I had held in such high regard during the Russian campaign, was to leave us and join the mounted Grenadiers of the Guard. His brigade, and that of General Corbineau, who had been given the position of aide-de-camp to the Emperor, were both put in charge of General Exelmans. General Wathiez was to replace Castex, and General Maurin to replace Corbineau. These three generals had however gone to France after the Russian campaign and I was the only colonel left, so General Sbastiani, to whose corps the new division was to be attached, ordered me to take over the command, which added a great deal of work to my regimental duties, for I had to make frequent visits, in appalling weather, to the cantonments of the other three regiments. The wound to my knee, although it had healed, was still painful and I did not know if I would be able to remain on duty until the end of the winter, when after a month General Wathiez returned to take up the command of the division.

A few days later, without my having asked, I was ordered to go to France to organise the large number of recruits and horses which had been sent to my regimental depot. The depot was in the department of Jemmapes, at Mons in Belgium, which was then part of the Empire . I left immediately and travelled quickly. I realised that as I was authorised to go to France on duty, it would not be acceptable for me to request even the shortest period of leave to go to Paris, so I welcomed the offer made by *Mme.* Desbrires, my mother-in-law, to bring my wife and my son to *Mons*. After a year of separation, during which I had experienced so many dangers, it was with the greatest pleasure that I once more saw my wife, and held in my arms our little Alfred, now eight months old. This was one of the happiest days of my life. The joy which I felt on holding my little son was increased by the recollection that he very nearly became an orphan on the day of his birth.

I spent the end of April and the months of May and June at the depot, where I was extremely busy. Many recruits had been sent to the 23rd, men of good physique and from a warrior race, for they mostly came from the neighbourhood of Mons, the former province of Hainault, from where the Austrians used to draw their finest cavalrymen, at the time when they possessed the low countries. These are people who love and care well for horses, but as the horses which come from this district are a little too heavy for Chasseurs, I obtained permission to buy some in the Ardennes, from where we obtained a fair selection.

I found at the depot some good officers and N.C.O.s, several of whom had been in Russia and had gone to the depot to recover from injuries or illness, and the ministry sent me some young officers from the school of cavalry at Saint-Cyr. From this material I made up various squadrons, which, although not perfect, could mingle without difficulty with the old cavalrymen from Russia whom I had left on the banks of the Elbe, and throughout whom they would be spread on their arrival. As soon as a squadron was ready it was sent off to join the army.

Chap. 23.

While I was busily engaged in rebuilding my regiment, as were many other colonels, mainly from the cavalry, who were in France for the same reason, hostilities broke out on the Elbe, which had been crossed by the allies.

The Emperor left Paris, and on the 25th of April he was at Naumbourg, in Saxony, at the head of 170,000 men, of whom only a third were French, a detachment of troops which had been sent to Germany having not yet arrived. The other two thirds of his army was formed of units from the Confederation of the Rhine, the majority of which were very reluctant to fight on his behalf. General Wittgenstein, who had gained some celebrity following our disaster at the Beresina, (although the weather did us far more harm than his manoeuvres), was in overall command of the Russian and German troops, a combined force of 300,000 men, which faced Napoleon's army on the 28th of April, in the region of Leipzig.

On the 1st of May there was a sharp engagement at Poserna, in an area where Gustavus Adolphus had died, during which Marshal Bessires was killed by a cannon-ball. The Emperor regretted his death more than did the army, which had not forgotten that it was the advice given to Napoleon by the Marshal, in the evening of the battle for Moscow, which had deterred him from achieving victory by committing his guards to the action; which had he done, it would have changed the outcome and led to the complete destruction of the Russian force.

The day after Bessires' death, while Napoleon was continuing his march towards Leipzig, he was attacked unexpectedly on the flank, by the Russo-Prussians, who had crossed the river Elster during the night. In this battle, which was given the name of the the Battle of Lutzen, there was some fierce fighting, in which the troops newly arrived from France showed the greatest courage, the marine regiments being particularly notable. The enemy, soundly beaten, withdrew towards the Elbe, but the

French, having almost no cavalry, were able to take few prisoners and their victory was incomplete. Nevertheless it produced a great moral effect in Europe, and above all in France, for it showed that our troops had retained their fighting qualities, and that only the frosts of Russia had overcome them in 1812.

The Emperor Alexander and the King of Prussia, after being present at Lutzen and witnessing the defeat of their armies, had gone to Dresden, from where they had to withdraw on the approach of the victorious Napoleon, who took possession of the town on the 8th of May, where he was shortly joined by his ally the King of Saxony. After a brief stay in Dresden, the French crossed the Elbe and pursued the Prusso-Russians, whose rear-guard they caught up with and defeated at Bischofswerda.

The Emperor Alexander, dissatisfied with Wittgenstein, assumed personal command of the allied armies, but having been defeated in his turn by Napoleon at Wurtchen, it seems likely that he recognised his lack of ability in this field, for he soon relinquished the position.

The Russo-Prussians having come to a halt and dug in at Bautzen, the French emperor ordered Ney to outflank their position, which resulted in a victory on the 21st of May, which lack of cavalry once more rendered incomplete though the enemy lost 18,000 men and fled in disorder.

On the 22nd, the French, in pursuit of the Russians, made contact with their rearguard at the pass of Reichenbach. What little cavalry Napoleon had was commanded by General Latour-Maubourg, a most distinguished soldier, who led it with such lan that the enemy were overwhelmed and abandoned the field after heavy losses. Those suffered by the French, though fewer, were most painful. The cavalry general, Bruyre, a fine officer, had both his legs carried away and died of this dreadful injury; but the saddest event of the day was the result of a cannon-ball which, after killing General Kirgener (brother-in-law of Marshal Lannes), mortally wounded Marshal Duroc, the grand marshal of the palace, a man liked by everyone, and Napoleon's oldest and best friend. Marshal Duroc survived for a few hours following his injury, and the Emperor who was at his side showed every sign of the deepest grief. Those who witnessed this melancholy scene, noted that the Emperor, who was forced to leave his friend by the demands of duty, parted from him in tears, having given him a rendez-vous in "A better world".

The French army now pressed on into Silesia, whose capital, Breslau (Wroclaw) it occupied on the 1st of June. The allies, and in particular the Prussians, much alarmed, realised that in spite of their boasts, they were unable, without help, to stop the French, and wanted to gain a respite in the hope that the Austrians would end their hesitation and join forces with them. They sent out envoys, given the task of soliciting an armistice which, subject to the mediation of Austria, would lead, they said, to a peace treaty. Napoleon thought that he should agree to this armistice, and so it was signed on the 4th of June, to last until the 10th of August.

While Napoleon was going from success to success, Marshal Oudinot was defeated at Luckau, and lost 1100 men. The Emperor hoped that during the armistice the numerous reinforcements from France which he was awaiting, particularly the cavalry which had been sorely missed, would make their appearance, and would take part in a new campaign if that became unavoidable. There were, however, several generals who regretted that the Emperor had not followed up his victory. They argued that if the armistice permitted us to build up our reserves, it did the same for the Russo-Prussians, who hoped that they would be joined by the Austrians, as well as by the Swedes, who were marching to their aid. The former were not yet ready, but they would have more than two months to organise and put into motion their numerous troops.

When at Mons I heard of the victories of Lutzen and Bautzen, I was sorry not to have been there, but my regrets were diminished when I found that my regiment had not been involved; it was, in fact, before Magdeburg on the road to Berlin. M.Lacour, a former aide-de-camp to General Castex had been posted as squadron commander to the 23rd, about the end of 1812, and he took command of the regiment in my absence. He was a brave man, who had acquired some education by reading, which gave him pretentions which were out of place in a military milieu; in addition to which his lack of experience as a commanding officer, resulted in the regiment suffering losses which should have been avoided, and of which I shall speak later. While I was at the depot, I gained as second squadron commander M. Pozac, a very fine officer in all respects who had been awarded a "Sabre of Honour" for his conduct at the battle of Marengo.

Towards the end of June, all the colonels who had been sent to France to organise the new forces, having completed this task, were ordered to return to their posts with the army, although hostilities would be suspended for some time. I was therefore forced to leave my family with whom I had passed so many happy days. Duty called and I had to obey.

I once more took the road to Germany, and went first to Dresden, to where the Emperor had summoned all the colonels in order to question them about the composition of the detachments they had sent to the army. There I learned something which annoyed me greatly. At the depot I had organised four superb squadrons of 150 men each. The two first of which (happily the smartest and best) had joined the regiment; the third had been taken, by Imperial decision, and sent to Hamburg to be incorporated in the 28th Chasseurs, one of the weakest regiments in the army. This was a lawful order, and I accepted it without complaint: but it was not the same when I was told that the 4th squadron which I had sent from Mons, having been noticed as it passed through Cassel, by Jrme, the King of Westphalia, this prince had found it so desirable that he had, on his own authority, enrolled it in his Guard. I knew that the Emperor, very irritated that his brother had taken it upon himself to make off with some Imperial troops, had ordered him to send them on their way immediately, and I had hopes that I would receive them; but King Jrme got hold of some of the Emperor's aides, who represented to his Majesty that as the King of Westphalia's Guard was composed entirely of Germans, who were not by any means to be relied upon, it was right that he should have a French squadron on whose loyalty he could count; in the second place the King had, at much expense, equipped the squadron with the brilliant uniform of Hussars of his Guard; and finally, that even without this squadron, the 23rd would still be the strongest regiment in the French cavalry. Whatever the reason, my squadron remained in the Westphalian guard, in spite of my loud protests. I could not get over this loss, and found it supremely unjust that I should be deprived of the fruits of my trouble and labour.

I rejoined my regiment not far from the Oder in the region of Zagan, where it was in cantonment in the little town of Freistadt, as was Exelman's division, of which it was a part.

During our stay in this area, a curious incident occurred. A trooper by the name of Tantz, the only bad character in the regiment, having got thoroughly drunk, threatened an officer who had ordered him to be put in the police cell. Put before a court-martial he was found guilty, condemned to death and the sentence confirmed. Now when the guard, commanded by Warrant-officer Boivin, went to fetch Tantz to take him to the place where he was to be shot, they found

The warrant-officer, a brave fellow, but one whose brains did not match his courage, instead of making him dress, told him to wrap himself in a cloak. However, having arrived on the draw-bridge across the large moat which surrounded the chteau, Tantz threw the cloak in the faces of the guard, leapt into the moat which he swam across, and having reached the other side made off to join the enemy on the opposite bank of the Oder. We never heard anything more of him... I broke the warrant-officer for being so careless, but he soon regained his rank, by an act of bravery which I shall describe shortly.

The squadrons which I had recently added to the regiment, brought its strength up to 993 men, of whom almost 700 had fought in the Russian campaign. The newly arrived soldiers were a well-built body of men who had nearly all come from the departmental legion of Jemmapes, which made it easier to train them as cavalrymen; I incorporated the newcomers in the older squadrons. Both sides were preparing for the coming struggle but our opponents had made good use of their time, and had presented us with a powerful adversary by persuading the Austrians to take up arms against us.

The Emperor Napoleon, whom numerous victories had accustomed to taking little account of his enemies, believed himself to be once more invincible, when he saw himself in Germany at the head of 300,000 men, but he did not examine sufficiently closely the composition of the forces with which he was about to oppose the whole of Europe united against him.

The French army had received an intake of fine quality recruits, and had never looked better; but with the exception of some regiments, the majority of these new soldiers had never been in action, and the disasters of the Russian campaign had generated an uneasy feeling in the corps, the effects of which were still felt. Our superb army was better suited to being put on show to obtain terms, than to being engaged at this moment in combat. Nearly all the generals and colonels, who saw the regiments at close quarters, were of the opinion that they needed some years of peace.

If one were to pass from the French army to an examination of those of her allies, one would see nothing but apathy, ill-will and the wish for an opportunity to betray France. Everything should have led Napoleon to treat with his enemies, and to do this he should have first settled with his father-in-law, the Emperor of Austria, by giving back to him Dalmatia, Istria, the Tyrol and some of the other provinces which he had seized in 1805 and 1809. Some concessions of this sort offered to Prussia would have quietened the allies who, it seems, were willing to return to Napoleon the colonies which had been taken from France and to guarantee his occupation of all the provinces this side of the Rhine and the Alps, and also upper Italy; but in return he would have to give up Spain, Poland, Naples and Westphalia. These terms were acceptable; but at a conference with the diplomats sent to discuss them, Napoleon was rude to M. Metternich, the principal member of the delegation, and sent them away without any concessions. It is said that as he saw them leave the palace of Dresden, he remarked "We'll give them a sound thrashing". The Emperor seemed to forget that the enemy armies were almost three times the size of his own forces. He had in fact no more than 320,000 men in Germany, while the allies could put in the line almost 800,000 fighting men.

The Emperor's birthday was on the 15th of August, but he ordered that it should be celebrated in advance, because the armistice ended on the 10th. The rejoicings of Saint-Napoleon's day then took place in the cantonments. This was the last time that the French army celebrated the birthday of its Emperor! There was not much enthusiasm, for even the least perceptive of officers was aware that we were on the brink of a catastrophe, and the worries of the commanders affected the morale of their subalterns. However each one prepared to do his duty, though with little hope of success, in view of the great inferiority in numbers of our army as opposed to the innumerable troops of the enemy. Already, among our allies of the Confederation of the Rhine, the Saxon General Thielmann had deserted with his brigade to join the Prussians, after trying to hand over to them the fortress of Torgau. Among our troops there was much uneasiness and lack of confidence.

It was at this time that one heard of the return to Europe of General Moreau who, condemned to banishment after the conspiracy of Pichegru and Cadoudal, had retired to America. The hatred which Moreau had for Napoleon made him forget the duty he owed to his country. He soiled his reputation by ranging himself with the enemies of France; however, it was not long before he paid the price of this infamous conduct.

Now an immense semi-circle was formed around the French army. A body of 40,000 Russians was in Mecklemberg; Bernadotte, the Prince Royal of Sweden, occupied Berlin and the surrounding district with an army of 120,000 men, composed of Swedes, Russians and Prussians. Two great Russian and Prussian armies, 220,000 men strong, of whom 35,000 were cavalry, were in Silesia between Schweidnitz and the Oder; 40,000 Austrians were stationed at Lintz, and the main Austrian army of about 140,000 men was concentrated in Prague; finally, a short distance behind this front line of 560,000 combatants, an enormous body of reserves was ready to march.

The distribution of his troops made by Napoleon was as follows: 70,000 men were concentrated around Dahmen in Prussia, to oppose Bernadotte; Marshal Ney with 100,000 occupied part of Silesia. A corps of 70,000 was in the region of Zittau. Marshal Saint-Cyr with 16,000 men occupied the camp at Pirna and gave cover to Dresden. Finally the Imperial Guard, 20 to 25,000 strong was spread round this capital, ready to go wherever was necessary. Including the troops left in the garrisons of the forts, the troops at Napoleon's disposal were infinitely fewer than those of the enemy. This enumeration did not include the forces left in Spain and Italy.

Chap. 24.

The French Emperor had divided his army into 14 Corps, called infantry, although they each contained at least a brigade of light cavalry. The commanding generals were as follows:-

1 Corps. Gen. Vandamme.

2 Corps. Marshal Victor.

3 Corps. Marshal Ney.

4 Corps. Gen. Bertrand.

5 Corps. Gen. Lauriston.

6 Corps. Marshal Marmont.

7 Corps. Gen. Reynier.

8 Corps. Prince Poniatowski.

9 Corps. Marshal Augereau.

10 Corps. (confined in Danzig) Gen. Rapp.

11 Corps. Marshal Macdonald.

12 Corps. Marshal Oudinot.

13 Corps. Marshal Davout.

14 Corps. Marshal Saint-Cyr.

Finally came the Guard, under the direct orders of the Emperor.

The cavalry was divided into 5 Corps, commanded by 1. Gen. Latour-Mauberg, 2. Gen. Sbastiani, 3. Gen. Arrighi, 4. Gen. Kellermann. 5. Gen. Milhau. The cavalry of the Guard was commanded by general Nansouty.

The army, as a whole, approved of some of these appointments but disapproved of others. They disliked such important posts being given to Oudinot, who had made more than one mistake during the Russian campaign, to Marmont, whose rashness had lost the battle of Arpiles, to Sbastiani, who did not seem equal to the task, and finally it was regretted that for a campaign which was to decide the destiny of France, the Emperor had seen fit to try out the strategic talents of Lauriston and Bertrand. The first was a good artillery officer, and the second an excellent engineer, but neither had directed troops in the field, and so lacked the experience needed to command an Army Corps.

Napoleon, recalling that when he was named as commander-in-chief of the army of Italy, he had hitherto commanded only some battalions, which had not prevented him from successfully filling the post, probably believed that Lauriston and Bertrand could do the same thing. But men of such universal talent as Napoleon are rare, and he could not hope that his new corps commanders could follow his example. It is thus that the personal affection which he felt for these generals led him to commit once more the error which he had previously made in giving command of an army to the artilleryman Marmont.

The history of past wars shows quite clearly that to be commander-in-chief, theoretical knowledge will not suffice, and with a very, very few exceptions, it is necessary to have served in an infantry or cavalry unit and to have commanded one in the rank of colonel, to be competent to direct masses of men in the field. This is a basic training which very few men can acquire as generals or as commanders of an army. Louis XIV never confided the command of troops in the open country to Marshal de Vauban, who was, however, one of the most able men of his century, and one presumes that if he had been offered the post Vauban would have turned it down in order to concentrate on his own specialty, which was the attack and defence of fortresses. Marmont and Bertrand, lacked this modesty, and the affection which Napoleon had for them prevented him from listening to any observations on the subject.

King Murat, who had gone to Naples after the Russian campaign, rejoined the Emperor at Dresden. The coalition, that is to say the Austrians, Russians and

Prussians, opened the campaign with an act of bad faith, unworthy of civilised nations. Although under the terms of the previous convention, hostilities should not have begun until the 16th of August, they attacked our outposts on the 14th, and put the greater part of their forces in motion after the defection of Jomini.

Until this time, only the two Saxon generals, Thielmann and Langueneau, had, shamefully, changed sides, but no general wearing French uniform had sullied it in such a manner. It was a Swiss, General Jomini, who was the first to do so. Jomini was a simple clerk, on a salary of 1200 francs, in the ministerial offices of the Republic of Helvetia, when, in 1800, General Ney was sent to Berne by the First Consul to discuss with the Swiss government the defence of their state, which was then our ally. The duties of the clerk Jomini, which involved dealing with confidential government documents, put him in contact with General Ney, who was thus in a position to appreciate his outstanding ability, and, yielding to his urgent requests, he arranged for him to admitted as lieutenant, and shortly captain, in the Swiss regiment which was being formed to serve with the French army. General Ney took an increasing interest in his proteg. He had him enrolled as a French officer, took him as an aide-de-camp and gave him the means to publish works which he had written on the art of war, works which, although over-valued, are not without some merit.

Thanks to protection of this kind, Jomini advanced rapidly to the rank of colonel and brigadier-general, and at the resumption of hostilities in 1813 was chief-of-staff to Marshal Ney. Seduced, however, by the extravagant promises made by the Russians, he deserted, in possession of much information about Napoleon's plans of campaign. It was fear that on hearing of this defection Napoleon would change these plans, that induced the allies to commence hostilities two days before the date agreed for the ending of the armistice. To the surprise of everyone, the Emperor Alexander rewarded the treacherous Jomini by taking him as an aide-de-camp, which is said to have outraged the delicate susceptibilities of the Austrian Emperor.

The information which Jomini was able to give the allies was a serious blow to Napoleon, for several of his units were attacked in the course of moving into position and had to give up a number of important points for lack of time to prepare their defence. However, the Emperor, whose plan it was to move into Bohemia, finding that his opponents were forewarned and on their guard against this, resolved to attack the Prussian army in Silesia, and re-engage in the offensive those troops which had been compelled to retreat before Blcher. In consequence Napoleon arrived at Lwenberg on the 20th of August, where he attacked a considerable force of the allies consisting of Prussians, Austrians and Russians. Various actions took place on the 21st, 22nd and 23rd, in the areas of Goldberg,Graditzberg and Bunzlau. The enemy lost 7000 men killed or taken prisoner, and retired behind the Katzbach.

During one of the numerous engagements which took place during these three days, Wathiez's brigade, which was pursuing the enemy, was held up by a wide and swift-flowing stream, a tributary of the Bobr. There was no way of crossing except by two wooden bridges about a quarter of a mile apart, which were covered by Russian artillery fire. The 24th Chasseurs, who had passed into the command of the gallant Colonel Schneit, having received the order to attack the left hand bridge, advanced to the assault with their usual courage, but it was a different matter when it came to the 11th (Dutch) Hussars, recently incorporated into the brigade. Ordered to take the right hand bridge, their Colonel M. Ligeard, the only Frenchman in the unit, called in vain on his troops to follow him, they were so overcome by fear that not one of them moved. As my regiment, which was in the second line, was being subjected to as much fire as the 11th Hussars, I hastened to the side of their colonel to give him some help in urging his men to attack the enemy artillery, which was the only way of stopping the cannonade, but when I saw that I would have no success, and that the cowardice of the Hollanders would result in many casualties in my regiment, I led my troops to the front of them and was about to move into the attack when I saw the bridge on the left collapse under the first section of men from the 24th, throwing them into the river where several men and horses were drowned. The Russians, during their withdrawal had prepared this trap by sawing so cunningly through the main timbers supporting the bridge that, unless one were warned, it was impossible to see what had been done.

The sight of this disaster made me fear that the same treatment had been given to the bridge towards which I was leading my men, so I called a halt in order to arrange an inspection. This was a dangerous undertakingr, for not only was the bridge within range of the enemy guns, but it was also within range of the muskets of an infantry battalion. I was about to call for a volunteer for this perilous task, when warrant-officer Boivin, whom I had recently demoted for negligently allowing the Chasseur condemned to death to escape, got off his horse and coming to me said, rather than risking the life of one of his comrades, would I please permit him to carry out the mission, in order to redeem his mistake. Pleased with this courageous declaration, I said, "Go then, and you will recover your epaulets at the end of the bridge!"

Boivin went forward and, ignoring cannon-balls and bullets, he examined the superstructure of the bridge and its supports and returned to assure me that it was in order and that the regiment could cross. I thereupon re-instated him in his rank. He remounted his horse and placing himself at the head of the squadron which was about to cross the bridge he led the way towards the Russians, who did not wait for us to attack, but withdrew smartly. The month following, when the Emperor reviewed the regiment and awarded several promotions, I had Boivin made a sous-lieutenant.

Our new brigade commander, General Wathiez, was able during the these various actions to win the affection and regard of the troops. As for the divisional commander, General Exelmans, we knew only his reputation in army circles which was that of a man of outstanding bravery; but he was also regarded as being somewhat unreliable. We had proof of this in an event which occurred at the re-commencement of hostilities.

At a time when the division was carrying out a withdrawal, to that he was about to lay a trap for the Prussian advance guard, ordered me to place at his disposal my elite company and 25 of my best marksmen, whom he put under the command of Major Lacour; then he put these 150 men in a meadow surrounded by woodland, and after telling them not to move without his permission, he went off and completely forgot them... The enemy arrived, and seeing the detachment abandoned in this manner, they halted, fearing that it had been put there to lure them into an ambush. To reassure themselves, they sent some individual men to slip into the wood, on the right and left, and when they heard no sound of gunfire, they gradually built up the number until they had completely surrounded our troopers. It was in vain that several officers pointed out to Major Lacour that this movement was going to cut off his retreat; Lacour, brave but lacking initiative, stuck rigidly to the order he had been given, without considering that General Exelmans might have forgotten him and that it might be as well to send someone to remind him, and at least to reconnoitre the terrain over which he might be able to retreat. He had been ordered to stay there, and he would stay there even if his men were killed or taken prisoner!

While Major Lacour was carrying out his instructions in the manner of a simple sergeant rather than that of a senior officer, the division marched into the distance. General Walthiez and I, when we saw that the detachment did not return, and not knowing how to contact General Exelmans, who was galloping across country, had serious misgivings. I then asked permission from General Walthiez to return to Major Lacour, and on receiving it I left at the gallop with a squadron and arrived just in time to see a most distressing sight, particularly for a commanding officer who cared for his soldiers.

The enemy, having infiltrated both flanks and even the rear of our detachment, had mounted a frontal attack by a greatly superior force, so that some 700 to 800 Prussian lancers surrounded our 150 men, whose only way of retreat was over a wretched footbridge of wooden planks which joined the two steep banks of a nearby mill-stream. Our horsemen could cross here only one by one so that there was congestion, and the elite company lost several men. A number of riders then noticed a large farmyard which they thought might lead to the mill-stream, and in the hope of finding a bridge they entered it, followed by the rest of the detachment. The stream did in fact, run past the farmyard, but it there formed the mill-pool, the banks of which were lined by slippery flagstones, making access extremely difficult for horses. This gave the enemy a great advantage, and in an attempt to capture all the French who had entered this huge yard, they closed the gates.

It was at this critical moment that I appeared on the other side of the stream with the squadron which I had hurriedly brought with me. I ordered them to dismount, and while one man held four horses, the rest, armed with their carbines, ran to the footbridge, which was guarded by a squadron of Prussians. The Prussians being on horseback and having only a few pistols as firearms, were unable to reply to the sustained fire from the carbines of our Chasseurs, and were forced to remove themselves to a distance of several hundred paces, leaving behind some forty dead and wounded.

308

The troops who had been shut in the farmyard wanted to take advantage of this momentary respite to force the main gate and make a rush for it on horseback; but I called to them not to attempt it, because to join me they would have had to cross the footbridge, which they could do only one by one, and at this point they would offer a target to the Prussians who would undoubtedly charge and destroy them. The river banks were garnished by many trees, amongst which an infantrymen can easily withstand the attacks of cavalry, so I placed the dismounted men along the riverside and once they were in communication with the mill's yard, I passed a message to the men there to dismount also, take their carbines, and while a hundred of them held off the enemy by their fire, the remainder could slip behind this protective screen and pass the horses from hand to hand over the footbridge.

While this manoeuvre, covered by the fire from a cordon of 180 dismounted Chasseurs, was proceeding in an orderly fashion, the Prussian lancers, furious that their prey was about to escape, tried to disorganise our retreat by a vigourous attack, but their horses, caught up in the willow branches, amid the numerous holes and pools of water, could scarcely move at a walk over the muddy ground, and could never reach our foot-soldiers, whose well aimed fire, directed at close range, inflicted on them heavy losses.

The Prussian major who led this charge, forcing his way boldly into the centre of our line, killed with a pistol shot to the head, Lieutenant Bachelet, one of my good regimental officers. I greatly regretted his loss, which was, however promptly revenged by the Chasseurs of his section, for the Prussian major, hit by several bullets, fell dead beside him.

The death of their leader, the numerous casualties they had suffered, and above all the impossibility of getting at us determined the enemy to give up the enterprise and they withdrew. I was able to pick up the wounded and make my retreat without being followed. My regiment lost in this deplorable affair an officer and nine troopers killed, and thirteen who were made prisoner, among whom was Lieutenant Marchal. The loss of these twenty-three members of the regiment I found all the more distressing because it served no useful purpose, and fell wholly on the finest soldiers in the unit, most of whom had been earmarked for decoration or promotion. I have never forgotten this undeserved setback. It resulted in our taking a poor view of General Exelmans, who got away with a reprimand from General Sbastiani and from the Emperor, who was influenced by his friendship with Murat. Old General Saint-Germain, a former commander, and almost the creator, of the 23rd Chasseurs, for whom he had retained much affection, having stated loudly that Exelmans deserved exemplary punishment, the two generals fell out and would have come to blows if the Emperor had not personally intervened. Major Lacour, whose incapacity had been largely responsible for this catastrophe, I no longer regarded with any confidence.

Chap. 25.

After the 21st, 22nd and 23rd of August, days on which we had defeated Field-marshal Blcher's corps, and forced him to retire behind the Katzbach, the Emperor gave orders for the follow-up on the next day. However, on hearing that the combined army of the allies, some 200,000 strong, commanded by Prince Schwartzenberg, had just emerged on the 22nd from the mountains of Bohemia and was heading for Saxony, Napoleon, taking his Guard as well as the cavalry of Latour-Maubourg and several divisions of infantry hastened by forced marches to Dresden, where Marshal Saint-Cyr had shut himself in with the troops he had hurriedly withdrawn from the camp at Pirna. On leaving Silesia the Emperor told Marshal Ney to follow him, and left Marshal Macdonald in charge of the large force which he left on the Bobr, that is to say the 3rd, 5th and 11th Infantry Corps and the 2nd \cavalry, with a powerful element of artillery, making a total of 75,000 men. The control of such a great body of combatants was too much for Marshal Macdonald, as subsequent events will show.

You must have noticed that the larger the number of troops involved, the less detail I give of their movements: firstly because this could require an enormous work, which I might not be able to complete, and secondly because it could make the reading of these memoirs too wearisome. I shall therefore be even more concise in my description of events in the War of 1813, in which 600,000 to 700,000 men took part, than I have been in describing previous campaigns.

On the 25th of August, the allies having surrounded the town of Dresden, whose fortifications were not proof against a major attack, the position of Saint-Cyr became critical for he had no more than 17,000 French troops to resist the immense numbers of the enemy. The latter, badly served by their spies, were unaware of the approaching arrival of Napoleon, and full of confidence in their superior numbers, they delayed the attack until the following day. This confidence was increased when they were strengthened by two Westphalian regiments who had deserted from King Jrme to join the Austrians.

The worried Marshal Saint-Cyr expected to be attacked on the morning of the 26th; but he was reassured as to the outcome of the struggle by the presence of the Emperor, who had arrived that very day at an early hour, at the head of the Guard and a numerous body of all arms. Soon after his arrival, the enemy, who still thought that they faced only Saint-Cyr's Corps, assaulted the town in force and captured several redoubts. The Russians and the Prussians, who now controlled the suburbs of Pirna, were attempting to break down the Freyberg gate when on the Emperor's orders it swung open to allow the emergence of a column of infantry of the Imperial Guard, the leading brigade of which was commanded by General Cambronne...It was as if the head of Medusa had appeared... The enemy recoiled horrified, their guns were captured at the double and the gunners killed on their mountings. Simultaneous sorties were made from all the gates of Dresden with the same results, and the allies, abandoning the redoubts they had taken, fled into the surrounding country where they were pursued by the cavalry to the foot of the hills. On this first day the enemy had 5000 men put out of action, and we took 3000 prisoners. The French had 2500 killed or wounded, amongst the latter there being five generals.

310

The next day it was the French army which took the initiative, although they had 87,000 fewer men than their adversaries. The action was at first fierce and sanguinary; but the rain which fell in torrents on the heavy soil soon covered the battle-field with pools of muddy water through which our troops moved with much difficulty on their advance towards the enemy. Nevertheless, advance they did, and the Young Guard had already driven back the enemy left, when Napoleon, having observed that Prince Schwartzenberg, the allies' commander-in-chief, had not given sufficient support to his left wing, overwhelmed it with an attack by Marshal Victor's infantry and Latour-Maubourg's cavalry.

King Murat, who was in command of this part of the line, was highly successful. He forced his way through the pass of Cotta and outflanking Klenau's corps, he separated it from the Austrian army and attacked it, sabre in hand, at the head of his carabiniers and Cuirassiers. Klenau was unable to withstand this fearsome charge, almost all his battalions were compelled to surrender, and two other divisions of infantry suffered the same fate.

While Murat was defeating the enemy left, their right wing was routed by the Young Guard, so that after some three hours, victory was assured and the allies beat a retreat towards Bohemia.

As a result of this second day of heavy fighting, the enemy left on the field of battle 18 flags, 26 cannons and 40,000 men, of whom 20,000 were prisoners. The main losses were suffered by the Austrian infantry, who had two generals killed, three wounded and two taken prisoner.

It may be remarked that at this epoch percussion caps were virtually unknown, and the infantry of all nations still used flint-lock muskets, which it was almost impossible to fire once the priming powder became wet. Now, as it had rained without ceasing for the whole day, this contributed largely to the defeat of the enemy infantry by our cavalry, and gave rise to an extraordinary incident.

A division of Cuirassiers, commanded by General Bordesoulle, found itself facing a strong Austrian infantry division formed into a square. Bordesoulle called on the enemy general to surrender, which he refused to do. Bordesoulle then pointed out to the Austrian that not one of his men's guns was capable of being fired, to which he replied that his men could defend themselves successfully with their bayonets, as the cavalry, whose horses were in mud up to their hocks, would be unable to charge them down. "Then I will blast your square with my artillery" "But you don't have any guns, they are stuck in the mud." "If I show you my cannons, which are behind my first regiment, will you then surrender?" "I would have no alternative, for I would have no means of defence."

The French general then brought to within thirty paces of the enemy a battery of six guns, the gunners with their slow-matches in their hands prepared to fire on the square. At this sight the Austrian general and his division laid down their arms.

The rain having prevented the infantry of both armies from using their muskets and greatly slowed the movements of the cavalry, it was the artillery which, in spite of the difficulty of manoeuvering on the rain sodden ground, played a decisive rle. In particular the French artillery, whose teams of horses Napoleon had doubled up, using animals from the headquarters wagons, which remained safely in Dresden. Our guns did great damage; it was one of their cannon-balls which struck Moreau.

It had been rumoured for some time that the once illustrious French general had returned to Europe and had joined the ranks of his country's enemies. Few people believed this, but it was confirmed in the evening following the battle of Dresden in a bizarre manner. Our advance-guard was in pursuit of the routed enemy when one of our Hussars saw, on entering the village of Notnitz, a magnificent Great Dane, which seemed to be searching in distress for its owner.

He took hold of the dog, and read on its collar the words "I belong to General Moreau." He was then told by the cur of the village that that General Moreau had undergone a double amputation in his house. A French cannon-ball had landed in the middle of the Russian general staff, it had struck one of the General's legs, and going through his horse had then struck the other. This had happened at the moment when the Austrian army had been defeated, and to prevent Moreau falling into French hands, the Emperor Alexander had arranged for him to be carried by some Grenadiers until, the pursuit having slackened, it was possible to dress his wounds and amputate both legs. The Saxon cur, who had witnessed this cruel operation, said that Moreau, who was well aware that his life was in danger, had repeatedly cursed the fate that had left him mortally wounded by a French missile, amongst the enemies of his country. He died on the 1st of September, and the Russians took away his body.

No one in the French army regretted the death of Moreau when it was known that he had taken arms against his country. A Russian envoy came to claim the dog on behalf of Colonel Rapatel, Moreau's aide-de-camp, who had stayed with him. It was returned but without the collar which was given to the King of Saxony and is now on display in Dresden.

As Prince Schwartzenberg, the commander of the enemy troops defeated at Dresden, had given Teplice as the rallying point for the remains of his defeated armies, the Austrians retreated through the valley of Dippoldiswalde, the Russians and the Prussians on the Telnitz road and the remnants of Klenau's corps via Freiberg. Napoleon accompanied the French columns which were pursuing the vanquished enemy as far as Pirna, but just before he arrived in that town, he was taken by a sudden indisposition, due perhaps to the fact that he had spent five days constantly on horseback, exposed to incessant rain.

It is one of the misfortunes of princes that there are always to be found in their entourage people who, to demonstrate their attachment, claim to be alarmed at the slightest indisposition and exaggerate the precautions which should be taken, which is what happened on this occasion. The master-of-horse, Caulaincourt, advised the

312

Emperor to return to Dresden, and the other great officers dared not give the much more sensible advice to continue to Pirna, which was no more than a league distant. The Young Guard was already there and the Emperor would have been able to have the rest which he required while remaining in a position to guide the movements of the troops in pursuit of the enemy, which he could not do from Dresden which was much further from the center of operations.

Napoleon then left to Marshals Mortier and Saint-Cyr the task of supporting General Vandamme, commander of 1st Corps, who, detached from the Grande Arme for three days, had defeated a Russian corps and now threatened the enemy rear. He had cut the road from Dresden to Prague and occupied Peterswalde, from where he dominated the Kulm basin and the town of Teplice, a most important point through which the allies had to make their retreat. However the return of the Emperor to Dresden nullified these successes and led to a disastrous reverse which contributed greatly to the fall of the Empire.

General Vandamme was fine and courageous officer who, already well-known from the earliest wars of the revolution, had been almost continually in command of various Corps during those of the empire; so that it was surprising that he had not yet been awarded the baton of a marshal; withheld perhaps because of his brusque and abrupt manner. His detractors said, after his defeat, that his desire to obtain this coveted honour had driven him, with no more than 20,000 men, to stand rashly in the path of 200,000 of the enemy, with the aim of barring their passage; but the truth is that having been informed by the Emperor's chief of staff that he would be supported by the armies of Marshals Saint-Cyr and Mortier, and been given a direct order to capture Teplice and so seal off the enemy's line of retreat, General Vandamme had perforce to obey.

Under the impression that he would be supported he descended boldly, on the 29th of August, towards Kulm from where, pushing enemy troops before him, he sought to reach Teplice; it is a certainty that if Mortier and Saint-Cyr had carried out the orders which they had been given, the Russian, Austrian and Prussian forces, stuck on the appalling roads, cut off from Bohemia and finding themselves attacked in front and in the rear, would have laid down their arms. Vandamme would have then been eulogised by the same people who have since blamed him.

However that may be, Vandamme arrived at Teplice on the morning of the 30th of August to be confronted by the division of Ostermann, one of the best of the Russian generals. Vandamme went confidently into the attack, as he saw, coming down from the heights of Peterwalde, and taking the route which he had taken the day previously, a body of troops which he took to be the armies of Mortier and Saint-Cyr, whose help the Emperor had promised him; but instead of friends these newcomers were two large Prussian divisions commanded by General Kleist, which, on the advice of Jomini, had passed between the corps of Mortier and Saint-Cyr without these two marshals taking any notice, such was the reluctance of Saint-Cyr to go to the aid of one of his colleagues. A reluctance which, on this occasion, spread to General Mortier. Neither of them budged and this at a time when their co-operation joined to the gallant efforts of Vandamme would have led to the total defeat of the enemy, whose columns of infantry, cavalry, artillery and baggage were piled up in disorder in the narrow passes of the high mountains which lie between Silesia and Bohemia.

In place of the help he was expecting, General Vandamme saw appear the two divisions of General Kleist, which instantly attacked him. Vandamme, continuing to fight the Russians of Ostermann in front of Teplice, turned round his rear-guard to face Kleist, whom he attacked furiously, but although the enemy was weakening, the huge reinforcements which they recieved, bringing their strength to around 100,000 men as opposed to Vandamme's remaining 15,000, made him think, in spite of his courage and tenacity, that he should retire towards the corps of Mortier and Saint-Cyr, whom he believed to be close at hand in accordance with what Prince Berthier had written to him on the Emperor's instructions.

On their arrival at the pass of Telnitz, the French found it occupied by General Kleist's divisions, who completely blocked their passage; but nevertheless, our battalions, preceded by the cavalry of General Corbineau who, in spite of the rough, mountainous terrain, had insisted on remaining the advance-guard, fell on the Prussians with such ferocity that they overcame them and broke through the pass after taking all the enemy guns, from which they took away only the horses because of the bad state of the roads.

Any soldier will be aware that such a success could be won only at the cost of many casualties, and after this savage engagement the strength of 1st Corps was greatly reduced. However, Vandamme, completely surrounded by forces ten times more numerous than his own, refused to surrender and placing himself at the head of two battalions of the 85th, the only ones left to him, he hurled himself into the midst of the enemy in a fight to the death. His horse was killed and a group of Russians seized him and made him prisoner. It is said that he was brought before the Emperor Alexander and his brother, the Grand Duke Constantin, and was rash enough to exchange insults with them. He was then taken to Wintka, on the frontier of Siberia, and did not see his country again until after the peace of 1814.

The battle of Kulm cost 1st Corps 2000 men killed and 8000 made prisoner, amongst whom was their commanding general. The 10,000 who were left managed to fight their way through the enemy lines to join Saint-Cyr and Mortier. Those two generals had gravely failed in their duty by not pursuing the beaten enemy and instead stopping — Saint-Cyr at Reinhards-Grimme and Mortier at Pirna — where they could hear the noise of the battle being fought by Vandamme.

It is surprising that from nearby Dresden Napoleon did not send one of his aides-de-camp, to make certain that Saint-Cyr and Mortier had gone to the aid of Vandamme, as he had ordered. The two marshals, having failed to carry out their orders, should have been court-martialled, but the French army, overwhelmed by the enormous number of enemies which Napoleon had raised against it, had reached such a point of exhaustion that had Napoleon wished to punish all those who failed in their duty, he would have had to dispense with the services of almost all his marshals. He therefore did no more than reprimand Saint-Cyr and Mortier.

He had an increasing need to conceal his disasters, for it was not only at Kulm that his troops had suffered a reverse, but at all points of the immense line which they occupied.

(Subsequent historical research has made it quite clear that as Napoleon was in control of the operations the two marshals were entirely correct in waiting to receive his instructions, as they did not know to where he intended them to go. As for the order to support Vandamme with two divisions, it did not arrive until the 30th, that is to say at a time when the catastrophe had already occurred, and no blame can be attributed to the marshals.)

Chap. 26.

It has been rightly said that in the last campaigns of the Empire , battles were rarely fought with any skill unless Napoleon himself was in command. It is regrettable that this great captain was not fully aware of this, and placed too much confidence in his lieutenants, of whom several were not up to the tasks which they presumed to undertake, as will be seen from some examples. Instead of ordering his corps commanders, when they were acting on their own initiative, to remain as much as possible on the defensive until he could come with a powerful reserve to crush the force facing them, the Emperor allowed them too much latitude, and as each one was jealous of his own reputation and wanted to have his personal Battle of Austerlitz, they often went ill-advisedly on the offensive and were defeated as a result.

This is what happened to Marshal Oudinot, to whom Napoleon had given a considerable army made up of the Corps of Bertrand and Reynier, in order to keep a watch on the numerous Prussian and Swedish troops stationed near Berlin under the command of Bernadotte, who had now become the Prince of Sweden. Marshal Oudinot was not as strong as his opponent and should have temporised, but the habit of advancing, the sight of the steeples of Berlin and the fear of not living up to the confidence Napoleon reposed in him, led him to push forward Bertrand's corps, which was repulsed, a setback which did not prevent Oudinot from persisting in his aim of taking Berlin. However he lost a major battle at Gross-Beeren and was forced to retire via Wittemberg, having suffered heavy losses.

A few days later, Marshal Macdonald, whom Napoleon had left on the Katzbach at the head of several army corps, thought that he also would take advantage of the liberty given him by the absence of the Emperor to attempt to win a battle, which would compensate for the bloody defeat which he had endured on the Trbia during the Italian campaign of 1799, but once more he was defeated.

Macdonald, although personally very brave, was constantly unfortunate in battle, not that he lacked ability but because, like the generals of the Austrian army, and in particular the famous Marshal Mack, he was too rigid and blinkered in his strategic

315

movements. Before the battle he drew up a plan of action which was almost always sound, but which he should have modified according to circumstances; this, however, his stolid temperament did not permit. He was like a chess player who, when he plays against himself, can make all the right moves, but does not know what to do when a real opponent makes moves which he had not foreseen. So, on the 26th of August, the day on which the Emperor was winning a resounding victory at Dresden, Macdonald lost the battle of Katzbach.

The French army, 75,000 strong, of which my regiment was a part, was drawn up between Liegnitz and Goldberg, on the left bank of the little river named the Katzbach,(Kaczawa) which separated them from several Prussian Corps commanded by Field-Marshal Blcher. The area which we occupied was dotted with small wooded hills, which, although practicable for cavalry, made movement difficult, but, by the same token, offered much advantage to the infantry. Now, as the main body of Macdonald's troops consisted of this arm, and he had only 6000 cavalry of Sbastiani's Corps, and as the enemy had 15 to 20,000 horse on the immense plateau of Jaur,(Jawor) where the ground is almost everywhere level, it was plainly Macdonald's duty to await the Prussians in the position which he occupied. In addition to this, the Katzbach does not have a steep approach on the left bank, where we were, but on the other side it does, so that to reach the plateau of Jaur one has to climb a high hill covered with rocks and affording only a steep and stony road.

The Katzbach, which runs at the foot of this hill has no bridges except at the few villages and only some narrow fords, which become unpassable on the least rise in the water-level. This river covered the French army front, which was greatly in our favour; but Marshal Macdonald wanted to attack the Prussians, and he abandoned this highly advantageous position and put the Katzbach at his back by ordering his troops to cross it at several points. Sbastiani's cavalry, of which Exelmans' division, which included my regiment, formed a part, were instructed to cross the river by the ford at Chemochowitz.

The weather, which was already threatening in the morning, should have warned the Marshal to put off the attack to another day, or at least to act rapidly. He did neither, and wasted precious time in giving detailed orders so that it was not until two in the afternoon that his columns began to move, and no sooner had they done so than they were overtaken by a tremendous storm which swelled the Katzbach and made the ford so difficult that General Saint-Germain's Cuirassiers were unable to cross.

Having arrived on the other bank, we climbed, by a narrow gully, a very steep slope which the rain had made so slippery that the horses were falling at every step. We had to dismount and did not get back into the saddle until we had reached the great plateau which dominates the valley of the Katzbach. There we found several divisions of our infantry, which the generals had wisely placed near the clumps of trees which are scattered over this plain; for, as I have said, the enemy were far stronger than us in cavalry, and had a further advantage in that the rain had made it impossible for the infantrymen to fire their weapons.

When we had arrived on this vast open space, we were astonished to see no signs of the enemy. The complete silence that reigned there seemed to me to conceal some kind of a trap, for we were certain that on the previous night Marshal Blcher was in this position with more than 100,000 men. It was, in my view, necessary to reconnoitre the countryside thoroughly before going any further. General Sbastiani thought differently; so as soon as Rousel d'Urbal's division was formed up, he despatched them into the distance, with not only their own guns but those belonging to Exelmans' division, which we had dragged onto the plateau with so much difficulty.

As soon as Exelmans, who had been separated from his troops, rejoined us as we emerged from the gully, and saw that Sbastiani had made off with his guns, he hurried after him to reclaim them, leaving his division without orders. The two brigades of which it was composed were some five hundred paces from one another, facing the same way and formed into columns by regiment. My regiment was at the head of Wathiez's brigade and had behind it the 24th Chasseurs. The 11th Hussars were in the rear.

The plateau of Jaur is so huge that although the Roussel d'Urbal division, which had gone ahead, was made up of seven regiments of cavalry, we could scarcely see them on the horizon. A thousand paces to the right of the column of which I was a part, was one of the clumps of trees which dot the plain. If my regiment had been on its own I would certainly have had this wood searched by a platoon; but as Exelmans, who was very jealous of his authority, had established it as a rule that no one was to leave the ranks without his order, I had not dared to take the usual precautions, and for the same reason the general commanding the brigade had felt obliged to do the same. This passive obedience was nearly fatal.

I was at the head of my regiment which, as I have said, was leading the column, when I suddenly heard a great outcry behind me; this arose from an unforeseen attack by a numerous body of Prussian lancers who, emerging unexpectedly from the wood, charged the 24th Chasseurs and the 11th Hussars, whom they took on the flank and threw into the greatest disorder. The enemy charge being on the oblique, had first struck the tail of the column, then the centre and was now threatening the head. My regiment was about to be hit on the right flank. The situation was critical, for the enemy was advancing rapidly. Confident in the courage and skill of all ranks of my cavalrymen, I ordered them to form line facing right at the full gallop.

This movement, so dangerous in the presence of the enemy, was carried out with such speed and accuracy that in the blink of an eye the regiment was in line facing the Prussians who, as they approached us obliquely, exposed a flank, which our squadrons took advantage of to get among their ranks where they effected great carnage.

When they saw the success obtained by my regiment, the 24th recovered from the surprise attack which had at first disorganised them, and rallying smartly they repelled the part of the enemy line which faced them. As for the 11th Hussars, composed entirely of Hollanders whom the Emperor had believed he could turn into Frenchmen by a simple decree, their commander found it impossible to lead them into a charge. But we were able to do without the assistance of these useless soldiers, for the 23rd and the 24th were enough to rout the three Prussian regiments which had attacked us.

While our Chasseurs were pursuing them, an elderly enemy colonel who had been unhorsed, recognising my rank by my epaulets, and fearing that he might be killed by one of my men, came to take refuge beside me where, in spite of the excitement of the action, no one would dare to strike him while he was under my protection. Although he was on foot, in the clinging mud, he followed for a quarter of an hour the hurried movements of my horse, supporting himself by a hand on my knee and repeating all the time "You are my guardian angel" I was truly sorry for the old fellow, for although he was dropping with fatigue he was unwilling to leave me, so when I saw one of my men leading a captured horse, I had him lend it to the Prussian colonel , whom I sent to the rear in the charge of a trusted Sous-officier. You will see that this enemy officer was not slow in showing his gratitude.

The plateau of Jaur now became the theatre for a desperate struggle. From each of the woods there emerged a horde of Prussians, so that the plain was soon covered by them. My regiment, whose pursuit of their opponents I had been unable to slow down, found itself before long facing a brigade of enemy infantry, whose muskets put out of action by the rain, could not fire a shot at us. I tried to break the Prussian square, but our horses, bogged down in the mud to their hocks, could move only at a slow walk, and without the weight of a charge it is almost impossible for cavalry to penetrate the close-packed ranks of infantry who, calm and well led, present a hedge of bayonets. We could go close enough to the enemy to speak with them and strike their muskets with the blades of our sabres, but we could never break through their lines, something which we could have done easily if General Sbastiani had not sent our brigade artillery elsewhere.

Our situation and that of the enemy infantry was really rather ridiculous for we were eye to eye without being able to inflict the least harm, our sabres being too short to reach the enemy, whose muskets could not be fired. We remained in this state for a considerable time, until General Maurin, the commander of a neighbouring brigade, sent the 6th Regiment of Lancers to help us. Their long weapons, outreaching the bayonets of the Prussians killed many of them and allowed not only the Lancers but also the Chasseurs of the 23rd and 24th to get into the enemy square, where they did great carnage. During the fighting, one could hear the sonorous voice of Colonel Perquit shouting in a very pronounced Alsation accent "Bointez! Lanciers, Bointez!"

The victory which we had won on this part of the vast battlefield was snatched from us by the unexpected arrival of more than 20,000 of Prussian cavalry who, after overwhelming the Roussel d'Urbal division, which had been so unwisely sent alone more than a league ahead of us, now came to attack us with infinitely greater numbers.

The approach of this enormous body of enemy troops was signalled by the arrival of General Exelmans who, as I have said, had briefly left his division to go almost unaccompanied to claim back from General Sbastiani his battery of artillery, which that General had so inappropriately despatched to join that of Roussel d'Urbal. Having been unable to find General Sbastiani, he arrived close to the leading division only to witness the capture of Roussel d'Urbal's guns and also his own, and to find himself involved in the utter rout of his colleague's squadrons. We had a warning of some disaster in the sight of our General, his appearance altered by the fact that he had lost his hat and even his belt. We hastened to recall our soldiers, who were busy sabring the enemy infantry which we had just broken into, but while we were engaged in forming them up in good order we were completely overrun by the many Prussian squadrons who were pursuing the debris of d'Urbal's division.

Instantly, Sbastiani's cavalry division, consisting at the most of 5 to 6000 men was confronted by 20,000 enemy horsemen who, as well as outnumbering us, had the advantage of being almost all of them Uhlans, that is to say armed with lances, while we had only a few such squadrons. So in spite of the stiff resistance which we put up, the groups which we formed were broken up by the Prussians, who drove us steadily back to the edge of the plain and to the verge of the steep descent into the gorge, at the bottom of which ran the river Katzbach.

We were met here by two divisions of French infantry, together with which we hoped to make a stand; but the muskets of our men were so wet that they would not fire, and they had no other means of defence but a battery of six guns and their bayonets, with which they momentarily arrested the Prussian cavalry; but the Prussian generals having brought up some twenty cannons, the French guns were instantly disabled and their battalions crushed. Then, cheering loudly, the twenty thousand enemy cavalry advanced on our troops and drove them in confusion towards the Katzbach.

This river which we had crossed in the morning with so much difficulty although it was not very deep, had been transformed into a raging torrent by the pouring rain which had continued ceaselessly throughout the whole day. The water, surging between the two banks, covered almost entirely the parapet of the bridge at Chemochowitz and made it impossible to discover if the ford at that point was still passable. However it was by those two points we had crossed in the morning, and it was to them that we went. The ford proved impassable for the infantry and a number were drowned there, but the great majority were saved by the bridge.

I gathered together my regiment, as much as was possible, and having been formed into tightly packed half-platoons which could give each other mutual support, they entered the water in reasonably good order and gained the other bank with the loss of only two men. All the other cavalry units took the same route, for in spite of the confusion inseparable from such a retreat, the troopers realised that the bridge had to be left for the infantry. I must confess that the descent of the slope was one of the most critical moments in my life... The very steep hillside was slippery under our horses feet, and they stumbled at every pace over numerous outcrops of rock. In addition, the constant hail of grape-shot which was hurled from the enemy guns made our position highly precarious. I came out of this without any personal accident, thanks to the courage, determination, and skill of my excellent Turkish horse, which by walking along the edge of precipices like a cat on a roof, saved my life, not only on this occasion but on several others. I shall mention this admirable creature later.

The French infantry and cavalry who had been driven down from the Jaur plateau thought themselves safe from their enemies once they had crossed the river, but the Prussians had sent a strong column to a bridge upstream of that at Chemochowitz, where they had crossed the Katzbach, so that having arrived on the bank which we had quitted in the morning, we were astonished to be attacked by squadrons of Uhlans. However, in spite of the surprise, several regiments, among which Marshal Macdonald in his report mentioned mine, unhesitatingly attacked the enemy...Nonetheless, I do not know what would have happened without the arrival of the division of General Saint-Germain. He had remained on the left bank of the river in the morning, and having in consequence taken no part in the fighting, found himself in full readiness to come to our aid. This division composed of two regiments of carabiniers, a brigade of Cuirassiers, and with six twelve pounders, fell furiously on the enemy and drove back into the river all those who had crossed with the aim of cutting off our retreat, and as there is nothing so terrible as troops who, having suffered a setback, resume the offensive, the troopers of Exelmanns' and d'Urbal's divisions slaughtered all whom they could reach.

This counter-attack did us much good, for it halted the enemy who, for that day, did not dare to follow us across the Katzbach. However, the French army suffered an immense disaster, for Marshal Macdonald having crossed the river by all the bridges and fords which there were between Liegnitz and Goldberg, that is to say on a line of more than five leagues, now found nearly all these crossing points cut off by flooding, the French army was extended in a long line with the Prussians at their back and facing an almost uncrossable river, so that the frightful scenes which I had witnessed on the Jaur plateau were reproduced at all points of the field of battle. Everywhere the rain prevented our infantry from firing and aided the attacks of the Prussian cavalry, four times more numerous than ours. Everywhere retreat was made highly perilous by the difficulty of crossing the flooded Katzbach. Most of those who tried to swim across were drowned, Brigadier-general Sibuet being among their number. We were able to save only a few pieces of artillery.

Chap. 27.

After the unhappy affair at the Katzbach, Marshal Macdonald, in an attempt to re-unite his troops, indicated as rallying points the towns of Bunzlau, Lauban, and Gorlitz. A pitch-dark night, rutted roads and continuous torrential rain made movement slow and very difficult; and many soldiers, particularly those of our allies, went astray or lagged behind.

Napoleon's army lost at the battle of the Katzbach 13,000 men killed or drowned, 20,000 prisoners and 50 cannons. A veritable calamity. Marshal Macdonald, whose faulty tactics had led to this irreparable catastrophe, although he forfeited the confidence of the army, was able to retain his personal esteem by the frankness and loyalty with which he admitted to his mistakes; for the day following the disaster he called together all the generals and colonels, and after engaging us to do all we could to maintain order, he said that every officer and man had done his duty, and there was only one person who was responsible for the loss of the battle, and that was himself; because, in view of the rain, he should not have left a well-broken terrain to go and attack, in a vast open space, an enemy who squadrons greatly outnumbered our own, nor, during a rain-storm, have put a river at his back. This contrite admission disarmed the critics, and everyone buckled to in order to help save the army, which retreated towards the Elbe via Bautzen.

Fate now seemed to be against us; for a few days after Marshal Oudinot had lost the battle of Gross-Beeren, Macdonald that of the Katzbach and Vandamme that of Kulm, the French forces suffered another major reverse. Marshal Ney, who had succeeded Oudinot in command of the troops who were destined to march on Berlin, not having a sufficiently powerful force to accomplish this difficult task, was defeated at Jutterbach (Jterbog) by the turncoat Bernadotte, and compelled to quit the right bank of the Elbe.

The Emperor came back to Dresden with his Guard. The various units under the command of Macdonald took up positions not far from that town, while Marshal Ney, having pushed back the Swedes to the right bank, concentrated his troops on the left bank at Dassau and Wittemberg. For almost a fortnight, between the end of September and the beginning of October, the French army remained almost motionless around Dresden. My regiment was in bivouac close to Veissig on the heights of Pilnitz, which were occupied by a division of infantry supported by the cavalry of Sbastiani and Exelmans.

Although there was no official armistice, the weariness of both sides led to a de facto suspension of hostilities, from which both parties profited to prepare for new and more terrible conflicts.

While we were in camp at Pilnitz, I received a letter from the colonel of Prussian cavalry to whom I had lent a horse after he had been captured and injured by the men of my regiment at the start of the battle of the Katzbach. This senior officer, named M. de Blankense, who had been freed by his own troops when things turned against us, was nonetheless grateful for what I had done, and to prove it he sent me ten Chasseurs and a lieutenant belonging to my regiment who had been left wounded on the battlefield and taken prisoner. M. de Blankense had seen that their wounds were dressed, and after caring for them for a fortnight he had obtained permission to have them led to the French outposts, with a thousand thanks to me, for having, as he assured me, saved his life. I believe he was right, but I was still touched by this expression of thanks from one of the leaders of our opponents.

During the time we were in this camp there took place a strange event which was witnessed by all the regiments. A corporal of the 4th Chasseurs, while drunk, had shown disrespect to an officer, and a Lancer of the 6th whose horse had bitten him and would not let go had struck it in the belly with some scissors which led to its death. Certainly the two men deserved to be punished, but only by proper disciplinary procedures. General Exelmans condemned them both to death on his own authority, and having ordered that the division should mount their horses, he drew them up in a huge square, one side of which was left open, where two graves were dug, to the side of which the two convicted men were led.

I had been away all night and returned to the camp in time to see these lugubrious preparations. I had no doubt that the prisoners had been tried and condemned, but I soon learned that this was not the case, and drawing near to a group formed by General Exelmans, the two brigadiers and all the regimental commanders, I heard M. Devence, Colonel of the 4th Chasseurs, and Colonel Perquit of the 6th Lancers beg General Exelmans to pardon the two culprits. General Exelmans refused to do so.

I have never been able to see an act which I consider unjust without expressing my indignation. It was perhaps wrong of me, but I addressed Colonels Devence and Perquit saying that it was an affront to their dignity that men of their regiments should be paraded through the camp as criminals when they had not had a proper trial, and I added "The Emperor has given no one the power of life or death, and has reserved for himself the right to grant pardon".

General Exelmans was sufficiently influenced by the effect produced by my outburst to announce that he would pardon the Chasseur of the 4th, but that the Lancer would be shot; that is to say he would pardon the soldier who had been disrespectful to his officer, but condemn to execution the one who had killed a horse.

In order to carry out this execution each regiment was asked to provide two N.C.O.s. but as they did not carry muskets, they would have to use those belonging to other soldiers. When this order reached me, I did not reply to my regimental sergeant-major, who took my meaning; so that no one from the 23rd presented himself to take part in the execution. General Exelmans noticed this but said nothing. Eventually a shot rang out, and all those present muttered with indignation. Exelmans ordered that, as was usual, the troops would be marched past the corpse. The march began. My regiment was second in the column and I was in some doubt whether I should make it march past the unlucky victim of Exelmans' severity when a great burst of laughter was heard from the 24th Chasseurs, who were in front of me and had already arrived at the scene of the execution. I sent a warrant officer to find out the cause of this unseemly mirth in the presence of the dead, and I soon discovered that the dead man was in remarkably good health!

The truth was that all that had happened was a theatrical performance staged to scare any soldiers who were tempted to indiscipline; a performance which included shooting a man with blanks. To keep the operation secret from the rank and file, our chief had formed the firing squad of sous-officers, to whom he had issued the blank

322

cartridges. However, to complete the illusion it was necessary for the troops to view the body, and Exelmans had told the Lancer who was to play the part to throw himself on his face at the sound of the shots and pretend to be dead, then to leave the army the next night, dressed as a peasant and with a sum of money which he had been given for the purpose; but the soldier who was a sharp-witted Gascon, had realised perfectly well that General Exelmans was exceeding his authority, and had no more right to have him shot without trial than he had to dismiss him from the army without a proper discharge, and so he remained standing when the shots were fired and refused to leave the camp without a pass which would guarantee him from arrest by the gendarmerie.

When I learned that it was this discussion between the General and the dead man which had produced the shouts of laughter from the 24th Chasseurs at the head of the column, I thought it better that my regiment did not take part in this comedy which seemed to me to be as much contrary to discipline as the misdemeanors it was supposed to punish or prevent. I therefore turned my squadrons about, and setting off at the trot I left this unhelpful scene and, returning to the camp, I ordered them to dismount. My example was followed by all the brigadiers and regimental commanders of the division, and Exelmans was left alone with the "dead man", who set off calmly down the road to the bivouac, where he tucked into a meal with his comrades amid much more laughter.

During our stay on the plateau of Pilnitz, the enemy, and above all the Russians, received many reinforcements, the main one, led by General Benningsen was of not less than 60,000 men, and was composed of the corps of Doctoroff and Tolsto and the reserve of Prince Labanoff. This reserve came from beyond Moscow and included in its ranks a large number of Tartars and Baskirs, armed only with bows and arrows.

I have never understood with what aim the Russian government brought from so far and at such great expense these masses of irregular cavalry, who having neither sabres nor lances nor any kind of firearm, were unable to stand up against trained soldiers, and served only to strip the countryside and starve the regular forces, which alone were capable of resisting a European enemy. Our soldiers were not in the least alarmed at the sight of these semi-barbarous Asiatics, whom they nick-named cupids, because of their bows and arrows.

Nevertheless, these newcomers, who did not yet know the French, had been so indoctrinated by their leaders, almost as ignorant as themselves, that they expected to see us take flight at their approach; and so they could not wait to attack us. From the very day of their arrival in sight of our troops they launched themselves in swarms against them, but having been everywhere repulsed by gunfire, the Baskirs left a great number of dead on the ground.

These losses far from calming their frenzy, seemed to excite them still more, for without any order and in all directions, they buzzed around us like a swarm of wasps, flying all over the place and being very hard to catch, but when our cavalry did catch them they effected a fearful massacre, our lances and sabres being immensely superior to their bows and arrows. All the same, as the attacks by these barbarians were incessant and the Russians supported them with detachments of Hussars to profit from the confusion which the Baskirs could create at various points on the line, the Emperor ordered the generals to be doubly watchful, and to make frequent visits to our advance posts.

Now both sides were preparing to renew hostilities which, as I have already said, had not been suspended by any agreement, but simply de facto. All was completely peaceful in my camp, and I had as usual taken off my coat and was preparing to shave in the open air before a little mirror nailed to a tree, when I was given a slap on the shoulder. As I was in the middle of my regiment, I turned round sharply to see who had used this familiarity with his commanding officer...I found myself facing the Emperor, who, wishing to examine some neighbouring positions without arousing the enemy, had arrived with only one aide-de-camp. As he was not accompanied by a detachment of his Guard, he was followed by squadrons chosen in equal numbers from all the regiments in the division, and having, on his orders, taken command of this escort, I spent the entire day at his side, and have nothing but praise for his kindliness.

When we were preparing to return to Pilnitz, we saw a horde of Baskirs hurrying towards us, with all the speed of their little Tartar horses. The Emperor, who had never before seen troops of this sort, stopped on a hillock and asked for the capture of some prisoners. To this end, I ordered two squadrons of my regiment to hide behind a clump of trees, while the remainder continued their march. This well-known ruse would not have deceived Cossacks, but it succeeded perfectly with the Baskirs, who have not the slightest notion of tactics. They passed close to the wood without sending anyone to inspect it, and were continuing to follow the column when they were unexpectedly attacked by our squadrons who, falling on them suddenly, killed a great number and took some thirty prisoners.

I had these brought to the Emperor, who, after examining them expressed his surprise at the spectacle of these wretched horsemen who were sent, with no other arms than bows and arrows, to fight European soldiers armed with sabres, lances, guns and pistols... These Tartar Baskirs had Chinese features and wore extravagant costumes. When we got back to the camp, my Chasseurs amused themselves by giving wine to the Baskirs who, delighted with this novel reception got drunk and expressed their joy by such extraordinary grimaces and capers that all the watchers, including Napoleon, were in fits of laughter.

On the 28th of September, after reviewing our army corps, the Emperor treated me with quite exceptional benevolence, for although he very rarely gave more than one reward at a time, he created me an officer of the Legion of Honour, a Baron, and awarded me a grant of money...He loaded favours on the regiment, saying that it was the only one of Sbastiani's corps which had maintained good order at the Katzbach, had captured some enemy guns and had driven off the Prussians whenever they met them.

The 23rd Chasseurs owed this distinction to the high praise of its conduct received by the Emperor from Marshal Macdonald who, after the debacle at the Katzbach, had sought refuge in the ranks of my regiment and had taken part in the fierce charges it made to drive the enemies back across the river.

After the review, when the troops were on the road to their camp, General Exelmans came to the front of the regiment and loudly complemented them for the recognition given by the Emperor to their courage. Then, turning to me, he embarked on a veritable, and exaggerated, eulogy of their colonel.

The French army now was concentrated in the area of Leipzig. All the enemy forces also proceeded to the town, around which their great number allowed them to form a huge circle, which contracted every day, and whose aim was obviously to hem in the French troops and cut off all means of retreat.

On the 14th of October there was a sharp encounter between the Austro-Russian advance-guard and our own; but after an indecisive result, both sides returned to their previous positions, and the action ended with one of the most ridiculous features of war, a cannonade which went on until nightfall, with no result but the loss of many men's lives.

The Emperor, after leaving at Dresden a garrison of 25,000 men commanded by Marshal Saint-Cyr, came to Leipzig, where he arrived on the morning of the 15th.

Chap. 28.

The exact details of the battle of Leipzig will never be known, partly because of the extent and complexity of the area over which fighting continued for several days, and partly because of the immense number of troops of different nations which took part in this memorable encounter. It is principally the documents relating to the French army which are missing, because several commanders of army corps and divisions, and some members of the general staff, having been killed or left in enemy hands, most of their reports have never been finished, and those which have been, reflect the inevitable haste and disorder surrounding their compilation. At Leipzig I was the colonel of a regiment, a part of a division whose movements I was bound to follow, so it was not possible for me to know what was happening elsewhere in the manner which it had been in previous campaigns, when as an aide-de-camp to various marshals, I was able to acquire a general view of operations while carrying orders to different parts of the battlefield. I must therefore, more than ever, limit my description to what is absolutely necessary for an understanding of the main events of the battle of Leipzig, the outcome of which had such a profound influence on the destinies of the Emperor, of France and of Europe.

The iron circle within which the allies were preparing to enclose the French army, had not yet completely surrounded Leipzig, when the King of Wurtemburg, a man of violence but honourable, thought it his duty to warn Napoleon that the whole of Germany, incited by the English, was about to rise against him, and that he had barely sufficient time to retire with the French troops behind the river Main, before all of the German Confederation abandoned him to join his enemies. He added that he himself, King of Wurtemburg, could not avoid doing likewise, as he was forced to accede to the demands of his subjects, who clamoured for him to go with the torrent of German public opinion and, breaking with Napoleon, range himself with the enemies of France.

The Emperor, shaken by this advice from the most able and most faithful of his allies, is said to have considered retiring towards the mountains of Thuringia and Hesse, to get behind the river Saale and there wait for the allies to attack him, where they would be at a disadvantage on the difficult terrain, heavily wooded and full of narrow passes.

This plan could have saved Napoleon; but it had to be executed quickly, before the enemy armies were completely united and near enough to attack us during the retreat. However, when it came to deciding to abandon a part of his conquests, the Emperor could not make up his mind. He was most unwilling to have it thought that he considered himself defeated because he sought refuge behind these inaccessible mountains. The over-boldness of this great captain was our undoing; he did not stop to consider that his army, weakened by numerous losses, contained in its ranks many foreigners who were waiting only for a favourable opportunity to betray him, and that it was liable to be overwhelmed by superior forces in the great open plains of Leipzig. He would have been wiser to lead it to the mountains of Thuringia and Hesse, which offered good defensive positions, and so nullify some of the numerical advantage of the royal coalition. In addition, the approach of winter and the need to feed their many troops would have soon compelled the enemies to separate, while the French army, its front and its flanks protected by the extreme difficulty of mounting an attack in a country bristling with natural obstacles, would have had behind it the fertile valleys of the Main, the Rhine and the Necker.

Such a position would at least have given us some time and perhaps tired the allies to the point of desiring a peace; but the confidence which Napoleon had in himself and in the valour of his troops overcame these considerations, and he elected to await his enemies on the plains of Leipzig.

This fatal decision had hardly been taken, when a second letter from the King of Wurtemburg informed the Emperor that the King of Bavaria, having suddenly changed sides had made a pact with the allies, and that the two armies, the Austrian and the Bavarian, in cantonment on the banks of the Inn, had joined into a single unit under the command of General de Wrde and were marching to the Rhine; and finally that, to his regret, he was compelled by force to join his army to theirs. In consequence, the Emperor could expect that soon 100,000 men would surround Mainz, and threaten the frontier of France.

At this unexpected news, Napoleon thought he should return to the project of retiring behind the Saale and the mountains of Thuringia; but it was too late, for already the main forces of the allies were in contact with the French army, and too close for it to be possible to carry out a retreat without being attacked in the course of this difficult operation. So the Emperor decided to stand and fight.... It was a disastrous decision, for the effective strength of the French troops and their allies amounted to no more than 157,000 men, of whom only 29,000 were cavalry, while Prince Schwartzenberg, the enemy generalissimo, disposed of a force of 350,000, of whom 54,000 were cavalry....

This huge army consisted of Russians, Austrians, Prussians, and Swedes, whom the former French Marshal Bernadotte was leading against his fellow countrymen and one-time brothers in arms. The total number of those engaged amounted to 507,000 without counting the troops left in fortresses.

The town of Leipzig is one of the most commercial and richest in Germany. It stands in the middle of a great plain which extends from the Elbe to the Harz mountains, to Thuringia and to Bohemia. Its situation has made it almost always the principal theatre for the wars which have bloodied Germany. A little river named the Elster, which is so small and shallow that one could call it a stream, runs from south to north through water-meadows in a slight valley as far as Leipzig. This watercourse divides into a great number of branches which are a real obstacle to the usual operations of war, and require a multiplicity of bridges for communication between the villages which edge the valley.

The Pleisse, another river of the same sort but even smaller than the Elster runs about a league and a half from the latter, which it joins under the walls of Leipzig.

To the north of the town is a small stream called the Partha which winds through a narrow valley and has at every pace fords or little bridges across it.

Leipzig, being at the confluence of these three streams and almost surrounded to the north and west by their multiple branches is the key to the terrain through which they run. The town, which is not very large, was at this period surrounded by an old wall in which were four large gates and three small ones. The road to Lutzen via Lindenau and Markranstadt was the only one by which the French army could communicate freely with its rear.

It is in the area of ground between the Pleisse and the Partha that the heaviest fighting took place. There, a noticeable feature is a small isolated hillock called the Kelmberg, known also as the Swedish redoubt, because in the thirty years war, Gustavus Adolphus built some fortifications at this spot, which dominates the surrounding countryside.

The battle of Leipzig began on the 16th of October 1813 and lasted three days; but the fighting on the 17th was infinitely more savage than that on the 16th and 18th.

Without wishing to go into the details of this memorable encounter, I think I should indicate the principal positions occupied by the French army, which will give a general idea of those of the enemy, since each of our army corps had facing it one and sometimes two of the enemy.

King Murat was in control of our right wing, the extremity of which was bounded by the Pleisse near the villages of Connewitz, Dlitz, and Mark-Kleeberg which were occupied by Prince Poniatowski and his Poles. Next to him and behind the market-town of Wachau was the corps of Marshal Victor. Marshal Augereau occupied Dsen.

These various corps of infantry were flanked and supported by several masses of Marshals Kellermann's and Michaud's cavalry.

The centre, under the direct command of the Emperor, was at Liebert-Wolkwitz. It was made up of the infantry corps of General Lauriston and Marshal Macdonald, having with them the cavalry of Latour-Maubourg and Sbastiani. My regiment which was part of this last general's corps, was positioned facing the hillock of Kelmberg, or the Swedish redoubt.

The left wing, commanded by Marshal Ney, comprised the infantry Corps of Marshal Marmont, and of Generals Souham and Reynier, supported by the cavalry of the Duc de Padoue. They occupied Taucha.

A body of 15,000 men under the command of General Bertrand was sent from Leipzig to guard the crossings of the Elster and the road to Lutzen.

At Probstheyda, behind our centre, was the reserve commanded by Marshal Oudinot and consisting of the Young and the Old Guard and Nansouty's cavalry.

The venerable King of Saxony, who had been unwilling to desert his friend the Emperor of France, remained in the town of Leipzig with his guard and several French regiments who were there to maintain order.

During the night of 15th-16th, Marshal Macdonald's troops were moved to concentrate in Liebert-Wolkwitz, leaving the area of the Kelmberg: but as there was no wish to abandon this position to the enemy before dawn, I was told to keep it under surveillance until first light. This was an operation of some delicacy, since I had to advance with my regiment to the foot of the hillock, while the French army retired for half a league in the opposite direction. I ran the risk of being surrounded and perhaps captured with all my men by the enemy advance-guard, whose scouts would not fail to climb to the top of the hillock as soon as the dawn light allowed them to see what was going on in the vast plains below them, which were occupied by the French army.

The weather was superb and, although it was night, one could see reasonably well by the light of the stars; but as in these circumstances it is much easier to see what is overhead than to see what is below one's feet, I brought my squadrons as close as possible to the hillock so that its shadow would conceal the riders, and after ordering silence and immobility, I awaited events.

The event which fortune had in store was one which could have changed the future of France and the Emperor and made my name for ever celebrated.

Half an hour before first light, three riders, coming from the direction of the enemy, climbed, at walking pace, the hillock of Kelmberg, from where they could not see us, although we could see clearly their silhouettes and hear their conversation. They were speaking in French, the one being Russian and the other two Prussians. The first, who seemed to have some authority over his companions, ordered one of them to go and inform their majesties that there were no Frenchmen at this spot, and they could climb up, for in a few minutes it would be possible to see the whole of the plain; but they should do this right away, in case the French sent sharp-shooters to the area.

The officer to whom these words were addressed observed that the escort was still a long way off. "What does it matter?" was the reply, "There is no one here but us". At these words my troops and I redoubled our attention, and soon we saw on the top of the hillock some twenty enemy officers, of whom one dismounted.

Although on setting up an ambush, I had no expectation of making any great capture, I had, however warned my officers that if we saw anyone on the Swedish redoubt, at a signal from me two squadrons would go round it, one to left and one to right, in order to encircle any enemy who had risked coming so close to our army. I had high hopes, when the over-keenness of one of my troopers ruined my plan. This man having accidently dropped his sabre, immediately took his carbine, and fearing that he would be late when I gave the order to attack, he fired into the middle of the group, killing a Prussian major. .

You may imagine how, in an instant, all the enemy officers, who had no other guard but a few orderlies, seeing themselves on the point of being surrounded, made off at the gallop. We dared not follow them too far for fear of falling ourselves into the hands of the approaching escorts. We did manage to capture two officers, from whom we could get no information, but I learned later from my friend, Baron de Stoch, who was a colonel in the guard of the Grand Duke of Darmstadt, that the Emperor Alexander of Russia and the King of Prussia had been among the group of officers who almost fell into French hands, an event which would have changed the destiny of Europe. However, fate having decided otherwise, there was nothing left for me to do but to withdraw smartly with my regiment to the French lines.

On the 16th of October at eight o'clock in the morning, the allied batteries gave the signal for the attack. A lively cannonade was directed at our lines and the allied army marched towards us from every point. The fighting commenced on our right, where the Poles, driven back by the Prussians, abandoned the village of Mark-Kleeberg.

At our centre the Russians and the Austrians attacked Wachau and Liebert-Wolkwitz six times and were repeatedly repulsed with great losses. The Emperor regretting, no doubt that he had abandoned that morning the Swedish redoubt which the enemy had occupied and from where their gunners rained down grape-shot, ordered its recapture, which was promptly carried out by the 22nd Light Infantry aided by my regiment.

Having obtained this first success, the Emperor, not being able to outflank the enemy wings because their superior numbers allowed them to present too long a front, decided to keep them occupied while he attempted to break through their centre. To this end, he sent Marshal Mortier to Wachau with two divisions of infantry, and Marshal Oudinot with the Young Guard. General Drout with sixty cannons aided the attack, which was successful.

For his part, Marshal Victor overcame and routed the Russian Corps commanded by Prince Eugne of Wurtemberg; but after suffering considerable losses, the Prince was able to rally his Corps at Gossa.

At this moment General Lauriston and Marshal Macdonald debouched from Liebert-Wolkwitz and the enemy was overthrown. The French then took possession of the wood of Grosspossnau. Geberal Maison was wounded in the taking of this important point.

It was in vain that the numerous Austrian cavalry commanded by General Klenau and aided by a host of Cossacks tried to restore the situation, they were defeated by General Sbastian's cavalry. This was a very fierce encounter; my regiment took part; I lost several men and my senior Major was wounded in the chest by a lance, having failed to protect himself by carrying his rolled cape.

Prince Schwartzenberg, seeing his line badly shaken, advanced his reserves to support it, which decided the Emperor to order a massive cavalry charge which involved the two corps of Kellermann and Latour-Maubourg as well as the Dragoons of the Guard. Kellermann overcame a division of Russian Cuirassiers, but taken on the flank by another division he had to fall back to the heights of Wachau after taking several enemy flags.

King Murat then advanced the French infantry and the fighting was renewed. The Russian Corps of the Prince of Wurtemberg was once more overwhelmed and lost twenty-six guns. This treatment resulted in the enemy centre yielding and it was about to give way when the Emperor of Russia who had witnessed the disaster, rapidly advanced the numerous cavalry of his guard which, encountering the squadrons of Latour-Maubourg in the state of confusion which always follows an all-out charge, repelled them in their turn and took back twenty-four of the guns which they had just captured. It was during this charge that General Latour-Maubourg had his leg carried away by a cannon-ball.

So far neither side had secured a marked advantage and Napoleon, to achieve a victory, had just launched against the enemy centre the reserve consisting of the infantry and cavalry of the Old Guard and a body of fresh troops newly arrived from Leipzig, when a regiment of enemy cavalry which had either deliberately or accidently got behind French lines created some alarm amongst the moving troops, who halted and formed a square so as not to be taken by surprise, and before it was possible to find out the cause of this alert, night had everywhere suspended military operations.

There had been other events on our extreme right. For the whole day General Merfeld had tried fruitlessly to secure a passage across the Pleisse, defended by Poniatowski's Corps and his Poles; however, towards the end of the day, he managed to take the village of Dlitz, which compromised our right wing; but the infantry Chasseurs of the Old Guard came from the reserve at the Pas de Charge and chased the Austrians back across the river, taking some hundreds of prisoners, among whom was General Merfeld who found himself for the third time in French hands.

Although the Poles had allowed the capture of Dlitz, the Emperor, to boost their morale, thought he should give the baton of a marshal of France to their leader, Prince Poniatowski, who did not enjoy the honour of bearing it for very long.

On the other side of the river Elster, the Austrian General Giulay had taken the village of Lindenau after seven hours of fierce fighting. The Emperor when told of this serious event, which compromised the way of retreat for the major part of his troops, ordered an attack by General Bertrand, who re-took the position by a vigourous bayonet charge.

On our left, the impatience of Ney nearly led to a major catastrophe. The Marshal who commanded the left wing which had been placed in position by the Emperor, seeing that by ten o'clock in the morning no enemy troops had appeared, sent, on his own authority, one of his army corps, commanded by General Souham, to Wachau, where there seemed to be an active engagement; but while this ill-considered movement was being carried out, the Prussian Marshal Blcher, who had been delayed, arrived with the Silesian army and captured the village of Mckern. Then Ney, deprived of a part of his force, and having at his disposal only Marmont's division, was compelled to withdraw to the walls of Leipzig and do no more than defend the suburb of Halle.

The French lost many men in this engagement, which also had a very disturbing effect on those of our soldiers who were in positions in front of or to one side of Leipzig, for they heard the sound of cannon and small-arms fire coming from behind them. However, at about eight in the evening, the fighting ceased in all parts and the night was peaceful.

Chap. 29.

This first day led to no decisive victory; but the French had the advantage, since with very much smaller numbers, they had not only held their own against the coalition, but had driven them off some of the ground they had occupied the day before.

The troops on both sides were preparing to renew the fighting on the following morning; but contrary to their expectations, the 17th passed without any hostile movement on the part of either side. The coalition was awaiting the arrival of the Russian Polish army, and the troops which were being brought by the Prince Royal of Sweden, Bernadotte, which would greatly increase their strength.

For his part Napoleon, now regretting his rejection of the peace offers which had been made to him two months previously during the armistice, hoped to have some result from a peace mission which he had sent the previous evening to the allied sovereigns through the Austrian General Comte de Merfeld, who had recently been taken prisoner.

Here could be seen a strange sequence of events. It was the Comte de Merfeld who sixteen years previously had come to ask General Bonaparte, then the commander of the army in Italy, for the armistice of Loben. It was he who had brought back to Vienna the peace treaty concluded between the Austrian government and the Directorate, represented by General Bonaparte. It was he who had carried to the French emperor, on the night following the Battle of Austerlitz, the proposal for an armistice made by the Austrian Emperor; now, as a remarkable turn of fate had brought General Merfeld once more into the Emperor's presence at a moment when he in his turn was in need of an armistice and peace, he had high hopes that this intermediary would return with the result he desired. However things had gone too far for the allied sovereigns to treat with Napoleon, from whom such a plea denoted the weakness of his position. So, although unable to conquer us on the 16th, they hoped to overcome us by a renewed effort with their superior numbers, and relied heavily on the defection of the German units which were still with us, and whose leaders, all members of the secret society, the Tugenbund, took advantage of the lull in hostilities of the 17th to agree on the manner in which they would execute their treacherous designs. The Comte de Merfeld's mission did not even receive a reply.

On the morning of the 18th, the coalition began its attack. The 2ndCavalry Corps, of which my regiment was a part, was placed as it had been on the 16th, between Liebert-Wolkwitz and the Kelmberg. The fighting, which broke out everywhere, was fiercest towards our centre, at the village of Probstheyda, which was attacked simultaneously by a Russian and a Prussian Corps who were driven off with tremendous losses. The Russians vigourously attacked Holzhausen, which Macdonald defended successfully.

About eleven o'clock, a cannonade was heard from behind Leipzig, in the direction of Lindenau, and we learned that at this point our troops had broken through the ring within which the enemy believed they could contain the French army, and that General Bertrand's corps was marching towards Weissenfeld in the direction of the

Rhine, without the enemy being able to stop him. The Emperor then ordered to evacuation of the equipment to Lutzen.

Meanwhile, the Leipzig plateau, around Connewitz and Lssnig, was the scene of a massive engagement; the earth shook with the noise of a thousand cannon, and the enemy tried to force a passage across the Pleisse. They were driven back, although the Poles managed to ruin some of the bayonet charges made by our infantry. Then the 1st French Cavalry Corps, seeing the Austrian and Prussian squadrons going to the aid of their allies, emerged from behind the village of Probstheyda and hurled themselves at the enemy, whom they overwhelmed and drove back to their reserves which were led by Prince Constantine of Russia. Defeated again at this spot the allies built up an immense force in order to capture Probstheyda, but this formidable mass had such a hot reception from some divisions of our infantry and the infantry Chasseurs of the Old Guard that they promptly withdrew. We lost there Generals Vial and Rochambeau. The latter had just been made a Marshal of France by the Emperor.

Bernadotte had not yet attacked the French and seemed, it was said, to waver; but at last urged on or even threatened by the Prussian Marshal Blcher, he decided to cross the Partha above the village of Mockau, at the head of his troops and a Russian corps which had been placed under his command. When a brigade of Saxon Hussars and Lancers which was positioned at this point saw the Cossacks who preceded Bernadotte approaching they marched towards them as if to give battle; but then, turning round suddenly and forgetting about their aged King, our ally who was in the midst of Napoleon's troops, the infamous Saxons aimed their muskets and cannons at the French.

This force led by Bernadotte, following the left bank of the Partha, headed for Sellerhausen which was defended by Reynier, whose corps was almost entirely made up of German contingents. Reynier having seen the desertion of the Saxon cavalry, distrusted their infantry, which he had placed next to the cavalry of Durette in order to restrain them; but Marshal Ney, with misplaced confidence, ordered him to deploy the Saxons and send them to assist a French regiment which was defending the village of Paunsdorf. The Saxons had gone only a little distance from the French, when seeing the Prussian ensigns in the fields of Paunsdorf they ran towards them at top speed, led by the shameless General Russel, their commander. Some French officers could not believe such treachery, and thought that the Saxons were going to attack the Prussians; so that General Gressot, Reynier's chief-of-staff rushed towards them to moderate what he thought was an excess of zeal, only to find himself confronted by enemies! This defection of an entire army corps produced a frightening gap in the French centre, and had the additional effect of raising the allied morale. The Wurtemberg cavalry promptly followed the example of the Saxons.

Not only did Bernadotte welcome the perfidious Saxons into his ranks, but he used their artillery to bolster up his own, which the former Marshal France now aimed at Frenchmen.

The Saxons had scarcely entered the enemy ranks when they celebrated their treachery by firing at us a hail of projectiles, many of which were directed to my regiment, for I lost some thirty men, among whom was Captain Bertain, an excellent officer who had his head taken off by a cannon-ball.

So now it was Bernadotte, a man for whom French blood had procured a throne, who was attempting to deliver to us the coup de grace.

Amid this general disloyalty, the King of Wurtemberg presented an honourable exception, for as I have said, he had informed Napoleon that circumstances forced him to renounce his friendship; but even after he had taken this final step, he ordered his troops not to attack the French without giving them ten days warning, and although he was now an enemy of France, he dismissed from his army the general and several officers who had handed over their troops to the Russians at the battle of Leipzig, and withdrew all their decorations from the turncoat regiments.

Probstheyda, however, continued to be the theatre of a most murderous struggle. The Old Guard, deployed behind the village, held itself in readiness to hasten to the aid of its defenders. Bulow's Prussian corps having attempted to push forward, was heavily defeated; but we lost in the action General Delmas, a distinguished soldier and a man of high principles who, having been involved with Napoleon since the creation of the Empire, had spent ten years in retirement, but asked to be returned to active service when he saw his country in danger.

Facing a terrible cannonade, and continual attacks, the French line remained steadfastly in position. Towards our left, Marshal Macdonald and General Sbastiani were holding the ground between Probstheyda and Sttteritz, in spite of numerous attacks by Klenau's Austrians and the Russians of Doctoroff, when they were assailed by a charge of more than 20,000 Cossacks and Baskirs, the efforts of the latter being directed mainly at Sbastiani's cavalry.

With much shouting, these barbarians rapidly surrounded our squadrons, against which they launched thousands of arrows which did very little damage because the Baskirs, being entirely irregulars, do not know how to form up in ranks and they go about in a mob like a flock of sheep, with the result that the riders cannot shoot horizontally without wounding or killing their comrades who are in front of them, but shoot their arrows into the air to describe an arc which will allow them to descend on the enemy. This system does not permit any accurate aim, and nine tenths of the arrows miss their target. Those that do arrive have used up in their ascent the impulse given to them by the bow, and fall only under their own weight, which is very small, so that they do not as a rule inflict any serious injuries. In fact the Baskirs, having no other arms, are undoubtedly the world's least dangerous troops.

However, since they attacked us in swarms, and the more one killed of these wasps, the more seemed to arrive, the huge number of arrows which they discharged into the air of necessity caused a few dangerous wounds. Thus, one of my finest N.C.O.s. by

334

the name of Meslin had his body pierced by an arrow which entered his chest and emerged at his back. The brave fellow, taking two hands, broke the arrow and pulled out the remaining part, but this did not save him, for he died a few moments later. This is the only example which I can remember of death being caused by a Baskir arrow, but I had several men and horses hit, and was myself wounded by this ridiculous weapon.

I had my sabre in my hand, and I was giving orders to an officer, when, on raising my arm to indicate the point to which he was to go, I felt my sabre encounter a strange resistance and was aware of a slight pain in my right thigh, in which was embedded for about an inch, a four foot arrow which in the heat of battle I had not felt. I had it extracted by Dr.Parot and put in one of the boxes in the regimental ambulance, intending to keep it as a memento; but unfortunately it got lost.

You will understand that for such a minor injury I was not going to leave the regiment, particularly at such a critical time... The reinforcements brought by Bernadotte and Blcher were determinedly attacking the village of Schnfeld, not far from where the Partha enters Leipzig. Generals Lagrange and Friederichs who were defending this important point, repelled seven assaults and seven times drove the allies out of houses they had captured. General Friederichs was killed during this action; he was a fine officer who among his other qualities, was the most handsome man in the French army.

Nevertheless, it looked as if the allies might take Schnfeld until Marshal Ney went to the aid of the village, which remained in French hands. Marshal Ney received a blow on his shoulder which forced him to leave the field of battle.

By nightfall the troops of both sides were, in most parts of the line, in the same positions which they had occupied at the beginning of the battle. In the evening my troopers and those of all the divisions of Sbastiani's cavalry tethered their horses to the same pickets which they had used for the three preceding days, and almost all the battalions occupied the same bivouacs. So this battle which our enemies have celebrated as a great success, was in fact indecisive, since being greatly inferior in numbers, having almost all the nations of Europe against us and harbouring a crowd of traitors in our ranks, we had not yielded an inch of ground. The English general, Sir Robert Wilson, who was in Leipzig in the rle of British representative and whose testimony cannot be suspected of partiality, said of this battle:-

"In spite of the defection of the Saxon army in the middle of the battle, in spite of the courage and perseverance of the allied troops, it proved impossible to take from the French any of the villages which they regarded as essential to their position. Night ended the fighting, leaving the French, and in particular the defenders of Probstheyda, in the well-earned position of having inspired in their enemies a generous measure of respect..."

After sunset, when it was beginning to grow dark, I was ordered to put a stop, at the front of my regiment, to the useless exchange of fire which usually goes on after a serious engagement. There is some difficulty in separating men on both sides who have been fighting each other, the more so because, to prevent the enemy from knowing what is going on, and making use of it to fall unexpectedly on our advance-posts, one cannot use drums or trumpets to instruct the infantrymen to cease fire and to form up to rejoin their regiments. A warning is given to platoon commanders, in quiet tones, and they then send sous-officiers to look silently for the small, scattered groups. As the enemy were doing the same, the firing gradually grew less and soon stopped entirely.

To make sure that no sentinel was forgotten and that this little withdrawal to bivouac was carried out in good order, it was my custom to have it supervised by an officer. The one who was on duty on this evening was a Captain Joly, a brave and well-trained officer, but inclined to be obstinate. He had given evidence of this trait some months before the battle when, given the job of distributing some officer's remounts which had been presented, on the Emperor's instructions, to those who had taken part in the Russian campaign, M. Joly, ignoring my advice and that of his friends, had selected for himself a magnificent light grey, which neither I nor my friends would have because of its striking colour, and which I had at first reserved for the trumpeters. So on the evening of the battle of Leipzig, while M. Joly, in carrying out his duty, was riding at a walk behind the lines of infantry, his horse stood out so clearly, in spite of the failing light, that it was picked out by the enemy and both horse and rider were seriously wounded. The captain had a musket ball through his body and died during the night in a house in the suburb of Halle, to where, on the previous evening, I had sent Major Pozac.

Although the latter's wound was not dangerous, he was grieved to think that the French army would probably leave and he would become a prisoner of the enemy, who would deprive him of the sabre of honour which he had been awarded by the First Consul after the battle of Marengo when he was still only a sous-officier; but I calmed his anxieties by taking charge of the precious sabre which was given into the care of one of the regimental surgeons, and handed back to Pozac when he returned to France.

Chap. 30.

The calm of the night having replaced in the fields of Leipzig the terrible battles which they had just witnessed, the leaders of both sides could examine their positions.

That of the Emperor Napoleon was the least favourable. If one could blame this great man for not retreating behind the Saale eight days before the battle, when he could have still avoided risking the safety of his army, which was threatened by infinitely more numerous forces, there is now even more reason to disapprove of his judgement when, at Leipzig, one sees him completely surrounded on the field of battle by his enemies. I use the word "completely" because, on the 18th, at eleven in the morning, Lichtenstein's Austrian corps seized the village of Kleinzschocher, on the left bank of the Elster, and for a time the route from Leipzig to Weissenfels, the only way of escape for the French, was cut and Napoleon's army entirely encircled.

It is true that this situation did not last for more than half an hour, but would Napoleon not have been wiser to avoid all the consequences which might have arisen from such an event by taking shelter behind the mountains of Thuringia and the river Saale before all the enemy forces could combine to surround him?

We now come to a very critical situation.... The French had held on to their positions for the three days of the battle, but this success had been achieved only at the expense of much blood, for in killed and wounded we had 40,000 casualties. It is true that the enemy had suffered 60,000, a figure greatly to their disadvantage, which was attributable to the persistence with which they attacked our entrenched positions. As, however, they had many more men than we did, having lost 40,000 we were proportionately much more weakened than they were.

In addition to this, the French artillery had fired during the three days 220,000 rounds, of which 95,000 were fired on the 18th, and there were no more than 16,000 rounds left in the reserves, that is to say enough to continue in action for only two hours. This shortage of ammunition which should have been foreseen before we engaged a powerful enemy so far from our frontiers, prevented Napoleon from renewing the battle, which he might possibly have won, and forced him to order a retreat.

This was a movement which it was very difficult to carry out, because of the nature of the terrain which we occupied, which was full of water-meadows and streams and traversed by three rivers, creating many narrow defiles which would have to be negotiated under the eyes and within close range of the enemy, who might easily throw our ranks into disorder during this perilous march.

There was only one means of assuring our retreat, and that was the construction of a large number of pathways and footbridges across the meadows, ditches and small streams, together with larger bridges across the Partha, the Pleisse and principally, over the Elster, which was joined by these various tributaries at the gates and even within the town of Leipzig. Now, nothing could have been easier than the creation of these indispensable means of passage, for the town and suburbs of Leipzig, barely a musket-shot away, offered a ready source of planks and beams, girders, nails and rope *etc*. The whole army believed that numerous crossing places had been made since their arrival before Leipzig and that these had been increased on the 16th and above all on the 17th, when the whole day had passed without any fighting. Well!... for a number of deplorable reasons and by unbelievable negligence, nothing whatsoever had been done... and among those official documents which we possess relating to this famous battle, one can find nothing, absolutely nothing, which would show that any measures had been taken to facilitate, in case of a retreat, the movement of the many columns which were in action beyond the obstructions formed by the rivers and the streets of Leipzig and its suburbs. None of the officers who escaped from the disaster, nor any of the authors who have written about it have been able to show that any of the senior staff of the army took steps to establish new crossing points or to ensure free use of those which existed. Only General Pelet, who is a great admirer of Napoleon and who, for this reason, is sometimes given to exaggeration, writing fifteen years after the battle, states that M. Odier, the deputy quartermaster of the Imperial Guard, told him several times that he was present when one morning (he does say on what day) the Emperor ordered a general on his staff to look into the construction of bridges and made him specially responsible for the task. General Pelet does not disclose the name of the general to whom the Emperor gave this order, although it would be most important to know it.

M. Fain, Napoleon's secretary, says in his memoirs "The Emperor ordered the construction in the neighbouring marshes of new pathways which would ease the passage of this long defile".

I do not know how much credit history will give to the accuracy of these assertions; but even supposing them to be true, there are those who think that the head of the French army should have done more than give an order to a general staff officer, who perhaps did not have at his disposal sappers or the necessary material, and that he should have given the responsibility for creating new crossing points to several officers, at least one from every regiment in each army corps, for it is plain that no one was doing anything. Here now is the truth of the matter, which is known to very few people.

The Emperor had for head of his general staff, Marshal Prince Berthier, who had never left him since the Italian campaign of 1796. He was capable, precise and loyal but having often suffered the effects of the imperial temper, he had developed such a fear of Napoleon's outbursts that he had decided never to take the initiative on any matter, never to ask any questions, and simply to carry out those orders he received in writing. This system which maintained good relations between the Major-general and his chief, was harmful to the interests of the army; for no matter how great the Emperor's energy and ability, it was impossible for him to see everything and undertake everything; and so if he overlooked something of importance nothing was done.

It seems that this is what happened at Leipzig, where, when almost all the marshals and generals had on several occasions, and particularly on the last two days, pointed out to Berthier how necessary it was to provide adequate ways out in the event of a retreat, his invariable reply had been "The Emperor has not ordered it." No materials were supplied, and so not a plank nor beam had been placed across a rivulet when, during the night of 18th-19th the Emperor ordered a retreat to Weissenfels and the river Saale.

The allies had suffered such heavy losses that they felt it impossible to renew the struggle. They did not dare to attack us afresh, and were on the point of retiring themselves when they noticed the heavy equipment of the army heading for Weissenfels via Lindenau, and realised that Napoleon was preparing to retreat.

Whereupon they took steps to place themselves in a position to profit from any opportunities which this movement might present to them.

The most unhappy moment of a retreat, particularly for a unit commander, is that when he has to leave behind those wounded whom he is compelled to abandon to the mercy of the enemy, who frequently does not have any and robs and murders those who are too badly injured to follow their comrades. However, since the worst of all things is to be left lying on the ground, I took advantage of the night to have my men pick up all the wounded from my regiment, whom I put in two adjoining houses, firstly to shield them from the drunken fury of the enemy, who would occupy the suburb, and secondly to allow them to help one another and keep up their spirits. An assistant surgeon, M.Bordenave, offered to remain with them. I accepted his offer, and after the peace I recommended this estimable doctor, whose care saved the lives of many men, for the award of the Legion of Honour.

The troops now began their march away from the battlefield where they had shown so much courage and shed so much blood. The Emperor left his bivouac at eight in the evening and went to the town where he stayed at a hostelry in the horse market,named "The Prussian Arms", and after giving some orders he went to visit the aged King of Saxony, whom he found preparing to follow him.

This King, a devoted friend, expected that to punish his unshakable adherence to the French Emperor, the allied sovereigns would seize his kingdom, but what grieved him more was the thought that his army had been dishonoured by deserting to the enemy. Napoleon was unable to comfort the good old man, and it was with difficulty that he persuaded him to remain in Leipzig, in the heart of his state, and send an envoy to the confederates to ask for terms.

When this emissary had left, the Emperor said adieu to the old King, the Queen and the Princess their daughter, a model of virtue who had followed her father even to face the guns of the enemy. The separation was made more unhappy when it was learned that the allies would make no promises about the fate reserved for the Saxon monarch, who would thus be at their mercy. He ruled over some fine provinces, an invitation to his enemies to be implacable.

About eight in the evening the retreat began, with the corps of Marshals Victor and Augereau, the ambulances, a part of the artillery, the cavalry and the IMperial Guard. While these troops filed through the suburb of Lindenau, Marshals Ney, Marmont and General Reynier guarded the suburbs of Halle and Rosenthal. The Corps of Lauriston, Macdonald and Poniatowski entered the town in succession and took up positions at the barriers which pierced the walls, all was thus arranged for a stubborn resistance by the rear-guard to allow the army to retreat in good order. Nevertheless, Napoleon wished to spare Leipzig the horrors which always result from fighting in the streets, and so he permitted the magistrates to address a request to the allied sovereigns asking them to allow, by an armistice of a few hours, the peaceful evacuation of the town. This proposal was rejected and the allies, hoping that the rear-guard might be thrown into a confusion by which they could profit, did not hesitate to expose to the risk of total destruction one of the finest towns in Germany.

Several French generals then suggested, indignantly, to Napoleon that he could assure the retreat of his army by massing it in the centre of the town and then setting fire to all the suburbs except that of Lindenau, by which our troops could leave while the fire held up the enemy.

In my opinion the allies' refusal to consent to an arrangement which would allow the retreat to be carried on without fighting, gave us the right to employ all possible means of defence, and fire being the most effective in such a situation, we should have used it; but Napoleon could not bring himself to do so, and this excessive magnanimity cost him his throne, for the fighting which I am about to describe resulted in the loss of almost as many men as the three days of battle in which we had just been involved, and worse even than that, it disorganised the army which would otherwise have arrived in France still a potent force. The stiff resistance which for three months the weak remnants put up against the allies is evidence enough of what we might have done if all the French fighting men who had survived the great battle had crossed the Rhine in good order with their weapons. France would probably have repelled the invaders.

That, however is not what happened, for while Napoleon with what I regard as misplaced generosity, refused to burn an enemy town in order to ensure the unopposed retreat of part of his army, the infamous Bernadotte, dissatisfied with the ardour displayed by the allies in destroying his fellow Frenchmen, launched all the troops under his command against the suburb of Taucha, captured it and from there reached the avenues of the town.

Encouraged by this example, Marshal Blcher and his Prussians, the Austrians and the Russians did the same and attacked from all sides the tail-end of the French, who were retreating towards the bridge at Lindenau. Finally, for good measure, a lively fusillade broke out near this bridge, the only way for our troops to cross the Elster. This fusillade came from the battalions of the Saxon guard who had been left in the town with their King, and who, regretting not to have deserted with the other regiments of their army, wanted to show their German patriotism by attacking from behind the French who were passing the chteau where their monarch was in residence.... It was in vain that the venerable prince appeared on the balcony, amidst the firing, crying out "Kill me, you cowards! Kill your King, so that I may not witness your dishonour!" The wretches continued to slaughter the French, while the King, going back to his apartments, took the flag of his Guard and threw it in the fire.

A parting stab in the back was given to our troops by a battalion of men from Baden who, being notorious cowards, had been left in the town during the battle to split logs for the fires of the bakery. These worthless Badeners, sheltered by the walls of the big bakery, fired from its windows on our soldiers, of whom they killed a great many.

340

The French fought back bravely from house to house and although the whole of the allied force was massed in the town filling the avenues and main streets our troops disputed every foot of ground as they retired towards the big bridge across the Elster at Lindenau.

The Emperor had difficulty in getting out of the town and reaching the outskirts through which the army was marching. He stopped and dismounted at the last of the smaller bridges, known as the mill bridge and it was then that he ordered the big bridge to be mined. He sent orders to Marshals Ney, Macdonald and Poniatowski to hold the town for a further twenty-four hours, or at least until nightfall, to allow the artillery park, the equipment and the rear-guard time to go through the suburb and across the bridges; but the Emperor had scarcely remounted his horse and gone a thousand paces down the road towards Ltzen when suddenly there was a massive explosion.

The big bridge across the Elster had been blown up.... Macdonald, Lauriston, Reynier and Poniatowski, with their troops as well as 200 artillery pieces were still on the streets of Leipzig and all means of retreat were now cut off. It was a total disaster!...

To explain this catastrophe, it was said later that some Prussian and Swedish infantrymen, for whom the Badeners had opened the Halle gate, had gradually worked their way to the region of the bridge where having joined some of the Saxon guard they had occupied some houses from which they started to fire on the French columns. The sapper charged with the responsibility of detonating the mine was deceived by this fire into thinking that the enemy had arrived and that the time had come for him to carry out his mission, and so he put a light to the fuse. Others blamed a colonel of the engineers named Montfort who, at the sight of some enemy infantrymen, had taken it on himself to order the detonation of the explosives. This last version was adopted by the Emperor and M. de Monfort was put on a charge and made a scapegoat for the fatal event, but it later became clear that he had nothing to do with it. However this may be, the army laid the blame once more on the Major-general Prince Berthier. It was justly claimed that he should have put the protection of the bridge in the hands of an entire brigade, whose general should have been made personally responsible for giving the order to blow it up, when he thought the moment had come to do so. Prince Berthier defended himself with his usual response "The Emperor had not ordered it!..."

After the destruction of the bridge, some of the French whose retreat was thus cut off, jumped into the Elster in the hope of swimming across. Several of them succeeded in doing so, Marshal Macdonald being among them; but the greater number, including among others Prince Poniatowski, were drowned, because after crossing the river they were unable to climb the muddy bank, which was lined by enemy soldiers.

Those of our soldiers who were trapped in the town and its suburbs aimed only to sell their lives as dearly as possible. They barricaded themselves behind the houses and fought all day and part of the night, but when their ammunition was exhausted they were forced to retire into their improvised defences where they were nearly all slaughtered! The carnage did not end until two o'clock in the morning.

The number of those massacred in the houses is given as 13,000, while 25,000 were taken prisoner. The enemy collected 250 cannons.

After describing in general the events which followed the battle of Leipzig, I shall now describe some of those which related particularly to my regiment and Sbastiani's cavalry corps to which it belonged. Seeing that we had for three consecutive days repelled the enemy attacks and maintained our positions on the field of battle, the men were greatly surprised and disgusted when, on the evening of the 18th we learned that because of shortage of ammunition we were about to retreat. We hoped that at least (and that appeared to be the Emperor's intention) we would go no further than across the river Saale to the proximity of the fortress of Erfurt, where we could renew our stocks of ammunition and recommence hostilities. So we mounted our horses at eight in the evening on the 18th of October, and abandoned the battlefield on which we had fought for three days and where we left the bodies of so many of our gallant comrades.

We had hardly left our bivouac when we ran into some of the difficulties arising from the failure of the general staff to make any arrangements for the withdrawal of such a large body of troops. At every minute the columns, particularly the artillery and cavalry, were held up by the need to cross wide ditches, bogs, and streams over which it would have been easy to put small bridges. Wheels and horses sank into the mud and the night being very dark there was congestion everywhere; our progress was therefore extremely slow, even when we were in the open country, and often completely arrested in the streets of the suburbs and the town. My regiment which was at the front of the column formed by Excelmans' division, which led this wearisome march, did not reach the bridge at Lindenau until four in the morning on the 19th. When we had crossed over, we were far from foreseeing the appalling catastrophe which would occur in a few hours.

Day broke. The fine, wide road was covered by troops of all arms, which showed that the army would still be of considerable strength on arriving at the Saale. The Emperor passed... but as he galloped along the side of the marching column, he did not hear the cheers which usually greeted his presence.... The army was displeased with the little effort which had been made to secure its retreat since leaving the battlefield. What would the troops have said if they had known of the inadequate arrangements made at the Elster, which they had just crossed, but where so many of their comrades would lose their lives?

It was during a halt at Markranstadt, a little town some three leagues from Leipzig, that we heard the explosion of the mine which destroyed the bridge; but instead of being alarmed, we rejoiced, for we all believed that the fuse would not have been lit until after the passage of all our columns, and in order to prevent that of the enemy.

342

During the few hours of rest which we had at Markranstadt, without being aware of the catastrophe which had occurred at the river, I was able to review our squadrons in detail and find out what losses we had suffered during the three days of conflict. I was dismayed! For they came to 149 men, of whom 60 were killed, among whom were two captains, three lieutenant and eleven N.C.O.s. A very large fraction of the 700 men with which the regiment had arrived on the battlefield on the morning of October the 16th. Nearly all the wounded had been hit by cannon-balls or grape-shot which, sadly, gave them little hope of recovery. My losses might have been doubled if I had not, during the battle, taken precautions to shield my regiment from cannon fire, as much as possible. This requires some explanation.

There are circumstances where the most humane of generals finds himself in the painful position of having to expose his troops openly to enemy fire; but it often happens that certain commanders deploy their men uselessly in front of enemy batteries, and take no steps to avoid casualties, although sometimes this is very easy, particularly for cavalry, who because of the rapidity of their movements can go swiftly to the point where they are required and take up the desired formation. It is when large masses of cavalry are involved on extensive battlefields that these measures of preservation are most required, and where, however, they are least employed.

At Leipzig, on the 16th of October, Sbastiani, commanding the 2nd Cavalry Corps, having placed his three divisions between the villages of Wachau and Liebert-Wolkwitz, and indicated to each divisional general roughly the position he should occupy, Exelman found himself placed on undulating ground intersected, as a result, by small ridges and hollows. The Corps formed a line of considerable length. The enemy cavalry, being a long way from us, could not take us by surprise. I took advantage of the hollows in the ground where our brigade was positioned to conceal my regiment which though formed up and ready for action, saw the greater part of the day pass without losing a single man, for the cannon-balls went over their heads while neighbouring corps suffered considerable casualties.

I was congratulating myself on having done this when General danger, ordered me, in spite of the representations of my brigade commander, to take the regiment a hundred paces forward. I obeyed, but in a short time I had a captain, M. Bertin, killed and some twenty men put out of action. I then had recourse to a different tactic: this was to send some troopers, well spaced out, to subject the enemy gunners to carbine fire. The enemy then advanced some infantrymen to counter this, and the two groups being involved in a fire-fight between the lines, the artillery could not use their guns for fear of hitting their own men. It is true that our gunners were in the same boat, but the cessation of gunfire in a minor corner of the battlefield was to our benefit, since the enemy had many more guns than we did. In addition to this, our infantry and that of the enemy being in action at the village of Liebert-Wolkwitz, the cavalry of both sides had to await the outcome of this savage fighting; it served no useful purpose for them to demolish one another by cannon fire, rather than leave the fighting to the infantrymen, who were for the most part only frightening the birds. My example was followed by all the regimental commanders of the other brigades, and the cannons opposite them too ceased fire, sparing the lives of many men. A greater number would have been spared if General Exelmans had not come and ordered the withdrawal of the men on foot, which was the signal for a hail of cannon-balls hurled at our squadrons. Fortunately the day was almost over.

It was now the evening of the 16th. All the colonels of cavalry belonging to 2nd Corps had found this method of sparing their men so effective that by common accord we all used it in the battle of the 18th. When the enemy started firing their cannons, we sent out our foot-soldiers, and as they would have captured the guns if they were not defended, the enemy had to send infantrymen to defend them, and so the guns were silenced on both sides. The commanders of the enemy cavalry which faced us, having probably realised what we were up to, started doing the same, so that on the third day the guns attached to the cavalry of both parties were much less used. This did not prevent vigourous cavalry engagements, but at least they were directed to the taking or holding of positions, in which we did not spare ourselves, but the cannonades aimed at stationary targets, which too often replace cavalry to cavalry actions, do nothing but kill good men for no useful purpose. This was something which Exelmans did not grasp, but as he was on the move all the time from one wing to the other, as soon as he had left a regiment the colonel sent out his foot-soldiers and the guns were silent.

All the cavalry generals, including Sbastiani, were so much persuaded of the advantages of this method, that eventually Exelmans was ordered not to irritate the enemy gunners by firing our guns at them, when the cavalry was only standing-to and had neither an attack nor a defence to undertake. Two years later I used the same tactics at Waterloo against the English guns and I lost far fewer men than I would have done otherwise: but now let us return to Markranstadt.

Chap. 31.

It was while the Emperor and the divisions which had come out of Leipzig were halted at this spot, that we heard the dreadful news of the destruction of the bridge at Lindenau, which deprived the army of almost all its artillery and half of its men, who were taken prisoner; and which delivered some thousands of our wounded comrades to the assaults and knives of the brutish enemy, full of liquor and encouraged to massacre by their unscrupulous officers! There was widespread grief! Each regretted the loss of a relative, a friend, some comrade in arms! The Emperor seemed appalled!...However, he ordered Sbastiani's cavalry to retrace their steps to the bridge, in order to gather and protect any stragglers who had been able to cross the river at some point, after the explosion.

In order to speed this help, my regiment and the 24th who were the best mounted in the corps were told to go ahead of the column and leave at a rapid trot. As General Wathiez was indisposed, and I was the next in seniority, I had to take command of the brigade.

When we had reached half way to Leipzig, we heard much gunfire, and as we approached the avenues we could hear the despairing cries of the unfortunate French, who having no means of retreat and no cartridges for their firearms, were unable to defend themselves, and hunted from street to street and house to house, were overwhelmed by numbers and disgracefully butchered by the enemy, mainly the Prussians, the Badeners and the Saxon guards.

It would be impossible for me to express the fury felt then by the two regiments which I commanded. All longed for vengeance and regretted that this was denied them, since the Elster, with its broken bridge, separated us from the assassins and their victims. Our anger was increased when we came across about 2000 Frenchmen, most of them without clothes and nearly all wounded, who had escaped death only by jumping into the river and swimming across in the face of the shots being fired at them from the opposite bank. Marshal Macdonald was among them; he owed his life to his physical strength and his ability as a swimmer. The Marshal was completely naked and his horse had been drowned, so I quickly found some clothes for him and lent him the spare horse which always came with me, which allowed him to go immediately to rejoin the Emperor at Markranstadt and to give him an account of the disaster of which he had been a witness, and in which one of the principal episodes had been the death of Prince Poniatowski, who had perished in the waters of the Elster.

The remainder of the French who had managed to cross the river had been obliged to discard their arms in order to swim, and had no means of defence. They ran across the fields to avoid falling into the hands of four or five hundred Prussians, Saxons and Badeners who, not satisfied with the blood-bath of the massacres in the town, had made a footbridge of beams and planks across the remaining arches of the bridge, and had come to kill any of our unfortunate soldiers whom they could find on the road to Markranstadt.

As soon as I caught sight of this group of assassins, I instructed Colonel Schneit of the 24th to combine with my regiment to form a vast semi-circle round them, and then sounded the charge.... The result was horrifying! The bandits, taken by surprise, put up very little resistance and there ensued a massacre, for no quarter was given.

I was so enraged at these wretches, that before the charge started I had promised myself that I would run my sabre through any of them I could catch, however when I found myself in their midst and saw that they were drunk and leaderless except for two Saxon officers who were fear-stricken at our vengeful approach, I realised that this was not a fight but an execution, and that it would not be a good thing for me to take part in it. I feared that I might find pleasure in killing some of these scoundrels, so I put my sabre back in its scabbard and left to our soldiers the business of exterminating these assassins, two thirds of whom were laid dead.

The remainder, including two officers and several Saxon guards, fled towards the debris of the bridge, hoping to recross the footbridge; but as they could cross only one by one and our Chasseurs were hard on their heels, they entered a large nearby inn and began to shoot at my men, helped by some Prussians and Badeners on the opposite bank.

As it seemed likely that the noise of firing would attract larger forces to the bank from where, without crossing the river, they could destroy my regiment by small-arms and cannon fire, I decided to bring matters to a conclusion, and ordered the majority of the Chasseurs to dismount and taking their carbines and plenty of ammunition to attack the rear of the inn and set on fire the stables and the hay loft. The assassins shut in the inn, seeing that they were about to be caught in the flames, tried to make a sortie; but as soon as they appeared in the doorway our Chasseurs shot them with their carbines.

It was in vain that they sent one of the Saxon officers to me to intercede; I was pitiless, and refused to treat as soldiers surrendering after an honourable defence, these monsters who had murdered our comrades who were prisoners of war. So the four to five hundred Prussians, Badeners and Saxons who had crossed the footbridge were all killed! I sent this information to General Sbastiani, who halted midway the other brigades of the Light Cavalry. .

The fire which we had lit in the forage store of the inn soon spread to the neighbouring houses. A major part of the village of Lindenau, which lines both sides of the road, was burned, delaying the repair of the bridge and the passage of enemy troops, bent on pursuing and harrying the retreating French army.

The mission being completed, I led the brigade back to Markranstadt, together with the 2000 French, who had escaped from the calamity at the bridge. Among them were several officers of all ranks; The Emperor questioned them on what they knew about the blowing up of the bridge and about the massacre of the French prisoners of war. It seems likely that this sorry tale made the Emperor regret that he had not taken the advice given him in the morning, to bar the enemy advance by setting fire to the suburbs, and even, if need be, the town of Leipzig itself, most of whose inhabitants had fled during the three day's battle.

In the course of this return to the bridge of Lindenau, the brigade which I was commanding suffered only three casualties, one of which was a member of my regiment; but it was one of my finest sous-officiers. He had been awarded the Legion of Honour and was named Foucher. A bullet wound, received at the inn had gone through both thighs, leaving four holes; but in spite of this serious injury the brave Foucher made the retreat on horseback, refused to enter the hospital at Erfurt, which we passed a few days later and remained with the regiment until we reached France. It is true that his friends and all the men in his platoon took great care of him, but he thoroughly deserved it.

As I left Leipzig, I was concerned about the fate of the wounded from my regiment, whom I had left behind, including Major Pozac; but luckily the distant suburb in which I had put them was not visited by the Prussians.

You have seen that during the last day of the great battle, an Austrian Corps tried to cut off our retreat by capturing Lindenau, through which passes the main road leading to Weissenfels and Erfurt, and how, on the Emperor's orders, they had been driven off by General Bertrand, who, after re-opening this route, had made his way to Weissenfels, where we rejoined him.

After the losses occasioned by the destruction of the bridge at Lindenau, it was impossible to think of stopping what remained of the army at the Saale, so Napoleon crossed the river.

A fortnight before the battle, this water-course had offered him an impregnable position, which he had spurned to risk a general engagement in open country, putting behind him three rivers and a large town, which presented obstructions at every step.... The great captain had relied too much on his "star" and on the incapacity of the enemy generals.

In the event, they made such serious mistakes that in spite of an immense superiority in numbers, they were not only unable, during a battle lasting three days, to take from us a single one of the villages we were defending. I have heard the King of Belgium, who was then serving with the Russian army, say to the Duc d'Orléans that on two occasions the allies were in such confusion that the order for a retreat was given: but then the situation changed and it our army which had to submit to the fortune of war.

After crossing the Saale, Napoleon thanked and dismissed those officers and soldiers of the Confederation of the Rhine, who either from some sense of honour or from lack of opportunity were still in our ranks. He even carried magnanimity so far as to allow them to retain their arms, although he was entitled to treat them as prisoners of war, since their sovereigns had joined the forces of our enemies. The French army continued its retreat to Erfurt, without anything happening but an encounter at Kosen, where a single French division defeated an Austrian army corps and took prisoner its commanding general the Comte de Giulay.

Led on always by the hope of a fighting return to Germany, and by the help which he would receive in such a case from the fortresses which he was now forced to leave behind him, Napoleon put a numerous garrison into Erfurt. He had left in Dresden 25,000 men, under the command of Saint-Cyr; at Hamburg 30,000 under Davout, and many strongholds on the Oder and the Elbe, manned in accordance with their importance. These garrisons comprised a loss in manpower to add to that due to the forts of Danzig and the Vistula.

I shall not repeat what I have already said about the disadvantages of deploying too many of one's troops to man forts which one is forced to leave behind. I shall merely point out that Napoleon left in the forts of Germany 80,000 men, not one of whom returned to France until after the fall of the empire, which they might perhaps have prevented, had they been defending our frontiers.

The arsenal at Erfurt was able to make good the loss of our artillery. The Emperor, who up till now had borne his reverses with stoical resignation, was however upset by the departure of his brother-in-law, the King Murat, who, with the excuse that he was going to defend his kingdom of Naples, abandoned Napoleon, to whom he owed everything.... Murat, at one time so brilliant in war, had done nothing much during this campaign of 1813. It is certain that, although he was in our ranks, he was carrying on a correspondence with M. de Metternich, the prime minister of Austria, who dangling before his eyes the example of Bernadotte, guaranteed, in the name of the allied sovereigns, the protection of his kingdom if he would join Napoleon's enemies. Murat left the French army at Erfurt and had scarcely arrived in Naples when he began preparations for war against us.

It was also at Erfurt that the Emperor learned of the audacious scheme of the Bavarians, his former allies, who, after deserting his cause, and joining with an Austrian Corps and several groups of Cossacks, had set off under the command of General the Comte de Wrde, whose ambition it was not only to stop the French army, but to make it captive, along with its Emperor.

General de Wrde marching parallel to us but at two days distance had already reached Wartzbourg with 60,000 men. He detached 10,000 to Frankfort and with the remaining 50,000 he went to the little fort of Hanau in order to bar the passage of the French. General de Wrde, who had fought on our side in Russia, thought that he would find the French army in the deplorable state to which cold and hunger had reduced those retreating from Moscow by the time they reached the Beresina, but we soon showed him that in spite of our misfortunes, we still had soldiers in good heart, and quite capable of defeating Austro-Bavarians.

General de Wrde, who did not know that the troops which we had fought at Leipzig, though following us were a long way behind, had become very bold and believed he could trap us between two fires. It was not possible for him to do so, though as several enemy corps were trying to mount an attack on our right by going through the mountains of Franconia, while the Bavarians stood in front of us the situation could have become serious.

Napoleon rose to the challenge and marched briskly towards Hanau, whose approaches are protected by thick forests and notably by the well-known pass of Gelnhausen, through which runs the river Kinzig. This river, whose banks are very steep, runs between two mountains which are separated by a narrow gap which allows the passage of the river, beside which has been made a fine main road, cut into the rock, and running from Fulde to Frankfort-on-main via Hanau.

Sbastiani's cavalry corps which had been the advance-guard from Weissenfels to Fulde, where one enters the mountains, should have been replaced by infantry at this point. I have never understood for what reason this well known principle of warfare was not followed in these grave circumstances; but to our astonishment, Exelmans' cavalry division continued to march in front of the army, led by my regiment and the 24th Chasseurs. I was in command of the brigade. We learned from the peasants that the Austro-Bavarian army already occupied Hanau, and that a strong division was facing the French, to dispute the passage of the defile.

My position, as commander of the advance-guard, was now very difficult; for how could I, without a single infantryman and with cavalry packed between two high mountains and an uncrossable torrent, fight troops on foot whose scouts, climbing up the rocks would shoot us at close range? I sent at once to warn the divisional general, but Exelmans could not be found. However I had been ordered to advance and I could not stop the divisions which were following me, so I continued my march until at a bend in the valley my scouts told me that they were in sight of a detachment of enemy Hussars. The Austro-Bavarians had made the same mistake as our leaders; for if the latter had sent cavalry to attack a long and narrow pass, where no more the ten or twelve horsemen could ride abreast, our enemies had sent cavalry to defend a position where a hundred sharpshooters could hold up ten regiments of cavalry. I was highly delighted to see that the enemy had no infantry, and as I knew from experience that when two opposing columns meet at a narrow spot, victory always goes to the one which, hurling itself at the head of the enemy, drives it back into the troops behind it, I launched at the gallop my elite company, of which only the leading platoon could engage the enemy; but they did so with such lan that the head of the Austrian column was overwhelmed and the rest thrown into such complete confusion that my troopers had only to take aim.

We continued the pursuit for more than an hour. The enemy regiment in front of us was that of General Ott. I had never seen such well turned out Hussars. they had come from Vienna, where they had been fitted with completely new uniforms, Their outfit, although a little theatrical, looked very handsome: the pelisse and dolman in white and the trousers and the shako in lilac; all clean bright and shining. One might have thought they were going to a ball, or to play in a musical comedy. This brilliant appearance contrasted somewhat with the more modest toilette of our Chasseurs, many of whom were still dressed in the worn clothing in which they had bivouacked for eighteen months, in Russia, Poland, and Germany, and whose distinguishing colours had been dimmed by the smoke of cannon and the dust of battlefields. However, under those threadbare garments were brave hearts and sturdy limbs. So the white pelisses of Ott's Hussars became horribly bloodstained, and this pretty regiment lost in killed and wounded more than 200 men without one of our Chasseurs having the smallest sabre cut, the enemy having always fled without ever turning to fight. Our Chasseurs took a large number of excellent horses and gold-braided pelisses.

Up until then everything had gone well, but as I galloped after the victors who pursued the vanquished, I was a bit worried about the end of this strange encounter, for the diminishing height of the mountains which bordered the Kinzig indicated that we were nearing the end of the valley, and it was likely that we would find ourselves in a small plain, full of infantry whose volleys and cannon fire would make us pay dearly for our success: but happily there was no such thing, and as we emerged from the pass we saw not a single infantryman, but only some cavalry, part of which comprised the main body of that section of Ott's regiment of Hussars, which we had so roughly manhandled and who in their panic continued their headlong flight, taking with them some fifteen squadrons, who retired to Hanau.

General Sbastiani then deployed his three divisions of cavalry which were soon supported by the infantry of Marshals Macdonald and Victor and several batteries. Then the Emperor with part of his guard, appeared and the rest of the French army followed.

It was now the evening of the 29th of October; we established our bivouacs in a nearby wood; we were only a league from Hanau and the Austro-Bavarian army.

Chap. 32.

Here now are the reasons why Exelmans dropped behind when we were going through the pass. Before we entered the valley, the scouts had brought to him two Austrian soldiers absentees from their unit, who were scrounging and drinking in an isolated village. Exelmans was having them questioned in German by one of his aides, when he was surprised to hear them reply in fluent French. One of these men, half drunk, and thinking it would do him good, announced that they were Parisians. As soon as he uttered these words, the general, furious that Frenchmen should take up arms against their fellow countrymen, ordered them to be immediately shot. The poor lad who had boasted of being French was about to be put to death, when his companion, sobered by this fearful spectacle, protested that neither of them had ever set foot in France, but having been born in Vienna to parents who, although they came from Paris, were naturalised Austrians, they were regarded as Austrian subjects and had been forced to join the regiment assigned to them. To prove this he showed his army record which confirmed the fact. Exelmans, yielding to the advice of his aides-de-camp, agreed to spare the innocent man.

At this stage, hearing the sound of firing, the General wished to reach the head of the column which I was commanding; but on his arrival at the mouth of the pass, he found it impossible to get through and take a place in the ranks because of the speed with which the two regiments were galloping after the enemy. After trying many times he was so jostled that he fell with his horse into the Kinzig and nearly drowned.

The Emperor, who was preparing for battle, took advantage of the night to reduce the amount of wheeled transport by sending all the baggage off to the right, in the direction of Coblentz, escorted by some battalions of infantry and the cavalry of Lefebvre-Denouettes and Milhau. This was a great relief to the army.

On the morning of the 30th, the Emperor had at his disposal only the infantry Corps of Macdonald and Victor, amounting to 5000 men, supported by Sbastiani's cavalry division.

In the direction from which we were coming, a large forest, through which the road runs, covers the approach to Hanau. The tall trees of this forest allow movement without much difficulty. The town of Hanau is built on the other side of the river Kinzig.

General de Wrde, although not lacking in military skill, had, however, made the serious mistake of placing his army where it had the river at its back, which deprived it of the support which it could have received from the fortifications of Hanau, with which he could not communicate except by the bridge of Lamboy, which was his only road of retreat. It is true that the position he occupied barred the way to Frankfort and to France, and he felt certain that he could prevent us from forcing a passage.

On the 30th of October at dawn the battle began, like a great hunting party. Some grape-shot and some small-arms fire from our infantry, together with a charge in open order by Sbastiani's cavalry, scattered the first line of the enemy, somewhat unskillfully placed at the extreme edge of the wood; but as one penetrated a little further, our squadrons could not operate except in the few clearings which they came across, only the Light Infantry followed in the steps of the Bavarians, whom they pursued from tree to tree to the end of the forest. At that point they had to stop, faced by an enemy line of forty thousand men, whose front was covered by eighty guns.

If the Emperor had had with him all the troops which he brought from Leipzig, a vigorous attack would have made him master of the Lamboy bridge, and General de Wrde would have paid dearly for his temerity, but Marshals Mortier and Marmont and General Bertrand, as well as the artillery, were held up by various passes, mainly that of Gelnhausen, and had not yet arrived. Napoleon had no more than ten thousand troops. The enemy should have taken advantage of this to attack us in force, but they did not dare, and this hesitation gave time for the artillery of the Imperial Guard to arrive.

As soon as General Drouet, their commander, had fifteen pieces in the field, he began firing, and his line grew in size until he had fifty cannons, which he advanced, firing continuously, although he still had very few troops behind him to give support; however it was not possible for the enemy to see through the thick smoke from the guns, that the gunners had little to back them up. Eventually the infantry Chasseurs of the Imperial Old Guard appeared, just as a gust of wind blew away the smoke.

At the sight of their busbies, the Bavarian infantry recoiled in fear. General de Wrde in an effort to stop this disorder at all costs, ordered all his cavalry, Austrian, Bavarian and Russian, to charge our artillery, and in an instant our battery was surrounded by a swarm of horsemen... but at the voice of their commander, General Drouet, who, sword in hand, set them an example in resistance, the French gunners, taking their muskets, remained calmly behind their guns, from where they fired point-blank at the enemy. Nevertheless, the great number of the latter would have eventually triumphed, had not, on the Emperor's order, all Sbastiani's cavalry, along with all that of the Imperial Guard , mounted Grenadiers, Dragoons , Chasseurs, Mamelukes, Lancers and Guards of Honour, hurled themselves furiously on the enemy cavalry, killing a great number and dispersing the rest.

Then, falling on the Bavarian infantry squares, they broke them and inflicted tremendous losses, at which stage the Bavarian army, put to rout, fled to the bridge over the Kinzig and to the town of Hanau.

General de Wrde was a brave man, so, before admitting himself beaten by forces half as numerous as his, he resolved to make another effort, and gathering all the troops remaining to him, he made a surprise attack on us. Suddenly a fusillade broke out and the forest rang once more to the sound of artillery; cannon-balls whistled through the trees, from which great branches fell with a crash....The eye sought in vain to pierce the depths of the wood; one could hardly see the flash of the guns, which lit, at intervals, the shade cast by the foliage of the huge beeches, beneath whose canopy we fought.

Hearing the noise made by this attack, the Emperor sent from his position the infantry Grenadiers of his Old Guard, led by General Friant who soon overcame this last effort of the enemy, who now hastily left the field of battle to re-group under the protection of the fort of Hanau, which they abandoned during the night, leaving behind a great number of wounded. The French occupied the fort.

We were no more than two short leagues from Frankfort, a considerable town, with a stone bridge across the Main. The French army would need to go along the bank of this river to reach Mainz and the frontier of France, which was a day's march from Frankfort; so Napoleon detached Sbastiani's corps and a division of infantry to go and occupy Frankfort, and to take over and destroy the bridge. The Emperor and the bulk of the army bivouacked in the forest.

The main road from Hanau to Frankfort runs along the right bank of the river Maine. General Albert, a friend of mine, who commanded the infantry which accompanied us, had been married, some years previously, at Offenbach, a charming little town, built on the left bank exactly opposite the spot where, after emerging from the woods of Hanau, we rested our horses on the immense and beautiful plain of Frankfort.

Finding himself so close to his wife and their children, General Albert was unable to resist the temptation to have news of them, and to reassure them of his well-being after the dangers he had encountered at the battles of Leipzig and Hanau. To do this he exposed himself to more risk, perhaps, than he had run during either of these sanguinary affairs, for advancing on horseback and in uniform to the edge of the river, in spite of our warnings, he hailed a boatman who knew him; but while he was chatting with this man, a Bavarian officer ran up with a picket of infantry who, aiming their weapons, prepared to shoot at the French general. However, a large body of citizens and boatmen crowded in front of the soldiers and prevented them from firing, for General Albert was very well liked in Offenbach.

352

As I looked at this town, to where I had come while fighting for my country, I did not dream that one day it would be my refuge from the proscription of a French government, and that I would spend three years there in exile.

After leaving the forest of Hanau to go on his way to Frankfort, the Emperor had hardly gone two leagues when he learned that fighting had broken out once more behind him. This was because the Bavarian general who, following his defeat the day before, had expected to be chased, with the Emperor at his heels, had taken reassurance from seeing the French army more concerned to reach the Rhine than to pursue him, and had launched a brisk attack on our rear-guard. However Macdonald, Marmont and Bertrand, who with their troops had occupied Hanau during the night, having allowed the Bavarians to attack them on that side of the Kinzig, received them with their bayonets, overwhelmed and massacred them. General de Wrde was seriously injured, and his son-in-law, Prince d'Oettingen was killed.

The command of the enemy army then devolved onto the Austrian General Fresnel who ordered a retreat, and the French army continued on its way peacefully towards the Rhine. We recrossed the river on the 2nd and 3rd of November 1813, after a campaign which included brilliant victories and disasterous defeats, the main cause of which, as I have said, was the mistake made by Napoleon when, instead of making peace in June, following the victories of Lutzen and Bautzen, he quarreled with Austria, which involved the Confederation of the Rhine, that is to say all of Germany, so that he soon had the whole of Europe ranged against him.

After we had returned to France, the Emperor spent only six days at Mainz, and then went to Paris, preceded by twenty-six flags taken from our enemies. The army disapproved of this rapid departure on the part of Napoleon. It was accepted that there were important political reasons which called him to Paris, but it was thought that he should have divided his time between his capital and the need to re-organise his army, and that he should have gone from one to the other to encourage the activity of each, for he should have learned by experience that in his absence little or nothing was done.

The last cannon shots which I heard in 1813 were fired at the battle of Hanau, where I nearly spent the last day of my life. My regiment carried out five charges, two on infantry squares, one on artillery and two on Bavarian cavalry; but the greatest danger I ran was when an ammunition wagon, loaded with mortar bombs, caught fire and exploded close to me. I have told how, on the Emperor's order, all the cavalry were in action at a particularly difficult moment. Now, in these circumstances, it is not good enough for a unit commander to send his troops blindly forward, a thing I have seen done on several occasions, but he must pay the closest attention to the ground over which his squadrons are about to pass, in case he sends them into bogs and marshes.

I was therefore, a few paces ahead, followed by my regimental staff and with my trumpeter at my side, who at a given command would signal to the various squadrons the obstacles which they would find in their way. Although the trees were widely spaced, the passage through the forest was difficult for the cavalry because the ground was littered with dead and wounded men and horses, arms, cannons and ammunition wagons, abandoned by the Bavarians. You can understand that in these conditions when one is galloping through shot and shell to reach the enemy one cannot always take much care of oneself, and I relied greatly on the intelligence and suppleness of my excellent and brave Turkish horse, Azolan. The little group which followed me had been much reduced by a blast of grape-shot which had wounded several of my orderlies and I had beside me only the trumpeter, a charming and good young man, when I heard from all along the line, cries of "Look out, Colonel!" And I saw ten paces away Bavariana ammunition wagon which one of our shells had set on fire.

A huge tree which had been knocked down by cannon-balls barred my way forward, and to go round it would have taken too long. I shouted to the trumpeter to duck, and crouching on my horse's neck, I urged him to jump the tree. Azolan leapt a long way, but not far enough to clear all the leafy branches in which his legs became entangled. The wagon was now in flames and the powder about to catch. I thought I was done for... when my horse, as if he realised our common danger, started bounding four or five feet into the air, getting always further from the wagon, and as soon as he was clear of the branches he galloped off with such speed that he really seemed to be "Ventre terre".

I was shaken when the explosion occurred, but it seemed I was out of range of the bursting shells for neither I nor my horse were touched.

Sadly it was not so for my poor young trumpeter, for when we resumed our march after the explosion we saw his body, mutilated by the shell fragments, and his horse also cut to pieces.

My brave Azolan had already saved my life at the Katzbach. I now owed him my life for the second time. I made much of him, and as if to show his pleasure he whinnied at the top of his voice. It is at times like these that one has to believe that some animals are more intelligent than is generally thought.

I greatly regretted the death of my trumpeter, who by his courage and his behaviour had made himself liked by all the regiment. He was the son of a teacher at the college in Toulouse, and had had a good education. He delighted in producing Latin quotations, and an hour before his death, the poor lad, having noticed that almost all the trees in the forest of Hanau were beeches, whose branches stretched out to make a sort of roof, had thought it a suitable occasion to declaim one of Virgil's eclogues, beginning:

"Tityre, tu patulae recubans sub tegmine fagi..."

which greatly amused Marshal Macdonald who happened to be passing and who exclaimed, "There's a jolly lad whose memory isn't upset by his surroundings; I'll bet it's the first time anyone has recited Virgil to the sound of enemy cannon fire!"

"Those who live by the sword, perish by the sword" says the scripture, and if this is not applicable to every soldier, it was to a great many under the Empire. For example, M. Guindet, who killed Prince Louis of Prussia in the fighting at Saalefeld, was himself killed at the battle of Hanau. It was no doubt the fear of meeting a similar fate which led the Russian General Czernicheff to run away from danger.

You may remember that in the first months of 1812, this officer, then a colonel, an aide-de-camp and favourite of the Emperor Alexander, came to Paris where he abused his position to corrupt two poor employees in the Ministry of War , who were executed for having sold to him situation reports on the French army, and that the Russian Colonel only escaped the penalty of the law by secretly fleeing the country. On his return to Russia, M.de Czernicheff, although he was a courtier rather than a soldier, was given the rank of general officer and the command of a division of 3000 Cossacks, the only Russian troops who appeared at Hanau where their leader played a rle which made him a laughing stock among the Austrians and Bavarians who were present at this engagement.

Czernicheff, as he marched towards us, spoke loudly of victory, believing that he had to face only soldiers who were sick and disorganised; but he changed his tune when he saw himself in the presence of the hardy and vigorous troops returning from Leipzig. General de Wrde had great difficulty in persuading him to enter the line, and as soon as he heard the fearsome cannonade of our artillery, he and his 3000 Cossacks trotted bravely off the field, to the cat-calls of the Austro-Bavarian troops, who witnessed this shameful conduct. When General de Wrde went personally to make some scathing observations, M. de Czernicheff replied that his regiment's horses needed feeding and that he was taking them for this purpose to nearby villages. This excuse was regarded as so ridiculous that for some time afterwards the walls of German villages were decorated by caricatures of M. de Czernicheff feeding his horses with bunches of laurels gathered in the forest of Hanau.

Once across the Rhine, the soldiers who made up the remains of the French army expected to see an end to their hardships as soon as they set foot on the soil of their motherland; but they were much mistaken, for the government, and the Emperor himself, had so much counted on success, and had so little foreseen that we might leave Germany, that nothing had been made ready at the frontier to receive and re-organise the troops. So, from the very day of our arrival at Mainz, the men and the horses would have gone short of food if we had not spread them out and lodged them with the inhabitants of nearby villages and hamlets; but since the first wars of the revolution, they had lost the habit of feeding soldiers, and complained vociferously, and it is true that the expense was too great for the communes.

As it was necessary to guard, or at least to watch over the immensely long frontier formed by the Rhine from Basle to Holland, we settled, as best we could the numerous sick and wounded in the hospitals of Mainz. All fit men rejoined the core of their regiments, and the various units of the army, which for the most part consisted only of a small cadre, were spread along the river. My regiment, together with what was left of Sbastiani's cavalry corps, went down the Rhine by short marches; but although the weather was perfect and the countryside charming, we were all deeply unhappy, for one could foresee that France was going to lose possession of this fine land, and that her misfortunes would not stop there.

My regiment spent some time in Cleves, next a fortnight in the little town of Urdingen, and then went on to Nimeguen. During this sad journey we were painfully affected by the sight of the inhabitants on the opposite bank, the Germans and the Dutch, tearing down the French flag from their steeples and replacing it with the flags of their former sovereigns. In spite of these gloomy reflections, all the colonels tried to re-organise the few troops which remained to them, but what could one do without clothing, equipment or replacement of arms?...

The need to provide food for the army compelled the Emperor to keep it dispersed, whereas to re-organise it would require the creation of large centres of concentration. We were therefore in a vicious circle. However, the allies, who should have crossed the Rhine a few days after us, to prevent our re-organisation, felt themselves still so weakened as a result of the hard blows we had delivered during the last campaign, that they needed time to recover.

They left us in peace for the months of November and December, the greater part of which I spent on the bank of the Rhine, in the ghost of the army corps commanded by Marshal Macdonald.

I was eventually ordered, as were the other cavalry colonels, to take all my dismounted men to my regimental depot for the task of building up new squadrons. The depot of the 23rd was still at Mons, in Belgium, and that is where I went. It was there that I saw the end of the year 1813, so filled with great events and in which I had had encountered many dangers and undergone so many trials.

Before I end my chronicle of the year, I ought to summarise briefly the final events of the campaign of 1813.

Chap. 33.

The German fortresses in which the retreating French had left garrisons were soon surrounded and in some cases besieged. Almost all surrendered. Four only were still holding out at the end of 1813.

The first of these was Hamburg, commanded by the intrepid Marshal Davout, who held on to this important fort until after the abdication of the Emperor, when the French government recalled the garrison to France; the second was Magdeburg, where General Le Marois, an aide-de-camp to the Emperor, also held out until the end of the war; the third was Wittemburg, defended by the elderly General Lapoype, and which was taken by assault on the 12th of the following January; and finally Erfurt, which had to capitulate for lack of food.

All the other fortresses beyond the Rhine, which the Emperor had wanted to keep, the most important of which were Dresden, Danzig, Stettin, Zamosk, Torgau and Modlin, were already in the hands of the enemy.

The circumstances surrounding the taking over of the first two of these fortresses do not reflect much honour on the allies. After the battle of Leipzig, Napoleon withdrew with the remains of his army, leaving at Dresden a corps of 25000 men commanded by Marshal Saint-Cyr, who tried by force of arms to cut a passage through the enemies who blocked his way. He drove them back several times but eventually overcome by stronger forces and short of food he was compelled to accept the honourable capitulation which was offered to him. This stipulated that the garrison would keep its arms, would not be made prisoners of war and would march back to France in day-long stages.

The Marshal wanted his troops to move as a corps and to bivouac all together at the same place, which would allow them to defend themselves in case of treachery; but the enemy generals pointed out that owing to the exhaustion of the countryside, it would be impossible to provide at any one place twenty-five thousand rations, and the French marshal had to accept this. He then agreed that his force should be divided into several small columns of 2 or 3000 men who would travel one or even two days apart.

For the first few days all went well, but as soon as the last French column had left Dresden, having handed over the fort and the munitions of war, the foreign generals announced that they did not have the authority to sign the capitulation without the agreement of their generalissimo, Prince Schwartzenberg, and as he did not approve, the agreement was null and void. They offered to allow our troops to return to Dresden in exactly the same state as they had been previously, that is to say with only enough food for a few days, a shortage which they had concealed from the enemy for as long as they occupied the place, and which, as it was now known to them, made the offer worthless.

Our troops were indignant at this odious lack of good faith, but what action could be taken by isolated detachments of 2 or 3000 men, whom the enemy had taken the precaution of surrounding by battalions of their own, before they could hear of the breakdown of the capitulation? Any resistance was impossible and our men were forced to lay down their arms.

To the treachery practised on the field of battle, was now added that of the breaking of agreements of capitulation. This did not prevent the Germans from celebrating a victory, for they regarded any measures, however despicable, as justified in order to defeat Napoleon. This new morality was put into operation at Danzig.

357

General Rapp had defended this place for a long time but having run out of food he was compelled to surrender on condition that the garrison would be allowed to return to France. However, in spite of a treaty signed by the Prince of Wurtemberg, the commander of the army which conducted the siege, the conditions were violated and the garrison of 16000 men were sent as prisoners to Russia where most of them died.

One of the most remarkable stories of this siege concerns a Captain de Chambure, who asked for and obtained permission to form an independent company, chosen from hand-picked volunteers. They engaged on the most daring ventures, going out at night and surprising enemy posts, getting into their entrenchments, into their camps, destroying their siege-works under the nose of their batteries, spiking their guns and going far into the country to capture or pillage their convoys. Chambure, having gone out one night with his men, surprised a Russian cantonment, set fire to an ammunition dump, destroyed several stores and killed or wounded one hundred and fifty men, for the loss of three of his own; and returned to the fort in triumph.

Now, however, let us return to examine the position of the French armies in December 1813.

Spain, the principal cause of all the catastrophes which marked the end of Napoleon's reign, had been stripped, in the course of the year, of all its best troops, which the Emperor had sent to reinforce the army in Germany. However, the effective strength of those who remained in the Iberian peninsula amounted to more than 100,000 men. A number which, although inadequate, would have contained the enemy if Napoleon had left the command to Marshal Soult; but as he most earnestly wished to make of his brother Joseph a general who could defend the kingdom which he had given him, it was to this prince, an estimable man but no soldier, that the Emperor entrusted the command of the armies of Spain. He gave him, it is true, as chief of staff and military advisor, Marshal Jourdan; but the Marshal was prematurely aged and had not been involved in active warfare since the first campaigns of the revolution. He was so worn out, both mentally and physically, that he inspired no confidence in the troops. So, in spite of the talents displayed by the generals who served under the orders of King Joseph, the Anglo-Portuguese army commanded by Lord Wellington and helped by Spanish guerrillas, caused us irreparable losses.

The French, under pressure at every point, had already been compelled to abandon Madrid, the two Castiles, and to recross the Ebro, to concentrate their main forces round the town of Vittoria. Attacked in this position by three times their number, they lost a battle; a loss which was made all the more disastrous by the fact that King Joseph and Marshal Jourdan had made no arrangements for the carrying out of a retreat, so that it became chaotic. The King's suite, the artillery parks, the many coaches of a crowd of Spaniards, who having taken sides with Joseph, sought to escape the vengence of their compatriots, the wagons of the treasury, of the military administration, *etc.*, *etc.*, all found themselves piled up in confusion, so that the roads were obstructed and the regiments had great difficulty in moving. However they did not lose their formation, and in spite of vigorous attacks by the enemy, the greater part of the army managed to reach Salvatierra and the road to Pamplona, by which the retreat was made.

The battle of Vittoria demonstrated the talent and courage of General Clausel, who rallied the army and gave it some direction. It was, however, an unhappy day. The French lost 6000 men killed, wounded or taken prisoner and left in the hands of the enemy a large part of their artillery and almost all their baggage.

Despite this set-back, the troops whose morale was excellent, could have remained in Navarre with the aid of the fortress of Pamplona and the Pyrénées mountains, but King Joseph ordered the continuation of the retreat and the crossing of the Bidassoa, where our rear-guard, commanded by General Foy, was ordered to blow up the bridge. So, from the end of June, we abandoned that part of the Spanish frontier; nevertheless, Marshal Suchet still held out in Aragon (The region of Zaragossa. Ed.) and Catalonia, and in the kingdom of Valencia; but the results of the battle of Vittoria had so much weakened us that when Wellington sent reinforcements to central Spain Suchet found it necessary to leave the town and the kingdom.

These events were taking place at a time when Napoleon was still triumphant in Germany. As soon as he was told of the state of affairs across the Pyrénées, he hastily revoked the powers which he had given to King Joseph and Marshal Jourden, and appointed Marshal l Soult commander of all the armies in Spain.

Soult, after re-organising the divisions, made a great effort to help the French garrison left in Pamplona, but in vain. They were forced to capitulate and Marshal Soult had to take his troops back across the Bidassoa. The fortress of San-Sebastian, governed by General Rey, held out for a long time; but was eventually taken by assault by the Anglo-Portuguese, who, ignoring the laws of humanity, robbed, raped and massacred the unfortunate inhabitants of this Spanish town, although they were their allies. The English officers made no attempt to stop these atrocities, which went on for three days, to the shame of Wellington, his generals and the English.

Marshal Soult defended the Pyrénées foot by foot and beat Wellington on several occasions; but the greater numbers at the latter's disposal allowed him unceasingly to take the offensive, so that he was able eventually to cross our frontier and set up his headquarters in Saint-Jean de Luz, the first town in France and a town which had never previously been lost, even during the defeats suffered by Francis I, or the disastrous wars of the end of the reign of Louis XIV.

It was evident that after the defection of the German troops at Leipzig, Marshal Soult could not hope to keep in the army of the Pyrénées several thousand soldiers from across the Rhine. They all went over to the enemy in a single night, thus augmenting Wellington's strength.

However, Marshal Soult, after concentrating several divisions below the ramparts of Bayonne, once more attacked the Anglo-Portuguese. On the 9th of December, at Saint-Pierre de Rube, there was a battle which lasted for five days, and was one of the bloodiest of the war, for it cost the enemy 16,000 lives and the French 10,000, but we were able to remain in position around Bayonne.

Before these events in the Pyrénées, Marshal Suchet, having learned of the reverses suffered by Napoleon in Germany, realised that it would be impossible for him to remain in the middle of Spain, and prepared to return to France. To do this he withdrew to Tarragon, where after taking the garrison into his army he blew up the ramparts. The retreat, although harried by the Spanish, was carried out in good order, and by the end of December 1813, Suchet and the troops under his command were established in Gerona.

To complete this examination of the position of the French armies at the end of 1813, one needs to recall that in the spring of that year, the Emperor, who distrusted Austria, had built up in the Tyrol and in his kingdom of Italy, a large army, the command of which he had given to his step-son Eugne de Beauharnais, the viceroy of the country. This prince was a good man, very gentle and greatly devoted to the Emperor, but although much more of a soldier than King Joseph of Spain, he lacked many of the qualities required to lead an army. The Emperor's affection for Eugne led him astray in this matter.

It was on the 24th of August, the day when the armistice between Napoleon and the allies was due to expire, that the Austrians abandoned their neutrality and declared themselves our enemies. The Italian troops continued to serve with us, but the Dalmatians (Croats) left us to join the Austrians. Prince Eugne had under his command a number of excellent lieutenants, but the fighting was never very strenuous because the commanders on both sides realised that the events in Germany would determine the outcome of the campaign. There were however, a number of actions, with various results. In the end the larger forces of the Austrians, who were shortly joined by an English contingent which disembarked in Tuscany forced the viceroy to lead the Franco-Italian army beyond the Adige.

In November came news of the defection of Murat the King of Naples. The Emperor to whom he owed everything, could not at first believe it. It was, however, only too true. Murat had joined forces with the Austrians, against whom he had fought for so long, and his troops already occupied Bologna. Such is the volatility of the Italians that everywhere they welcomed with acclamation the Austro-Neapolitans, whom they had previously detested and whom they would soon hate even more. By December, the vice-roi's army of only 43,000 men, occupied Verona and its surroundings.

The Emperor, seeing the whole of Europe combined against him, could not fail to realise that the first condition which a peace would demand of him would be the re-installment of the Bourbons on the throne of Spain. He decided therefore to do of his own volition what he would be forced to do later: he set free King Ferdinand, who had been detained at Valancay, and ordered Suchet's army to retire behind the Pyrénées.

360

Thus, at the end of 1813, we had lost all of Germany, all of Spain, and the greater part of Italy. Wellington's army, which had crossed the Bidassoa and the western Pyrénées, was encamped on French soil and threatening Bayonne, Navarre and Bordeaux.

Chap. 34.

I began the year 1814 at *Mons*. Where I did not undergo such physical dangers as I had done in previous years, but where I suffered much more mentally.

As I had left, at Nimeguen, all the troopers of my regiment who still had horses, I had none at Mons, where the depot was situated, except dismounted men, for whom I was trying to get horses from the Ardennes, when events prevented this.

On the 1st of January, the enemies, after hesitating for three months before invading France, crossed the Rhine at several points, the two most important of these being firstly at Kaub, a market town situated between Bingen and Coblentz, where a rocky gorge greatly reduces the width of the river, and then at Basle where the Swiss handed over the stone bridge, in violation of their neutrality, a neutrality which they maintain or abandon according to their interests.

It is estimated that some five to six hundred thousand allied soldiers entered a France exhausted by twenty-five years of war, half of whose troops were prisoners in foreign lands, and many of whose provinces were ready to defect on the first suitable occasion. Amongst which was that containing the department of Jemmapes, of which Mons was the principal town.

This huge area of rich country which had been annexed to France, firstly "de facto" by the war of 1792, and then by right after the treaty of Amiens, had been so accustomed to this union that after the disasters of the Russian campaign, it had shown great enthusiasm and made considerable sacrifices to help the Emperor to put his troops back on a sound footing. Men, horses, equipment, clothing... it had complied with all demands without a murmur; but the losses we had suffered in Germany had discouraged the Belgians, and I found the attitude of the populace had completely changed. They loudly regretted the paternal government of the house of Austria, under which they had lived for so long, and were most anxious to separate themselves from France, whose continual wars were ruining their trade and industry. In a word, Belgium awaited only a favourable moment to revolt, an event which would be the more serious for us because, by its geographical situation the province was in the rear of the weakened army corps which we still had on the Rhine. The Emperor sent some troops to Brussels, whom he placed under the command of General Maisons, a capable and very determined man. Maisons, having, visited several departments, recognised that Jemmapes, and particularly the town of Mons, was the most disaffected. There was there, open discussion of the possibility of taking up arms against the weak French garrison, something which its commander general "O"... could not have prevented, for the old general, stricken by gout, and lacking in energy, who had been born in Belgium, seemed afraid to earn the dislike of his compatriots. General Maisons suspended him from duty and gave me the command of the department of Jemmapes.

My job was made more difficult because, after the inhabitants of Lige, those who live in Borinage are the boldest and most turbulent in all Belgium, and to control them I had only a small unit of 400 conscripts, a few gendarmes and 200 unmounted cavalrymen from my regiment, among whom there were some fifty men who were born in the area and who, in case of trouble, would join the insurgents. I could rely entirely only on the other 150 Chasseurs, who born in France, and having been in action with me, would have followed me anywhere.

There were some good officers; those in the infantry, and in particular the battalion commander, were very willing to back me up.

I could not, however, disguise the fact that if it came to blows, the two sides were not equally matched. From the hotel where I stayed I saw every day 3 or 4,000 peasants and workmen from the town, armed with big sticks who gathered in the main square to listen to speeches from former Austrian officers, all of them wealthy nobles, who had quitted the service on the union of Belgium with France, and now spoke out against the Empire, which had loaded them with taxes, taken their children to send them to the wars, *etc.*,etc. These speeches were listened to with all the more attention, in that they were delivered by great landed proprietors, and addressed to their tenants and employees, over whom they wielded much influence.

Add to this that each day brought news of the advance of our enemies, who were approaching Brussels, driving before them the debris of Marshal Macdonald's Corps. All the French employees left the department to take refuge in Valenciennes and Cambrai. Finally the mayor of Mons, M. Duval of Beaulieu, an honourable man, thought it his duty to warn me that neither my feeble garrison nor myself were safe in the midst of an excited and numerous population, and that I would be wise to leave the town, a move which would not be opposed since my regiment and I had always lived at peace with the inhabitants.

I was aware that this proposition came from a committee composed of former Austrian officers, which had instructed the mayor to put it to me, in the hope that I would be intimidated. I resolved then to show my teeth, I said to M. Duval that I would be most grateful if he would summon the town council and the leading citizens, and that I would then give my reply to the proposals which he had brought me.

Half an hour later, all the garrison were armed, and when the municipal council accompanied by the wealthiest citizens had assembled in the square, I mounted on horseback, in order to be heard by all, and after I had told the mayor that before talking with him and his council, I had an important order to give to my troops, I told my men about the suggestion which had been made that we should abandon, without a struggle, the town which had been put in our care.

They were most indignant, and said so loudly! I added that I could not conceal the fact that the ramparts were broken down at several points, and a lack of artillery would make defence difficult against regular troops, though if need be we would do our best; but that if it was the inhabitants of the town and the countryside who rose against us, we would not confine ourselves to defence, we would attack with all the means at our disposal, for we would be dealing with revolutionaries. As a consequence I was ordering my men to take over the church tower, from where, after a delay of half an hour and three rolls on the drums they would fire on the occupants of the square, while patrols would clear the streets by shooting, mainly at those who had left their work in the country to come and do us harm. I added that if it came to fighting, I would order, as the best means of defence, the setting on fire of the town, in order to keep the inhabitants busy, and I would shoot at them continually to prevent its extinction.

This speech may seem a little drastic, but consider the critical position in which I found myself; with no more than 700 men, few of whom had seen action, no expectation of reinforcements, and surrounded by a multitude which increased in size by the moment, for the officer in charge of the detachment sent to the church tower told me that the roads leading to the town were full of miners from the pits of Jemmapes, heading for the town of *Mons*. My little troupe and I were at risk of being wiped out if I had not taken decisive action. My address had produced a marked effect among the rich noblemen, the promoters of this disturbance, and also among the townspeople, who began to disperse; but as the peasants did not budge, I brought up two ammunition wagons to issue a hundred cartridges to each soldier, and when they had loaded their weapons, I ordered the three rolls on the drums, the prelude to the fusillade.

At this frightening sound, the huge crowd which filled the square began to run in tumult to the neighbouring streets, where each one rushed to find shelter, and a few moments later the leaders of the Austrian party, with the mayor at their head, came to clutch at my hand and beg me to spare the town. I agreed on the condition that they would send immediately to tell the miners and workmen to go back to their homes. They hastened to comply, and the elegant young men who were the best mounted, jumped on their fine horses and went out through all the city gates to meet the mob which they sent back to their villages without any opposition.

This passive obedience confirmed me in my opinion that the disturbance had powerful backers, and that my garrison and I would have been held prisoner, had I not frightened the leaders by threatening to use all means, even fire rather than hand over to rioters the town confided to my charge.

The Belgians are very fond of music, and it so happened that there was a concert to be given that evening, to which I and my officers had been invited, as was M.de Laussat the prefect of the department.

We agreed that we should go there as usual, which was the right decision, for we were received with cordiality, at least on the surface. While talking to the nobles, who had been behind the disturbance, we put it to them that it was not for the populace to decide by rebellion the fate of Belgium, but rather for the contending armies; and it would be folly on their part to incite the workmen and peasants to shed their blood, in order to hasten by a few days a solution which would presently become evident.

An elderly Austrian general, who had retired to Mons, his birthplace, then said to his compatriots that they had been wrong to plot the seizure of the garrison, for that would have resulted in much damage to the town, as no soldiers would lay down their arms without a fight. They all agreed that this assessment was correct, and from that day forward the garrison and the townsfolk lived peacefully together as in the past. The people of Mons even gave us a few days later a striking demonstration of their support.

As the allied armies advanced, a crowd of partisans, mainly Prussians, disguised themselves as Cossacks, and driven by the desire for plunder they grabbed anything which had belonged to the French administration, and had no hesitation in seizing the goods of even non-military French citizens.

A large band of these imitation Cossacks, having crossed the Rhine and spread out on the left bank, had reached as far as the gates of Brussels, and had pillaged the imperial chteau of Tervueren, from where they took all the horses of the stud farm which the Emperor had installed there; then, splitting into smaller groups, these marauders infested Belgium. Some of them came to the department of Jemmapes, where they tried to stir up the populace, but when they did not succeed in doing so, they put this down to the fact that Mons, the principal town of the region, had not supported them because of the terror inspired by the colonel in command of the garrison. Whereupon they decided to capture or kill me, but in order not to awaken my suspicions by employing too great a number of men for this exploit, they limited the number to three hundred. It appeared that the leader of these partisans had been well briefed, for, knowing that I had too few men to guard the old gates and ancient, partly demolished, ramparts, he took his men, during a dark night, to the rampart, where the major part of them dismounted and made their way silently through the streets to the main square and the Hotel de la Poste, where I had at first stayed. However, since I had heard of the crossing of the Rhine by the enemy, I had gone every evening to the barracks, where I spent the night surrounded by my troops. It was as well that I had done so, for the German Cossacks surrounded the hotel and rifled through all the rooms. Then, furious at not finding any French officers, they set on the inn-keeper, whom they robbed and maltreated, and whose wine they drank until both officers and soldiers were drunk.

A Belgian, a former corporal in my regiment, named Courtois, for whom I had obtained a decoration as one of my bravest soldiers, arrived at this moment at the hotel. This man, born at Saint-Ghislain near Mons, had lost a leg in Russia the previous year, and happily I had been able to save him by securing means for him to return to France. He was so grateful for this that during my stay in Mons in the winter of 1814, he came often to visit me, and on those occasions he dressed in the uniform of the 23rd Chasseurs which he had once so honourably worn. Now, it so happened that on the night in question, Curtois, while returning to the house of one of his relatives where he had been staying, saw the enemy detachment heading in the direction of the hotel, and although the gallant corporal knew that I did not sleep there, he wanted to be sure that his colonel was in no danger, so he went to the hotel, taking with him his relative.

At the sight of the French uniform and the Legion of Honour, the Prussians shamefully grabbed the crippled man and tried to snatch the cross of the Legion from him. When he resisted, the Prussian Cossacks killed him and dragged his body into the street before continuing their drinking.

Mons was so large in comparison to my small garrison, that I had taken refuge in the barracks and having arranged my defences for the night at this spot, I had forbidden my men to go near the main square, although I had been told that the enemy were there, because I did not know their strength and feared that the local populace would combine with them; but when the townspeople heard of the murder of Courtois, their fellow countryman and one regarded with affection by all, they resolved to be revenged, and forgetting their complaints against the French, they sent a deputation, comprising the brother of the dead man and some of the leading citizens, to ask me to put myself at their head in order to drive away these "Cossacks".

I was well aware that the pillage and excess at the Hotel de La Poste inspired in every bourgeois fear for his family and his house, which motivated them to expel the Cossacks as much as the death of Curtois, and that they would have acted very differently if, instead of robbers and assassins, it had been regular troops who had entered the town. Nonetheless I thought it my duty to take advantage of the good-will of those inhabitants who were prepared to take up arms to help us. I then took part of my troop and set off for the square, while the remainder, in charge of the battalion commander, who knew the town well, I sent to lie in wait at the breach in the wall through which the Prussian Cossacks had entered.

At the first shots fired by our people at these rogues, there was a great tumult in the hotel and the square. Those who were not killed took to their heels, but many got lost in the streets and were finished off one by one. As for those who reached the place where they had left their horses tied up to trees in the promenade, they ran into the battalion commander, who greeted them with a withering fusillade. At daylight we counted in the town and in the old breach more than 200 dead, while we had not lost a single man because our adversaries, fuddled by wine and strong liquor had offered no defence. Those of them who escaped into the country were caught and killed by the peasantry, who were enraged at the death of the unfortunate Curtois, who was something of a local celebrity, and who, given the name of "Jambe de bois", had become as dear to them as General Daumesnil, another "Jambe de bois". was to the working class of Paris.

I do not cite this fighting in Mons as something to be particularly proud of, for with the national guard, I had twelve or thirteen hundred men compared to the three hundred of the Prussians; but I thought it worth recording this bizarre encounter to demonstrate the volatility of the masses, which is displayed by the fact that all the peasants and coal miners of Borinage who a month previously had come in a mass to exterminate or at least disarm the few Frenchmen remaining in Mons, had come to join us to oppose the Prussians because they had killed one of their compatriots. I greatly regretted the death of the brave Courtois, who had fallen victim to his regard for me.

The most important trophy from our victory was the three hundred horses which the enemy abandoned. They nearly all came from the region of Berg and were of very good quality so I took them into my regiment, for which this unexpected provision of remounts was extremely welcome.

I passed a further month at Mons, whose inhabitants treated us perfectly well despite the approach of the enemy armies. However their continued advance meant that the French were forced not only to abandon Brussels but the whole of Belgium, and recross the frontiers into their motherland. I was ordered to take my regimental depot to Cambrai where, with the horses which I had taken from the Prussian Cossacks I was able to remount 300 good troopers who had returned from Leipzig, and make two fine squadrons, which commanded by Major Sigaldi, were sent to the army which the Emperor was assembling in Champagne. There they upheld the honour of the 23rd chasseuers, particularly at the battle of Champaubert, where the gallant Captain Duplessis, an outstanding officer, was killed.

I have always favoured the lance, a lethal weapon in the hands of a good cavalryman. I asked for and obtained permission to distribute to my squadrons some lances which artillery officers had been unable to carry away when they left the forts on the Rhine. They were so much appreciated that several other cavalry units followed my example, and were glad to have done so.

The regimental depots were obliged to cross to the left bank of the Seine to avoid falling into the hands of the enemy, mine went to Nogent-le-Roi, an arrondissment of Dreux. We had a fair number of troopers but almost no horses. The government was making great efforts to collect some at Versailles, where it had created a central cavalry depot commanded by General Prval.

The General, like his predecessor General Bourcier, knew much more about remounts and organisation than he did about war, in which he had rarely been involved. He did his utmost to fulfil the difficult task which the Emperor had given him; but as he could not improvise horses or equipment, and as he would not send out detachments until they were fully organised, departures were not very frequent. I grumbled, but no colonel could return to his unit without the permission of the Emperor, who to conserve his resources, had forbidden the employment of more officers in any unit than was justified by the number of men they had to command. It was therefore useless for me to beg General Prval to let me go to Champagne. He fixed my departure for the end of March, at which time I would lead to the army a draft composed of mounted men from my own depot and several others.

366

Until this time I was authorised to live in Paris with my family, for M. Caseneuve, my second-in-comand could take care of the 200 men who were still at Nogent-le-Roi, which I could reach if necessary, in a few hours. So I went to Paris, where I spent the greater part of March, which, although I was with those I loved most, was one of the most miserable months of my life. The imperial government, to which I was attached, and which I had for so long defended at the cost of my blood, was everywhere crumbling. The armies of the enemy, spreading from Lyon, occupied a large part of France, and it was easy to see that they would soon arrive at the capital.

Chap. 35.

The Emperor's greatest antagonists are forced to admit that he excelled himself in the winter campaign which he conducted in the first three months of 1814. No previous general had ever shown such talent, or achieved so much with such feeble resources. With a few thousand men, most of whom were inexperienced conscripts, one saw him face the armies of Europe, turning up everywhere with these troops, which he led from one point to another with marvellous rapidity.

Taking advantage of all the resources of the country in order to defend it, he hurried from the Austrians to the Russians, and from the Russians to the Prussians, going from Blcher to Schwarzenberg and from him to Sacken, sometimes beaten by them, but much more often the victor. He hoped, for a time, that he might drive the foreigners, disheartened by frequent defeats, from French soil and back across the Rhine. All that was required was a new effort by the nation; but there was general war-weariness, and there was in all parts, and particularly in Paris, plotting against the Empire.

There are those who have expressed surprise that France did not rise in mass, as in 1792, to repel the invader, or did not follow the Spanish in forming, in each province, a centre of national defence.

The reason is that the enthusiasm which had improvised the armies of 1792 had been exhausted by twenty-five years of war, and the Emperor's over-use of conscription, so that in most of the departments there remained only old men and children. As for the example of Spain, it is not applicable to France, where too much influence has been allowed to Paris, so that nothing can be done unless Paris leads the way, whereas in Spain each Province was a little government and was able to create its own army, even when Madrid was occupied by the French. It was centralisation which led to the loss of France.

It is no part of the task which I have set myself, to relate the great feats performed by the French army during the campaign of 1814, to do so I would have to write volumes, and I do not feel inclined to dwell on the misfortunes of my country. I shall content myself by saying that after disputing, foot by foot, the territory between the Marne, the Aube, the Sane and the Seine, the Emperor conceived a daring plan which, if it had succeeded, would have saved France. This was to go, with his troops, by way of Saint-Dizier and Vitry towards Alsace and Lorraine, which by threatening the rear of the enemies, would make them fear being cut off from their depots and finding themselves without any route of retreat. This would decide them to withdraw to the frontier while they still had the opportunity.

However, to ensure the success of this splendid strategic movement, it required the fulfilment of two conditions which failed him. These were the loyalty of the high officers of state, and some means of preventing the enemy from seizing Paris if they ignored the movement of the Emperor towards their rear and launched an attack on the city.

Sadly, loyalty to the Emperor was so much diminished in the Senate and the legislative body, that there were leading members of these assemblies, such as Tallyrand, the Duc de Dalberg, Laisn and others, who through secret emissaries informed the allied sovereigns of the dissatisfaction among the upper-class Parisians with Napoleon, and invited them to come and attack the capital.

As for defences, it must be admitted that Napoleon had not given this sufficient thought, and they were limited to the erection of a spiked palisade at the gates on the right bank, without the provision of any positions for guns. As the garrison, formed by a very small number of troops of the line, of invalids, veterans and students from the polytechnic was insufficient to even attempt resistance, the Emperor, when he left the capital in January to go and head the troops assembled in Champagne, confided to the National Guard the defence of Paris, where he left the Empress and his son. He had called together at the Tuileries the officers of this bourgeois militia, who had responded with numerous vows and bellicose undertakings to the rousing speech which he addressed to them. The Emperor named the Empress as Regent and appointed as overall commander his brother Joseph the ex-King of Spain, the pleasantest but most unsoldierlike of men.

Napoleon, under the illusion that he had thus provided for the safety of the capital, thought that he could leave it for some days to its own devices, while he went with those troops which still remained to him to carry out the project of getting behind the enemy. He left for Lorraine about the end of March; but he had been on his way for only a few days, when he learned that the allies, instead of following him as he had hoped, had headed for Paris, driving before then the weak debris of Mortier's and Marmont's corps who, positioned on the heights of Montmartre, attempted to defend the city without any help from the National Guard except an occasional infantryman.

This alarming news opened Napoleon's eyes; he turned his troops to march towards Paris, for where he set out immediately.

On the 30th of March, the Emperor, riding post and with no escort, had just passed Moret when a brisk cannonade was heard; he held on to the hope of arriving before the allies entered the capital, where his presence would certainly have had a remarkable effect on the population, who were demanding arms. (There were one hundred thousand muskets and several million cartridges in the barracks of the

Champ de Mars, but General Clarke, the Minister for War, would not allow their distribution.)

On his arrival at Fromenteau, only five leagues from Paris, the Emperor could no longer hear gunfire and he realised that the city was in the hands of the allies, which was confirmed at Villejuif. Marmont had, in fact signed a capitulation which delivered the capital to the enemy.

As danger approached, the Empress and her son, the King of Rome, had gone to Blois, where they were shortly joined by King Joseph, who abandoned the command which the Emperor had given him. The troops of the line left by the Fontainebleau gate, a route by which the Emperor was expected to arrive.

It is not possible to describe the agitation which seized the city whose inhabitants, divided by so many different interests, had been surprised by an invasion which few of them had foreseen... As for me, who had expected it, and who had seen at close quarters the horrors of war, I was most anxiously thinking of a way to ensure the safety of my wife and our young child, when the elderly Marshal Srurier offered a shelter for all my family at Les Invalides, of which he was the governor. I was comforted by the thought that as everywhere the homes for old soldiers had always been respected by the French, the enemy would act in the same way towards ours. I therefore took my family to the Invalides and left Paris, before the entry of the allies, to report to General Prval at Versailles. I was given command of a small column made up of available cavalrymen from my own regiment and from the 9th and 12th Chasseurs.

Even if the allies had not marched on Paris, this column was due to be assembled at Rambouillet, and it is to there that I went. I found there my horses and my equipment, and I took command of the squadrons which had been allotted to me. The road was full of the carriages of those who were flying from the capital. I was not surprised by that; but I was unable to understand where the great number of troops of all arms came from, which one saw arriving from all directions in detachments, which if they had been combined would have formed a corps of sufficient size to hold up the enemy at Montmartre, and allow time for the army which was hurrying from Champagne and Brie to arrive and save Paris. The Emperor misled by his Minister for War, had given no instructions regarding the matter, and was probably unaware that he still had so great a capacity for defence at his disposal, a description of which follows, taken from Ministry of War documents.

There were at Vincennes, the military school of the Champ de Mars and the central artillery depot some four hundred cannons with ammunition and 50,000 muskets. As for men, there were the troops brought by Marshals Marmont and Mortier, which together with troops gathered from other sources including 20,000 workmen, nearly all of them old soldiers, who had volunteered to help defend the city, amounted to some 80,000.

It would have been possible for Joseph and Clarke to assemble this force in a few hours and to defend the city until the arrival of the Emperor and the army which was following him.

Joseph and Clarke had forty-eight hours warning of the enemy approach, but did nothing, and as a final act of incompetence, at the moment when the enemy troops were attacking Romainville, they sent 4000 men of the Imperial Guard to Blois, to reinforce the escort of the Empress, which was already quite big enough.

When the Emperor learned that Paris had capitulated and that the two small corps of Marmont and Mortier had left, and were retiring towards him, he sent them orders to take up positions at Essonnes, seven leagues from Paris and mid-way between that city and Fontainebleau. He went himself to this last town, where were arriving the heads of the columns coming from Saint-Dizier, an indication that he intended to march on Paris as soon as his army was gathered together.

The enemy generals have later stated that if they had been attacked by the Emperor, they would not have risked a battle, with the Seine behind them and also the great city of Paris, with its million inhabitants, which might rise in revolt at any moment during the fighting and barricade the streets and the bridges, thus cutting off their line of retreat. So they had decided to draw back and camp on the heights of Belleville, Charonne, Montmartre and the slopes of Chaumont, which dominate the right bank of the Seine and the route to Germany, when new events in Paris kept them in the city.

M. de Tallyrand, a former bishop now married, who had always appeared to be devoted to the Emperor, by whom he had been loaded with riches and made prince of Benevento, Grand Chamberlain, etc., etc., felt his pride injured when he was no longer Napoleon's confidant, and the minister directing his policy. So, after the disasters of the Russian campaign, he had put himself at the head of an underground conspiracy, which included all the malcontents from every party, but mainly the Faubourg Saint-Germain, that is to say the high aristocracy, who, after appearing at first submissive and even serving Napoleon in the time of his prosperity, had become his enemy and without openly compromising themselves, attacked, by all means, the head of government.

These people, guided by Tallyrand, the most cunning and scheming of them all, had been waiting for an occasion to overthrow Napoleon. They realised that they would never have a more favourable opportunity than that offered by the occupation of the country by a million and a half enemies, and the presence in Paris of all the crowned heads of Europe, most of whom had been grossly humiliated by Napoleon at one time or another. Napoleon, however, though greatly weakened, was not yet entirely beaten, for, apart from the army which he had with him, and with which he had performed prodigies, there was Suchet's army, between the Pyrénées and the Haute-Garonne, there were troops commanded by Marshal Soult, there were two fine divisions at Lyon, and finally, the army in Italy was still formidable, so that in spite of the occupation of Bordeaux by the English, Napoleon might still assemble

370

considerable forces and prolong the war indefinitely, by raising a population, exasperated by the exactions of the enemy.

Tallyrand, for his part, realised that if they gave the Emperor time to bring to Paris the troops who were with him, he might beat the allies in the streets of the capital, or withdraw to some loyal provinces, where he might continue the war, until the allies were exhausted and ready to make peace. In the view of Tallyrand and his friends, it was therefore necessary to change the government. Here there arose a great difficulty, for they wanted to restore the Bourbons to the throne, in the person of Louis XVIII, while other parts of the country wanted to retain Napoleon, or at most to install his son.

The same difference of opinion existed amongst the allied sovereigns. The kings of England and Prussia were on the side of the Bourbons, while the emperor of Russia, who had never liked them, and who feared that the antipathy felt by the French nation towards these princes and the migrs would lead to a fresh revolution, was inclined to favour Napoleon's son.

To cut short these discussions, and decide the question by making the first move, the astute Tallyrand, in an attempt to force the hand of the foreign sovereigns, arranged for a group of about twenty young men from the Faubourg Saint-Germain to appear on horseback in Louis XV square, decked with white cockades, and led by Vicomte Talon, my former comrade in arms, from whom I have these details. They went towards the mansion in the rue Saint-Florentin occupied by the Emperor Alexander, shouting at the top of their voices "Long live King Louis XVIII! Long live the Bourbons! Down with the tyrant!"

The effect produced on the curious gathering of onlookers by these cries, was at first one of astonishment, which was quickly succeeded by threats and menaces from the crowd, which shook even the boldest of the cavalcade. This first royalist demonstration having been unsuccessful, they repeated the performance at various points on the boulevards. At some places they were booed, at others applauded. As the entry procession of the allied sovereigns approached, and as the Parisians need a slogan to animate them, the one produced by Vicomte Talon and his friends rang in the ears of the Emperor Alexander throughout the whole day, which permitted Tallyrand to say to that monarch in the evening, "Your Majesty can judge for himself with what unanimity the nation desires the restoration of the Bourbons!"

From that moment, although his supporters greatly outnumbered those of Louis XVIII, as the events of the following year would show, Napoleon's cause was lost.

End of Volume 2, The Memoirs of General the Baron de Marbot. Translated by Oliver.C.Colt

771617

Printed in Great Britain by
Amazon.co.uk, Ltd.,
Marston Gate.